Development Economics
Volume III

The International Library of Critical Writings in Economics

Series Editor: Mark Blaug

Professor Emeritus, University of London
Consultant Professor, University of Buckingham
Visiting Professor, University of Exeter

This series is an essential reference source for students, researchers and lecturers in economics. It presents by theme an authoritative selection of the most important articles across the entire spectrum of economics. Each volume has been prepared by a leading specialist who has written an authoritative introduction to the literature included.

A full list of published and future titles in this series is printed at the end of this volume.

Development Economics
Volume III

Edited by

Deepak Lal

Professor of Political Economy
University College London
and James S. Coleman Professor
in International Development Studies
University of California, Los Angeles

An Elgar Reference Collection

Published by
Edward Elgar Publishing Limited
Gower House
Croft Road
Aldershot
Hants GU11 3HR
England

Edward Elgar Publishing Limited
Distributed in the United States by
Ashgate Publishing Company
Old Post Road
Brookfield
Vermont 05036
USA

CIP catalogue records for this book are available from the British Library and the US Library of Congress.

ISBN 1 85278 196 3 (4 volume set)

Printed and bound in Great Britain by Bookcraft, Bath

Contents

Acknowledgements

The editor and publishers wish to thank the following who have kindly given permission for the use of copyright material.

American Economic Association for articles: Jagdish N. Bhagwati and Anne O. Krueger (1973), 'Exchange Control, Liberalization and Economic Development', *American Economic Review*, **LXIII** (2), 419–27; Anne O. Krueger and Baran Tuncer (1982), 'An Empirical Test of the Infant Industry Argument', *American Economic Review*, **LXXII**, 1142–52; Anne O. Krueger (1978), 'Alternative Trade Strategies and Employment in LDCs', *American Economic Review*, **LXVIII** (2), 270–74; Anne O. Krueger (1974), 'The Political Economy of the Rent-Seeking Society', *American Economic Review*, **LXIV**, 291–303.

Basil Blackwell Ltd. for articles: M.A.M. Smith (1977), 'Capital Accumulation in the Open Two-Sector Economy', *Economic Journal*, **87** (346), 273–82; H. Myint (1958), 'The "Classical Theory" of International Trade and the Underdeveloped Countries', *Economic Journal*, **LXVIII**, 317–37; James Riedel (1984), 'Trade as the Engine of Growth in Developing Countries, Revisited', *Economic Journal*, **94**, 56–73; Irving B. Kravis (1970), 'Trade as a Handmaiden of Growth: Similarities Between the Nineteenth and Twentieth Centuries', *Economic Journal*, **LXXX**, 850–72; M. June Flanders (1964), 'Prebisch on Protectionism: An Evaluation', *Economic Journal*, **LXXIV** (2), 305–26.

Canadian Journal of Economics for article: Alan V. Deardorff (1984), 'An Exposition and Exploration of Krueger's Trade Model', *Canadian Journal of Economics*, **XVII** (4), 731–46.

Elsevier Science Publishers B.V. for articles: Jagdish N. Bhagwati, Richard A. Brecher and T.N. Srinivasan (1984), 'DUP Activities and Economic Theory', *European Economic Review*, **24**, 291–307; Howard Pack and Larry E. Westphal (1986), 'Industrial Strategy and Technological Change: Theory Versus Reality', *Journal of Development Economics*, **22**, 87–128.

Indian Economic Review for articles: I.M.D. Little (1971), 'Trade and Public Finance', *Indian Economic Review*, **6** (2), 119–32; T.N. Srinivasan (1989), 'Recent Theories of Imperfect Competition and International Trade: Any Implications for Development Strategy?', *Indian Economic Review*, **XXIV** (1), 1–23.

The Nobel Foundation for article: W. Arthur Lewis (1980), 'The Slowing Down of the Engine of Growth', *American Economic Review*, **LXX**, 555–64.

The World Bank for articles: Deepak Lal and Sarath Rajapatirana (1987), 'Foreign Trade Regimes and Economic Growth in Developing Countries', *World Bank Research Observer*, 2 (2), 189–217; Enzo R. Grilli and Maw Cheng Yang (1988), 'Primary Commodity Prices, Manufactured Goods Prices, and the Terms of Trade of Developing Countries: What the Long Run Shows', *World Bank Economic Review*, 2 (1), 1–47.

University of Chicago Press for article: M. Bronfenbrenner (1960), 'A Simplified Mahalanobis Development Model', *Economic Development and Cultural Change*, IX (1), 45–51; Deepak Lal (1972), 'The Foreign-Exchange Bottleneck Revisited: A Geometric Note', *Economic Development and Cultural Change*, 20 (4), 722–30; Jagdish Bhagwati and V.K. Ramaswami (1963), 'Domestic Distortions, Tariffs and the Theory of Optimum Subsidy', *Journal of Political Economy*, LXXI, 44–50; W.M. Corden (1966), 'The Structure of a Tariff System and the Effective Protective Rate', *Journal of Political Economy*, LXXIV, 221–37; Robert E. Baldwin (1969), 'The Case Against Infant-Industry Protection', *Journal of Political Economy*, 77, 295–305.

Every effort has been made to trace all the copyright holders but if any have been inadvertently overlooked the publishers will be pleased to make the necessary arrangement at the first opportunity.

In addition the publishers wish to thank the library of the London School of Economics and Political Science and The Alfred Marshall Library, Cambridge University for their assistance in obtaining these articles.

Introduction to Volumes III and IV

In 1965, J.R. Hicks noted, 'Underdevelopment economics is a vastly important subject, but it is not a formal or theoretical subject. It is a practical subject which must expect to call upon any branch of theory (including non-economic, for instance sociological, theory) which has any relevance to it. If there is any branch of economic theory which is especially relevant to it, it is the theory of International Trade.' (Hicks, 1965, pp.3–4.) And so it has proved in the evolution of development economics over the last four decades. International trade theory has been one of the most productive sources of insights into the process and policies for development.

Historically the international economy has been of vital importance in economic development for three reasons. First, because international trade has been a powerful 'engine of growth' for some countries and not for others (or so it has been argued by Nurkse (1961)), and it is important to discuss the reasons for this differing pattern. Second, many developing countries were originally integrated into the world economy through trade and commerce and the accompanying colonialism. Many writers (for example, Myrdal (1958), Balogh (1963), Emmanuel (1972)) have insisted that their present backwardness is in part due to the unequal partnership foisted on them by their imperial masters – with developing countries specializing in primary commodities and developed countries specializing in manufactures. Third, and linked to this, is the age-old controversy about the relative merits of Free Trade and Protection.

The most fiercely contested debates have concerned the effects of the world economy on developing economies, and how developing countries can best cope with them. The old controversies over the relative merits of free trade and protection for a developing country (going back to the arguments of Hamilton and List for protection of the then late developers – the USA and Germany) continue to rage in debates on the appropriate public policies towards foreign trade, foreign capital and industrialization in the Third World. Developments in theory, which have been stimulated mainly by the problems of developing countries (particularly those in the modern theory of trade and welfare) and the divergent experiences of developing countries (from following alternative policies) have however, hopefully narrowed the distance between the protagonists. This distance is ultimately based on a deeper difference in *Weltanschauung* which goes back to fundamental disputes about the role of the State (or socialism versus capitalism). (Lal (1983)) So questions concerning the feasibility and desirability of planning are never far from the surface of debates concerning the appropriate policies for a small open developing economy. These debates have been further enlivened and enriched in recent years by a more systematic exploration of the nature of the State in different developing countries, within the theoretical perspective which goes under the name of the 'new' political economy. In these two final volumes of these readings, I have put together the major articles which I recommend (with the caveats noted in the General Introduction) to my students to enable them to form their own views on these continuing controversies.

Trade and Growth

The starting point for a theoretical consideration of the developing country in an open economy, is the modern theory of comparative costs associated with the names of Hecksher, Ohlin and Samuelson (HOS). The simplest static version considers a two-good, two-factor model of a perfectly competitive economy, and shows how the country's pattern of trade reflects its relative factor endowments. It will import/export the good which uses its relatively scarce/abundant factor most intensively. In addition the theory's normative conclusion is that irrespective of a country's specific social welfare function, there are gains from trade, as the removal of trade barriers expands the feasible set of consumption possibilities, and thence welfare.[1] Questioning of the assumptions of the theoretical case for the classical gains from trade provides the various arguments for departures from free trade. Even within the classical theory it was recognized by Mill, Bickerdike, Edgeworth and Marshall that a country which bulked large in foreign trade could garner a larger share of the cosmopolitan gains through trade restrictions. This optimum tariff argument (see Johnson (1953) for its detailed modern statement) is still recognized as a valid qualification to the free trade case. However, its relevance for developing countries which are by and large 'small' in relation to world trade and hence unable to influence their terms of trade, is limited (but see Sections II and IV below).

A continuing criticism has been the static nature of the classical case for free trade – based on given factor endowments, and the comparative costs they represent. As economic development inevitably leads to changes in factor endowments and thence the country's future comparative advantage, the static theory was declared to be irrelevant, as it was not dynamic. Chapter I by Smith shows in a compact manner how this criticism has been met by adding features of the neo-classical growth model to the standard HOS model of static comparative advantage. (Also see Johnson's Wicksell Lectures (Johnson (1968))

Further developments of the HOS model incorporating features of particular importance to developing countries are contained in the next two readings. Anne Krueger in her Graham Lectures (Krueger (1977)) introduced a model which included land as a third factor of production, as she argued that land-based agriculture was still of great importance in developing countries. She proposed a model in which (as in the dual economy) there is an agricultural sector which uses land and labour, and a manufacturing sector which uses capital and labour. Capital and land are specific to their respective sectors, but labour is mobile between them. She thus married the HOS model of the pure theory of international trade to the so-called Ricardo–Viner specific factors model which was most clearly formulated by Jones (1971). This three factor model is outlined in Chapter 2, by Deardorff. It shows that there is a richer menu of development paths and their associated factor price implications than in the HOS model. Leamer (1987) has recently extended the Krueger model into a fully fledged three-factor, multi-commodity model of an open economy, and also provided a very useful pedagogic device (the Leamer triangle) to expound its workings. In a recently completed multi-country study of the political economy of poverty, equity and growth in 21 developing countries, this framework proved useful in classifying countries according to their factor endowments, and in drawing lessons about their different development paths. In particular, the typical efficient development path of a labour abundant economy for example, Korea, Taiwan, Hong Kong, Singapore) may not be replicated in land abundant countries (for example, Brazil, Argentina). (See Lal and Myint (forthcoming)). Also the Leamer triangle has been used in Lal (1989) to explain the otherwise puzzling political economy of post-war Latin American industrialization.

Whilst the Lewis model, with its purported surplus of labour has bewitched many development economists, its relevance has been questioned by Myint, who has had the land abundant (and relatively labour scarce) South East Asian peasant export economies in his ken. His classic model of the 'vent for surplus' to explain the development of these economies is in Chapter 3.

The collapse of world trade during the Great Depression led to a profound 'trade pessimism' amongst both theorists and practitioners of economic development, after the Second World War. Nurkse (1961) produced the most notable challenge to the classical case for a liberal order for foreign trade and payments. He emphasized the importance of world demand in determining the gains from trade, whereas the classical theory had emphasized the domestic supply side, with the major benefits from free trade flowing from the more efficient use of available resources. Nurkse argued that whereas international trade had been an engine of growth for the new white settler countries – USA, Canada, Argentina and Australia – in the nineteenth century, this engine was not available to developing countries because of the low income elasticity of demand for their exports of tropical products. Nor did he expect developing countries to be able to export manufactures, partly because of inherent difficulties in industrializing backward countries, and partly because of the protectionism that would be provoked by any surge of Third World imports into the First. Irving Kravis (Chapter 4) questions Nurkse's reading of history, particularly his demand orientated view that international trade was an engine of growth in the nineteenth century for the countries of new settlement. He argues that there were important differences in their performance, which can only be explained by their differing supply responses to similar external stimuli. Trade, he argues, is better looked upon as the handmaiden rather than the engine of growth.

The spectacular growth performance of a number of countries in South East Asia collectively known first as the Gang of Four,[2] then as the Baby Tigers and then as NICs (newly industrialized countries) – South Korea, Taiwan, Hong Kong and Singapore – belied the post war trade pessimism of development economists. As Little–Scott–Scitovsky (1970) showed in a magisterial work, their policies of maintaining a virtual free trade regime had led to unprecedented export growth, which moreover, based as it was on intensive use of their most abundant factor of production, labour, was also highly equitable. Their spectacular export performance occurred against the backdrop of an unprecedented boom in world trade. This followed the gradual removal of the tariff barriers that had been erected by developed countries since the Great Depression. These reductions were made during various rounds of trade negotiations under the General Agreement of Tariffs and Trade (GATT). (see Blackhurst, Marian & Tumlir (1977))

This post war boom – which has been called a 'Golden Age' – ended abruptly in 1973, with the raising of oil prices by the newly formed cartel of oil producers (OPEC). The turbulence in the world economy over the subsequent decades – with a further rise in oil prices in 1979 followed by a long term decline in their real value, gyrating primary commodity prices, volatility in capital flows and their associated real rates of interest, led to another round of 'export pessimism', based once again on a refurbished 'engine of growth' type of view. The most polished version is Arthur Lewis's Nobel Lecture in Chapter 5, whilst Chapter 6 by Riedel is a detailed refutation.

The Terms of Trade

The lessons drawn about the dangers of specializing in primary commodities following the collapse of their prices in the 1930s, and combined with a simple dichotomy between those developing countries specialized in the production of primary commodities, and those developed in manufactures, has held a strange fascination for development economists. Prebisch (1959) and Singer (1950) produced theories which purported to show that there would be an inexorable tendency for a decline in the terms of trade of free trading, primary product exporting developing countries. This would imply that free trade on the classical prescription would lead to their immiserization, and hence their policy prescriptions that developing countries should adopt policies of forced import substituting industrialization behind a wall of tariff and quota protection. Chapter 7 by June Flanders presents a theoretically coherent account of the Prebisch argument, as well as a critique.

Meanwhile, there has been an interminable statistical debate about what has happened to the terms of trade of developing countries. It was shown early on by Lipsey (1963) that changes in the relative prices of primary commodities and manufactured goods in world trade were not synonymous with the barter terms of trade of developing countries, as many developed countries – notably the USA, Australia and Canada – were also primary product exporters. Nor could a decline in a country's commodity terms of trade be taken to lead necessarily to a welfare loss, as the income terms of trade (which also took account of the volume of exports and not just their relative price) were equally important in forming this judgment. Chapter 8, by Grilli & Yang presents the most up-to-date and authorative statistical analysis of the historical series. It shows that the possible fall after World War II of net barter terms of trade in developing countries has been more than compensated by a steady improvement in their income terms of trade.

Moreover, as Bhagwati (1956) had shown in a seminal article on the pure theory of international trade, faced with a secular decline in a country's terms of trade, immiserizing growth could be prevented by imposing an optimal export tax (the optimum tariff).[3] There was no welfare justification for any further trade restrictions or for forced import substitution.

Foreign Exchange Constraints

The belief in a secular decline in the terms of trade of developing countries and the export pessimism associated with it, reached its apotheosis in the theory of the foreign exchange constraint or bottleneck propounded by Chenery and Strout (1966) and McKinnon (1964). It was now assumed that developing countries were faced by a fixed import capacity because of a complete inelasticity of export earnings. Hence even if they were willing to save more, they could not transform the incremental savings into effective investment because of the impossibility of obtaining the complementary imported inputs that were required for domestic investment. Foreign capital, particularly foreign aid was shown to be doubly productive. Not only did it supplement domestic savings, but even more importantly it allowed the foreign exchange bottleneck to be broken. The extremely implausible assumptions on which this view was based were soon noted (see Bruton (1969), Bhagwati (1966)). Chapter 9 by Lal provides a simple intertemporal general equilibrium model, which pinpoints the highly implausible conditions concerning trading possibilities and substitutability in the production and consumption sets of the economy, which must hold *simultaneously* for a foreign exchange bottleneck to occur. The assumption of a lack of substitutability in production and/or consumption sets, which means they are 'kinky', underlies the views of the 'structuralist' school of development economists. A spirited and detailed critique of their views is in Little (1982).[4]

Suppose, however, that a country was in a strict foreign exchange bottleneck, and moreover had no access to foreign capital, how could it break out of the foreign exchange constraint? This was the question the so-called Feldman–Mahalanobis model of development sought to answer. Feldman's model had been produced in 1928 and subsequently used by Stalin to justify his strategy of forced industrialization based on the development of heavy industry (see Domar (1957)). In the 1950s, given the prevailing export pessimism, Indian planners too were searching for a model of self-sustained growth which assumed a fixed import capacity. Mahalanobis, a physicist who was an advisor to Nehru, independently rediscovered the Feldman model. It formed the intellectual basis for India's Second Five Year Plan. Chapter 10 by Bronfenbrenner lucidly outlines the model and provides a critique. The model shows that, to raise and sustain future (long run) consumption levels, a country faced by a fixed import capacity should produce all the goods it can which would otherwise have been imported. This means that it should also import substitute vertically into heavy industry. Whilst this strategy is implemented, current consumption would have to be drastically curtailed.[5]

Whilst the Feldman model might have been relevant for the Soviet Union during its period of 'capitalist encirclement' when it could plausibly be argued that it faced limited foreign trade possibilities, the relevance of the Mahalanobis model to post-war Indian conditions is highly dubious. It has left an 'inward looking' bias to Indian economic policy which has blighted Indian development prospects for over four decades (see Bhagwati and Desai (1970), Bhagwati and Srinivasan (1975), Lal (1980a and 1988)).

Theory and Practice of Protection

Whilst development theorists and policy makers were finding more and more grounds for departing from the classical liberal framework which emphasized the importance of an open trading and payments regime, there were a few voices, most notably Viner (1953), and Haberler (1950 and 1959), which sounded a note of caution, and upheld the old classical virtues.[6] The rising tide of protectionism in developing countries as well as theoretical developments in welfare economics, led to new insights in trade theory, beginning with a seminal article by Haberler (1950). As part of this theoretical renaissance the modern theory of trade and welfare emerged, developed most fully in Meade (1955). In the classical argument, the case for free trade had been closely allied with that for *laissez-faire*. The modern theory maintains that even though the case for *laissez-faire* may be invalid, because government intervention may be required to correct distortions in the working of the domestic price mechanism, this does not invalidate the case for free trade. Arguments for protection are usually based on the need to deal with domestic distortions. But these are better dealt with through appropriate domestic taxes and subsidies. Protection which taxes and discriminates against foreign transactions will be worse, because it creates various other 'byproduct' distortions in dealing with the primary domestic distortion.

The seminal article which sets out this theory of optimal subsidy as contrasted with protection to deal with the 'domestic distortions' most commonly adduced by protectionists, is Chapter 11 by Bhagwati and Ramaswami. Whilst Johnson (1965) provides the most succinct statement of this modern theory of trade and welfare, Corden (1974) remains the most comprehensive and accessible discussion of all aspects of trade policy in a 'second best' world!

This modern theory was empirically validated by the multi-country comparative study by Little, Scitovsky and Scott (1970) on *Industry and Trade in Some Developing Countries*. Chapter 12 by Little, shows why (and how) the whole question of tariff protection to deal with domestic distortions can be looked upon as a part of public finance. This is important because without lump sum taxation, financing domestic subsidies will also lead to 'byproduct' costs associated with distortionary taxation. Little shows how in most practical cases, the 'second best' argument would still favour the 'domestic subsidy' rather than the 'tariff protection' route to deal with the domestic distortions adduced by protectionists.

An important aspect of the tariff structure in many countries is the cascading of tariff rates on imports by stage of production. Thus raw materials usually have a lower tariff rate than intermediate inputs which in turn have lower rates than finished goods. The nominal rate of protection offered to the finished good will then understate the true or 'effective' protection offered to the factors of production employed in its production. Chapter 13 by Corden is one of the articles that pioneered the concept of effective protection. The concept has been widely used subsequently as a diagnostic tool to assess the prima-facie resource allocation effects of tariff structures in numerous developing countries (see for instance Balassa (1971)).[7] Governments may have set nominal tariffs or quotas (with varying implicit nominal tariff rates over time) to achieve their stated objective of protecting particular industries. But the actual incentives will be determined by the relative profitabilities associated with the pattern of effective protection, which as it is unintended can usually be found to have no economic rationale whatsoever, and often actually to conflict with the stated aims. Thus India for instance sought to promote heavy industry and to penalize consumer good production through a complex system of foreign trade and industrial controls. But the pattern of effective protection these interventions engendered, led to the relative profitability in producing consumer goods to be substantially higher than that for capital goods, thus sabotaging the chosen strategy (see Lal (1980)).

Import Substituting Industrialization

By the 1970s there seemed to be an emerging consensus, based both on theory and practice, of the superiority of what came to be called an 'outward orientated' strategy of development in contrast to the 'import substituting', 'inward looking' policies that most developing countries had adopted in the 1950s and 1960s. The example of the NICs proved important.

However, in the 1980s there has been a *dirigiste* backlash amongst trade theorists and development economists. One tactic has been to steal the prime exhibits in the empirical cupboards of the liberal trade proponents – South Korea and Taiwan – as examples of efficient *dirigisme*.[8] The other has been to provide sophisticated new arguments for protection based on various novel twists to the classical infant industry and optimal tariff type arguments for protection.

Chapter 14 by Baldwin presents a classic modern examination of the hoary infant industry argument for protection, and finds it wanting. Chapter 15 by Pack and Westphal attempts a sophisticated rehabilitation, which is claimed to be in consonance with South Korean practice. Its success is said to have been based on a sophisticated policy of selective intervention to promote industries where increasing returns and pecuniary external economies were important. Their argument based on pecuniary externalities can however be questioned because of the Pareto-irrelevance (in Buchanan–Stubbeline terminology) of pecuniary as contrasted with technological externalities (see Baumol and Oates (1975) for a clear headed treatment of the issues).

As regards the argument for intervention based on increasing returns and dynamic external economies, a necessary condition for its desirability (which should ideally be in the form of domestic subsidies rather than trade protection) is that the inputs per unit of output decrease more rapidly (that is its total factor productivity (TFP) increases) both relative to foreign competitors and other domestic industries. In addition, it is also necessary that the discounted present value of the losses incurred during an industry's infancy are sufficiently recouped when it is grown up, to yield at least the social rate of return to investment in the economy. The Reading by Krueger and Tuncer provides a test of these necessary conditions for justifiable intervention on infant industry grounds for a sample of Turkish industry, and does not find them to be met. A survey by Bell et al. (1984) of the TFP performance of infant industries in a number of developing countries also provides little empirical support for the infant industry type arguments, nor does the evidence cited in Page (1990).

Chapter 17 by Srinivasan is a critical survey of the relevance of the 'new' trade theories which emphasize the importance of increasing returns, imperfect competition and strategic behaviour for trade policy in developing countries.[9] He is sceptical of its relevance, and of the claims made by some (for example, Helliner (1985)) that it controverts the case made in the 1960s and 1970s for outward oriented trade regimes in developing countries.

Beginning with the OECD sponsored study by Little, Scitovsky and Scott of industry and trade in developing countries, the method of comparative historical research has been productively applied to various policy problems of importance for developing countries. the next two readings provide summaries of two of these major comparative studies undertaken in the 1970s. The first was directed for the NBER by Jagdish Bhagwati and Anne Krueger on exchange control, liberalization and economic development. (The volumes by Krueger (1978) and Bhagwati (1979) provide detailed syntheses of the findings.) The project was concerned with delineating the complex anatomy of exchange control regimes, and their resource allocation and growth implications. Chapter 18 by Bhagwati and Krueger is a summary of their preliminary findings.

The second comparative study also sponsored by the NBER and directed by Anne Krueger, sought to analyse 'the extent to which employment and income distribution are affected by the choice of trade strategies and by the interaction of trade policies with domestic policies and market distortions' (Krueger (1983)). Chapter 19 provides a summary of the findings.

More recently, a large comparative study undertaken by the World Bank[10] sought to understand the process – including the impediments – through which a country makes the transition from a distorted to a liberal trade regime. This included questions about the proper sequencing of the various components of the trade liberalization and stabilization programmes. Papageorgiou, Choksi and Michaely (1990) provides a succinct summary of the findings, while a more detailed synthesis is in Michaely, Papageorgiou, and Choksi (1991). As no article summarizing the findings of this study was available for reprinting in these readings, it may be useful to quote some of their findings on liberalizing trade regimes.

First, there is nothing in a country's basic economic profile (its size, per capita income, and so on) that need put reform out of reach. Second, apparently unhelpful initial circumstances can work to the advantage of reform if they make it possible for governments to be bolder than they would otherwise have been. Third, the short term costs of reform, if any, are small. Economies adjust to a more open trade regime more quickly than has generally been thought. So the economic benefits of liberalisation are not unduly postponed: they begin to arrive almost at once . . . for reform to succeed, a small group of factors – each entirely within the government's control – appears to really count: The program should be bold and it should start with a bang. Any quantitative restrictions should be rapidly dismantled. Where appropriate, the program should begin with a substantial real depreciation of the currency. And there must be a stable macroeconomic environment. Almost every program that has followed these four simple rules has succeeded'. (Michaely, Papageorgiou and Choksi, 1991, pp. 40–41)

An important new perspective on development policy and thinking was provided by an application of what has come to be called the 'new' political economy (or public choice) in the United States (see Buchanan and Tullock (1962), Olson (1965)) to trade policy in developing countries. One of the pioneers of public choice, Gordon Tullock (1967) had pointed out that the conventional measures of the deadweight losses associated with tariffs and monopolies was much larger than conventionally measured. It not only included the so-called Harberger triangle (the net consumer surplus lost as a result of the artificial raising of consumer prices by the tariff) but also the whole of the tariff revenue. For in a competitive market (including that for political goods) economic agents would lobby for the revenues associated with tariff protection. With perfect competition amongst these rent seekers, the whole value of the perceived rents or revenues would be competed away, with the rent seekers (in aggregate) wastefully spending (in time or financial resources like bribes) the full expected value of the rents. Chapter 20 by Anne Krueger is a fuller development of this rent-seeking model with applications to the control regimes in Turkey and India.

In a series of papers Bhagwati has rechristened and extended the notion of rent-seeking. Chapter 21 by Bhagwati, Brecher and Srinivasan demonstrates the wide relevance of what he calls directly unproductive activities (DUP), and integrates the notion into the standard general equilibrium model of international trade. (For further developments including critiques of the rent-seeking and DUP approaches, readers might refer to two collections of essays, Rowley, Tollison and Tullock (eds) (1988) and Collander (ed.) (1984)).

Finally, Chapter 22, by the editor and Rajapatirana critically surveys the empirical studies that have sought to adjudicate in the continuing controversies surrounding the appropriate trade regime for developing countries.

Stabilization in an Open Economy

The Real Exchange Rate, the Balance of Payments and the Dutch Disease.

Perceived problems in dealing with the balance of payments were a major reason, in practice, for the institution of exchange control regimes in most developing countries. Balance of payments disequilibria can occur because of various internal or external shocks to the economy. There has been much confusion about the role of exchange rate changes in the subsequent process of adjustment. Volume IV begins with a seminal article by Salter (Chapter 1) which clarifies the process and sets out what has come to be called the Australian model of a small open economy. This model distinguishes between traded and non-traded goods and makes their relative price (or its inverse) the 'real exchange rate', a key determinant in the process of balance of payments adjustment. Salter also provides a simple diagram which is a valuable pedagogical tool in thinking about the multifaceted problems associated with the causes of, and cures for balance of payments disequilibria in a simple general equilibrium framework.

During the turbulent period in the world economy during the 1970s and 1980s, and with the onset of the Third World debt crisis, problems of stabilization came to the forefront of policy concern in many developing countries. Both the World Bank and the IMF were increasingly called in to design and finance so-called stabilization and structural adjustment programmes. These combined liberalization of trade and financial markets with macroeconomic stabilization of the economy. Chapter 2 provides a simple analytical framework which combines the Australian model of 'real' adjustment with a simple model of the monetary economy to allow the real effects of these stabilization and structural adjustment programmes to be assessed. A fuller and more general treatment of the determinants of that key relative price – the real exchange rate – in the adjustment process is provided in Edwards, Chapter 3. Also see his more comprehensive treatment in Edwards (1989).

The Australian model is also useful in thinking through the consequences of what has been called the Dutch Disease, which infected many developing countries (and developed ones too, for example, the UK and Holland, with their large oil and natural gas based windfalls). This disease refers to the effects of foreign exchange windfalls – large rises in oil or other primary commodity prices, large foreign aid inflows, or capital inflows based on remittances of migrant workers in the Gulf are the major sources in developing countries – on the real exchange rate and thence on the structure of production in the domestic economy. Corden and Neary (1982) is the seminal article which provides a rigorous framework for thinking through the problems that arise in the rest of the economy with a boom in the traded goods sector. Chapter 4 by Corden provides a succinct review of the literature on the Dutch Disease.

Inflation, Stabilization and Liberalization

The establishment of an independent central bank and the associated monetary independence was seen as a hallmark of political independence by most developing countries. On gaining independence most ex-colonies eschewed the rigid 'gold standard' type monetary arrangements, represented for instance by the colonial currency board systems (see Walters (1987) for a concise discussion), in favour of monetary systems where domestic monetary conditions no longer reflected the developments in the country's balance of payments. In practice this allowed the Treasury to obtain access to the Central Bank's printing presses, which led in many countries to historically unprecedented rates of inflation. Furthermore, with the purported aim of directing investment into socially productive lines, credit was rationed administratively through various devices leading to what has been called a financially repressed economy (see Mckinnon (1973), Shaw (1973)). With real interest rates for depositors being kept artificially low, and with a wide dispersion in effective real rates for borrowers, both the level of domestic savings and the allocation of investment were adversely affected (see Fry (1978 and 1982) and the useful collection of essays in Coats and Khatkhate (1980)).

In the 1980s, particularly in the context of the debt crisis and the adoption of various IMF and World Bank programmes, many countries (particularly in Latin America) sought to liberalize their economies through programmes which liberalized repressive trade regimes, reduced financial repression, removed price controls, privatized or closed loss making public enterprises and also sought macroeconomic stability through eliminating budget deficits, controlling the money supply and maintaining realistic exchange rates. An important issue thrown up by these reform efforts has been that of the proper sequencing of these various reforms of a repressed economy. There were few unequivocal success stories, and even in the two most notable cases – Chile and Bolivia – it took a long time to set their houses in order (see Edwards and Edwards (1987) for a discussion of the Chilean, and Sachs and Morales (1988) for the Bolivian stabilization and liberalization programmes).

Nevertheless, particularly in Latin America and amongst theorists of a structuralist perspective, the older debates about the structural causes of inflation in the course of development and the need for so-called 'heterodox' stabilization programmes continues. (For a recent statement of this viewpoint see Taylor (1988)). The readings in this section provide some of the flavour of a burgeoning literature on these issues of inflation, stabilization and liberalization.

Chapter 5 by Harberger presents a lucid outline of what can be termed the 'monetarist' argument about the causes and consequences of inflation. Chapter 6 by Olivera presents the clearest theoretical statement of the alternative structuralist diagnosis. Chapter 7 by Corbo and de Melo is a succinct summary of the reasons for the differing outcomes of the various reform efforts undertaken since the 1970s in the countries of the Southern Cone in Latin America (also see Edwards and Teitel (eds) (1986)). Finally Chapter 8, by Lal, attempts to explain in terms of the 'new' political economy, why countries get into the 'crises' which require drastic treatment in the first place, and also discusses the conditions under which a successful liberalization is likely to be undertaken. It also discusses the correct sequencing of the various reforms within the standard liberalization package. Edwards (1984), and Choksi and Papageorgiou (eds) (1986) should be consulted for more detailed discussions of the sequencing issue and for a contrary viewpoint.

Commodity Price Instability

Since the collapse of primary commodity prices during the Great Depression, apart from the fears about a secular decline in their terms of trade, developing countries have also been concerned about the volatility in the prices of primary commodities. It has been claimed that the resulting instability of export earnings impedes growth. This has led to calls for developing countries, even with a comparative advantage in producing primary commodities, to delink themselves from the world economy and/or to establish international buffer stock type commodity agreements to stabilize international commodity prices. The first option was recommended (but only in part because of the problem of export earnings instability) by the 'dependencia' theorists (on which more below). The second was the centrepiece of what became the demand under the aegis of UNCTAD (in the 1970s) for the establishment of a worldwide commodity price stabilization scheme under the banner of the Common Fund.

Mcbean (1966) was an important early study which questioned the adverse effects on growth of primary commodity price and export earnings instability. Chapter 9 by Brundell et al. extends an earlier statistical study by Massell (1970) and finds that instability of export earnings is explained as much by the inward looking policies pursued by many developing countries, as the structuralist factors emphasized by many development economists.

UNCTAD was dominated by the latter viewpoint, ever since its inception under Prebisch's leadership. It went on in the 1970s to promote an integrated programme for primary commodities as part of the Third World's demand for a New International Economic Order (NIEO). A thorough analysis of this scheme is in Newberry and Stiglitz (1981). Chapter 10 presents their theoretical framework for analysing the impact of price stabilization rules, and its links to earlier analyses. (Also see Henderson and Lal (1976) for a critical evaluation of the UNCTAD proposals.) The conclusions of their massive book on the subject are worth quoting:

> . . . although the market does not necessarily provide an efficient allocation of resources, we believe that the gains to be had from a commodity price stabilisation program are likely to be small, and that most of the benefits in risk reduction maybe had by improving the workings of the market, for example, by making futures markets more readily accessible (directly or indirectly) to small producers. This is not to say that a commodity programme will have little extra effect compared with improving the working of the market, for it may have quite different distributional consequences, but it does say that commodity programmes are likely to be a relatively expensive way of improving efficiency. (Newberry and Stiglitz (1981), p.445).

Besides stabilizing prices around a given trend, the UNCTAD commodities programme also aimed to raise the trend price of primary commodities. If a successful cartel of primary commodity producers could be organized on the lines of OPEC, then on optimum tariff grounds a case could be made for the co-ordinated exercise of the exporters monopoly power in foreign trade. Its success would however depend upon the acceptance of supply restrictions by the cartel's members. This, as the example of OPEC amply demonstrates, has been the Achilles heel of such cartels, because of the incentives to cheat on their supply quotas by the cartel's members. Henderson and Lal (1976) provide an alternative which may be more incentive-compatible to achieve the same end, namely an agreed set of national export taxes on the relevant commodities. However, despite the passions aroused, the practical relevance of these schemes, devised to exercise the collective monopoly power of Third World primary product exporters, is likely to be limited, partly because of the limited number of commodities it would be feasible to cover, and in part because of past diversification few Third World countries exports are currently dominated by primary products.

Foreign Capital

The role of foreign capital – both commercial flows and concessional aid – in promoting development has aroused controversy throughout the post-war decades. Chapter 11 by the editor surveys the earlier literature on the purported effects of both direct foreign investment and foreign aid – the principal forms of capital inflows into developing countries until the first oil price rise of 1973.[11]

With the emergence of large current account surpluses in OPEC countries after 1973 – which they placed on deposit in Western commercial banks – there was an explosion of commercial bank lending to Third World countries, particularly in Latin America, in the 1970s. Much of this borrowing was at variable interest rates by governments or underwritten by them. These sovereign loans turned sour when the deflation of the late 1970s led to an unprecedented rise in world interest rates, and a decline in primary product prices flowing from the reduction in global demand. Mexico's moratorium on its debt repayments in 1982 precipitated the 'debt crisis' which has continued ever since to haunt many developed country commercial banks, their governments and those in borrowing countries.

There has been a continuing debate about the merits of some form of debt forgiveness, based on the notion that the debt crisis was due to the inability rather than the unwillingness to pay of sovereign borrowers. Chapter 12 by Eaton, Gersovitz and Stiglitz provides a lucid analysis of the economics of sovereign debt. They show why it is to be expected that a country will be unwilling to pay its sovereign loans well before they are unable to do so. Studies of the debt crisis have burgeoned. Mention may be made of Smith and Cuddington (eds) (1985), Cline (1984), and Sachs (ed.) (1989) amongst others.

Chapters 13 to 15 all deal with foreign aid, which remains highly controversial. The rationale for foreign aid has changed over the years. Humanitarian, political and purely economic justifications have been provided for transferring capital on concessionary terms through bilateral or multilateral official agencies to Third World governments. As a result of the widespread defaults on Third World bonds in the 1930s, Western capital markets were in effect shut to developing country borrowers after the Second World War. The US 'blue sky' laws forbade US financial intermediaries from holding foreign government bonds, whilst most European markets were closed by pervasive exchange controls. This provided some justification for official flows (to overcome this artificial closing of commercial markets to developing countries) but at *commercial interest rates*.

As the political and humanitarian arguments, as well as economic ones – based for instance on the purported existence of the foreign exchange bottleneck – for foreign aid have become weaker over the years, a new economic argument for official flows has been developed. This is based on the need to overcome the cessation of private capital flows because of the 'debt overhang' in many highly indebted countries, and the difficulty in practice of separating the commitments flowing from 'old' to 'new' debt. Chapter 13 by Krueger outlines this economic argument for official flows at commercial rates, as well as that for concessional official aid based on the difficulties encountered by countries with weak fiscal systems in financing the social and physical infrastructure which is required in the process of development.

Chapter 14 by Bauer and Yamey presents a sceptical view of the benefits of foreign aid. They argue that far from being productive, because of the politicization of domestic and international economic life it inexorably promotes, foreign aid erodes the basic individualistic economic framework for efficient development which promotes entrepreneurship, productivity, and thrift – the mainsprings of growth.

With growing 'aid fatigue' amongst donors, a number of recent attempts have been made to assess the economic benefits of past foreign aid, and to counter the arguments of the critics (see Cassen et al. (1986), Mosley (1987), Krueger, Michalopoulos and Ruttan (1989), Lele and Nabi (eds) (1991)). Chapter 15 by Mosley is an example of this genre. It finds that 'it is impossible to establish any statistically significant correlation between aid and the growth rate of GNP in developing counries' (ibid, p.636). But with well entrenched aid lobbies and bilateral and multilateral aid bureaucracies, whose self interest demands the continuance of official capital flows to the Third World, this historically peculiar form of capital flow is likely to continue.

Developing Countries in the World Economy

An important tendency in both development theory and practice has been to externalize the problems of developing countries. Neo-imperialism or neo-colonialism have been blamed for their backwardness (as in the dependency literature), or for the supposedly unfair workings of the international economy (as discussed in many of the preceding readings). This tendency culminated in the demand by developing countries under the aegis of the United Nations for a 'New International Economic Order' (NIEO). A report prepared under the chairmanship of the former West German Chancellor Willy Brandt became the major manifesto for the NIEO. Chapter 16 by David Henderson is a critique of its proposals (also see Grassman and Lundberg (eds) (1981), Bhagwati (ed.) (1977), Corden (1979), Lal (1978)).

With the growing acceptance of an outward oriented development strategy, one fear that was voiced (Cline (1982), Streeten (1982)) was that if all developing countries tried to follow the export led growth strategy of the Far Eastern NICs, the developed countries would not allow this surge of Third World imports into their economies. It was claimed that there is a fallacy of composition in generalizing the East Asian experience to the rest of the developing world. Chapter 17 by Ranis is a robust critique of this view.

As we have seen, the links between North and South in an interdependent world economy have been a major concern of development economics since its inception. In fact a whole sub-field of North–South models has mushroomed. (A good survey is by Findlay (1984), who has also been an important contributor to this area.) Chapter 18 by the editor and van Wijnbergen presents a model of these global interactions which emphasizes the financial links that have become important with the growing integration of world capital markets. It emphasizes the impact on the world economy of the competition for world savings between the public sectors in developed and developing countries, and explains changes in global interest rates as well as in the developing country–developed country terms of trade by the consequent global 'crowding out' of investment by public sectors worldwide!

Development Planning

Development planning was a major part of the subject matter of development economics till the mid 1970s. A prima-facie case for systematic government intervention is provided by the theory of market failure. (Arrow (1970) still provides the clearest and most concise account. Also see Sen (1983), Hahn (1984).) There was a famous debate in the 1930s between Lange and Lerner on one side and Hayek and von Mises on the other, about the feasibility of centralized planning (see Hayek (ed.) (1935)). This was prompted by the adoption by the USSR of centralized planning in the inter-war years. Lange (1938) and Lerner (1944) had argued that a planned economy could overcome the unavoidable imperfections of a market economy,[12] by simulating the workings of a competitive economy on their computers and legislating the outcomes through direct administrative controls on the economy. Hayek and von Mises claimed this was a mirage, because no central planner could acquire the requisite information to simulate the workings of a competitive economy, nor would they be able to provide the necessary incentives to achieve productive efficiency by replacing the market with mandarins. Both theory and practice (with the universal collapse of erstwhile centrally planned economies in the late 1980s) have vindicated Hayek and Mises (also see Dasgupta (1980), Lal (1987a)). So in a sense the heat has gone out of the old debates as all three worlds currently rush to the market!

Nevertheless, as public investment remains of importance (and is likely to continue to be so, at least for infrastructure), some rational planning of this investment will be required. Chapter 19 by Manne provides a lucid survey of development planning models developed in the 1950s and 1960s, some of which are still useful in thinking of the perspective planning type problems which are part of the problem of formulating a sensible public sector investment plan.[13]

A second development associated with the planning syndrome of the 1950s and 1960s was the development of complex systems of investment appraisal for public sector investments. Three major systems were promoted: those due to UNIDO (Dasgupta, Marglin and Sen (1972), Little and Mirrlees (1974), and Harberger (1972)). A comparison of these various methods is provided in Lal (1974), whilst Dreze and Stern (1987) and Squire (1989) provide general surveys of the subsequent literature, and Little and Mirrlees (1991) provide a reappraisal of their methodology and its contemporary relevance.

All these systems sought robust second-best rules for shadow pricing inputs and outputs in economies where there are both policy induced (trade protection, price controls) and endogenous (dualistic labour markets) distortions in the working of the price mechanism. After all the heat and dust that the technical discussion of the rival merits of these various brands raised, one robust second-best rule which emerged was for the valuation of traded commodities (even in highly protected economies) – the so-called 'world prices rule' due to Little and Mirrlees.[14] Chapter 20 by Srinivasan and Bhagwati examines the validity of this rule in the standard trade-theoretic framework and shows its robustness as compared with various other investment criteria that have been proposed.

Finally, Chapter 21 by Wellisz is a *tour de horizon* of the theory and practice of planning in its heyday, and an early statement of the view that planning needs to be confined to the rational deployment of macroeconomic policy instruments and the provision of those public goods which only the State can provide – internal and external security, a legal system for delineating and enforcing property rights, and possibly social overhead capital in the form of public health and education.

One offshoot of the second-best welfare economics underlying the project evaluation rules developed in the early 1970s, was the recognition that they were relevant for the determination of the pricing policies of public enterprises as well as in the design of fiscal policy (see Little and Scott (1976), Lal (1980a), (1980b)). The fullest development of this strand of the planning literature is in Newberry and Stern (1987), and applications are in Ahmad and Stern (1991). The optimal tax rules due to Ramsey (1927), which flow from this literature are based on the notion of the neutrality of taxation – in the sense of reducing the deadweight consumer surplus losses associated with any form of non-lump sum taxation. By contrast there is an older classical definition of neutrality recently championed by Harberger (1987) which questions the desirability of the Ramsey optimal tax rules. Moreover, once the assumption that the State implementing these optimal taxes consists of Platonic Guardians is questioned, then such revenue-maximizing taxation will not be in the interests of citizens as the 'new' political economy has shown (see Brennan and Buchanan (1980), Lal (1990)). But this leads on to an area which is currently on the frontiers of research, and which is discussed briefly in the next section.

Political Economy and Institutions

The disenchantment with planning has been paralleled by a growing awareness amongst development economists that the implicit assumptions about the character of the State on which this case for planning within the 'welfare economics' framework was predicated is not universally valid. These assumptions concerned the omniscience, omnipotence and most importantly the benevolence of governments. The technical debates concerning the feasibility of planning had already provided sufficient reason to question the omniscience of governments, if for no other reason than the recognition of the irreducible uncertainty surrounding any investment which necessarily entails giving hostages to fortune. The obvious difficulties that governments of developing countries had in enforcing controls and even in raising taxes (see Kaldor (1963)) shattered any belief in their omnipotence, even if they were authoritarian. But the really important question mark over their presumed character concerns their benevolence.

This is where the 'new' political economy is of importance. It takes a more even-handed view of the motives of the State and its citizens. It extends the same self-regarding motives ascribed by economists to producers and consumers to their governors. This surprisingly has considerable explanatory power as Chapter 22 by Findlay on the nascent applications of the 'new' political economy to developing countries shows.[15]

The new institutional economics is another major recent development which is being applied fruitfully to developing countries. We have already examined one strand of this literature in the context of rural institutions in Volume I. This strand provides a rationale for various institutions within the context of the economics of imperfect information. Stiglitz (1986) provides a summary of the findings of this research effort. An equally important strand of the new institutional economics has developed from the 'transactions costs' (and property rights) approach (see Coase (1988), Demsetz (1967), North and Thomas (1973), Williamson (1985)). (A useful collection of essays on the economics of property rights is Furubotn and Pejovich (1974).) One of the major proponents of this approach, who has also applied it to economic history is Douglas North. Chapter 23 provides a succinct summary of the application of this framework in explaining the divergent institutional development of the USA and Latin America. Finally, Chapter 24 by Bardhan both puts the new institutional economics into perspective (in terms of Walrasian theory) and also provides a critique.

The readings in this last section should demonstrate the continuing intellectual excitement that the economics of developing countries can provoke. More than most subdisciplines in economics, it is still concerned with nearly all the Grand Questions of social science. Given the obvious interactions between political, social and economic factors, in the process of development, its study necessarily forces interdisciplinary thoughts – of thinking as a social scientist and not merely as an economist! It thus redresses some of the narrow specialization which since the Second World War has splintered the social sciences into narrow compartments.

In his famous memorial to Alfred Marshall, Keynes wrote:

> Good or even competent economists are the rarest of birds. An easy subject, at which very few excel! The paradox finds its explanation, perhaps, in that the master-economist must possess a rare *combination* of gifts . . . He must be mathematician, historian, statesman, philosopher – in some degree. He must understand symbols and speak in words. He must contemplate the particular in terms of the general, and touch abstract and concrete in the same flight of thought. He must study the present in the light of the past for the purposes of the future. No part of man's nature or his institutions must lie entirely outside his regard. He must be purposeful and disinterested in a simultaneous mood; as aloof and incorruptible as an artist, yet sometimes near the earth as a politician. (Keynes (1925), p.12)

Of no part of economics is this more true than development economics.

Notes

1. A compact diagrammatical analysis of the modern theory of the gains from trade, which also incorporates the case of a large country which can influence its terms of trade, and which should levy the optimal tariff is Baldwin (1952).
2. A term invented by Ian Little for its obvious ironic reference!
3. In a two-good model of an open economy as Lerner (1936) demonstrated, a tax on imports is equivalent to a tax on exports and *vice versa*, as both lower the relative price of exports to imports.
4. There is also a neo-Marxist literature on trade and development. One strand argues that such trade must involve unequal exchange, see Emmanuel (1972). A devastating critique is in Samuelson (1976). Another strand argues that such trade leads to dependency, hence the South should delink from the North. The proponents of this view amongst others are Amin (1976), Frank (1967), Cardoso and Faletto (1979). A critique of their views from the Left is in Smith (1980), and Warren (1973) whilst Diaz-Alejandro (1978) provides a critique from a more mainstream position.
5. For further elaboration of the model see Raj and Sen (1961).
6. Also see Cairncross (1962) for a very sensible evaluation of the *dirigisme* being propounded in the 1950s.
7. See Corden (1971) for a comprehensive discussion of the theory of protection.
8. See for instance A. Amsden (1989), R. Wade (1990). Well may the liberal economist sigh with Shakespeare's Antonio: 'The Devil can cite scripture for his purpose', (The Merchant of Venice)!
9. A clear and accessible account of the conclusions drawn by the trade theoretic literature on the gains from trade when there are increasing returns and imperfect competition is in Markusen and Melvin (1984).
10. The other comparative studies initiated as part of the same research programme at the World Bank and currently completed or nearing completion are on agricultural pricing (whose preliminary results are reported in Reading 28 in Volume 2 of these readings), on the political economy of poverty, equity and growth (Lal and Myint (1991)) and on macro-economic adjustment (being codirected by R. Cooper, M. Corden, I. Little and S. Rajapatirana).

11. See Lal (1990) for a more recent survey of capital flows and development, which also considers the burgeoning literature associated with the 'debt crisis' of the 1980s in the Third World.
12. These imperfections were unavoidable because of the impossibility of creating complete markets for all commodities, indexed by time, place and state of nature – which is required for a *laissez-faire* economy to be Pareto-efficient.
13. Though whether there is *any* role for public investment, even in infrastructure remains an open question. See the excellent book by Roth (1987) which shows how many of the traditional public utilities and services could be and have been privatized at various times and places in the past.
14. For my own afterword on what has emerged from these debates on project evaluation see Lal (1987b).
15. My own attempts at using the insights of the 'new' political economy are in Lal (1988) (1989a and b) and Lal and Myint (1991). A stimulating historical application of the 'endogenous tariff' type political economy theorizing to various historical situations in currently developed countries by a political scientist is Rogowski (1989). Other important work in this genre is by Bates (1981 and 1983). Also see the collection of essays in Bates (ed.) (1988) and Stigler (ed.) (1988).

References

Ahmad, E. and Stern, N.H. (1991), *Tax Reform and Development*, Cambridge.

Amin, S. (1976), *Unequal Development*, Sussex: Harvester.

Amsden, A. (1989), *Asia's Next Giant: South Korea and Late Industrialisation*, New York: Oxford University Press.

Arrow, K.J. (1970), 'Political and economic evaluation of social effects and externalities' in J. Margolis (ed.), *The Analysis of Public Output*, Columbia, New York: NBER.

Balassa, B. (1971), *The Structure of Protection in Developing Countries*, Baltimore: Johns Hopkins University Press.

Baldwin, R.E. (1952), 'The New Welfare Economics and gains in international trade', *Quarterly Journal of Economics*, LXVI (1), February, 91–101, reprinted in Caves and Johnson (eds) (1968).

Balogh, T. (1963), *Unequal Partners*, 2 vols, Oxford: Blackwells.

Bates, R. (1981), *Markets and States in Tropical Africa*, Berkeley: University of California Press.

Bates, R. (1983), *Essays on the Political Economy of Rural Africa*, Cambridge.

Bates, R. (ed.) (1988), *Towards a Political Economy of Development*, Berkeley: University of California Press.

Baumol, W.J. and Oates, W.E. (1975), *The Theory of Environmental Policy*, New York: Prentice-Hall.

Bell, M., Ross-Larsen, B. and Westphal, L.E. (1984), 'Assessing the performance of infant industries', *Journal of Development Economics*, 16, Sept/Oct.

Bhagwati, J.N. (1956), 'Immiserising Growth: A geometrical note', *Review of Economic Studies*, June.

Bhagwati, J.N. (1966), 'The nature of balance of payments difficulties in developing countries' in *Measures for Trade Expansion of Developing Countries*, Tokyo: Japan Economic Research Centre.

Bhagwati, J. (ed.) (1977), *The New International Economic Order*, Cambridge, Mass: MIT.

Bhagwati, J. (1979), *Anatomy and Consequences of Trade Control Regimes*, Cambridge, Mass: NBER, Ballinger.

Bhagwati, J. and P. Desai (1970), *India – Planning for Industrialisation*, Oxford.

Bhagwati, J. et al. (eds) (1971), *Trade, Balance of Payments and Growth*, Amsterdam: North Holland.

Bhagwati, J. and Srinivasan, T.N. (1975), *Foreign Trade Regimes and Economic Development – India*, Columbia, New York: NBER.

Blackhurst, R., Marion, N. and Tumlir, J. (1977), *Trade Liberalisation, Protectionism and Interdependence*, GATT studies in International Trade, No.5, November, Geneva: GATT.

Blackhurst, R., Marion, N. and Tumlir, J. (1978), *Adjustment, Trade and Growth in Developed and Developing Countries*, GATT studies in international trade no.6, September, Geneva: GATT.

Brennan, G. and Buchanan, J.M. (1980), *The Power to Tax*, Cambridge.

Bruton, H. (1969), 'The two-gap approach to aid and development', *American Economic Review*, **59**, June, 439–46.

Buchanan, J.M., and Tullock, G. (1962), *The Calculus of Consent*, Michigan: Ann Arbour.

Cairncross, A. (1962), *Factors in Economic Development*, London: Allen and Unwin.

Cardoso, F.H. and Faletto, L. (1979), *Dependency and Development in Latin America*, Berkeley: University of California.

Cassen, R., et al. (1986), *Does Aid Work?*, Oxford: Clarendon Press.

Caves, R.E. and Johnson, H.G. (1968), *Readings in International Economics*, American Economic Association, London: Allen and Unwin.

Chenery, H. and Strout, A.M. (1966), 'Foreign Assistance and Economic Development', *American Economic Review*, **56**, September, 679–733.

Choksi, A. and Papageorgiou, D. (eds) (1986), *Economic Liberalisation in Developing Countries*, Oxford: Blackwell.

Cline, W.R. (1982), 'Can the East Asian model of development be generalised?', *World Development*, **10** (2), February, 81–90.

Cline, W.R. (1984), *International Debt: systemic risk and policy response*, Washington DC: Institute for International Economics.

Coase, R. (1988), *The Firm, the Market and the Law*, Chicago.

Coats, W.L. and Khatkhate, D.R. (eds) (1980), *Money and Monetary Policy in Less Developed Countries*, Oxford: Pergamon.

Collander, D.C. (ed.) (1984), *Neoclassical Political Economy*, Cambridge, Mass: Ballinger.

Corden, W.M. (1971), *The Theory of Protection*, Oxford: Clarendon Press.

Corden, W.M. (1974), *Trade Policy and Economic Welfare*, Oxford.

Corden, W.M. (1979), *The NIEO Proposals: A Cool Look*, Thames Essays No.21, London: Trade Policy Research Centre.

Corden, W.M. and Neary P. (1982), 'Booming sector and de-industrialisation in a small open economy', *Economic Journal*, **92**, December, 825–48.

Dasgupta, P. (1980), 'Decentralisation and Rights', *Economica*, **47** (2), May, 107–23.

Dasgupta, P., Marglin, S. and Sen, A.K. (1972), *Guidelines for Project Evaluation*, UNIDO, New York: United Nations.

Demsetz, H. (1967), 'Toward a theory of property rights', *American Economic Review*, **57**, May, 347–59, reprinted in Furubotn and Pejovich (eds) (1974).

Diaz-Alejandro, C. (1978), 'Delinking North and South: Unshackled or Unhinged' in A. Fishlow et al., *Rich and Poor Nations in the World Economy*, New York: McGraw Hill.

Domar, E. (1957), *Essays in the Theory of Economic Growth*, New York: Oxford University Press.

Dreze, J. and Stern, N.H. (1987), 'The theory of cost-benefit analysis', in A. Auerbach and M. Feldstein (eds), *Handbook of Public Economics*, Amsterdam: North Holland.

Edwards, S. (1984), *The Order of liberalisation of the external sector*, Princeton Essays in International Finance, No.156, International Finance Section, Princeton.

Edwards, S. (1989), *Real Exchange Rates, Devaluation and Adjustment – exchange rate policy in developing countries*, Cambridge, Mass: MIT.

Edwards, S. and Edwards, A.C. (1987), *Monetarism and Liberalisation – the Chilean experience*, Cambridge, Mass: Ballinger.

Edwards, S. and Larrain, F. (eds) (1989), *Debt, Adjustment and Recovery: Latin America's Prospects for Growth and Development*, Oxford: Blackwell.

Edwards, S. and Teitel, S. (eds) (1986), 'Growth, Reform and Adjustment: Latin America's trade and macroeconomic policies in the 1970s and 1980s', *Economic Development and Cultural Change*, **34** (3), April.

Emmanuel, A. (1972), *Unequal Exchange*, New York: Monthly Review Press.

Findlay, R. (1984), 'Growth and Development in trade Models', in R.W. Jones and P.B. Kenen (eds), *Handbook of International Economics*, **1**, Amsterdam: North Holland.

Frank, A.G. (1967), *Capitalism and Underdevelopment in Latin America*, New York: Monthly Review Press.

Fry, M.J. (1978), 'Money and capital or financial deepening in economic development?', *Journal of Money, Credit and Banking*, **10** (4), November, 465–72.

Fry, M.J. (1982), 'Models of financially repressed developing economies', *World Development*, September.

Furubotn, E.G. and Pejovich, S. (eds) (1974), *The Economics of Property Rights*, Cambridge, Mass: Ballinger.

Grassman, S. and Lundberg, E. (eds) (1981), *The World Economic Order: Past and Present*, London: Macmillan.

Harberler, G. (1950), 'Some problems in the pure theory of international trade', *Economic Journal*, LX, June, 223–40, reprinted in Caves and Jones (eds) (1968).

Haberler, G. (1959), *International Trade and Economic Development*, 50th Anniversary Commemorative Lectures, National Bank of Egypt, Cairo, 1959. Reprinted (1988) with a new introduction, International Centre for Economic Growth, San Francisco: ICS press.

Hahn, F.H. (1984), 'Reflections on the Invisible Hand', in his *Equilibrium and Macroeconomics*, Oxford: Blackwell.

Harberger, A.C. (1959), 'The fundamentals of economic progress in underdeveloped countries: using the resources at hand more effectively', *American Economic Review*, 49 (42), 134–46.

Harberger, A.C. (1971), 'Three basic postulates for applied welfare economics: an interpretative essay', *Journal of Economic Literature*, 9, 785–97.

Harberger, A.C. (1972), *Project Evaluation*, Chicago.

Harberger, A.C. (1987), 'Neutral taxation', in Eatwell, Milgrom and Newman (eds), *The New Palgrave*, London: Macmillan.

Hayek, F.A. (ed.) (1935), *Collectivist Economic Planning*, London, Routledge.

Helliner, G. (1985), 'Industrial Organisation, Trade and investment: a selective literature review for developing countries', paper presented at conference on 'Industrial organisation, trade and investment in N. America', Mexico: Merida.

Henderson, P.D. and Lal, D. (1976), 'UNCTAD IV, the commodity problem and international economic reform', *ODI Review*, no.2.

Hicks, J.R. (1965), *Capital and Growth*, Oxford: Clarendon Press.

Johnson, H.G. (1953), 'Optimum tariffs and retaliation', *Review of Economic Studies*, XXI (55), 142–53, reprinted (1958), in his *International Trade and Economic Growth*, London: Allen and Unwin.

Johnson, H.G. (1965), 'Optimal trade interventions in the presence of domestic distortions' in R. Baldwin et al. (eds), *Trade, Growth and the Balance of Payments*, Chicago.

Johnson, H.G. (1968), *Comparative Cost and Commercial Policy – theory for a Developing World Economy*, Wicksell lectures 1968, Stockholm: Almqvist and Wiksell.

Jones, R.W. (1971), 'A three factor model in theory, trade and history' in J. Bhagwati et al. (eds).

Kaldor, N. (1963), 'Will underdeveloped countries learn to tax?', *Foreign Affairs*, January, reprinted (1964), in his *Essays in Economic Policy*, London: Duckworth.

Keynes, J.M. (1925), 'Alfred Marshall' in A.C. Pigou (ed.), *Memorials of Alfred Marshall*, London: Macmillan.

Krueger, A.O. (1977), *Growth, Distortions and Patterns of Trade Among Many Countries*, Princeton Studies in International Finance, no.40, Princeton: International Finance Section.

Krueger, A.O. (1978), *Liberalisation Attempts and Consequences*, NBER, Cambridge, Mass: Ballinger.

Krueger, A.O. (1983), *Trade and Employment in Developing Countries 3 – Synthesis and Conclusions*, Chicago: NBER.

Krueger, A.O., Michalopoulos, C. and Ruttan, V. (1989), *Aid and Development*, Baltimore: Johns Hopkins University Press.

Lal, D. (1974), *Methods of Project Analysis*, World Bank Occasional Papers No. 16, Baltimore: Johns Hopkins University Press.

Lal, D. (1978), *Poverty, Power and Prejudice – the North–South Confrontation*, Fabian Research Series No. 340, London: Fabian Society.

Lal, D. (1980a), *Prices for Planning*, London: Heinemann Educational Books.

Lal, D. (1980b), 'Public Enterprises' in J. Cody, H. Hughes, and D. Wall (eds), *Policies for Industrial*

Progress in developing countries, Oxford.

Lal, D. (1983), *The Poverty of 'Development Economics'*, Hobart paperback no.16, Institute of Economic Affairs, London, and expanded edition, 1985, Harvard.

Lal, D. (1987a), 'Markets, mandarins and mathematicians', *The Cato Journal*, **7** (1), 43–70.

Lal, D. (1987b), 'Comment' on A.C. Harberger's Pioneers lecture, in G.M. Meier (ed.), *Pioneers in Development*, 2nd series, New York: Oxford University Press.

Lal, D. (1988), *The Hindu Equilibrium*, 2 vols, Oxford: Clarendon Press.

Lal, D. (1989a), 'After the Debt crisis: Modes of Development for the longer run in Latin America', in Edwards and Larrain (eds).

Lal, D. (1989b), 'The political economy of industrialisation in primary product exporting economies: some cautionary tales', in N. Islam (ed.), *The Balance between Industry and Agriculture in Economic Development*, **5** – *Factors influencing change*, International Economic Association, London: Macmillan.

Lal, D. (1990a), *Fighting Fiscal Privilege – towards a fiscal constitution*, SMF paper no.7, London: Social Market Foundation.

Lal, D. (1990b), 'International Capital flows and economic development', in Scott and Lal (eds) (1990).

Lal, D. and H. Myint (1991), 'The Political Economy of Poverty, Equity and Growth', mimeo, London.

Lange, O. and Taylor, F.M. (1938), *On the Economic Theory of Socialism*, Univ. of Minnesota, reprinted 1964, McGraw Hill.

Leamer, E. (1987), 'Paths of development in the three factor n good general equilibrium model', *Journal of Political Economy*, **95** (5), October.

Lele, U. and Nabi, I. (eds) (1991), *Transitions in Development – the role of aid and commercial flows*, International Centre for Economic Growth, San Francisco: ICS Press.

Lerner, A.P. (1936), 'The symmetry between import and export taxes', *Economica*, **3** (11), August, 306–13.

Lerner, A.P. (1944), *The Economics of Control*, London: Macmillan.

Lipsey, R.E. (1963), *Price and Quantity Trends in the Foreign Trade of the United States*, Princeton.

Little, I.M.D. (1982), *Economic Development*, New York: Basic Books.

Little, I.M.D. and Mirrlees, J.A. (1974), *Project Appraisal and Planning for Developing Countries*, London: Heinemann Educational Books.

Little, I.M.D. and Mirrlees, J.A. (1990), 'Project appraisal and planning twenty years on', *Proceedings of the World Bank Annual Conference on Development Economics, 1990*, 351–82.

Little, I.M.D., Scitovsky, T. and Scott, M.Fg. (1970), *Industry and Trade in Some Developing Countries*, Oxford.

Little, I.M.D. and Scott, M.Fg. (eds) (1976), *Using Shadow Prices*, London: Heinemann Educational Books.

Markusen, J. and Melvin, J. (1984), 'The gains from trade theorem with increasing returns to scale' in H. Kierzkowski (ed.), *Monopolistic Competition and International Trade*, Oxford: Clarendon Press.

Massell, B.F. (1970), 'Export Instability and economic structure', *American Economic Review*, **60** (4), September, 618–30.

McBean, A. (1966), *Export Instability and Economic Develoment*, Cambridge, Mass: Harvard.

Mckinnon, R. (1964), 'Foreign exchange constraints in economic development', *Economic Journal*, June.

Mckinnon, R. (1973), *Money and Capital in Economic Development*, Washington DC: Brookings.

Meade, J.E. (1955), *Trade and Welfare*, Oxford.

Michaely, M., Papageorgiou, D. and Choksi, A. (1991), *Lessons of Experience in the Developing World*, Oxford: Blackwell.

Mosley, P. (1987), *Overseas Aid*, Brighton: Wheatsheaf.

Mueller, D.C. (1979), *Public Choice*, Cambridge.

Myrdal, G. (1958), *Economic Theory and Underdeveloped Regions*, Bombay: Vora and Co.

Newberry, D.M.G. and Stern, N.H. (eds) (1987), *The Theory of Taxation for Developing Countries*, New York: Oxford University Press.

Newberry, D.M.G. and Stiglitz, J.E. (1981), *The Theory of Commodity Price Stabilisation*, Oxford: Clarendon Press.

North, D. and Thomas, R. (1973), *The Rise of the Western World*, Cambridge.

Nurkse, R. (1961), *Equilibrium and Growth in the World Economy*, Harvard.

Olson, M. (1965), *The Logic of Collective Action*, Harvard.

Papageorgiou, D., Choksi, A. and Michaely, M. (1990), *Liberalising Foreign Trade in Developing Countries – the lessons of experience*, Washington DC: World Bank.

Prebisch, R. (1959), 'Commercial policy in underdeveloped countries', *American Economic Review*, May.

Raj, K.N. and Sen, A.K. (1961), 'Alternative patterns of growth under conditions of stagnant export earnings', *Oxford Economic Papers*, **13** (1), February, 43–52.

Ramsey, F.P. (1927), 'A contribution to the theory of taxation', *Economic Journal*, **37** (1), March, 47–61.

Rogowski, R. (1989), *Commerce and Coalitions*, Princeton.

Roth, G. (1987), *The Private Provision of public services in developing countries*, New York: Oxford University Press.

Rowley, C.K., Tollison, R.D. and Tullock, G. (eds) (1988), *The Political Economy of Rent-Seeking*, Boston: Kluwer.

Sachs, J. (ed.) (1989), *Developing Country Debt and the World Economy*, Chicago: NBER.

Sachs, J. and Morales, J.A. (1988), *Bolivia: 1960–1986*, International Centre for Economic Growth, San Francisco: ICS Press.

Samuelson, P.A. (1976), 'Illogic of neo-Marxian doctrine of unequal exchange' in D.A. Belsey et al. (eds), *Inflation, Trade and Taxes*, Ohio State University.

Scott, M.Fg. and Lal, D. (eds) (1990), *Public Policy and Economic Development*, Oxford: Clarendon Press.

Sen, A.K. (1983), 'The Profit Motive', *Lloyds Bank Review*, January.

Shaw, E. (1973), *Financial Deepening in Economic Development*, New York: Oxford University Press.

Singer, H. (1950), 'The distribution of gains between borrowing and investing countries', *American Economic Review*, May.

Smith, G.W. and Cuddington, J.T. (eds), (1985), *International Debt and the Developing Countries*, Washington DC: World Bank.

Smith, S. (1980), 'The ideas of Samir Amin: Theory or tautology?', *Journal of Development Studies*, **17** (1), October, 5–21.

Squire, L. (1989), 'Project evaluation in theory and practice', in H. Chenery and T.N. Srinivasan (eds), *Handbook of Development Economics*, **2**, Amsterdam: North Holland.

Stigler, G. (ed.) (1988), *Chicago Essays in Political Economy*, Chicago.

Stiglitz, J. (1986), 'The new development economics', *World Development*, **4** (2), February, 257–65.

Streeten, P. (1982), 'A cool look at "outward-looking" strategies for development', *World Economy*, **5** (1), March, 159–70.

Taylor, L. (1988), *Varieties of Stabilisation Experiences*, Oxford: Clarendon Press.

Tullock, G. (1967), 'Welfare costs of tariffs, monopolies and theft', *Western Economic Journal*, **5**, June, 224–32.

Viner, J. (1953), *International Trade and Economic Development*, Oxford.

Wade, R. (1990), *Governing the Market: Economic Theory and the role of government in East Asian Industrialisation*, Princeton.

Walters, A. (1987), 'Currency Boards', in Eatwell, Milgrom and Newman (eds), *The New Palgrave – A Dictionary of Economics*, London: Macmillan.

Warren, B. (1973), 'Imperialism and Capitalist Accumulation', *New Left Review*, Sept/Oct.

Williamson, O. (1985), *The Economic Institutions of Capitalism*, New York: Free Press.

Part I
Trade and Growth

[1]

The Economic Journal, **87** (*June* 1977), 273–282

Printed in Great Britain

CAPITAL ACCUMULATION IN THE OPEN TWO-SECTOR ECONOMY[1]

The aim of this paper is largely expository. The version of the two-sector model used by Jones (1965) and Caves and Jones (1973, pp. 182–5) is a compact and comprehensible framework in which the standard results of static international trade theory can be demonstrated. By a slight modification to the model, endogenous capital accumulation may be considered, and from one basic relationship it is possible to prove the principal results which have emerged from the recent development of the theory of trade and growth. The golden rule of capital accumulation is naturally of central importance in the analysis, but it turns out that in a large open economy the rule has to be formulated with some care. Some new results on trade and growth in large economies are presented.

I. THE BASIC MODEL

The model is the standard two-sector model, with one of the outputs being a pure investment good, the other being a pure consumption good.

Production levels of the goods are respectively Q_I and Q_C; and I and C denote domestic absorption levels. The investment good is taken as the numeraire, and the price of the consumption good is p. The capital and labour inputs available are K and L; the rental rate on capital is r and the wage rate is w.

A full-employment, perfectly competitive open economy with balanced trade satisfies the following relations:

$$K = a_{KI} Q_I + a_{KC} Q_C, \tag{1}$$

$$L = a_{LI} Q_I + a_{LC} Q_C, \tag{2}$$

$$1 \leqslant r a_{KI} + w a_{LI} \tag{3}$$

with equality if $Q_I > 0$,

$$p \leqslant r a_{KC} + w a_{LC} \tag{4}$$

with equality if $Q_C > 0$,

$$p(C - Q_C) + I - Q_I = 0. \tag{5}$$

Equations (1) and (2) are full-employment conditions; perfect competition requires (3) and (4); and (5) is the statement of balance-of-trade equilibrium. The coefficients a_{MN} measure the amount of input M required in the production of one unit of output Q_N. They are chosen so as to minimise the cost of production, that is they minimise $r a_{KN} + w a_{LN}$ subject to $f^N(a_{KN}, a_{LN}) = 1$, where f^N is the constant-returns-to-scale production function of Q_N. Optimal choice of technique is easily shown to give rise to the equations

$$0 = r \, da_{KN} + w \, da_{LN} \quad (N = I, C) \tag{6}$$

[1] I am grateful for helpful comments on an earlier version of this paper from John Black and John Martin.

(which hold trivially in the case of no choice of technique), so that changes in p, r and w must satisfy

$$0 = dra_{KI} + dwa_{LI} \tag{7}$$

if $Q_I > 0$, and

$$dp = dra_{KC} + dwa_{LC} \tag{8}$$

if $Q_C > 0$; these equations being obtained from the total differentiation of (3) and (4) and from (6).

The value of national income is

$$Y = I + pC \tag{9}$$

$$= Q_I + pQ_C \tag{10}$$

$$= rK + wL, \tag{11}$$

where (10) follows from (5), and (11) from (1)–(4). The labour force grows exogenously at the rate n, so steady state requires investment at a level which makes the capital stock grow at the rate n also:

$$I = nK, \tag{12}$$

and from (9), (11) and (12) we have

$$pC = (r - n)K + wL. \tag{13}$$

Taking the total differential of (13) with L constant enables us to compare steady states with different saving rates and different relative prices. (1), (2), (7) and (8) allow the elimination of the input prices:

$$dpC + pdC = (r - n)\,dK + drK + dwL \tag{14}$$

$$= (r - n)\,dK + dpQ_C, \tag{15}$$

which implies

$$pdC = (r - n)\,dK + dp(Q_C - C). \tag{16}$$

This equation plays a central role throughout the paper.

In a closed economy $Q_C = C$, and in an open economy which is so small as to have no influence on its terms of trade $dp/dK = 0$. In either case, (16) implies that across steady states dC/dK has the sign of $(r - n)$, which is the standard "golden rule" result on the effect of capital accumulation on steady state consumption.

In a large open economy, however, a rise in K will lead to an increased net export of the more capital-intensive product, implying an endogenous change in p, so that dC/dK depends not only on $(r - n)$ but also on the "terms of trade effect" $(Q_C - C)\,dp/dK$.

This fact seems first to have been noted by Bertrand (1975). It may seem paradoxical, for the golden rule is accepted as a result of complete generality. There is, however, an interpretation of the apparent paradox as a standard second-best proposition. Free trade is not the optimal trade policy for a large country. If the optimal trading rule is not applied, there is no reason to suppose that the usual rule for optimal savings will continue to be valid. (Negishi (1972, pp. 174–7) has demonstrated in the case of a small country the converse proposition that in the absence of optimal savings, the free-trade rule for optimal trade no longer holds.) What we should expect, however, is that with an optimum tariff, the standard relationship between consumption and capital accumulation will be restored.

The formal argument is as follows. (The derivation of the optimum tariff follows the lines of the analysis in Caves and Jones (1973, pp. 244–7).) Let net exports of the consumption good be $E_C = Q_C - C$, and let the domestic price of the consumption good be π, which will, in general, be different from the world price p. Relationships (1), (2), (3), (5), (6) and (7) continue to apply, but (4) and (8) hold with p replaced by π, which modified relationships are denoted by (4') and (8') below. The value of national income at domestic prices is

$$Y = I + \pi C \tag{17}$$

$$= Q_I + \pi Q_C + (p - \pi)\, E_C \tag{18}$$

$$= rK + wL + (p - \pi)\, E_C, \tag{19}$$

using (5), (3), (4'), (1) and (2). Taking differentials for constant K and L and using (7), (8'), (1) and (2) gives

$$dI + \pi dC = -d\pi C + dr K + dw L + (dp - d\pi)\, E_C + (p - \pi)\, dE_C \tag{20}$$

$$= -d\pi C + d\pi Q_C + (dp - d\pi)\, E_C + (p - \pi)\, dE_C \tag{21}$$

$$= dp E_C + (p - \pi)\, dE_C. \tag{22}$$

The tariff is at its optimal level if the value of income is maximised at domestic prices, which implies $dI + \pi dC = 0$, so that

$$dp E_C + (p - \pi)\, dE_C = 0, \tag{23}$$

an optimum tariff formula which may be more familiar in the form

$$\pi = p + E_C \frac{dp}{dE_C} = \frac{d(p E_C)}{dE_C}, \tag{24}$$

showing the equality of the domestic price ratio and the slope of the foreign offer curve.

In steady state (12) continues to hold but (17) and (19) imply that (13) is replaced by

$$\pi C = (r - n)\, K + wL + (p - \pi)\, E_C \tag{25}$$

so that across steady states

$$\pi dC = -d\pi C + dr K + dw L + dp E_C - d\pi E_C + (r - n)\, dK + (p - \pi)\, dE_C \tag{26}$$

$$= (r - n)\, dK \tag{27}$$

from (21), (22) and (23).

Recalling that the optimum tariff in a small economy is zero, (27) allows us to state a general result that in the comparison of steady states in an open economy *imposing an optimum tariff, dC/dK has the sign of $(r - n)$.*

II. COMPARATIVE DYNAMICS: CAPITAL–LABOUR RATIO CONSTANT

The equation (16) above can form the basis of an analysis of the effects of trade in a two-sector economy under alternative assumptions about capital accumulation. In this section I assume that the capital–labour ratio is the same in trade as in autarky.

In the short run, the inputs K and L are in fixed supply. It is a standard proposition of the two-sector model of production that a rise in the relative price of one good induces an increase in its production. This is usually shown as a shift along

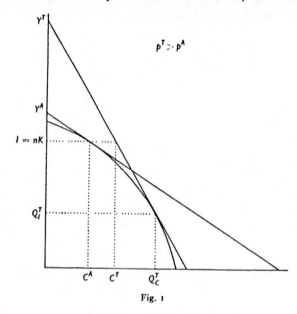

Fig. 1

the transformation curve. A formal proof uses (1)–(4) and the fact that input coefficients are chosen to minimise costs to establish the inequality

$$(p^1 - p^2)(Q_C^1 - Q_C^2) \geqslant 0, \tag{28}$$

which is the desired result, where 1 denotes the situation before and 2 the situation after the relative price change.

Let the world price of the consumption good be p^T and the autarky price be p^A. If initially $p^T > p^A$, so the country has a comparative advantage in the consumption good, then Q_C rises above Q_C^A and Q_I falls below Q_I^A. But if we wish the economy to remain in steady state with the same K/L ratio, (12) requires that I remains the same, so that $Q_I - I$ becomes negative and $Q_C - C$ positive, from (5). Hence (16) with $dK = 0$ shows that as p rises from p^A to p^T, *if* the economy invests just enough to remain in steady state, then consumption is increased by trade. This case is illustrated in Fig. 1.

The same is true, *a fortiori*, if the economy were to impose an optimum tariff. For, if π^0 and p^0 are the domestic and foreign prices when the optimum tariff is imposed, then if the country is a net exporter of consumption goods, it must be the case that $p^O > \pi^O > p^A$, as illustrated in Fig. 2. (26) implies that with K and L constant

$$\pi dC = dp E_C + (p - \pi)\, dE_C \tag{29}$$

and in the movement from autarky to the optimum tariff equilibrium p rises, E_C rises, and $p - \pi$ becomes positive, so that the economy attains steady state with a permanently increased level of consumption.

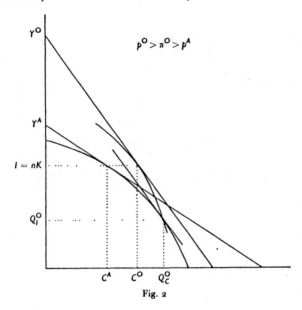

Fig. 2

The fact that these new equilibria, attainable immediately as a result of trade, are steady states and therefore sustainable into the future is a clear indication of the existence of gains from trade. Consumption at every point in time will be higher than on the autarky steady state path.

The alternative case in which $p^T < p^A$ can be analysed similarly. The comparative advantage in the investment good leads Q_C to fall below Q_C^A and Q_I to rise above Q_I^A. $Q_C - C$ becomes negative because $Q_I - I$ becomes positive. Again, equation (16) with $dK = 0$ shows that if the economy is to remain in steady state, consumption will rise; and, again, consumption rises also in the case of an optimum tariff being imposed. These two cases are shown in Figs. 3 and 4.

III. COMPARATIVE DYNAMICS: SAVING RATE CONSTANT

The effect of trade on steady state consumption if the saving rate is the same in trade as in autarky is easy to deduce from the results of the previous section. Again equation (16) is the key, though now it is used in a different way. What I do here is make more precise the argument sketched out in Smith (1976, section 7), and extend it to the case of a large economy. The first step is to compare

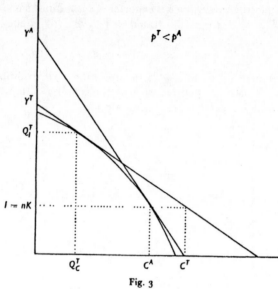

Fig. 3

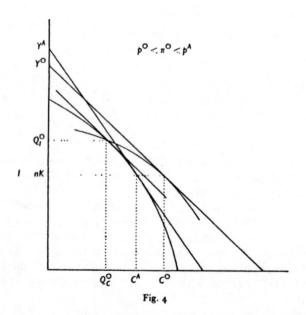

Fig. 4

the steady state analysed in the previous section with the steady state with the same saving rate as the autarky equilibrium.

In contrast with the previous section, the direction of comparative advantage is important. If $p^T > p^A$, then, in the obvious notation, for fixed K and L

$$Y^A = I^A + p^A C^A < I^A + p^T C^A < r^T K + w^T L = I^T + p^T C^T = Y^T, \qquad (30)$$

where (30) follows from the same type of argument as establishes (28). The fact that $Y^A < Y^T$ means that if, as in Section II, I were to be held constant, the saving rate would be reduced from $s = I^A/Y^A = nK^A/Y^A$ to $s' = nK^A/Y^T$. The free trade steady state with the same capital–labour ratio as the autarky steady state has a lower saving rate.

If, therefore, when trade opens up the saving rate is kept at s, capital will accumulate faster than the labour growth rate. The economy will move towards a steady state with a higher value of K/L than the steady state of Section II.

When an optimum tariff is imposed, $(p^O - \pi^O) E_C$ is positive. If $\pi^O > p^A$, (17)–(19), and the type of argument used to establish (30) imply, in the obvious notation, that

$$Y^A < I^A + \pi^O C^A < r^O K + w^O L < r^O K + w^O L + (p^O - \pi^O) E_C = Y^O. \quad (31)$$

Now, equation (16) (or in the case of the optimum tariff, equation (27)) can be used to compare the open steady state with saving rate s' with the open steady state with saving rate s. Accumulation will raise consumption if r exceeds n, in a small economy or in a large economy imposing an optimum tariff. Consumption falls if r is less than n.

In a large open economy with free trade, there is a terms-of-trade effect that must be taken into account, and its sign will depend on which good is the more capital-intensive.

Conversely, if $p^T < p^A$, $Y^T < Y^A$ in the short run and there will be decumulation, which in a small country, equation (16) tells us, will lower or raise consumption as $(r - n)$ is positive or negative. In a large free trade economy, there is again a terms-of-trade effect to be taken additionally into account.

In a large economy imposing an optimum tariff for which $\pi^O < p^A$, Y^O may be larger or smaller than Y^A. The gain from the tariff may outweigh the effect on the value of income of the shift along the transformation curve. Then, (27) shows that dC/dK depends only on $(r - n)$, but we cannot tell whether K will rise or fall.

Figs. 1–4 show the effect of trade on the value of income under the assumption about saving made in Section II. The corresponding diagrams for the case of fixed saving rates would be slightly different but would show qualitatively similar changes in Y.

What I have done so far is to compare the steady state with the same saving rate as in autarky and the steady state with the same capital–labour ratio as in autarky. To compare the autarky steady state with saving rate s and the trade steady state with the same saving rate, we have to put the above argument together with the analysis of Section II.

Before listing the results, one more observation must be made. The terms of trade effect may obviously outweigh the effect of capital accumulation or decumulation, especially if $(r - n)$ is close to zero. But it cannot outweigh the effect, analysed in Section II, of the initial opening up of trade. This is because, as Deardorff (1974) has shown, if the autarky steady state is stable (a necessary condition for this type of comparative dynamics to be meaningful), then the direction of comparative advantage will not be reversed by capital accumulation or decumulation. Equation (16) implies that when we compare p^A and the *final* value of p^T the second term must be positive.

Thus we obtain the following results:

(i) In a small economy with initial comparative advantage in the consumption good, the initial gain in consumption represented by the possibility of immediately attaining steady state with saving rate s' is reinforced by the subsequent effects of capital accumulation if r exceeds n throughout the transition towards the asymptotic steady state.

(ii) In a small economy with initial comparative advantage in the investment good, the initial consumption gain may, if r exceeds n, be counteracted by the effects of capital decumulation.

(iii) In a large free trade economy, the effects of terms of trade changes may reinforce or counteract the effects of capital accumulation or decumulation, but, if the autarky steady state was stable, the total effect is as in (i) or (ii) above.

(iv) In a large open economy imposing an optimum tariff, with initial comparative advantage in the consumption good, the effects are as in (i) above.

(v) In a large open economy imposing an optimum tariff, with initial comparative advantage in the investment good, the initial consumption gain may be followed by either capital accumulation or decumulation, the effects of this depending on the sign of $(r-n)$.

These results extend somewhat the results of Johnson (1971), Vanek (1971), Deardorff (1973), Togan (1975), and Bertrand (1975).

IV. COMPARATIVE DYNAMICS: PROFIT RATE CONSTANT

I turn now to the final comparison: of trade and autarky steady states which have the same profit rate. One special feature of this case is that, because of the factor price equalisation theorem, complete specialisation is likely to occur, but the basic relations of the model, we have seen, continue to apply.

Suppose that when trade opens up the country has a comparative advantage in the more capital-intensive product. (I assume no factor intensity reversals.) We have seen that one short-run effect is to change the value of income, but there will also be a change in factor prices: the profit rate will rise and the wage rate fall. This is the Stolper–Samuelson theorem, which is easily confirmed from (7) and (8). To move from this steady state to a steady state with the lower, autarky, profit rate, a rise in the capital–labour ratio is required. If the country is small so that the world price is given, the Rybczynski theorem (which follows from (1) and (2)) implies that there will be increased production of the more capital-intensive good (and it is clear from (3) and (4) that there will be complete specialisation if the rest of the world has the same technology).

If the country is large and does not impose an optimum tariff, the eventual equilibrium price will be different from the initial world price, but the direction of comparative advantage must be the same and the above argument still holds.

The final effect on consumption levels is deduced by using (16) to compare the autarky steady state and the free trade steady state with the same profit rate. The second term in (16) must be positive: it encompasses the initial effect of the opening-up of trade and the terms of trade effect, if any. The first term has the sign of $(r-n)$.

The optimum tariff case is rather like the small-country case. From (29) we have seen that the opening-up of trade with the imposition of an optimum tariff raises the level of C. If the domestic price π^0 is such as to induce increased production of the capital-intensive product, then, as above, there will be capital accumulation and, from (27), its effect has the sign of $(r-n)$.

Thus, if the target profit rate satisfies $r \geqslant n$, both the free trade steady state and the optimum tariff steady state have higher consumption levels than the autarky steady state with the same profit rate. If $r < n$, the total effect on consumption is ambiguous.

A similar argument applies to the case where the country has its comparative advantage in the more labour-intensive product, but now trade leads to decumulation so that it is when $r \leqslant n$ that trade leads to increased steady state consumption, while if $r > n$, the total effect is of ambiguous sign.

In Smith (1976, section 6), I drew a distinction between the "static" and "intertemporal" effects of trade: the "static" effects being the effects associated with the price changes between autarky and trade, the "intertemporal" effects being the effects of changes in the capital stock. In the model presented here, this distinction is neatly illustrated in equation (16) where the first term is the "intertemporal" effect, the second is the "static" effect. This model also shows the possibility of an alternative dichotomy, between the short-run effect analysed in Section II and the capital accumulation effects analysed above.

V. TWO COMMENTS

(*a*) Since at several points in Sections III and IV the possibility arises of trade reducing steady state consumption, even when $r \geqslant n$ and when trade policy is optimal, it should be emphasised that this is not to be taken as contradicting the usual gains from trade propositions. Section II has shown us that trade always implies a potential Pareto improvement in the sense that consumption at each point in time is increased. Sections III and IV show that, depending on the saving objective, actual consumption may be unequally distributed over time. It is easy to confirm that when $r \geqslant n$, trade can reduce steady state consumption only by boosting consumption in the short run. We have the usual result that trade benefits some and harms others: here the "some" are the early time periods of the open economy, the "others" are the later time periods.

(*b*) The basic model of Section I is easy to generalise to more than two sectors, and the result of Section II is also clearly a general result, but the comparative dynamics results of Sections III and IV do not generalise. (In Smith (1976) I have shown how some fundamental aspects of this model carry over to input–output and vintage technologies, but how, similarly, only the simplest forms of such technologies give determinate comparative dynamic results.) The model is therefore to be taken as providing illustrative and, perhaps, instructive examples of how trade may affect the intertemporal allocation of consumption rather than precise predictions about the real world.

VI. CONCLUSIONS

A glance at Sections III and IV will show the impossibility of giving a brief summary of results, and even there a complete list of possible cases is not given. The fact is that there is, in a way typical of trade theory, a range of different cases to be considered. My aim here has not been to attempt to present a simple and memorable taxonomy of results. It has been to present methods by which results can be obtained and thereby make the theory of trade and growth more accessible. There are several features of those methods worth recalling in conclusion.

(i) The equation (16) is a crucial relationship, allowing one to discuss the effects of price changes, both exogenous and endogenous, and of capital accumulation, under alternative savings assumptions.

(ii) The steady state which is immediately attainable on the opening up of trade is an important benchmark in the analysis.

(iii) Although the terms of trade effect of capital accumulation in large economies seems at first likely to complicate the analysis, it turns out that this effect is always dominated by the effects of the initial price change resulting from the opening up of trade, and also that the analysis is easily extended to the case of the imposition of an optimum tariff, in which case the terms of trade effect is eliminated.

M. A. M. SMITH

London School of Economics

Date of receipt of final typescript: October 1976

REFERENCES

Bertrand, T. J. (1975). "The Gains from Trade: an Analysis of Steady State Solutions in an Open Economy." *Quarterly Journal of Economics*, vol. 89 (4), pp. 556–68.

Caves, R. E. and Jones, R. W. (1973). *World Trade and Payments.* Boston: Little Brown and Company.

Deardorff, A. V. (1973). "The Gains from Trade in and out of Steady-state Growth." *Oxford Economic Papers*, N.S. vol. 25 (2), pp. 173–91.

Deardorff, A. V. (1974). "Trade Reversals and Growth Stability." *Journal of International Economics*, vol. 4 (1), pp. 83–90.

Johnson, H. G. (1971). "Trade and Growth: a Geometrical Exposition." *Journal of International Economics*, vol. 1 (1), pp. 83–102.

Jones, R. W. (1965). "The Structure of Simple General Equilibrium Models." *Journal of Political Economy*, vol. 73 (6), pp. 557–72.

Negishi, T. (1972). *General Equilibrium Theory and International Trade.* Amsterdam: North Holland.

Smith, M. A. M. (1976). "Trade, Growth and Consumption in Alternative Models of Capital Accumulation." *Journal of International Economics*, vol. 6 (4), pp. 371–84.

Togan, S. (1975). "The Gains from International Trade in the Context of a Growing Economy." *Journal of International Economics*, vol. 5 (3), pp. 229–38.

Vanek, J. (1971). "Economic Growth and International Trade in Pure Theory." *Quarterly Journal of Economics*, vol. 85 (3), pp. 377–90.

[2]

An exposition and exploration of Krueger's trade model

ALAN V. DEARDORFF / University of Michigan

Abstract. This paper provides a diagrammatic exposition of Anne Krueger's (1977) model of developing country trade and within that context examines the effects of tariffs on real factor rewards, with and without international capital mobility. The model has an agricultural sector employing labour and land, plus a manufacturing sector producing several goods using labour and capital. It is shown that without capital mobility the effects of tariffs on the real returns to all three factors are largely well defined but very sensitive to the pattern of specialization. With mobile capital, however, a tariff on any produced good raises the real wage.

Interprétation et développement du modèle de commerce international d'Anne Krueger. Ce mémoire propose une présentation graphique du modèle de commerce international pour un pays en voie de développement développé par Anne Krueger. Dans ce contexte, l'auteur examine l'effet des droits de douane sur la rémunération des facteurs de production dans l'hypothèse de mobilité internationale du capital mais aussi dans l'hypothèse où une telle mobilité n'existe pas Le modèle met en scène un secteur agricole qui utilise les facteurs travail et terre et un secteur manufacturier qui produit plusieurs biens en utilisant les facteurs travail et capital. On montre que si l'on assume que le capital est immobile, les effets des droits de douane sur les rendements réels des trois facteurs de production sont en gros bien définis, mais ces résultats dépendent d'une manière dramatique du pattern de spécialisation. Quand on postule que le capital est mobile, cependant, un droit de douane sur n'importe quel bien produit va accroître le niveau du salaire réel.

INTRODUCTION

In her 1977 Graham lecture Anne Kruger described a model of specialization and trade among many countries that she suggested was particularly appropriate for developing countries. The model is also useful for developed countries, however, and provides a nice synthesis of two strands within the pure theory of international trade: the Heckscher–Ohlin model and the specific factors model. In this paper I will elaborate on the exposition of her model, focusing in particular on an issue that she

For their helpful comments on earlier drafts of this paper, I would like especially to thank Anne Krueger, Richard Porter, and Robert Stern, as well as other participants in the Research Seminar in International Economics at Michigan and the 1983 NBER summer institute on international economics An anonymous referee also made useful suggestions did not address: the effects of trade policy on factor prices, especially in capital-scarce developing countries.

Consider, for example, how tariffs will affect wages in a developing country. Three answers suggest themselves, based on theories of international trade. First, the Stolper–Samuelson theorem, in the two-dimensional Heckscher–Ohlin model, suggests that a tariff in a labour-abundant developing country will lower the real wage of labour.[1] Second, a specific-factors model with only labour mobile between industries gives an ambiguous effect of a tariff on the real wage, depending on what workers consume.[2] Finally, a model such as MacDougall's (1960), with international investment, suggests that a tariff can benefit labour by attracting more foreign capital for it to work with.[3]

The Krueger model is particularly appropriate for sorting out these possibilities because it is a hybrid of the Heckscher–Ohlin and specific-factors models. Thus, it gives scope for both of the first two effects of a tariff mentioned above. In addition, one can add a simple form of international capital mobility to the model and thus evaluate MacDougall's argument.

Throughout the paper I examine only countries that are small enough to take international prices as given. Also, I simply assume that a tariff raises the domestic price above the world price by its full amount. For a tariff alone this is appropriate only if the good is imported both with and without the tariff. The results of this paper therefore apply to non-prohibitive tariffs on imported goods.[4] Alternatively, however, the results also apply without such a qualification if the policy is not a tariff by itself, but rather a tariff accompanied by an equal subsidy to exports of the same good. This policy combination does raise the domestic price above the world price, whether the good is exported, imported, or neither.[5]

This is an analysis of factor prices. It is not an analysis of welfare, even for groups within the economy. A change in a factor's real return may imply a similar change in the welfare of the factor's owners, but only if two conditions are met. First, the owners of the factor must own *only* the one factor and not any other. Second, the owners must not experience a change in taxes or transfer payments vis-à-vis government, or any changes in the benefits they derive from public goods. With a tariff or export subsidy it is impossible for the second of these conditions to be met for all factor owners, since something must be done with the tariff revenue and a subsidy must be financed.

In the second section I describe the Krueger model, including a geometric analysis

---

1 See Stolper and Samuelson (1941) or any textbook on international economics
2 Modern interest in the specific-factors model dates from Jones (1971) and Samuelson (1971) If labour's preferences are typical of the economy as a whole, then Ruffin and Jones (1977) establish a presumption that a tariff will lower the real wage.
3 In essentially a one-sector model, MacDougall (1960) showed how a capital inflow would raise the wage of labour and informally suggested a tariff as one cause of the capital inflow itself. He did not evaluate the combined effects of the tariff plus the capital inflow.
4 When capital is perfectly mobile, Mundell (1957) has shown in a two-sector Heckscher–Ohlin model that any positive tariff is prohibitive In the Krueger model this need not be the case.
5 The results do *not* apply to an export subsidy alone, which would not change prices to consumers. The necessary modifications in the argument for this case should be obvious

to make her results more accessible. Also, since later results depend crucially on a country's patterns of specialization and trade, I shall delineate how these depend on factor endowments and tastes.

In the third section I analyse the effects of a tariff. As might be expected, effects on real wages can conform to either the Stolper–Samuelson or the specific-factors predictions described above, depending on the pattern of specialization. In addition, real wages may rise if the tariff is levied on more labour-intensive imports. Also, the model generates effects on rental prices of both capital and land.

Finally, I introduce international capital mobility in the fourth section. A tariff then can indeed raise real wages unambiguously, and regardless of the capital intensity of the imported good. The increase normally accompanies an inflow of capital, but it can also occur with an outflow of capital if the tariff shifts specialization to a more labour-intensive good.

A VIEW OF THE MODEL

Developing countries differ greatly in levels of development. To describe them a trade model should therefore permit greater variety in relative factor endowments than is possible in the standard two-by-two Heckscher–Ohlin (H–O) model of international trade. In addition, the exclusive focus of the H–O model on manufactured goods is also inappropriate in most developing countries. The additional availability of employment in a large agricultural sector is surely important for the effects of tariffs on factor prices, particularly the wage.

Recognizing these needs, Krueger (1977) proposed a variant of the H–O model that is a hybrid of it with the specific-factors model.[6] Her model includes an agricultural sector that employs labour and land plus a manufacturing sector that employs labour and capital.[7] Capital and land are immobile between sectors, but capital is mobile *within* the manufacturing sector, which is modelled as capable of producing any of a large number of manufactured goods. These can be traded internationally, with a large number of countries among which factor prices are assumed to be unequal. The agricultural good – call it food – is also trade internationally.

Technologies in both agriculture and manufacturing are identical internationally and display constant returns to scale. Goods and factors are priced competitively, so that goods prices, together if necessary with factor endowments, determine factor prices in each country. Factor endowments are assumed to differ enough among countries to prevent factor price equalization even in the manufacturing sector. Thus

6 The simple H–O model and the specific-factors model are both special cases of a generalized Heckscher–Ohlin model, in which there are arbitrary numbers of goods, factors, and countries The generalized model retains some but not all of the properties of the simple model See Deardorff (1979, 1982) and Ethier (1983). The Krueger model, too, is a special case of the generalized H–O model.

7 The names 'land' and 'capital' are to indicate that these factors are not mobile between the agricultural and manufacturing sectors and need not otherwise have the properties of actual land and capital. The factor 'land,' in particular, could be thought of as representing a variety of factors that are specific to agriculture, including agricultural capital

734 / Alan V. Deardorff

world prices are such that, without interference, no country could produce more than a subset of the manufactured goods.

Countries at different levels of development may, depending also on their endowments of land, produce and perhaps export more or less capital-intensive manufactured goods. Also, unless they have very extreme factor endowments, they will import a variety of manufactured goods, some more capital intensive, and some less, than what they produce themselves. Finally, with exports of food also possible, a country with much land might import *all* manufactured goods, even when it produces only one of them.

All this can be seen in figure 1. The figure combines Lerner–Pearce unit-value-isoquants for determining specialization within the manufacturing sector with the beaker-shaped diagram of the specific-factors literature. Together the two panels determine specialization and factor prices for a country with given factor endowments and facing given (free trade) prices of all goods.

To see how it is done, consider first the top panel, which is similar to figures in Deardorff (1979). Given world prices of three manufactured goods, p_1, p_2, and p_3, unit-value isoquants are drawn as M_1, M_2, and M_3 and are then connected by common tangents to form their convex hull.[8] This hull acts as a unit-value isoquant for manufacturing as a whole. Its slope indicates the ratio of the wage, w, to the rental on capital, r_K, that is implied by the marginal products of these factors in manufacturing. Along straight segments of the hull two goods[9] are produced in the sector, and marginal products of both factors are invariant with respect to small changes in the sector's employment of capital and labour.[10] Along curved portions of the hull, on the other hand, only one manufactured good is produced and marginal products of factors decline as their employment increases.

Given the capital stock $\bar{K}$, therefore, one can infer the behaviour of the manufacturing-sector wage as the level of employment in that sector, L_M, is varied. Moving to the right along the horizontal line at $\bar{K}$ in the top panel, one passes into and out of regions of specialization and non-specialization. For levels of manufacturing employment below L^0, for example, the sectoral capital-labour ratio is above the minimum k_3 needed for specialization in M_3. In this region the manufacturing wage, which is the value of labour's marginal product in manufacturing, $V_L{}^M$, is also its value marginal product in producing only M_3. As L_M rises in this region, the capital-labour ratio in M_3 falls, and so must the manufacturing wage. This is shown by the curve w_M in the lower panel.

When L_M rises above L^0, the manufacturing sector begins production of M_2 as well

8 The diagram can easily accommodate more than three goods, but three can make the points in this paper.
9 I assume that world prices permit production of no more than two manufactured goods in any freely trading country. With only three manufactured goods in the sector, this is necessary in order to permit factor prices to differ internationally With a larger number of goods that would not be necessary The reader may think of figure 1 as including many additional undrawn isoquants, tangent to the hull along the straight segments
10 This of course is the familiar phenomenon of the factor-price equalization theorem of Samuelson (1949)

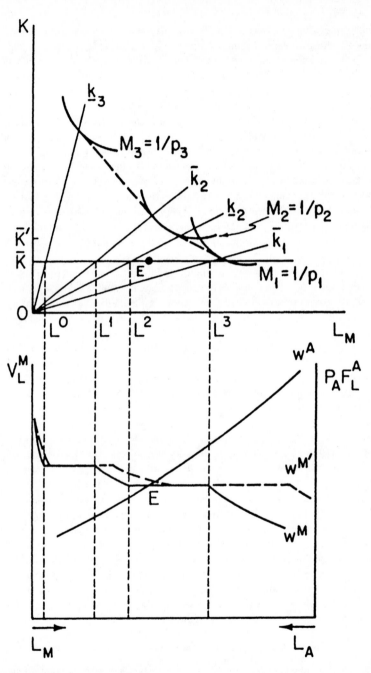

FIGURE 1

736 / Alan V. Deardorff

as M_3. Factor prices become fixed, since the capital-labour ratio in the sector can now fall without changing the ratios $\bar{k}_1$ and $\bar{k}_2$ employed in each of the two industries. Thus the manufacturing wage in the lower panel becomes flat throughout this region of non-specialization – that is, between L^0 and L^1. Proceeding further to the right, the sector alternates between specialization and non-specialization, and the w_M curve below alternates downward sloping and horizontal segments.

Once constructed in this way, the w_M curve can be combined with another curve representing the agricultural wage, w_A, to determine the equilibrium allocation of labour between the sectors. This is the usual beaker-shaped diagram of the specific-factors model. The horizontal dimension of the beaker is the labour endowment, $\bar{L}$. Agricultural employment, L_A, is measured leftwards from the right-hand wall of the beaker. The agricultural wage must equal the value of the marginal product of labour in agriculture, $P_A F_L^A$. Given the endowment of land, $\bar{T}$, which is specific to that sector, and given also the world price of the agricultural good, P_A, that marginal product is a decreasing function of agricultural employment, as drawn.

Labour-market equilibrium with free mobility of labour between sectors requires the same wage in both. Thus equilibrium is at E, where the w_M and w_A curves intersect. The pattern of specialization can be inferred from the segment of the w_M curve in which this intersection appears, and other behaviour in the manufacturing sector can be found in the upper panel.[11] As drawn, for example, the equilibrium entails production of both M_1 and M_2, using capital-labour ratios $\bar{k}_1$ and $\bar{k}_2$ in their production.

The diagram lends itself readily to comparative-static analysis and yields conclusions about effects of growth on trade that were a subject of Krueger's paper. For example, an increase in the capital stock to $\bar{K}'$ shifts the w_M curve proportionately rightward, to w_M'. As drawn, this causes manufacturing to specialize completely in M_2. However, it is also clear that, for other initial equilibria, some capital accumulation can occur without changing the pattern of specialization, the wage, and total manufacturing employment. Note the contrast to the simpler specific factors model where accumulation of either specific factor necessarily raises the wage.

Comparison of economies with different endowments of land can also be done, although I leave the diagram to the reader. An increase in land shifts the w_A curve upward and causes an unambiguous decline in manufacturing employment, together with Rybczynski-like effects on separate manufacturing outputs in regions of nonspecialization.[12] One can easily derive Krueger's interesting conclusion that a country with little capital may none the less produce quite capital-intensive manufactured goods if it is also well endowed with land.

Since the pattern of specialization will turn out to be crucial for the effects of a tariff, a more formal picture of how factor endowments determine specialization may

---

11 The point E in the upper panel could be used as the upper-right corner of an Edgeworth Box, showing allocation of capital and labour between industries M_1 and M_2.
12 For example, as manufacturing employment falls in the region between L^2 and L^1, output of M_2 rises and output of M_1 falls, much as in Rybczynski (1955)

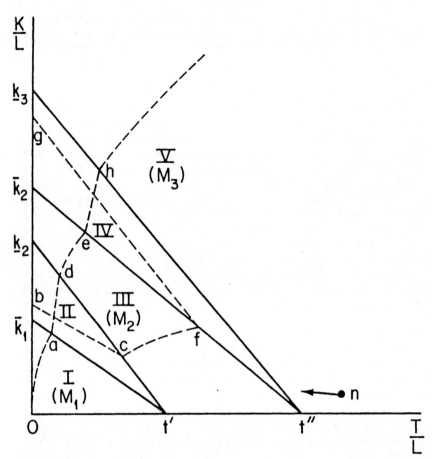

FIGURE 2

be useful. This picture is shown in figure 2, which can be derived from figure 1. Here the space of per capita land and capital endowments is divided into five regions, each corresponding to a different pattern of specialization. These regions are delineated by heavy straight lines that connect various industry factor ratios. For example, in region II both M_1 and M_2, as well as the agricultural good, are produced. Since relative factor prices are fixed throughout this region, factors are employed in the same ratio for a given industry everywhere within it. Thus this region is the triangle bounded by $\bar{k}_1$ and k_2 on the K/L axis and by a single value t' of the land-labour ratio on the T/L axis.[13]

13 The boundaries of these regions can be derived from the full-employment condition for labour For example, at the lower bound of region II the economy produces only M_1 and food, the former with capital-labour ratio $\hat{k}_1$, and the latter with land-labour ratio t' Thus full employment requires $(K/\hat{k}_1) + (T/t') = L$. This can be solved to yield $(K/L) = \hat{k}_1 - (\hat{k}_1/t')(T/L)$, which defines the (linear) lower bound of region II.

738 / Alan V. Deardorff

From these regions the roles of relative capital and land endowments are obvious. Large amounts of either capital or land put the economy in region v, where only the most capital-intensive manufactured good, M_3, is produced. Likewise one can picture the process of development as described by Krueger. A land-poor country would start in region I. As it accumulates capital it moves up in the diagram, passing through each region of specialization.[14]

There is also another possibility that was not noted by Krueger. Suppose that a land-rich, capital-poor country accumulates *both* capital and labour over time as its population grows. Then even though the capital-labour ratio may grow, the country may still move to specialization in *less* capital intensive manufactured goods. This may be seen in figure 2, by extending the path shown as starting at point *n* ultimately into region *I*. Along this path the labour force is growing, since T/L is falling, and the capital stock is growing somewhat faster than the labour force, since K/L is rising. This is possible because the rate of growth of labour in manufacturing is not the same as its rate of growth in the economy as a whole. If labour in agriculture grows more slowly – as it must, given fixed land – then the capital-labour ratio in manufacturing can fall even as it rises for the economy as a whole.[15]

It is of interest, too, to determine the pattern of trade, which depends on demand as well as supply. In figure 2, I have sketched approximate boundaries dividing exports from imports for two of the four goods. These are drawn under an assumption about demand that, at free-trade prices, approximately one-quarter of income is spent on each of the four goods.

The curve *Oadehi* indicates trade in the agricultural good. Below the curve more than one quarter of output is agricultural and food is exported. Above, it is imported.

The curve *bcfg*, with the vertical axis, encloses the region in which the middle manufactured good, M_2, is exported. It includes only points where M_2 is produced and, therefore, parts of regions II, III, and IV only. But it does not include *all* of any region. Even in region III, where manufacturing produces only M_2, the economy as a whole also produces food. If the endowment of land is large relative to capital, the manufacturing sector will be unable to satisfy domestic demand for M_2, even when completely specialized.[16,17]

EFFECTS OF TARIFFS

Consider now the effects of price increases due to tariffs.[18] These can occur for any good, but I focus primarily on that manufactured good, M_2, of intermediate capital intensity. A rise in p_2 captures all the qualitative effects of any manufactured-good

14 The diagram can be used over time only if world prices – and therefore presumably everything else abroad – are constant over time. However, the results here are valid in more general terms for growth at home *relative* to growth abroad

15 Note however that if capital grows strictly faster than labour, then movement into regions other than v can be only temporary, since K/L will eventually surpass k_3

16 The boundaries of these regions are linear in regions II and IV, but generally non-linear elsewhere.

17 With a larger number of manufactured goods, there would be a large number of non-specialization triangles There would be export regions for each good, and these would tend to become narrower and extend closer to the T/L axis as the number of goods goes up

18 Or tariffs cum export subsidies as explained above

price increase, including what one would find in a model with a larger number of goods. I also briefly note the effects of an increase in the price of the agricultural good.

A rise in the price of M_2 shifts the unit-value isoquant for M_2 radially inward, as shown in figure 3. The common tangents with the other two isoquants also adjust, rotating to maintain their tangencies. This alters all the capital-labour ratios at which these tangencies occur and thus changes the boundaries of all regions of specialization. The central region, for specialization in M_2, expands, while those for both M_1 and M_3 contract.

Factor prices are also altered by the price change in much of the diagram. Within regions of non-specialization these are most easily inferred from marginal products in M_1 and M_3, since their prices have not changed. In the lower region where M_1 and M_2 are produced, the capital-labour ratio in M_1 must fall. Thus, at world prices the wage falls and the rental on capital rises. Just the opposite happens in the upper non-specialization region, since k rises in M_3. Finally, in the central region, where only M_2 is produced, all marginal products in terms of M_2 remain constant for given capital-labour ratios. Since the domestic price of M_2 has risen, however, both w and r_K rise in terms of world prices by the amount of the price increase.

These partial equilibrium effects on the wage are shown in the lower panel of figure 3 as altering the shape of the w_M curve from $w_M{}^0$ to $w_M{}'$. The horizontal portions of the curve shift vertically – one up, one down – while the downward sloping centre portion shifts up vertically by the amount of the price increase.

Obviously the ultimate effects on both the wage and other factor prices depend crucially on where the initial equilibrium happens to lie. Several cases need to be considered, represented in the figure by alternative positions of the w_1 curve. I consider only cases in which the price change is too small to move the economy from one region of specialization to another. Larger changes are therefore combinations of the cases considered below. The results for all cases are summarized in table 1.

Tariff on a non-produced good
Perhaps the simplest case is a tariff on a good that is not produced at all. This is the case in figure 3 if the agricultural wage curve is $w_A{}^0$ and the initial equilibrium is at E_0.[19] Here M_2 is not produced. If that continues to be true with the tariff, then the equilibrium does not move and all factor prices remain constant in nominal terms. All factor prices fall, however, in real terms, since p_2 has gone up.

Tariff on the only produced manufactured good[20]
If the economy is completely specialized in producing M_2 and remains so with the tariff, then the nominal wage rises but by less than p_2, while the rental on capital rises more than p_2 and the rental on land falls. This is the case for the initial equilibrium E_1

19 The same result would obtain, of course, for a w_A curve much higher than all those shown, intersecting $w_M{}'$ in its left-most sloping portion

20 For a tariff alone, complete specialization may make it unlikely that the policy will affect prices at all, since the good is likely to be exported That is not inevitable, however, as already noted in figure 2 Alternatively, the results of this case apply independently of the pattern of trade if the tariff accompanies an export subsidy on the same good

740 / Alan V. Deardorff

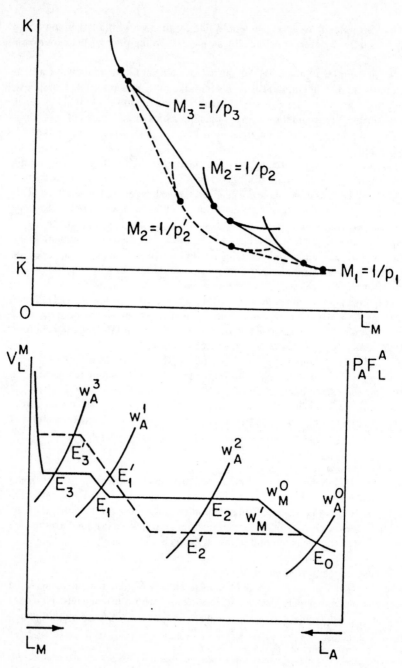

FIGURE 3

TABLE 1

Effects of a non-prohibitive tariff (or tariff-cum-export subsidy) on real factor rewards

Tariff on	Specialization region in figure 2	Effect on real price of		
		labour	capital	land
Manufactured good – M_2				
Not produced	I or V	–	–	-
Only produced	III	?	+	–
Capital-intensive (of two produced)	II	–	+	? or +
Labour-intensive (of two produced)	IV	+	–	–
Agricultural good				
M sector specialized	I, III, or V	?	–	+
M sector not specialized	II or IV	–	–	–

+ = Factor price rises relative to all goods
– = Factor price falls relative to all goods
? = Factor price rises relative to some goods and falls relative to others

which moves with the tariff to E_1'. Labour is reallocated from agriculture to manufacturing, just as in the specific-factors model. Labour's marginal product rises in agriculture and falls in M_2, while the marginal products of land and capital move in the opposite directions, giving the results just described. Thus, in this case real rentals rise for capital and fall for land, while the effect on the real wage is ambiguous.[21]

Tariff on the more capital-intensive of two produced goods
If the manufacturing sector is not specialized, as at E_2 in figure 3, and the tariff raises the price of the more capital intensive of the produced goods, then the results conform to the Stolper–Samuelson prediction that I mentioned at the outset. Movement in figure 3 is from E_2 to E_2'. The wage falls absolutely and therefore in real terms, while the real rental on capital increases. Also, as employment in agriculture expands, the rental on land rises but not perhaps by as much as p_2. Thus the effect on the real rental of land is ambiguous.

Tariff on the more labour-intensive of two produced goods
I have already noted, as did Krueger, that even a fairly labour-abundant country may, if it has a good deal of land, import at least some goods that are more labour intensive than its exports. If it also produces such a good (as, incidentally, it will if the tariff is large enough), then the Stolper–Samuelson prediction regarding tariffs on such an import is exactly reversed. Thus, in figure 3, suppose that equilibrium is initially at E_3 and moves to E_3' owing to a tariff on M_2. Now the wage rises even relative to p_2, since labour's marginal product in M_2 goes up, and the rental on capital falls absolutely. Here, too, since labour leaves the agricultural sector, the rental on land also falls absolutely.

21 As in Ruffin and Jones (1977), this ambiguity might be resolved by considering the preferences of workers In this case, however, the presumption favours an improvement in the real wage, since the tariff has raised the price of only one of many manufactured goods

742 / Alan V. Deardorff

Tariff on the agricultural good

A last case to consider is a tariff (or tariff cum subsidy) that raises the price of the agricultural good. Although not shown in the figure, this shifts the w_A curve upward. The effects, as can be verified, depend on whether manufacturing is completely or incompletely specialized. In the former case the results are exactly those of the specific-factors model: real rentals fall for capital and rise for land, while the effect on the real wage is ambiguous. If manufacturing is not specialized, however, then all factor prices remain constant in terms of world prices and all fall in real terms, since the domestic price of the agricultural good has risen. The results here are analogous to those above for a tariff on a good that is not produced at all.[22]

The conclusion of this section is that tariffs can have any of a large variety of effects on factor prices, even before we introduce international capital mobility. The results are quite predictable, however, and can be understood individually in terms of the Stolper–Samuelson and specific-factors contributions that came before. Which of the results apply depends on the pattern of specialization. Since this was delineated in terms of factor endowments in figure 2, I have identified the various cases in table 1 by the regions of figure 2 into which they fall.[23]

CAPITAL MOBILITY

Consider now MacDougall's (1960) argument that a tariff might attract foreign investment and thus raise the wage. One might suspect, adding mobile capital to the model, that this would occur, if at all, only for particular specialization patterns. It turns out, however, that this must occur so long as the protected good is initially produced.[24]

To model capital mobility I now assume that the country has access to unlimited international capital at a rate of return, r^*, measured at world prices. To be consistent with internationally unequal factor prices, I must assume that r^* is particular to the host country rather than prevailing worldwide.[25] For example, r^* might incorporate a risk premium reflecting the country's political environment.[26]

Fixing $r = r^*$ means fixing the capital-axis intercept of the unit isocost line, since

22 There is an intriguing variant of this result if the price increase is due to an export subsidy that is *not* accompanied by a tariff Consumers then will import at the unchanged world price, and all factor prices will be constant in real terms Any effect on welfare will be due exclusively to the tax that must be levied to finance the subsidy

23 Note, however, that these regions were drawn for free trade A tariff will shift their boundaries.

24 Studies of tariffs with capital mobility, beginning with Mundell (1957), have typically made the assumptions that would otherwise be needed for trade to equalize factor prices. As a result, perfect capital mobility eliminates trade whenever tariffs are positive Alternatively, as in Brecher and Diaz Alejandro (1977), capital is allowed to be only partially mobile and the effects of tariffs remain largely those of Stolper and Samuelson. The result here was also noted in a specific-factors model by Brecher and Findlay (1982)

25 If the latter were true and if technology were everywhere identical for all manufactured goods, then prices would have to be such as to line up all unit-value isoquants tangent to a single unit isocost line. The argument of this section would still be formally valid, but the model would look implausible.

26 Mundell (1957) also mentions a perfectly elastic supply of foreign capital at a rate above that prevailing abroad.

this intercept measures $1/r$.[27] Given the prices of the goods and their corresponding unit-value isoquants, the wage of labour must be such as to place the unit-isocost line, with intercept $1/r^*$, tangent to the convex hull of the unit-value isoquants. Capital will flow into or out of the country as necessary to achieve whatever capital-labour ratio in the manufacturing sector is consistent with full employment at this wage.

Since prices and r^* together determine a unique unit-isocost line, the wage must be independent of manufacturing employment, and the manufacturing wage curve in the beaker diagram becomes a horizontal line. Its height is the reciprocal of the labour-axis intercept of the unit-isocost line, as can also be seen from the unit cost equation.

All this is shown in figure 4. At initial prices the solid unit-value isoquants, M_1, M_2, and M_3, obtain. Given a return to capital, r^*, the wage must be w_0 for production of some good to break even and none to make a profit. As drawn, this good happens to be M_1 and the sector completely specializes in M_1, employing capital and labour in the ratio k^0 in the manufacturing sector.

In the lower panel the w_M curve is horizontal, initially at level w_0. With the usual w_A curve, the equilibrium is at E_0 with L_M^0 units of labour employed in manufacturing. What makes this feasible is the variability of capital, which flows into or out of the country as necessary until its ratio to L_M^0 is exactly k^0.

Consider now a tariff (or tariff *cum* export subsidy) that raises the domestic price of M_2. Since, as drawn, M_2 was not initially produced, a small tariff is possible without altering any levels of production. Such a tariff, like the first case in table 1, would simply lower the real prices of all domestic factors.[28] A larger tariff, however, will cause some changes, as shown in figure 4.

Here the tariff shifts the M_2 unit-value isoquant to M_2', inside the initial unit-isocost line. To maintain r^*, the isocost line must pivot on its vertical intercept so as to be tangent to M_2'. This raises the wage from w_0 to w_1, shifting the w_M curve in the lower panel upward to w_M'. The new equilibrium is at E_1 and involves the following changes. Labour moves from agriculture manufacturing. The capital-labour ratio in this case also goes up – to k^1 – requiring, therefore, a quite substantial capital inflow. The wage rises in nominal terms, and the rental on land falls both absolutely and in real terms.

The real wage is ambiguous here, but only because the tariff has changed the pattern of specialization. In general, a tariff on a good that is already produced must *raise* the real wage regardless of the capital intensity of the good. For example, once M_2 is produced, any further increase in its price makes the unit-isocost line steeper. This means a rise in the wage-rental ratio, a rise in the cost-minimizing capital-labour ratio in that industry, and a rise, therefore, in the marginal product of labour in producing M_2. Thus the wage rises relative to p_2 and rises even more relative to other prices, which have not changed.

This is true regardless of the capital intensity of the good bearing the tariff. In

27 The unit isocost line is defined by $wL + rK = 1$ On the K-axis, $L = 0$ and thus $K = 1/r$
28 The owners of imported capital, who presumably consume abroad at world prices, experience no change

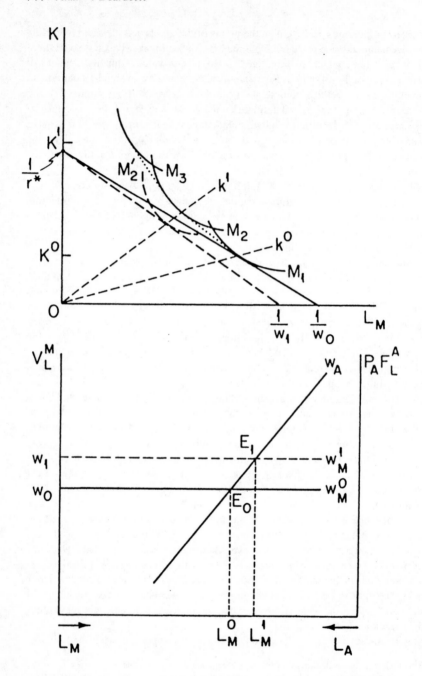

FIGURE 4

figure 4 a tariff on M_1 would have this effect immediately. A tariff on M_3 would have this effect eventually, once the tariff first becomes large enough to start production of M_3.

The result also does not depend on the tariff inducing a capital inflow. One can construct a case in which the economy initially produces a more capital-intensive good than in figure 4, say M_2. A large enough tariff on more labour-intensive M_1 can then lower the manufacturing-sector capital-labour ratio sufficiently to require a capital outflow, even though employment there is rising.

CONCLUSION

This model yields quite clear results for the effects of tariffs on factor prices. However these results do depend, clearly but dramatically, on patterns of specialization. Without capital mobility, one cannot make any sweeping generalizations about how protection affects factor prices, such as that protection is harmful to abundant factors and beneficial to scarce factors, as Stolper and Samuelson argued in a simpler context. Too much depends on the capital intensity of protected goods compared with other goods that are produced; and with many traded manufactured goods, most countries will import both more and less capital-intensive goods than they produce.

Capital mobility, on the other hand, can limit outcomes considerably. With an infinitely elastic supply of capital from abroad, a tariff on any good that is produced will, regardless of its capital intensity, raise the real wage. While the assumptions here are extreme, this result certainly points to the importance of international factor movements in determining the effects of protection.[29]

REFERENCES

Brecher, R.A. and C.F. Diaz Alejandro (1977) 'Tariffs, foreign capital and immizerizing growth,' *Journal of International Economics* 7, 317–22

Brecher, R.A. and R. Findlay (1982) 'Tariffs, foreign capital and national welfare with sector-specific factors.' Carleton Economic Papers No. 82-18, February

Deardorff, A.V. (1979) 'Weak links in the chain of comparative advantage.' *Journal of International Economics* 9, 197–209

— (1982) 'The general validity of the Heckscher–Ohlin Theorem.' *American Economic Review* 72, 683–94

Ethier, W.J. (1983) 'Higher dimensional trade theory.' Chap. 3 of R.W. Jones and P.B. Kenen, eds, *Handbook of International Economics*, vol. 1 (Amsterdam: North-Holland)

Jones, R.W. (1971) 'A three-factor model in theory, trade, and history.' In J.N. Bhagwati, R.W. Jones, R.A. Mundell, and J. Vanek, eds, *Trade, Balance of Payments and Growth: Essays in Honor of Charles P. Kindleberger* (Amsterdam: North Holland)

Krueger, A.O. (1977) 'Growth, distortions, and patterns of trade among many countries.' *Princeton Studies in International Finance*, No. 40 (Princeton, NJ: Princeton University)

MacDougall, G.D.A. (1960) 'The benefits and costs of private investment from abroad: a theoretical approach.' *Economic Record*, Special Issue (March); reprinted in R.E. Caves

29 The result derived here for capital mobility is not, incidentally, at all peculiar to the Krueger model. It can be derived in any of a variety of more familiar models.

746 / Alan V. Deardorff

and H.G. Johnson (1968), *Readings in International Economics* (Homewood, IL: Richard D. Irwin, Inc.)

Mundell, R.A. (1957) 'International trade and factor mobility.' *American Economic Review* 57, 321–35

Ruffin, R J. and R.W. Jones (1977) 'Protection and real wages: the neoclassical ambiguity.' *Journal of Economic Theory* 14, 337–48

Rybczynski, T.M. (1955) 'Factor endowments and relative commodity prices.' *Economica* 22, 336–41

Samuelson, P.A. (1949) 'International factor-price equalization once again.' *The Economic Journal* (June), 181–97

— (1971) 'Ohlin was right.' *Swedish Journal of Economics* 73, 365–84

Stolper, W. and P.A. Samuelson (1941) 'Protection and real wages.' *Review of Economic Studies* 9, 58–73

[3]

THE "CLASSICAL THEORY" OF INTERNATIONAL TRADE AND THE UNDERDEVELOPED COUNTRIES[1]

THERE has recently been a considerable amount of controversy concerning the applicability of the "classical theory" of international trade to the underdeveloped countries.[2] The twists in this controversy may be set out as follows. The critics start with the intention of showing that the "nineteenth-century pattern" of international trade, whereby the underdeveloped countries export raw materials and import manufactured goods, has been unfavourable to the economic development of these countries. But instead of trying to show this directly, they concentrate their attacks on the "classical theory," which they believe to be responsible for the unfavourable pattern of trade. The orthodox economists then come to the defence of the classical theory by reiterating the principle of comparative costs which they claim to be applicable both to the developed and the underdeveloped countries. After this, the controversy shifts from the primary question whether or not the nineteenth-century pattern of international trade, as a historical reality, has been unfavourable to the underdeveloped countries to the different question whether or not the theoretical model assumed in the comparative-costs analysis is applicable to these countries. Both sides then tend to conduct their argument as though the two questions were the same and to identify the "classical theory" with the comparative-costs theory.

It will be argued in this paper that this has led to the neglect of those other elements in the classical theory of international trade which are much nearer to the realities and ideologies of the nineteenth-century expansion of international trade to the underdeveloped countries. In Sections I and II we shall outline these elements and show that they are traceable to Adam Smith and to some extent to J. S. Mill. In Section III we shall show how one of Adam Smith's lines of approach can be fruitfully developed to throw a more illuminating light on the past and present patterns of the international trade of the underdeveloped countries than the conventional theory. In Section IV we shall touch upon some policy implications of our analysis and show certain weaknesses in the position both of the orthodox economists and of their critics.

[1] This paper has benefited from comments by Sir Donald MacDougall, Professor H. G. Johnson, R. M. Sundrum and G. M. Meier.

[2] Of the very extensive literature on the subject, we may refer to two notable recent works, the first stating the orthodox position and the second the position of the critics: J. Viner, *International Trade and Economic Development*, and G. Myrdal, *An International Economy*.

I

The neglected elements in the classical theory of international trade may
be traced to Adam Smith, particularly to the following key passage in the
Wealth of Nations:

> " Between whatever places foreign trade is carried on, they all of
> them derive two distinct benefits from it. It carries out that surplus
> part of the produce of their land and labour for which there is no demand
> among them, and brings back in return for it something else for which
> there is a demand. It gives a value to their superfluities, by exchanging
> them for something else, which may satisfy a part of their wants, and
> increase their enjoyments. By means of it, the narrowness of the home
> market does not hinder the division of labour in any particular branch
> of art or manufacture from being carried to the highest perfection. By
> opening a more extensive market for whatever part of the produce of
> their labour may exceed the home consumption, it encourages them to
> improve its productive powers, and to augment its annual produce to
> the utmost, and thereby to increase the real revenue and wealth of
> society " (Vol. I, Cannan ed., p. 413).

There are two leading ideas here. (i) International trade overcomes
the narrowness of the home market and provides an outlet for the surplus
product above domestic requirements. This develops into what may be
called the " vent for surplus " [1] theory of international trade. Later we
hope to remove some of the prejudice aroused by this " mercantilist "
sounding phrase. (ii) By widening the extent of the market, international
trade also improves the division of labour and raises the general level of
productivity within the country. This develops into what may be called
the " productivity " theory. We shall be mainly concerned with the " vent
for surplus " theory and the light it throws upon the growth of international
trade in the underdeveloped countries in the nineteenth century. But
first it is necessary to consider the " productivity " theory briefly.

The " productivity " doctrine differs from the comparative-costs doctrine
in the interpretation of " specialisation " for international trade. (*a*) In the
comparative costs theory " specialisation " merely means a movement along
a static " production possibility curve " constructed on the given resources
and the *given techniques* of the trading country. In contrast, the " productivity " doctrine looks upon international trade as a dynamic force which, by
widening the extent of the market and the scope of the division of labour,
raises the skill and dexterity of the workmen, encourages technical innova-

---

[1] This term is borrowed from Professor J. H. Williams, who in turn quoted it from a passage in
J. S. Mill's *Principles*, in which Mill was criticising this particular aspect of Smith's theory of international trade. Professor Williams is the only modern economist to sponsor this " crude " doctrine.
While he is mainly concerned with the loss to a country on being deprived of the export market for
its surplus product, we shall pay special attention to the gain to a hitherto isolated underdeveloped
country on obtaining a " vent " for its surplus productive capacity. Cf. J. H. Williams, " The
Theory of International Trade Reconsidered," ECONOMIC JOURNAL, June 1929, pp. 195–209.

tions, overcomes technical indivisibilities and generally enables the trading country to enjoy increasing returns and economic development.[1] This distinction was clearly realised by J. S. Mill, who regarded the gains in terms of comparative-costs theory as direct gains and the gains in terms of Adam Smithian increases in productivity as "indirect effects, which must be counted as benefits of a high order." Mill even went on to extend this doctrine to countries at "an early stage of industrial advancement," where international trade by introducing new wants "sometimes works a sort of industrial revolution" (*Principles*, Ashley ed., p. 581). (*b*) In the comparative costs theory "specialisation," conceived as a reallocation of resources, is a completely reversible process. The Adam Smithian process of specialisation, however, involves adapting and reshaping the productive structure of a country to meet the export demand, and is therefore not easily reversible. This means that a country specialising for the export market is more vulnerable to changes in the terms of trade than is allowed for in the comparative-costs theory. We shall come back to this point later.

In the expansive mental climate of the late nineteenth century the "productivity" aspect of international specialisation completely dominated the "vulnerability" aspect. At a semi-popular level, and particularly in its application to the underdeveloped countries, Smith's "productivity" doctrine developed beyond a free-trade argument into an export-drive argument. It was contended that since international trade was so beneficial in raising productivity and stimulating economic development, the State should go beyond a neutral and negative policy of removing barriers to trade and embark on a positive policy of encouraging international trade and economic development. Under its influence, many colonial governments went far beyond the strict *laissez-faire* policy in their attempts to promote the export trade of the colonies.[2] Further, although these governments were frequently obliged to use "unclassical" methods, such as the granting of monopolistic privileges to the chartered companies or the taxing of the indigenous people to force them to take up wage labour or grow cash crops, they nevertheless sought to justify their policy by invoking the Adam Smithian doctrine of the benefits of international division of labour. This partly explains why some critics have associated the "classical theory" with "colonialism" and why they have frequently singled out Adam Smith for attack instead of Ricardo, the founder of the official classical free-trade theory.

It is fair to say that Smith's "productivity" doctrine is instructive more

---

[1] Cf. *op. cit.*, Chapters II and III, Book I. This aspect of Smith's theory has been made familiar by Professor Allyn Young's article on "Increasing Returns and Economic Progress," ECONOMIC JOURNAL, December 1928, pp. 527–42.

[2] See for instance, L. C. A. Knowles, *The Economic Development of the British Overseas Empire*, Vol. I, pp. 119–20, 248–9 and 486–7. However, in Section IV below we shall argue that, in spite of the attention they have received, these export-drive policies were not successful enough to cause a significant "export-bias."

in relation to the ideological than to the actual economic forces which characterised the nineteenth-century expansion of international trade to the underdeveloped countries.   It is true, as we shall see later,[1] that both the total value and the physical output of the exports of these countries expanded rapidly.   In many cases the rate of increase in export production was well above any possible rate of increase in population, resulting in a considerable rise in output per head.   But it is still true to say that this was achieved not quite in the way envisaged by Smith, viz., a better division of labour and specialisation leading on to innovations and cumulative improvements in skills and productivity per man-hour.   Rather, the increase in output per head seems to have been due: (i) to once-for-all increases in productivity accompanying the transfer of labour from the subsistence economy to the mines and plantations, and (ii) what is more important, as we shall see later, to an increase in working hours and in the proportion of gainfully employed labour relatively to the semi-idle labour of the subsistence economy.

The transfer of labour from the subsistence economy to the mines and plantations with their much higher capital–output ratio and skilled management undoubtedly resulted in a considerable increase in productivity. But this was mostly of a once-for-all character for a number of reasons.   To begin with, the indigenous labour emerging from the subsistence economy was raw and technically backward.   Moreover, it was subject to high rates of turnover, and therefore not amenable to attempts to raise productivity. Unfortunately, this initial experience gave rise to or hardened the convention of " cheap labour," which regarded indigenous labour merely as an undifferentiated mass of low-grade man-power to be used with a minimum of capital outlay.[2]   Thus when the local labour supply was exhausted the typical reaction was not to try to economise labour by installing more machinery and by reorganising methods of production but to seek farther afield for additional supplies of cheap labour.   This is why the nineteenth-century process of international trade in the underdeveloped countries was characterised by large-scale movements of cheap labour from India and China.[3]   This tendency was reinforced by the way in which the world-market demand for raw materials expanded in a series of waves.   During the booms output had to be expanded as quickly as possible along existing lines, and there was no time to introduce new techniques or reorganise production; during the slumps it was difficult to raise capital for such purposes.

[1] See footnotes on pp. 324 and 327 below.   See also Sir Donald MacDougall's *The World Dollar Problem*, pp. 134–43.   Sir Donald's argument that the productivity of labour in the underdeveloped countries has been rising faster than is generally assumed is mainly based on figures for productivity *per capita*.   These figures are not inconsistent with our argument that on the whole the expansion of the export production has been achieved on more or less constant techniques and skills of indigenous labour, by increasing working hours and the proportion of gainfully employed labour rather than by a continuous rise in productivity per man-hour.

[2] Cf. S. H. Frankel, *Capital Investment in Africa*, pp. 142–6, and W. M. Macmillan, *Europe and West Africa*, pp. 48–50.

[3] Cf. Knowles, *op. cit.*, pp. viii and 182–201.

This failure to achieve Adam Smith's ideal of specialisation leading on to continuous improvements in skills can also be observed in the peasant export sectors. Where the export crop happened to be a traditional crop (*e.g.*, rice in South-East Asia), the expansion in export production was achieved simply by bringing more land under cultivation with the same methods of cultivation used in the subsistence economy. Even where new export crops were introduced, the essence of their success as peasant export crops was that they could be produced by fairly simple methods involving no radical departure from the traditional techniques of production employed in subsistence agriculture.[1]

Thus instead of a process of economic growth based on continuous improvements in skills, more productive recombinations of factors and increasing returns, the nineteenth-century expansion of international trade in the underdeveloped countries seems to approximate to a simpler process based on constant returns and fairly rigid combinations of factors. Such a process of expansion could continue smoothly only if it could feed on *additional* supplies of factors in the required proportions.

II

Let us now turn to Smith's " vent for surplus " theory of international trade. It may be contrasted with the comparative-costs theory in two ways.

(*a*) The comparative-costs theory assumes that the resources of a country are given and fully employed before it enters into international trade. The function of trade is then to reallocate its given resources more efficiently between domestic and export production in the light of the new set of relative prices now open to the country. With given techniques and full employment, export production can be increased only at the cost of reducing the domestic production. In contrast, the " vent for surplus " theory assumes that a previously isolated country about to enter into international trade possesses a surplus productive capacity[2] of some sort or another. The function of trade here is not so much to reallocate the given resources as to provide the new effective demand for the output of the surplus resources which would have remained unused in the absence of trade. It follows that export production can be increased without necessarily reducing domestic production.

[1] Thus A. McPhee wrote about the palm-oil and ground-nut exports of West Africa: " They made little demand on the energy and thought of the natives and they effected no revolution in the society of West Africa. That was why they were so readily grafted on the old economy and grew as they did " (*The Economic Revolution in West Africa*, pp. 39–40). Some writers argue that there was a studied neglect of technical improvements in the peasant sector to facilitate the supply of cheap labour to other sectors. Cf., for example, W. A. Lewis, " Economic Development with Unlimited Supplies of Labour," *Manchester School*, May 1954, pp. 149–50. For a description of imperfect specialisation in economic activity in West Africa see P. T. Bauer and B. S. Yamey, " Economic Progress and Occupational Distribution," Economic Journal, December 1951, p. 743.

[2] A surplus over domestic requirements and *not* a surplus of exports over imports.

(*b*) The concept of a surplus productive capacity above the requirements of domestic consumption implies an inelastic domestic demand for the exportable commodity and/or a considerable degree of internal immobility and specificness of resources. In contrast, the comparative-costs theory assumes either a perfect or, at least, a much greater degree of internal mobility of factors and/or a greater degree of flexibility or elasticity both on the side of production and of consumption. Thus the resources not required for export production will not remain as a surplus productive capacity, but will be reabsorbed into domestic production, although this might take some time and entail a loss to the country.

These two points bring out clearly a peculiarity of the " vent-for-surplus " theory which may be used either as a free-trade argument or as an anti-trade argument, depending on the point of view adopted. (*a*) From the point of view of a previously isolated country, about to enter into trade, a surplus productive capacity suitable for the export market appears as a virtually " costless " means of acquiring imports and expanding domestic economic activity. This was how Adam Smith used it as a free-trade argument. (*b*) From the point of view of an established trading country faced with a fluctuating world market, a sizeable surplus productive capacity which cannot be easily switched from export to domestic production makes it " vulnerable " to external economic disturbances. This is in fact how the present-day writers on the underdeveloped countries use the same situation depicted by Smith's theory as a criticism of the nineteenth-century pattern of international trade. This concept of vulnerability may be distinguished from that which we have come across in discussing the " productivity " theory of trade. There, a country is considered " vulnerable " because it has adapted and reshaped its productive structure to meet the requirements of the export market through a genuine process of " specialisation." Here, the country is considered " vulnerable " simply because it happens to possess a sizeable surplus productive capacity which (even without any improvements and extensions) it cannot use for domestic production. This distinction may be blurred in border-line cases, particularly in underdeveloped countries with a large mining sector. But we hope to show that, on the whole, while the " vulnerability " of the advanced countries, such as those in Western Europe which have succeeded in building up large export trades to maintain their large populations, is of the first kind, the " vulnerability " of most of the underdeveloped countries is of the second kind.

Let us now consider the " vent-for-surplus " approach purely as a theoretical tool. There is a considerable amount of prejudice among economists against the " vent-for-surplus " theory, partly because of its technical crudeness and partly because of its mercantilist associations. This may be traced to J. S. Mill, who regarded Smith's " vent-for-surplus " doctrine as " a surviving relic of the Mercantile Theory " (*Principles*, p. 579).

The crux of the matter here is the question: why should a country isolated from international trade have a surplus productive capacity? The answer which suggests itself is that, given its random combination of natural resources, techniques of production, tastes and population, such an isolated country is bound to suffer from a certain imbalance or disproportion between its productive and consumption capacities. Thus, take the case of a country which starts with a sparse population in relation to its natural resources. This was broadly true not only of Western countries during their mercantilist period but also of the underdeveloped countries of South-East Asia, Latin America and Africa when they were opened up to international trade in the nineteenth century. Given this situation, the conventional international-trade theory (in its Ohlin version) would say that this initial disproportion between land and labour would have been equilibrated away by appropriate price adjustments: *i.e.*, rents would be low and relatively land-using commodities would have low prices, whereas wages would be high and relatively labour-using commodities would have high prices. In equilibrium there would be no surplus productive capacity (although there might be surplus land by itself) because the scarce factor, labour, would have been fully employed. Thus when this country enters into international trade it can produce the exports only by drawing labour away from domestic production. Now this result is obtained only by introducing a highly developed price mechanism and economic organisation into a country which is supposed to have had no previous economic contacts with the outside world. This procedure may be instructive while dealing with the isolated economy as a theoretical model. But it is misleading when we are dealing with genuinely isolated economies in their proper historical setting; it is misleading, in particular, when we are dealing with the underdeveloped countries, many of which were subsistence economies when they were opened to international trade. In fact, it was the growth of international trade itself which introduced or extended the money economy in these countries. Given the genuine historical setting of an isolated economy, might not its initial disproportion between its resources, techniques, tastes and population show itself in the form of surplus productive capacity?

Adam Smith himself thought that the pre-existence of a surplus productive capacity in an isolated economy was such a matter of common observation that he assumed it implicitly without elaborating upon it. But he did give some hints suggesting how the " narrowness of the home market," which causes the surplus capacity, is bound up with the underdeveloped economic organisation of an isolated country, particularly the lack of a good internal transport system and of suitable investment opportunities.[1] Further his concept of surplus productive capacity is not merely a matter of surplus land by itself but surplus land combined with surplus labour; and the

[1] *Op. cit.*, Vol. I, pp. 21 and 383. This is similar to what Mrs. J. Robinson has described as " primitive stagnation." Cf. *The Accumulation of Capital*, pp. 256–8.

surplus labour is then linked up with his concept of "unproductive" labour. To avoid confusion, this latter should not be identified with the modern concept of "disguised unemployment" caused by an acute shortage of land in overpopulated countries. Although Smith described some cases of genuine "disguised unemployment" in the modern sense, particularly with reference to China, "unproductive" labour in his sense can arise even in thinly populated countries, provided their internal economic organisation is sufficiently underdeveloped. In fact, it is especially in relation to those underdeveloped countries which started off with sparse populations in relation to their natural resources that we shall find Smith's "vent-for-surplus" approach very illuminating.

III

Let us now try to relate the "vent-for-surplus" theory to the nineteenth-century process of expansion of international trade to the underdeveloped countries. Even from the somewhat meagre historical information about these countries, two broad features stand out very clearly. First the underdeveloped countries of South-East Asia, Latin America and Africa, which were to develop into important export economies, started off with sparse populations relatively to their natural resources. If North America and Australia could then be described as "empty," these countries were at least "semi-empty." Secondly, once the opening-up process had got into its stride, the export production of these countries expanded very rapidly, along a typical growth curve,[1] rising very sharply to begin with and tapering off afterwards. By the Great Depression of the 1930s, the expansion process seems to have come to a stop in many countries; in others, which had a later start, the expansion process may still be continuing after the Second World War.

There are three reasons why the "vent-for-surplus" theory offers a more effective approach than the conventional theory to this type of expansion of international trade in the underdeveloped countries.

(i) The characteristically high rates of expansion which can be observed in the export production of many underdeveloped countries cannot really be explained in terms of the comparative-costs theory based on the assumption of given resources and given techniques. Nor can we attribute any significant part of the expansion to revolutionary changes in techniques and increases in productivity. As we have seen in Section I, peasant export

---

[1] For instance, the annual value of Burma's exports, taking years of high and low prices, increased at a constant proportional rate of 5% per annum on the average between 1870 and 1900. Similar rates of expansion can be observed for Siam and Indonesia (Cf. J. S. Furnivall, *Colonial Policy and Practice*, Appendix I; J. H. Boeke, *The Structure of Netherlands Indian Economy*, p. 184; and J. C. Ingram, *Economic Change in Thailand since 1850*, Appendix C). African export economies started their expansion phase after 1900, and the official trade returns for the Gold Coast, Nigeria and Uganda show similar rates of increase after that date, although the expansion process was arrested by the depression of the 1930s.

production expanded by extension of cultivation using traditional methods of production, while mining and plantation sectors expanded on the basis of increasing supplies of cheap labour with a minimum of capital outlay. Thus the contributions of Western enterprise to the expansion process are mainly to be found in two spheres: the improvements of transport and communications [1] and the discoveries of new mineral resources. Both are methods of increasing the total volume of resources rather than methods of making the given volume of resources more productive. All these factors suggest an expansion process which kept itself going by drawing an increasing volume of hitherto unused or surplus resources into export production.

(ii) International trade between the tropical underdeveloped countries and the advanced countries of the temperate zone has grown out of sharp differences in geography and climate resulting in absolute differences of costs. In this context, the older comparative-costs theory, which is usually formulated in terms of qualitative differences [2] in the resources of the trading countries, tends to stress the obvious geographical differences to the neglect of the more interesting quantitative differences in the factor endowments of countries possessing approximately the same type of climate and geography. Thus while it is true enough to say that Burma is an exporter of rice because of her climate and geography, the more interesting question is why Burma should develop into a major rice exporter while the neighbouring South India, with approximately the same type of climate and geography, should develop into a net importer of rice. Here the " vent-for-surplus " approach which directs our attention to population density as a major determinant of export capacity has an advantage over the conventional theory.[3]

(iii) Granted the importance of quantitative differences in factor endowments, there still remains the question why Smith's cruder " vent-for-surplus " approach should be preferable to the modern Ohlin variant of the comparative-costs theory. The main reason is that, according to the Ohlin theory, a country about to enter into international trade is supposed already to possess a highly developed and flexible economic system which can adjust its methods of production and factor combinations to cope with a wide range of possible variations in relative factor supplies (see Section II above). But in fact the economic framework of the underdeveloped countries is a

---

[1] This is what Professor L. C. A. Knowles described as the " Unlocking of the Tropics " (*op. cit.*, pp. 138–52).

[2] Cf. J. Viner, *International Trade and Economic Development*, pp. 14–16.

[3] Those who are used to handling the problem in terms of qualitative differences in factors and differential rent may ask: why not treat the surplus productive capacity as an extreme instance of " differential rent " where the transfer cost of the factors from the domestic to export production is zero? But this does not accurately portray the situation here. The transfer cost of the factors is zero, not because land which is used for the export crop is not at all usable for domestic subsistence production but because with the sparse population in the early phase there is no demand for the surplus food which could have been produced on the land used for the export crop. As we shall see, at a later stage when population pressure begins to grow, as in Java, land which has been used for export is encroached upon by subsistence production.

much cruder apparatus which can make only rough-and-ready adjustments. In particular, with their meagre technical and capital resources, the under-developed countries operate under conditions nearer to those of fixed technical coefficients than of variable technical coefficients. Nor can they make important adjustments through changes in the outputs of different commodities requiring different proportions of factors because of the inelastic demand both for their domestic production, mainly consisting of basic foodstuff, and for their exportable commodities, mainly consisting of industrial raw materials. Here again the cruder " vent-for-surplus " approach turns out to be more suitable.

Our argument that, in general, the " vent-for-surplus " theory provides a more effective approach than the comparative-costs theory to the inter-national trade of the underdeveloped countries does not mean that the " vent-for-surplus " theory will provide an exact fit to all the particular patterns of development in different types of export economies. No simple theoretical approach can be expected to do this. Thus if we interpret the concept of the surplus productive capacity strictly as pre-existing surplus productive capacity arising out of the original endowments of the factors, it needs to be qualified, especially in relation to the mining and plantation sectors of the underdeveloped countries. Here the surplus productive capacity which may have existed to some extent before the country was opened to inter-national trade is usually greatly increased by the discovery of new mineral resources and by a considerable inflow of foreign capital and immigrant labour. While immigrant labour is the surplus population of other under-developed countries, notably India and China, the term " surplus " in the strict sense cannot be applied to foreign capital. But, of course, the exist-ence of suitable surplus natural resources in an underdeveloped country is a pre-condition of attracting foreign investment into it. Two points may be noted here. First, the complication of foreign investment is not as damaging to the surplus-productive-capacity approach as it appears at first sight, because the inflow of foreign investment into the tropical and semi-tropical underdeveloped countries has been relatively small both in the nineteenth century and the inter-war period.[1] Second, the nineteenth-century pheno-menon of international mobility of capital and labour has been largely neglected by the comparative-costs theory, which is based on the assumption of perfect mobility of factors within a country and their imperfect mobility between different countries. The surplus-productive-capacity approach at least serves to remind us that the output of mining and plantation sectors can expand without necessarily contracting domestic subsistence output.

The use of the surplus-productive-capacity approach may prove in particular to be extremely treacherous in relation to certain parts of Africa,

[1] Cf. R. Nurkse, " International Investment To-day in the Light of Nineteenth Century Experience," ECONOMIC JOURNAL, December 1954, pp. 744–58, and the United Nations Report on *International Capital Movements during the Inter-war Period.*

where mines, plantations and other European enterprises have taken away from the tribal economies the so-called " surplus " land and labour, which, on a closer analysis, prove to be no surplus at all.   Here the extraction of these so-called " surplus " resources, by various forcible methods in which normal economic incentives play only a part, entails not merely a reduction in the subsistence output but also much heavier social costs in the form of the disruption of the tribal societies.[1]

When we turn to the peasant export sectors, however, the application of the " vent-for-surplus " theory is fairly straightforward.   Here, unlike the mining and plantation sectors, there has not been a significant inflow of foreign investment and immigrant labour.   The main function of the foreign export–import firms has been to act as middlemen between the world market and the peasants, and perhaps also to stimulate the peasants' wants for the new imported consumers' goods.   As we have seen, peasant export production expanded by using methods of production more or less on the same technical level as those employed in the traditional subsistence culture. Thus the main effect of the innovations, such as improvements in transport and communications [2] and the introduction of the new crops, was to bring a greater area of surplus land under cultivation rather than to raise the physical productivity per unit of land and labour.   Yet peasant export production usually managed to expand as rapidly as that of the other sectors while remaining self-sufficient with respect to basic food crops.   Here, then, we have a fairly close approximation to the concept of a pre-existing surplus productive capacity which can be tapped by the world-market demand with a minimum addition of external resources.

Even here, of course, there is room for differences in interpretation.   For instance, there is evidence to suggest that, in the early decades of expansion, the rates of increase in peasant export production in South-East Asian and West African countries were well above the possible rates of growth in their working population.[3]   Given the conditions of constant techniques, no significant inflow of immigrant foreign labour and continuing self-sufficiency with respect to the basic food crops, we are left with the question how these peasant economies managed to obtain the extra labour required to

[1] Cf. The United Nations Report on the *Enlargement of the Exchange Economy in Tropical Africa*, pp. 37 and 49–51.

[2] It may be noted that the expansion of some peasant export crops, notably rice in South-East Asia, depended to a much greater extent on pre-existing indigenous transport facilities, such as river boats and bullock carts, than is generally realised.

[3] For instance, cocoa output of the Gold Coast expanded over forty times during the twenty-five year period 1905–30.   Even higher rates of expansion in cocoa production can be observed in Nigeria combined with a considerable expansion in the output of other export crops.   Both have managed to remain self-sufficient with regard to basic food crops (cf. West African Institute of Economic Research, *Annual Conference*, Economic Section, Achimota, 1953, especially the chart between pp. 96 and 98; *The Native Economies of Nigeria*, ed. M. Perham, Vol. I, Part II).   In Lower Burma, for the thirty-year period 1870–1900, the area under rice cultivation increased by more than three times, while the population, including immigrants from Upper Burma, doubled. (Cf. also, Furnivall, *op. cit.*, pp. 84–5.)

expand their export production so rapidly.   A part of this labour may have
been released by the decline in cottage industries and by the introduction
of modern labour-saving forms of transport in place of porterage, but the gap
in the explanation cannot be satisfactorily filled until we postulate that even
those peasant economies which started off with abundant land relatively to
their population must have had initially a considerable amount of under-
employed or surplus labour.   This surplus labour existed, not because of a
shortage of co-operating factors, but because in the subsistence economies,
with poor transport and little specialisation in production, each self-sufficient
economic unit could not find any market outlet to dispose of its potential
surplus output, and had therefore no incentive to produce more than its
own requirements.   Here, then, we have the archetypal form of Smith's
" unproductive " labour locked up in a semi-idle state in the underdeveloped
economy of a country isolated from outside economic contacts.   In most
peasant economies this surplus labour was mobilised, however, not by the
spread of the money-wage system of employment, but by peasant economic
units with their complement of " family " labour moving *en bloc* into the
money economy and export production.

The need to postulate a surplus productive capacity to explain the rapid
expansion in peasant export production is further strengthened when we
reflect on the implications of the fact that this expansion process is inextric-
ably bound up with the introduction of the money economy into the subsistence sectors.   To the peasant on the threshold of international trade,
the question whether or not to take up export production was not merely a
question of growing a different type of crop but a far-reaching decision to
step into the new and unfamiliar ways of the money economy.

Thus let us consider a community of self-sufficient peasants who, with
their existing techniques, have just sufficient land and labour to produce
their minimum subsistence requirements, so that any export production can
be achieved only by reducing the subsistence output below the minimum
level.   Now, according to the conventional economic theory, there is no
reason why these peasants should not turn to export production if they have a
differential advantage there, so that they could more than make up for their
food deficit by purchases out of their cash income from the export crop.
But, in practice, the peasants in this situation are unlikely to turn to export
production so readily.   Nor is this " conservatism " entirely irrational, for
by taking up export production on such a slender margin of reserves, the
peasants would be facing the risk of a possible food shortage for the sake of
some gain in the form of imported consumers' goods which are " luxuries "
to them.   Moreover, this gain might be wiped off by unfavourable
changes in the prices of both the export crop they would sell and the foodstuffs they would have to buy and by the market imperfections, which would
be considerable at this early stage.   Thus, where the margin of resources is
very small above that required for the minimum subsistence output, we

should expect the spread of export production to be inhibited or very slow, even if there were some genuine possibilities of gains on the comparative costs principle.[1]

In contrast, the transition from subsistence agriculture to export production is made much easier when we assume that our peasants start with some surplus resources which enable them to produce the export crop *in addition* to their subsistence production. Here the surplus resources perform two functions: first they enable the peasants to hedge their position completely and secure their subsistence minimum before entering into the risks of trading; and secondly, they enable them to look upon the imported goods they obtain from trade in the nature of a clear net gain obtainable merely for the effort of the extra labour in growing the export crop. Both of these considerations are important in giving the peasants just that extra push to facilitate their first plunge into the money economy.

Starting from this first group of peasants, we may picture the growth of export production and the money economy taking place in two ways. Firstly, the money economy may grow extensively, with improvements in transport and communications and law and order, bringing in more and more groups of peasants with their complements of family labour into export production on the same "part-time" basis as the first group of peasants. Secondly, the money economy may grow intensively by turning the first group of peasants from "part-time" into "whole-time" producers of the export crop.[2] In the first case, surplus resources are necessary as a lubricant to push more peasants into export production at each round of the widening circle of the money economy. Even in the second case, surplus resources are necessary if the whole-time export producers buy their food requirements locally from other peasants, who must then have surplus resources to produce the food crops above their own requirements. Logically, there is no reason why the first group of peasants who are now whole-time producers of the

[1] Of course, this argument can be countered by assuming the differences in comparative costs to be very wide. But, so long as export production requires withdrawing some resources from subsistence production, some risks are unavoidable. Further, remembering that the middlemen also require high profit margins at this stage, the gains large enough to overcome the obstacles are likely to arise out of surplus resources rather than from the differential advantages of the given fully employed resources. The risk of crop-failure is, of course, present both in subsistence and export production.

[2] In either case the expansion process may be looked upon as proceeding under conditions approximating to constant techniques and fixed combinations between land and labour once equilibrium is reached. The distinctive feature of peasant export economies is their failure to develop new and larger-scale or extensive methods of farming. It is true that in subsistence agriculture "fixed factors," such as a plough and a pair of bullocks, were frequently used below capacity, and one important effect of cash production was to increase the size of the holding to the full capacity of these "fixed factors." But this may be properly looked upon as equilibrium adjustments to make full use of surplus capacity rather than as the adoption of new and more land-using methods of production. Increasing the size of holding to make a more effective use of a pair of bullocks is different from the introduction of a tractor! Our assumption of constant techniques does not preclude the development of large-scale ownership of land as distinct from large-scale farming.

export crop should buy their food requirements locally instead of importing them. But, as it happens, few peasant export economies have specialised in export production to such an extent as to import their basic food requirements.

The average economist's reaction to our picture of discrete blocks of surplus productive capacity being drawn into a widening circle of money economy and international trade is to say that while this " crude " analysis may be good enough for the transition phase, the conventional analysis in terms of differential advantages and continuous marginal productivity curves must come into its own once the transition phase is over. Here it is necessary to distinguish between the expansion phase and the transition phase. It is true that in most peasant export economies the expansion process is tapering off or has come to a stop, as most of the surplus land suitable for the export crop has been brought under cultivation. This, of course, brings back the problem of allocating a fixed amount of resources, as we shall see in the next section when we consider issues of economic policy. But even so, the surplus-productive-capacity approach is not entirely superseded so long as the transition from a subsistence to a fully developed money economy remains incomplete. In most underdeveloped countries of Asia and Africa [1] this transition seems not likely to be over until they cease to be underdeveloped.

The continuing relevance of the surplus-productive-capacity approach may be most clearly seen in the typical case of a peasant export economy which with its natural resources and methods of production has reached the limit of expansion in production while its population continues to grow rapidly. According to the surplus-productive-capacity approach, we should expect the export capacity of such a country to fall roughly in proportion as the domestic requirement of resources to feed a larger population increases. This common-sense result may, however, be contrasted with that obtainable from the conventional theory as formulated by Ohlin. First, it appears that the Ohlin theory puts to the forefront of the picture the *type* of export, *i.e.*, whether it is more labour-using or land-using as distinct from the total export capacity measured by the ratio of total exports to the total national output of the trading country. Secondly, in the Ohlin theory there is no reason why a thickly populated country should not also possess a high ratio of (labour-intensive) exports to its total output.

The ideal pattern of trade suggested by the Ohlin theory has a real counterpart in the thickly populated advanced countries of Europe, which for that very reason are obliged to build up a large export trade in manufactures or even in agriculture as in the case of Holland. But when we turn to the thickly populated underdeveloped countries, however, the ideal

[1] Cf. the United Nations Report cited above on the *Enlargement of the Exchange Economy*. Even in the most developed peasant export economies the money economy has not spread to the same extent in the market for factors of production as in the market for products.

and the actual patterns of international trade diverge widely from each other.   Indeed, we may say that these countries remain underdeveloped precisely because they have not succeeded in building up a labour-intensive export trade to cope with their growing population.   The ratio of their export to total production could, of course, be maintained at the same level and the pressure of population met in some other way.   But given the existing conditions, even this neutral pattern may not be possible in many underdeveloped countries.   Thus, in Indonesia there is some evidence to suggest that the volume of agricultural exports from the thickly populated Java and Madura is declining absolutely and also relatively to those of the Outer Islands, which are still sparsely populated.[1]   Of course, there are other causes of this decline, but population pressure reducing the surplus productive capacity of Java seems to be a fundamental economic factor; and the decline spreads from peasant to plantation exports as more of the plantation lands, which were under sugar and rubber, are encroached upon by the peasants for subsistence production.[2]   In general, given the social and economic conditions prevailing in many underdeveloped countries, it seems fair to conclude that the trend in their export trade is likely to be nearer to that suggested by the surplus-productive-capacity approach than to that suggested by the theory of comparative costs.[3]

IV

This paper is mainly concerned with interpretation and analysis, but we may round off our argument by touching briefly upon some of its policy implications.

(i) We have seen that the effect of population pressure on many under-developed countries, given their existing social and economic organisation, is likely to reduce their export capacity by diverting natural resources from export to subsistence production.   If we assume that these natural resources have a genuine differential advantage in export production, then population pressure inflicts a double loss: first, through simple diminishing returns, and secondly, by diverting resources from more to less productive use.

[1] Cf. J. H. Boeke, *Ontwikkelingsgang en toekomst van bevolkings-en ondernemingslandbouw in Neder-landsch-Indie* (Leiden, 1948), p. 91.   I owe this reference to an unpublished thesis by Mr. M. Kidron.

[2] The same tendency to transfer land from plantation to subsistence agriculture may be observed in Fiji with the growing population pressure created by the Indian immigrant labour originally introduced to work in the sugar plantations.   The outline is blurred here by the decline in the sugar industry.   The reason why this tendency does not seem to operate in the West Indies is complex. But it may be partly attributable to the tourist industry, which helps to pay for the food imports of some of the islands.

[3] The surplus-productive-capacity approach also partly helps to explain why underdeveloped countries, such as India, which started off with a thick population tend to retain large and persistent pockets of subsistence sectors in spite of their longer contacts with the world economy, while the subsistence sectors in thinly populated countries, such as those in West Africa, tend to disappear at a faster rate in spite of their much later start in international trade.

Thus, if Java has a genuine differential advantage in growing rubber and sugar, she would obtain a greater amount of rice by maintaining her plantation estates instead of allowing them to be encroached upon by peasants for subsistence rice cultivation. The orthodox liberal economists, confronted with this situation, would, of course, strongly urge the removal of artificial obstacles to a more systematic development of the money economy and the price system. Now there are still many underdeveloped countries which are suffering acutely from the economic rigidities arising out of their traditional social structure and/or from discriminatory policies based on differences in race, religion and class. Here the removal of barriers, for instance, to the horizontal and vertical mobility of labour, freedom to own land and to enter any occupation, etc., may well prove to be a great liberating force.[1] But our analysis has suggested that it is much easier to promote the growth of the money economy in the early stage when a country is newly opened up to international trade and still has plenty of surplus land and labour rather than at a later stage, when there are no more surplus resources, particularly land, to feed the growth of the money economy. Thus in a country like Java there is a considerable amount of artificial restriction, customary or newly introduced, which the liberal economists can criticise, *e.g.*, restriction on land ownership. But given the combination of population pressure, large pockets of subsistence economy and traditional methods of production which can no longer be made more labour-intensive, it seems very doubtful whether the mere removal of artificial restrictions can do much by itself without a more vigorous policy of state interference. The truth of the matter is that in the underdeveloped countries where, for various reasons described above, the exchange economy is still an extremely crude and imperfect apparatus which can make only rough-and-ready responses to economic differentials, it may require a considerable amount of state interference to move toward the comparative-costs equilibrium. Thus given that Java has genuine differential advantages in the production of rubber and sugar, a more optimal reallocation of her resources may require, for instance, the removal of her surplus population either to the thinly populated Outer Islands or to industries within Java and a vigorous export-drive policy supplemented by bulk purchase and subsidies on the imported rice. Here we come to a fundamental dilemma which is particularly acute for the orthodox liberal economists. On a closer examination it turns out that their free-trade argument, although ostensibly based on the comparative-costs principle, is buttressed by certain broad classical presumptions against protection and state interference :[2] *e.g.*, the difficulty of selecting the right

[1] This is why the case for the "liberal" solution is strong in places such as East and Central Africa, where due both to the general backwardness of the indigenous population and the presence of a white settler population, both types of rigidity prevail (cf. *The Royal Commission Report on East Africa*).

[2] Cf. J. Viner, *International Trade and Economic Development*, pp. 41–2. See also Sidgwick, *Principles of Political Economy*, Book III, Chapter V.

industry to protect, the virtual impossibility of withdrawing protection once given, the tendency of controls to spread promiscuously throughout the economic system strangling growth, and so on. These presumptions gain an added strength from the well-known administrative inefficiency and sometimes corruption of the governments of some underdeveloped countries. Thus even if we believe in the " nineteenth-century pattern " of international trade based on natural advantages, how can we be sure that the state is competent enough to select the right commodities for its export-drive policy when it is considered incompetent to select the right industry for protection?

(ii) We have seen that the rapid expansion in the export production of the underdeveloped countries in the nineteenth century cannot be satisfactorily explained without postulating that these countries started off with a considerable amount of surplus productive capacity consisting both of unused natural resources and under-employed labour. This gives us a common-sense argument for free trade which is especially relevant for the underdeveloped countries in the nineteenth century: the surplus productive capacity provided these countries with a virtually " costless " means of acquiring imports which did not require a withdrawal of resources from domestic production but merely a fuller employment for their semi-idle labour. Of course, one may point to the real cost incurred by the indigenous peoples in the form of extra effort and sacrifice of the traditional leisurely life [1] and also to the various social costs not normally considered in the comparative-costs theory, such as being sometimes subject to the pressure of taxation and even compulsory labour and frequently of having to accommodate a considerable inflow of immigrant labour creating difficult social and political problems later on. One may also point to a different type of cost which arises with the wasteful exploitation of natural resources.[2] But for the most part it is still true to say that the indigenous peoples of the underdeveloped countries took to export production on a voluntary basis and enjoyed a clear gain by being able to satisfy their developing wants for the new imported commodities. Thus our special argument for free trade in this particular context still remains largely intact. The orthodox economists, by rigidly insisting on applying the comparative-costs theory to the underdeveloped countries in the nineteenth century, have therefore missed this simpler and more powerful argument.

[1] It may be formally possible to subsume the surplus-productive-capacity approach under the opportunity-cost theory, by treating leisure instead of foregone output as the main element of cost. But this would obscure the important fact that the underdeveloped countries have been able to expand their production very rapidly, not merely because the indigenous peoples were willing to sacrifice leisure but also because there were also surplus natural resources to work upon.

[2] The social cost of soil erosion can be very great, but this may be caused not merely by an expansion of export production but also by bad methods of cultivation and population pressure. The problem of adequately compensating the underdeveloped countries for the exploitation of their non-replaceable mineral resources belongs to the problem of the distribution of gains from trade. Here we are merely concerned with establishing that the indigenous peoples do obtain some gains from trade.

(iii) We have seen in Section I that the deep-rooted hostility of the critics towards the " classical theory " and the nineteenth-century pattern of international trade may be partly traced back to the time when Western colonial powers attempted to introduce export-drive policies in the tropical underdeveloped countries; and tried to justify these policies by invoking the " classical theory " of free trade and the Adam Smithian doctrine of international trade as a dynamic force generating a great upward surge in the general level of productivity of the trading countries. To the critics, this appears as a thinly disguised rationalisation of the advanced countries' desire for the markets for their manufactured products and for raw materials. Thus it has become a standard argument with the critics to say that the nineteenth-century process of international trade has introduced a large " export bias " into the economic structure of the underdeveloped countries which has increased their " vulnerability " to international economic fluctuations.

In Section II we have seen that once we leave the ideal world of the comparative costs theory in which the resources not required for the export market can be re-absorbed into domestic production, every country with a substantial export trade may be considered " vulnerable." Thus a country may be said to be vulnerable because it has built up a large ratio of export to its total production simply by making use of its pre-existing surplus productive capacity. *A fortiori*, it is vulnerable when it has genuinely improved upon its original surplus productive capacity. How does the idea of " export bias " fit into our picture?

The term " export bias " presumably means that the resources of the underdeveloped countries which could have been used for domestic production have been effectively diverted into export production by deliberate policy. The implication of our surplus-productive-capacity approach is to discount this notion of " export bias." In the peasant export sectors, at the early stage with sparse populations and plenty of surplus land, the real choice was not so much between using the resources for export production or for domestic production as between giving employment to the surplus resources in export production or leaving them idle. In the later stage, when the population pressure begins to increase as in the case of Java, we have seen that the bias is likely to develop against, rather than in favour of, the export sector. Even when we turn to the mining and plantation sectors, it is difficult to establish a significant " export bias " in the strict sense. Here the crucial question is: how far would it have been possible to divert the foreign capital and technical resources which have gone into these sectors into the domestic sector? The answer is clear. For a variety of reasons, notably the smallness of domestic markets, few governments of the underdeveloped countries, whether colonial or independent, have so far succeeded in attracting a significant amount of foreign investment away from the extractive export industries to the domestic industries. In criticising the colonial governments it should be remembered that the only choice open to them was whether to attract a greater or a smaller amount of foreign investment within the export sector and not whether to attract investment for the domestic or the export sector.

This is not to deny that the colonial governments had a strong motive for promoting export production. Apart from the interests of the mother country, the individual colonial governments themselves had a vested interest in the expansion of foreign trade because they derived the bulk of their revenues from it.[1] In their search for revenue they have pursued various policies designed to attract foreign investment to the mining and plantation sectors, such as granting favourable concessions and leases, favourable tariff rates for rail transport, taxation policy designed to facilitate the supply of labour, provision of various technical services, etc.[2] But on the whole it is still true to say that the most important contribution of the colonial governments towards the expansion of the colonial exports is to be found, not in these export-drive policies, but in their basic services, such as the establishment of law and order and the introduction of modern transport, which enabled the pre-existing surplus productive capacity of the colonies to be tapped by the world market demand. If we wish to criticise the export-drive policies of the colonial governments it would be more appropriate to do so, not on the ground of " export bias " but on the ground that they may have diverted too great a share of the gains from international trade and of the public services of the colonies to the foreign-owned mines and plantations at the expense of indigenous labour and peasant export producers.

It may be argued that we have given too strict an interpretation of the " export-bias " doctrine which is merely meant to convey the general proposition that, whatever the exact cause, the nineteenth-century process of international trade has landed many underdeveloped countries with a large ratio of raw materials exports to their total national products, making it desirable to reduce their " vulnerability " to international economic fluctuations. But the trouble is that the " export bias " doctrine tends to suggest that the raw-materials export production of the underdeveloped countries has been artificially over-expanded, not merely in relation to their domestic sector, but absolutely. Given the strong feelings of economic nationalism and anti-colonialism in the underdeveloped countries, this can be a very mischievous doctrine strengthening the widespread belief that to go on producing raw materials for the export market is tantamount to preserving the " colonial " pattern of trade. Thus already many underdeveloped countries are giving too little encouragement to their peasant

[1] This is true for the governments of most underdeveloped countries, whether colonial or independent, past or present.

[2] For a discussion of the question of the possible export bias through the operation of the 100% sterling exchange system of the colonies, see A. D. Hazlewood, " Economics of Colonial Monetary Arrangements," *Social and Economic Studies*, Jamaica, December 1954.

export sectors by diverting too much of their capital and technical resources to industrial-development projects, and are also crippling their mining and plantation export sectors by actual or threatened nationalisation and various restrictions and regulations. The effect is to reduce their foreign-exchange earnings so urgently needed for their economic development. Of course, no competent critic of the nineteenth-century pattern of international trade would ever suggest the drastic step of reducing exports absolutely; some would even concede the need for vigorous export drive policies.[1] But having built up a pervasive feeling of hostility and suspicion against the " nineteenth-century " or the " colonial " pattern of international trade, they are not in a position to ram home the obvious truths: (*a*) that, even on an optimistic estimate of the possibilities of international aid, the underdeveloped countries will have to pay for the larger part of the cost of their economic plans aiming either at a greater national self-sufficiency or at the export of manufactured goods; (*b*) that the necessary foreign exchange for these development plans can be earned by the underdeveloped countries at the present moment only by the export of raw materials (though not necessarily the same commodities for which they were supposed to have a differential advantage in the nineteenth century); and (*c*) that therefore to pursue their development plans successfully it is vitally important for them to carry out the " export-drive " policies, which in their technical properties may not be very different from those of the colonial governments in the past.[2] In trying to carry out their development plans on the foreign-exchange earnings from raw-materials export they would, of course, still be " vulnerable "; but this should be considered separately as a problem in short-term economic stability[3] and not as a criticism of the nineteenth-century pattern of international trade in relation to the long-term development of the underdeveloped countries. From a long-term point of view, even countries which have successfully industrialised themselves and are therefore able to maintain their population at a higher standard of living by building up a large export trade in manufactures, such as Japan or the

[1] Cf., for example, Gunnar Myrdal, *An International Economy*, p. 274.

[2] Colonial governments have frequently defended their export-drive policies as the means of taxing foreign trade to finance services needed for internal development. But because they were colonial governments, their motives were suspect. At first sight we might imagine that the new independent governments of the underdeveloped countries would be free from this disability. But unfortunately, given the atmosphere of intense nationalism and anti-colonialism, this is not true. In some cases the hands of the newly independent governments seem to be tied even more tightly, and economic policies admitted to be desirable are turned down as " politically impossible." Here those economists who regard themselves as the critics of the classical theory and the nineteenth-century pattern of international trade have a special responsibility. Instead of dealing tenderly with the " understandable " emotional reactions which they have partly helped to create, they ought to be emphatic in pointing out the conflicts between rational considerations and " understandable " mental attitudes. The underdeveloped countries are too poor to enjoy the luxury of harbouring their emotional resentments.

[3] Cf. the United Nations Report on *Measures for International Economic Stability* and Myrdal's comments on it, *op. cit.*, pp. 238–53.

thickly populated countries of Western Europe, will continue to be " vulnerable." [1]

H. MYINT

Oxford.

[1] It is particularly in relation to the thickly populated advanced countries of Western Europe which have specialised and adapted their economic structure to the requirements of the export market that Professor J. H. Williams found Adam Smith's " vent-for-surplus " approach illuminating. We have, in this paper, interpreted the " surplus " more strictly in its pre-existing form without the improvements and augmentation in productive capacity due to genuine " specialisation." (Cf. J. H. Williams, " International Trade Theory and Policy—Some Current Issues," *American Economic Review, Papers and Proceedings*, 1951, pp. 426-7.)

[4]

TRADE AS A HANDMAIDEN OF GROWTH: SIMILARITIES BETWEEN THE NINETEENTH AND TWENTIETH CENTURIES[1]

THERE is a widely held view that international trade served as an engine of growth for the periphery countries in the nineteenth century but that it cannot be counted upon to serve a similar function for the developing countries of the twentieth century. It is probably no exaggeration to say that this interpretation of the past and assessment of the present has been a major influence in the formulation of post-Second World War economic policy in the developing countries of the world. Furthermore, since development in to-day's world is much more a matter of conscious direction and effort, current trade-pessimism theory is a matter of great practical importance. The widespread and largely uncritical acceptance of this theory has led to inward-oriented development policies and, more recently, as the limits of import substitution have become more obvious, to an emphasis on the *external* forces limiting the ability of the L.D.C.s to increase their export proceeds.

A full investigation of the contrasts and similarities between the rôle of trade in promoting the economic growth of developing countries in the nineteenth and twentieth centuries would be a monumental task. In this paper we attempt only to examine some of the more important empirical evidence that has a bearing on the generalisations about the trade-growth nexus of the past and present.

This evidence, it is argued below, does not support any simple generalisations about the dominant rôle of trade in the success stories of nineteenth-century growth. Export expansion did not serve in the nineteenth century to differentiate successful from unsuccessful countries. Growth where it occurred was mainly the consequence of favourable internal factors, and external demand represented an added stimulus which varied in importance from country to country and period to period. A more warranted metaphor that would be more generally applicable would be to describe trade expansion as a handmaiden of successful growth rather than as an autonomous engine of growth.

Neither does the evidence provide a basis for the view that external conditions for to-day's developing countries are less favourable than nine-

[1] Most of the work on this paper was performed during the author's tenure as a Guggenheim Fellow. The aid of a grant from the National Science Foundation and the use of the facilities of the Maurice Falk Foundation for Economic Research in Israel are also gratefully acknowledged. Tzve Bodey and Linda Robson assisted with the statistical materials. The author benefited from the comments of Arthur Bloomfield, Richard Easterlin, Charles Kindleberger, Robert Lipsey and Wilfred Malenbaum.

teenth-century markets were for the periphery countries of that time.[1]   In to-day's world, trade can still play the handmaiden rôle in the growth of developing countries.[2]

I. The Engine-of-growth Hypothesis

The historical engine-of-growth and current trade-pessimism theory was most systematically set forth by Ragnar Nurkse.[3]   His reading of nineteenth-century history (*i.e.*, 1815–1914 [44, p. 284]) was that the large increases in the exports of new countries in temperate latitudes were attributable mainly to favourable demand conditions.   It was " the tremendous expansion of western Europe's, and especially Great Britain's, demand . . . for foodstuffs and raw materials " that provided " the basic inducement that caused them [especially the United States, Canada, Argentina and Australia] to develop." " Trade in the Nineteenth Century . . . was above all an engine of growth " [44, pp. 242–3].   Even in the nineteenth century, however, the pattern did not work for all periphery areas.   It was primarily in the potential granaries of the world where the mechanism triggered growth; other areas were relatively neglected by the expansion of export demand and the flow of capital, or developed dual economies [44, p. 289].

Nurkse did not oppose trade in principle as an engine of growth for to-day's developing countries, but he was pessimistic about its availability to the developing countries.   The world's industrial centres were no longer " exporting " their own growth rates to primary producing countries, owing to such factors as low income elasticities of demand, the rise of synthetics and the importance of home primary product output in the advanced countries (especially in the United States).   Prospects for exports of manufactures from the developing countries to the industrial centres were also poor, both because of the " formidable " obstacles to the attainment of a minimum level

---

[1] Nothing in this paper, however, is intended to deny the justice of many of the complaints of the developing countries about the commercial policies of the developed countries.   By preventing market access for commodities such as textiles and sugar, which L.D.C.s could produce competitively in free markets, and by imposing tariffs that are progressive with the stage of processing, the United States and other developed countries make it more difficult for the L.D.C.s to develop their economies along efficient lines and frustrate the developed countries' avowed objectives for the world economy.   Nevertheless, it is argued below, the large and rapidly growing income and trade of the developed countries have still been providing market opportunities for L.D.C.s, which, though less favourable than they should be, are quite substantial relative to those that were available to the developing countries of the nineteenth century.

[2] A greater contrast between the nineteenth and twentieth centuries in the rôle of trade may be found in the extent to which the emerging countries of both periods were open to one of the major indirect benefits of trade—viz., the rôle of international competition in limiting the development of high-cost inefficient industries.   (Cf. [25, pp. 10 f.] and Keesing [29].)   Tariffs, the protective instruments of the nineteenth century, did not, even when high, sever the link between the domestic and the world price structure as completely as do quantitative controls, which are widely employed in addition to high tariffs in most twentieth-century developing countries.

[3] See his " Balanced and Unbalanced Growth " and " Patterns of Trade and Development," reprinted in [44].   " Patterns . . " contains his two Wicksell Lectures, one of which was the famous " Contrasting Trends in Nineteenth and Twentieth Century World Trade."

of efficiency in the former countries and because of unfavourable commercial policies in the latter [44, pp. 244, 299, 308–14].

Other writers, notably Prebisch and Myrdal, went beyond Nurkse's pessimism about the adequacy of markets and claimed that free trade would be an impediment to the economic advance of the poor countries, the former basing his argument on an alleged secular deterioration in the terms of trade [48] and the latter on the claim that trade would tend to perpetuate or even create backward sectors in the underdeveloped countries [41].

It was his empirical finding that " growth through trade " was no longer possible that led Nurkse to prescribe balanced growth—*i.e.*, a " linked progress " in farming and manufacturing [44, p. 315] and diversification within manufacturing " enough to overcome the frustration of isolated advance " [44, p. 252]. " This export lag is a basic assumption without which balanced growth is untenable or pointless " [44, p. 279].

Nurkse's reference to supply factors in the course of rejecting the possibility of manufactured goods exported by developing countries is one of the few passages in his treatment of trade and development in which supply is admitted to the discussion. He was, of course, aware that he was concentrating only on part of the story. " It is not suggested that the trade-and-investment relationship is the only explanation of their rapid growth in the past. There are other factors, but these lie outside our present subject " [44, p. 288]. Despite this and a few other caveats, Nurkse assigned a primary role to trade in the nineteenth-century growth. As he himself pointed out, his analysis and his conclusions were based on " the causal predominance of demand conditions " [44, p. 299].

Although a wide variety of alternative hypotheses about the relationship of trade and growth was advanced before and after Nurkse's essays, the policy implications of Nurkse's explanation corresponded to the inclinations of influential writers, advisers and government officials in Latin America, where the collapse of export proceeds in the 1930s had made a lasting impression, and in Asia and Africa, where newly independent countries tended to equate exports, especially primary product exports, with colonialism or at least with an undesired dependence on ex-colonial powers. Thus, despite the early doubts expressed by Haberler [25] and Cairncross [8],[1] Nurkse's contrast between trading opportunities in the nineteenth and twentieth centuries has been repeatedly cited down to the present day as justification for inward-oriented development programmes stressing import substitution. The acceptance of Nurkse's views has also led to an emphasis upon external demand factors rather than on internal structural or supply factors in accounting for the lag of L.D.C. exports or in considering the possibilities of L.D.C. export expansion.[2]

[1] See also the writings of Charles Kindleberger, who has stressed the variety of response in growth rates to foreign trade stimuli [31, esp. Chap. 12] and [30].

[2] For a recent example of an official United Nations document in which the contrast between nineteenth- and twentieth-century conditions was cited, see [51, pp. 6–7].

Now, more than two decades after the Second World War, enough experience has accumulated to make it possible to assess at least tentatively the relative rôles of demand and supply factors in the export performance of L.D.C.s. As a background for this assessment, we begin by examining nineteenth-century experience in the light of Nurkse's hypothesis.

II. The Nineteenth-century Experience

The hypothesis of nineteenth-century growth induced by export demand might be examined in terms of the historical records of three groups of countries—those new countries that did in fact experience rapid growth, those periphery countries whose *per capita* incomes did not rise rapidly and the centre countries. For each type of country we may ask what historical phenomena we might expect to be able to observe if the hypothesis were correct, and then see the extent to which these expectations are borne out.

A. *From the Vantage Point of the Successful Countries*

The successful countries upon which Nurkse based his generalisation about the rôle of trade in the nineteenth century were a small number of new countries in the " regions of recent settlement "; he mentioned Argentina, Australia, Canada, New Zealand, South Africa, the United States and Uruguay.

If Nurkse was right—if the growth of these countries was dominated by external demand—we should expect to find at least some of the following features in their economic history: (1) a large and/or growing share of exports in domestic production; (2) an association between the timing of changes in exports and in G.N.P. with the latter following the former; (3) a concentration of exports in sectors marked by relatively rapid growth and/or rapid growth of industries linked to the export industries; (4) the attraction of foreign capital to export industries or to industries supported by them.

Of the seven countries mentioned by Nurkse, the United States at least shows few signs of export-dominated growth.[1] Exports remained a small and relatively constant proportion of G.N.P. (6 or 7%). Changes in exports tended to lag behind changes in G.N.P. Exports were concentrated in agriculture, which was characterised by lower output per man[2] and by slower growth than the rest of the economy.[3] Foreign capital was attracted by domestically generated growth (railroads, the most important area of foreign investment, earned only a small fraction—less than 5% in 1890—of

---

[1] This conclusion and the statements in the rest of the paragraph are based upon a study of the rôle of foreign trade in United States growth which will be published in another article. The most persuasive case for the contrary position has been set out by D. North [42] for the period before the Civil War. See also Baldwin [2], Easterlin [16], Fishlow [20], Temin [50], and Williamson [57].

[2] Value added per worker in agriculture varied from 64 to 76% of the average for all commodity-producing sectors, without trend, in the census years (ten years apart) from 1839 to 1899 [22].

[3] The share of agriculture in commodity output declined from 69% in 1839 to 33% in 1899 [22].

their revenues from moving agricultural exports), and in any case foreign capital, though it financed significant fractions of United States net capital formation during certain periods,[1] contributed only about 5 or 6% of the total over the century preceding the First World War taken as a whole.

It has not been possible for the writer to study each of the other six countries in the same way as the United States, and the Nurkse thesis may well fit their economic history better than it does that of the United States. However, it is not unlikely that some qualifications, at least, would have to be made for one or more of these countries.[2] In Australia, for example, the course of growth appears also to have been dominated mainly by internal conditions, though Australia was much more dependent on outside financing than the United States (cf. Butlin [6, p. 5]). More exceptions would be found if attention were paid to the quality of growth. Argentina, for example, seems to conform to the Nurkse hypothesis of export-led nineteenth-century growth [18], but if account is taken of such factors as the distribution of income and the establishment of conditions fostering innovation nineteenth-century Argentina is not a success story. The difference in these respects from the United States cannot be ascribed to external factors: the two countries enjoyed roughly similar rates of export expansion and were exporting similar products in the last half of the nineteenth century. The reasons must be sought in internal factors such as the way in which land was distributed and the quality of the labour force.

B. *The Standpoint of the Unsuccessful Periphery Countries*

The implication of the external demand hypothesis is that the expansion of nineteenth-century trade served as an engine of growth for some countries but by-passed others. Nurkse did remark that the impact of trade was sometimes to produce a " lop-sided " pattern of development as in the dual economies of South-East Asia; this, he observed, was better than no growth, but it showed the limitations of the external trade and investment engine when other conditions of progress were absent [44, p. 289].

Actually, it is the presence or absence of the " other conditions of progress " referred to by Nurkse in passing that is the crux of success or failure in economic growth. The " other conditions " were present in the United States, and the expansion of trade was a very helpful but not essential factor in growth. They were absent in many other areas and, despite the fact that

---

[1] Foreign funds were very important in the 1830s and also significant in the 1850s, but there were no net inflows in the 1820s and 1840s. In the post-war period, for which better estimates are available, the peak periods were 1869–76 and 1882–93 when net foreign capital amounted to 15·5 and 10·3%, respectively, of net capital formation [57, p. 142]. All in all, the United States experience strongly supports the assessment made by Professor Cairncross that foreign investment accompanied and reinforced growth rather than provided the early stimulus [9, p. 43].

[2] Aside from Australia and Argentina, mentioned in the text, the prevailing opinion in favour of the Nurkse hypothesis has recently been challenged by Chambers and Gordon and the orthodox view defended by Dales, McManus and Watkins [10].

some of these places shared in the expansion of world trade, they did not develop.

In fact, in the three or four decades preceding the First World War the trade expansion of the underdeveloped countries was almost as rapid as that of the developed areas—36% per decade as against 40% (see Table 2). At least some of the countries not successful in the growth league, such as India and Ceylon, enjoyed expansions in exports during the second half of the nineteenth century that seem to have been of the same order of magnitude as those of a number of Nurkse's regions of recent settlement, including the United States and Canada.[1] India, incidentally, was also a major importer of capital at least in the latter part of this period [4].

Furthermore, the importance of foreign trade relative to G.N.P. was rising more rapidly in the underdeveloped regions than in the developed countries [48, p. 15].

The failure of these areas to develop cannot then be attributed to the fact that they did not share in the nineteenth-century expansion of world trade. Some were like the American South in that they were producers of primary products which were much in demand in Europe, and trade did not serve as an engine of growth because " the other conditions " were lacking. It would take us far afield to try to do more than speculate briefly about the nature of these conditions. Nurkse was in a sense assuming that the conditions were associated with empty lands, although he submerged this factor in the course of emphasising external demand. Even among the empty regions, however, there were differences in the extent and quality of growth, and at least one country that does not fit into the empty region category, Japan, was a spectacular growth success. Surely any adequate explanation must include the social factors that influence a society's capacity to transform itself such as those that determine attitudes towards work and reward.[2]

[1] The point may be illustrated by the following ratios of export volume from one date to another:

Dates.	United States.	India.	Dates.	United States.	Ceylon
1880 to 1835	8·33	7·53	1850–59 to 1830–39	2·48	9·42
1900 to 1880	2·16	1·84	1900–9 to 1850–59	6·48	5·18

The terminal figures for United States and Indian ratios are two-year averages (the given year and the year following). These export data and the generalisations in the text are based on United States sources already cited and on Firestone [19], Lim [37, p. 248], Dutt [14, II, pp. 114, 248 and 386] and Vaishney [49, p. 447]. The export data for India prior to 1900 and for Ceylon were crudely deflated through the use of Imlah's index for United Kingdom import prices. It might be added that the rate of growth in real national income was about 1·1% per annum (0·5% *per capita*) in India between 1857–63 and 1906–14 (Mukerji in [49, pp. 686 and 701–2]), while the United States growth in real G.N.P. was about 3·8% per annum (1·6% *per capita*) in the fifty-year period beginning in 1849–58 [36, p. A–37].

[2] Suggestive in this connection is the inverse correlation among Latin American countries, pointed out to the author by Richard Easterlin, between ranks with respect to *per capita* incomes and proportions of Indians in the population. The Spearman coefficient is 0·45 (significant at the 0·05% level) for 16 countries, based on population data cited by [3, p. 461], and E.C.L.A. estimates of 1960 *per capita* real G.N.P. given by S. N. Braithwaite [5, p. 129]).

C. *Viewed from the Centre*

We turn now to the situation in the centre country and ask what circumstances we might expect to find if it were true that a steep secular rise in its demand for primary products was being transmitted to the periphery countries.

One way that the spillover idea of growth could work would be for the centre to maintain a constant propensity to import but to have a higher growth rate than the periphery. Actually growth rates were lower for the centre: the growth of total product in France and the United Kingdom was less than half the United States rate between 1823 and 1863, and in the following half century only slightly more than half the United States rate. In the latter period the growth rate for eight European countries[1] was 2·2% per annum compared with 3·7% for the United States, Canada and Australia.

Another way the centre countries could have exported their growth was to allow their import propensities to rise. Such increases did in fact occur; the proportions of imports to total product expanded, for example, from 12·1% in 1827–35 to 24·6% in 1900–13 for the United Kingdom, from 6·3% in 1825–34 to 27·8% in 1905–13 for France, and from 6% in 1840 to 20·5% in 1910–13 in Germany [35]. Even so, it is far from clear that the rate of growth of imports by the centre countries from the periphery exceeded the rate of product growth in the latter. The volume of the centre's total imports did not expand as rapidly, and it is doubtful that the difference was made up by a redistribution of origins in favour of the periphery countries.[2]

Of course, a higher rate of growth in exports to the centre as compared with total product growth is not a necessary condition for export-led growth in the periphery countries. However, the lower rate of export growth fits in with other circumstances which suggest that rapid growth in the periphery may have served more to stimulate growth in the centre than vice versa.

[1] United Kingdom, France, Netherlands, Germany, Norway, Sweden, Denmark and Italy. All data from Kuznets [36, 1–3 and appendix tables].

[2] In the United Kingdom, for example, the volume of net imports grew at 4·0% per annum between 1823 and 1863 and at 3·2% from 1863 to 1913 (computed from B. R. Mitchell and P. Deane [40, pp. 328–9]), while in Western Europe the import volume expanded at 3·0 % per annum between 1874 and 1913 (computed from Maddison [38, pp. 63–4]). The statement in the text about the absence of a strong shift in favour of periphery areas in the origins of the centre's imports is based on the following United Kingdom data on computed values of imports:

Source.	Ratio of imports in 1912–13 to imports in 1854–55.
North-west and central Europe	5·97
United States	5·04
British North America	6·40
Australia	8·43
India	4·30

The initial two-year period was taken because it is the earliest for which data are given in the source (computed from Mitchell and Deane [40, pp. 317–27]).

Some basis for this viewpoint is offered, at least for the period beginning with the 1840s, by Imlah's conclusion that British imports tended to lag after British exports [26, p. 165]. For the period from 1870 to 1914, A. G. Ford found that exports were the proximate cause of fluctuations in British income, and that British overseas lending was one significant influence upon British exports [21].

It is even possible that the United States and other periphery countries benefited more from the lack of growth at the centre than from growth. This is suggested by Cairncross' findings of a see-saw relationship between British home and foreign investment after 1870 [7, Chapters VII and VIII]. He also concluded that high rates of emigration were associated with high levels of foreign and low levels of domestic investment, and Easterlin has presented data suggesting that for given rates of natural increase, lagged emigration rates from European countries in the latter half of the nineteenth century were inversely correlated with *per capita* income levels.[1]

A second kind of evidence we might find if the main change that brought about economic development in the periphery had been a spurt in the centre's demand for foodstuffs, would be that the centre's traditional suppliers would also share in the expansion. If, on the other hand, the main factors at work were internal growth and transformation in one or a few periphery countries the shares in the centre's imports of the successful new countries would rise.

At least in the case of wheat, one of the major primary products to which Nurkse was referring, the shares of the new countries in United Kingdom imports rose rapidly, while the shares of two of the traditional suppliers (France and Germany) declined and that of a third (Russia) revealed no trend [47, p. 146]. Between the 1840s and the 1890s the United States share in particular registered a gain of 39 percentage points, while the combined shares of Germany and France declined by 36 percentage points. The rapid internal development of the United States—particularly the settlement of western lands, the coming of the railroad and, in the last quarter of the century, the reduction of ocean freights—made large quantities of United States grain available at low prices.[2] It was these low prices that enabled American grain to push its way not only into the United Kingdom market, which had been opened by the repeal of the Corn Laws in 1846, but also in the closing decades of the century into continental markets, producing successful demands for protection in France and Germany [11, pp. 181, 211; 30].

[1] However, Easterlin did not find evidence of a correlation between the trend of emigration and changes in *per capita* income level in individual countries, and he concludes by agreeing with the earlier view of Kuznets that the main factor affecting the flow of emigration was the swings in economic conditions in the United States [15]. See also Arthur Bloomfield's discussion of " pull " factors in the United States and " push " influences in the United Kingdom in determining United Kingdom emigration and capital flows to the United States [4].

[2] The low prices had at root a large cost advantage that the United States grower had over his European counterpart; one estimate, quoted by the United States Commissioner of Agriculture in his annual report for 1883, placed United States costs at one-third less than the average cost in Europe [43, p. 272].

It might also be argued that the external demand hypothesis would lead us to expect that the growth in exports should cater to increments in foreign (*i.e.*, centre) demand rather than displace foreign production. To the extent that foreign production is displaced, it is more likely that the increased exports are attributable to changes in supply conditions in the new country.

For nearly thirty years after the repeal of the Corn Laws British imports did serve mainly to supplement domestic production. Domestic agriculture enjoyed prosperity; acreage in cultivation actually expanded, and rents and land values rose [26, pp. 182–3]. But then the situation changed swiftly; British wheat production dropped by 60% between 1873 and 1894 [45, p. 165] and the United States accounted for nearly 80% of the increase in United Kingdom imports between 1870s and 1890s. United States farm costs had long been lower, but it was not until the cheapening of transport costs that British growers lost the protection that distance had given them. This can, of course, be interpreted as an increase in the demand for United States wheat, but to the extent that the development of the West and the building of railroads rather than the advent of the steamship were responsible, it can be said that the reason for the large increases in United States wheat exports to the United Kingdom in the 1870s was that United States supply conditions, viz., the capacity of the United States economy to produce goods in the West and to move them cheaply, had changed.

This reconnaissance in the comparative study of nineteenth-century growth suggests that there is little basis for a broad generalisation connecting favourable external demand conditions created by an expansionary centre with successful economic development at the periphery. The idea that there was a powerful expansionary impact from the centre's demand for food and raw materials, which was the main factor generating growth, can be true, if at all, for but a few countries. It is not so clear to what degree expansionary impulses emanated primarily from the centre, nor was export expansion by periphery countries the differentiating factor determining the extent and quality of their growth.

This is not to deny that trade was often a stimulating factor. In the United States, for example, export markets buoyed up the agricultural sector, the availability of European grain markets and European capital encouraged the building of the railroads, and cheap European implements and other manufactures could be purchased. Some cyclical expansions, most clearly before the Civil War, were sparked by increases in foreign demand. In addition, ideas, new methods of production and well-qualified additions to the labour force were obtained from Europe.

Perhaps the most important rôle played by trade is one that cannot be measured by trade statistics, viz., that a relatively open market enabled the growing country to find its areas of comparative advantage and to avoid the development of insulated, high-cost, inefficient sectors. In their direct impact, however, trade and capital movements were supplementary factors;

they were handmaidens not engines of growth.   The mainsprings of growth were internal; they must be sought in the land and the people, and in the system of social and economic organisation.

III.   Twentieth-century Trade Opportunities

A good case can be made for the proposition that the twin legacies of colonialism and of the Great Depression are still potent forces in affecting L.D.C. policies towards industrialisation, import-substitution and trade. The changes in the structure of production started in the 1930s and encouraged first by war-time shortages and later by the rationalisations of the trade pessimists left many Latin American L.D.C.s less free to pursue close links with the world economy, even had they wished it.   Many African and Asian L.D.C.s are in a similar position, although the beginning of the process has usually been more recent.

While it is easy to understand and to sympathise with the factors that led to programmes of import-substitution in the 1930s, that period is not very relevant to the prospects facing the developing countries to-day.   In assessing the trading opportunities of these countries we shall concentrate on the period since the Second World War.   It is quite possible that the extraordinary rate of growth of the past two decades will not be maintained, and we may therefore appear to be in danger of falling into the same error of extrapolating the recent past into the future, only with opposite conclusions from those of the trade pessimists.   Yet there are several reasons for dwelling on these recent decades.

In the first place the war and immediately preceding depression years were atypical from an historical standpoint; the long-run record shows trade growing faster than world production, while these periods, like the First World War, show it growing more slowly.   For almost any set of terminal dates usually employed by historians to mark off the periods of the last century and a half, trade will be found to have held its own or more probably to have expanded relative to production, provided that the years of war and depression be excluded or, if included, placed within long spans of time.[1]

[1] For example, the following per decade growth figures from Kuznets [48, p. 4]:

Period.	World trade, %.	Product of rapidly growing countries.	
		%.	Countries.
1840–70	64·4	29·1	United Kingdom, France, United States
1870–1900	35·4	36·6 ⎱	Above plus Germany, Belgium, Norway, Denmark,
1881–1913	39·5	32·7 ⎰	Sweden, Canada
1913–28	22·1	24·3 ⎫	
1928–63	31·9	35·0 ⎬	Above plus Netherlands, Switzerland, Japan, Italy
1913–63	28·9	31·7 ⎭	

Comparisons between the two columns should allow for the fact that total world output increased more slowly than the figures given in the second column, since the latter pertain to countries whose growth rates were relatively high.

Secondly, the basic economic forces that have in the past given such a strong impetus to trade expansion are still at work and may be expected to operate in the future. The cheapening of transport, the growing standardisation of patterns of world consumption and the ever-increasing importance of economics of scale as more powerful and more expensive machinery is placed in use seem to augur for a continued growth in world trade.[1] Perhaps recent rates cannot be sustained, and trade is obviously vulnerable to unfavourable governmental policies, but even these may be expected to be more and more difficult to maintain in a shrinking world.

Finally, the L.D.C. export lag is a post-war phenomenon; in earlier periods or over longer periods, between 1913 and 1953, for example, the trade of less developed areas grew faster than that of the centre [8].

A. *Trading Opportunities for L.D.C.s*

The general proposition that the current world offers fewer market opportunities to the L.D.C.s of to-day than the nineteenth century offered to its periphery countries cannot be confronted with evidence unless it is reformulated so as to specify more precisely the means by which we are to gauge the " market opportunities." Several possible measures suggest themselves.

In the most general sense, opportunities may be considered in terms of the size or rate of growth of the markets of the centre relative to the economic size of the countries yet to be developed. Some very rough calculations concerning relative G.N.P.s of the centre and periphery countries suggest that one hundred years ago the ratio was about 2 to 1, whereas it is about 4·5 to 1 to-day.[2] Many questions could be raised about price deflation and the inclusions and exclusions of countries from each group, but it seems unlikely that refinements of the data could alter the conclusions. It is clear that the markets of to-day's centre countries loom much larger relative to the output of the L.D.C.s than was the case in the nineteenth century. Also, post-Second World War markets have expanded about twice as fast per annum as in the nineteenth century, with the increase between 1950 and 1965 being equivalent to more than four times the 1950 aggregate G.N.P. of the L.D.C.s.

But it may be objected that much of the increase in the developed countries' G.N.P. may have consisted of services and other goods which are not readily traded, or that the propensities of the developed countries to trade have been declining for commercial policy or other reasons. Thus what has

---

[1] R. N. Cooper concludes after examining the evidence that inter-regional trade in the United States has probably not declined in relative importance with the long-run growth of the American economy [12].

[2] Calculations for the nineteenth century were based on Kuznets data [36] for 8 European countries as the " centre " (see note 1, p. 856) and United States, Canada, Australia and Japan as the " periphery." Twentieth-century " centre " includes developed countries [53] and twentieth century " periphery " includes to-day's developing countries [46].

actually happened to the volume of world trade may be a more relevant measure of the opportunities confronting to-day's developing countries.

An effort has been made to place long-run movements in world trade in perspective in Table I. The first column shows the figures cited by Nurkse

TABLE I

Percentage Changes per Decade in the Volume of World Trade, Selected Periods,
1820–1966

	Nurkse. (1)	Kuznets. (2)	Maddison. (3)	G.A.T.T. (4)
1820–50		50		
1850–80	55	50		
1880–1913	35		37	
1913–1928			22	
1928–37/38			−2	−3
1929–48			−1	−2
1928–58	16		23	16
1928–66				32
1948–53			79	85
1948–66				95
1953–66				99

Note: All data are based on exports except Kuznets' which are based on exports and imports.
Source:
Col. 1. Nurkse [44, p. 290].
Col. 2. Kuznets [35, p. 4].
Col. 3. Maddison [38, Table 24]. (Export figure for 1880 extrapolated from 1881 on the basis of world imports.)
Col. 4. G.A.T.T. [24, p. 20; 23, 1952, 1955 and 1966].

to substantiate his view that world trade was tending downwards. Subsequent columns suggest that the expansion of world trade following the Second World War is of unprecedented magnitude; it is very unlikely that there were any fifteen- or twenty-year periods in the nineteenth century in which the volume of world trade was nearly doubling on a per decade basis. The increase from an annual average of $59·3 billion in 1948–51 to $158·1 billion in 1963–66 is equivalent, roughly, to about $89 billion in 1960 prices;[1] it was very large compared to the L.D.C.s' aggregate product of $142 billion in 1950 and $289 billion in 1965.

But the main fire of the trade pessimists has been directed neither at the size of growth of aggregate markets (*i.e.*, G.N.P.) nor at the rate of growth of total world trade. Their chief concern has been with the position of the developing countries in the expansion of world trade. However, the relevant record, set out in Table II, does not suggest that post-war export growth for

[1] Trade converted to 1960 prices on the basis of unit value indexes. Data from G.A.T.T. [23].

TABLE II

Development of World Exports of Primary Products and Manufactures,
Originating in Developed and Underdeveloped Areas, 1876–80 to 1966

	Millions of dollars. (current prices)				Rate of growth per decade.		
	1876– 80. (1)	1913. (2)	1953. (3)	1966. (4)	1876–80 to 1913. (5)	1913 to 1953. (6)	1953 to 1966. (7)
Total trade							
All countries . . .	6,010	19,159	68,410	170,800	39	43 (41)†	102 (104)
Developed . . .	4,562	14,871	47,980	135,080	40	40 (40)	122 (126)
Underdeveloped . .	1,448	4,233	20,410	35,720	36	50 (42)	54 (37)
Primary products							
All countries . .	3,720	12,176	35,800	64,560	40	39 (35)	57 (50)
Developed . . .	2,307	8,310	17,980	35,820	44	32 (31)	70 (74)
Underdeveloped . .	1,413	3,866	17,820	28,740	33	51 (41)	44 (20)
Manufactured goods							
All countries . .	2,290	6,928	31,320	103,130	37	48	150
Developed . . .	2,255	6,561	28,880	96,270	36	48	152
Underdeveloped . .	35	367	2,450	6,870	96	49	121
Shares of:	%.	%.	%.	%.			
Primary products * .	62	64	53	38			
Underdeveloped in— .							
Total exports . .	24	22	30	21			
Primary exports .	38	32	50	45			
Manufactured exports	2	5	8	7			

* Shares in sum of primary and manufactured exports; total exports usually contain small amount that could not be allocated to one or the other of the categories.
† Growth rates in parentheses are for exports excluding fuels.

Notes to Table 2
Columns 1 and 2: Based on Yates [58, Tables A–19, A–21 and A–23]. The developed countries include the United States and Canada, Europe, Oceania and Japan. In 1876–80, however, data for Oceania and Japan were not separated from that of the underdeveloped continents.
Columns 3 and 4: Based on U.N. [54]. No attempt has been made to adjust the 1953 figures for developed countries exports upwards for revisions made in the later issue, which did not contain 1953 data; for 1955 the later issue reported developed country exports at a figure that was 3·75% higher than the figure in the earlier issue. The data exclude exports to or from centrally planned economics.
Column 5: Calculated from columns (1) and (2).
Column 6: Calculated from data in Yates (*idem*), which excludes Iron Curtain countries.
Column 7: Calculated from columns (3) and (4).

L.D.C.s has been low by historical standards.[1] Indeed, the growth rate for total underdeveloped area exports is higher than those either of the developed

[1] [56, pp. 554 and 546.] Data are given in Table II exclusive of fuels because writers inclined towards trade pessimism often treat oil-producing countries as a special case and dwell upon the problems of the other developing countries. However, it is difficult to see why the external demand for oil represents less of a trade-conferred stimulus to growth than the external demand for cotton or wheat did for the United States in the nineteenth century. (Cf. Cairncross [8, pp. 194–5].) Incidentally if fuels are excluded from both the recent data for the developing countries and the pre-First World War data for the United States and Canada the export growth rate of the former would still be slightly higher.

or underdeveloped areas of the halcyon era preceding the First World War.[1] It is also well above the 43% per decade rate of growth in United States exports between 1876–80 and 1913, when trade was supposed to have been an engine of growth.

There is little evidence of poor rates of growth of primary product trade relative to the past, and it cannot be said that the developed countries have failed to provide growing markets for primary products [54]:

| | Rates of growth per decade (1953–66) in exports to developed countries from | | |
	All areas.	Developed.	Underdeveloped.
Current Values:			
All primary products . . .	62	74	48
All excluding fuel	50	76	19
1958 prices:			
All primary products . . .	68	77	60
All excluding fuel	53	76	25

What can be said is that the developing countries have not been sharing fully in the booming world markets of the post-war period. Their share of world exports declined from 30% in 1953 to 21% in 1966, and their share in primary exports from 50 to 45% between the same dates. (If fuels are excluded the declines are from 26 to 16% and from 47 to 35% respectively.) Can this lag be attributed to unfavourable demand conditions? Or is it more plausible to think that the fault lay with the supply conditions in the L.D.C.s?

B. *Factors in the L.D.C.s' Declining Share*

One important consideration is the pervasive pessimism about trade prospects engendered by the experience of the 1930s and fostered by the trade pessimists. This may well have represented a case of a self-fulfilling forecast; it is possible that only the enormous growth of world markets prevented a real debacle in L.D.C. exports. Pessimism about prospects for foreign-exchange earnings from traditional exports often led to policies that directly or indirectly shifted incomes out of agriculture and into the public or industrial sector; these policies included tariffs and other trade restrictions designed to encourage import substitution in the manufacturing sector, over-valued currencies or multiple exchange rates, and direct taxes and subsidies. The traditional export sectors were not given normal incentives to

---

[1] Comparisons based on growth in quantum show the recent export growth of the developing countries relative to the past in an even more favourable light. This is a dubious advantage, since it reflects an unfavourable movement in their relative export prices. However, there is reason to believe that the available data exaggerate the extent of the developing countries' deterioration in terms of trade [34].

expand and were saddled with high costs for their manufactured and imported inputs, and the entire agricultural sector, with whatever potential it may have had for developing new exports in a world with more and more people to feed, was placed under similar handicaps. Within the manufacturing sector, the varying and unpredictable effects of changes in quantitative restrictions, subsidies, import fees, multiple exchange rates and the like placed a premium on business leadership that could deal with the administrative maze rather than leadership that would turn its energies to low-cost production. The isolation of the economy from the world price structure through quantitative restrictions weakened or removed competitive pressures, and the small size of the home market often meant high costs in any case. Not only did these circumstances militate against exports, except those that the Government considered it economic to encourage, but the possibility for the spontaneous development of new export industries was made remote.[1]

Such factors must surely have played a rôle in the decline in the L.D.C.s' share of primary markets. The decline cannot be ascribed completely to unfavourable markets for commodities produced wholly or mainly in the L.D.C.s. These products—viz., coffee, tea, cocoa, tin, bananas and spices—account for only around a quarter of the value of L.D.C. primary product exports exclusive of fuel. The other three-quarters, according to an U.N.C.T.A.D. classification, face competition from substitute or like commodities produced in the developed countries [53, Table I-1]. It is in these categories, particularly grains, fruits, vegetables, and oils and oil seeds, that the L.D.C.s lost market opportunities.

Secondly, the possibility that new export industries might be found has generally in the past received little weight in the strategy for growth adopted by many L.D.C.s. Their tendency to assess trade prospects solely in terms of the outlook for primary products currently produced in developing countries implicitly assumes a high degree of rigidity in the structure of production which can be broken only by cutting off the economy from world prices and markets.

Now it is very unlikely that such high rates of trade growth would have been achieved either in the pre-1913 United States or in post-Second World War Europe if the export expansion had been confined to products already exported. Unless a country is lucky in that it has oil or some other product which foreigners want and can come with their technology to produce or with their money to buy, trade, like economic growth in general, depends on the ability to shift into different lines of production. It can hardly be hoped that the world will always increase its consumption of coffee and cocoa *pari*

---

[1] This series of consequences has been described many times both with reference to specific countries and in general terms. For a recent example see [27, pp. 42 ff and 107 ff]. For a description of the " precocious " widening of the scope of industrial activity in Latin American countries. see Felix in [1, pp. 370–401, esp. pp. 382 f.]. Anne Krueger has raised the possibility in correspondence that the expansion of United States wheat exports in the nineteenth century might never have occurred had the dollar been overvalued.

passu with its real income.   World consumption of cotton did not increase in this way, and the growth of the United States would have been much slower if it had been unable to shift so readily into other lines of production and other sources of export earnings.   Some current analyses (*e.g.*, [52, p. 17]) explaining the lag of L.D.C. agricultural exports behind those of the developed countries in terms of commodity composition (*i.e.*, the former products with inelastic and the latter products with elastic demands), while correct in a certain narrow descriptive sense, would have had their analogue a century or more ago if someone had despaired of the future of United States exports on the grounds that cotton exports, which accounted for half of the total in the decade before the Civil War, were destined to increase more slowly than world trade in wheat, which then accounted for only 6% of United States exports [56, pp. 545, 547].[1]

What the recent experience of the L.D.C.s shows is not a failure of external demand but that the internal problems of supply, inherent in underdevelopment, particularly when biased against trade by policy measures, cannot be automatically resolved even by extraordinarily favourable external demand conditions.

C.   *Successful Exporters among the L.D.C.s*

It is difficult to put this interpretation to a rigorous test, but some evidence can be mustered to suggest that supply rather than demand factors played the dominant rôle.

To start with, it is important to realise that the lagging overall export growth rate of the L.D.C.s conceals a wide variety of experience.   The poor export performance of a few large L.D.C.s, such as India, Pakistan, Argentina and Brazil, with 1963–66 export proceeds no more than 25% above the 1948–51 level, did much to pull the average down.

At the opposite extreme from these big L.D.C.s were a number of small countries whose export expansion met the 6% per annum (79% per decade) growth rate that Prebisch considered necessary to achieve the United Nations Development Decade target of 5% per annum growth in income [51, pp. 3–4].   Altogether 29 out of the 69 L.D.C.s for which export proceeds are readily available for the period 1948–66 fall in this category, but we excluded 7 of them from the list of " successful " exporters in Table III because they were oil exporters (choosing to err in favour of the trade pessimist school).   The first 13 countries on the list had higher export growth rates than the industrial countries as a whole.[2]

---

[1] Not all of the policy measures in the L.D.C.s that inhibit adjustment to world demand arise out of import-substitution motivations.   Some, like the policies in Brazil which have continued to make coffee production profitable relative to other crops despite official diversification objectives [32], arise from the problem, unfortunately not unknown in the United States and other developed countries, of politically potent vested interests.

[2] One of the star performers, the Republic of Korea, is excluded from our list of countries because data for our base years were not available in the source used.

TABLE III

L.D.C.s with Successful Export Performance, 1948–51 to 1963–66

	Percent increase per decade.		Percent increase per decade.
Israel	315	Jordan	119
Nicaragua	192	British Guiana	115
Taiwan	187	Panama	112
Jamaica	180	Ethiopia	105
Liberia	168	El Salvador	100
Equatorial Africa	144	Mozambique	93
Sierra Leone	136	Ecuador	89
Peru	133	Guatemala	85
Surinam	126	East Cameroons	85
Lebanon	123	Angola	84
Rhodesia, Malawi and Zambia	120	Kenya	83

Source: I.M.F. [28].

One factor that may limit the significance of the findings is that all of the successful exporters are small countries which had small export proceeds to start with. Yet, despite the intuitive appeal of the argument that it should be relatively easy for a small country to attain large export increases, the results cannot be entirely set aside on this ground.

From the supply side, it is not easy to say why a small country should find it easier than a large one to achieve a given percentage increase in its exports. On the demand side, it may appear plausible to think that a country with large initial exports will run into more private and governmental obstacles in, say, doubling its exports than will a country with small initial exports. Sierra Leone, with exports of $24 million in 1948–51, could more than triple them by 1963–66, but would foreign competitors and foreign governments not put up a stiffer battle against a similar increase in India's exports from its starting level of $1·4 billion in 1948–51? An affirmative answer seems plausible, but it also implies, viewed solely from the demand side, that India should have found it easier to expand than, say, France with an initial level of $3·0 billion. (Actually, India's 1963–66 exports were 25% higher than in 1948–51; France's 221% higher.)[1]

In any case, since most developing countries are small (both in terms of population and exports), even if it is granted· that the significance of the findings is limited to small countries, they are still relevant to all but a hand-ful of the L.D.C.s.

Furthermore, there is a tendency for countries that have been successful exporters to have had more rapid growth in real product. For 37 of the non-

---

[1] Nevertheless, both in our sample of countries and in the findings of other investigators there is an inverse relationship between the size of L.D.C.s' initial exports and their rate of growth in exports. Spearman's coefficient of rank correlation for the 37 countries is 0·39, and significant at the 0·01 level. (See footnote below for the basis for selecting the countries.) De Vries reports a similar finding [13].

oil exporting L.D.C.s, for example, Spearman's coefficients of rank correlation between increases in exports and increases in real G.N.P. between
1950–52 and 1963–65 was 0·51.[1]

This raises the question of whether success in export growth is due primarily to favourable conditions which increase both exports and G.N.P. or
mainly to favourable internal conditions which produce both growth and a
more competitive position in world markets.   If the former is the case we
may expect to find the varying fortunes of the L.D.C.s explained by the
behaviour of world markets for their traditional exports; if, on the other
hand, supply conditions, whether spontaneous or brought about by policies
favourable to trade, are the main sources of difference we should find that
the successful exporters increased their relative shares in their traditional
exports and diversified the commodity composition of their exports.

A recent G.A.T.T. study [23, 1965, p. 27] throws some light on this
question at least for part of our period (1959–61 to 1964–65).   The G.A.T.T.
analysis, which we summarise in Table IV, showed for each L.D.C. what its

TABLE IV

Analysis of Varying Export Performance of L.D.C.s, 1959–61 to 1964–65

Export performance group.	Average indexes * for groups of countries.					
	Number of countries. (1)	Total export earnings. (2)	World market factor. (3)	Competitiveness factor. (4)	Diversification factor. (5)	Own performance indicator. (6)
Superior	22	177·6	122·9	133·4	112·5	147·0
Middle	15	140·0	122·7	106·6	108·3	114·6
Inferior	21	108·8	118·5	95·2	102·0	96·9
All: mean		143·0	121·9	112·6	107·6	120·5
median		142	120	107	103	112

Source: G.A.T.T. [23, 1966, p. 27].   * 1964–65 as percentage of 1959–61.

export performance would have been had its exports changed only in response to changes in the world demand for its traditional exports (*i.e.*, if it
had maintained a constant share in world markets for each product); we
have called this the " world market factor " (col. 3).   The G.A.T.T. study
also calculated how each country's exports would have changed if total world
trade for each traditional export had remained constant, with only the
shares of different L.D.C.s being allowed to change, as in fact they did; this

[1] The countries and dates were selected because data for real G.D.P. were conveniently available in the O.E.C.D. publication [46].   The correlation coefficient is significant at the 0·01 level.
The association in L.D.C.s between growth in G.D.P. and growth in exports has been previously
noted by a number of writers.   See, for example, R. Emery [17], who argues that while exports and
growth are interdependent, a rise in exports generally stimulates growth rather than vice versa.   A
close association between growth and exports was found for manufacturing for the period 1899–1959
for 7 developed countries or areas by Maizels [39, pp. 217–24].

is labelled as the " competitiveness factor " (col. 4) in our table. What we have called the " diversification factor " (col. 5) was computed by G.A.T.T. as the residual change in a country's export proceeds which is left after account is taken of the first two factors; it is equivalent to the ratio of the share of traditional exports in the country's total exports in the initial period to the share of the same products in the terminal period.[1] At the risk of some oversimplification, we may take the world market factor as a reflection of the rôle of external demand factors in changes in export proceeds and take the product of the competitiveness and diversification factors as the country's " own performance indicator " (col. 6), that is, the part played by its increased competitiveness and product diversification. The L.D.C.s are classified for our purposes in three groups, those with greater increases in export proceeds between 1959–61 and 1964–65 than the industrial countries as a group had, those with increases less than the average for all L.D.C.s and the remaining group of L.D.C.s with middle positions with respect to export performance.

The results suggest that export success did not depend primarily on the world market factor. The largest difference among the groups is in the competitiveness factor; that is, the successful performers among the L.D.C.s were differentiated from the less successful primarily by increases in their shares in world markets for their traditional exports rather than by good fortune in world demand for their particular exports.[2] The successful exporters tended also to have done better at diversification, but the margins of superiority on this account were much smaller.

Furthermore, the countries with high " own performance indicators " tended to be countries that had high growth rates; for 39 countries for which real product growth rates were available there was a 0·51 Spearman coefficient between ranks with respect to the export indicator and ranks with respect to the growth rate (significant at the 1% confidence level).

An examination of the connection between export performance and export diversification for 21 countries over a longer period of time produced an $\bar{r}^2$ of 0·22 [33]. The measure of diversification used for each country in this analysis was the ratio of the Hirschman index of concentration (the square root of the sum of the squared percentage shares of each export

[1] The outcome of such analyses is, of course, affected by the selection of the traditional products and of the commodity classifications. A more inclusive list of " traditional products " and the use of broad classifications usually tend in practice to diminish the rôle of diversification in the outcome. However, once these decisions are taken, whatever errors are imparted cannot be assigned to one of the categories, as the G.A.T.T. report implies, simply because it is computed as a residual; the G.A.T.T. estimate of the diversification factor is therefore not inherently less reliable than the estimates of the other two factors. It should perhaps be added that in the G.A.T.T. analysis no separate account is taken of differences in the prosperity of each country's traditional geographical markets.

[2] This implies that some successes may have been obtained at the expense of the shares of others among the 58 included countries or of L.D.C.s not included in the G.A.T.T. study, but this need not have been the case in principle, since, as previously noted, more L.D.C. exports compete with developed countries' exports too.

category) in 1952 to the index in 1965. There is a hint in the data that export diversification was associated with a high G.D.P. growth rate; the r^2 was 0·12 for the 21 countries, but, unlike the coefficient with respect to export performance, this one fell short of significance at the 5% confidence level.

It seems quite unlikely that external demand conditions can account for the correlation between export performance and diversification. It is more probable that the reasons for the differences are to be found in the differences in internal factors that determine the mobility of resources and that therefore promote growth in general.

IV. Conclusions

International trade cannot provide a differential diagnosis to explain the varying growth records of countries in the nineteenth century. The United States, the greatest success story of the nineteenth century and the best documented case, owed the pattern and speed of its development mainly to internal factors, while trade expanded just as rapidly for some countries, such as India and Ceylon, that did not experience fast growth.

This is not, of course, to deny that it is helpful to a developing country to have a strong external demand for a commodity that it can advantageously produce—such as cotton, wheat, oil or coffee. It is to deny that the presence of such a demand is a necessary or sufficient condition for growth or even for trade to play a helpful role in growth. It is to say that trade is one among many factors affecting growth, and that it is unlikely to be the dominant variable in many instances. The exaggeration of the past rôle of trade has often served to heighten the contrast drawn with allegedly less favourable present-day world markets and thus to minimize the potential rôle of trade for to-day's developing countries. The term " engine of growth " is not generally descriptive and involves expectations which cannot be fulfilled by trade alone; the term " handmaiden of growth " better conveys the notion of the rôle that trade can play. One of the most important parts of this handmaiden rôle for to-day's developing countries may be to serve as a check on the appropriateness of new industries by keeping the price and cost structures in touch with external prices and costs.

With respect to the opportunities afforded to developing countries by world markets, it is the similarities between the nineteenth and twentieth centuries rather than the contrasts that are notable. If anything, external demand, by almost any measure, has been larger relative to the economic size of to-day's L.D.C.s than in the former period.

The post-war export performance of the L.D.C.s as a group is not unfavourable by historical standards; their exports in the last two decades have expanded at rates comparable to those of the exports of the countries of recent settlement in the late nineteenth century when trade was supposed to be serving as an engine of growth.   This expansion occurred to a large extent as a result of an enormous increase in world demand and in many instances in the face of L.D.C. policies unfavourable to trade expansion.

It is only when compared with the export performance of the advanced countries that the L.D.C. record looks bad.   Such a comparison suggests that the L.D.C.s have not on the whole taken full advantage of world trade opportunities, often incorrectly attributing their difficulties to unfavourable external conditions when the more important problems have been at home. The limited evidence available indicates that the L.D.C.s that have shared more fully in the growth of world trade do not owe their export successes to the passive acceptance of favourable markets for their traditional products; rather they have succeeded in raising their shares in these markets and in diversifying their exports.   The implication is that internal factors affecting the mobility of resources rather than external demand conditions account for good export performance, and the positive association between export performance and growth in real G.N.P. lends further support to this view.

IRVING B. KRAVIS

University of Pennsylvania.

REFERENCES

1. W. Baer and I. Kerstenetzky, eds., *Inflation and Growth in Latin America* (Homewood, Ill., 1964), pp. 290–318.
2. R. E. Baldwin, " Patterns of Development in Newly Settled Regions," *Manchester School*, May 1956, Vol. 24, pp. 161–79.
3. G. I. Blanksten, " The Politics of Latin America," in G. A. Almond and J. S. Coleman, eds., *The Politics of Developing Areas* (Princeton, N.J., 1960).
4. A. I. Bloomfield, *Patterns of Fluctuation in International Investment Before 1914.* Princeton Studies in International Finance, No. 21 (Princeton, N.J., 1968).
5. S. N. Braithwaite, " Real Income Levels in Latin America," *Review of Income and Wealth*, June 1968, Series 14, pp. 113–82.
6. N. B. Butlin, *Investment in Australian Economic Development, 1861–1900* (Cambridge, 1964).
7. A. K. Cairncross, *Home and Foreign Investment, 1870–1913* (Cambridge, 1953).
8. —— " Patterns of Trade and Development," *Kyklos*, 1960, reprinted in *Factors in Economic Development* (London, 1960), pp. 190–203.
9. —— " The Contribution of Foreign and Domestic Capital to Economic Development," *International Journal of Agrarian Affairs*, April 1961, pp. 39–74.
10. E. J. Chambers and D. F. Gordon, " Primary Products and Economic Growth: An Empirical Measurement," *Journal of Political Economy*, August 1966. (See also the comment by Dales, McManus and Watkins and the authors' *Rejoinder*, same *Journal*, December 1967.)
11. J. H. Clapham, *Economic Development of France and Germany, 1815–1914* (Cambridge, England, 1936).
12. R. N. Cooper, " Growth and Trade; Some Hypotheses About Long-term

Trends," *Journal of Economic History*, December 1964, Vol., 24, pp. 609–28.

13. B. A. De Vries, *The Export Experience of Developing Countries*, World Bank Staff Occasional Papers Number Three (Washington, 1967).

14. R. Dutt, *The Economic History of India: 1857–1956* (Bombay, 1965).

15. R. A. Easterlin, " Influences in European Overseas Emigration Before World War II," *Economic Development and Cultural Change*, April 1961, Vol. 9, pp. 331–51.

16. R. A. Easterlin, Review of North [42], *Journal of Economic History*, March 1962, 22, pp. 122–6.

17. R. Emery, " The Relation of Exports and Economic Growth," *Kyklos*, 1967, Vol. 20, pp. 470–86.

18. A. Ferrer, *The Argentine Economy* (Berkeley and Los Angeles, 1967).

19. O. J. Firestone, *Canada's Economic Development, 1867–1957*, Income and Wealth, Series VII (London 1958).

20. A. Fishlow, " Antebellum Interregional Trade Reconsidered," *American Economic Review*, May 1964, Vol. 54, pp. 352–64.

21. A. G. Ford, " Overseas Lending and Internal Fluctuations: 1870–1914," *Yorkshire Bulletin of Economic and Social Research*, May 1965, Vol. 17, pp. 19–31.

22. R. Gallman, " Commodity Output, 1839–1899," in *Trends in the American Economy in the Nineteenth Century*, National Bureau of Economic Research Conference on Income and Wealth, Vol. 24 (Princeton, 1960).

23. Geneva Agreement on Tariffs and Trade, *International Trade*. Annual (Geneva).

24. Geneva Agreement on Tariffs and Trade, *Trends in International Trade*. October 1958 (Geneva).

25. G. Haberler, *International Trade and Economic Development* (Cairo, 1959).

26. A. H. Imlah, *Economic Elements in the Pax Britannica* (Cambridge, Mass., 1958).

27. International Monetary Fund, *Annual Report, 1967.* (Washington).

28. International Monetary Fund, *International Financial Statistics*, Supplement to 1965/66 issues, and January 1968 issue (Washington).

29. D. B. Keesing, " Outward-Looking Policies and Economic Development," ECONOMIC JOURNAL, June 1967, pp. 303–20.

30. C. P. Kindleberger, " Group Behavior and International Trade," *Journal of Political Economy*, February 1951, pp. 30–46.

31. C. P. Kindleberger, *Foreign Trade and the National Economy* (New Haven, Conn., 1962).

32. I. B. Kravis, " International Commodity Agreements to Promote Aid and Efficiency: The Case of Coffee," *Canadian Journal of Economics*, May 1968, pp. 295–317.

33. I. B. Kravis, *External Demand and Internal Supply Factors in LDC Export Performance*, U.S. AID Summer Research Project (Washington, D.C., 1969).

34. I. B. Kravis, and R. E. Lipsey, *Price Competitiveness in World Trade.* New York, forthcoming.

35. S. Kuznets, " Quantitative Aspects of the Economic Growth of Nations: X Level and Structure of Foreign Trade: Long Term Trends," *Economic Development and Cultural Change*, Vol. 15, No. 2, Part II, January 1967.

36. S. Kuznets, " Level and Variability of Rates of Growth," 1968 (processed).
37. Y. Lim, " Trade and Growth: The Case of Ceylon," *Economic Development and Cultural Change*, January 1968, Vol. 16, pp. 245–60.
38. A. Maddison, " Growth and Fluctuation in the World Economy," *Banca Nazionale del Lavoro Quarterly Review*, June 1962, Vol. 61, pp. 63–4.
39. A. Maizels, *Industrial Growth and World Trade* (Cambridge, England, 1963).
40. B. R. Mitchell and P. Deane, *Abstract of British Historical Statistics* (Cambridge, England, 1962).
41. G. Myrdal, *Economic Theory and Under-Developed Regions* (London, 1957).
42. D. North, *The Economic Growth of the U.S., 1790–1860* (New York, 1966).
43. E. G. Nourse, *American Agriculture and the European Market* (New York, 1924).
44. R. Nurkse, *Equilibrium and Growth in the World Economy*, G. Haberler and R. M. Stern, eds. (Cambridge, Mass., 1961).
45. M. Olson, Jr., and C. C. Harris, Jr., " Free Trade in ' Corn': A Statistical Study of the Process and Production of Wheat in Great Britain from 1873 to 1914," *Quarterly Journal of Economics*, February 1959, Vol. 73, pp. 145–68.
46. Organization for Economic Cooperation and Development Centre, *National Accounts of Less Developed Countries, Preliminary* (Paris, February 1967).
47. W. Page, ed., *Commerce and Industry, Tables of Statistics for the British Empire from 1815*, Vol. 2 (London, 1919).
48. R. Prebisch, " The Economic Development of Latin America and its Principal Problems," *Economic Bulletin for Latin America*, February 1962, pp. 1–22.
49. V. B. Singh, ed., *Economic History of India: 1857–1956* (Bombay, 1965).
50. P. Temin, " The Causes of Cotton-price Fluctuations in the 1830's," *Review of Economics and Statistics*, 1967, Vol. 49, pp. 463–70.
51. United Nations Conference on Trade and Development, *Towards a New Trade Policy for Development*. Report by the Secretary General (New York, 1964).
52. United Nations Conference on Trade and Development, *UNCTAD Commodity Survey, 1966* (New York, 1966).
53. United Nations Conference on Trade and Development, Second Session, " The Development of an International Commodity Policy," TD/8/Supp. 1. November 14, 1967.
54. United Nations, *Monthly Bulletin of Statistics*, New York, November 1965 and November 1967.
55. U.S. Agency for International Development, *G.N.P. Growth Rates and Trend Data*, March 31, 1967, RC-W-138 (Wash., D.C.).
56. U.S. Bureau of the Census, *Historical Statistics of the U.S., Colonial Times to 1957* (Washington, D.C., 1960).
57. J. G. Williamson, *American Growth and the Balance of Payments, 1820–1913* (Chapel Hill, N.C., 1964).
58. P. L. Yates, *Forty Years of Foreign Trade* (New York, 1959).

[5]

The Slowing Down of the Engine of Growth

By W. Arthur Lewis*

Let me begin by stating my problem. For the past hundred years the rate of growth of output in the developing world has depended on the rate of growth of output in the developed world. When the developed grow fast, the developing grow fast, and when the developed slow down, the developing slow down. Is this linkage inevitable? More specifically, the world has just gone through two decades of unprecedented growth, with world trade growing twice as fast as ever before, at about 8 percent per annum in real terms, compared with 0.9 percent between 1913 and 1939, and less than 4 percent per annum between 1873 and 1913. During these prosperous decades, the less developed countries (*LDC*s) have demonstrated their capacity to increase their total output at 6 percent per annum, and have indeed adopted 6 percent as the minimum average target for *LDC*s as a whole. But what is to happen if the more developed countries (*MDC*s) return to their former growth rates, and raise their trade at only 4 percent per annum: is it inevitable that the growth of the *LDC*s will also fall significantly below their target? My purpose is not to predict what is going to happen, but to explore existing relationships and how they may change.

The extraordinary growth rates of the two decades before 1973 surprised everybody. We knew that the world economy experiences long swings in activity; that world trade, for example, grew faster between 1830 and 1873 than it grew between 1873 and 1913, that is to say, between 4 and 5 percent before 1873, compared with between 3 and 4 percent after 1873. But a jump to 8 percent was inconceivable.

*Princeton University. This article is a revised version of the lecture W. A. Lewis delivered in Stockholm, Sweden, December, 1979, when he received the Nobel Prize in Economic Science. The article is copyright © the Nobel Foundation 1979. It is published here with the permission of the Nobel Foundation.

Some people were even more surprised by the performance of the *LDC*s. In 1950 these people were sceptical of the capacity of *LDC*s to grow rapidly because of inappropriate attitudes, institutions, or climates. The sun was thought to be too hot for hard work, or the people too spendthrift, the government too corrupt, the fertility rate too high, the religion too other worldly, and so on. This kind of analysis has now almost completely gone from the literature. In discussions at the end of the 1940's, noting that the *U.S.* national income per head had grown at about 2 percent a year over long periods, and noting that *LDC* populations were growing at about 1 percent, economists in United Nations circles were boldly discussing the possibility that the *LDC* growth rate might be 3 percent. The United Nations at the end of the 1950's fixed 5 percent as the target for the 1960's, meaning by "target" something that was unattainable but inspirational. Then to everybody's surprise UN figures showed 5 percent being averaged already by the middle 1960's. So the target was raised to 6 percent for the 1970's, but the figures showed 6 percent already in the early 1970's, and the UN was just getting ready to fix 7 percent for the 1980's when the recession started in 1974. I do not vouch for the accuracy of any of these performance figures, but I think *LDC*s have demonstrated beyond doubt their capacity to use physical and human resources productively.

The fast pace of world trade also played havoc with development theory. The collapse of international trade in the 1930's had seemed irreversible, so much so that Keynes had even declared that we didn't need much of it anyway. So in the 1940's and 1950's we created a whole set of theories which make sense if world trade is stagnant—balanced growth, regional integration, the two-gap model, structural inflation—but which have little relevance in a world where trade is growing at 8 percent per annum. Also many countries, basing their policies on the same assumption, oriented inwards mainly towards import substitution. The fact that world trade was growing rapidly was not universally recognized until the second half of the 1960's. Then nearly every country discovered the virtues of exporting. Now we are in danger of being caught out again. Since 1973 the growth rate of world trade has halved, and nobody knows whether this is temporary or permanent. But most of our economic writing continues to assume implicitly that a return to 8 percent is only just around the corner.

I

Let me come back to the relationship between *MDC*s and *LDC*s. The principal link through which the former control the growth rate of the latter is trade. As *MDC*s grow faster, the rate of growth of their imports accelerates and *LDC*s export more. We can measure this link. The growth rate of world trade in primary products over the period 1873 to 1913 was 0.87 times the growth rate of industrial production in the developed countries; and just about the same relationship, about 0.87, also ruled in the two decades to 1973.[1] World trade in primary products is a wider concept than exports from developing countries, but the two are sufficiently closely related for it to serve as a proxy. We need no elaborate statistical proof that trade depends on prosperity in the industrial countries. More interesting is the evidence that the relationship was quantitatively the same over a hundred years, so that the two-thirds increase in the rate of growth of exports of primary products from *LDC*s was no more or less than could be predicted from the increased rate of growth of *MDC* production.

Most interesting is that the coefficient is less than one, viz. 0.87. This means that if the engines of growth were industrial pro-

duction in *MDC*s and exports of primary products in *LDC*s, then the *MDC* engine was beating slightly faster than the *LDC* engine. The effects of equal beating would not necessarily be exactly the same. And there are side effects that strengthen the connection. When the beat is faster the terms of trade are expected to be more favorable to the *LDC*s (though that did not happen this time). The domestic market prospers, so *LDC* industrialization for the domestic market is speeded; this happened. The *MDC*s relax their barriers to imports of manufactures, so this trade accelerates as well. Foreign capital flows into minerals, manufactures, and infrastructure. And foreign countries take more migrants, so that the homeward flow of remittances to *LDC*s is larger in prosperous times.

Putting it all together, including the fact that industrial production grew faster in *LDC*s than in *MDC*s, it is not surprising that the rate of growth of gross domestic product was just about the same in *LDC*s and in *MDC*s over the quarter of a century ending in 1973, namely about 5 percent per annum. Since *LDC* population was growing faster than *MDC* population, there is a big gap in the growth rates of output per head, about 4 percent in *MDC*s, against 2.5 percent in *LDC*s. The performance of *LDC*s was remarkable in absolute terms, but the gap between *MDC*s and *LDC*s in income per head continued to widen rapidly.

Now we come to our dilemma. The objective of most people who are concerned with these matters is to narrow the per capita gap between *MDC*s and *LDC*s. But how is one to do this if they are linked to equal growth of total output? One might perhaps conceive a lower rate of growth of *MDC*s. Many *MDC* voices are calling for this—the environmentalists, the persons who fear exhaustion of exhaustible resources, the advocates of greater grace and leisure in our lives, and others. But if the *MDC* growth rate falls, the *LDC* growth rate will fall too, and *LDC*s will get the worst of it, since the terms of trade will move against them. Given the link, it is in the interest of *LDC*s that the *MDC*s should grow as rapidly as they can.

[1]For data, see my *Growth and Fluctuations 1870–1913*, pp. 175–76.

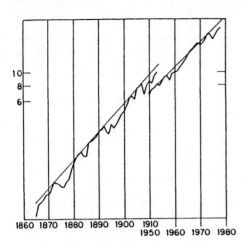

FIGURE 1. U.S. INDUSTRIAL PRODUCTION,
1865-1913 AND 1950-78

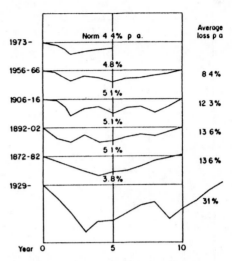

FIGURE 2. U.S. GREAT DEPRESSIONS: DEVIATION
OF ACTUAL FROM "CAPACITY" INDUSTRIAL
PRODUCTION

Three questions come to mind. First, what is likely to happen to the speed of *MDC* growth? Secondly, can *LDC*s maintain fast growth even in face of a decline of *MDC* growth? And thirdly, is it desirable that *LDC* development depend on rapid growth of exports to *MDC*s? My main purpose in this paper is to consider the second question, but I shall also briefly explore the first. The third question, on the desirability of *LDC/MDC* trade, may be left to another occasion.

II

Many people now assert that the world economy has made one of those major turns that it makes from time to time, as it did in 1873 when world trade settled into a growth rate only about two-thirds of that of the preceding half-century. However, part of the evidence they adduce is merely evidence of cyclical and not secular decline—high unemployment rates, low profits,[2] low invest-

ment ratios, low savings, and a slower growth rate of productivity are the familiar elements of cyclical downswing, and throw no light-term trends.

Over the past century, the United States has experienced a series of Great Depressions, each of which took ten years to complete itself, except for that of 1929, which took twelve years. The starting points of these depressions were 1873, 1893, 1907, 1929, 1957, and 1974. Figure 1 shows *U.S.* industrial production on a semilogarithmic scale, where the straight lines indicate the rate of growth along the peaks, and the potential output at that rate.[3] The difference

---

[2]Evidence of a decline in the profits ratio, often cited, is hard to interpret. In the United States, industrial production runs along a ceiling when the ratio of manufacturers' profits to sales is around 5 percent (after tax). The ratio averaged 4.8 over 1951-56 and 5.1 over 1966-69, which were also years of full employment (less than 4 percent unemployed). The basis of

the series changes between 1973 and 1974; on the new basis, the ceiling would be about 6 percent. That the profit ratio averaged 5.4 in 1976 and 5.3 in 1977 merely indicates, along with elevated unemployment, the continuance of cyclical deficiency in those years. Series from the *Economic Report of the President*.

[3]From 1923, the index is that of the Federal Reserve Board. Prior to 1913, the index is that of Edwin Frickey, as amended by the National Bureau of Economic Research statisticians. For references, see my *Growth and Fluctuations 1890-1913*, pp. 272-73. Construction is excluded. The charts are semilogarithmic. The slope of the straight line from 1872 to 1906 indicates growth at 5.1 percent per annum; that from 1951 to 1973

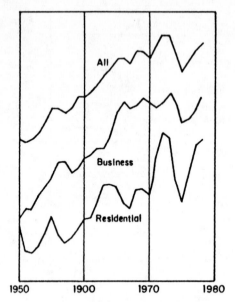

1950   1900   1970   1980

FIGURE 3. U.S. CONSTRUCTION

between actual and potential output is shown in Figure 2 for each of these Great Depressions separately.[4] The depression at the top of the figure is the one we are now experiencing. It seems to conform to pattern. For example, as is well known, these Great Depressions are associated with similar long fluctuations in construction activity. Figure 3 shows that this association is unchanged, despite Moses Abramovitz's optimistic prediction to the contrary; deep depressions in both business and residential construction are at the heart of our current depression.[5] Again, suggestions that the *U.S*

---

indicates growth at 4.4 percent per annum. In Figure 1, the position of the lower curve in relation to the upper reflects that industrial output in 1956 was 20 percent less than it would have been if it had grown at 4.4 percent per annum since 1913. The interwar curve is omitted. Its familiar shape would show output rising at 3.8 percent per annum before 1929, then plunging into the Great Depression.

[4] The depression of 1929 is of such a different magnitude from the rest that it has been taken out of its sequence, and put at the bottom of the figure.

[5] Expenditure on structures at 1972 prices; Tables B2 and B7 of the *Economic Report of the President*. It can be seen in Figure 2 that the two postwar depressions are notably less deep than the pre-1913 depressions.

economy was overheated at the end of 1978 (year 5) seem implausible—they confuse lack of capacity due to many years of low construction in face of rising population, with lack of capacity due to high demand. Shortage of capacity after years of depression is what triggers a new investment boom. If the past repeats itself, a spurt of activity in the early 1980's (growth at 6 to 7 percent per annum) should bring *U.S.* industrial production back on to its prosperity line by 1983. This does not rule out the possibility of a minor fluctuation in the interim. There is, of course, no basis for predicting that the past will repeat itself, but equally there is no basis for predicting that this depression will go on forever.[6]

If then we reject all evidence that can be explained by six years of depression, we are left with a number of arguments that are being advanced to suggest that the prosperity of 1950–73 was special and not repeatable. I shall merely list them, because to pursue each of them would take us too far off course. Here are the leading six:

1. The fast growth of Europe after World War II was due to catching up on a backlog of innovations whose feasibility and profitability the United States had demonstrated by 1950, but whose utilization had been delayed in Europe by two world wars and the Great Depression — telephones, automobiles, refrigerators, television, aeroplanes, and so on. This backlog, it is claimed, is now exhausted.

2. There is no new innovation of Schumpeterian magnitude to take its place. This proposition could be established only by hindsight; expenditure on research and development by private industry may have declined, but this may only be a cyclical event.

3. Western Europe's reserves of surplus labor in agriculture, petty retailing, and

---

[6] The National Bureau of Economic Research has trained us to think of the Kitchin as the reference cycle (forty months), so any depression that extends beyond eighteen months feels like the end of the world. Our economic journalists have even lower horizons, since they seldom get beyond comparing this year with last. We cannot understand what is happening without at least a ten-year perspective.

elsewhere, which facilitated rapid expansion of industry and other high-level occupations is now exhausted, and immigration of cheap labor from Southern Europe will not be resumed.

4. We shall run into a shortage of minerals; of copper, tin, bauxite, and others, because transnational companies and LDC governments cannot agree on terms for new investment; and of oil because of OPEC's conservation policies. This imbalance is one of the two primary sources of inflation. The other primary source is the spiralling of prices as organized groups bargain for an annual increase in income of at least 5 percent (plus last year's increase in prices) in an economy where productivity rises by 3 percent per annum or less. Attempts to control inflation through controlling the money supply touch neither of these primary sources, unless pushed to the level of 15 percent unemployment, which is not politically feasible. Whether the monetary authorities opt for stagflation or for massive unemployment, the rate of growth is slowed.

5. The preference of consumers in rich countries for services rather than manufactured commodities will result in relative decline of the industrial population. Among the effects of this may be a decline in the rate of growth of imports of primary production.

6. High levels of taxation may diminish initiative, enterprise, and the rate of growth.

I list these propositions neither to support them nor to controvert them, but only to remind us that the world economy has had long periods of prosperity (like 1850 to 1873) and long periods of relative stagnation (say 1913 to 1950) so that there is nothing strange in the idea that the next two or three decades may turn out to be difficult. But there is also nothing strange in the idea that they may turn out to be rather prosperous.

III

In what follows I shall assume that industrial production in MDCs grows more slowly than it was growing before 1973, and that the imports of these countries grow only at 4 percent a year, over the next twenty years. This is not a prediction; it is merely the assumption whose consequences we are seeking to analyze.

I shall also assume that LDCs want their GDP to grow at 6 percent per annum, and that this requires their imports to grow at 6 percent. This linkage follows from the further assumption that the individual LDC will not become more self-sufficient, perhaps because it is too small; though LDCs as a group will have to be more self-sufficient. No importance attaches to whether the figure for imports is the same as the figure for the growth of gross domestic product; all that matters is that the growth rate of exports from LDCs is assumed to be significantly higher than the rate of growth of imports of LDC commodities into MDCs. The LDCs will continue to pay for some of their imports out of proceeds of transfers, including foreign aid and private foreign investment, but we shall assume that this still leaves LDCs needing, say, a 6 percent growth rate for exports, while MDCs are assumed to increase their imports from LDCs only at 4 percent a year. The problem is how to reconcile these two growth rates.

There could theoretically be a simple way, namely for LDCs to have an ever increasing share of MDC imports, but we have closed this door. The main link between MDC and LDC economies has been the MDC demand for LDC primary commodities. This has been a link in terms of physical volume, not much affected by prices. The LDCs could not sell significantly more primary produce by reducing prices; on the contrary, they would earn substantially less purchasing power as the terms of trade deteriorated. The LDCs could earn more by reducing the volume or by joining together in raising prices. The direct effect of these actions would be to reduce output, but this could be offset by investing the extra earnings judiciously. However none of this seems to be in the cards; so we shall assume that our problem cannot be solved by accelerated or decelerated production of primary commodities normally exported to MDCs.

What about manufactures? These are now nearly 40 percent of the exports of the non-OPEC LDCs, and are still their fastest growing export. Could the whole problem be solved simply by increasing the growth rate of manufactured exports to *MDC*s, in substitution for primary products? I shall assume that this cannot be done, since if it can be done my paper ends abruptly. Also I do not think that it can be done. The *MDC*s are willing to let in manufactured exports when they are prosperous, since they then have many growing industries that can take in people displaced by imports. Our assumption that the *MDC* growth rate is low rules out this possibility. It would indeed be more appropriate to assume that *MDC*s will take less manufactures from *LDC*s rather than more.

Our basic assumptions therefore are that *LDC*s need to have their exports grow at 6 percent a year, but *MDC*s will increase their imports from *LDC*s only at 4 percent a year. What is to happen to the growth of *LDC* output?

Let me concede at once that from the standpoint of the individual *LDC* it matters not at all what the *MDC* growth rate may be. Given resources and flexibility, it can always sell more to *MDC*s. However, it thereby displaces some other *LDC*'s trade. What one can do cannot be done by all.

At the level of arithmetic this problem now has only one solution. If total sales from *LDC*s increase at 6 percent, while sales to *MDC*s increase at 4 percent, sales to the rest of the world (given weights of seven to three) must increase initially at about 11 percent per annum. Ignoring the socialist countries, which could help by buying much more from *LDC*s but won't, the *LDC*s can solve the problem only by accelerating sharply their trade with each other.

Inter-*LDC* trade is still rather small— about 19 percent of the exports of non-OPEC *LDC*s.[7] The percentage did not change significantly over the two decades to 1973 despite all the effort that was put into creating and servicing regional trade institutions. Can this trade take up the slack left by *MDC*s as *MDC*s slow down?

The answer is in the affirmative. Currently the *LDC*s depend on the *MDC*s for food, fertilizers, cement, steel, and machin-

ery. Taken as a group, *LDC*s could quickly end their dependence for the first four, and gradually throw off their dependence for machinery. They also import a considerable quantity of light manufactures for which they are not in any sense dependent (some $31 billion in 1977, compared with $47 billion of engineering products). They could quickly rid themselves of these, and more gradually throw off their dependence for machinery.

The *LDC*s are capable of feeding themselves now, if they adopt appropriate agrarian policies and, as our eleven new international tropical agricultural research institutes give us better varieties and improved technology, output should more than keep up with population. The problem is to get through the period while the birth rate remains obstinately high to the less-frightening times when the birth rate will have dropped below twenty per thousand. It may be a near thing, but we should make it.

As for fertilizers, cement, and steel, these are made by applying standard technology to raw materials that are widely available outside the *MDC*s. Machinery is more bothersome because important parts of this trade involve economies of scale, continually improving technology, and patented or secret knowledge. However, several *LDC*s are moving into this field, and already machinery is 15 percent or more of the output of manufactures in at least eight *LDC*s (India, Brazil, Singapore, Chile, Korea, Argentina, Mexico, and Israel).[8] The *LDC* exports of engineering products are also growing rapidly, and contrary to popular belief, already exceed *LDC* exports of textiles and clothing in value. There is no reason why *LDC*s as a group should not become nearly self-sufficient in standard types of equipment.

If all this scope exists for inter-*LDC* trade, why have the regional customs unions not been more successful? Note three reasons.

First, a region is not a homogenous area. Some countries are much more

---

[7]Trade data in this and the next two paragraphs are from GATT, *International Trade 1977–78*.

[8]Share of machinery in manufactures calculated from United Nations, *Yearbook of Industrial Statistics 1976*.

advanced than others in industrial competitiveness, to an almost inconceivable extent. These advanced countries attract more new industries than the less advanced, who feel exploited by the customs union. The union then survives only if costly measures are taken to placate the less advanced, and these measures are difficult to negotiate.

Secondly, the usefulness of the union is maximized in sharing out industries with substantial economies of scale, extending over the whole regional market. Each country is anxious to keep for itself all those industries that can attain the economies of scale within the national market. Destruction of any of these industries by competition from another member of the union causes a political uproar. The union is therefore safest when it does not require internal free trade in all commodities, but instead concentrates on those few "integration" industries as they are called which need the whole regional market. Even this more modest task is hard to negotiate if each member country is to have its fair share of integration industries.

The third reason why the customs unions have not done better is that their basic assumption—that a country should trade most with its next-door neighbors—is no longer true in these days of very low transport costs. For reasons of climate, soil, and history, the next-door neighbor is probably in the same business, and not a potential customer or supplier. He is equally poor, and therefore offers an equally limited market. The LDCs developing new industrial products are drawn to large rich LDC markets rather than to those of their neighbors. Frankly, in the 1950's and 1960's, aggressive developers did not much need the support of customs unions; these offer more to their members when world trade is stagnant than when it is booming.

It follows, therefore, that in the situation we are analyzing, where world trade decelerates, customs unions would be more highly prized and would be made more effective, especially in regard to large-scale industries with region-wide economies of scale. But even so, the leading commodities that LDCs would now have to produce to a greater

extent for each other cannot be shared out between next door neighbors on a political basis. Food, fertilizers, cement, steel, and fuel pick their locations more in terms of raw material availability, and machinery will come in the first instance from those LDCs that already have a substantial industrial base. This new LDC trade would be worldwide, just as European and U.S. trade are worldwide.

IV

I am therefore arguing that it is physically feasible for LDCs to maintain a high rate of growth even if MDCs decide otherwise for themselves. How does physical feasibility translate into an effective economic framework?

One way would be to follow the customs union route, with LDCs giving preferential treatment to imports from other LDCs. The nucleus of this exists already in the Protocol Relating to Trade Negotiations among Developing Countries which came into force in 1973, with the blessing of GATT, and which provides for negotiated preferential arrangements among sixteen of the bigger and more advanced LDCs. The philosophy of such an arrangement is in line with the spirit of Bretton Woods, which recognized the rights of countries to impose restrictions on other countries which were tending persistently to run balance-of-payments surpluses, as would be the situation if the LDCs were growing faster than the MDCs. One may doubt however whether such different countries will get very far along the route of preferential concessions. If they are to prefer each other's goods, this will have to be because they are competitive in price with those of MDCs.

In the economist's model this competitiveness would come about automatically. The LDCs would run a balance-of-payments deficit because of the MDC slowdown, yet persist in their own rapid growth instead of slowing down themselves. Adjustment comes in the old gold standard version through an outflow of gold that reduces their price levels; or in the modern versions by devaluation, which has the same effect. The real world is more complicated. Inflation is universal, but aggressive sellers of manufactures have to keep their prices down; so this set of *LDC*s would need special emphasis on inflation controls. Devaluation cannot be avoided when prices cease to be competitive, but is palliative rather than curative in situations when it triggers further increases in domestic costs that reinstate the differential that it was meant to eliminate. The *LDC*s have the same problem as the *MDC*s: the domestic price level can no longer be controlled merely by twirling general controls such as the rate of interest, or the supply of money, or the rate of exchange for the currency. They too now experience the cost-push element in price determination, for which the only remedy is some sort of incomes policy. We expect more from the economic system than our grandparents did in the nineteenth century, by way of full employment and faster growth, and should not be surprised that the economic system requires more from us, by way of supporting institutions.

These new aggressive *LDC*s, exporting machinery to each other, may also have problems in financing their trade. Nearly every *LDC* has a separate currency. We are envisioning Nigeria selling cereals to India for rupees, with which it buys machinery from Brazil. Some kind of clearing agreement may become necessary; otherwise *LDC* traders will tend to do business with each other in one or more *MDC* currencies, and will be constrained by the relative scarcity of such currencies. Perhaps the International Monetary Fund would straighten this out. A more serious problem will be to finance the export of capital goods from one *LDC* to another, since the seller is expected to help finance the buyer. It is not likely that the *LDC* exporters can do this on their own. We must assume that they will be allowed to raise untied loans in the *MDC* financial markets, perhaps using the regional development banks as intermediaries to a greater extent than is now the case.

But the real problem is not whether *LDC*s can become competitive and hold their own in each other's markets. Problems of pricing and foreign exchange can work themselves

out in the world market. The real problem is whether *LDC*s will persist in rapid growth despite the slowdown of the *MDC*s. If the economy is still dependent, the balance-of-payments weakness will pull it down; but if it has attained self-sustaining growth, the weakness in the foreign exchanges merely launches a drive to export to other *LDC*s, and the weakness in the balance of payments is then only transitional.

If a sufficient number of *LDC*s reach self-sustaining growth, we are into a new world. For this will mean that instead of trade determining the rate of growth of *LDC* production, it will be the growth of *LDC* production that determines *LDC* trade, and internal forces that will determine the rate of growth of production. Not many countries are ready to make this switch. India is an obvious possibility, along with some of the other subscribers to the Protocol of 1973. It is not possible for all *LDC*s to make this switch and neither is it necessary, for if leading *LDC*s grow fast and import heavily, they will substitute to some extent for the former rapid growth of *MDC*s. For those who use the language of center and periphery, this means that a number of countries leave the periphery and join the center. Or if they are specially linked to each other by preferential trade and currency arrangements, one may even speak of the creation of a new center consisting of former peripheral nations that have built a new engine of growth together.

The shadow on this picture is what happens to those *LDC*s whose best option has been to export raw materials to *MDC*s. Our exercise starts from the assumption that the growth rate of *MDC* demand is reduced, so these face surpluses and unfavorable terms of trade. We have provided an escape for *LDC*s that can turn to exporting food or manufactures, but we have not assumed that the new core *LDC*s will substitute for the *MDC*s by drinking more coffee or tea, or using more rubber and jute. This solution therefore involves some hardships for the less adaptable *LDC*s, constrained by climate or by the small size of their markets. A framework for helping them exists already in the IMF's compensatory financing, and in the EEC's STABEX support; but these are meant for temporary fluctuations. Bigger and more persistent support would be required.

Transnational corporations would probably play some part in the establishment of this new inter-*LDC* trading network. The cadre of domestic entrepreneurs is adequate in the more advanced industrial *LDC*s to manage most of the range of light consumer goods and light engineering products. One of our main concerns, however, is to diminish reliance on *MDC*s for heavy machinery and such, and this extends into fields where experience is limited. Since we are assuming that the market will send out price signals favoring production in *LDC*s, whether because of tariffs or of currency adjustments, transnational corporations will be eager to preserve their markets by establishing subsidiaries behind the protective barrier. Hostility to such corporations is universal and their influence is diminishing in most sectors, especially in mining, public utilities, distribution, and finance; but not in manufacturing, where judging by advertisements in the *New York Times* and the financial press, *LDC* governments are only too anxious to invite the participation of transnational corporations. There are plenty of restrictions—on the hiring of expatriate staff, on percentages of equity owned by foreigners, on borrowing in the local market, on technology, and so on. Also, in many cases joint ownership with local capitalists or with government agencies is prescribed. A government anxious to promote industrialization and a corporation anxious to preserve or extend its market find common ground.

The awkward part of the exercise is to sustain the momentum of 6 percent growth through the transition from dependence on *MDC* trade to dependence on *LDC* markets. During this transition the leading industrial *LDC*s must establish their footholds in each others' markets, as well as those of other *LDC*s; also the agrarian changes must occur which both feed the urban population and present a growing market for its goods and

services. It is possible that some of the leading *LDC*s can take this in their stride, just as German industrialists launched their trade drive in the 1880's, followed by the United States after 1895, by Japan in the 1930's, and more recently by Brazil. They do not have to begin with machinery, since *LDC*s still import so much light manufactures from *MDC*s. They can start here and move more gradually into machinery.

At the other extreme, it is also possible that there is simply not yet enough entrepreneurial steam in the leading *LDC*s to make this transition without a supporting framework. I have already mentioned the main international elements of such a framework, namely preferential tariff and currency arrangements. The domestic element consists of the maintenance of home demand in the face of stagnant world trade in primary products, so that the economy can continue to go forward instead of collapsing. Much of the responsibility for maintaining momentum then falls on the government, given its large share of the cash economy, and also the extent to which it regulates or supports the private sector. It has to carry the responsibility for a large investment program (private and public) in human and physical capital. This responsibility could not be carried without external aid. The *MDC*s would have to be in a mood to say: we will not give you more trade; here for a while is more aid instead.

The recession that started in 1974 has now lasted long enough for *LDC*s to consider the possibility that *MDC*s intend to maintain rates of *GNP* growth which will allow world trade to expand only at around 4 percent a year. This would be a major blow to *LDC* growth aspirations, unless new steps were taken to support rising participation of *LDC*s in *LDC* trade. I have been trying to analyze what these steps might be. They ought to figure prominently in current North-South negotiations, but in fact they do not, since these negotiations tacitly assume that high *MDC* growth rates will soon be resumed. Perhaps this assumption will turn out to be correct; economics does not foretell the future. For the least, *LDC*s should be discussing among themselves in what directions they would wish to go, prior to negotiations with the *MDC*s.

Of course, the problems tackled in this paper would not arise at all if *MDC*s were willing to allow *LDC*s a greater share of *MDC* markets. This would be the logical evolution of a situation where *LDC*s grow faster than *MDC*s; trade with *LDC*s should become an ever-increasing portion of *MDC* trade. We live in a strange world. Through the 1960's and 1970's, *MDC*s have been dismantling their barriers to each other's trade while increasing their barriers to *LDC* trade. Since imports of manufactures from developing countries are only 2 percent of the consumption of manufactures in OECD countries, this indicates exceptional sensitivity to minor change. Lack of sensitivity, on the other hand, characterizes the failure of developed countries to recognize that dependence is mutual, in that the non-OPEC *LDC*s take 20 percent of OECD exports, and could therefore by their prosperity help a little to sustain OECD prosperity. It can hardly be an OECD interest to force the *LDC*s into discriminating against OECD sources.

Nor would these problems arise if the *MDC*s would return to the attack on mass poverty within their own borders which they launched so successfully in the 1950's and 1960's, and have now abandoned; since what we all really need is that world trade recapture its growth rate of 8 percent a year. But that is a different story.

REFERENCES

M. Abramovitz, "The Passing of the Kuznets Cycle," *Economica*, Nov. 1968, *35*, 349–67.

W. Arthur Lewis, *Growth and Fluctuations 1870–1913*, London; Boston 1978.

GATT, *International Trade 1977–78*, Geneva 1978.

United Nations, *Yearbook of Industrial Statistics 1976*, Vol. 1, New York 1978.

UNCTAD, *Handbook of International Trade and Development Statistics, Supplement 1977*, New York 1978.

U.S. Council of Economic Advisers, *Economic Report of the President*, Washington, various years.

[6]

The Economic Journal, **94** (*March* 1984), 56–73
Printed in Great Britain

TRADE AS THE ENGINE OF GROWTH IN DEVELOPING COUNTRIES, REVISITED*

James Riedel

In his 1979 Nobel lecture, W. Arthur Lewis (1980) analysed the consequences of a slowdown of the engine of growth in developing countries (LDCs) and proposed a strategy to revive it. The engine, according to Lewis, is trade, which in the past was fueled by industrial growth in developed countries. The slowdown is attributed to what some believe is a secular decline in the rate of economic growth in developed countries since the mid-1970s. The only way to keep the engine of LDC growth beating at a satisfactory rate, so the argument goes, is to turn to an alternative source of fuel. This, Lewis argues, lies in trade among the developing countries, which he asserts can 'take up the slack left by MDCs (more developed countries) as MDCs slow down' (1980, p. 560).

Pessimism about demand for LDC exports in developed countries' markets is a recurrent theme in the development literature. Also familiar is the approach taken by Lewis to dismiss past successes of LDCs in world trade by declaring the alleged engine of past growth to be no longer operating satisfactorily. The intellectual foundations of the import-substitution strategy laid in the 1950s by Prebisch, Myrdal and, most importantly, Nurkse rested on similar grounds. Arguing that the demand for 'periphery' countries' exports in the 20th century is far weaker than it was in the 19th century, trade was dismissed as an engine of growth, a function Nurkse alleged it had served in the 19th century. The solution prescribed in the 1950s was to look inward, in effect, to scrap the trade engine altogether. Lewis' remedy, coming two decades later when most import-substitution possibilities in many LDCs have been all but exhausted, retains the trade engine but seeks an alternative source of fuel to drive it.

The classic critique by Irving Kravis (1970) of Nurkse's thesis of trade as a faltering engine of growth showed that 'Export expansion did not serve in the nineteenth century to differentiate successful from unsuccessful countries' (p. 850). This followed from two findings: first, that successful 19th century countries showed few signs of export dominated growth; second, that unsuccessful periphery countries enjoyed export expansion in the second half of the 19th century of the same order of magnitude as the temperate regions of recent settlement. This led Kravis to conclude that 'A more warranted metaphor

* This paper was written while I was consultant to the World Bank, Economic Analysis and Projections Department. The views expressed in the paper are my own and should not be attributed to the World Bank. Invaluable research assistance was provided by Irma Jacobsen and Jean Rosenheim; the paper expertly typed by Karen Adams. Helpful comments on an earlier draft entitled 'Lewis on trade as the engine of growth in developing countries' were provided by Chris Delgado, Angus Hone, Helen Hughes, Peter Miovic, Morris Morkre, Larry Westphal and Martin Wolf. I would also like to acknowledge useful comments and criticisms on the earlier draft by Professor Arthur Lewis, but this should in no way be construed to imply his endorsement of the views expressed in this paper. The usual caveat applies.

that would be more generally applicable would be to describe trade expansion as a handmaiden of successful growth rather than as an autonomous engine of growth' (p. 850).

The critique of Lewis' thesis of trade as an engine of growth presented in this paper follows a different tack. The principal focus is not the proposition that LDC growth in recent decades was driven by trade. Rather, since Lewis' point of departure is the economic slowdown in developed countries, the focus is the proposition that LDC exports are fuelled by prosperity in developed countries. The paper is divided into two parts. The first examines the theoretical basis of the trade engine theory. The objective is to identify the assumptions which establish developed country growth as the main driving force of LDC exports and growth. The mechanics of the trade engine are shown to hinge on extreme assumptions about LDC export supply and demand parameters.

The second part of the paper assesses the empirical relevance of the trade engine theory, considering in particular the implications of far-reaching changes in the composition of LDC exports over the last two decades. These changes, it is argued, have significantly weakened any mechanical link that might once have existed between the export growth of many LDCs and prosperity in the developed countries. The quantitative relationship which Lewis believes to have remained the same over a hundred years, and takes as the cornerstone of this thesis, is shown to be largely a statistical artifact, applicable if at all to a diminishing number of developing countries which export primarily raw materials.

A final point deserves mention before proceeding. Since this paper stresses the implications of LDC export diversification, mainly into manufactures, the charge could be made that it talks past Lewis, Findlay and those whose theories assume a division of the world into an industrialised North and a primary producing South. Lewis' empirical analysis, for that matter, uses world trade in primary products as a proxy for LDC exports. It would be too easy and perhaps unfair simply to take issue with this obviously imprecise proxy, even though in drawing his conclusions Lewis is not careful to limit their applicability by the extent to which LDCs individually or as a whole are dependent on exports of primary products. In fact, the view that LDC export prospects in general (i.e. not just of primary products) are tied to economic prosperity in developed countries is held widely, if not by Lewis himself.[1] For those reasons, it is useful to assess the trade engine theory broadly, and not just in terms of its applicability to primary exports. By looking at the issues more broadly one can see very clearly how misleading it has become to dichotomise the world falsely into developed countries as producers and exporters of industrial goods, and LDCs as producers and exporters of primary products.

---

[1] A typical expression of this view is contained in the I.B.R.D.'s *World Development Report, 1978* (p. 13): 'Since the industrialized countries demand for imports depends on their income their economic growth is very important to the export and growth prospects of developing countries.'

I. THEORY

The theory of trade as an engine of growth is founded on the premise that there exists a stable, mechanical relationship between economic growth in developed countries and export growth in developing countries Lewis describes the relationship as follows:

> The growth rate of world trade in primary products over the period of 1873 to 1913 was 0·87 times the growth rate of industrial production in the developed countries; and just about the same relationship, about 0·87, also ruled in the two decades to 1973.... We need no elaborate statistical proof that trade depends on prosperity in the industrial countries (Lewis, 1980, p. 556).[1]

It is obvious that this view of strict dependence of LDC export growth on income growth in developed countries implies very limited substitutability between the products LDCs produce and export and those produced in developed countries. In other words, it admits very little scope for LDCs to engage in price competition by which means they could conceivably expand exports despite slowdown in developed countries by claiming a larger share of the DC market. Lewis rules out price competition explicitly, arguing that 'The main linkage between MDC [more developed countries] and LDC economies has been MDC demand for LDC primary commodities. This has been a link in terms of physical volume not much affected by price' (Lewis, 1980, p. 559).[2]

In recent years several attempts have been made to model rigorously the trade engine theory (e.g. Findlay, 1980 and Taylor, 1981). Not surprisingly, these exercises begin by hypothesising complete specialisation in MDCs and LDCs, which implies that LDC and MDC products compete only as gross substitutes in the budget constraint of each country.[3] The foundation of the trade engine having thus been laid, further assumptions are then required to ensure that it is the MDCs that play the role of engine and the LDCs that are pulled along behind. In Findlay (1980), for example, this is done by assuming, first, that only the MDC good can be used for investment, thereby conditioning growth in LDCs by the willingness of MDCs to accept their exports; and second, that the (consumption) good produced in LDCs is available in perfectly elastic supply, thereby establishing that the price of the LDC export is determined exclusively by the LDC cost of production, and that the quantity of LDC export is determined exclusively by the level of expenditure in developed countries.[4] These assumptions also ensure, of course, that attempts by LDCs to

---

[1] Lewis (1980, p. 556) states that 'World trade in primary product is a wider concept than exports from developing countries, but the two are sufficiently closedly related for it to serve as a proxy.'

[2] Likewise, the major criticism levelled at Nurkse's trade engine thesis by Cairncross (1960) was Nurkse's failure to take into account 'the price factor'.

[3] The closest Lewis comes to providing an explicit model of the relationship is in his Wicksell Lecture (1969) which analyses determinants of the terms of trade in the context of a two region model with LDCs specialised in a 'tropical' product, coffee, and MDCs in a 'temperate' product, steel, with both producing food which serves as the numeraire. Also see Findlay (1981).

[4] Perfectly elastic supply derives from the surplus labour assumption for which Lewis' pathbreaking work is well known (Lewis, 1954).

generate growth internally will be negated by adverse movements in the terms of trade.

The assumptions on which the trade engine theory is based are of course extreme, and purposely so since they serve to make rigorous modelling tractable. Obviously, by choosing different assumptions, one could produce a consistent model to yield very different results. However, given that our objective is to reach an understanding of the 'real world' relevance of Lewis' thesis, it may be more enlightening to eschew hard theoretical results in favour of a looser framework which allows the focus to shift to matters of degree – that is, where specialisation is a matter of degree, product differentiation is a matter of degree and where supply elasticities are a matter of degree.

Such a framework is in fact provided by the standard Walrasian model of world trade used extensively in global modelling exercises. The procedure is to solve a simultaneous system of supply and demand functions which yield a set of reduced-form equations defining the relationship between the market clearing price and quantity of exports and each of the exogenous variables that enter into the determination of supply and demand.[1] The reduced-form coefficient describing the particular relationship between income growth in one region (e.g. MDCs) and export volume in another (e.g. LDCs) is found to be a complex expression of all the supply and demand parameters of the system. It is easily shown that the coefficient measuring the impact of a given change in MDC income on the quantity exported of a given LDC product will be greater, other things equal:

- the greater the LDC share of the MDC market for the good;
- the lower the elasticity of substitution between competing products in the market;
- the greater the income elasticity of demand;
- the lower the elasticity of supply of competing products; and
- the greater the elasticity of supply of LDC products.

Since the values of these parameters vary from product to product, one would reasonably expect the relationship between aggregate export performance and growth in developed countries to vary among developing countries due to differences in export composition, among other reasons. If developing countries are considered as a whole, as is the usual practice, then one would expect the relationship between MDC growth and LDC export performance to change over time as the composition of LDC exports changes. Constancy in the relationship which Lewis observes over a hundred year span and takes as the cornerstone of his thesis would, therefore, in this more general theoretical framework appear to be an empirical anomaly. Explaining this apparent anomaly and analysing how the last three decades of economic change in LDCs have altered the relationship is the aim of the next part of the paper.

---

[1] See Armington (1969) and Deppler and Ripley (1978).

II. EMPIRICAL EVIDENCE

Structural Changes in LDC Exports

A look at the aggregate data on LDC trade would seem to dispel very quickly concerns based on the notion that LDCs are dependent on exports of agricultural products. As Table 1 shows, two dramatic changes have occurred in the structure of LDC exports to reduce the share of agricultural products (food and raw materials) to something only slightly greater than 20 % of total exports. One is the doubling of the share of fuels from 25 % of exports in 1955 to 53 % in 1978, a phenomenon largely attributable to OPEC-administered oil price increases since 1973. The other change, far more profound in terms of the issues addressed in this paper, is the rise of manufactured exports. The three-fold increase in the share of manufactures in LDC exports is not, as in the case of fuel, mainly a price phenomenon. Rather it is the fundamental consequence of three decades of sometimes painful and costly industrialisation efforts in developing countries. Moreover, although the largest part of the expansion of manufactured exports has been accounted for by a small number of relatively small countries, the potential for all developing countries to share in the trade in manufactures distinguishes it from the oil boom, which can only be enjoyed by a few. For these reasons, and because major oil exporting LDCs can no longer be considered to be constrained by their ability to export (whatever other problems they face), the following analysis focuses on non-fuel exports and countries other than those that earn most of their foreign exchange from oil. (Hereafter reference to total exports should be understood to mean total non-fuel exports.)

Table 1

The Structure of LDC Exports: Selected Years 1955–78 (Percentages)

	1955	1960	1970	1978
Total exports	100	100	100	100
Food	36·5	33·6	26·5	16·4
Agricultural raw materials	20·5	18·3	10·0	4·8
Minerals, ores	9·9	10·6	12·3	4·6
Fuels	25·2	27·9	32·9	52·8
Manufactures*	7·7	9·2	17·7	20·9
Total non-fuel exports	100	100	100	100
Food	48·9	46·7	39·5	34·8
Agricultural raw materials	27·4	25·3	14·9	10·1
Minerals, ores	13·3	14·6	18·3	9·7
Manufactures*	10·4	12·8	26·4	44·4
Share of MDCs in Exports of LDCs				
Total non-fuel exports	76·3	74·3	71·9	65·4
Food	79·0	77·7	74·0	65·6
Agricultural raw materials	74·3	67·8	64·4	61·8
Minerals, ores	94·5	92·0	89·2	78·0
Manufactures*	45·9	54·0	61·2	63·3

* Manufactures = SITC 5 to 8 less 68.
Source: UNCTAD, Handbook of Trade and Development Statistics, 1972, 1979, 1980.

Were LDCs a homogeneous group of countries sharing similar production and trade structures, the aggregate data alone might allow one to dismiss as unrealistic the models discussed above. In fact, LDCs share few common economic characteristics other than per capita income below some arbitrarily set level.[1] Not surprisingly, therefore, the aggregate data mask a wide diversity of export structures among LDCs. Four political entities in East Asia (South Korea, Taiwan, Hong Kong and Singapore) alone in 1978 accounted for more than 60 % of total LDC manufactured exports, but alas only about 3 % of the total population of developing countries.[2] These four entities, together with Lebanon and Macao, are the only LDCs in which manufactures account for as much as 75 % of exports.

In the rest of the developing world, primary products, the traditional mainstay, are still the predominant export. However, as shown in Fig. 1, even among countries relying heavily on primary exports, manufactures are claiming an ever larger share. Among the 52 sample countries represented in Fig. 1, the average share of manufactures in non-fuel exports rose from 7·4 % in 1960 to 18 % in 1978.[3] Moreover, it is particularly important to note that the increased share of manufactures was claimed totally from the share of the single largest primary commodity in total exports, thereby gaining the maximum in export diversification from the expansion of manufactures.

The picture presented in Fig. 1 is, however, also misleading because even within this group of countries, success in diversifying exports has been widely different. Among the 52 countries, eleven managed to raise the share of manufactures from an average of 15 % in 1960 to almost 40 % in 1978.[4] This group of 'balanced exporters', which includes most of South Asia, Egypt, Brazil, Mexico and some smaller Latin American countries (see Appendix 1), and accounts for about two-thirds of the population of the developing world, appears to have severed dependence on the single largest traditional primary export. As shown in Fig. 2, the average decline in the percentage share of primary exports was almost totally accounted for by the decline of the single largest commodity export.

Developing countries in which primary exports continue to account for 80 % or more of the total exports are large in number but relatively small in size, and together account for only about one-third of the population of developing countries.[5] However, even among these countries important differences regarding export diversification deserve mention. Among the countries still exporting predominantly primary products, only the African countries appear to have been unable to make much headway toward breaking dependence on the traditional, single largest primary export (see Fig. 3). As shown in Fig. 4,

---

[1] The World Bank, judging from the *World Development Report*, 1980, set it in 1978 at $3,500, though apparently other factors are involved since Ireland with per capita income of $3,470 is considered developed while Israel with $3,500 is not.

[2] The unavailability of data prevents us from including the People's Republic of China within the group of LDCs.

[3] The sample includes all but some of the smallest LDCs for which data were not consistently available over the period of investigation.

[4] A trade weighted average for the eleven would put the share of manufactures above 50%.

[5] Excluding China.

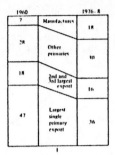

Fig. 1. Average export structure for total sample of LDC (52 countries).

Fig. 2. Average export structure for balanced exporters (11 countries).

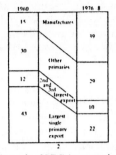

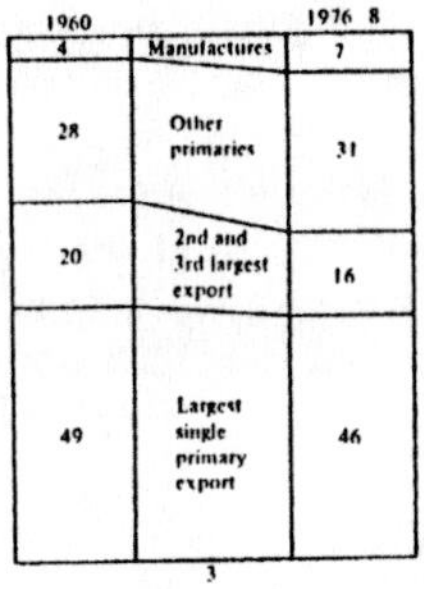

Fig. 3. Average export structure for African primary exports (20 countries).

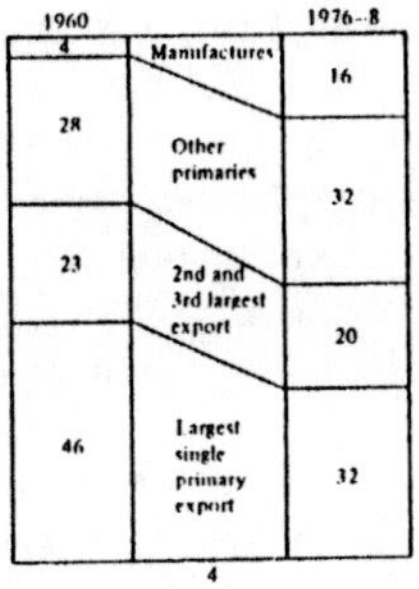

Fig. 4. Average export structure for non-African primary exporters (23 countries).

Note: Country groupings are given in Appendix 1.

Source: M. Wolf, 'LDC Exports – Key Features of Past Performance – unpublished mimeo, February 1978; World Bank, Commodity Trade and Price Trends, 1973, 1980; Handbook of International Trade and Development Statistics, 1979.

non-African primary exporters have reduced the share of the single largest export from 46% to 32%, both by expansion of manufactures and by diversification within the primary exports, most of which occurred in the 1970s.

In summary, significant changes have occurred in the structure of exports in developing countries, particularly those outside Africa. Dependence on a single primary export, a key characteristic of the pre-war colonial economy, has been greatly eroded. Secondly, manufactures are rapidly claiming an ever larger share of exports in most developing countries, and already have a share in exports almost equal to primary products in countries representing the majority of the population in the developing world.

Market Shares of LDC Exports

Export diversification in developing countries has many implications, but how has it affected the link between the LDC exports and economic prosperity in developed countries? One thing it has not changed is LDC dependence on MDC markets, for as shown in Table 1, LDCs have come to depend on MDC markets as much for manufactures as for primary exports. The answer lies not in shifting markets but in analysis of the competitive position of different LDC exports within the MDC market. A crucial assumption of the trade engine theory, it will be recalled, is that of complete specialisation, which implies limited substitutability between the goods LDCs supply and those produced domestically in developed countries. Suppose to start with we follow Lewis in assuming away manufactures and focus only on primary exports. Is the assumption of complete specialisation by LDCs in 'tropical' or 'broadly non-competing' primary products reasonable?

One very tentative approach to this question is to attempt a classification of LDC primary exports into 'directly competing' and 'broadly non-competing' categories. The problem of course is that most 'tropical' products have substitutes of some sort in developed countries and some have very close substitutes. The procedure in Table 2 was to classify as broadly non-competing those products for which the LDC share of world exports exceeds 80%. This criterion is obviously arbitrary and in some important instances is very misleading. For example, exception had to be made for sugar, in which LDCs dominate world exports but account for less than half of MDC consumption. The figures reported in Table 2, therefore, are intended only to give a rough indication of the relative importance of so-called 'tropical' products in LDC exports.[1]

Tropical products, as shown in Table 2, have long been of secondary importance in LDC primary exports to developed countries.[2] In 1962, the share of non-competing products was little more than one-third of total primary exports and only about one-fourth of total non-fuel exports. Measured in current prices, the share of non-competing products rose to almost 40% of total primary exports in 1978; however, due to the expansion of manufactures, non-competing products fell to less than 20% of total non-fuel exports in 1978. The rising share in primary exports is shown in Table 2 to have been due to an increase in the relative price of non-competing products; for in constant 1970 prices the share of non-competing products in 1978 was 7 percentage points below the 1962 level.

The experience of African LDCs is again shown, in Table 2, to diverge from that of other LDCs. Whereas the volume share of non-competing primary exports in total primary and total non-fuel exports has fallen for the aggregate of all LDCs, it has steadily increased for African LDCs. Indeed, the very category accounting for the largest part of the incremental decline in the share of non-competing exports for LDC total, beverages, accounts for the largest part of the incremental increase in the share of non-competing products in

---

[1] See Appendix 2 for a listing of products classified as broadly non-competing. The terms 'tropical' and 'broadly non-competing' are used interchangeably.

[2] Because of the unavailability of disaggregated LDC export data over the entire period covered in Table 2, it was necessary to use DC import data. Since MDCs account for about two-thirds of LDC primary commodity exports, the figures in Table 2 can be considered to broadly reflect the structure of total LDC non-fuel primary commodity exports.

primary exports of African LDCs. This suggests that African LDCs, while failing to share in the expansion of manufactures exports, have begun to take over the commodities being abandoned by more successful developing countries that have made or are making the transition.

Turning to manufactures, there is no question that LDCs play a minor role in MDC markets despite growth in the volume of manufactures exports to developed countries in excess of 12 % per year over the last two decades. Table 3 shows the shares of LDC exports in apparent consumption of developed countries aggregated at the ISIC 2-digit level. For 1979, the average share was only 3·4 %, up from a mere 1·7 % in 1970. Disaggregating to the 5-digit ISIC level, Hughes and Waelbroeck found only four categories (leather, knitted apparel, furs and jewellery) out of a total of more than 150 in which the LDC share of the MDC market exceeded 25 %. In clothing and electrical machinery, the fastest growing categories, LDC market shares in 1979 were 14·1 and 4·1 % respectively.

Table 2

The Shares of Broadly Non-competing and Directly Competing LDC Exports of Non-fuel Primary Commodities to MDCs: 1962, 1970, 1978

(Figures in parentheses are shares in 1970 prices.)*

Commodity group	1962 Total LDCs	1962 Africa	1970 Total LDCs	1970 Africa	1978 Total LDCs	1978 Africa
Broadly non-competing†	34·2 (39·8)	25·9 (25·9)	33·3	26·2	39·3 (32·3)	43·3 (30·6)
Food stuffs	22·0 (27·6)	14·6 (17·4)	21·1	18·4	27·5 (21·6)	32·8 (22·6)
Of which beverage	17·0 (21·0)	12·4 (12·1)	15·1	15·3	21·4 (14·6)	30·1 (20·0)
Ag raw material	9·3 (8·0)	5·6 (4·8)	8·5	3·4	7·8 (5·7)	3·1 (2·0)
Metals and minerals	2·9 (4·2)	5·7 (3·7)	3·9	4·4	4·0 (5·0)	7·4 (6·0)
Directly competing‡	65·7 (60·2)	74·1 (74·1)	66·4	73·3	60·8 (67·7)	56·8 (69·4)
Food stuffs	32·5	39·3	29·4	22·2	33·3	21·8
Ag raw materials	14·6	10·8	9·5	8·6	9·1	9·4
Metals and minerals	18·6	24·0	27·5	42·5	18·4	25·6
Total non-fuel primary	100	100	100	100	100	100

* In computing constant price shares, individual price indexes for each non-competing product were used to derive 1970 dollar values of LDC exports of each non-competing product. The aggregate non-fuel primary export deflator was used to obtain total non-fuel primary exports in 1970 dollar prices. The constant price shares for total directly competing exports were derived residually. Since individual price indexes were not available for directly competing products, constant price shares could not be derived.

† A list of commodities classified as broadly non-competing is given in Appendix 2.

‡ The values of directly competing exports were computed as the residual difference between the total and the sum of commodities defined as non-competing.

Sources: IBRD computer tapes of GATT trade data system; World Bank, 'Commodity trade and price trends,' August 1980; UN, *Monthly Bulletin of Statistics*, Special Table F, July 1980.

Table 3

LDC Shares in Apparent Consumption of Manufactured Goods in Industrialised Countries by Major Product Groups: 1970, 1975, 1979

Group (ISIC code)	1970	1975	1979
Food, beverages and tobacco (31)	3·4	3·5	3·9
Clothing, textiles and leather (32)	2·7	6·0	9·6
Wood products (33)	1·8	2·1	3·8
Paper and printing (34)	0·1	0·2	0·4
Chemicals (35)	2·0	3·0	3·4
Non-metallic minerals (36)	0·3	0·6	1·0
Basic metal (37)	3·2	0·9	2·0
Machinery (38)	0·3	0·9	2·0
Miscellaneous (39)	3·0	10·3	18·2
Total manufacturing (3)	1·7	2·4	3·4

Source: Hughes H. and Waelbroeck, J. 'Can the growth of developing countries exports keep growing in the 1980's?' *The World Economy*, vol. 4, no. 2 (June, 1981), pp. 127–47.

It might be argued, that although LDC market shares are low in manufactures, the developed countries' threshold of tolerance for LDC penetration of their markets is equally low. Such arguments surfaced in the mid-1970s during a period of resurgence of industrial protectionism. However, a recent study sponsored by the World Bank on the political economy of protectionism in developed countries has failed to find any significant correlation between the level or rate of change of market penetration and the incidence of protectionism. Moreover, the continuation of LDC market penetration since 1974 suggests that 'The actual impact of the new protectionism of the 1970s ... [was] not as large as was initially thought probable' (Hughes and Waelbroeck, 1981, p. 143).

To summarise, the elasticity assumptions on which the trade engine theory is based apply best to traditional LDC exports of broadly non-competing, tropical commodities. Such products, however, have been shown to constitute a relatively small and declining share of exports in most developing countries. Although reliable estimates of demand elasticities for LDC manufactures in developed countries are not available, given the present small share of the market claimed by LDCs, one can reasonably assume that demand elasticities are extremely high for most LDC manufactures.[1] The changing composition of LDC exports should, therefore, have weakened the external constraint on LDC export growth. Yet, as Lewis measures it, the link appears remarkably stable over time, in fact, 'quantitatively the same over a hundred years' (1980, p. 556).

The Statistical Link

The appropriate procedure for measuring the link between MDC income growth and LDC export growth, as suggested in the earlier theoretical discus-

---

[1] Evidence in support of this assumption is found in Grossman (1978) and Riedel (1983).

sion, is simultaneous estimation of supply and demand equations for LDC exports. The enormous complexity of demand and supply relationships, however, makes this approach methodologically infeasible and generally restricts analysis to highly reduced-form relationships. Lewis first measured the link, for example, by regressing the logarithm of the quantum index of world trade in primary products (X_A), which he takes as a proxy for LDC exports, on the logarithm of an index of world production of manufactures (I_M), which he takes as a proxy of developed countries prosperity. Using data for the period 1881 to 1929, Lewis obtained a regression coefficient of 0·87.[1] This coefficient may be interpreted as a measure of the income elasticity of demand, only if one assumes, as he does, that relative price changes are unimportant and export supply is infinitely elastic. If these assumptions prove invalid then the meaning of the coefficient is problematic and its value may be expected to be unstable.

Lewis (1980, p. 556) states that 'just about the same relationship, about 0·87, also ruled in the two decades to 1973', and the evidence he cites (1978, p. 175) is the ratio (0·864) of the average annual growth rate from 1950/52 to 1969/71 of quantum trade in primary products (5·1 %) to world production of manufactures (5·9 %). A similar coefficient is obtained using regression techniques to estimate the relationship for the recent period. Using data for the period 1953 to 1977 yields the following result (t statistics in parentheses):

$$\log X_F = -1·179 + 0·832 \log I_M$$
$$(7·822)\ (36·541)$$

$$R^2 = 0·982; \quad SEE = 0·043; \quad DW = 0·467,$$

where

$$X_F = \text{volume index of world exports of primary products}[2]$$

and

$$I_M = \text{index of production of manufactures in developed countries.}[3]$$

Remarkable as the similarity is between the slope coefficient Lewis obtained for the period 1881–1929 and that which we obtain for the period 1953–77, evidence of highly significant autocorrelation in the latter results suggests caution in concluding, as Lewis has, that the relationship was quantitatively the same over a hundred year period. An inspection of the residuals of the regression equation reveals that primary exports were generally underestimated by the regression equation in the 1950s and 1970s and overestimated in the 1960s.

To test whether the relationship was significantly different in the three decades, the regression was re-estimated with intercept and slope dummy

---

[1] This result was first reported in Lewis, 1952, p. 111.

$$\text{Log } X_A = 0·1238 + 0·8702 \log I_M.$$

No regression test statistics accompanied this result. The United States and U.S.S.R. were excluded from I_M so as to improve the fit.

[2] Source: U.N. *Monthly Bulletin of Statistics*, Special Table F, selected issues.

[3] Source: U.N. *Growth of World Industry*, 1980.

variables for the 1950s and 1970s included. The following result was obtained (*t* statistics in parentheses):

$$\log X_{F} = 2 \cdot 697 + \underset{(15 \cdot 646)}{0 \cdot 599} \log I_{M} + \underset{(4 \cdot 040)}{0 \cdot 423} (D_{50} \log I_{M})$$

$$+ \underset{(4 \cdot 574)}{0 \cdot 477} (D_{70} \log I_{M}) - \underset{(-4 \cdot 125)}{2 \cdot 673} D_{50} - \underset{(-4 \cdot 411)}{3 \cdot 213} D_{70}$$

(10·679) (15·646)

$$R^2 = 0 \cdot 996; \quad SEE = 0 \cdot 022; \quad DW = 1 \cdot 968,$$

where

$D_{50} = 1$ for observations 1953–59 and zero otherwise.

$D_{70} = 1$ for observations 1970–77 and zero otherwise.

Note the coefficient for ($\log I_{M}$) is that which would obtain were the regression estimated for the period 1960–69 alone, and the coefficients for ($D_{50} \log I_{M}$) and ($D_{70} \log I_{M}$) measure differences in the slope estimates for the 1950s and 1970s, respectively, relative to the 1960s.[1]

These results indicate that the relationship was statistically significantly lower in the 1960s than in the other two decades. In the 1950s and 1970s a close to one-to-one relationship held, while in the 1960s the coefficient (0·599) was significantly lower. Instability of this magnitude clearly belies any simple mechanical relationship. However, given the proxies used for MDC prosperity and LDC exports, it is difficult to discern what underlies the observed shifts in the coefficient, much less what the coefficient indeed measures.

Focusing on the last two decades, available data allow the link to be defined more precisely. Table 4 reports the results of similar regression analyses of the relationship between MDC real GDP and the volume of LDC non-fuel exports, disaggregated by major commodity groups (manufactures, raw materials and food). As before, dummy variables are included to test the statistical significance of shifts in the regression coefficients over time. The coefficient of ($D \log Y$) measures the difference between the coefficient for the 1970s and the 1960s, the associated *t* statistics indicating the statistical significance of the difference.

Consider first the results for total non-fuel exports. Regression 1 indicates that over the entire period total exports grew more than proportionately to MDC income. Again, however, positive autocorrelation of the error terms suggests the relationship was not uniform over the estimation period. As regression 2 shows the slope coefficient more than doubled in the 1970s.[2] That this shift is attributable to the rapid expansion of manufactures exports in the 1970s is revealed in regressions 3 and 4. Even in the 1960s, LDC exports of manufactures grew almost twice as fast as MDC real GDP, but in the 1970s, despite a general slowdown of growth after 1973, LDC exports maintained their rapid pace, growing more than four times (4·08 = 1·87 + 2·21) as fast as MDC real GDP.

---

[1] The intercept dummies, D_{50} and D_{70}, have no particular economic interpretation.

[2] Additional tests, not reported here, found no significant shift in the slope coefficient after 1970; rather the break in the relationship for total non-fuel exports and manufactures occurred about 1970.

Table 4

Regression of LDC Export Volumes (X) on MDC Real GDP (Y): 1960 to 1978

$$(\log X_t = a_0 + a_1 \log Y_t + a_2 D \log Y_t + a_3 D + e_t.)$$

Dependent variable	Independent variables*				R^2	D.W.
	Const.	Log Y†	$D \log Y$‡	D‡		
(1) Volume of total non-fuel exports	−1·354 (−4·664)	1·272 (22 060)	—	—	0 964	0·286
(2) (SITC 0–9 except 3)	−0·609 (−2 755)	0 863 (18 857)	0 884 (9 260)	−4·441 (−9·019)	0·996	1·876
(3) Volume of manu-factures exports (SITC 5–9 except	−8·827 (12·097)	2 877 (19 849)	—	—	0 956	0·240
(4) 68)	−4·011 (−6·422)	1·873 (14·503)	2 210 (8 201)	−11·111 (−7·966)	0·993	1·753
(5) Volume of raw materials exports	0·974 (12·097)	0·788 (11·998)	—	—	0·888	0·701
(6) (SITC 2+4+68)	0·181 (0·334)	0·951 (8·490)	−0·883 (−3·776)	4·573 (3·792)	0·935	1·667
(7) Volume of food	1·681 (10·855)	0·627 (20·390)	—	—	0·958	1·937
(8) exports (SITC 0+1	2·311 (7·593)	0·495 (7·868)	0·152 (1·158)	0·729 (−1·077)	0·965	2·354

* t — statistics in parentheses.
† Y — Index of real US Dollar GDP of 'OECD-North' countries; i.e. OECD excluding Greece, Portugal, Spain and Turkey.
‡ D = 1 for observation 1970–8 and zero otherwise.
Sources: 'Prospects for real growth and inflation in OECD North countries' World Bank, Economic Analysis and Projections Department, Nov. 5, 1980; U.N., *Monthly Bulletin of Statistics*, Special Table F and G, UNCTAD, *Handbook of International Trade and Development Statistics*, various years, Table A. 8.

The thesis that prosperity in developed countries fuels exports of developing countries clearly cannot be applied to manufactures, that is unless one is prepared to argue that a radical shift in preferences favouring LDC manufactures occurred in the 1970s.[1] Since manufactures' share in MDC consumption is declining secularly, and further, since the mid-1970s witnessed a rise of protectionism against developing countries' exports, if anything the opposite would seem to be the case. Nor can it be argued that the growth of exports in the 1970s was maintained by finding markets outside the developed countries, since as shown in Table 1 the share of MDCs in LDC exports has been steadily

[1] This is not to imply that Lewis believes that LDC exports of manufactures bear a fixed relationship to MDC income. Lewis simply ruled out rapid manufactures export growth on grounds, first, that 'The main link between MDC and LDC economies has been the MDC demand for LDC primary commodities' (1980, p. 59) and, second, that protectionism would halt LDC manufactures export growth if MDCs go into recession.

increasing. The evidence, therefore, suggests that supply rather than demand factors have principally determined LDC export performance in manufactures.[1]

The relationship between MDC income and LDC exports of raw materials (regressions 5 and 6) is also found to be unstable, but the shift is in the opposite direction to that of manufactures. While a one-to-one relationship is observed in the 1960s, virtually no relationship between MDC income and LDC raw materials exports is found in the 1970s. As shown in Table 5, however, this shift can be traced in part to a change in underlying demand parameters as well as to a change in LDC supply of raw materials to the world market. Columns 1 and 2 of Table 5 show that MDC consumption of cotton and iron ore, two of the LDCs' most important raw material exports, has declined at a far faster rate than can be explained by the general slowdown of economic growth. The failure of MDC consumption of these commodities to keep up with the slowing pace of economic activity is clearly attributable to the decline of the cotton textile and steel industries in developed countries, which in turn is in part the consequence of increased competition from developing countries. At the same time, rapid industrial expansion in developing countries has accelerated internal consumption of key raw material exports (as shown in columns 3 and 4). In addition to shifts in the pattern of global consumption of raw materials, however, LDC production, especially cotton and iron ore, declined in the 1970s. The combined effect of these changes has therefore been to weaken the link between the level of economic activity in developed countries and export performance of LDCs.

The one major commodity group for which a stable export relationship to MDC real GDP is observed is food. Food, in particular beverages (coffee, tea and cocoa), were traditionally the mainstay of LDC exports and not accidentally are central to Lewis' theorising about the trade engine. Even though the coefficient measuring the link to MDC income (regression 7, Table 4) is somewhat

Table 5

Compound Annual Growth Rates of the Volume of MDC and LDC Consumption and LDC Production of Selected Raw Materials: 1960–78 (percentages)

| | Consumption | | | | Production LDCs | |
| | MDCs | | LDCs | | | |
Commodity	1960–70	1970–78	1960–70	1970–78	1960–70	1970–78
Cotton	−1·3	−2·9	3·4	3·2	3·4	0 8
Rubber	2·8	1·7	6 3	7·9	4·0	2·8
Copper	4·1	2·1	5 6	8·1	2·9	4·3
Iron ore	3·8	0 2	6·0	7·1	7·7	0·8

Source: World Bank, *Price Prospects for Major Primary Commodities,* Report no. 814-80, January, 1980.

[1] This is the main conclusion reached in numerous case studies of individual countries' experience in the 1960's and 1970's. See Little *et al.* (1970); Bhagwati (1978); Krueger (1978); Donges and Riedel (1977).

Table 6

*Regressions of the Volume of Selected LDC Food Exports (X)
on MDC Real GDP (Y): 1960 to 1978*

$$(\log X_i = a_0 + a_1 \log Y_i + a_2 D \log Y_i + a_3 D + e_i.)$$

Dependent variable	Independent variables*				R^2	D.W.
	Const.	Log Y†	D log Y‡	D‡		
(1) Volume of coffee exports	6.703 (16.654)	0.262 (3.301)	—	—	0.368	1.571
(2)	5.703 (6.521)	0.469 (2.604)	-0.648 (-1.948)	3.322 (1.930)	0.431	2.072
(3) Volume of cocoa exports	6.810 (14.878)	0.036 (0.398)	—	—	0.052	1.552
(4)	6.619 (6.814)	0.073 (0.366)	-0.688 (-1.849)	3.616 (1.891)	0.097	1.906
(5) Volume of tea exports	4.374 (27.862)	0.407 (13.134)	—	—	0.910	2.156
(6)	4.764 (13.026)	0.326 (4.336)	0.075 (0.538)	-0.356 (-0.495)	0.907	2.063
(7) Volume of sugar exports	5.714 (11.407)	0.691 (6.975)	—	—	0.737	1.756
(8)	7.986 (7.865)	0.220 (1.053)	0.732 (1.889)	-3.630 (-1.817)	0.794	2.456
(9) Volume of copra exports	12.225 (11.707)	-1.028 (-4.981)	—	—	0.584	2.139
(10)	12.221 (4.781)	-1.027 (-1.954)	-0.075 (-0.773)	0.399 (0.794)	0.524	2.143
(11) Volume of groundnuts exports	15.125 (13.037)	-1.647 (-7.181)	—	—	0.748	0.998
(12)	7.769 (4.341)	-0.121 (-0.329)	-2.215 (-3.232)	10.916 (3.099)	0.886	2.290

* t = Statistics in parentheses.
† Y = Real GDP of OECD North.
‡ D = 1 for observations for 1970–8, zero otherwise.
Source: Y: Same as Table 4.
X: World Bank, *Commodity Trade and Price Trends*, August, 1980.

lower (i.e. 0·65) than Lewis computes using total world agricultural exports as a proxy, it does appear exceptionally stable over time.

Stability of the link proves deceptive, however, when one examines the behaviour of individual commodity exports within the food aggregate.[1] Table 6 presents the results of regression analysis of the relationship between MDC real GDP and the volume of major LDC food exports (coffee, cocoa, tea, sugar, copra and groundnuts). Of the six commodities, only tea and sugar exports bear the hypothesised relationship to income in developed countries. Cocoa

---

[1] The constancy of the aggregate coefficient for food could be more than fortuitous were it the result of a gross expenditure constraint. However, since LDC exports account for a small share of food consumption, in MDCs the gross expenditure presumably does not constitute the binding constraint on aggregate LDC food exports.

exports exhibit no relationship to MDC income, while for copra and ground-nuts the relationship is negative, and hence inexplicable in terms of the 'engine' theory.

Coffee, the single most important LDC food export, is also found to bear a weak relationship to MDC real GDP. This observation is consistent with the evidence from econometric studies of the world coffee market which invariably come up with extremely low price and income elasticities of demand for coffee.[1] For certain major markets, including the United States, the estimated income elasticity of demand approaches zero. Among the implications of this is that the slowdown of economic growth in developed countries will mean very little to the already relatively dismal growth prospects for coffee exporters.

III. CONCLUSION

The theory of trade as an engine of growth in developing countries is, as its name suggests, highly mechanistic. Trade, viewed as an engine, serves simply to transmit growth impulses from developed to developing countries. Mechanical efficiency of an engine requires that the gearing of interconnecting parts be tightly fitted. Lewis' observation of a stable hundred year link between growth in developed countries and primary exports of developing countries, geared at the ratio 0·87, is taken as evidence that the trade engine is mechanically efficient, and that therefore a slowdown of one part (developed country growth) leads mechanically to a slowdown of connecting parts (LDC trade and, connected to that, LDC growth).

There can be no doubt that economic prospects in one region of the world affect those in other regions, and it is certainly not the aim of this paper to argue anything to the contrary. What we take issue with is the proposition that the economic relationship between developed and developing countries can be defined adequately in terms of simple mechanical linkages. Measures of linkage obtained by regressing LDC exports on MDC income prove far too unstable to be interpreted reasonably as mechanical gears of an engine of growth. Highly reduced-form analysis which ignores the influence of relative price changes and shifts in supply, however convenient methodologically, cannot provide an adequate basis for explaining the impact of economic slow-down in developed countries on LDC trade, much less LDC growth.

It is ironic that those who appeal to the notion of trade as an engine of growth invariably do so to justify a policy of reducing reliance on trade, arguing that the engine has broken down. This was the approach, in the 1950s, of Nurkse, Prebisch and Myrdal in laying the foundations of the import-substitution strategy. Their prognosis was proved wrong by the experience of the 1960s and 1970s in which countries pursuing outward-looking strategies of development uniformly out-performed those pursuing the prescribed inward-looking strategy.[2]

---

[1] See Singh *et al.* (1977) and de Vries (1979).
[2] Bhagwati (1978), Balassa (1978), and Michaely (1978) show that a high positive correlation exists between export growth and economic growth across LDCs.

Equally wrong, however, was their reading of history, which as Kravis convincingly argues, shows trade to have been the 'handmaiden' rather than the engine of growth in the nineteenth century.

This paper has not taken up the question of whether trade, however propelled, served as the engine of LDC growth in recent decades. However, if the premise that LDC exports are externally driven is rejected, it is difficult to maintain the notion of trade as an engine, for it then becomes impossible to distinguish the input to the engine from the output. No similar dilemma is encountered with a more organic view of economic interrelationships in which trade and growth are more properly regarded as interdependent aspects of a single, evolutionary process. The metaphor of trade as a handmaiden of growth is, of one adopts such a view, more theoretically appealing and more likely to be applicable to the experience of the 1960s and 1970s.

The Johns Hopkins University

Date of receipt of final typescript: June 1983

APPENDIX 1

52 sample countries – primary commodities exporters

11 balanced exporters	21 non-African predominantly primary commodity exporters	20 African predominantly primary commodity exporters
Bangladesh	Afghanistan	Central African Empire
Barbados	Argentina	Chad
Brazil	Bolivia	Cameroon
Egypt	Burma	Ethiopia
Haiti	Chile	Gambia
India	Columbia	Ghana
Jordan	Costa Rica	Ivory Coast
Mexico	Dominican Republic	Kenya
Pakistan	El Salvador	Liberia
Tunisia	Guatemala	Mali
Uruguay	Guyana	Morocco
	Honduras	Mozambique
	Jamaica	Niger
	Malaysia	Senegal
	Nicaragua	Somalia
	Paraguay	Sudan
	Peru	Tanzania
	Philippines	Uganda
	Sri Lanka	Zaire
	Thailand	Zambia
	Turkey	

APPENDIX 2

Broadly non-competing non-fuel primary commodities

Foodstuffs	Agricultural raw materials	Metals and minerals
Beverages	Jute	Copper
Cocoa	Natural rubber	Bauxite
Coffee	Sisal	Natural phosphates
Tea	Silk	
Bananas	Nonconiferous logs	
Spices		
Copra		
Groundnuts		
Palm oil		
Coconut oil		

REFERENCES

Armington, Paul S. (1969). 'A theory of demand for products distinguished by place of production', *IMF Staff Papers*, vol. 15, no. 1, (March), pp. 159–78.

Balassa, Bela (1978). 'Exports and economic growth'. *Journal of Development Economics*, vol. 5, no. 2, (June), pp. 181–9.

Bhagwati, Jagdish, (1978). *Foreign Trade Regimes and Economic Development: Anatomy and Consequences of Exchange Control Regimes*, Cambridge, Mass.: Ballinger Publishing Co.

Cairncross, A. K. (1960). 'International trade and economic development', *Kyklos*, vol. 13, no. 4, pp. 545–58.

Deppler, Michael P. and Ripley, Duncan M. (1978). 'The world trade model: merchandise trade', *IMF Staff Papers*, vol. 25, no. 1, (March), pp. 147–206.

Donges, J. B. and Riedel, J. (1977). 'The expansion of manufacturing exports in developing countries; an empirical assessment of supply and demand issues', *Weltwirtschaftliches Archiv*, vol. 113, no. 1, pp. 58–87.

Findlay, Ronald (1980). 'The terms of trade and equilibrium growth in the world economy', *American Economic Review*, vol. 70, no. 3, (June), pp. 291–9.

—— (1981). 'The fundamental determinants of the terms of trade', in S. Grassman and E. Lundberg (eds.), *The World Economic Order: Past and Prospects*, London: Macmillan Press Ltd., pp. 425–57.

Grossman, Gene M. (1978). 'Import competition from developed and developing countries', Unpublished Mimeo, (October).

Hughes, Helen and Waelbroeck, J. (1981). 'Can developing-country exports keep growing in the 1980s?' *The World Economy*, vol. 4, no. 2, (June), pp. 127–47.

International Bank for Reconstruction and Development/The World Bank, *World Development Report 1980*. Washington, D.C. 1980.

Kravis, Irving B. (1970). 'Trade as the handmaiden of growth: similarities between the nineteenth and twentieth centuries', ECONOMIC JOURNAL, vol. 80, (December), pp. 850–72.

Krueger, Anne (1978). 'Growth distortions and patterns of trade among many countries', *Princeton Studies in International Finance*, no. 40.

Lewis, W. Arthur (1952). 'World production, prices and trade, 1870–1960', *The Manchester School of Economics and Social Sciences*, (May), pp. 105–38.

—— (1954). 'Economic development with unlimited supplies of labour', *Manchester School of Economics and Social Studies*, vol. 22, (May), pp. 139–91.

—— (1969). *Aspects of Tropical Trade, 1883–1965*, Stockholm: Almquist and Wiksell.

—— (1980). 'The slowing down of the engine of growth', *American Economic Review*, vol. 70, no. 4, (September), pp. 555–64.

Little, I. M. D., Scitovsky, T. and Scott, M. (1970). *Industry and Trade in Some Developing Countries*, London: Oxford University Press.

Michaely, Michael (1977). 'Exports and growth: an empirical investigation', *Journal of Development Economics*, vol. 4, pp. 49–54.

Myrdal, G. (1957). *Economic Theory and Underdeveloped Regions*, London: Duckworth.

Nurkse, Ragnar (1959). *Patterns of Trade and Development*, Stockholm: Almquist and Wiksell.

Prebisch, Raoul (1950). *The Economic Development of Latin America and its Principle Problems*. New York: UN Economic Development for Latin America.

Riedel, James (1983). 'Export price and volume adjustment to fluctuations in world income case study of a small open economy', in M. Dutta, ed., *Studies in U.S.–Asian Economic Relations*, forthcoming in 1983.

Singh, Shamsher, de Vries, Jos, Hulley, J. and Yeung, P. (1977). *Coffee, Tea and Cocoa: Market Prospect and Development Lending*, Baltimore: John Hopkins University Press.

Taylor, Lance (1981). 'South-North trade and Southern growth: bleak prospects from the structuralist point of view', *Journal of International Economics*, vol. 11, pp. 589–602.

de Vries, Jos (1979). 'The world coffee economy: an econometric analysis', International Bank for Reconstruction and Development, (December).

Wolf, M. (1978). 'LDC exports – key features of past performances', Unpublished Mimeo, (February).

Part II
The Terms of Trade

7

PREBISCH ON PROTECTIONISM: AN EVALUATION [1]

In the area of international trade and payments theories, one of the most important issues to-day, from the point of view of relevance to contemporary world problems and application to policy-making decision, is that of determining the optimum commercial policy of under-developed or, more euphemistically, " developing " countries. Specifically, there has in recent years been much discussion of the desirability of such countries adopting a policy of protecting and/or subsidising domestic industry, substituting home production for imports of at least some manufactured goods. The importance of the question and the way in which it is ultimately resolved is fairly obvious,[2] and it is not surprising that the debate has been lively; nor is it surprising that the discussion has acquired, at times, ideological overtones, involving issues of planning *vs.* the market mechanism, social justice, colonialism, unintentional " neo-colonialism " and the like. Many professional economists have addressed themselves to this problem, but none seems to have attracted as much attention among his colleagues nor have had so widespread an influence on thinking outside the profession as Professor Raul Prebisch, until recently the Executive Secretary of the United Nations Economic Commission for Latin America and presently Secretary-General of the United Nations Conference on Trade and Development. Because of the interest which his pronouncements have evoked, it is worth some time and effort to examine his arguments more thoroughly than has heretofore been done; for, interestingly enough, though his writings have been much discussed, most of this discussion revolves around only one part of his multi-faceted argument, and much of it stems from a misinterpretation of even that one part. In what follows we propose to discuss his work and to show that there is not one single " Prebisch thesis " or model, but many, and that it is by no means obvious that they are consistent with one another.

It is usual to begin a critical evaluation of a writer's work by summarising it, but one of the implications of our contention that there are a number of " Prebisch theses " is that his work, by its very nature, defies any attempt to

[1] The author wishes to thank the following people for helpful comments and suggestions, but absolves them from all responsibility: Irma Adelman, Nathan Rosenberg, Vernon Ruttan and Rubin Saposnik.

[2] Interest in the issue has been growing; one sees increasingly frequent reference to it in elementary text-books and semi-popular books in economics written " for the intelligent layman." *Vide, e.g.,* Benjamin Higgins, *United Nations and U.S. Foreign Economic Policy* (Homewood: Richard D. Irwin, 1962), pp. 38 ff. At the same time there has been increasing discussion and recognition of the problem among policy-makers and their advisors. For one example (from a large and rapidly growing host of studies and reports) see *Economic Developments in South America,* a Report of the Subcommittee on Inter-American Economic Relationships of the Joint Economic Committee, Congress of the United States, Washington, July 1962, especially Chapter VII, " The Dilemma Presented by Dependence upon Limited Export Commodities."

present a single, simple, summary statement of it. There have, indeed, been many exegeses of his text, but in the main these have involved emphasis on one or two aspects of his argument, ignoring the others. It is necessary, therefore, to consider his arguments one by one.' The discussion that follows will be based on the two well-known and oft-cited essays, which will be referred to as Prebisch I [1] and Prebisch II [2] respectively.

The most frequently heard view of Prebisch's thesis is that peripheral countries have experienced (and presumably will continue to experience) long-run deterioration in their terms of trade with the centre and that they should counteract this by imposing tariffs on industrial imports. Much of the discussion,[3] therefore, has dealt with the questions of whether in fact the terms of trade of the periphery did fall; and if they fell, what were the reasons for the decline (alleged differences in market structure between peripheral and central countries being the most oft-mentioned issue here). It should be noted, incidentally, that a careful reading of Prebisch shows him to be much less of an " autarkist " than either his detractors or his supporters seem to think.[4]

One of our purposes here is to discover what in the Prebisch model(s) would tend to cause a deterioration in the periphery's terms of trade. Another is to find the connection between the declining terms of trade and the protectionism he proposes. In other words, what precisely are the

---

[1] *The Economic Development of Latin America and its Principal Problems*, Economic Commission for Latin America (Lake Success, New York: United Nations, Department of Economic Affairs, 1950).

[2] " Commercial Policy in the Underdeveloped Countries," *American Economic Review, Papers and Proceedings*, Vol. XLIV (May 1959), pp. 251–73.

[3] *Vide, e.g.*, Gottfried Haberler, " Terms of Trade and Economic Development," in *Economic Development for Latin America*, Howard S. Ellis, Ed. (London: Macmillan, 1961), pp. 275–97; Paul T. Ellsworth, " The Terms of Trade between Primary Producing and Industrial Countries," *Inter-American Economic Affairs*, Vol. X (Summer 1956); Werner Baer, " The Economics of Prebisch and ECLA," *Economic Development and Cultural Change*, Vol. X (January 1962), pp. 169–82, and also a Comment by M. June Flanders in a forthcoming issue of the same journal.

[4] Chapter VI of Prebisch I is entitled " The Limits of Industrialization." On pp. 45 and 46 particularly he warns of the danger of " . . . sacrificing part of [Latin America's] exports in order to increase industrial production as a substitute for imports." And again: " Nevertheless, exports can be sacrificed to an illusory increase in real income long before the possibilities of intensifying productivity or of utilizing all the manpower available have been exhausted." In Prebisch II he speaks of the need for " . . . a definite readjustment of commercial policy based on the clear recognition that, instead of trying to crystallize the existing pattern of peripheral imports, an effort should be made to help promote these *changes in composition* which are indispensable for fostering the rate of economic development." (P. 265. Italics added.) " Imports from the centers will continue to depend on Latin American exports to them—a clearly passive situation. The only changes—and these will be very important indeed—will take place in *import composition*, and through them countries will specialize in industrial products as well as agricultural ones. Without the [Latin American] common market, there will be a continued tendency by each country to try to produce everything— say from automobiles to machinery—under the sheltering wing of very high protection." (P. 268. Italics added.) There are many more statements to the same effect, but those cited above are sufficient to show that Prebisch's protectionism is tempered by a sincere concern with allocative efficiency and that (at least part of the time) he views tariffs as primarily a device to allocate scarce earnings of foreign exchange, not as a means for altering the level of trade. This second point is very important, and we shall return to it below.

benefits which the periphery can be expected to reap from protectionism? In broad categories, there are three types of benefits which Prebisch seems to expect.

One is the "rationing" effect, noted in footnote 4 on p. 306. In Prebisch I this is closely tied in with the world-wide "dollar shortage," so that tariffs are simply one method of rationing limited supplies of United States dollars (p. 3; Chapter III; Chapter IV). In 1950, of course, Prebisch was not the only economist who was misled into expecting the dollar shortage to continue for ever—or at least for a very long time. By Prebisch II the dollar shortage has dropped from the discussion, but he is still disturbed by the low import coefficient of the United States (p. 266) and the low capacity to import, because of inadequate foreign-exchange earnings, of the Latin American countries (p. 267). The high income elasticity of demand for imports into the periphery combined with the low income elasticity of demand for imports into the centre will force the periphery to achieve balance-of-payments equilibrium by either of the unattractive alternatives of growing more slowly than the centre, or of restraining its demand for imports, preferably by imposing tariffs. Now, the latter alternative may well be the less unpleasant of the two, but a tariff system designed to ration scarce foreign exchange, not to decrease the total demand for imports, cannot be expected to cause an improvement in the terms of trade. At best it might slow down future deterioration in the terms of trade.[1]

This brings us to Prebisch's second type of benefit from protectionism, that of preventing further deterioration in the terms of trade (or reversing past losses?) by "countervailance."[2] As we shall see, this raises a number of highly complicated issues regarding what Prebisch is really assuming as to market structure, income distribution and wage-rate determination in the periphery and the centre respectively. But there are also some "macro" problems involved. The usual "monopoly" argument for tariffs[3] is presented in terms of a two-country model. Now, even if we assume, with Prebisch, that there is only one centre country and one peripheral country, and even if we assume that they are of roughly comparable economic size, we must recognise that in fact the centre's biggest customer is itself, not the periphery. That is, if we think of two "countries," the centre and the periphery, "domestic" demand will have a greater influence on the prices of

---

[1] This would be the case if the imposition of tariffs, by preventing the demand for imports from rising as much as it otherwise would, discouraged the tendency for the periphery's exports to increase, causing a decline in the price of exports. This, as we shall see, rests not on the assumption of price inelasticity of demand for peripheral exports, but rather on the reasonable assumption that the periphery as a whole is a monopolist in the world market for its exports, so that larger quantities of exports can be sold only at declining prices. Prebisch states, laudably, that he is interested only in what happens to all the peripheral countries as a group (Prebisch II, p. 260), but the clarity of his analytical discussion is frequently marred by his failure to specify when he is referring to a single country and when he is considering the total periphery as a unit.

[2] Cf. Werner Baer, *op. cit.*

[3] *Vide, e.g.*, the now classic discussion by Tibor Scitovsky, "A Re-consideration of the Theory of Tariffs," *The Review of Economic Studies*, Vol. IX (Summer 1942), pp. 89-110.

export goods, relatively to foreign demand, in the centre than it will in the periphery. Hence, protection in the periphery cannot be expected to cause a significant reduction in the prices of its imports.[1] Furthermore, Prebisch insists that protection should be highly " selective " (Prebisch II, p. 257). But then the industrial product (or products) to be protected will be different in each peripheral country. Thus the " countervailing " effects of the tariffs will be diffused among many industries in many countries of the centre, and will thus be even less likely to influence the prices of industrial imports.[2]

There is one further difficulty with the " countervailance " argument, in terms of consistency with other parts of the model. The past deterioration of the terms of trade of the periphery is attributed in large measure to the downward inflexibility of prices and wages in the centre as contrasted with the periphery.[3]

If this is so, a downward shift in the periphery's demand function for centre exports will result in making the centre worse off, through unemployment, without making the periphery better off through improvement in the terms of trade. (We need not delve into the subtle and esoteric question of the disutility of envy—or the utility to be derived from seeing one's neighbour worse off than before. There is absolutely no indication that Prebisch would regard such a situation as an improvement from the point of view of the periphery.) In fact, by lowering the income and employment levels in the centre this would actually hurt the periphery by reducing the demand for its exports; however small the income elasticity of demand for imports in the centre may be, there is no reason to expect it to be negative.

The third category of benefits from protection, according to Prebisch, is an " allocative " one. This, like the first, is only indirectly associated with the simple terms of trade argument, and it will be discussed more fully when we examine the formal model(s) in detail.

There is one important expected benefit from protection which Prebisch does not discuss systematically; however, he mentions it at several points, though only incidentally. This is the whole class of benefits that may accrue

[1] This point has nothing to do with differences in income elasticity or price elasticity of demand for primary products as compared with industrial products. It is analogous to an attempt by a group of, say, a few hundred automotive engineers to raise their real wages by buying fewer automobiles in the hope that this will lead to a decline in automobile prices.

[2] Prebisch I is specifically concerned only with Latin America. Prebisch II purports to embrace the whole world (p. 251), but many of his arguments are relevant only to Latin America, and at least implicitly he is apparently thinking primarily of Latin America *vis-à-vis* the United States. Within this framework his countervailance argument is stronger, as far as the importance of the peripheral country, both as a buyer and as a seller, is concerned. However, since Prebisch himself does not restrict the applicability of his arguments to the Western Hemisphere, and since commentators generally assume that his proposals are meant to be valid and useful on a global scale, it is reasonable to assess them on that basis.

[3] Prebisch I, Chapter II. It is interesting that this particular argument does not reappear in Prebisch II. This may be due to a decline in its importance, in Prebisch's view, or else to the brevity of the second paper. In any case, it is an important part of the argument in Prebisch I; and the attention it has received in the commentaries justifies our consideration of it here.

to a country which is industrialised—the changes in economic " structure," the flexibility, vitality, the changes in social structure and " personality " of a country that many people are convinced comes with, and only with, an increase in the proportion of industrial production to total output of a country. There has been much written on this subject, and many of the arguments are highly plausible. Those who advocate protectionism for this type of reason may well be right. But it is important to note and remember that this is independent of, and very different from, any of the arguments Prebisch advances.[1]

As suggested above, only a part of Prebisch's argument in favour of some protection in the periphery devolves on the assertion that " . . . the great industrial centres not only keep for themselves the benefit of the use of new techniques in their own economy, but are in a favourable position to obtain a share of that deriving from the technical progress of the periphery " (Prebisch I, p. 14). We shall argue that the validity of this assertion is not necessary as a support of his policy recommendations. Nevertheless, this notion is worth examining carefully, for two reasons. First, because this is the part of his analysis that has attracted the most attention and the greatest amount of comment, both critical and favourable. It seems to many writers, and apparently to Prebisch himself, to be the main line of his argument, upon which the validity of everything else he says depends. And secondly, it is that part of his argument which elicits the most emotional response, again both from critics and supporters.[2] The notion that, whether deliberately or not, the developed countries have " exploited " the periphery and will, unless counteracting measures are taken, continue to do so, is not one to be passed over lightly.

Let us examine first the argument presented in Prebisch I (pp. 8–14). Table 2 (p. 11) is a hypothetical illustration of both the actual and the " ideal " " . . . distribution of the benefits of technical progress between the

---

[1] The name of Hans W. Singer is frequently joined with that of Prebisch in discussion of the issue. In his paper " The Distribution of Gains between Investing and Borrowing Countries," *American Economic Review, Papers and Proceedings,* Vol. XL. (May 1950), pp. 473-85, he does enunciate what is commonly referred to as " the Prebisch thesis." But he also stresses, and elaborates on, the importance, in a dynamic context, of industrialisation *per se.* He argues, for example, that " . . . the most important contribution of an industry is not its immediate product . . . and not even its effects on other industries and immediate social benefits . . . but perhaps even further its effect on the general level of education, skill, way of life, inventiveness, habits, store of technology, creations of new demand, etc. And this is perhaps precisely the reason why manufacturing industries are so universally desired by underdeveloped countries; namely, that they provide the growing points for increased technical knowledge, urban education, the dynamism and resilience that goes with urban civilization, as well as the direct Marshallian external economies. No doubt under different circumstances commerce, farming, and plantation agriculture have proved capable of being such ' growing points,' but manufacturing industry is unmatched in our present age " (pp. 476-77).

[2] Note, for example, the very angry tone of Gunnar Myrdal's exposition of this view, in *An International Economy, Problems and Prospects* (New York: Harper and Brothers, 1956), pp. 230 ff., esp. p. 235, where he goes so far as to attribute to Prebisch " . . . a sort of ' good loser's ' gallantry which is scarcely representative." It should be noted, however, that Myrdal's own defence of protectionism also appeals, more coolly, to considerations of rationing scarce foreign exchange and the like.

centre and the periphery, . . . in which it is assumed that the indexes of productivity, per man, are greater [rise more] in industry than in primary production. For the sake of simplification, both are supposed to make an equal contribution to the finished product." (This last assumption is difficult to interpret in the light of differential rates of productivity change in the two kinds of activity.) In the illustration productivity *per man* in primary production increases by 20% as a result of technical progress. In the centre technical progress in industrial production raises productivity by 60%. Since industry and primary production contribute equally to the value of the final product, productivity per man, in world output of finished products, rises by 40%. Now, he says, if all productivity changes are reflected in declining prices, and (money?) income does not rise at all, primary producers experience an increased purchasing power of 16·7% per unit of primary product. Since, with a given work force, they can now produce 20% more output, their total buying power of finished goods, that is, their total real income, has risen by 40%. In the centre, on the other hand, the purchasing power of a unit of output has fallen to 87·5% of its original value. But since a given number of workers can now produce 60% more than previously, the total real income of the centre has risen by 40%, and the centre and the periphery have shared equally the fruits of the technical progress. " The benefits of technical progress would thus have been distributed alike throughout the world, *in accordance with the implicit premise of the schema of the international division of labour*, and Latin America would have had no economic advantage in industrializing. On the contrary, the region would have suffered a definite loss, until it had achieved the same productive efficiency as the industrial countries."[1]

This argument seems to be based on the factor-price equalisation theorem, but it is a fallacious and naïve interpretation. Quite apart from the many well-known restrictions to any *practical* application of that theorem to the " real world,"[2] Prebisch's hypothetical example involves a mis-application of the results of that theorem. As he does elsewhere, he seems to be identifying wages with personal income, that is, assuming that there is only one factor of production in the world, labour. If that is the case, however, the factor-price equalisation theorem is not relevant[3] and the equalisation of income

---

[1] Prebisch I, p. 8. Italics added. The last sentence in the quotation is hard to understand in view of the benefits which would have accrued to the periphery from the technical progress of the centre.

[2] *Vide, e.g.*, Paul Samuelson, " International Factor Price Equalisation Once Again," ECONOMIC JOURNAL, Vol. LIX (June 1949), pp. 193–7; for a more detailed discussion see James E. Meade, *Trade and Welfare* (London: Oxford University Press, 1955), Chapters XXI, XXII, XXIII.

[3] If there is only one factor of production, then one of the following must be true: (*a*) There is something called " atmosphere," " conditions of production," " climate " or " state of technology," which is not an economic factor because it is free, but which differs between one country and another. In that case there is no reason why wages or—what is the same thing in this situation—*per capita* income should be equal. The single factor, " labour," will be more productive in the country with favourable " atmosphere " than in the other. (*b*) There is no difference between countries in " atmosphere," " state of technology," etc. In this case there could never be any difference in

throughout the world is not an " . . . implicit premise of the schema of the international division of labour." Alternatively, if there are two factors of production the theorem is valid only when both countries produce both commodities. This is a difficult assumption to make when one country is the periphery and the other is the centre; in any case, Prebisch, in the example we are discussing, specifically assumes that there is complete specialisation.

Prebisch seems to be arguing here: (1) that " technical progress," defined by him as an increase in productivity per man, just " happens " and is not the result of an increase in any other input; the benefit derived from such progress, then, is presumably analogous to " unearned " land rent; and (2) that from the point of view of justice and equity in distribution, such " unearned " benefits should be distributed equally throughout the world. Both of these propositions are highly questionable. The opportunity cost of technical progress is by no means negligible, even if we include only the direct outlay for research and development made by private business in the countries of the centre. Nor should one ignore the benefits of the centre's progress which accrue to the periphery by means other than the decline in the prices of final products which Prebisch argues should have taken place; the opportunity for peripheral countries to exploit such natural resources as rubber, for example, grew in the first place out of the development in the centre of industries requiring such primary products as inputs.[1] In any case, however, neither of the propositions stated above follows naturally, as Prebisch argues, from the traditional theory of comparative advantage and international specialisation.

Having contrasted what he thinks " should " have happened with what in fact, he asserts, did happen, namely the movement of the terms of trade against, rather than in favour of, the periphery, Prebisch goes on to explain the mechanism by which this took place.

> " The existence of this phenomenon cannot be understood, except in relation to trade cycles and the way in which they occur in the centres and at the periphery, since the cycle is the characteristic form of growth of capitalist economy, and increased productivity is one of the main factors of that growth " (p. 12).

---

factor returns, even if there were no trade. (It may be, in fact, that this is really what Prebisch has in mind, since, as we shall see below, his argument implies that technical progress is a costless activity and its benefits should be distributed equally throughout the world.) In fact, in such a case there is little reason for international trade to exist at all. Leontief has shown that trade will take place even when costs are identical, if tastes are different. But his argument rests on the concavity of the production possibilities curve, which in turn requires either that there be two factors of production or that both goods be produced under conditions of decreasing returns (to scale), which is difficult to imagine in a one-factor world. See Wassily W. Leontief, " The Use of Indifference Curves in the Analysis of Foreign Trade," *Quarterly Journal of Economics*, Vol. XLVII (May 1933), pp. 493–503.

[1] Prebisch himself makes this point, but dismisses it. " The increased productivity of the industrial countries certainly stimulated the demand for primary products and thus constituted a dynamic factor of the utmost importance in the development of Latin America. That, however, is distinct from the question discussed below." Prebisch I, p. 8. We would willingly agree that it is distinct, but not that it is therefore irrelevant.

At this point profits come into the picture, not, however, as a return to a factor of production, but rather as a windfall due to temporary emergence of excess demand.

> " As prices rise, profits are transferred from the entrepreneurs at the centre to the primary producers of the periphery. The greater the competition and the longer the time required to increase primary production in relation to the time needed for the other stages of production, and the smaller the stocks, the greater the proportion of profits transferred to the periphery. Hence follows a typical characteristic of the cyclical upswing; prices of primary products tend to rise more sharply than those of finished goods, by reason of the high proportion of profits transferred to the periphery.
>
> " If this be so, what is the explanation of the fact that, with the passage of time and throughout the cycles, income has increased more at the centre than at the periphery?
>
> " There is no contradiction whatsoever between the two phenomena. The prices of primary products rise more rapidly than industrial prices in the upswing, but also they fall more in the downswing, so that in the course of the cycles the gap between prices of the two is progressively widened " (p. 13).

What he must mean here, though not explicitly stated, is that the fall in prices in the downswing (in the periphery as compared with the centre) is greater than the relative rise in the upswing (in the centre as compared with the periphery). Otherwise there would not be the long-run ratchet effect that he speaks of. This is subsequently explained in terms of the wage mechanism at the centre. Some of the rising profits in the upswing are mopped up by higher wages;[1] in the downswing wages are rigid, however, so that prices of raw materials are forced down by more than the previous rise. But greater price–wage rigidity at the periphery would not alleviate the difficulty; it would, in fact, intensify it,

> " . . . since, when profits in the periphery did not decrease sufficiently to offset the inequality between supply and demand in the cyclical centres, stocks would accumulate in the latter, industrial production contract, and with it the demand for primary products. Demand would then fall to the extent required to achieve the necessary reduction in income in the primary producing sector " (pp. 13–14).

There is a peculiar asymmetry here. The rigidity of wages in the periphery, if it existed, would result in a decline in employment, presumably, as demand for primary products decreased. Thus income would be decreased in the

---

[1] " During the upswing, part of the profits are absorbed by an increase in wages, occasioned by competition between entrepreneurs and by the pressure of trade unions. When profits have to be reduced during the downswing, the part that had been absorbed by wage increases loses its fluidity, at the centre, by reason of the well-known resistance to a lowering of wages." Is it generally accepted that this " well-known resistance " existed throughout the period he refers to, from the 1870s to the 1930s? (Prebisch I, p. 13).

periphery by means of unemployment rather than by means of lower prices and real wages. This reasoning is unobjectionable, but surely it should be applied also to the centre. It is not, however. In the centre, *per capita* income is identified, apparently, with wages and the terms of trade, that is, with real wages, and no allowance is made for the declining income *per capita* which is the obvious concomitant of mass unemployment (p. 13).

In Prebisch II (pp. 258–61) the " . . . process of transfer of real income through the deterioration in the terms of trade " (p. 258) is explained in terms of " productivity ratios " and " technological densities " rather than differences in market structure between the periphery and the centre. The basic concept involved here stems from Graham's [1] notion of a list of products, ranked in order of the degree of comparative advantage, the commodity at the top of the list being that in which the country has the greatest comparative advantage. Prebisch applies this by comparing the " productivity ratio |which] expresses the relationship of physical productivity per man between the periphery and the center " with the wage ratio (p. 258). There is, of course, only one wage ratio [2] and there are as many productivity ratios as there are commodities. A commodity will be exported by the periphery only if the productivity ratio is equal to or greater than the wage ratio. In order for it to export (or stop importing) a commodity for which the productivity ratio is less than the wage ratio wages must fall. However, Prebisch goes on to argue that the difference in productivity between the " best " and the " marginal " export good is transferred " to the center through the free play of market forces " (pp. 258–9). But this assertion is valid only under highly restrictive assumptions. To determine the gains from trade by comparing wage ratios with ratios of physical productivity per man is possible only if labour is the sole factor of production and wage costs, therefore, the total cost of production. The parenthetical comment (p. 259) that land rental is excluded " to avoid complications . . . since it cannot be transferred " is, to say the least, ingenuous. Economists make simplifying assumptions all the time, of course, but this one is analogous to " simplifying " a study of oligopoly by assuming that there is only one firm! A comparison of wage ratios and productivity ratios might be admissible as a rough index of comparative advantage if: (*a*) both countries produced the goods that entered into trade, and (*b*) if they produced them with roughly the same combinations of labour with other inputs. (Even this is questionable in this instance, since Prebisch himself, as we have noted previously, argues that there is a significant " profit " element included in wages in the centre but not in the

[1] Frank D. Graham, " The Theory of International Values Re-examined," *Quarterly Journal of Economics*, Vol. XXVIII (November 1923), pp. 54–86.

[2] Prebisch does not, in his formal analysis, make use of the notion of " dualism " in the economy of the periphery, in the sense of non-competing groups in the labour market. He does make references to " low productivity domestic services," which seem to be the source of the indefinitely large reserve of redundant man-power, but the existence of this group does not prevent him from speaking throughout of a single wage-rate. For a further discussion of this problem see p. 6.

periphery.) [1] Thus, it is impossible to say that the productivity of labour (or of anything else) in coffee production is four times as high in Brazil as in Canada, because nobody knows what the productivity of labour in coffee production is in Canada. Furthermore, it would be wrong to say that if productivity per man in beef production in Argentina is three times as high as in the United Kingdom and wages in Argentina are half as high as in the United Kingdom, then beef must cost one-sixth as much in Argentina as in the United Kingdom. It would be wrong, because we know from this nothing about the relative amounts (and costs) of non-labour inputs—land, feed, shelter, etc., involved in beef production in the two countries. In fact, in such a case one could not even say with certainty that Argentina would export beef to the United Kingdom. Furthermore, if the world did indeed have only one factor of production, then the situation would be symmetrical, and the centre would also be transferring to the periphery its differential productivity for all exports for which the productivity ratio is higher than the wage ratio. In order, then, for the periphery to be at a disadvantage in this respect it would be necessary to show either that *only* at the periphery are there no factors of production other than labour or else that there is a systematic tendency for the periphery to have a greater " productivity surplus " than the centre over and above the productivity in the last, infra-marginal export commodity. This is an empirical question, but apparently it is Prebisch's belief that there is in fact a tendency for the periphery to have a greater " productivity surplus " than the centre. This is clearly what he means when he talks about " disparities in technological densities " (p. 262).

This can best be explained by supposing that there are ten commodities, *A . . . J*, such that the ratio of Country *P*'s productivity to Country *C*'s productivity is highest for commodity *A* and lowest for commodity *J*. Then Graham's conclusions are: (1) that country *P* is better off in trade the smaller the number of commodities (in addition to *A*) that it actually exports, that is, the less far down the list it has to go in exporting in order to pay for its imports; but (2) *ceteris paribus*, *P* is better off the closer together the internal productivity ratios, A/B, B/C, C/D, etc. The closer together the productivities (in Prebisch's terminology, the more dense the technology), the less deterioration in its terms of trade a country will have to suffer in response to an increase in its demand for imports or a decrease in foreign demand for its current exports.

Suppose *P* is exporting *A* and *B* and importing commodities *C* through *J*. Now as productivity (in general?) in the periphery increases and growth

---

[1] This is implicitly the assumption involved in Sir Donald McDougall's study, but he was comparing exports from the United Kingdom and the United States to third countries. This is quite a different matter. In the first place he was by definition confining himself to commodities produced in both countries. Secondly, productive techniques in the United Kingdom and the United States are likely to be more similar than in the United Kingdom and Brazil, for example. See G. D. A. MacDougall, " British and American Exports: A Study Suggested by the Theory of Comparative Costs," ECONOMIC JOURNAL, Vol. LXI (December 1951), pp. 697–724; Vol. LXII (September 1952), pp. 487–521.

occurs, there is surplus man-power in the periphery which must be employed by producing C domestically. Real wages must drop accordingly to maintain the equality of the wage ratio with the (marginal) productivity ratio. Since P's technology is sparse (*i.e.*, not " dense "), the decline in the productivity as it moves to producing C is large. Since wages constitute the only cost of production, according to Prebisch, the price in terms of foreign currency of all exports must fall proportionately, and the " differential productivity " of labour in the production of A and B is transferred abroad. But protection of C, the marginal industry, will not cure the transfer abroad of the productivity differential of A as compared to B which had been taking place all along. Furthermore, protection of this type is not only necessarily permanent, as Prebisch recognises it to be, it is also self-propagating. If P imposes a tariff on the import of C, Prebisch argues, then if productivity in the production of commodity C increases and protection is maintained, P can raise wages throughout. But if this is done, then B can no longer be exported without protection or subsidisation. So that protection, far from being temporary, must increase over time. Presumably Prebisch would argue that this would not be the case because productivity would also increase in B. But if that were the case, then wages could have been raised without the protection. This may be impossible, however, because of the surplus man-power (which, we shall argue, is the real villain of the piece); but then the increase of productivity in C will also generate surplus man-power, and it will be necessary to extend protection to D, and so on.

As noted, the real problem seems to lie with the surplus man-power; Prebisch seems to be thinking of an indefinitely large, and growing, population, with no relation whatever (even, apparently, at " subsistence " wages) between the wage-rate and the supply of labour. It is possible to make a strong case for protection in such a situation in order to stimulate, or at least permit, industrialisation, because of the beneficial social effects (and social external economies), including amelioration of the tendency towards population explosions. But this has nothing to do with the transfer-of-income argument.

Furthermore, it is not obvious why the surplus man-power should not be successfully utilised in the production of goods which are likely to be domestic goods regardless of the terms of trade (within any reasonably expected limits to the terms of trade) because of high transport costs: construction of all sorts, including that of social overhead capital, or various types of services.[1] Nor is it obvious why there should not be an increase in agricultural production for domestic consumption, since poor nutrition and near-starvation are ubiquitous problems in peripheral countries. One is tempted to speculate that the objection to both of these alternatives would be in terms of the desirability of industrialisation as such. And again, it should be emphasised

---

[1] Surely there is no need for services to be confined to the " low productivity domestic services " with which Prebisch is justifiably concerned. Education, for example, is one obvious alternative.

that the desire for industrialisation is a respectable motive for protection, but is quite independent of the arguments Prebisch employs.

Thus far we have discussed essentially two versions of Prebisch's argument, both dealing with the notion that the periphery transfers abroad the fruits of its technological progress through deterioration in its terms of trade. In one instance this is due to the fact that prices and wages are flexible upward in the centre but not in the periphery; in the other case it is due to the "technological density" of the centre as compared with the periphery. There is yet a third branch of the argument [1] which is stated in Prebisch II (pp. 252–60). Assume that the centre and the periphery are growing at the same rate—presumably *per capita* income is increasing at the same annual rate in both. Then, at a given set of price levels and exchange rates, the periphery will tend to develop a balance-of-payments deficit because its marginal propensity to import is higher than that of the centre. It is therefore necessary to effect import substitution, which is " . . . defined here as an increase in the proportion of goods that is supplied from domestic sources and not necessarily as a reduction in the ratio of imports to total income " (p. 253). (It is difficult to comprehend this definition.) One fairly obvious way to achieve this is through devaluation, which Prebisch discusses at some length. The " usual " type of objection to devaluation in such a system would be to argue that it would fail to increase foreign-exchange earnings if the demand for exports were inelastic with respect to price. Prebisch holds the view that price elasticity of demand for primary products is indeed low (p. 256), but this is not an important part of his argument. (The significance of price-inelastic demand for primary products has been given much more attention in the " commentaries " than in Prebisch's own work.)

The objection to devaluation, in Prebisch's view, is that it will stimulate exports from the periphery beyond the point which is socially optimal from the point of view of any one peripheral country. Higher internal prices for exports (initially) would encourage an increase in the output of exports. Higher internal prices of imports would also encourage domestic production of import-substitutes. But exports would increase too much, because the perfectly competitive firms producing exports would equate marginal cost with price, whereas socially the appropriate calculation would be an equation of marginal cost with marginal revenue. Since the domestic prices of exports would fall (from the initial post-devaluation peak—whether they would fall to levels lower than before devaluation is not clear), social marginal revenue would be less than price. Since for some, at least, of the world's primary products, the demand function facing any individual exporting *country* is probably close to infinitely elastic, the assumption here must be that all the

---

[1] There are others, but these are mentioned in passing, somewhat sporadically, rather than developed systematically. It should be noted that many of Prebisch's " asides " are extremely perceptive, thought-provoking and, in our opinion, more useful and relevant to the problem than much of the " formal " analysis.

peripheral countries are pursuing the same policy [1] and that either: (1) exports are produced under conditions of perfect competition in each country; or (2) the decision-making unit in each country is ignoring the policy being carried out in the other countries exporting the same commodity. One of these is essential to the mechanism, since supply of exports (which is the same thing, in Prebisch's model, as the output of exportables) is a function of price, not of marginal revenue.

For a " demonstration " that devaluation would lead to an increase in exports beyond the socially optimum point, the reader is referred to the Appendix (Prebisch II, pp. 269–73). The analysis here, however, is extremely difficult to follow. First, he is referring here, not to the response to devaluation, but rather to

"... how the process of spontaneous industrialization might operate according to the classical mechanism, assuming that there is free mobility of labor and unrestricted competition. We are concerned here only with the alternative employment of the surplus manpower in export production and industrial activities: for the sake of simplicity, other aspects will be overlooked " (p. 269).

Some of these " other aspects," however, would seem to be fairly important. Thus for the sake of " simplicity " it must be assumed that there is no domestic demand for the export good, nor for any (agricultural or primary) product which may be a very close substitute on the supply side for the export commodity. (Nor, *a fortiori*, can there be any new export good which is a close substitute in supply for existing exports.) All production not devoted to export must be industrial production. But even within this somewhat restrictive simplification it is not clear what the process is. " Spontaneous industrialization " is not defined. All we know is that we start from a position in which there is some industrial production (which is able to compete with imports in the home market) and there is a given quantity of " surplus man-power " which needs to be employed. Presumably productivity (in export(?)industry(?) both(?)) has risen, so that with output constant there is redundant labour. The issue therefore is that of allocating this surplus labour between primary production for export and industrial production for home consumption.

Some additional production for export can take place without any decline in export prices. The extent to which this is possible depends upon the rate of growth at the centre and the centre's income elasticity of demand for

---

[1] Prebisch makes this explicit on pp. 260-1, and states that he is "... considering the general need of the peripheral countries for industrialization." On this score he is commendably unselfish and would (justifiably) reject Kindleberger's criticism that he is ignoring " the competitive effect." Part of this " competition " could be directed, according to Kindleberger, at the developed countries, which are presumably fair game. But Kindleberger argues also that " an underdeveloped country can expand its sales if it can out-produce its fellow underdeveloped countries," and this solution Prebisch refuses to consider. See Charles P. Kindleberger, *Economic Development* (New York: McGraw-Hill, 1958), p. 247.

imports of the primary product in question. Beyond a certain point, more exports can be sold only at lower prices. (There really should be no distinction made. The only significance of the point—point 0 in Prebisch's diagram—is that before that point is reached export prices are lower than they would otherwise have been; after the point is reached prices are actually falling.) It should be noted again that this does not depend on the demand for primary products being inelastic with respect to price. A larger output can be sold only at declining prices whenever the demand is less than infinitely elastic. Since marginal physical productivity is constant and profits *per unit* are constant (p. 271), wages are less than prices by a constant amount and the decline in export prices forces wages down in the export-producing sector. Since labour is mobile (and presumably, homogeneous) this forces wages down in the industrial sector as well, making additional, previously extra-marginal, industries competitive with imports. Equilibrium is attained when the average product in export production (which is declining because prices of exports are falling) equals the average product in industry (which is declining because as industrial production expands output is expanded and extended to activities where productivity is lower and lower).[1] Wages, of course, are the same throughout, equal in each sector to average product less a constant. But marginal income per person in the export sector is less than wages and less than marginal (equal to average) income in industry. The reason for this is the declining price of exports, which means that marginal revenue is less than price. In industry, on the other hand, " . . . marginal income per person is the same as *per capita* income, from the point of view of the economy as a whole. . . . The fall of wages has brought also a decline of prices in existing industries; but this involves a purely internal transfer, whereas in export activities there is an external loss of income which reduces the increment of income due to the employment of the surplus manpower " (p. 272). The socially optimum allocation would be to stop increasing export production where marginal product in exports is equal to average product in industry. This can be achieved only by some interference with the free market. The problem, then, is not that the centre's demand is price- or income-inelastic—greater elasticity would postpone the day of reckoning, perhaps, but would not avert it. The problem stems from the fact that exports are produced under perfectly competitive conditions (which may be a valid assumption for parts of Latin America, but surely not for many other countries in the periphery); and that they are produced under conditions of constant marginal physical productivity of labour, which, for primary products, seems inconceivable.

When we apply this analysis to the effects of a devaluation the problem

---

[1] Elsewhere, Prebisch seems to feel that undertaking industrial activity will *raise* average productivity. For example, in Prebisch I, p. 15, we read: " As productivity increases with industrialization, wages will rise, thus causing a comparative increase in the prices of primary products. In this way, as its income rises, primary production will gradually obtain that share of the benefits of technical progress which it would have enjoyed had prices declined."

of explaining the origin of the "spontaneous industrialization" is removed. The immediate effect of the devaluation is to raise the domestic prices of both exports and imports. Export production is therefore stimulated, as is the production of at least some of the import-competing goods. Since, as we have noted, there seems always in Prebisch's world to be a redundancy of labour, both of these sectors are able to increase simultaneously. The argument, then, is that the response of the free market to the devaluation would involve an increase in the output of exports that was larger than the optimum and, correspondingly, an increase in the output of industrial, import-competing goods, that was smaller than optimum. It is worth recalling what assumptions underlie this analysis.

1. The labour force is perfectly homogeneous and perfectly mobile.
2. The periphery as a whole is a monopolist in the market for its exports, or at any rate a sufficiently important seller so that it is faced with a downward-sloping demand curve.
3. The export commodity is produced under perfectly competitive conditions *or* the producers of the export commodity (whether private enterprise, government-owned or directed by governmental or para-governmental agencies, such as a marketing board) in each country ignore the fact that other peripheral countries producing the same commodity are also executing the same policies of devaluation and expansion of exports.
4. All increased output of the export commodity must be exported. Thus, not only is there no stock-piling of the commodity by marketing boards, but there is no domestic consumption of the export commodity, or else the domestic demand for the export commodity is totally inelastic with respect to both price and income.
5. Exports are produced under conditions of constant returns to scale.
6. Exports are produced under conditions of constant marginal physical productivity of labour, which in turn implies either: (*a*) that labour is the only factor of production; or (*b*) that the supply of the other factors of production is infinitely elastic at the prevailing price, which is the "constant unit profit" mentioned above.

It is hardly necessary to point out that this is a rather formidable set of assumptions. The objections to assumptions 5 and 6, particularly in the case of agricultural and primary production, are obvious. Assumption 4 may be a reasonable approximation for some countries and some products in the form in which we have stated it here. But if it is interpreted more broadly it raises a host of new questions. For the assumption that exports are not consumed at home is the same as the statement that there are two sectors in the economy, an industrial, import-competing sector, and a primary-producing, export sector. This is not a "dual economy" problem, since

Prebisch raises neither the questions concerned with technological dualism, differences in factor substitutability and the like,[1] nor those involving non-competing groups in the labour market. But the importance of assuming that there are two—and no more than two—sectors is that it limits the number of alternatives available. There is always redundancy in the labour market (though this does not affect the wage level) which can be employed only in the industrial sector, where it runs up against competition from imports which can be overcome only by protection or subsidisation, or else in the export sector, where it runs into decreasing real returns due to the transfer of income abroad which results from the decline in price of exports. As we have noted previously, there is no room in his discussion for an increase in the output of " domestic goods," such as construction, with high transport costs; or of agricultural products for home consumption, which may be very close substitutes in production for the export commodity; or of " social overhead capital "; or, for that matter, of new exports which may be close substitutes in production for existing export goods. On the other hand, there are a number of instances in which Prebisch does seem to be thinking of a third sector (Prebisch I, p. 18, *e.g.*) which consists of domestic services and the like, and in which productivity is very low, so that output in that sector should not be encouraged. In fact, in a number of cases it is this third sector which seems to be the source of the apparently indefinitely large supply of man-power.

An even more troublesome, though related problem, is the question of the wage-determination mechanism. In the discussion of the disadvantages resulting from not having " technological density " and in the model presented in the Appendix which we have just examined, it seems clear that the real wage is equal to marginal (which equals the average) product in the export industry. Since this is constant, real wages in fact depend on the terms of trade. As the price of exports falls, wages fall, and this allows industrial activity, where productivity is lower, to expand. But elsewhere there is the notion that wages are determined by overall, or average, productivity, in the whole economy, as illustrated in footnote 1 on p. 318 and in the following:

> " It was pointed out at the beginning of this section that there are two ways of increasing real income. One is through an increase in productivity and the other through a readjustment of income from primary production so as to lessen the disparity between it and income of the great industrial countries.
>
> " The second result can be achieved only in so far as the first is accomplished. As productivity and the average real income from industry increase in the Latin-American countries, wages in agriculture

[1] *Vide*, *e.g.*, R. S. Eckaus, " The Factor-Proportions Problem in Under-Developed Areas," *The American Economic Review*, Vol. XLV (September 1955), pp. 539–65; Dale W. Jorgenson, " The Development of a Dual Economy," ECONOMIC JOURNAL, Vol. LXXI (June 1961), pp. 309–34.

and primary production in general will have to rise, as they have in other countries " (Prebisch I, p. 47).

These quotations are from Prebisch I, and it is, of course, possible that Prebisch's views changed during the years intervening between publication of the two essays. But whatever the reason, it is clear that there is a difference between the two views of the wage-determination mechanism which needs to be explained. Furthermore, there seems to be a difference in Prebisch's estimation of the productivity in industry in the two cases. If overall productivity rises as a result of industrialisation, productivity in industry must be higher than in the production of exports, in which case it is not clear why there is a need for protection of industry. There are two possible explanations for this. One is that Prebisch is implicitly going from a static to a dynamic analysis (which, incidentally, he does frequently throughout both papers) and the rise in productivity which results from industrialisation is a long-run result of the working-out of the external economies of industrialisation and its overall socio-economic effects, that is, the infant industry, or " infant economy " argument. A different explanation is that the higher productivity resulting from industrialisation results from the elimination, or at any rate the diminution, of the third sector, the low productivity domestic services. This is implied elsewhere in Prebisch I (p. 18). But this brings us back to the question of why this third sector cannot consist of " domestic goods " with high transport costs, of agricultural production for home consumption and/or of high-productivity services. What is more serious, there is the problem of how to explain the existence of such a sector in an economy in which labour is mobile and the wage-rate uniform. If productivity in that sector is so low, why does labour not move out of it and into the production of exports until the wage level in exports is brought down (through falling exports prices) to that prevailing in domestic service?

Almost all of the preceding discussion has been directed at the formal, analytical structure of Prebisch's arguments. As we stated at the beginning, there is not one, single model, but several. In this sense, we would argue, Prebisch has fallen short of making his case because he has over-stated it. The obvious question then is, can we ferret out from his argument a single, " minimum " model which would be sufficient to justify the policies he proposes? The following is a simplified version which we believe to be logically consistent and sufficient. Its acceptability depends, of course, on its empirical relevance.

Consider two countries, P and C, which are alike with respect to rate of growth of population, rate of increase in *per capita* income (hence rate of increase in productivity per man and in the real wage-rate) and technological density. At the existing exchange rate and wage-rates in the two countries all of P's exports are primary products and all of C's exports are industrial goods. The only difference is that with growth in income the world demand function for C's industrial exports is rising faster than the world demand function for P's primary exports. As a result, an ever-increasing proportion of P's incremental population *must* be allocated to industrial production, while in C an ever-increasing proportion of the incremental population *can*—and will—be allocated to industrial production. But P's industrial output can compete (in P's home market) with imports from C only if, through changes in the exchange rate or in the wage-rate, P accepts a deterioration in its terms of trade. Thus part of the increase in productivity in P accrues to C. So far there has been no need to appeal to differences in market structure, the mechanism of wage determination or any other asymmetrical imperfections in the working of the market mechanism and perfect competition.

Analytically, the only question remaining is whether there is any tendency for the decline in the terms of trade to stop. Prebisch does not address himself explicitly to this problem, but one gets the impression that he considers the decline in the terms of trade to be a continuing process. There seem, however, to be two equilibrating forces at work. First, as the proportion of the labour force employed in industrial production in P increases, the demand for imports of industrial goods from C should increase at a decreasing rate. Secondly, the fact that the terms of trade for P are declining means that real income *per capita* is not growing as rapidly as in C, so that even with a high income elasticity of demand for imports the absolute increments in imports demanded by P should eventually equal the growth in demand for its exports. Prebisch himself is aware of the latter tendency (Prebisch II, pp. 253–4), but argues that as a result the periphery's growth rate will be less than it would be if the demand for its exports were more income-elastic (or more price-elastic) or the demand for imports less income-elastic. This, indeed, is the heart of the " Prebisch thesis," and, we repeat, it stems from the assumption of different income elasticities of demand, not from alleged differences in market structure and the wage–price mechanism.

The problem thus far is essentially a balance-of-payments problem. Because of the disparities in income elasticities, income in P cannot grow as rapidly as income in C without generating a chronic deficit in the balance of payments. (The protectionism this suggests is of the " exchange-rationing " type discussed on p. 307. Tariffs, multiple exchange rates, or various types of discriminatory controls are frequently proposed—as relatively simple alternatives to more difficult alterations in the internal tax structure—to prevent the high-income groups from " frittering away " precious foreign-exchange reserves by exporting flight capital or importing luxury consumer goods. It would, indeed, be interesting to know the relationship between the apparently high income elasticity of demand for imports and the shape of the income distribution in P.) But the question still remains how fast real income *per capita could* grow in the absence of the balance-of-payments constraint. We are back to the traditional welfare propositions of international trade theory. Ignoring, as Prebisch does, a number of extremely important considerations, such as institutional patterns, the propensity to save and invest, the distribution of income, etc., the absolute growth at any one time is clearly a function of the level of real income. Furthermore, if our goal is to maximise income at some future date it is not obvious that maximising the rate of growth over the relevant time interval is the most appropriate means to that end. A slower rate of growth of a higher level of income may be better. If " the free play of market forces " dictates an increase in exports, and if this maximises P's income at any—and every—given point in time, this may be preferable to having a lower level of income which is growing at a more rapid rate.[1] Here the empirical questions of world (not domestic) market structure enter. The difficulty is that the periphery (as a group) is a monopolist but not a monopsonist: the world price of its imports is not a function of its demand for imports; and the demand for its exports is likewise independent of its demand for exports. But, though the demand *function* for P's exports is independent of what P does, the *price* of P's exports is directly dependent on the amount it offers for sale on the world market.[2] In a static context this is the only possible interpretation of Prebisch's statement (Prebisch II, p. 255): " It is not really a question of comparing the industrial costs with import prices but of comparing the increment of income obtained in the expansion of industry with that which could have been obtained in export activities had the same productive resources been employed there." The two comparisons will yield the same solution (if the international market is in equilibrium) *unless* marginal value product is less than the average in exports and equal to the average (or less, but with a smaller differential) in domestic industrial production, and import prices are not affected. (In a dynamic framework the quoted sentence can be interpreted as a statement of the infant industry argument.)

We can therefore characterise the basic Prebisch thesis as consisting of two components: (1) A " balance-of-payments " problem, with demand for imports in P tending to grow faster than import demand in C, so that equilibrium can be achieved only if P grows more slowly than C. This problem arises from C's inelastic demand (for imports from P) with respect to *income*. (2) A " real income " problem. This is frequently stated as C's price-inelastic demand for imports from P, but more correctly should be attributed to P's monopolistic position in the world market, which causes the demand for her exports to be less than infinitely elastic with respect to price. The result of this is that the " free market," responding to existing relative prices, misallocates resources in P between export industries and import-competing

---

[1] This increase in exports may, of course, stop short of complete specialisation, since production of exports may begin to run into decreasing returns. Cf. Prebisch II, p. 263, discussing " . . . forces . . . of a Ricardian character." This, incidentally, is one of the many examples of Prebisch's " asides " belying the naïveté of his assumptions and " simplifications " in the formal analysis.

[2] The terminology is not Prebisch's, but this is clearly implied in the analysis in the Appendix to Prebisch II, for example.

industries, so that aggregate real income in P is not maximised. (It should be remembered, however, that this misallocation is the result of two assumptions about market structure, both of which are necessary: (1) the monopolistic position of P in the world market *and* either (2) perfect competition among producers of the export good in each P-country, or (3) perfectly competitive behaviour on the part of decision-makers in each P-country, each assuming that output of its export good remains constant in the other countries of the periphery.)

What remains is a number of empirical questions which must be investigated in order to determine whether the model we have just stated is relevant to the real world. A reasonably careful study of these questions would constitute at least one additional paper, and we shall not attempt it here. We shall, however, indicate the direction that should be followed in such an investigation and the realms that need to be explored.

The " balance-of-payments " component of our " modified Prebisch model " rests on the assumption of a high income elasticity of demand for imports into the periphery and a low income elasticity of demand for imports into the centre. As to the former, even if it proves, on the basis of historical data, to be valid, it is necessary, from a policy-making point of view, to determine the reasons for it. One obvious cause, in the past, for the " scarcity " of foreign exchange in peripheral countries was the capital flight and the high propensity to import of the high-income groups in those countries.[1] A related question is to what extent the high propensity to import has been " programmed " by government development plans requiring large imports of capital goods.[2] This is not to say that such imports are " unjustified," but the question remains whether they should be " built in " to the model as a parameter in describing the economic behaviour of the periphery.

A second question, frequently raised in discussions of the alleged differences in income elasticity of demand facing exporters in the centre as compared with the periphery, pertains to the working of Engel's law. Clearly this applies, if at all, only to the food exports of the periphery (and of the centre, be it remembered), not to industrial raw materials. Empirical studies indicate that Engel's law probably holds, and that income elasticity of demand for food is less than one. But a corollary of this, also indicated empirically, is that the income elasticity of demand for food is higher among lower-income groups than for high-income groups.[3] As peripheral countries grow, then, an increasing demand for food may compete with growing imports for increasing expenditures. Additionally, a growing demand for the export goods for domestic consumption might be expected, in some

---

[1] Prebisch makes several references to this, among them Prebisch I, pp. 29, 40.

[2] Cf. Fritz Machlup, " Three Concepts of the Balance of Payments and the So-Called Dollar Shortage," ECONOMIC JOURNAL, Vol LX (March 1950), pp. 46–68.

[3] This is one of the results of a cross-sectional study by Hendrik S. Houthakker, " An International Comparison of Household Expenditure Patterns, Commemorating the Centenary of Engel's Law," *Econometrica*, Vol. 25 (October 1957), pp. 532–51.

countries of the periphery at any rate, to mitigate the misallocation effect with which Prebisch is concerned, since for that part of the domestic output which is consumed domestically, marginal revenue must be equal to average revenue, just as it is in the industrial sector; there is no " transfer abroad " involved. Furthermore, since Engel's law applies to expenditures for housing as well as for food, the possibility of diverting demand from imports to domestic goods as income rises increases in scope, since this is an industry in which, as yet, transport costs are high enough to preclude all but a very small amount of international trade.

Probably more important, for present purposes, than the validity of Engel's law is the question of the low income elasticity of demand, in the centre, for imports of industrial materials. It is not difficult to believe that this elasticity is, in fact, not high. (It has been suggested that it has a value approximately equal to one.) But Prebisch's purported demonstration that it is low (Prebisch I, pp. 24 ff.) is open to question on a number of counts. First, he speaks only of the United States, which for obvious reasons (such as sheer size, diversity of economic regions and resource endowments) has in general a low foreign-trade component in national income. Secondly, he speaks of the long-range decline in the import coefficient of the United States. We would argue: (*a*) that marginal, rather than average, propensity to import is important here; (*b*) that it is the marginal propensity to import *raw materials* that matters, rather than total imports; and (*c*) that the period Prebisch is considering, 1919–48, would be expected to contain more years of declining than of rising imports as a share of national income. Since almost two-thirds of the period are accounted for by the Great Depression and by the Second World War and the immediate post-war period, the overall decline in the import coefficient shown in Prebisch's Table V (Prebisch I, p. 24) is not at all surprising.[1]

One of the causes to which the supposed low income-elasticity of demand for raw materials in the centre is frequently attributed is the development of synthetic substitutes. We do not dispute this argument, but it should be noted that one of the effects of the appearance of substitutes is to make the *price* elasticity of demand higher. In the case of rubber and certain textiles, for example, one would expect the present price elasticity of demand to be very high indeed.

Related to the question of domestic production of food is that of the possibilities of diversification of exports, especially by the development of

---

[1] A study has been made for several countries by Calvin Patton Blair, *Fluctuations in United States Imports from Brazil, Colombia, Chile, and Mexico, 1919–1954* (Austin: Bureau of Business Research, the University of Texas, 1959). He concludes that " . . . results do indicate a common general tendency: the United States propensity to import [as a function of gross national product] from each of the four countries shifted downward during the depression and its aftermath, to be lifted again by the stimulus of war demand; and in no case did the import function return to its prewar position " (pp. 33-4). That the function should have risen during the war, while Prebisch's table shows the import coefficient rising only after the end of the war, is, of course, not unexpected, since Prebisch's data are for total imports, from all sources.

joint products or vertical expansion.[1] Both this and the possibilities of increased food production are illustrated by the following statement with respect to Ghana:

> " The draft [of a seven-year development plan] states that ' Ghana's agriculture has been unable to keep up with the domestic demand for food.' Emphasis will, therefore, be placed first on agricultural development: expenditure of £G10·8 million on state farms is expected to increase food production to such an extent that food imports costing £G23 million can be eliminated. In industry there will be more emphasis on the processing of raw materials. At least half of Ghana's cocoa exports are to be in the form of processed cocoa rather than of cocoa beans. Timber is to be converted into wood products, plywood, and chipboard. By 1970, it is expected that production of alumina from local bauxite will approach the requirements of the aluminum smelter at Tema."[2]

Clearly, both this type of extension of the export list as well as the readiness with which resources can be shifted from export production to supplying food for domestic consumption will vary greatly from one peripheral country to another. This problem of the extent to which generalisation is possible, however, is equally applicable to Prebisch's analysis. As we have previously noted, there are a number of points in his argument at which what Prebisch has observed in Latin America is not obviously relevant for other parts of the periphery. In this connection, as in many others in economic analysis, aggregation is a tool which has greater power than fineness.

M. June Flanders

Purdue University,
Lafayette, Indiana.

---

[1] Michael Michaely, in his study of concentration in trade, has concluded that " . . . there is no association between the intensity of price fluctuations of exports and the extent of specialization in exports of primary goods. What may have led to the belief that such an association does exist is the disregard of the degree of commodity concentration. . . . It is only because exporters of primary goods are usually countries with highly concentrated exports that they appear to be more vulnerable to violent price fluctuations " (*Concentration in International Trade* (Amsterdam: North-Holland Publishing Company, 1962), p. 78). Michaely's discussion of The Implications of Economic Development (Chapter 6) is, in general, extremely thoughtful and apt. He seems to feel that on the whole the obstacles to development presented by fluctuations in the terms of trade have been exaggerated, though he recognises the problem. He is concerned primarily with the problems raised by *fluctuations* in the terms of trade rather than with the question of long-run deterioration, and for this reason we have not dealt with his arguments at greater length. His work, however, is highly suggestive and could well serve as a guide to further empirical study of *trends* in prices and terms of trade.

[2] Quoted in International Monetary Fund, *International Financial News Survey*, Vol. XV, No. 14, April 12, 1963, p. 121.

8

THE WORLD BANK ECONOMIC REVIEW, VOL. 2, NO. 1: 1-47

Primary Commodity Prices, Manufactured Goods Prices, and the Terms of Trade of Developing Countries: What the Long Run Shows

Enzo R. Grilli and Maw Cheng Yang

The authors revisit in this article the empirical foundation of the alleged secular decline in the prices of primary commodities relative to those of manufactures. They use a newly constructed index of commodity prices and two modified indexes of manufactured good prices, and find that from 1900 to 1986 the relative prices of all primary commodities fell on trend by 0.5 percent a year and those of nonfuel primary commodities by 0.6 percent a year. They thus confirm the sign, but not the magnitude, of the trend implicit in the work of Prebisch. But even the more limited secular decline shown by their relative price indexes may be magnified by an incomplete account of quality improvements in manufactures. They then show that the evolution of the terms of trade of nonfuel primary commodities is not the same as that of the net barter terms of trade of non-oil-exporting developing countries. Finally, they find that despite the decline that has probably occurred during the current century in the terms of trade of nonfuel primary commodities, the purchasing power of total exports of these products has increased considerably. Similarly, the fall that may have occurred after World War II in the net barter terms of trade of developing countries seems to have been more than compensated for by the steady improvement in their income terms of trade.

An important focus of the analysis of commodity price movements has been on the distribution of gains from commodity production between producers and consumers. Transposed to the international domain, this type of analysis has focused on the long-term movements in the net barter terms of trade of developing countries, taken as an indicator of the distribution of gains from trade between commodity producers in developing countries and commodity consumers in industrial countries. Alternatively, and sometimes at the cost of some confusion, attention has been placed on the long-term trends in the prices of

Enzo R. Grilli is Chief Economist, Economic Advisory Staff, the World Bank. Maw Cheng Yang is an economist in the Bank's International Economics Department. In preparing this article, they received valuable assistance from many colleagues in the World Bank, in the Statistical Office of the United Nations, and in the U.S. Bureau of Labor Statistics. Takamasa Akiyama, Riccardo Faini, Christian Moran, Denis Richard, Theophilos Priovolos, and H. Singer offered many useful observations and comments on the draft. B. Salimi helped greatly in collecting the basic data.

internationally traded primary commodities relative to those of manufactured products.

The contours of the controversy about the alleged long-term deterioration in the (net barter) terms of trade of developing countries, which was generated by the early work of Prebisch and Singer, are too well known to need another review here (see United Nations 1949; Prebisch 1950; Singer 1950; Lewis 1952; Viner 1953; Kindleberger 1956; Ellsworth 1956; Baldwin 1955, 1966; Morgan 1959; Meier 1958, 1963; Maizels 1970; Streeten 1974; Ray 1977; Macbean and Balasubramanyan 1978; and Kravis and Lipsey 1974, 1981). The empirical evidence available so far on the long-term movements in the prices of primary and manufactured products has also been recently revisited (Spraos 1980 and Sapsford 1985).

However, a common problem of the analyses that have focused on the long-run trends in the terms of trade of developing countries, or on the long-run trends in the relative prices of primary commodities, has been the inadequacy of the basic price data. Long-term movements in the terms of trade of developing countries were either inferred from those of certain industrial countries or from the movements in the prices of primary commodities relative to those of manufactured products (the so-called primary commodity terms of trade) without accounting for changes in the volume or composition of exports of the developing countries. Both practices obviously suffer from serious shortcomings. Yet instead of generating caution, the paucity of the available empirical evidence generated a tendency in the opposite direction: strong conclusions were derived from evidence that was weak in both accuracy and economic significance.

In this article we attempt, first of all, to solidify the empirical evidence on the prices of internationally traded goods, with special attention to nonfuel primary commodity prices. We go on to examine the long-run movements in the prices of nonfuel commodities relative to those of manufactures. We then investigate the statistical relationship between the movements in the relative prices of nonfuel primary commodities and those in the net barter terms of trade of developing countries at the aggregate, regional, and country levels. We also look at the evidence on the long-term movements in the purchasing power of total primary commodity exports (and in the income terms of trade of developing countries after World War II) to put in perspective the question of the gains from trade accruing to developing countries that depend on nonfuel primary commodities. We finally examine the various possible effects of growth on the relative prices of primary commodities. In this context, we review the theoretical and empirical validity of the classical economists' argument on the long-run movements in the "real prices" of primary products.

I. EXISTING AND NEW EVIDENCE ON LONG-TERM COMMODITY PRICE MOVEMENTS

There are several indexes of nonfuel commodity prices, but only the *Economist* Index (EI) and the W. A. Lewis Index (WALI1) cover a sufficient amount of time to be useful in analyzing commodity price movements in the long run (Lewis 1952; and *The Economist* 1974).[1] Both indexes, however, suffer from considerable drawbacks. The commodity coverage of the EI has been revised several times in its long history, and its weights reflect the relative values of commodities in the import trade of industrial countries. The WALI1 stops in 1938 and, instead of international market quotations, is based on export unit values of selected countries. The EI, moreover, does not include fuel prices, whereas the WALI1 does.

The available empirical evidence on long-term movements in the prices of manufactured goods is also limited. There is an index prepared by W. A. Lewis (WALI2) that goes back to 1870, but it has two gaps, which roughly correspond to the two world wars (Lewis 1952). Another index, constructed by Maizels (AMI), covers about the same period as the WALI2, but it is reported only as averages of selected subperiods (Maizels 1970). There is, finally, the possibility of constructing yet another index from U.N. sources (Manufacturing Unit Values, United Nations; MUVUN) covering the period after 1900, but there are two gaps in this index for 1914–20 and 1939–47 (United Nations 1969, 1974). All these indexes are based on unit values of exports for a selected number of industrial countries.

Confronted with the alternative of recomputing the EI on a different weight system and with uniform commodity coverage over time or of computing a new index of nonfuel commodity prices, we chose the second and built a U.S. dollar index of prices of twenty-four internationally traded nonfuel commodities, beginning in 1900 (figure 1). The basic version of this new index (Grilli-Yang Commodity Price Index; GYCPI) is base-weighted, with 1977–79 values of world exports of each commodity used as weights.[2] It therefore reflects the movements over time of the international prices of a given basket of primary commodities. We computed three additional versions of this index. The first two (GYCPI′ and GYCPI″) differ from the basic version in the weighting systems used to construct them, whereas the third (GYCPI′′′) is also different in commodity coverage, as fuels are included in the sample (Grilli and Yang 1987).

Given the impossibility of computing a new price index of manufactures going back to 1900, we opted for a modified version of the MUVUN, constructed by filling its two gaps by interpolation, using export and import unit values of manufactured goods of the United States and the United Kingdom as indicators.[3] The modified U.N. index (MUV) reflects the unit values of exports of

1. The *Economist* Index begins in 1860 and is regularly updated and reported by the compiler. See, for example, *The Economist*, March 2, 1964, and September 6, 1973. The W. A. Lewis Index of commodity prices starts in 1870 and goes up to 1938. It is largely based on price data reported by Schlote (1938), complemented by data from the League of Nations (1945). A more complete analysis of these indexes is in Grilli and Yang (1987).

2. This new index covers the prices of 54 percent of all nonfuel commodities traded in the world in 1977–79 (49 percent of all food products, 83 percent of all nonfood agricultural products, and 45 percent of all metals). The GYCPI and its components are shown in appendix I.

3. For the years 1915 to 1920, the interpolation was made by first regressing the MUV index (in percentage terms) on the index of export and import unit values of manufactures of the United States and

Figure 1. *Index of Nonfuel Primary Commodity Prices (GYCPI), 1900–86*

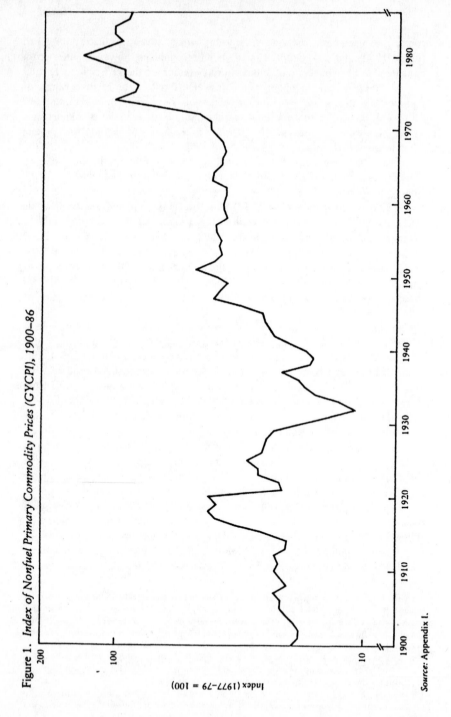

Index (1977–79 = 100)

Source: Appendix I.

manufactures of a number of industrial countries. It has variable weights that reflect the relative importance of the various types of manufactures in international trade. These were updated every five to seven years until 1938 and changed again in 1959, 1963, 1970, 1975, and 1980 (United Nations 1969, 1972, 1976, 1982, and 1987).

In addition to this index of unit values of manufactures exported by industrial countries, we derived an index of domestic prices of manufactured products in the United States (United States Manufacturing Price Index; USMPI) by netting out energy, timber, and metal prices from the U.S. wholesale price index of industrial commodities (USMPIO) to eliminate overlap with goods in primary commodities indexes and rescaling it (Grilli and Yang 1987). This index is also useful as a reference, for it gives an idea of the relationship between prices and unit values of exports that existed over time and of the reasonableness of the results obtained from the interpolation procedure used to fill the gaps in the MUVUN. These two indexes of manufactured goods "prices" show a very close trend growth from 1900 to 1986 equal to 2.49 percent a year for the MUV and 2.48 percent a year for the USMPI (figure 2).[4] The MUV, however, is slightly more erratic than the USMPI. Its average percentage deviation from trend over the 1900–86 period is 6.2 percent, whereas that of the USMPI is 5.1 percent.

The USMPI and MUV were used to compute two sets of relative prices (or "real" prices) of nonfuel primary products from 1900 to 1986. Measuring, for example, the long-term movements in the relative prices of nonfuel commodities in terms of a wholesale price index or in terms of an index of unit values of trade of manufactures obviously carries different meanings. The first set of relative prices (GYCPI/USMPI) measures the evolution of the purchasing power of nonfuel primary commodities in terms of a basket of tradable goods valued at domestic prices.

In open economies, wholesale price trends should reflect rather closely those of the international prices of the same products. This should be even more so when the time period under consideration is long enough to accommodate possible short-run deviations in the movements of tradable versus nontraded goods prices. Yet, how far one can rely on the law of one price through time is still an open question, given the obstacles to free trade in manufactures that have existed (and still exist) and the possibility that producers of manufactures facing different market conditions domestically and abroad can successfully and persistently employ price discrimination across markets. In our use of the USMPI, the degree of openness of the U.S. economy could also be considered insufficient to

the United Kingdom (in percentage terms) obtained by averaging the subindexes and then by extrapolating the values of the MUV index on the basis of the estimated equation. For the years 1939 to 1947, the interpolation was made using the same procedure, but the MUV was regressed only against the index of import and export unit values of manufactures of the United States.

4. These are semilog trends, corrected for serial correlations using a maximum-likelihood procedure. Both are statistically significant at the 5 percent confidence level or above.

Figure 2. *Indexes of Manufactured Goods Prices (MUV and USMPI), 1900–86*

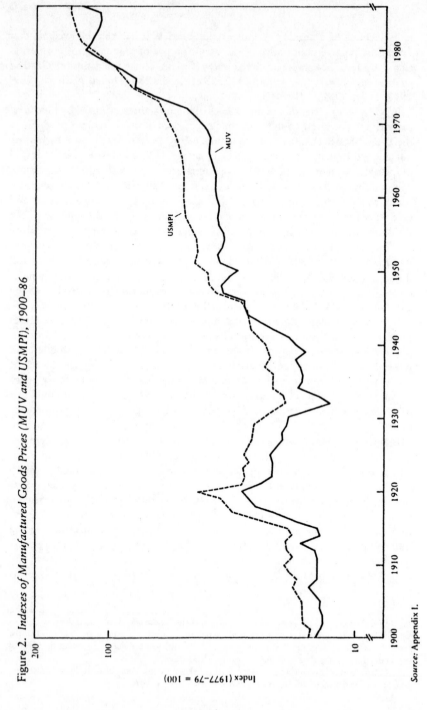

Index (1977–79 = 100)

Source: Appendix 1.

warrant the use of U.S. tradable goods prices as proxies for internationally traded goods prices. In making this choice we have "traded off" in favor of an index (USMPI) with a coverage of manufactured goods prices which could be carefully checked and sufficiently narrowed to allow a clear differentiation between the two baskets of goods of which the relative prices were to be measured (nonfuel primary commodities and manufactures). This would not have been possible if we had chosen instead the U.K. wholesale price index because of the greater openness of the U.K. economy.

The second set of relative prices (GYCPI/MUV) measures the evolution of the purchasing power of a basket of nonfuel primary commodities in terms of traded manufactures, valued at "international prices." This type of measurement raises questions about the representativeness of trade unit values as proxies for international prices. In addition, the meaning of the time movements of the ratio of primary commodities and manufactures prices is clouded by the fact that technical progress may have differential effects on the price trends of the two types of goods.

The basic issues are quite familiar. They have to do with the appropriate construction of trade unit values, and how to adequately account for the introduction of new items in the basket of traded manufactures and the "upward bias" carried by manufactured good prices or unit values whenever they incorporate the effects of technical progress that significantly improves their quality (Viner 1953; Baldwin 1955, 1966; Meier 1958, 1963; Morgan 1959; Kravis and Lipsey 1974, 1981). In comparing primary commodities and manufactured goods prices over time, the measurement risks are those implicit in the nonhomogeneity of the two sets of prices and of the two baskets of goods of which the prices are measured. These issues deserve attention, and we will return to them in the last section of this article.

Finally, neither set of relative prices that we have calculated can be taken as an adequate proxy of the net barter terms of trade of developing countries (Px/Pm), because the total price index of exports of developing countries (Px) contains more than primary commodities and the total price index of imports of developing countries (Pm) contains more than manufactures. In addition, the trend shown by any index of the net barter terms of trade should not be taken, in itself, as an adequate indicator of the real income effects of trade over time. A negative trend would not automatically mean that real income has also fallen in time. The sign of the income effect would in fact depend not only on the reasons for the decline in the net barter terms of trade, but also on what happened to the purchasing power of total exports. The latter, moreover, should not be mistaken for the purchasing power of a given basket of exports. To reflect the real income effects of trade, one has to account simultaneously for the movements in the relative prices of exports and for the quantity of exports. The income terms of trade $(Px\,Qx/Pm)$ is a measure of this type that reflects the purchasing power of total exports in terms of imports.

8   THE WORLD BANK ECONOMIC REVIEW, VOL. 2, NO. 1

II. Long-Term Trends in the Relative Prices of Nonfuel Primary Commodities: The Main Aggregates

Since 1900 nonfuel commodity prices seem to have declined substantially relative to those of manufactured goods sold in the United States, as well as to those of manufactured goods exported by industrial countries. The GYCPI/USMPI series shows a negative exponential trend of 0.57 percent a year over the 1900–86 period. The GYCPI/MUV series shows a trend decline of 0.59 percent a year over the same period (table 1).

Reweighting the GYCPI (still on a 1977–79 basis) to account specifically for the importance of developing countries in world trade of nonfuel primary commodities yields a new index (GYCPI′) that does not differ significantly from the original one. The weights in GYCPI′ are the value share of developing countries' exports of each commodity, instead of the value shares of world exports of each commodity. The purchasing power of the basket of nonfuel primary commodities exported by developing countries measured by the GYCPI′/MUV appears to have fallen on trend by 0.67 percent a year since 1900. If the GYCPI′/USMPI is taken as a measure, the trend decline is 0.66 percent a year.

A further check on the tracking stability of our original index was conducted by recomputing it using as weights the value shares of commodities in world

Table 1. *Aggregate Trends in the Relative Prices of Primary Commodities, 1900–86*

Relative price index		Intercept ($\hat{\alpha}$)	Coefficient of time ($\hat{\beta}$)	Regression statistics[a]			
				R^2	SEE	F	DW
ln GYCPI/MUV	=	4.9810* (67.7)	−0.00589* (−4.11)	0.82	0.11	394.9	1.74
ln GYCPI/USMPI	=	4.7554* (41.9)	−0.00567* (−2.60)	0.81	0.10	359.1	1.38
ln GYCPI′/MUV	=	4.9650* (46.6)	−0.00669* (−3.23)	0.77	0.13	282.2	1.94
ln GYCPI′/USMPI	=	4.7526* (31.2)	−0.00665* (−2.29)	0.75	0.12	253.9	1.61
ln GYCPI″/MUV	=	5.1249* (65.4)	−0.00669* (−4.38)	0.80	0.12	332.3	1.71
ln GYCPI″/USMPI	=	4.8889* (44.4)	−0.00629* (−2.96)	0.79	0.11	314.7	1.39
ln GYCPI‴/MUV	=	5.0057* (48.4)	−0.00518* (−2.58)	0.74	0.13	242.6	1.52
ln GYCPI‴/USMPI	=	4.7821* (32.3)	−0.00501* (−1.77)	0.74	0.12	236.6	1.25

t values in parentheses.

* = significant at the 10 percent confidence level or above.

Note: The estimated model is ln GYCPI$_t$ = $\alpha + \beta t_i + u_i$, where t_i is a time trend. All time series are trend-stationary; ordinary least squares (OLS) estimates are based on annual data. A maximum-likelihood procedure was used to correct for serial correlation.

a. SEE = standard error of the estimate. DW = Durbin-Watson statistic.

trade in 1913, 1929, 1937, 1959, 1963, 1970, 1975, and 1980. These different weights closely reproduce those of MUV. Using this new index (GYPCI") based on given-year weights, one finds that the purchasing power of nonfuel primary commodities in terms of manufactures declined since 1900 at an annual rate of 0.63 percent to 0.67 percent depending on whether the USMPI or MUV is used as a measure of manufactured goods prices.

Finally, if one includes fuel prices in the index of primary commodities (GYCPI'''), using the same variable weights as in the GYCPI" to account for the considerable changes that have intervened over time in the relative importance of fuels in world trade, the rate of decline in the prices of *all* primary commodities relative to those of manufactures (GYCPI''' /MUV) becomes 0.52 percent a year. The inclusion of coal and oil prices in the basket of primary commodities for which prices are tracked over time does not change the sign of the trend shown by this index relative to that of unit values of manufactures. The relative prices of *all* primary commodities appear to have fallen on trend since 1900 at only a slightly less rapid rate than those of nonfuel commodities.

The trend rate of decline in GYCPI''' /MUV is closer in absolute value to that of the W. A. Lewis indexes (WALI1/WALI2) for 1871–1938 (0.46 percent a year) than to that implicit in the Prebisch data for 1876–1938 (0.95 percent a year). The original U.N. series, which covers prices of "other goods" (including fuels) in addition to the prices of manufactures, shows in turn a trend rate of decline in the relative prices of these other goods (0.73 percent a year) that falls between that of the GYCPI''' /MUV and the Prebisch index (W. A. Lewis 1952; Prebisch 1950; and United Nations 1969). Our results therefore strongly support the inference made by Spraos (1980) about Prebisch's original data: the price series he used exaggerated the adversity of the trends in the relative prices of all primary products. Yet our data indicate, from the beginning of the present century to date, a cumulative trend fall of about 40 percent in the market prices of nonfuel primary commodities relative to those of manufactured products and a cumulative trend decline of about 36 percent in the market prices of all primary commodities.[5]

A question that naturally arises is whether the exponential time trends that we computed can be considered acceptable measures of the underlying long-term trends. There is no rigorous answer to this question. Yet at least three sets of issues need to be addressed. The first regards the specification of the time regression model that we used, and the statistical acceptability of the estimates derived from it; the second pertains to the stability over time of the estimated time trend coefficients; the third has to do with the "legitimacy" of the starting point.

As shown by Nelson and Kang (1983), the use of time as an independent variable in regression models is not appropriate when the dependent variable

---

5. The cumulative decline for the various relative price indexes for 1900–86 are: GYCPI/MUV, 39.8 percent; GYCPI/USMPI, 38.7 percent; GYCPI'/MUV, 43.9 percent; GYCPI'/USMPI, 43.6 percent; GYCPI"/MUV, 43.4 percent; and GYCPI'''/MUV, 35.6 percent.

10   THE WORLD BANK ECONOMIC REVIEW, VOL. 2, NO. 1

follows a difference-stationary process (DSP). Conversely, it is appropriate when the dependent series follows a trend-stationary process (TSP). We used a test suggested by Dickey and Fuller (1979) to verify the trend stationarity of our relative price series and found them belonging to a TSP. The (semilog) time regression model that we used thus is correctly specified in all cases and the standard tests can be performed to judge the statistical significance of the estimated time coefficients.

First-order serial correlation, however, was to be consistently present in all the estimated time regressions. It would be expected in the price series under review, insofar as they reflect the influence of random factors (such as the two world wars, several local wars, periods of droughts affecting agricultural prices) spread over several years. We corrected for it using a maximum-likelihood procedure. The time coefficients of the regression models in their corrected version (shown in table 1) maintain statistical significance, whereas the standard error of the estimate (SEE), the F, and Durbin-Watson (DW) statistics of the regressions improve substantially with respect to the results obtained from the regressions uncorrected for serial correlation.

The second set of issues that remains to be dealt with pertains to the validity of the assumption of continuous and constant trend growth implicit in the exponential time models that we estimated. The possibility that the negative growth path shown, for example, by the GYCPI/MUV or by GYCPI'''/MUV may not have remained constant over time cannot be ruled out by simply looking at the statistical significance of its ordinary least-squares (OLS) estimates.

Examination of the residuals of the semilog time regressions, as well as a priori knowledge of the exogenous factors that may have caused a structural break in the price series, indicated the possibility of breaks at three points in time: 1921, 1932, and 1945, three of the troughs shown by the series. Various tests were performed to check on the stability of the estimated time coefficients of the GYCPI/MUV and GYCPI'''/MUV regressions.

First we tested for shifts in the slope and the intercept of the estimated time trends using a dummy variable procedure suggested by Gujarati (1970a, 1970b). Then we tested for the possibility of a change in slope, assuming no discontinuity in the time trend, by using the piecewise regression procedure suggested by Suits, Mason and Chan (1978) to estimate the time trend of the GYCPI/MUV and GYCPI'''/MUV. The models used and the results obtained are shown in appendix II. The main conclusion from this analysis is that no clear break seems to have occurred since 1900 in negative trends shown by the indexes of the relative prices of either nonfuel or all primary commodities.

The third set of issues has to do with the "legitimacy" of the starting point (the year 1900) of our estimated long-term trends. The cyclical instability in commodity prices is significantly greater in the first forty years covered by our series than in the subsequent ones. World War I and the great economic depression of the early 1930s seem to have generated such strong cycles in commodity prices that fitting a trend to these prices beginning in 1900 may lead to results that are largely dependent on starting points.

Given the nature of the problem, the usual empirical rule that is applicable is to extend the data sample backward. This option was precluded to us, for the range of price data necessary to do so is not available. A check on the trend of individual price series that go beyond 1900 would seem to indicate that, with very few exceptions, our starting year was quite appropriate. Yet we conducted a further check by comparing the estimated price trends of the GYCPI/MUV and GYCPI′′′/MUV with those of the two available commodity price indexes that go beyond 1900: the EI and WALI1, deflated by a common index of manufactured goods prices—the WALI2 (figure 3).

This double comparison is necessary because the GYCPI and EI do not include the prices of fuels, whereas the GYCPI′′′ and WALI1 include them. Over the 1870–1900 period, the annual trend of EI/WALI2 is 0.48 percent, whereas that of WALI1/WALI2 is 0.52 percent. These trends compare quite closely with those respectively shown by GYCPI/MUV (0.59 percent) and GYCPI′′′/MUV (0.51 percent) over the 1900–86 period. Although not conclusive per se, these comparisons of price tendencies before and after 1900 tend to support the notion that the trends in the prices of primary commodities relative to those of manufactured products that we computed after 1900 should not have been much affected by their starting years.

III. Long-Term Trends in the Relative Prices of the Principal Nonfuel Commodity Groups

Taking advantage of the possibility of breaking the GYCPI into its three main components (food prices—GYCPIF, nonfood agricultural raw material prices—GYCPINF, and metal prices—GYCPIM), we computed the trends in the prices of these subcategories of nonfuel commodities relative to those of manufactures. Our results show that over the 1900–86 period the decline in relative prices of nonfuel commodities was not uniform across commodity groups (table 2). Metal and nonfood agricultural product prices (relative to MUV) show a much stronger long-term trend rate of decline than agricultural food prices (0.82 percent and 0.84 percent respectively, versus 0.36 percent a year). Thus, not all producers of nonfuel primary commodities experienced the same falling trend in the purchasing power of a given volume of their products over the past eighty-six years. The export product mix has made some significant difference (figures 4–7).

But there are further significant differences. The negative trend in the GYCPIF/MUV is the composite of a strong positive trend (0.63 percent a year) in the relative price index of tropical beverages (GYCPIBEV/MUV, comprising coffee, cocoa, and tea), and of a negative trend of similar magnitude (0.54 percent a year) in the relative price index of agricultural food products strictly defined (GYCPIOF/MUV) (table 2). The relatively larger weight of other food in the aggregate index (GYCPIF) swamps the effect of secularly rising prices of tropical beverages (especially coffee and cocoa) relative to those of manufactured products. Among all the subcategories of nonfuel commodities, tropical beverages are the only one showing rising relative prices over time. This contrasts rather clearly

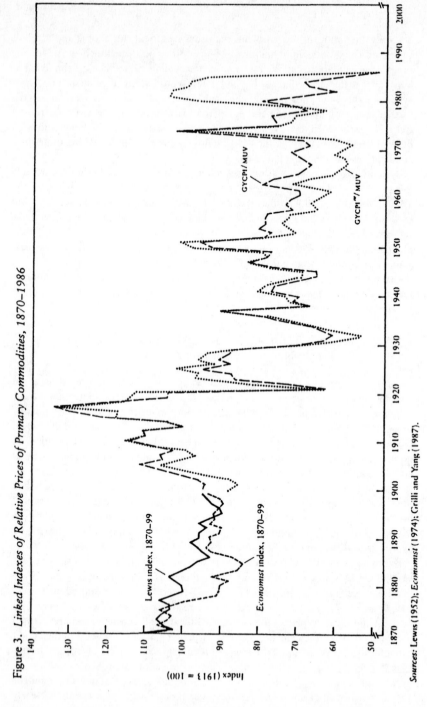

Figure 3. Linked Indexes of Relative Prices of Primary Commodities, 1870–1986

Index (1913 = 100)

Sources: Lewis (1952); Economist (1974); Grilli and Yang (1987).

Table 2. *Trends in the Relative Prices of the Principal Nonfuel Primary Commodity Subgroups, 1900–86*

Relative price index	Intercept (α̂)	Coefficient of time (β̂)	Regression statistics			
			R^2	SEE	F	DW
Food:						
In GYCPIF/MUV	4.8328*	−0.00357*	0.72	0.13	215.5	1.73
	(57.5)	(−2.17)				
Nonfood agricultural:						
In GYCPINF/MUV	5.1259*	−0.00817*	0.78	0.12	306.3	1.74
	(55.9)	(−4.57)				
Metals:						
In GYCPIM/MUV	5.1214*	−0.00841*	0.77	0.12	286.2	1.52
	(34.7)	(−2.98)				
Food:						
In GYCPIF/USMPI	4.5973*	−0.00320	0.72	0.13	214.8	1.46
	(39.7)	(−1.43)				
Nonfood agricultural:						
In GYCPINF/USMPI	4.8933*	−0.00777*	0.77	0.12	276.7	1.56
	(38.2)	(−3.15)				
Metals:						
In GYCPIM/USMPI	4.9129*	−0.00820*	0.76	0.12	264.6	1.49
	(28.4)	(−2.50)				
Tropical beverages:						
In GYCPIBEV/MUV	3.7192*	0.00630*	0.50	0.17	84.8	1.75
	(26.20)	(2.29)				
Nonbeverage Foods:						
In GYCPIOF/MUV	5.0642*	−0.00543*	0.70	0.15	198.2	1.63
	(53.08)	(−2.92)				
Cereals:						
In GYCPICE/MUV	5.2782*	−0.00683*	0.71	0.15	193.8	1.64
	(56.33)	(−3.74)				
Tropical beverages:						
In GYCPIBEV/USMPI	3.4880*	0.00678*	0.51	0.17	84.5	1.74
	(21.83)	(2.20)				
Nonbeverage foods:						
In GYCPIOF/USMPI	4.8280*	−0.00506*	0.70	0.14	194.1	1.38
	(38.58)	(−2.09)				
Cereals:						
In GYCPICE/USMPI	5.0320*	−0.00620*	0.69	0.15	186.5	1.46
	(45.23)	(−2.87)				

t values in parentheses.

* = significant at the 10 percent confidence level or above.

Note: The estimated model is In GYCPI$_i$ = α + βt_i + u$_i$, where t_i is a time trend. All time series are trend-stationary; OLS estimates are based on annual data. A maximum-likelihood procedure was used to correct for serial correlation.

Figure 4. *Indexes of Relative Prices of Nonfuel Primary Commodities, 1900–86*

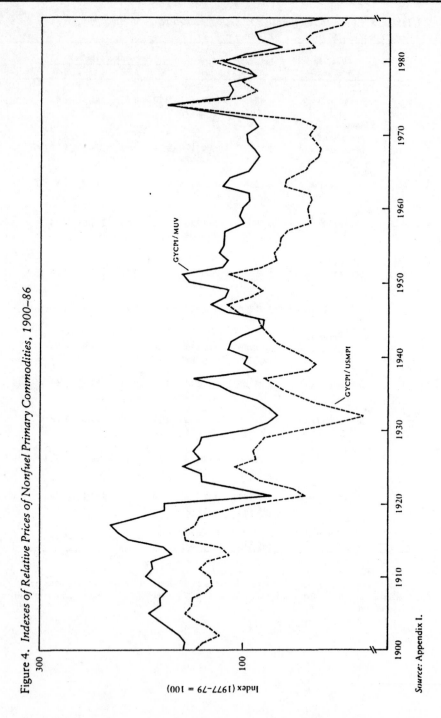

GYCPI/MUV

GYCPI/USMPI

Index (1977–79 = 100)

Source: Appendix I.

Figure 5. *Indexes of Relative Prices of Food Commodities, 1900–86*

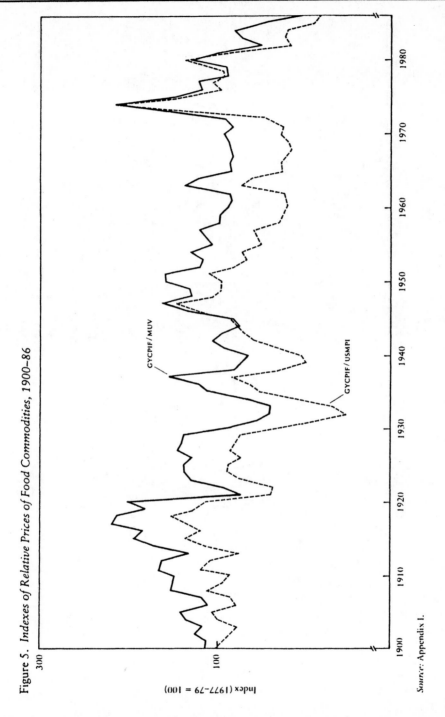

GYCPIF / MUV

GYCPIF / USMPI

Index (1977–79 = 100)

300

100

1900   1910   1920   1930   1940   1950   1960   1970   1980

Source: Appendix I.

Figure 6. *Indexes of Relative Prices of Nonfood Agricultural Commodities, 1900–86*

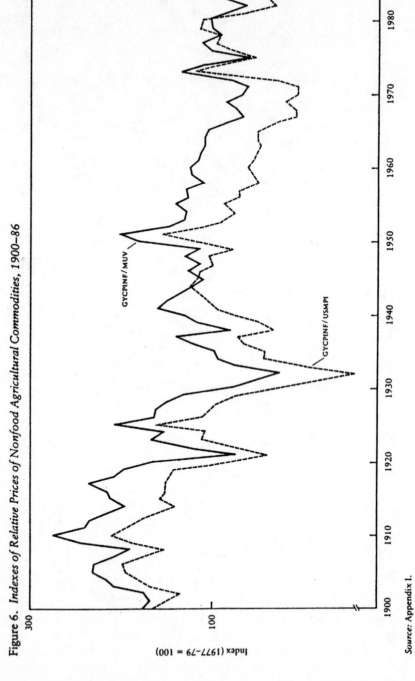

GYCPINF/MUV

GYCPINF/USMPI

Index (1977–79 = 100)

1900   1910   1920   1930   1940   1950   1960   1970   1980

300

100

Source: Appendix I.

Figure 7. *Indexes of Relative Prices of Metals, 1900–86*

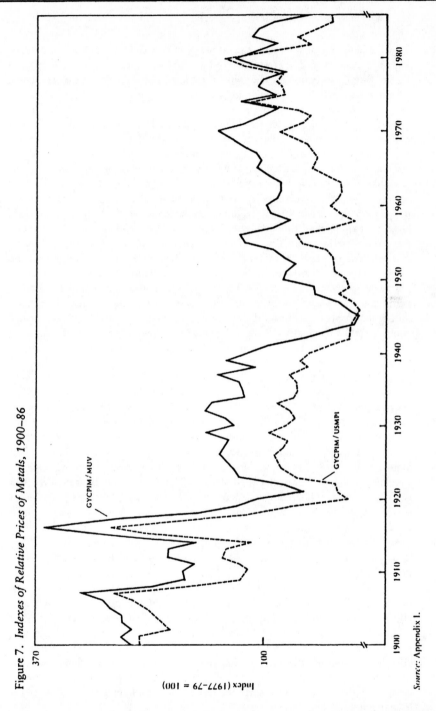

18 THE WORLD BANK ECONOMIC REVIEW, VOL. 2, NO. 1

with the behavior of the relative price index of cereals (GYCPICE/MUV, comprising wheat, maize, and rice), which exhibits a long-term falling trend (table 2 and figures 8–10). To gauge the economic significance of these relative price trends, it should be recalled that developing countries are the sole exporters of tropical beverages but are large net importers of most other foods, particularly cereals. Therefore, in drawing inferences between the trends in the purchasing power of commodities and the net barter terms of trade of developing countries, considerable care must be exercised, even when commodity prices are broken down into various subgroups and examined at a fairly high level of disaggregation.

Unlike food prices, whose trends have to be interpreted with great care, nonfood agricultural commodity prices appear to have fallen strongly and steadily relative to internationally traded manufactures. Developing countries are large net exporters of these commodities. Since 1900, the purchasing power of these products in terms of manufactures has fallen on trend by more than 50 percent. The rather devastating effect of synthetic product substitution on the prices of nonfood agricultural raw materials also becomes evident if one looks at the trend over the 1953–86 period (figure 6). It was in the mid-1950s that petroleum-based synthetic products began to exercise strong downward pressure on natural rubber and natural fiber prices (cotton, jute, wool). This pressure continued throughout the 1960s, and contrary to widely held expectations, the two oil shocks of the 1970s do not seem to have significantly modified the falling trend in the prices of nonfood agricultural commodities relative to those of manufactures.

The negative trend present in the relative prices of metals from 1900 to 1986, however, is not uniform over time. A clear break in the price trend occurs in the early 1940s (figure 7). Developing countries are large net exporters of minerals and metals, even though these commodities are also exported in large amounts by resource-rich industrial countries, such as Australia, Canada, and the United States. From 1900 to about 1941, the GYCPIM/MUV shows a strong negative trend (1.7 percent a year). Between 1942 and 1986 the trend turns positive (0.5 percent a year). The rising trend of the GYCPIM/MUV after 1941 was even stronger until the early 1970s. During a period of more than thirty years, metal producers seem to have been able to capture, in terms of realized prices, a good deal of the benefits deriving from the productivity gains that were achieved. And these have been considerable, at both the extraction and refinery stages (Kendrick 1961).

Seen against the rise in productivity realized in the past half-century, this increase in the "real" prices of metals implies rather clearly the existence of effective forms of market control by producers. The market power of the few multinational corporations that long dominated the production, smelting, and primary processing of many metals seems to have been brought to bear quite effectively. However, the weakening in the role played by multinational corporations in the production of metals relative to that of newly formed national companies that has occurred since the late 1960s may have already changed, at least in part, this historical pattern.

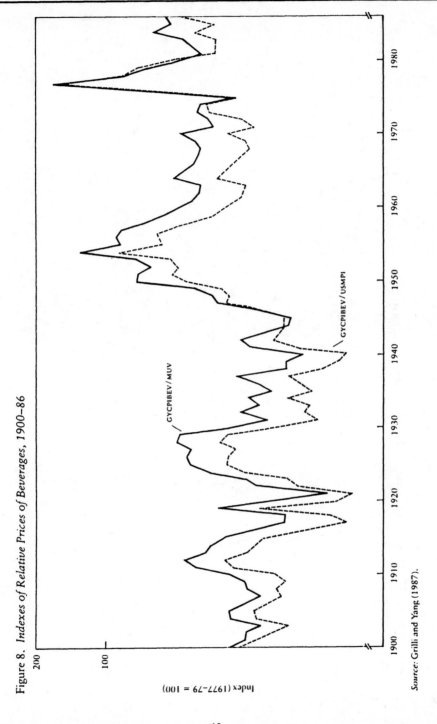

Figure 8. *Indexes of Relative Prices of Beverages, 1900–86*

Index (1977–79 = 100)

GYCPIBEV/MUV

GYCPIBEV/USMPI

Source: Grilli and Yang (1987).

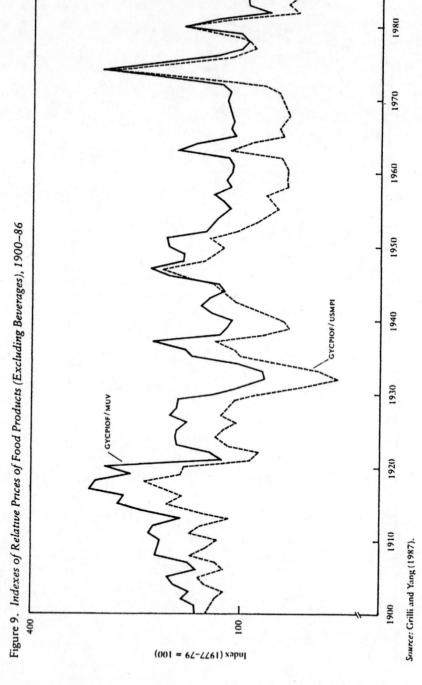

Figure 9. *Indexes of Relative Prices of Food Products (Excluding Beverages), 1900–86*

Index (1977–79 = 100)

GYCPIOF / MUV

GYCPIOF / USMPI

Source: Grilli and Yang (1987).

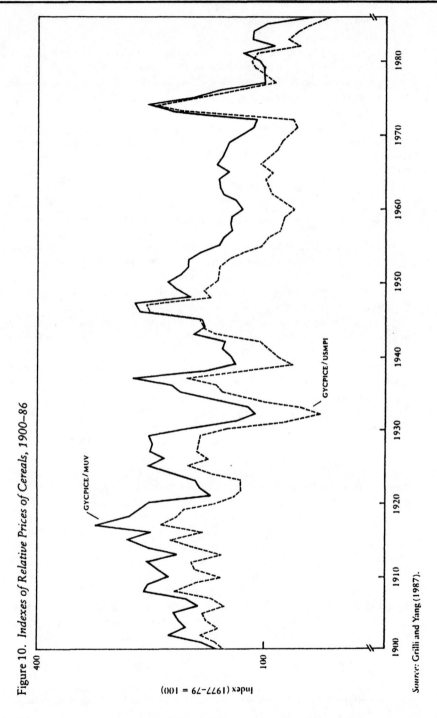

Figure 10. *Indexes of Relative Prices of Cereals, 1900–86*

Index (1977–79 = 100)

GYCPICE/MUV

GYCPICE/USMPI

400

100

1900   1910   1920   1930   1940   1950   1960   1970   1980

Source: Grilli and Yang (1987).

22   THE WORLD BANK ECONOMIC REVIEW, VOL. 2, NO. 1

The expansion in the number of independent producers (often state-owned companies in developing countries) has in itself complicated the global supply management problem.[6] The divergent productive strategies often pursued at the national level have further increased the difficulties faced by producers in keeping an effective hold on the market. What probably used to be a game quietly and effectively played by a few decisionmakers has now become a semipublic international political affair. The case of copper is highly representative of this trend. The weakening in the real prices of metal that has become evident in the mid and late 1970s is in part the reflection of this reduced ability of metal suppliers to influence the markets.

IV. COMMODITY PRICES AND TERMS OF TRADE OF DEVELOPING COUNTRIES

As previously indicated, the trend decline in the relative prices of primary commodities that seems to have occurred from 1900 to 1986 cannot be taken without qualification as a proxy for the evolution of net barter terms of trade of developing countries during the same period. This is the case, quite apart from the possibility that the decline in either the GYCPI/MUV or the GYCPI′′′/MUV may be overstated, given that some of the increase in the MUV may be caused by new manufactured products entering international trade or by improvements in the quality of existing ones. Developing countries, aside from exporting primary commodities and importing manufactures, have traditionally also exported manufactures and imported primary commodities. Moreover, the share of manufactures in the exports of developing countries has increased substantially over the years, going from an estimated 3.7 percent in 1899 to 21.1 percent in 1979 (Grilli 1982).

Statistical evidence relative to the post–World War II period shows, for instance, that the net barter terms of trade of non-oil-exporting developing countries are positively related to the ratio of prices of nonfuel commodities and manufactures (GYCPI/MUV) and are negatively related to the ratio of prices of oil and manufactures (OILP/MUV). The net barter terms of trade of non-oil-exporting developing countries improve on average when nonoil commodity prices rise, relative to manufactured good prices, and worsen when oil prices go up relative to those of manufactures, but the partial elasticity of the net barter terms of trade with respect to the GYCPI/MUV is only a fraction of one. The estimated relationships for various periods after 1950 are shown in table 3.

On the basis of the results obtained for the aggregate of developing countries from 1953 to 1983, the only period for which data on developing countries' terms of trade are available, the observed 40 percent decline in the relative prices of their nonfuel primary commodities since the turn of the century would imply,

---

6. Supply diffusion was helped by the breaking up of vertical integration in the industry after the first oil shock of 1973 and by the "security of supply" policies followed by large industrial countries. Japan, for example, encouraged through government finance the entry of new quasi-independent suppliers of metals in developing countries. We are indebted to Kenji Takeuchi for bringing this point to our attention.

Table 3. *Commodity Prices and Terms of Trade of Non-Oil-Exporting Developing Countries: Regression Results*

Group of countries, continent, or country	Constant term ($\hat{\alpha}$)	GYCPI MUV ($\hat{\beta}$)	OILP MUV ($\hat{\gamma}$)	R^2	SEE	DW	Rho	Years
		Coefficient			Regression statistics			
TOT: all								
non-oil-exporting	3.6301*	0.2786*	0.0890*	0.82	0.036	1.45	0.73	1953–83
	(10.4)	(3.55)	(−4.05)					
	3.5382*	0.3125*	0.1009*	0.82	0.039	1.60	0.63	1965–83
	(8.63)	(3.37)	(−4.22)					
TOT: Africa	3.0006*	0.4033*	0.0957*	0.88	0.046	1.62	0.91	1955–83
	(7.03)	(3.98)	(−2.41)					
	2.7077*	0.5472*	0.1569*	0.87	0.047	1.42	0.54	1965–83
	(4.46)	(3.98)	(−5.19)					
TOT: Southeast Asia[a]	2.4243*	0.5691*	0.1599*	0.92	0.061	1.84	0.80	1955–83
	(4.11)	(4.27)	(−3.80)					
	3.7206*	0.3409*	0.1400*	0.88	0.035	1.73	0.38	1965–83
	(7.27)	(3.02)	(−6.92)					
TOT: Latin America[b]	3.4199*	0.3681*	0.1764*	0.85	0.056	1.11	0.89	1965–83
	(6.11)	(2.72)	(−2.22)					
TOT: Korea	5.8968*	0.1807*	0.1354*	0.96	0.026	1.90	0.36	1965–83
	(21.3)	(−2.98)	(−12.7)					
TOT: Yugoslavia	5.2472*	0.1224*	0.0243*	0.79	0.015	1.77	—	1965–83
	(34.8)	(−3.49)	(−5.36)					
TOT: India[c]	5.1586*	0.0863	−0.1851*	0.80	0.056	1.49	0.48	1953–80
	(7.76)	(0.56)	(−6.04)					

t values in parentheses.

* = significant at the 10 percent confidence level or above.

— Uncorrected.

Note: The estimated model is $\text{TOT}_t = \alpha + \beta\,(\text{GYCPI}/\text{MUV})_t + \gamma\,(\text{OILP}/\text{MUV})_t + u_t$, where TOT_t = terms of trade of country(ies)/continent; $\text{GYCPI}/\text{MUV}_t$ = prices of nonfuel commodities relative to those of manufactures; and OILP/MUV_t = prices of oil relative to those of manufactures. OLS estimates are based on annual data; Cochrane-Orcutt serial correlation correction is used throughout. Equations are estimated in the levels of logarithms of all the variables. Country definitions and TOT data are from IMF *International Financial Statistics* and *Supplements on Trade and Prices.* "Korea" refers to the Republic of Korea.

a. Southeast Asia includes Malaysia, Philippines, Sri Lanka, and Thailand (recomputation of regional TOT index follows IMF weighting procedures).

b. Latin America includes Central America as well as South America. Data on TOT for Latin America are available only from the early 1960s onward and cover uniformly only a selected number of countries. No regression starting from the 1950s could be estimated as in the case of Africa, Southeast Asia, and all non-oil-exporting developing countries. A dummy variable for the 1976–77 coffee boom years was used in the regression. It has the right sign, and it is statistically significant.

c. India TOT data are available only to 1980. A dummy variable for the 1977 boom in tea prices was used in the regression. It has the right sign, and it is statistically significant.

other things being equal, a cumulative decline in non-oil-exporting developing countries' terms of trade of about 11 percent. Yet although there is no a priori reason to think that the set of statistical relationships bearing on the determination of net barter terms of trade of developing countries may have differed between the pre– and the post–World War II periods, the relative importance of

24   THE WORLD BANK ECONOMIC REVIEW, VOL. 2, NO. 1

the individual components of these movements has probably changed over time in a manner which suggests that these results may understate the extent of the decline in the terms of trade over the earlier period. The post–World War II period did witness the sharpest increase in the relative importance of manufactured products in the total exports and of oil in the total imports of non-oil-exporting developing countries. In previous years, when dependence on nonfuel primary commodity exports and manufactured product imports was more pronounced, the nexus between net barter terms of trade and nonfuel commodity prices might have been stronger (that is, the value of $\hat{\beta}$ for all non-oil-exporting developing countries in table 3 might have been higher than 0.28). Over the entire 1900–86 period the cumulative decline in non-oil-exporting developing countries net barter terms of trade corresponding to a 40 percent decline in the GYCPI/MUV may therefore have been greater than 11 percent, but in any case a fraction of the measured cumulative trend decline in GYCPI/MUV.

If we restrict our attention to the 1953–83 period, our analysis shows that non-oil-exporting commodity price changes remained an important influence on the net barter terms of trade of African and Southeast Asian countries, but were less important in the case of Latin American countries (table 3). Moreover, although the relative importance of nonoil commodity prices seems to have increased in recent years in the case of Africa, the opposite seems to have occurred for Southeast Asia. For Southeast Asian countries, which succeeded in diversifying their exports into manufactures, changes in nonfuel commodity prices are becoming a less important determinant of their net barter terms of trade movements. For African countries, increasingly dependent on traditional commodity exports, the movement is in the opposite direction.

At the country level, the relationship between nonfuel commodity prices and net barter terms of trade is even more diversified. Not only does the intensity of the (positive) relationship between these two variables differ, but its sign is reversed in some cases. For natural-resource-poor countries that have become principal exporters of manufactures, such as the Republic of Korea and Yugoslavia, a decline in the relative prices of nonfuel primary commodities tends to improve their net barter terms of trade. These countries behave now like industrial countries. India, conversely, constitutes an interesting intermediate situation: changes in nonfuel primary commodity prices relative to those of manufactures do not seem to affect significantly net barter terms of trade in one direction or another. Oil prices, however, are shown to be negatively related to net barter terms of trade changes in a consistent and significant way across the spectrum of non-oil-exporting developing regions and countries.

This analysis of the links between nonfuel commodity prices and net barter terms of trade of non-oil-exporting developing countries in the post–World War II period shows how difficult it is to draw valid conclusions over time and across countries, even from seemingly solid aggregate relationships. The inference remains possible that those developing countries that have continued to export primarily nonfuel commodities and import mostly manufactured products may have faced secularly worsening net barter terms of trade; but this needs to be qualified in both extent and significance.

Although the extent of the terms of trade loss suffered by any developing country or group of countries is largely an empirical question, the economic significance of any such loss is a more complex issue. If there exists an aggregate positive relationship between net barter terms of trade changes and profitability in commodity production, and between profitability in the commodity sector and investments, a secular deterioration in the relative prices of primary products may have had the consequence of holding down the growth potential of these countries via lower investment rates. Such a secular deterioration may also have led to distorted investment patterns, wherever resource mobility was constrained by lack of alternatives or by domestic price policies that did not reflect market forces.

The link between worsening net barter terms of trade and worsening sector profitability depends critically on factor productivity. It is only when reduction in the input of factors per unit of output does not fully compensate for the decline in relative output prices, and the returns to the factors employed in the primary commodity-producing sectors may diminish over time, that overall output growth is limited by lower profitability and underinvestment. The existence of such circumstances, however, is a factual question which is not only time- and country-specific but also probably specific to various export subsectors within the same country.

Even for those developing countries whose commodity and net barter terms of trade may have shown a secularly deteriorating trend, the conclusion that trade has been harming their growth should not be drawn solely on the basis of this type of evidence. Country- and sector-specific information is needed to measure the possible compensating effects of productivity growth in agriculture and mining. Even in the presence of deteriorating commodity terms of trade and net barter terms of trade, single factoral terms of trade may have moved in the opposite direction. At the global level—that is at the level at which our analysis of relative prices has been conducted—no strong evidence exists on secular factor productivity trends in the agriculture and mining sectors of non-oil-exporting developing countries. The growth-constraining effects of deteriorating commodity and net barter terms of trade, via production, for those developing countries that mainly export nonfuel primary products and mainly import manufactures thus remain indeterminate.

The reduction in real income (or purchasing power) evidenced by falling commodity and net barter terms of trade may also have constrained the growth possibilities of non-oil-exporting developing countries, and especially of those that have remained most dependent on nonfuel commodity exports, given that their capacity to import capital goods and other essential inputs was thereby reduced. Here, too, caution must be exercised in drawing conclusions from price evidence alone. The total real income effect of trade, under less than full employment conditions, depends on export quantities as well as on relative export

26   THE WORLD BANK ECONOMIC REVIEW, VOL. 2, NO. 1

prices. Under these conditions, a fall in purchasing power occurs only if the growth of export volumes is not enough to offset the decline in relative prices.

The evidence on the size of the real income effects of trade on developing countries is much stronger than evidence on the production effects. Both direct and indirect indicators point to a positive real income effect over time. The purchasing power of exports of all primary commodities in terms of manufactures increased at a trend rate of 4.5 percent a year from 1900 to 1913. Between 1921 and 1938 its growth was much smaller (0.4 percent a year), but still positive, notwithstanding the unfavorable trend of relative prices, which declined at 1.2 percent a year. In the period between 1955 and 1983 growth resumed strongly, with a trend rate of 4.2 percent a year. The purchasing power of developing countries' exports of nonfuel primary commodities also rose in the post–World War II period—at 2.8 percent a year between 1955 and 1983—as export volumes grew strongly (3.2 percent a year) in the face of a mild decline in relative prices (-0.4 percent a year). If oil is included in the sample, growth of purchasing power of commodity exports becomes even stronger (United Nations 1969; UNCTAD 1972, 1976, 1983, 1984; IMF 1982, 1985).

The direct evidence on the behavior of the income terms of trade of non-oil-exporting developing countries is even more persuasive from the early 1950s onward (Wilson, Sinha and Castree 1969). More recent data show that these improved on trend by 5.3 percent a year between 1953 to 1983, a period during which the net barter terms of trade of developing countries declined at about 0.6 percent a year, but overall export quantities rose at almost 6 percent a year. These trends are represented in figure 11, which shows the long-run tendency of the purchasing power of exports of primary products to grow in terms of manufactures.

In the presence of a strong improvement in the purchasing power of commodity exports and in the income terms of trade of non-oil-exporting developing countries, the negative welfare significance of falling relative prices of nonfuel primary commodities should not be overstated. Nor does there appear to be any strong reason to infer from available evidence either that trade per se or trade in nonfuel primary products has in the aggregate been harmful to countries specializing in their production. Obviously, immiserizing growth might have occurred in specific commodities or in specific periods, but its existence cannot be assumed. It must instead be proven and possibly explained in terms of the balance between autonomous factor supply growth (and/or technical progress), market structures, and government price and investment policies affecting output in the export sector. More important, one has to keep in mind that gains from trade are dynamic, far reaching in their effects, and cumulative over time. They go well beyond the direct production and real income effects of terms of trade changes.

V. THE EFFECT OF GROWTH ON RELATIVE PRIMARY COMMODITY PRICES: DID CLASSICAL ECONOMISTS GO WRONG?

The observed decline in the prices of nonfuel primary commodities relative to those of manufactures appears to contradict the tightly held belief of classical

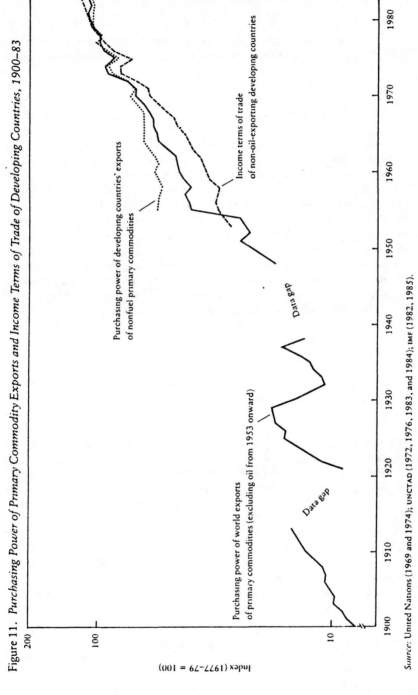

Figure 11. *Purchasing Power of Primary Commodity Exports and Income Terms of Trade of Developing Countries, 1900–83*

Source: United Nations (1969 and 1974); UNCTAD (1972, 1976, 1983, and 1984); IMF (1982, 1985).

27

economists that the expected outcome had to be in the opposite direction. Diminishing returns in primary commodity production and growing population, viewed against the effects of increasing specialization and technological progress in manufacturing, led these economists to expect a falling tendency in the prices of manufactures relative to those of raw materials (Ricardo 1817; Torrens 1821; Mill 1848).

The validity of the position of the classical economists not only remained virtually unquestioned throughout the nineteenth century but was reaffirmed in the current century by modern economists such as Keynes. Constant returns to scale in industry and decreasing returns in agriculture, along with population growth, Keynes argued, would have caused in the long run a decline in the relative prices of manufactured products and thus of the net barter terms of trade of the European countries (Keynes 1912, 1920). This is a conclusion that neoclassical trade theorists would find hard to accept without a precise specification of the shape of the production functions, in a situation where the greater capital intensity of manufacturing production relative to that of agricultural production is normally assumed to exist. It is only by postulating a relatively faster growth of capital (and not labor) in the manufacturing exporting sector, and by assuming away technical progress, that the presumption of deteriorating terms of trade of Europe could have been built on neoclassical grounds.

Yet notwithstanding the apparent theoretical shakiness of the classical economists' case, the Ricardian tradition on terms of trade developments was not seriously challenged until quite recently, with orthodox neoclassical economists not only sitting more or less on the sidelines, but alternating in their judgments on the very importance of the concept of terms of trade.[7] Prebisch and Singer independently—if almost simultaneously and much along the same lines—provided the economic rationale for the counterthesis that terms of trade were bound to deteriorate for developing countries exporting primary commodities and importing manufactured products from industrial countries. Though couched in seemingly unconventional terms, the original Prebisch-Singer counterargument in its essence is based on orthodox economic concepts. If productivity growth systematically shifts the supply curve for primary commodities to the right more than that for manufactured products, and income growth systematically shifts the demand curve for manufactures to the right more than that for primary commodities, the relative price of primary commodities in terms of manufactured goods will tend to decline over time (and to the extent that developing countries export primary products and import manufactures, their net barter terms of trade will tend to fall).

Cast in these terms, the original Prebisch-Singer conclusion on terms of trade between primary commodities and manufactures seems inescapable. Because the

---

7. Viner (1937) and Kindleberger (1956), among others, have stressed the importance of terms of trade changes, whereas economists such as Graham (1948) have not hesitated to call the terms of trade an irrelevant concept.

point on the higher income elasticity of demand for manufactured products is hardly debatable, what remains to be explained is why productivity growth has a different impact on the supply schedule of primary commodities with respect to that of manufactures. Prebisch and Singer assume competitive market structure in the case of primary commodities and oligopolistic market structure in the case of manufactures (Prebisch 1950; Singer 1950). This assumption is used to explain why the distribution of productivity gains between primary commodity producers and producers of manufactures is uneven (manufacturers would reap the benefits of the gains in terms of rising returns to factors of production, while primary commodity producers would pass it on to consumers in the form of falling prices). However, the device of resorting to the notion of different market structures and referring to the differential effects of productivity under oligopoly, although plausible on the surface, breaks down when one considers that productivity growth can hardly be taken as given and is probably in itself a function of the market form.

If the options for innovation are positively related to the size of the firm, which is much larger under oligopolistic market conditions than under competitive conditions, the rate of technical progress would tend to be greater under oligopolistic (or monopolist) market conditions than under free competition (Sylos-Labini 1956). If this is the case, and there is considerable empirical evidence that shows at least that firm concentration and productivity growth are positively related (Greer and Rhoades 1976; Scherer 1984), then the simple comparative static conclusions regarding prices and output under monopolistic or oligopolistic market conditions, as compared to competitive conditions, are no longer applicable. Output growth would also tend to expand faster under the push of technical progress in noncompetitive markets, a point that had not escaped Schumpeter (Schumpeter 1942).

Pending a more comprehensive analysis of the actual effects of growth on the terms of trade, it is incorrect to suggest that our empirical results on long-term relative price trends of nonfuel primary commodities simply validate the original Prebisch-Singer thesis (with which they appear to be compatible) and invalidate the classical conclusion (with which they appear to be incompatible). Other explanations of the empirical results that we obtained can be found outside both the classical and the original Prebisch-Singer models.

Within the neoclassical model of trade, if growth occurs in the export sector of developing countries and is the consequence of growth in factor endowments (say labor, producing labor-intensive goods), supplies of exports will rise and, other things being equal, developing countries' terms of trade will worsen. The size of the terms of trade effect will depend on elasticity conditions. If growth in exports occurs as a consequence of technical progress in the export sector, the effects will be similar.

Outside the neoclassical framework, one can find models of relations among unequal trading partners that would lead to the conclusions that developing countries' terms of trade are bound to decline (Emmanuel 1969; Amin 1973).

Singer himself has recently come close to this unorthodox tradition of unequal development, which strongly emphasizes the importance of the asymmetry that exists between different types of countries, instead of (or together with) the differences between various types of commodities (Singer 1975).

Methodological, as well as theoretical, explanations can also be put forward to explain the outcome of falling terms of trade. Exponential trends, such as those that we estimated to examine the basic tendencies shown by the relative prices of nonfuel primary commodities, are not always appropriate to depict an underlying reality that is changing significantly over time. An example of this can be found in the trend in the relative prices of metals in the 1900–86 period, which shows a clear primary tendency to fall, but a secondary tendency in the opposite direction. If one computes a parabolic (or log-parabolic) trend for the GYCPIM/MUV, the second term of the fitted parabola is found to be positive and statistically significant, whereas the first term is negative and statistically significant (table 4).[8] The explanatory power of the log-parabolic time model is also superior to that of the exponential model. No other subgroup of nonfuel commodity prices shows significant parabolic or log-parabolic trends over the period.

Such a time profile of the relative prices of nonrenewable resources such as metals can be thought of as the result of two sets of forces affecting their long-run costs of production: on the one hand, technological improvements make it possible to lower directly the unit costs of production of these commodities (for example, new mining and smelting techniques) or to augment the possibilities of producing them (for example, access to new lands and new ore deposits); on the other, limitations are imposed by the finiteness of available physical resources and the effects of decreasing returns (beyond a certain point). The impact of the first set of forces, which has so far been dominant and has tended to push down the real prices of metals, may have been progressively offset by the impact of the second set of forces, the net effect of which is in the opposite direction. Classical economists may have underestimated the extent and possibly the effects of emerging technical progress, and thus misjudged the "length of the long-run," but may still be on the right track in terms of the direction of expected changes in the relative prices of many primary commodities in the longer term.

VI. STATISTICAL LIMITS OF THE PRESENT RELATIVE PRICE ESTIMATES

The question that arises at this point is how reliable are the aggregate price indexes that were used here to measure long-term commodity and manufactured price movements. We have little doubt about the representativeness of the non-

---

8. Slade (1982) found evidence of a parabolic time pattern of prices at the level of single metals. She showed that this pattern is consistent with a model of long-run price determination where price equals marginal extraction costs and the rate of change of price is equal to that of marginal cost because of changes in technology, plus the discount rate times the rent.

Table 4. Quadratic Trends in the Relative Prices of the Principal Nonfuel Primary Commodity Subgroups, 1900–86

Relative price index	Intercept ($\hat{\alpha}$)	Linear coefficient of time ($\hat{\beta}_1$)	Quadratic coefficient of time ($\hat{\beta}_2$)	Regression statistics			
				R^2	SEE	F	DW
Tropical beverages: GYCPIBEV/MUV	42.859* (3.59)	0.21190 (0.34)	0.00187 (0.27)	0.08	11.73	3.6	1.80
Nonbeverage foods: GYCPIOF/MUV	149.67* (8.23)	−0.11903 (−0.12)	−0.00601 (−0.57)	0.14	20.67	6.8	1.80
Nonfood agricultural: GYCPINF/MUV	173.71* (10.60)	−1.4919* (−1.74)	0.00540 (0.57)	0.31	15.73	18.9	1.74
Metals: GYCPIM/MUV	208.25* (12.31)	−3.7843* (−4.26)	0.03035* (3.11)	0.39	18.96	27.27	1.43
Tropical beverages: ln GYCPIBEV/MUV	3.7854* (19.12)	0.00151 (0.15)	0.00005 (0.48)	0.50	0.17	42.30	1.75
Nonbeverage foods: ln GYCPIOF/MUV	4.9667* (35.90)	0.00145 (0.20)	−0.00008 (−0.98)	0.70	0.15	99.53	1.65
Nonfood agricultural: ln GYCPINF/MUV	5.1384* (40.03)	−0.00905 (−1.34)	0.00001 (0.14)	0.79	0.13	152.21	1.73
Metals: ln GYCPIM/MUV	5.3570* (39.00)	−0.02609* (−3.63)	0.00020* (2.58)	0.81	0.12	184.07	1.47

t values in parentheses.

* = significant at the 10 percent confidence level or above.

Note: The estimated model is ln $GYCPI_t = \alpha_0 + \beta_1 t_t + \beta_2 t_t^2 + u_t$. All time series are trend-stationary, and OLS estimates are based on annual data. A maximum-likelihood procedure was used to correct for serial correlation.

fuel commodities price index that we built. Within the class of index to which it belongs, the tracking behavior of the GYCPI should be more than acceptable, given its coverage, the care taken in choosing representative quotations for each of the twenty-four products included in it, and the results of the various experiments that were conducted to test its sensitivity to different weight schemes. The MUV, on the other hand, is an index of unit values of exports and thus potentially open to more serious questions about its ability to represent market prices.

Although comparison with the USMPI, which represents domestic prices of tradable manufactured products in the United States, seems to confirm the broad representativeness of the MUV as an indicator of long-term trends in manufactured good prices, the appropriateness of the use of the MUV is still open to doubt on account of possible differences between unit values of exports and international market prices. Available empirical evidence on international prices of manufactured goods is still limited. Kravis and Lipsey have built an index of manufactured good prices (KLI) covering the 1953–77 period and the same SITC product categories as are included in the MUV. Compared with the MUV, this new price index shows a much smaller cumulative increase over the period (127 percent as opposed to 153 percent), leading them to conclude that the U.N. unit value index overestimates the growth of prices of internationally traded manufactured goods (Kravis and Lipsey 1981).

The KLI, however, shows a markedly different behavior from that of the MUV only from 1973 onwards. From 1953 to 1972, KLI and MUV movements are remarkably close to one another: their cumulative increase at end points is respectively 41.1 percent and 45.6 percent. It is only in the following five years, characterized by severe monetary and exchange rate turmoil in the world economy and by a major supply shock (1973–74), that the two indexes apparently diverge widely. The KLI shows an increase of 60.7 percent (at end points), whereas the MUV goes up by 73.9 percent.

This strong divergence of the two indexes after 1972 is magnified by several factors. The KLI, apart from its different construction, covers only the prices of manufactures exported by six industrial countries—Canada, the Federal Republic of Germany, Japan, the Netherlands, the United Kingdom, and the United States—whereas the MUV reflects the unit value of exports of five additional countries—Belgium, France, Italy, Sweden, and Switzerland. Of this latter group, the first four are countries that experienced relatively high inflation rates, reflected in part in their faster-than-average growth in the dollar unit values of the manufactures that they exported after 1972.

Moreover, Kravis and Lipsey have complete price information only up to 1975.[9] A strict comparison between the two indexes is thus possible only for the 1973–75 period and should be conducted not on the basis of the overall U.N. MUV index, but of a subindex including the same six countries covered in the KLI. When this is done, one finds that over the 1953 to 1972 period the two indexes show a very similar behavior: the KLI increases by 41.1 percent at end points and the modified MUV by 43.9 percent. Between 1973 and 1975 the KLI increases by 46.1 percent, whereas the modified MUV increases by 59.5 percent. The difference is still large, but we feel that no strong conclusion can be reached on the basis of the behavior of the two indexes over such a short and atypical period of time. The problem of the representativeness of export unit value therefore remains. On the basis of available evidence, it seems that its practical importance may have been exaggerated.

9. Prices for the Netherlands in 1976 and 1977 are missing from KLI, and German prices are not available for 1977 (Kravis and Lipsey 1981, table 2).

The remaining open question regarding our measures of long-term relative price changes has to do with the so-called quality bias, which is potentially worrisome, particularly in the case of manufactured goods. The quality bias has two dimensions. The first has to do with the rate of increase in the number of new manufactured products entering trade, causing changes in the internal composition of the various commodity groups over time. The second has to do with the direct improvement in the quality of the same goods whose prices are measured over time. Even if it were possible to keep unchanged over time the basket of manufactured goods whose prices are to be measured and to deal in this way with the problem of new goods, part of the increase shown by the index would simply represent the effects of improvements in the quality and performance of existing goods.

Some quality improvement of this type should also be reflected in the prices of primary commodities. Our index is based on uniform weights and a single representative market quotation for each product. Quality improvements in commodities such as tea, coffee, rubber, cotton, and vegetable oils did occur over time, even if they are not fully reflected in our index. If quality improvements could be measured by averaging market quotations of various grades and by accounting for the changes in their relative importance, one could presume that such a price index would be positively affected over time by quality improvements. An index of export unit values would also reflect this effect. Yet it can be reasonably assumed that manufactured goods prices reflect more of this upward drift on account of both changes in composition and quality improvement of traded goods. The question that arises is how much more. The empirical evidence on this point is still very scarce.

Kravis and Lipsey have recently constructed an index of U.S. prices of machinery and transport equipment (SITC7) and corrected it for quality improvements, showing that the quality bias accounted for about a quarter of the cumulative price increase over the 1953–76 period (Kravis and Lipsey 1981, table 3). They are inclined to think that a quality bias of such magnitude may be common to the price indexes of SITC7 manufactures exported by the major industrial countries over the same period. We find it hard to accept this assumption, given that for this group of manufactured goods—which includes electrical, electronic, and telecommunication equipment—and for most of the time period covered by this Kravis and Lipsey index, the rate of technological change has probably been faster in the United States than elsewhere.

Whatever may be the merit to this objection to the geographical representativeness of this U.S.-based index, using it to correct for quality improvements across the spectrum of manufactures, as Kravis and Lipsey do, necessitates the acceptance of an even stronger assumption: that the quality improvment factor present in the prices of SITC7 manufactures be considered representative of that of all other categories, from chemical products (SITC5), to manufactured goods classified chiefly by material (SITC6), to miscellaneous manufactures (SITC8). We find that there is no logical or empirical basis for accepting this assumption of equal rate of technological change in such different categories of goods. If anything, one would be prone to assume the opposite, that is, that the quality improvement factor reflected in the prices of SITC7 manufactures may be much larger than that reflected in the prices of SITC5, SITC6, and SITC8 manufactures.

Our conclusion is that the cumulative trend decline shown by the relative price indexes of nonfuel primary commodities that we computed over the 1900–86 period cannot be assumed away simply resorting to either the notion of unit value bias or of quality bias. The available evidence to the contrary is neither totally persuasive nor sufficiently precise to cast overwhelming doubt on it.

VII. Conclusions

Our new series indicate that, relative both to the prices of manufactured goods traded within the United States and to the export unit values of manufactures from industrial countries, nonfuel commodity prices have fallen considerably between 1900 and 1986. A cumulative trend decline of about 40 percent, though possibly magnified by the relatively greater effect of quality improvements on the prices of manufactured products, probably reflects a net fall in the purchasing power of a given basket of nonfuel primary commodities during the past century. No strong evidence of change was found in the negative trend shown over this period by our index of nonfuel commodity prices deflated by the index of unit value of exports of manufactures.

The long-run tendencies in the relative prices of the major subgroups of nonfuel primary commodities, however, are far from uniform. Nonfood agricultural raw materials appear to have sustained the steadiest reduction in purchasing power in terms of manufactured products. Metals, conversely, though showing the strongest overall negative trend in their relative prices over the current century, did experience a precipitous fall until the early 1940s and a strong inversion of that tendency since then. Agricultural food products, considered together, exhibit a substantially smaller trend decline in their relative prices than that of the other two major commodity groups. The trend in the aggregate of food product prices, however, is the result of sharply different within-group tendencies. Beverage prices have increased substantially over time relative to those of manufactures, while those of other food products, including cereals, have declined markedly over the same period.

We also found that the prices of all primary commodities (including fuels) relative to those of traded manufactures declined by about 36 percent over the 1900–86 period, at an average annual rate of 0.5 percent. These results tend to confirm those of Lewis, which were derived using different price information and over a different time period. The results also indicate, however, that the decline in the net barter terms of trade of all primary commodities shown by the data used by Prebisch represents a considerable overstatement of the long-term trend.

The average rate of decline of about 0.6 percent a year in the relative prices of nonfuel commodities that we found over the 1900–86 period does not indicate a similar rate of decline in the net barter terms of trade of non-oil-exporting developing countries. These countries in fact have exported over time increasing amounts of fuel products and manufactures, in addition to nonfuel commodities, and always have imported fuels and nonfuel primary commodities, in addition to manufactures. We found that in the post–World War II period, other things being equal, a decline of 1 percent in the relative prices of nonfuel primary commodities is associated with a 0.28 percent decline in the net barter terms of trade of non-oil-exporting developing countries considered as a whole. It is conceivable that in the earlier part of the century the value of this partial elasticity might have been higher, because of the lower share of manufactures in their exports and of oil in their imports. But to judge even notionally the extent of the effective fall that might have taken place since 1900 one should not forget that: (a) the cumulative trend decline that we observed in our price data may have been somewhat exaggerated by an imperfect account of quality improvements in manufactures, and (b) considerable differences in the relationships between net barter terms of trade and relative prices of nonfuel primary commodities are evident both at the regional and at the country level.

Even greater caution needs to be exercised in drawing conclusions on gains from trade for the developing countries on the basis of export price information alone. Although a deterioration in net barter terms of trade indicates a reduction in real income gains, with respect to a situation of unchanged terms of trade, the actual magnitude of the real income effect over time also depends critically on export quantities. The assumption of constant full employment of resources is not tenable in the analysis of the effects of trade over time. Available evidence indicates that, even if one disregards trade in manufactures and fuels, exports of nonfuel primary commodities by developing countries have grown in terms of volume at appreciably positive rates since 1900. This has given rise to a positive growth in the total purchasing power of nonfuel commodity exports. In the post–World War II period, moreover, available empirical evidence on the income terms of trade of non-oil-exporting developing countries indicates that consistent and substantial gains were obtained by them.

The extent of production effects of falling relative prices of primary commodities is uncertain, given the lack of evidence on long-term factor productivity growth in the agricultural and mining sectors of the developing countries. The presumption, however, is that the negative effects of declining real export prices may have been at least in part mitigated by productivity growth.

There is no comprehensive empirical analysis of the effects of growth on the net barter terms of trade of primary commodities. What can be said about the reasons for this apparent secular deterioration in the relative prices of primary commodities therefore is limited. The simple primary trends that we measured appear to go against the expectations of classical economists regarding the rela-

36   THE WORLD BANK ECONOMIC REVIEW, VOL. 2, NO. 1

tive price movements of manufactured goods and instead to be consistent with the original Prebisch-Singer counterargument. It is not difficult, however, to show how these empirical findings can be theoretically explained outside both the classical and the original Prebisch-Singer frameworks. Neoclassical analysis of the effects of growth on relative trade prices offers numerous possible alternative explanations, and so does unequal development theory.

APPENDIX I. PRICE INDEXES OF PRIMARY COMMODITIES AND MANUFACTURES

Year	GYCPI	GYCPI'	GYCPI''	GYCPI'''	MUV	USMPI	GYPIF	GYPINF	GYCPIM
1900	19.309	20.748	20.391	19.214	14.607	15.382	15.587	21.310	27.778
1901	18.236	18.802	18.765	17.604	13.858	15.169	14.716	19.292	27.522
1902	18.145	17.703	18.772	17.532	13.483	16.180	15.209	19.268	25.518
1903	19.006	19.808	20.543	19.099	13.483	16.340	14.634	22.860	26.668
1904	20.586	21.790	22.220	20.581	13.858	16.393	16.444	24.450	27.526
1905	21.621	23.101	23.765	21.938	13.858	16.499	16.924	26.226	29.150
1906	21.610	23.344	23.877	22.054	14.607	17.032	15.422	27.547	31.726
1907	22.757	23.489	23.793	22.070	15.356	17.883	16.672	25.967	36.699
1908	20.427	20.670	22.570	20.970	14.232	17.245	18.276	22.291	24.245
1909	21.554	23.244	25.506	23.541	14.232	18.575	18.143	28.973	20.822
1910	22.630	26.053	26.618	24.561	14.232	19.373	18.088	32.924	21.026
1911	21.909	24.722	25.328	23.385	14.232	17.830	19.498	28.122	19.923
1912	22.640	24.911	26.023	24.077	14.607	18.948	19.739	28.188	23.176
1913	20.461	21.817	23.443	21.820	14.607	19.161	17.149	25.440	23.134
1914	20.210	20.383	23.579	21.933	13.858	18.130	19.509	22.239	19.291
1915	24.468	23.140	26.851	25.012	14.232	18.594	22.292	24.388	31.321
1916	31.933	29.920	32.753	30.710	17.603	24.105	26.497	30.897	50.327
1917	39.396	33.817	44.339	41.277	20.974	31.419	37.074	40.257	45.271
1918	42.028	36.036	47.002	43.852	25.468	33.943	43.861	42.841	35.121
1919	39.208	34.348	48.802	46.069	26.966	35.334	39.902	43.292	30.853
1920	41.951	40.925	50.275	48.313	28.839	44.141	47.052	39.641	29.684
1921	21.356	18.987	26.111	24.911	24.345	28.689	21.602	21.605	20.219
1922	21.910	20.047	28.973	27.213	21.723	28.020	21.147	24.771	19.919
1923	26.407	26.013	33.632	31.482	21.723	28.638	25.234	29.989	24.587
1924	26.521	24.951	33.292	31.066	21.723	27.350	26.086	28.365	25.066
1925	29.381	28.716	36.139	33.563	22.097	28.123	26.637	36.978	26.315
1926	25.758	24.828	30.987	28.854	20.974	27.402	24.250	28.691	25.962
1927	25.143	23.462	30.585	28.450	19.850	26.355	24.677	26.823	24.028
1928	24.423	21.756	30.216	28.012	19.850	26.327	24.217	25.393	23.585

(Table continues on the following page.)

APPENDIX I. CONTINUED

Year	GYCPI	GYCPI'	GYCPI''	GYCPI'''	MUV	USMPI	GYPIF	GYPINF	GYCPIM
1929	23.266	20.637	26.437	24.516	19.101	25.882	23.098	22.332	25.210
1930	18.277	15.365	19.797	18.570	18.727	23.935	17.838	16.949	21.655
1931	13.610	11.282	13.977	13.240	15.356	21.441	12.675	12.308	18.479
1932	10.797	8.9658	10.685	10.150	12.734	19.156	9.7342	8.9577	16.883
1933	12.591	10.490	13.650	12.893	14.232	19.691	10.833	12.357	18.388
1934	15.763	13.522	17.523	16.513	16.854	21.609	14.522	16.427	18.591
1935	17.294	14.592	18.781	17.631	16.479	21.468	17.465	16.229	18.383
1936	18.418	15.659	20.491	19.213	16.479	21.723	18.369	18.348	18.677
1937	21.361	17.501	24.733	22.798	16.854	23.561	21.988	20.366	20.931
1938	16.552	14.025	18.504	17.389	17.603	22.472	16.105	16.198	18.474
1939	16.019	14.369	18.551	17.324	16.105	22.697	14.267	17.499	19.188
1940	17.237	15.230	20.407	19.100	17.603	23.219	15.063	20.547	18.932
1941	20.093	18.263	23.857	22.337	18.727	24.913	18.288	24.844	18.452
1942	23.073	21.359	27.217	25.403	21.723	27.010	22.419	27.716	18.039
1943	24.283	21.319	29.168	27.193	24.345	27.264	23.905	29.094	18.132
1944	25.243	21.912	30.246	28.222	27.715	27.469	24.816	30.786	18.132
1945	25.832	22.643	31.109	29.021	28.464	27.864	26.186	30.112	18.232
1946	31.232	26.216	36.901	34.182	28.839	30.603	34.314	32.688	19.485
1947	40.389	34.875	45.858	42.408	34.831	37.474	46.952	37.349	24.709
1948	38.722	35.114	44.106	41.895	35.581	40.044	41.107	40.934	27.980
1949	35.845	32.359	41.753	39.009	33.333	39.557	38.930	35.727	26.479
1950	39.263	38.393	47.761	44.316	30.337	40.858	40.130	45.060	27.767
1951	48.093	47.245	58.834	54.094	35.955	45.348	47.929	58.702	32.466
1952	40.508	39.284	46.741	43.925	36.704	44.134	40.623	45.983	31.825
1953	37.897	36.348	42.910	36.998	35.206	44.386	38.289	40.839	32.214
1954	38.565	39.134	43.612	37.620	34.457	44.657	39.738	39.797	33.066
1955	38.233	39.165	44.655	38.450	34.831	45.447	36.107	42.537	38.267
1956	39.895	40.585	45.133	39.075	36.330	47.517	38.747	41.517	40.977
1957	40.108	41.108	45.080	39.227	36.704	49.149	40.525	42.372	35.376

Year									
1958	36.231	35.998	40.368	35.226	36.330	49.742	36.235	38.647	32.546
1959	37.113	35.951	42.153	36.144	36.330	50.514	35.926	40.667	35.379
1960	37.327	36.183	42.312	35.965	37.079	50.490	35.305	41.799	36.781
1961	36.466	34.491	40.374	34.605	37.453	50.267	34.917	40.424	35.242
1962	36.486	34.275	40.715	34.888	37.453	50.310	35.377	39.893	34.734
1963	41.419	41.656	46.842	39.787	37.453	50.229	44.723	39.084	34.747
1964	41.046	39.962	45.517	38.659	38.202	50.502	42.774	39.782	37.620
1965	38.119	35.314	40.953	35.063	38.951	50.918	36.429	39.990	40.499
1966	37.935	34.192	40.766	34.879	39.700	51.891	37.325	37.445	40.568
1967	36.846	33.593	39.162	33.585	39.700	52.713	36.830	33.813	41.509
1968	37.431	34.033	39.357	33.605	39.326	53.973	36.718	34.620	43.914
1969	39.761	37.565	42.378	36.046	40.449	55.521	38.322	37.459	47.712
1970	42.201	40.421	43.668	37.161	42.697	57.627	41.381	36.438	53.500
1971	42.324	39.919	43.429	37.397	45.318	59.583	42.051	37.638	50.293
1972	46.625	45.176	50.407	43.318	48.689	61.325	47.037	43.823	49.613
1973	69.472	63.184	76.502	65.043	58.801	63.977	74.123	69.054	55.720
1974	102.41	104.01	111.28	103.46	71.161	74.371	123.33	74.718	79.813
1975	85.156	83.693	91.786	88.288	79.026	83.260	97.598	65.807	76.090
1976	83.110	83.077	85.553	83.775	78.652	87.946	85.707	78.946	81.408
1977	93.125	98.295	92.723	90.871	86.517	92.641	96.064	90.681	87.752
1978	93.627	93.165	93.198	91.662	98.876	99.163	94.159	94.173	91.149
1979	113.25	108.54	114.54	120.82	114.61	108.20	109.78	115.15	121.10
1980	138.83	140.34	155.33	182.10	125.47	119.65	142.99	126.49	144.72
1981	117.94	112.00	128.81	183.92	119.10	130.30	120.38	108.87	124.21
1982	96.784	90.110	100.51	178.32	115.73	135.62	92.364	96.727	110.54
1983	102.78	95.356	107.86	163.00	110.49	138.31	97.566	103.15	118.37
1984	103.54	94.533	104.21	159.30	108.61	142.54	99.686	105.29	112.81
1985	91.268	82.578	92.665	151.62	109.59	144.91	87.022	90.490	105.59
1986	88.358	84.059	90.788	93.759	130.30	144.36	84.013	86.026	105.34

Note: GYCPI, GYCPI' and GYCPI'' = indexes of prices of nonfuel primary commodities; GYCPI''' = index of prices of all primary commodities; MUV = index of unit values of exports of manufactures from industrial countries; USMPI = index of wholesale prices of manufactures in the United States; GYCPIF, GYCPINF, GYCPIM = index of prices of food, nonfood agricultural raw materials and metals (sub-indexes of GYCPI).

Source: Grilli and Yang (1987).

40   THE WORLD BANK ECONOMIC REVIEW, VOL. 2, NO. 1

APPENDIX II
TESTS ON THE STABILITY OF THE ESTIMATED TIME TREND OF GYCPI/MUV

Given that both the GYCPI/MUV and the GYCPI'''/MUV price series show three possible common breaks in 1921, 1932, and 1945, we tested first for equality between the estimated coefficients of the regression covering the years before the possible break and those of the regression for the years subsequent to it. To do so we used the dummy variable procedure suggested by Gujarati (1970a, 1970b). This test involves the OLS estimates of the following single regression model:

(1) $$\ln (P_c/P_m)_i = \alpha_0 + \beta_l t_i + \alpha_l D_i + \beta_2 (D_i t_i) + u_i$$

where P_c/P_m is either GYCPI/MUV or GYCPI'''/MUV, t_i is a time trend, and D_i is a dummy variable $= 0$ up to (but excluding) the year of break, and $= 1$ in subsequent years.

In this model α_l is the differential intercept coefficient, and β_2 is the differential slope coefficient. The standard statistical significance tests can be performed on their estimated values ($\hat{\alpha}_l$ and $\hat{\beta}_2$) to judge whether the two regressions implicit in this model have a common intercept, a common slope, or both.

The regression results, shown in appendix tables 1 and 3, indicate that there is no strong evidence of parameter shifts, in terms of either slope or intercept, of the estimated trend lines of the GYCPI/MUV and the GYCPI'''/MUV at any of the assumed break points. None of the $\hat{\alpha}_l$ and $\hat{\beta}_2$ parameters is statistically significant at at least the 10 percent level.

After testing for shifts in the slope and intercept of the estimated exponential time trend of the GYCPI/MUV and GYCPI'''/MUV, we tested for the possibility of a change in slope, assuming no discontinuity in the time trends, by using the following piecewise model (Suits, Mason, and Chan 1978):

(2) $$\ln (P_c/P_m) = \alpha_0 + \beta_l t_i + \beta_2 (t_i - t^*) D_i + u_i$$
where t_i is a time trend; D_i is a dummy variable $= 1$ when $t_i > t^*$, and $= 0$ when $t_i < t^*$; and t^* is the threshold year.

In this model β_1 gives the slope of the first segment of the regression line, while $(\beta_1 + \beta_2)$ gives the slope of the second segment of the regression line. The threshold years are 1921, 1932, and 1945. The hypothesis of no break in the slope of the regression lines at the threshold years can be tested by looking at the statistical significance of $\hat{\beta}_2$.

The results, shown in appendix tables 2 and 4, again indicate that at none of the possible break years is there evidence that a break may have actually occurred in the regression lines.[10] The statistical significance of the $\hat{\beta}_2$ coefficients in either lines 2-1 to 2-3 or lines 4-1 to 4-3 is consistently below 10 percent.

---

10. We also tested for multiple structural breaks but found no evidence of them.

Appendix table 1. *Dummy Variable Analysis of Trends in the Relative Prices of Nonfuel Primary Commodities, 1900–86*

Relative price index	Intercept ($\hat{\alpha}_0$)	Coefficient of dummy ($\hat{\alpha}_1$)	Coefficient of time ($\hat{\beta}_1$)	Coefficient of time and dummy ($\hat{\beta}_2$)	Regression statistics			
					R^2	SEE	F	DW
1-1 ln GYCPI/MUV	4.89149* (51.3)	-0.12237 (-0.90)	0.01262* (1.83)	-0.01521* (-2.07)	0.80	0.09	108.9	1.55
1-2 ln GYCPI/MUV	5.05227* (51.7)	-0.24853 (-1.37)	-0.00908* (-1.90)	0.00596 (1.04)	0.74	0.11	77.3	1.69
1-3 ln GYCPI/MUV	5.03845* (63.0)	-0.08256 (-0.34)	-0.00900* (-3.20)	0.00377 (0.80)	0.74	0.11	76.8	1.71

* = significant at the 10 percent confidence level or above.

Note: t values in parentheses.

The estimated model is ln GYCPI/MUV, $= \alpha_0 + \alpha_1 D_i + \beta_1 t_i + \beta_2 (D_i t_i) + u_i$, where t_i is a time trend, D_i is a dummy variable $= 0$ up to 1920 in 1-1, 1931 in 1-2, and 1944 in 1-3 and $= 1$ in subsequent years; OLS estimates on annual data; a maximum-likelihood procedure was used to correct for serial correlation.

41

Appendix table 2. *Piecewise Regression Analysis of the Trends in the Relative Prices of Nonfuel Primary Commodities, 1900–86*

Relative price index	Intercept ($\hat{\alpha}_0$)	Coefficient of time ($\hat{\beta}_1$)	Coefficient of time and dummy ($\hat{\beta}_2$)	Regression statistics			
				R^2	SEE	F	DW
2-1 ln GYCPI/MUV	5.01402* (50.7)	-0.00838 (-1.57)	0.00313 (0.49)	0.74	0.11	114.9	1.72
2-2 ln GYCPI/MUV	5.04433* (57.3)	-0.00943* (-2.64)	0.00544 (1.08)	0.74	0.11	116.0	1.71
2-3 ln GYCPI/MUV	5.01496* (59.2)	-0.00746* (-2.78)	0.00358 (0.70)	0.74	0.11	115.2	1.71

* = significant at the 10 percent confidence level or above.

Note: t values in parentheses.

The estimated model is ln GYCPI/MUV$_t$ = $\alpha_0 + \beta_1 t_t + \beta_2 (t_t - t^*) D_t + u_t$, where t is a time trend, D_t is a dummy variable = 0 up to 1920 in 2-1, 1931 in 2-2 and 1945 in 2-3 and = 1 in subsequent years, and t^* = 1921 in 2-1, 1932 in 2-2, and 1945 in 2-3. OLS estimates on annual data; a maximum-likelihood procedure was used to correct for serial correlation.

Appendix table 3. *Dummy Variable Analysis of Trends in the Relative Prices of All Primary Commodities, 1900–86*

Relative price index	Intercept ($\hat{\alpha}_0$)	Coefficient of dummy ($\hat{\alpha}_1$)	Coefficient of time ($\hat{\beta}_1$)	Coefficient of time and dummy ($\hat{\beta}_2$)	Regression statistics			
					R^2	SEE	F	DW
3-1 ln GYCPI'''/MUV	4.87483* (33.3)	-0.05912 (-0.28)	0.01711* (1.68)	-0.01937* (-1.75)	0.73	0.12	72.6	1.37
3-2 ln GYCPI'''/MUV	5.06205* (37.7)	-0.29885 (-1.19)	-0.00667 (-1.03)	0.00520 (0.66)	0.68	0.13	58.4	1.50
3-3 ln GYCPI'''/MUV	5.05007* (42.4)	-0.21785 (-0.61)	-0.00739* (-1.81)	0.00490 (0.69)	0.68	0.13	57.0	1.51

* = significant at the 10 percent confidence level or above.

Note: t values in parentheses.

The estimated model is ln GYCPI'''/MUV$_t$ = $\alpha_0 + \alpha_1 D_t + \beta_1 t + \beta_2 (D_t t_t) + u_t$, where: t_t is a time trend, and D_t is a dummy variable = 0 up to 1920 in 3-1, 1931 in 3-2, and 1944 in 3-3 and = 1 in subsequent years. OLS estimates on annual data; a maximum-likelihood procedure was used to correct for serial correlation.

43

Appendix table 4. *Piecewise Regression Analysis of the Trends in the Relative Prices of All Primary Commodities, 1900–86*

Relative price index	Intercept $(\hat{\alpha}_0)$	Coefficient of time $(\hat{\beta}_1)$	Coefficient of time and dummy $(\hat{\beta}_2)$	Regression statistics			
				R^2	SEE	F	DW
4-1 ln GYCPI'''/MUV	4.99781* (36.9)	−0.00481 (−0.67)	−0.00030 (−0.03)	0.68	0.13	86.0	1.52
4-2 ln GYCPI'''/MUV	5.05294* (40.1)	−0.00803 (−1.58)	0.00455 (0.63)	0.68	0.13	86.5	1.51
4-3 ln GYCPI'''/MUV	5.04872* (43.4)	−0.00728* (−1.98)	0.00493 (0.70)	0.68	0.13	86.5	1.51

* = significant at the 10 percent confidence level or above.

Note: t values in parentheses.

The estimated model is GYCPI'''/MUV$_t$ = $\alpha_0 + \beta_1 t + \beta_2 (t_t - t^*) D_t + u_t$, where t is a time trend, D_t is a dummy variable = 0 up to 1920 in 4-1, 1931 in 4-2, and 1945 in 4-3 and = 1 in subsequent years, and t^* = 1921 in 4-1, 1932 in 4-2, and 1945 in 4-3. OLS estimates on annual data; a maximum-likelihood procedure was used to correct for serial correlation.

References

Amin, Samir. 1973. *Le Développement Inégal.* Paris: Editions de Minuit. (English ed., New York: Monthly Review Press, 1976.)

Baldwin, R. E. (1955). "Secular Movements in the Terms of Trade." *American Economic Review, Papers and Proceedings* 45, no. 2 (May): 259–69.

———. 1966. *Economic Development and Growth.* New York: Wiley.

Dickey, D. A., and W. A. Fuller. 1979. "Distribution of the Estimators for Autoregressive Time Series with a Unit Root." *Journal of the American Statistical Association* 74, no. 366 (June): 427–31.

The Economist, March 2, 1974.

Ellsworth, P. T. 1956. "The Terms of Trade between Primary Producing Countries and Industrial Countries." *Inter-American Economic Affairs* 10, no. 1 (Summer): 47–65.

Emmanuel, A. 1969. *L'Echange Inégal.* Paris: F. Maspero. (English ed., New York: Monthly Review Press, 1972.)

Graham, F. 1948. *Theory of International Values.* Princeton, N.J.: Princeton University Press.

Greer, D. F., and S. A. Rhoades. 1976. "Concentration and Productivity Changes in the Long and the Short Run." *Southern Economic Journal* 43, no. 2 (October): 1031–44.

Grilli, Enzo R. 1982. *Materie Prime ed Economia Mondiale* (Primary Commodities and the World Economy). Bologna: Il Mulino.

Grilli, Enzo R., and Maw Cheng Yang. 1987. "Long-Term Movements of Non-Fuel Commodity Prices: 1900–86." World Bank International Economics Department Working Paper. Washington, D.C. Processed.

Gujarati, D. 1970a. "Use of Dummy Variables in Testing for Equality between Sets of Coefficients in Two Linear Regressions: A Generalization." *American Statistician* 24, no. 5 (December): 18–22.

———. 1970b. "Use of Dummy Variables in Testing for Equality between Sets of Coefficients in Two Linear Regressions: A Note." *American Statistician* 24, no. 1 (January): 50–52.

IMF (International Monetary Fund). 1982. *International Financial Statistics: Supplement on Trade Statistics.* Washington, D.C.

———. 1985. *International Financial Statistics.* Washington, D.C.

Kendrick, J. W. 1961. *Productivity Trends in the United States.* Princeton, N.J.: Princeton University Press.

Keynes, J. M. 1912. "Board of Trade Tables for 1900–1911." *Economic Journal.* (Reprinted in *The Collected Writings of J. M. Keynes,* vol. XI.)

———. 1920. *The Economic Consequences of the Peace.* New York: Harcourt, Brace and Howe.

Kindleberger, C. P. 1956. *The Terms of Trade: A European Case Study.* Cambridge, Mass.: MIT Press.

Kravis, I. B., and R. L. Lipsey. 1974. "International Trade and Price Proxies." In N. D. Ruggles, ed., *The Role of the Computer in Economic and Social Research in Latin America.* New York: National Bureau of Economic Research.

———. 1981. "Prices and Terms of Trade for Developed Country Exports of Manufactured Goods." National Bureau of Economic Research Working Paper 774. New York.

46   THE WORLD BANK ECONOMIC REVIEW, VOL. 2, NO. 1

Processed. Also published in Bela Csikos-Nagy, Douglas Hagve and Graham Hall, eds., *The Economics of Relative Prices,* pp. 415–45. New York: St. Martin's, 1984.

League of Nations. 1945. *Industrialization and Foreign Trade.* Geneva.

Lewis, W. A. 1952. "World Production, Prices and Trade, 1870–1960." *Manchester School of Economics and Social Studies* 20, no. 2 (May): 105–38.

Macbean, A., and V. N. Balasubramanyan. 1978. *Meeting the Third World Challenge.* London: Macmillan.

Maizels, A. 1970. *Growth and Trade.* Cambridge, Eng.: Cambridge University Press.

Meier, G. M. 1958. "International Trade and International Inequality." *Oxford Economic Papers* 10, no. 3 (October): 277–89.

———. 1963. *International Trade and Development.* New York: Harper & Row.

Mill, J. S. 1848. *Principles of Political Economy.* London: John W. Parker (Repub. by Pelican Classics. Harmondsworth, Eng.: Penguin, 1970).

Morgan, T. O. 1959. "The Long-Run Terms of Trade between Agriculture and Manufacturing." *Economic Development and Cultural Change* 8, no. 1 (October): 1–23.

Nelson, C. R., and H. Kang. 1983. "Pitfalls in the Use of Time as an Explanatory Variable in Regressions." National Bureau of Economic Research Technical Working Paper 3. New York. Processed.

Prebisch, R. 1950. *The Economic Development of Latin America and Its Principal Problems.* New York: United Nations.

Ray, G. F. 1977. "The Real Price of Primary Products." *National Institute Economic Review,* no. 81 (August): 72–76.

Ricardo, D. 1817. *Principles of Political Economy and Taxation.* London: John Murray. (Repub. by Pelican Classics. Harmondsworth, Eng.: Penguin, 1971.)

Sapsford, D. 1985. "The Statistical Debate on the Net Barter Terms of Trade between Primary Commodities and Manufactures: A Comment and Some Additional Evidence." *Economic Journal* 95, no. 379 (September): 781–88.

Scherer, F. M. 1984. *Innovation and Growth: Schumpeterian Perspectives.* Cambridge, Mass.: MIT Press.

Schlote, W. 1938. *Entwicklung und Strukturwandlungen des Englischen Aussenhandels von 1700 bis zur Gegenwart.* Jena: Gustav Fisher. (English translation: *British Overseas Trade from 1700 to 1930s,* Oxford: Blackwell, 1952).

Schumpeter, J. 1942. *Capitalism, Socialism, and Democracy.* New York: Harper.

Singer, H. 1950. "The Distribution of Gains between Investing and Borrowing Countries." *American Economic Review, Papers and Proceedings* 40, no. 2 (May): 473–85.

———. 1975. "The Distribution of Gains from Trade and Investment—Revisited." *Journal of Development Studies* 11, no. 4 (July): 376–82.

Slade, M. E. 1982. "Trends in Natural-Resource Commodity Prices: An Analysis of the Time Domain." *Journal of Environmental Economics and Management* 9, no. 2 (June): 122–37.

Spraos, J. 1980. "The Statistical Debate on the Net Barter Terms of Trade between Primary Commodities and Manufactures." *Economic Journal* 90, no. 357 (March): 107–28.

Streeten, P. 1974. "World Trade in Agricultural Commodities and the Terms of Trade with Industrial Goods." In N. Islam, ed., *Agricultural Policy in Developing Countries.* London: Macmillan.

Suits, D. B., A. Mason, and L. Chan. 1978. "Spline Function Fitted by Standard Regression Method." *Review of Economics and Statistics* 60, no. 1 (February): 132–39.

Sylos-Labini, P. 1956. *Oligopolio e Progresso Tecnico.* Torino: Einaudi Editore. (English translation: *Oligopoly and Technical Progress.* Cambridge, Eng.: Cambridge University Press, 1962).

Torrens, R. 1821. *An Essay on the Production of Wealth.* London: Longman, Hurst, Rees, Orme, and Brown. (Republished by A. M. Kelly, New York, 1965).

United Nations. 1969 and 1974. *Statistical Yearbook.* New York.

———. 1972, 1976, 1982, and 1987. *Monthly Bulletin of Statistics.*

———. 1949. "Post War Price Relations in Trade between Underdeveloped and Industrialized Countries." Economic and Social Council, Doc. E/CN.1/Sub.3/W5. Processed.

UNCTAD (United Nations Conference on Trade and Development). 1972, 1976, 1983, 1984. *Handbook of International Trade and Development Statistics.* Geneva: United Nations.

Viner, Jr. 1937. *Studies in the Theory of International Trade.* New York: Harper.

———. 1953. *International Trade and Economic Development.* Oxford: Oxford University Press.

Wilson, T., R. P. Sinha, and J. R. Castree. 1969. "The Income Terms of Trade of Developed and Developing Countries." *Economic Journal* 74, no. 316 (December): 813–32.

Part III
Foreign Exchange Constraints

[9]

The Foreign-Exchange Bottleneck Revisited:
A Geometric Note*

Deepak Lal
University College, London

In the recent literature on economic development, the notion that the growth of developing countries is limited by a foreign-exchange constraint which is independent of a savings constraint has gained wide currency.[1] This view implies that for many developing countries there is a redundancy of "ex ante" domestic savings, imposed by the limited availability of foreign exchange to the economy. The resulting two-gap analysis in terms of independent savings and foreign-exchange constraints has been enshrined in the UNCTAD philosophy as presented by Prebisch in "Towards a New Trade Policy for Development,"[2] and has formed the basis of the theoretical models of McKinnon[3] and Chenery and Strout.[4] More recently, the basic assumptions of these models have come under attack.[5] The purpose of this note is to integrate these criticisms in terms of a simple model which (*a*) rigorously shows the minimal assumptions needed to give rise to an independent foreign-exchange bottleneck, (*b*) distinguishes between

* I am indebted to the following for helpful comments and discussion on an earlier paper ("Foreign Exchange Bottlenecks, Balance of Payments, Investment Criteria, and the Optimum Pattern of Trade and Production," mimeographed [Oxford, 1967]) in which the basic model of this paper was first presented: Sir Roy Harrod and Messrs. M. F. Scott, F. L. Seton, and J. F. Wright.

[1] J. P. Lewis, *Quiet Crisis in India* (Washington, D.C.: Brookings Institution, 1962); S. B. Linder, *Trade and Trade Policy for Development* (London: Pall Mall Press, 1967); I. M. D. Little and J. Clifford, *International Aid* (London: Allen & Unwin, 1965); G. Myrdal, *Asian Drama* (New York: Twentieth Century Fund, 1968); I. G. Patel, "Trade and Payments Policy for a Developing economy," in *International Trade Theory in a Developing World*, ed. Roy F. Harrod and Douglas C. Hague (London: Macmillan, 1963); W. B. Reddaway, *The Development of the Indian Economy* (London: Allen & Unwin, 1952); United Nations, "Towards a New Trade Policy for Development," *Report by the Secretary General of UNCTAD*, 1964.

[2] United Nations (n. 1 above).

[3] R. I. McKinnon, "Foreign Exchange Constraints in Economic Development," *Economic Journal* 74 (June 1964): 308–409.

[4] H. B. Chenery and A. M. Strout, "Development Alternatives in an Open Economy," *American Economic Review* 56 (September 1966): 679–733.

[5] H. J. Bruton, "The Two-Gap Approach to Aid and Development," *American Economic Review* 59 (June 1969): 439–46; V. Joshi, "Savings and Foreign Exchange Constraints," mimeographed (Oxford, 1969), to be published in a forthcoming volume in honor of Lord Balogh.

Deepak Lal

strict and partial foreign-exchange constraints and foreign-exchange shortages, and (*c*) integrates the concept of a foreign-exchange bottleneck with traditional international trade theory and neoclassical growth theory.

The basic model I shall develop is a combination of (1) the classic two-period, capital theoretic, one-good Fisher model and (2) a simple extension of the well-known two-good, two-factor, neoclassical international trade model.

We first construct a simple two-period, one-good model, in which all imports are inputs into production.

Consider an economy whose aggregate output is represented by a composite good X (which may be thought of as corn). It can be consumed, saved and invested (there are no Keynesian effective-demand-type problems in the economy), and exported. Production of X (corn) requires inputs of itself, an imported input M (which can be thought of as tractors), and labor which is paid in X (corn). Hence, the aggregate-production function of the economy can be described by isoquants drawn in X-M (corn-tractor) space.

Three assumptions relating to the transformation possibilities open to the economy must hold simultaneously in such an economy for there to be a foreign-exchange constraint which is independent of a savings constraint to increasing future output of X (corn).

First, along any isoquant, the technology does not permit any substitutability, after a point, of domestic for foreign inputs in the production of X.[6] *Second*, the domestic rate of transformation of X into M is zero. The domestic good cannot be converted into the imported input domestically, the transformation being only possible through trade. *Third*, the foreign rate of transformation of X into M is zero, after a certain stage, for movements along the foreign-offer curve. The economy is faced by a complete inelasticity of export earnings and, hence, a fixed import capacity.

Figure 1 illustrates the model. The amount of domestic output (of X) saved in any period is measured along the horizontal axis. The quantity of the imported input (M) available to the economy is measured on the vertical axis. Say the amount of savings is given by OS_2. From our second assumption, we know that M can only be acquired through trade. Thus, from S_2 we can draw the foreign-offer curve which shows the amounts of M the economy can obtain in exchange for X through foreign trade. The shape of this offer curve is determined by the third of our above assumptions. As far as point P, the curve is a straight line, which assumes that at first X can be exchanged for M at constant terms of trade, given by the slope of S_2P. After P, the terms of trade steadily worsen. After point C, any further exports of X result in a lowering of the total imports of M. Line OM_1 represents the maximum amount of the imported input (M) the

---

[6] The converse does not hold, since foreign inputs can be substituted for domestic inputs indefinitely.

Economic Development and Cultural Change

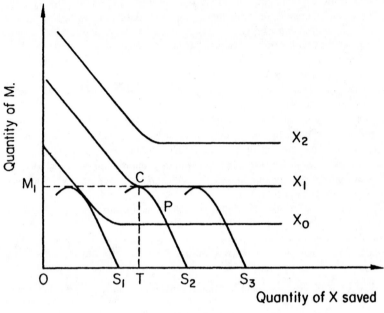

FIG. 1

economy can acquire through trade, by exporting S_2T of X, leaving OT of X to be combined with OM_1 of M for producing domestic output (of X) in the next period.

Furthermore, for any given amount of savings (OS_d), there will be an identically shaped offer curve (or factor-availability curve), which can be derived by shifting the origin to the right (if $S_d > S$) or to the left (if $S_d < S$). These are the curves S_3 and S_1, respectively.

In the same quadrant, we can also depict the amount of domestic output (of X) which can be produced in the next period, given differing quantities of current inputs of X and M. These are shown by the X isoquants, whose shape is derived from the first of our above assumptions —namely, that after a certain stage there is nonsubstitutability of domestic for foreign inputs—so that the isoquants become horizontal. As foreign inputs can be substituted indefinitely for domestic inputs, the isoquants cut the vertical axis. As drawn, it is also assumed that the rate of substitution of domestic for foreign inputs is constant for a certain portion of the isoquants, and then this rate falls, until it becomes zero at the point where the isoquants become horizontal.

From the diagram, it can be readily seen that there will be one isoquant which is tangential to any given S-offer curve. This point gives the highest attainable isoquant (maximum output of X) consistent with any given level of savings and hence S-offer curve. It will thus be the point of opti-

Deepak Lal

mum trade and production, given the amount of domestic savings, the foreign-offer curve, and the technology. Thus, given savings OS_2, the economy would export S_2T of X in exchange for OM_1 of M, which would be combined with OT of X to give output X_1 in the next period.

Suppose that our economy wants to achieve an output target in the next period, represented by the X_2 isoquant. For this purpose, it is willing to save, say, OS_3. From the diagram, it is clear that it will not be able to achieve any output greater than that represented by isoquant X_1. Any extra savings beyond OS_2 which the economy may be willing to undertake will be insufficient to raise output of X in the next period beyond the X_1 level. The economy is in a strict foreign-exchange bottleneck. Foreign exchange imposes a prior and independent constraint to domestic savings to achieving any output target greater than X_1, even though potential savings are greater than OS_2.[7]

It is important to note that *all* the three assumptions we have made to derive figure 1 must hold simultaneously. If any one of them is relaxed while the other two hold, there will no longer be an independent foreign-exchange constraint to increasing output. This can be readily verified from figure 2.[8]

[7] The Chenery-Strout and McKinnon bottleneck models can be readily interpreted in terms of figure 1. These linear models, in their simplest forms, assume a single aggregate ratio of imports to total output and a single aggregate capital-output ratio for the economy. This implies that in figure 1 the output isoquants will be straight lines (as shown in the accompanying figure 2a). To the left of the line OP', the isoquants will be a set of parallel lines of 45-degree slope, reflecting the constant trade-off between savings and foreign exchange when the savings constraint is binding and foreign-capital inflow is a supplement to domestic savings. To the right of OP' they will be horizontal and parallel to the savings axis, reflecting the binding foreign-exchange constraint, namely, that increased savings alone are insufficient to raise output. If the level of completely stagnant exports earnings is given by EPX (this corresponds to the fixed import capacity OM_1 in figure 1), then, without any inflow of foreign capital, the highest attainable level of output in the next period would be given by the isoquant X_0. If a higher level of output is desired—say, that given by isoquant X_1—then foreign-capital inflow of EF_1 will be needed if the foreign-exchange constraint is binding. If, on the other hand, it is the savings constraint which is binding, so that the economy's savings are limited to OS and the associated export earnings are OE, and if again the desired output goal is given by isoquant X_1, then foreign-capital inflow of EF_2 will be needed to achieve the desired output goal. Figure 2a also illustrates the further property of these linear bottleneck models, namely, that the productivity of foreign-capital inflows is greater when an economy is bound by the foreign-exchange constraint than by the savings constraint. For, given that the economy is at P, a capital inflow of EF_1 is needed to put it on isoquant X_1 if the foreign-exchange constraint is binding, while an inflow of EF_2 is required if the savings constraint is binding. It can be readily seen that EF_2 must always be greater than EF_1, given the assumptions embodied in the shapes of the X isoquants. Hence, the productivity of foreign-capital transfers will be higher in the foreign-exchange bottleneck situation than in the case of a savings constraint.

[8] Relaxing the first assumption implies that the isoquants no longer become horizontal. Clearly, then, output can be increased with increased savings. Similarly, if the third assumption is relaxed, then there will no longer be a fixed import capacity, and, as long as the marginal rate of transformation along the offer curve remains positive, again no independent foreign exchange constraint can arise. Finally, if the second assumption is relaxed and import substitution of M is possible, then, as long

Economic Development and Cultural Change

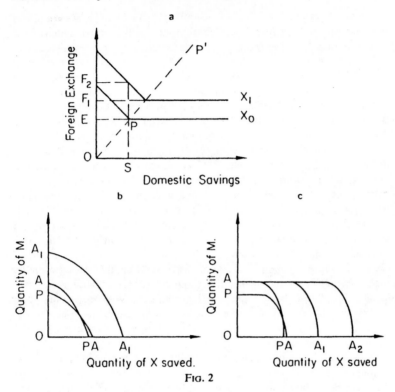

Fig. 2

Finally, there is a *fourth* assumption which must also hold before a strict foreign-exchange constraint can arise. Given a social welfare function, or planners' preference between present and future consumption, the

as the domestic rate of transformation does not fall to zero, there will not be an independent foreign-exchange constraint. This last point is illustrated by the accompanying figures 2*b* and 2*c*. The curve *PP* in figure 2*b* is the domestic-production-possibility curve for transforming *X* into *M*. The total availabilities of *X* and *M* available for producing *X* in the next period, given a level of current savings *OP*, are represented by the total availabilities frontier *AA*, which is obtained by combining the domestic-transformation curve and the foreign-offer curves to generate the familiar Baldwin envelope. The isoquants are not drawn into the diagrams, but they are the same as in figure 1. Any point on the *AA* envelope has the same slope as the associated production point on the domestic-transformation frontier. Thus, as long as the rate of transformation on the *PP* curve does not fall to zero, even though the rate of transformation on the foreign-offer curve does fall to zero, the rate of transformation on the envelope will remain positive. This implies that, with a positive domestic rate of transformation, the successive availabilities frontiers for higher levels of savings will continue to have the convex shape of A_1A_1, and so, although the isoquants became horizontal, future output could always be increased with higher savings. It is only if the domestic rate of transformation falls to zero, so that the availabilities envelope becomes flat at a certain stage, as in figure 2*c*, that increased savings will not lead to an increase in the availability of *M* and, hence, increased output of *X* in the next period.

Deepak Lal

marginal utility of present consumption must fall to zero before the rate of transforming present into future consumption falls to zero. This is illustrated by figure 3. Line OC represents total current output, which can be either consumed or saved and invested to provide output in the next period. The CY curve shows the output which can be obtained in the next period, given different levels of current savings. The latter are measured by distances moving to the left from C on the horizontal axis. The curve CY is derived from the points of tangency between the X isoquants and the S-offer curves in figure 1. There are diminishing returns in terms of future output to increasing current savings until, at a savings level $CT (= OS_2$ in fig. 1), the CY curve becomes flat, implying that no further increase in the next period's output is possible by increasing current savings.[9]

So far in our discussion, we have assumed that there was some exogenously given output target to be achieved in the next period; and, clearly, if this is greater than OY, then it will be unattainable even though society may be willing to give up present consumption greater than CT. This was the strict foreign-exchange-bottleneck case. However, we need to say something more about how such a target could be laid down. Formally, the problem facing society (or the planners) is to maximize a specified intertemporal utility function whose arguments are weighted consumption at different dates, subject to the transformation possibilities open to the economy for transforming present consumption into future consumption. In our two-period model, society's preference for present and future consumption can be represented by social indifference curves in figure 3. The shape of these indifference curves is crucial for deciding whether or not the economy is on the foreign-exchange-bottleneck section of the transformation curve. It will be on this section if the indifference curves are of the shape of the $Y_1 Y_1$ curve in figure 3. This implies that society (or the planners) place no value on present consumption beyond the $O1 (= YA)$ level, at which point (A) the indifference curve becomes horizontal. Clearly, as long as A is to the left of B, society will not be able to transform value-less present consumption into future output (and consumption), and it is limited entirely by the complete lack of transformation possibilities (both domestic and foreign) for converting present consumption into future consumption beyond OT. All transformation possibilities have been exhausted before any further cuts in present consumption come to represent a positive cost. It is this redundancy of ex ante savings (present consumption foregone) which constitutes the case of an economy in a strict foreign-exchange bottleneck, and for this both the transformation curve and the highest attainable indifference curve must be horizontal at their point of tangency.

If the transformation-possibilities curve CY does not become horizontal, or if A lies at or to the right of B, then it cannot be said that the economy

---

[9] It is obvious that figure 3 is the well-known two-period Fisher diagram, except for the particular shapes of the transformation and social indifference curves.

Economic Development and Cultural Change

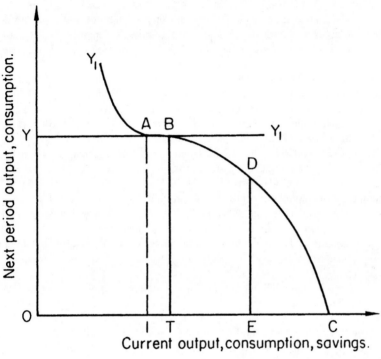

FIG. 3

is in a strict foreign-exchange bottleneck. Furthermore, given that the shape of the transformation curve is *CY*, if the marginal utility of present consumption is always positive, then the indifference curves will not become horizontal and will be tangential to the *CY* curve to the right of *B*. Again, the economy cannot be said to be in a strict foreign-exchange bottleneck. In all these cases, there is no redundancy of ex ante savings which characterizes the strict foreign-exchange-bottleneck situation. I shall label these cases as a "partial foreign-exchange bottleneck," for reasons which will soon be apparent. Thus, we have established that, for a strict foreign-exchange bottleneck to arise, it is also necessary that the marginal utility of present consumption fall to zero before the rate of transformation between present and future consumption falls to zero.

It should be noted that, in both the strict and partial foreign-exchange-bottleneck cases, the economy is doing the best it can, in the sense that it is operating on the given transformation frontier at a point of tangency with the highest attainable social indifference curve. Also, in both cases we have assumed that planners can enforce any savings level they consider desirable. The two cases differ only with respect to the redundancy of potential domestic savings. In the strict bottleneck case, there is such a

Deepak Lal

redundancy, in the sense that society can get no increase in future output from the increasing current savings. In the partial bottleneck case, however, there is no such redundancy of ex ante domestic savings. Society can get an increase in future output, but, given the social utility function, the marginal utility of the increase in future output made possible by the transformation possibilities is less than the marginal utility of present consumption which has to be foregone to obtain this increase.

A third case which needs to be distinguished is the pure savings-constrained situation. Such a case is depicted by the point D in figure 3. It is now assumed that the planners cannot cut domestic consumption beyond the level OE. This minimum-consumption level may be given by the inability of the planners to control domestic consumption through taxation or by political constraints. In such a case, as long as the point of tangency of the highest attainable social indifference curve and the transformation curve is to the left of D, the economy will be in a pure savings bottleneck, since it has transformation possibilities open to it which provide the means for reaching a higher level of social welfare, the only limitation being society's inability to generate the requisite amount of savings.

The label "partial" foreign-exchange bottleneck, applied to the second of the three cases distinguished above, needs a few words of justification. First, note that the term "foreign-exchange bottleneck," even for the "strict" case, is misleading. For the bottleneck relates to all transformation possibilities, both domestic and foreign, as well as to the lack of substitutability of domestic for imported inputs in domestic production. The reason for labeling the second of our cases a "partial" bottleneck is due to the characteristic it shares with the strict foreign-exchange-bottleneck case, namely, that, even though ex ante savings can be increased, the transformation possibilities open to the economy at the relevant points of tangency with a social indifference curve do not make such savings worthwhile. This is different from the case of a pure savings bottleneck, where it is difficulties in raising savings rather than limited transformation possibilities which prevent any rise in future output. However, the partial foreign-exchange bottleneck case is similar to the pure savings-bottleneck case insofar as there is no redundancy of ex ante savings as in the strict foreign-bottleneck situation. If the society did manage to save more, future output could be increased.

Summarizing the discussion so far, for a strict foreign-exchange bottleneck to exist, all opportunities for import substitution and for increasing export earnings must be exhausted, the import content of current production should be unalterable, and the marginal utility of present consumption must be zero. All these conditions must hold simultaneously. There will then be an ensuing redundancy of ex ante savings due to the complete lack of any transformation possibilities for converting present into future consumption in the economy. In a partial foreign-exchange

Economic Development and Cultural Change

bottleneck, there is no such redundancy of potential savings, but the transformation possibilities are limited (though not completely absent), so that it is not socially desirable to increase savings. In a pure savings bottleneck, there is no redundancy of potential savings; there are favorable transformation possibilities but an inability to raise savings beyond a certain level, even though such increased savings would be socially desirable.

Finally, it is important to distinguish between a foreign-exchange bottleneck and a foreign-exchange shortage. The latter can arise if overvalued exchange rates are maintained, as they often are in developing countries. Then, at the official exchange rate, there will be excess demand for foreign exchange, which will appear as a foreign-exchange shortage. It is obvious that it would be erroneous to deduce that growth in a country suffering from a foreign-exchange shortage in the above sense was constrained by foreign exchange in either the strict or partial senses distinguished above. A foreign-exchange shortage reflects a disequilibrium in the foreign-exchange market, and, in order to deduce whether such a shortage is also accompanied by a strict foreign-exchange bottleneck, it would be necessary to demonstrate that all four assumptions necessary to generate such a bottleneck did in fact hold.

[10]

A SIMPLIFIED MAHALANOBIS DEVELOPMENT MODEL*

M. Bronfenbrenner
University of Minnesota

The Mahalanobis Model

Dr. P. C. Mahalanobis is Director of the Indian Statistical Institute in Calcutta and Editor of the international statistical journal Sankhya. Originally trained as a physicist and eminent primarily as a mathematical statistician, he scorns the title of economist. He nevertheless became more than any other single man the guiding spirit of the Second Five Year Plan of his native India. What is yet more remarkable, his leadership was equally in evidence on the ideological and on the technical side.

Few formal models of economic development have therefore been as influential for policy in any country as the neo-Marxist ones devised by Mahalanobis in connection with the Indian Second Five Year Plan. Mahalanobis' thinking is distilled in a series of three papers in Sankhya; this note concentrates upon the first of these.[1] His work had been to some extent anticipated by other Marxist writers,[2] his mathematical exposition was highly elliptical, and his papers ap-

---

* While retaining all responsibility for errors and omissions, the writer acknowledges the assistance of other members of the University of Minnesota Workshop in Economic Development, particularly Professor Anne O. Krueger.

1. P. C. Mahalanobis, "Some Observations on the Process of Growth of National Income," Sankhya, XII, 1952, pp. 307-312; "The Approach of Operational Research to Planning in India," ibid., XVI, 1955, pp. 3-62; "Draft Plan-Frame for the Second Five-Year Plan," ibid., pp. 63-89. These articles, written following a visit by Mahalanobis to the Soviet Union, presumably embody some of what Mahalanobis considers the lessons of both Marxist theory and Soviet experience.

2. Mahalanobis may to some extent have been influenced by the British Marxian economist Maurice Dobb, whose "Note on the So-Called Degree of Capital-Intensity of Investment in Under-Developed Countries," though published originally in 1954, was written during and after service as an economic consultant in India. Dobb's completely literary essay may be found in Chapter VII of his On Economic Theory and Socialism, New York, International Publishers, 1955.

As Professor E. D. Domar has pointed out, Mahalanobis' work was also foreshadowed in part by the neglected Soviet economist G. A. Feldman as early as 1928, although there is no evidence that Mahalanobis knew of Feldman's paper. See Domar, "A Soviet Model of Growth," in Essays in the Theory of Economic Growth, New York, Oxford University Press, 1957, particularly note 13, page 230.

46   MAHALANOBIS DEVELOPMENT MODEL

peared in a statistical rather than an economic journal. For all these reasons Mahalanobis' models have received in the West less attention than they deserve in view of their influence in India, and through India on other developing countries. [3]

This note is based on Mahalanobis' original two-sector presentation of 1953. The writer develops a simpler model with the principal properties of the Mahalanobis one, and in a form accessible to economists without extensive mathematical training.[4] Except where statements are made to the contrary, our assumptions and conclusions are intended to parallel his. Critical comments on the model developed here are also intended to apply to the Mahalanobis original.

The Income Growth Equation

Let income during any period t be denoted by Y_t, and let it be the sum of contemporaneous investment (I_t) and consumption (C_t). In other words, $Y_t = I_t + C_t$. Let the magnitudes of investment and consumption I_t and C_t be related to the capital stock K_{t-1} of the end of the preceding period, in such wise that:

$$I_t = \lambda_i \beta_i K_{t-1} \qquad \text{and} \qquad C_t = \lambda_c \beta_c K_{t-1}$$

The terms in λ may be called allocations. A certain proportion of capital is allocated by the market (or by an economic plan) to investment or to consumption goods. The sum of the allocations $\lambda_i + \lambda_c$ must equal unity. Furthermore, since saving and investment are equal ex post, a higher λ_i requires also a higher saving ratio while a higher λ_c permits greater present consumption. As for the terms in β, these are gross productivities of capital, and are also fractional in the real world. There is, however, no condition on their sum.

We follow Mahalanobis in defining I and C as including raw materials and parts, so that they represent the outputs of investment and consumption goods with their respective subsidiaries. In this they differ from the Marxian "departments" I and II of Das Kapital.[5] This reconstitution restricts I largely to the output of heavy industry. Industry producing not only clothing but other textiles, not only food but cans and bottles, is included in C.

Mahalanobis' model, and also this one, assumes that the entire national income is produced domestically. The economy is or should become independent of outside sources for "fundamental" goods of all sorts. Mahalanobis' model, and also this one, assumes the entire economic problem to be one of supply. There are no demand equations. There is no need to worry about demand, at least in a poor country like India. The Plan, meaning the Government, will ab-

---

3. See however Ryutaro Komiya, "A Note on Professor Mahalanobis' Model of Indian Economic Planning," Review of Economics and Statistics, XLI, 1959, pp. 29-35, and literature cited therein.

4. The Komiya critique (cited in the preceding note) is based on Mahalanobis' later and more complex four-sector expansion.

5. Interestingly enough, Feldman also reorganized the Marxian "departmental" structure in the same way in his 1928 article. Compare Domar, op. cit., pp. 226-228.

sorb or distribute any surpluses that may arise. These two assumptions are of course subject to question not only for India but to a larger extent for other countries without India's range of resource endowments.[6]

We have however departed from Mahalanobis by introducing explicitly the capital stock $\underline{K}$, although he sees capital as the strategic limitation on production in both the investment and consumption sectors of the economy. Instead of $\underline{K}$, Mahalanobis uses expressions involving the sum of the series:

$$I_o + I_1 + \ldots + I_t = \alpha_o Y_o + \alpha_1 Y_1 + \ldots + \alpha_t Y_t$$

where the α terms are propensities to save and invest. The use of these series complicates Mahalanobis' subsequent mathematics. More important, it involves the assumption that $\underline{K}_o$, the base period capital stock, is negligibly small.

Let us define both $\underline{Y}_t$ and $\underline{Y}_{t-1}$ in terms of our definitions of $\underline{I}$ and $\underline{C}$.

$$Y_t = (\lambda_i \beta_i + \lambda_c \beta_c) K_{t-1}$$

$$Y_{t-1} = (\lambda_i \beta_i + \lambda_c \beta_c) K_{t-2}$$

This enables us to define the growth rate of income $\underline{g}$ (not used by Mahalanobis):

$$g = \frac{Y_t - Y_{t-1}}{Y_{t-1}} = \frac{(\lambda_i \beta_i + \lambda_c \beta_c)}{(\lambda_i \beta_i + \lambda_c \beta_c)} \frac{(K_{t-1} - K_{t-2})}{K_{t-2}}$$

But the difference between the two capital stocks is simply $\underline{I}_{t-1}$, which we have defined as $(\lambda_i \beta_i K_{t-2})$. Substituting this value for $(K_{t-1} - K_{t-2})$ and carrying out all cancellations, we obtain an extremely simple result:

$$g = \lambda_i \beta_i \qquad (1)$$

which says that the growth rate depends only upon the allocation of capital to investment industries and upon its productivity there.

Equation (1) can be rewritten as a difference equation:

$$Y_t - Y_{t-1} = \lambda_i \beta_i Y_{t-1}$$

whose solution is:[7]

$$Y_t = Y_o (1 + \lambda_i \beta_i)^t$$

or in terms of $\underline{Y}_1$ and $\underline{K}_o$:

$$Y_t = (\lambda_i \beta_i + \lambda_c \beta_c) K_o (1 + \lambda_i \beta_i)^{t-1} \qquad (2)$$

---

6. Komiya, op. cit., p. 31 f., has expanded these critical observations in fuller detail.

7. The difference equation can be rewritten:

$$Y_t - (1 + \lambda_i \beta_i) Y_{t-1} = 0.$$

(continued on page 48)

48   MAHALANOBIS DEVELOPMENT MODEL

Equation (2) corresponds to a more complex result of Mahalanobis:[8]

$$Y_t = Y_o \left[1 + \alpha_o \frac{\lambda_i \beta_i + \lambda_c \beta_c}{\lambda_i \beta_i} \left\{ (1 + \lambda_i \beta_i)^t - 1 \right\} \right]$$

Both (2) and the Mahalanobis equivalent can be used to show that income will eventually be higher with a high λ_i than with a low one, even though capital may be more productive in the consumption goods industries. This paradox

---

Let $Y_t = aX^t$, where $\underline{X}$ is a dummy variable without economic meaning. Substituting this value for Y_t, we find:

$$X = (1 + \lambda_i \beta_i)$$

while $\underline{a}$ becomes equal to $\underline{Y_o}$ in order that $a(1 + \lambda_i \beta_i)^o$ be equal to the known value $\underline{Y_o}$ in the base period.

For a fuller explanation written with the needs of economists in mind, see W. J. Baumol, Economic Dynamics, Second Edition, New York, Macmillan, 1959, Ch. 9.

8. Mahalanobis, "Rate of Growth of National Income," op. cit., equation (1), p. 309.

While Mahalanobis leaves this formula underived, a derivation is given below. If data for period $\underline{o}$ are already determined, we know for period 1:

$$Y_1 = Y_o + (\lambda_i \beta_i + \lambda_c \beta_c) I_o$$

$$I_o = \alpha_o Y_o$$

Therefore:

$$Y_1 = Y_o \left[1 + \alpha_o (\lambda_i \beta_i + \lambda_c \beta_c) \right]$$

For period 2, the productivity of investment has been increased by the factor $(1 + \lambda_i \beta_i)$ by which the investment goods sector has been expanded in period 1, and we now have:

$$Y_2 = Y_o \left[1 + \alpha_o (\lambda_i \beta_i + \lambda_c \beta_c) (1 + \lambda_i \beta_i) \right]$$

For period 3, if we allow for two periods of building up the investment goods sector:

$$Y_3 = Y_o \left[1 + \alpha_o (\lambda_i \beta_i + \lambda_c \beta_c) \left\{ (1 + \lambda_i \beta_i) + (1 + \lambda_i \beta_i)^2 \right\} \right]$$

And finally, for period t:

$$Y_t = Y_o \left[1 + \alpha_o (\lambda_i \beta_i + \lambda_c \beta_c) \left\{ (1 + \lambda_i \beta_i) + (1 + \lambda_i \beta_i)^2 + \dots + (1 + \lambda_i \beta_i)^{t-1} \right\} \right]$$

The expression within curled brackets is a geometric series whose sum is:

$$\left[(1 + \lambda_i \beta_i)^t - 1 \right] + (\lambda_i \beta_i)$$

Substituting this result yields the Mahalanobis formula at once.

ECONOMIC DEVELOPMENT AND CULTURAL CHANGE   49

Mahalanobis illustrates by assuming β_i and β_c to be 0.1 and 0.3 respectively, and working out alternative growth patterns for λ_c of 0.1 ($\lambda_c = 0.9$) and λ_i of 0.3 ($\lambda_c = 0.7$). We shall use the same coefficients to derive the same paradox.

With λ_i equal to 0.1, equation (2) may be written as (2-a); with λ_i equal to 0.3, it becomes (2-b):

$$Y_t = .28 \; K_o \; (1.01)^{t-1} \qquad\qquad (2\text{-a})$$

$$Y_t = .24 \; K_o \; (1.03)^{t-1} \qquad\qquad (2\text{-b})$$

For low values of $\underline{t}$, (2-a) gives higher values for income than (2-b), but for higher values of $\underline{t}$ (2-b) forges ahead. The critical value of $\underline{t}$ at which (2-a) and (2-b) give equal values of Y_t is 8.86 periods.[9] For the long view (nine periods or longer) (2-b) does better, without regard to the initial value of the capital stock.

Returning to equation (1) for the growth rate $\underline{g}$, we obtain at once another result on which Mahalanobis lays great stress,- the minimum value of λ_i consistent with a "respectable" rate of growth. If 3 percent per period is the growth rate required to remain ahead of the "population explosion" and increase per capita income perceptibly in India, and if Mahalanobis' estimate of .10 for β_i is approximately correct, it follows at once that λ_i must be at least .30. Mahalanobis' own suggested minimum of .33 is slightly higher than this. For higher minimal growth rates, λ_i is correspondingly still higher.

The allocation of saving and investment between capital and consumption goods should also correspond to the country's saving ratio, although this feature does not enter the Mahalanobis model explicitly. The higher is λ_i, in other words, the higher must be the saving ratio α_t required to support it without strain. There is undoubtedly a maximum value of λ_i beyond which the population could not survive in the early years of the growth process. This exogenous condition is known to (or at least estimated by) the economic planner and is also excluded from the model itself. A dilemma of many development plans is the possibility that the maximum λ_i which the populace will accept without heavy doses of propaganda laced with terror may be less than the minimum λ_i for a growth rate which keeps ahead of population expansion. A model of the Mahalanobis type brings out this dilemma, but suggests no method of avoiding it. When it occurs, the model provides no choice between stagnation and dictatorship.

The Consumption Growth Equation

Still following Mahalanobis' lead, we can derive a growth equation for consumption as well as for income as a whole. Here again we shall find the Mahala-

---

9. To obtain the critical value of $\underline{t}$, equate the logarithms of the right hand sides of (2-a) and (2-b):

$\log 0.28 + \log K_o + (t-1) \log 1.01 = \log 0.24 + \log K_o + (t-1) \operatorname{Log} 1.03$

and solve as a linear equation for $(t-1)$.

Mahalanobis, ibid., p. 309, uses 15 years as his critical value of $\underline{t}$. He also believes β_c to be less than three times β_i, but wishes to avoid suspicion of biasing the arithmetical results in his own favor.

50 MAHALANOBIS DEVELOPMENT MODEL

nobis paradox holding, with the level of consumption eventually increased by concentration upon investment goods industries even when capital is more productive in consumption goods industries.

As in our previous development of the income growth equation, we have:

$$C_t = \lambda_c \beta_c K_{t-1}$$

$$C_{t-1} = \lambda_c \beta_c K_{t-2}$$

If we define g' as the rate of growth of consumption, we obtain the result:

$$g' = \frac{C_t - C_{t-1}}{C_{t-1}} = \frac{(\lambda_c \beta_c)}{(\lambda_c \beta_c)} \frac{(K_{t-1} - K_{t-2})}{K_{t-2}}$$

Again the difference between the two capital stocks is I_{t-1}, defined above as $(\lambda_i \beta_i K_{t-2})$. Substituting this value for $(K_{t-1} - K_{t-2})$ and carrying out all cancellations, we obtain the simple and interesting result:

$$g' = \lambda_i \beta_i \tag{3}$$

which says that the growth rate of consumption is identical to that of income, and also depends only upon the allocation of capital to investment industries and to its productivity there.

Like equation (1), equation (3) may be rewritten as a difference equation:

$$C_t - C_{t-1} = \lambda_i \beta_i C_{t-1}$$

whose solution is:

$$C_t = C_o (1 + \lambda_i \beta_i)^t$$

or in terms of $\underline{C}_1$ and $\underline{K}_o$:

$$C_t = (\lambda_c \beta_c) K_o (1 + \lambda_i \beta_i)^{t-1} \tag{4}$$

To derive the Mahalanobis paradox, let us again assume β_i and β_c to be 0.1 and 0.3 respectively, and work out alternative growth patterns for λ_i of 0.1 ($\lambda_c = 0.9$) and λ_i of 0.3 ($\lambda_c = 0.7$).

With λ_i equal to 0.1, equation (4) may be rewritten as (4-a); with λ_i equal to 0.3, it becomes (4-b):

$$C_t = .27 K_o (1.01)^{t-1} \tag{4-a}$$

$$C_t = .21 K_o (1.03)^{t-1} \tag{4-b}$$

For low values of $\underline{t}$, (4-a) gives higher values for consumption than (4-b), but for higher values (4-b) forges ahead. The critical value of $\underline{t}$, at which (4-a) and (4-b) give equal values of C_t, is 29.10 years without regard to the value of $\underline{K}_o$. As expected, this is substantially longer than the corresponding interval for income as a whole, which we derived as 8.86 years. Mahalanobis' estimate of the critical period for consumption is also 29 years. [10]

10. Mahalanobis, ibid., p. 310.

Equation (3) gives a minimum value of λ_i if consumption per capita is to expand appreciably despite population growth. For consumption as well as for income as a whole, this minimum investment-goods allocation is 0. 3 on Mahalanobis' numerical assumptions.

Possible Expansion

Comments have been made upon the autarchic character of the Mahalanobis model. Although no doctrinaire believer in economic isolation, Mahalanobis sees advantages for India in this feature. It serves both as a safeguard against political pressures and as insurance against interruption of import supplies by international conflict. More generally, however, it may be well to expand the model to include as a third sector the export industries, and likewise to include the contributions to income of the imports which are paid for by exports. We would then have:

$$Y_t = I_t + C_t + X_t$$

where X_t represents the output of export industries and their subsidiaries. We might also write for $\underline{I}_t$, $\underline{C}_t$, and $\underline{X}_t$ three separate equations, retaining the Mahalanobis assumption that supply (rather than demand) is the strategic limitation on output in all three sectors:

$$I_t = \lambda_i \beta_i \ K_{t-1} + \mu_i \gamma_i \ X_{t-1}$$

$$C_t = \lambda_c \beta_c \ K_{t-1} + \mu_c \gamma_c \ X_{t-1}$$

$$X_t = \lambda_x \beta_x \ K_{t-1} + \mu_x \gamma_x \ X_{t-1}$$

Here the terms in μ represent allocations of imports, either by the market or by an economic plan. The terms in γ represent their productivities; when final products are imported, the corresponding γ term is unity.

This model makes imports depend upon the exports of the preceding period. If trade is balanced, the sum of the three terms in μ is unity; if there is a trade deficit, this sum will exceed unity, and if there is a surplus it will fall short of unity. The sum of the three terms in λ is however equal to unity in any case.

Elementary experimentation with this slightly more complex and realistic expansion calls in question some of the cocksure certainties of models like the Mahalanobis one. A large λ_x rather than a large λ_i, concentration of capital on exports rather than industrialization, may be called for when the μ and γ coefficients are large, making imports efficient inputs for domestic production. Furthermore, a large λ_c rather than a large λ_i, concentration of capital on consumption rather than investment goods, may be called for when μ_i and γ_i exceed μ_c and γ_c, making it most efficient to use foreign sources of investment goods. [11] Elaboration of this point, however, calls for an essay in criticism and more advanced mathematics, whereas this note aims at simplified restatement and exposition.

---

11. Komiya, op. cit., p. 31 and note 8, develops this point more fully, using the later four-sector Mahalanobis model.

Part IV
Theory and Practice of Protection

[11]

DOMESTIC DISTORTIONS, TARIFFS AND THE THEORY OF OPTIMUM SUBSIDY[1]

JAGDISH BHAGWATI AND V. K. RAMASWAMI
Indian Statistical Institute, New Delhi

THERE is confusion of varying degrees in the current literature on trade theory concerning the desirable form of intervention in foreign trade when the economy is characterized by domestic distortions (divergences of the commodity price ratios from the corresponding marginal rates of substitution). For instance, the age-old debate over whether tariffs or subsidies should be used to protect an infant industry is still carried on in terms of the respective political and psychological merits of the two forms of protection while their relative economic advantages are assumed not to point in the direction of a definite choice.[2]

Three questions about the use of tariffs when domestic distortions exist need to be distinguished here. (1) Is a tariff necessarily superior to free trade (that is, can a tariff rate always be found that yields a welfare position not inferior to that produced by free trade)? (2) Is a tariff policy necessarily superior to any other form of *trade* policy? (3) If the choice can be made from the entire range of policy instruments, which is the optimal economic policy?

In Section I we state the general theory that provides the answers to these three questions. In the light of this theory, we examine the propositions advanced in the two central contributions to trade theory in this field: Haberler's justly celebrated 1950 *Economic Journal* paper[3] and Hagen's recent analysis of wage differentials.[4] Sections II and III examine these two analyses. Section IV concludes with some observations concerning the relative advantages of tariffs and subsidies from the practical viewpoint.

I. GENERAL THEORY

The three questions posed here can be effectively answered by analyzing the characteristics of an optimum solution. Thus, for instance, the optimum tariff argument can be stated elegantly in terms of these characteristics. The achievement of an optimum solution is characterized by the equality of the foreign rate of transformation (FRT), the domestic rate of transformation in production (DRT), and the domestic rate of substitution in consumption (DRS). If the country has monopoly power in trade, a competitive free trade solution will be characterized by $DRS = DRT \neq FRT$. By introducing a suitable tariff, a country can achieve $DRS = DRT = FRT$. A subsidy (tax)

[1] An early draft of this paper was read to seminars at Massachusetts Institute of Technology, the University of Chicago, and Stanford University by one of the authors. C. P. Kindleberger and H. G. Johnson have made useful suggestions.

[2] For instance, C. P. Kindleberger in his *International Economics* (Homewood, Ill.: Richard D. Irwin, Inc., 1958), as does also G. Haberler in his *Theory of International Trade* (Glasgow: William Hodge & Co., 1936), states the economic argument in favor of subsidies and tariffs without stating definitely that one is invariably superior to the other from the economic viewpoint.

[3] G. Haberler, "Some Problems in the Pure Theory of International Trade," *Economic Journal*, LX (June, 1950), 223–40.

[4] E. Hagen, "An Economic Justification of Protectionism," *Quarterly Journal of Economics*, LXXII (November, 1958), 496–514.

DISTORTIONS, TARIFFS AND THE THEORY OF OPTIMUM SUBSIDY   45

on the domestic production of import-ables (exportables) could equalize *DRT* and *FRT* but would destroy the quality of *DRS* with *DRT*. Hence it is clear that a tax-cum-subsidy on domestic produc-tion is necessarily inferior to an optimum tariff. Moreover it may be impossible in any given empirical situation to devise a tax-cum-subsidy that would yield a solu-tion superior to that arrived at under free trade.

By analogy we can argue that, in the case of domestic distortions, *DRS* = *FRT* ≠ *DRT* under free trade. A suit-able tariff can equalize *FRT* and *DRT* but would destroy the equality between *DRS* and *FRT*. Hence it is clear that no tariff may exist that would yield a solu-tion superior to that under free trade. A suitable tax-cum-subsidy on domestic production, however, would enable the policy-maker to secure *DRS* = *FRT* = *DRT* and hence is necessarily the opti-mum solution. Hence a tariff policy is also necessarily inferior to an optimum tax-cum-subsidy policy. And the same argument must hold true of trade sub-sidies as well since they also, like tariffs, are directed at *foreign* trade whereas the problem to be tackled is one of *domestic* distortion.

Three propositions, therefore, follow in the case of domestic distortions. (*a*) A tariff is not necessarily superior to free trade. (*b*) A tariff is not necessarily su-perior to an export (or import) subsidy. (*c*) A policy permitting the attainment of maximum welfare involves a tax-cum-subsidy on domestic production. Just as there exists an optimum tariff policy for a divergence between foreign prices and *FRT*, so there exists an *optimum subsidy* (or an equivalent tax-cum-subsidy) poli-cy for a divergence between domestic prices and *DRT*.

II. HABERLER ON EXTERNAL ECONOMIES

A divergence between the domestic commodity price ratios and the marginal rates of transformation between com-modities may arise from what are usually described as "external economies." These may take various forms.[5] It is most fash-ionable at the moment to discuss the ex-ternal economies arising from the inter-dependence of investment decisions.[6]

Haberler analyzes this problem in terms of the standard two-good, two-factor model of trade theory, using geo-metrical methods. Haberler is aware that a tariff is not necessarily superior to free trade. However, he is in error concerning the relative advantages of tariffs and trade subsidies. Further, he does not dis-cuss the optimum economic policy under the circumstances.

Haberler distinguishes between two sit-uations according to whether the domes-tic production of importables rises or falls (what he calls the direction of "speciali-zation"). We shall analyze each case separately.

Case 1.—In the former case, illustrated here in Figure 1*a*, *AB* is the production possibility curve. The discrepancy be-tween the domestic price ratio and the domestic rate of transformation (*DRT*)

[5] According to Haberler, "there may be a devia-tion between social and private cost due to external economies or diseconomies, i.e. due to certain cost-raising or cost-reduction factors which would come into play if one industry expanded and the other contracted—factors which for some reason or other are not, or not sufficiently, allowed for in private cost calculations" ("Some Problems . . . ," *op. cit.*, p. 236).

[6] This has been analyzed in the context of inter-national trade by J. Bhagwati, "The Theory of Com-parative Advantage in the Context of Under-devel-opment and Growth," *Pakistan Development Review*, II, No. 3 (Autumn, 1962), 339-53. See also H. Chenery, "The Interdependence of Investment De-cisions," in Moses Abramovitz *et al.*, *The Allocation of Economic Resources* (Stanford, Calif.: Stanford University Press, 1959).

46   JAGDISH BHAGWATI AND V. K. RAMASWAMI

leads to self-sufficiency equilibrium at *S*. Free trade, at the *given* international price *PF*, leads to production at *P*, consumption at *F*, export of agricultural goods, and a deterioration in welfare.[7]

The following comments are warranted. First, although Haberler does not state this explicitly, it can be shown that prohibitive protection may make the country worse off (Fig. 1*b*). Second, it follows from Section I that *no tariff* may be superior to free trade (this is implicit, we think, in Haberler's statements elsewhere in his paper). Finally, the optimum result could be achieved by a

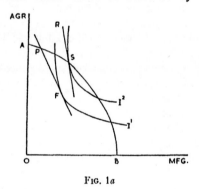

Fig. 1*a*

policy of tax-cum-subsidy on domestic production. Such a policy is illustrated in Figure 1*c* where the tax-cum-subsidy eliminates the divergence between commodity prices and *DRT* and brings production to *P'* and consumption to *F'*.

Case II.—Haberler distinguishes the other case by arguing that the self-sufficiency price ratio *RS* may be less steep than the *given* foreign price ratio *PF*. Here the production point is shifted to the right by free trade.[8] In this case, Haberler argues that "the country would

specialize in the 'right' direction but not sufficiently. *It would after trade be better off than before, but it would not reach the optimum point.... In that case an export or import subsidy (rather than a tariff) would be indicated.*"[9]

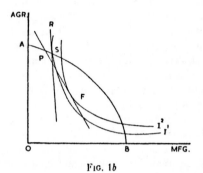

Fig. 1*b*

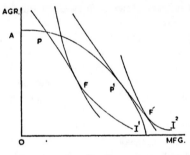

Fig. 1*c*

While Haberler is right in arguing that a movement to the right of *S*, when free trade is introduced, will necessarily be beneficial, his conclusion that an export

---

[7] Haberler wrongly seems to imply that the country must export agricultural goods in this case. There is no reason, *once there is a domestic distortion*, why a country should necessarily export the commodity that is cheaper than abroad in the absence of trade.

[8] This, of course, is erroneous, as noted in n. 7. Haberler implies that under free trade manufactures will now become the exported good. Haberler also describes this case as characterized by specialization in the "right" direction. He is right if, by this, he means that the movement of the production point to the right of *S*, caused by free trade, will necessarily improve welfare. He is wrong, however, if he means that the commodity exported will be that which would have been exported if the divergence did not exist.

[9] Haberler, "Some Problems ...," *op. cit.*, p. 237. Our italics.

(or import) subsidy is indicated and would be preferable to a tariff is erroneous in every rigorous sense in which it may be understood. First, it cannot be argued that the optimal solution when the policy used is an export (or import) subsidy will be necessarily superior to that when the policy used is a tariff. As argued in Section I, both policies are handicapped as they seek to affect *foreign* trade whereas the distortion is *domestic;* there is no reason why one should necessarily be better than the other. Second, nor can one maintain that an export (or import) subsidy will necessarily exist that will be superior to free trade, just as one cannot maintain that a tariff necessarily will be available that is superior to free trade. Third, the optimum solution again is to impose a tax-cum-subsidy on domestic production.

Case III.—Hagen on wage differentials. —A divergence between *DRT* and the domestic price ratio, arising from factor-market imperfections in the form of intersectoral wage differentials, has been discussed in relation to trade policy by Hagen. Before we proceed to Hagen's analysis, certain observations concerning the circumstances in which differential remuneration causes a distortion are in order.

The observed wage differentials between the urban and rural sector may *not* represent a genuine distortion. For instance, they may reflect (1) a utility preference between occupations on the part of the wage-earners, or (2) a rent (on scarce skills), or (3) a return on investment in human capital (by training), or (4) a return on investment in the cost of movement (from the rural to the urban sector). There *would* be a distortion, however, where the differential is attributable to (5) trade-union intervention, or (6) prestige-cum-humanitarian grounds

("I must pay my man a decent wage") that fix wages at varying levels in different sectors. Two other types of explanations may also be discussed: (7) Hagen argues that the differential occurs in manufacture because this is the advancing sector and growing activities inevitably have to pay higher wages to draw labor away from other industries. While this "dynamic" argument appears to provide support for the distortionary character of the differential, there are difficulties with it. For instance, the fact that a differential has to be maintained to draw labor away may very well be due to the cost of movement.[10] (8) A more substantive argument is that the rural sector affords employment to non-adult members of the family whereas, in the urban sectory, the adult alone gets employment (owing to institutional reasons such as factory acts). Hence, to migrate, an adult would need to be compensated for the loss of employment by the non-adult members of his family.[11] If this is the case, there is certainly a market imperfection (assuming that individual preferences rather than collective preferences, expressed in legislation, are relevant) and hence distortion.[12]

[10] Other difficulties also arise when the argument is used in conjunction with a static analysis. These will be discussed later.

[11] This hypothesis was suggested to us by D. Mazumdar.

[12] This "distortion," unlike the others, involves a contraction of the labor force as labor moves from one sector to another. Hence, the following analysis does not apply and a fresh solution, incorporating a changing labor supply, is called for. Note here also that the wage differential variety of distortion is quite distinct from the distortion caused when, although the wage is identical between sectors, it differs from the "shadow" optimal wage. This distinction has been blurred by recent analysts, especially W. A. Lewis, "Economic Development with Unlimited Supplies of Labor," *Manchester School*, XXII (May, 1959), and H. Myint, "Infant Industry Arguments for Assistance to Industries in

In the following analysis, we shall assume that the wage differential represents a genuine distortion while remaining skeptical about the degree to which such distortions obtain in the actual world.[13] We will also adopt Hagen's analytical framework of a two-commodity, two-factor model and a *constant* wage differential. The assumption of constancy of the wage differential raises some difficulties, probably with reasons (3) and (6) but certainly with reason (7), on which Hagen mainly relies. As will be seen presently, Hagen's analysis involves the *contraction* of manufactures after the introduction of trade; if the wage differential is due to the fact that manufactures are expanding and drawing labor away, it should surely reverse itself during the transition from autarky to free trade. The difficulty is that Hagen, in relying upon reason (7) while using traditional trade analysis, is illegitimately superimposing a dynamic argument upon a comparative statics framework. To analyze the distortion arising from reason (8) one needs an explicitly dynamic analysis. Hence, the following analysis applies, strictly speaking, only to distortions produced by reasons (5) and (6).

Hagen concludes that a tariff is superior to free trade when the *importable manufacturing* activity has to pay the higher wage.

As a result of the wage disparity, manufacturing industry will be undersold by imports when the foreign exchanges are in equilibrium. Protection which permits such industry to exist will increase real income in the economy. However, a subsidy per unit of labour equal to the

wage differential will increase real income further, and if combined with free trade will permit attaining an *optimum optimorum*.[14]

Hagen works successively with two models that differ only in the assumption concerning the number of factors of production. Since the first model has only one factor and is only a special case of the second, two-factor model, we shall concentrate here on the latter. It is assumed that all the standard Paretian conditions obtain except for the wage differential. We begin with Hagen's analysis and then comment on it.

In Figure 2a, *AQB* is the production possibility curve on the assumption of a wage uniform between the two sectors. *APB* is the production possibility curve, assuming the given wage differential.[15] The wage differential against manufac-

---

[13] the Setting of Dynamic Trade Theory" (paper presented to a conference on "Trade in a Developing World," International Economic Association, September, 1961). Also see Bhagwati, *op. cit.*

[13] A. Kafka, "A New Argument for Protectionism," *Quarterly Journal of Economics*, LXXVI (February, 1962), 163–66.

[14] *Op. cit.*, p. 498. Hagen himself does not state explicitly that he is confining the analysis to the case where the differential operates against the importable activity. If the differential were to work in the contrary direction, the results would naturally have to be modified radically.

[15] The reader can satisfy himself as to the "shrinking in" of the production possibility curve by manipulating the Edgeworth box diagram. The careful reader of Hagen's paper will note that Hagen draws the "shrunk-in" production possibility curve so that it is convex (in the mathematical sense). This, however, is a property that does not necessarily follow from the assumptions made, and it is possible to produce counter-examples of concavity, although we have not been able to produce a general mathematical proof. (When this paper was read at Stanford, Paul David drew attention to A. Fishlow and P. David's "Optimal Resource Allocation in an Imperfect Market Setting," *Journal of Political Economy*, LXIX [December, 1961], 529–46, for a proof of this proposition. These writers have also anticipated our criticism concerning Hagen's confusion of statics and dynamics.) We shall use the convex curve, however, as it enables us to state our propositions in terms of equalities and without bothering about second-order conditions; the substance of the propositions *that interest us here* is unaffected by this complication. The divergence between the commodity price ratio and the domestic rate of transformation, which also results from the wage differential, needs a rigorous proof, which can be found by the reader in Hagen, *op. cit.*, pp. 507–8.

tures, aside from reducing the production feasibilities, will make the commodity price ratio, at any production point on APB, steeper than the rate of transformation along APB so that the price ratio understates the profitability of transforming agriculture into manufactures. PT being the foreign price ratio, the economy produces at P and consumes at F under free trade. Under self-sufficiency, however, the relative price of manufactures being higher, the economy would produce and consume at S and be better

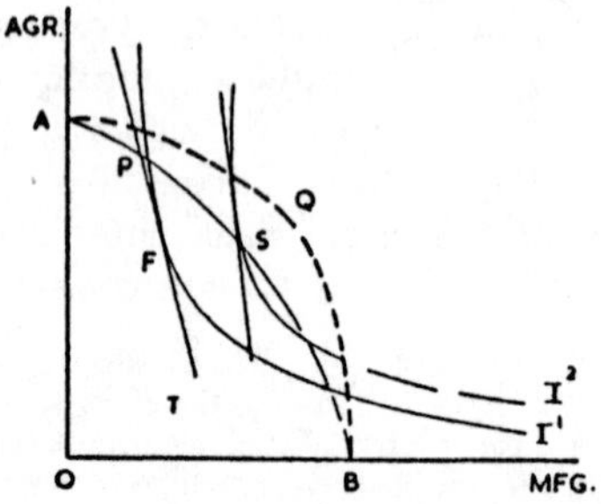

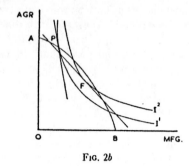

Fig. 2b

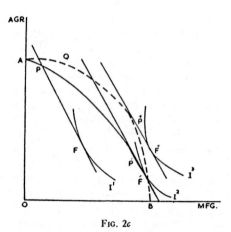

Fig. 2a

off. From this, Hagen concludes: "Protection of manufacturing from foreign trade will increase real income."[16]

However, the conclusion must be rectified. First, as illustrated in Figure 2b, where the contrary possibility is shown, prohibitive protection is not necessarily superior to free trade. Second, it may further be impossible, as argued in Section I, to find any level of tariff (or trade subsidy) that is superior to free trade. Third, a tax-cum-subsidy on the domestic production of the commodities, which eliminates the divergence between the price ratio and DRT (along APB) would necessarily yield a better solution than protection. In Figure 2c, F' represents the consumption and P' the production reached by the pursuit of such a tax-cum-

[16] Hagen, *op. cit.*, p. 510.

subsidy policy.[17] Finally, a policy of tax-cum-subsidy on labor use would achieve equilibrium production at P'' and consumption at F'' in Figure 2c and produce the "first-best" result, as recognized by Hagen.

Fig. 2c

Note that, in contrast to the case of external economies, the optimum tax-cum-subsidy on domestic production, while superior to protection or trade subsidy,

[17] In relation to this point, it is also worth noting that the standard procedure adopted by several tariff commissions, of choosing a tariff rate that just offsets the differential between the average domestic cost at some *arbitrary*, given production of the existing units and the landed (c.i.f.) cost, is not necessarily correct. There is no reason why the tariff rate which just offsets this differential is necessarily the tariff rate which is optimum from the viewpoint of economic policy.

JAGDISH BHAGWATI AND V. K. RAMASWAMI

does not yield the *optimum optimorum* in the wage-differential case. The reason is straightforward. The wage differential causes *not merely* a domestic distortion but *also* a restriction of the production possibility curve. A tax-cum-subsidy on domestic production measure will, therefore, merely eliminate the domestic distortion but not restore the economy to the Paretian production possibility curve (AQB). It will thus achieve the equality of FRT and DRS with DRT along *the restricted production possibility curve* (APB) and hence constitute the optimal solution when the wage differential cannot be directly eliminated. Where, however, a direct attack on the wage differential is permitted, the fully optimal, "first-best" solution can be achieved by a policy of tax-cum-subsidy on factor use.

III. CONCLUSION

We have argued here that an optimum subsidy (or a tax-cum-subsidy equivalent) is necessarily superior to any tariff when the distortion is domestic. It may be questioned, however, whether this advantage would obtain in practice. This question, of course, cannot be settled purely at the economic level. A fully satisfactory treatment of this issue would necessarily involve disciplines ranging from politics to psychology. However, by way of conclusion, we think it would be useful to consider a few arguments that are relevant to the final, realistic choice of policy.

1. The contention that the payment of subsidies would involve the collection of taxes which in practice cannot be levied in a non-distortionary fashion is fallacious. A tax-cum-subsidy scheme could always be devised that would *both* eliminate the estimated divergence and collect taxes sufficient to pay the subsidies.

2. The estimation problem is also easier with subsidies than with tariffs. The former involves estimating merely the divergence between the commodity price ratio and DRT (at the relevant production point). The latter must extend the exercises necessarily to the estimation of the relevant DRS (which involves locating both the right level of income *and* the relevant consumption point).

3. The political argument has usually been claimed by free traders to favor the payment of subsidies under external economy arguments like infant industries. It is thought that it would be difficult to pay a subsidy longer than strictly necessary whereas a tariff may be more difficult to abolish. It must be pointed out, however, that this argument also pulls the other way because, precisely for the reasons which make a subsidy difficult to continue, a subsidy is difficult to choose in preference to a tariff.

[12]

Trade and Public Finance

(A Memorial Lecture for V. K. Ramaswami, given at the
Delhi School of Economics, November, 1970)[1]

No permanent Civil Servant, since J. S. Mill, has made such a contribution to theoretical economics as V. K. Ramaswami. Mill was not strictly a Civil Servant, but he had a full-time job at India House, from 1823-1858. I do not know if this is coincidence, or whether practical concern for India also stimulates contemplation. There are very few other contenders for this prize of mine. In the same field of optimum trade theory, C.F. Bickerdike, a permanent U.K. Civil Servant, made a path-breaking contribution in the *Economic Journal* of 1906.[2] But he was not prolific. D. Bensusan Butt, for long a Treasury official, is another candidate deserving mention. But I have no doubt that the quality and number of Ramaswami's contributions justify my first remark. I am sure, however, that he would not have liked me to speak of his achievements without mentioning his frequent collaborators, Jagdish Bhagwati and T.N. Srinivasan. It is something of a joke that these three authors have published in all seven possible combinations of B. R. and S.

Academically speaking, Ramaswami was an economist of the 1960's. I do not mean merely that most of his output was during those years. I think it is correct to say that the style of most academic work on developing countries changed significantly between the 1950's and 1960's. Economists in the 1950's—anyway those working on developing country problems—tended to assume, by and large, that both producers and consumers—whether in agriculture or industry—in developing countries were unresponsive to price changes. Everything was very inelastic—so price changes would affect income distribution much more than they would result in beneficial shifts in production or consumption. Farmers might even have perverse reactions. Industrial entrepreneurs were non-existent, or mere converted traders with all their supposed faults; they would need tremendous jolts or fabulous rewards to make them do anything. So, with the apparent success of the U.K. economy in wartime, and with the

---

1. This is a slightly improved version of the lecture actually delivered. I am indebted to M.FG. Scott for helping to improve it.
2. C.F. Bickerdike, 'The Theory of Incipient Taxes', *Economic Journal*, 1906.

120   I. M. D. LITTLE

Russian example also in mind, planning was stressed. Emphasis was also laid on the exploitative or one-sided nature of trade relations with developed countries. The horrors of the great depression were still in people's minds and so was the war—both of which resulted in import starvation. So trade was distrusted, and export pessimism was also rife. There were calls for a new economics especially suited to developing countries. It was a decade of appeals for unorthodoxy.

There was no trace of this in Ramaswami's writing. Almost all his work is concerned with showing how the price mechanism can best be adapted to serve national ends. The presumption is that it works well. He was also entirely relaxed about foreign trade. One should, of course, try to influence the developed countries to behave well, and to make unreciprocated concessions. But their remaining malpractices need not, and should not, stop the developing countries from making the best of the world as it is.

He saw early and clearly that tariffs and import controls were not, in the main, a method of defence against trade threats, but a means of reallocating resource within the developing country. He was also orthodox and neo-classical in his methods. He used and developed traditional trade models to get his results. He robustly paid no heed to the capital theory war, and cheerfully wrote $P = f (K, L)$, and even derived the marginal product of capital from it. I sympathize with him, for it seems to me that if one can get some useful insight from disputable methods — and I believe Ramaswami did, for instance in his *Economica* 1968 article on "Factor Movements"[3], then one need not fuss too much about the dispute.

I have said he was an economist of the 1960s. For, during this last decade, most economic writing on developing countries has become more orthodox. Indeed, many economists have critically concerned themselves with both theoretical and empirical analyses of the policies evolved in the 1950's. Ramaswami's work, apart from his very first paper, was entirely theoretical; but it was in tune with more empirical work and with events. For the 1960s have seen, in many developing countries, though not in India, a decline in the use of central planning through controls, and a growth in the rational use of prices as a means of achieving national ends—this later subject being Ramaswami's chief interest, as it is, indeed, mine also.

3. V. K. Ramaswami, 'International Factor Movements and the National Advantage', *Economica*, August 1968.

Now let me touch in more detail on what, in my opinion, were some of his most important contributions. Perhaps the most important, in his *JPE* 1963 article, with Bhagwati, was that one should 'go to the heart of the matter'. To put it in their own words "intervention should be aimed directly to the point at which the distortion or externality occurs".[4] This seems very obvious now, and I think it was implied in some writing on welfare economics, especially in James Meade's *"Trade and Welfare"*. But it had not been sufficiently stressed, and therefore it was still not recognised in much writing on trade theory, let alone, of course, by trade officials or negotiators. Indeed, for 167 years, from Alexander Hamilton in 1791 to E. E. Hagen in 1958, domestic distortions were used as an argument for protection. There was a grain of truth in these justifications. Some low level of protection must produce a better result than *laissez-faire* in the face of domestic distortions, provided there are not also external distortions (this is a result of the three horses working in harness together—the troika, Bhagwati, Ramaswami, and Srinivasan).[5] But it was a misleading grain of truth, for domestic distortions cannot appropriately be said to justify protection if better policies are at hand. Also, the externalities implicit in any valid statement of the infant industry argument, even combined with an undesirably high level of wages in manufacturing, could hardly justify the very high levels of protection which reigned in some now industrialized countries during the second half of the 19th century, and the first quarter of this century.

In addition to stressing the first-best solution, Ramaswami contributed a number of interesting second-best results. For instance, even if there is a case for a revenue tariff, nevertheless any tax on the imported inputs used in exports should be rebated.[6] This justifies a practice which has, I am sure rightly, been increasingly adopted by the developing countries (although sometimes the procedures are so clumsy and unreliable that exporters fail to collect their due, with a result that exports remain inhibited).

4. J. Bhagwati and V. K. Ramaswami, 'Domestic Distortions, Tariffs and the Theory of Optimum Subsidy', *J.P.E.*, February 1963.
5. J. Bhagwati, V. K. Ramaswami, and T.N. Srinivasan, 'Domestic Distortions, Tariffs, and the Theory of Optimum Subsidy: Some Further Results', *J.P.E.*, November/ December 1969.
6. V. K. Ramaswami and T.N. Srinivasan, 'Optimal Subsidies and Taxes when some Factors are Traded', *J.P.E.*, July/August 1968.

I have drawn a diagram of the model used to produce this result (see Diagram I). This diagram shows no tax obstacle impeding the flow

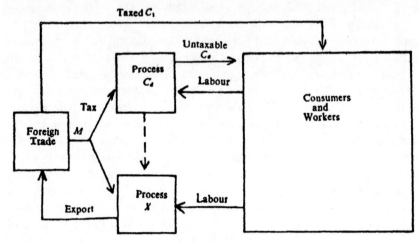

Diagram I.

$X \rightarrow FT \rightarrow M \rightarrow X$, where M stands for metal which flows into both domestic processes.

In intuitive terms, the reason is that this is entirely a non-consumption flow: since the main objective of taxation is to restrain consumption, only harm would result from impeding such a flow. But note that in this model the export has as inputs only domestic labour and an import. There are no domestic material inputs which themselves use taxed imported inputs (this complication is easily introduced into the model by drawing an arrow from the C_d process to the X process. One could think of C_d as being both a consumption good and a producer good, like electricity, paper, or furniture). I guess it can be proved all right that tariffs on the indirect imports resulting from the operation of a productive activity should also be rebated. But this would require difficult and not altogether objective calculations, and so might be deemed to be administratively impossible. Indeed, I am not aware that this kind of rebate of indirect taxes is actually given. If such rebates of taxation on indirect imports are ruled out, then I doubt whether this Ramaswami-Srinivasan result would any longer hold good. This would be a pity! I am sure that T.N. Srinivasan will quickly resolve this doubt.

Another point to note in the diagram is that the $M \rightarrow C_d$ flow is taxed, although M is an intermediate good. But this is only because the flow $C_d \rightarrow$ consumers is not taxable, ex-hypothesi. How does this link up with the Diamond-Mirrlees result[7] that only consumers' goods should be taxed? There is no conflict, because, in the latter model, all consumers' goods are taxable. Clearly a lot depends on what is taxable, and what is not. I shall revert to this later.

Meanwhile let me now recapitulate what seems in tariff theory to be the state of play—as Ramaswami left it. Here I am going to ignore national monopoly power, because this is a well-worked field, and it is generally accepted that inelasticities of foreign supply and demand can constitute a good reason for import and export taxes. Apart from this, with one exception which I shall mention later, there can be no argument for protection, given any conventional utility function, if the first best solution by way of domestic taxes and subsidies is attainable. The result I have just talked about is a specially strong case of denial of this last condition—for no domestic indirect taxes are allowed in this model. But we must ask whether it may not be rather generally true that optimum domestic taxes and subsidies cannot be imposed. One must take notice here of the argument that a tariff may be desirable because domestic taxes, to pay for the subsidization required to remove the domestic distortion, are themselves distorting. Of course, this is not always the case. One can reasonably posit optimal self-financing tax-cum-subsidy arrangements in some cases. But how generally can one do this? I believe that the economic literature has been a little cavalier in saying that if the distortion is such and such, then a subsidy on such and such is optimal. I have no doubt that this thought was crossing the mind of our chairman, Dr. I. G. Patel, even before I enunciated it!

Let us concentrate on the argument for some protection of manufacturers because a factor of production, e.g. labour, costs manufacturers more than its cost to society. The first-best solution is to subsidise that factor, provided it can be shown that the tax required to pay the subsidy, or the reduction in government expenditure if no tax is raised, does not upset some other condition of optimality. Thus Meade has written "This (first-best) argument, however, tacitly assumes that there are no problems involved in raising the revenue for the payment of the subsidy . . . . But . . . the fact that taxes imposed for the purpose of raising revenue themselves cause divergencies between values and costs is a conflicting factor."[8] It should be noted that Meade did not consider

7. P. Diamond and J. Mirrlees, 'Optimal Taxation and Public Production', parts I and II, *A.E.R.* 1971.
8. J. E. Meade, *Trade and Welfare*, pp. 230-31.

the possibility of reducing government expenditure to pay for the subsidy. It seems to follow that there may be a public finance reason for protection, and I do not think this view has been completely exploded by the work of Ramaswami and others.

In a recent book by T. Scitovsky, M.FG. Scott, and myself, the authors went, I believe, a little further and argued that protection could be justified essentially only for *administrative* reasons.[9] This is different from saying 'for public finance reasons', where these latter include the fact that raising taxes may destroy some optimum condition.

The authors further argued that these administrative reasons are weak. I would like to submit our arguments here, because economists tend only to comment on articles, even if they read books. But I shall also carry the argument a little further than in the book. Let us assume that all domestically produced goods are as taxable as imports of them. I shall also assume that the government has imposed what would be an optimum indirect tax system if there were no distortions within the productive processes. This implies that all rates of indirect tax are believed to be just at the level that they should be, taking account of the elasticity of demand, of any distorting effects of the tax on private decisions, of the wealth of the consumers of each good, and, in general, of all the benefits which flow from both public and private expenditure. Initially, there is no protection—i.e., excise taxes are all at the same level as customs duties.

We consider an economy in this impossible position because one can easily make viable comparisons only with optimum situations. Thus, if taxes are not optimal then, whatever tax-subsidy schemes are suggested for the purpose of curing a particular distortion, the issue can always be confused by saying that the tax could have been better used to correct some other distortion or disequilibrium.

Now the government of our country suddenly decides that manufacturing needs encouragement because of some factor distortion, and considers protection. In the book, we argued that there was no *prima facie* case for or against instituting the protection by raising the customs duty as compared with lowering the domestic excise tax (or subsidizing the domestic production if the optimal tax, before protection was considered, was held to be zero). In this respect I now want to make a stronger

---

9.   Ian Little, Tibor Scitovsky, and Maurice Scott, *Industry and Trade in some Developing Countries*, Oxford University Press, 1970, pp. 135-144.

statement and argue that *lowering* the excise tax (or subsidizing) is very probably the best way of instituting the protection from a purely public finance point of view. Let us first suppose that the government wants to encourage the production of one particular good. It may do this with or without protection. Either way production is 'subsidized', but in the case of protection the price of the good is simultaneously raised by the unit value of the 'subsidy'. Diagram II illustrates this. Letting p

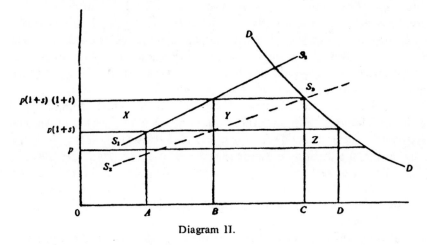

Diagram II.

be the cif price, at which supply is perfectly elastic, the initial position is domestic production of OA with both foreign and domestic goods incurring a sales tax of s. It is desired to raise production to OB. One can do this by paying a proportional 'subsidy' of $\frac{t}{1+t}$ to domestic producers, so that with production of OB their marginal cost is reduced from $p(1+s)(1+t)$ to $p(1+s)$; i.e., the supply curve is lowered from $S_1 S_1$ to $S_2 S_2$. Alternatively one can raise the price to $p(1+s)(1+t)$ by putting on a tariff of t.

The sole relevant difference is that the tariff method raises the price, and makes some difference to government revenue, as compared with the 'subsidy' method.[10] It is an economically irrelevant difference that in one case the producers receive the rectangle marked X from the public, while in the other case they get it from the government.

10. We put 'subsidy' in inverted commas, since it may or may not involve an actual subsidy. The net-of-sales-tax marginal cost at B is $p(1+t)$, and this has to become $p(1+s)$: therefore, the actual tax or subsidy is $\frac{t-s}{1+t}$.

So the best method depends on balancing the effects of the price rise against the change in revenue. With the 'subsidy' method there is a direct loss of revenue of X, and there are no indirect effects since there is no price change. With the tariff method there is a price change, so that the change in actual revenue depends on many circumstances: it should be noted that it is *not*, in general, an increase equal to the rectangle marked Y. This would only (except fortuitously) be the case if the original optimum tax (s) was zero, and if all other (optimum) taxes were also zero—an eventuality which can be ruled out. If s is positive, the tax revenue raised on this particular good is the rectangle Y *less* the rectangle Z. But the effects of substitution must also be allowed for. Tax receipts on other goods may fall or rise as a result of expenditure being switched to or from the protected good.

One extreme (but not, perhaps, in practice uncommon) possibility is worth mentioning. Suppose the optimum sales tax was a maximum revenue tax (after allowing for the effect of substitution on tax receipts). In that event, the tariff would reduce revenue by more than the subsidy ($X+Y-Z$ is negative). Raising the price of the good would both reduce revenue and make consumers worse off. By subsidizing instead, the government can both increase its other expenditure and secure lower consumers' prices.

It is also worth considering the opposite extreme—where the optimum tax is zero. This is likely to be the case of an intermediate good, or a final good much consumed by the poor. In the former case, taxation generally has no point in terms of the final objectives of economic policy, unless the final goods produced by the intermediate are administratively untaxable or difficult to tax. Since such taxation distorts production decisions, it would, therefore, normally be better to increase tax rates on final goods to pay for the protection desired. In the latter case, it is quite likely that the beneficial effects of government expenditure are less than the loss of welfare which would result from increasing the prices of such goods. Against this argument it may be objected that, if this is true, the good should in principle have been subsidized. This objection is valid if the difficulties involved in subsidizing are ignored, and we would argue that the absence of subsidization does not imply that raising the price of such goods rather than reducing government expenditure (or raising other taxes) might not reduce welfare. It is worth noting that when governments desire to encourage the domestic production of such goods—intermediates (including capital goods and raw materials) and those consumed by the poor—they are in fact more inclined to use subsidization. The subsidization of agriculture in the U.S.A. and the U.K. and elsewhere, though not in the *EEC*, is the prime example.

Thus the most plausible cases for those who would argue that protection should be instituted by raising a tariff, are those where the optimum rate of tax is positive but less than the maximum revenue rate[11]. In these cases the tariff may not increase actual revenue, but it will at least yield a lower revenue loss than the subsidy method. In these cases we rely on the following very general argument (which really applies to all cases). The introduction of a reason for encouraging an industry, which therefore requires some significant financial support, disturbs the previous optimum set of taxes and government expenditures: consequently an optimum reshuffle is required. This cannot consist solely of raising the price of one particular good, for the familiar reason of a loss of consumers' surplus. The optimum reshuffle must consist of marginal increases in all existing taxes and reductions in existing expenditures. Since taxation on any one good is a very small part of total revenue, this implies that the 'subsidy' to producers (the newly discovered item of desirable expenditure) should be paid for by marginal changes everywhere, and not by a significantly large increase in the price of that particular good. In other words, protection is better instituted by a 'subsidy' (any desirable increase in the price being negligible).

It may seem strange that I have started by assuming an optimum level of taxation. Is it not true to say that much protection has come about as a result of instituting tariffs on goods which were previously untaxed, but which should have been taxed? No doubt! But this case is very easy to deal with. If the tariff represents an optimal level of taxation,

---

11. These cases may arise either (*a*) when the optimum tax is already relatively high, but demand is still inelastic, or (*b*) when the optimum tax is relatively low, and demand is elastic. If the optimum tax is average, meaning by this that switches of expenditure to or from other goods as a result of the price rise would have no effect on revenue, then the elasticity does not matter. This can be seen as follows. The actual increase in cost to the consumer of the quantity of good *A* bought after the price rise can be thought of as being paid for by reductions in the amount of *A* itself as well as other goods purchased. The division of these reductions between *A* and other goods is irrelevant if the tax on *A* and the average tax (weighted by the quantity changes) on other goods are equal. It is tempting to think that a modest increase in tax from, say, zero, if demand is very inelastic, and therefore distortion effects small, must be one of the tax rises most likely to be beneficial. Actually it will reduce revenue as spending is switched away from more highly taxed things.

it is obvious that there can be no public finance reason for not raising the same level of taxation on domestic production, and paying it back as a subsidy to the employment of some factor of production.

I now generalize. If the level of taxation on a good is optimal, it is always better to institute protection by reducing the domestic rate of tax. If the level is suboptimal, protection is best instituted by raising a tariff. But, in the former case, it is better still not to reduce the domestic rate of tax, but instead to keep it on and pay a subsidy which goes to the heart of the distortion. In the latter case, it is better still to increase the domestic tax to the same level as the tariff, and pay the resultant extra proceeds back in the form of a subsidy which also goes to the heart of the matter. Protection, by which I mean a lower rate of tax on the domestic product than on imports, is thus a correct policy only if the subsidy which goes to the heart of the matter is a subsidy on the product.[12] This implies not only a lower sales tax than import duty, but also an export subsidy equal to the difference in the rates. It is promotion as well as protection. However, I believe this to be an exceptional case, for it seems likely that beneficial externalities mostly flow through employment of some factor or other. People educate each other and disseminate information more than machines.

Some readers may feel at this point that I have cheated by considering the case of a particular good. What if the government believes that the whole of manufacturing industry requires encouragement? Does this not strengthen the case for protection? We can try to deal with this contention by thinking in terms of a three-good economy consisting of (a) a manufacture, which is both imported and produced, and is not consumed extensively by the poor; (b) food, which is produced both for home consumption, and for export where the demand is assumed to be perfectly elastic; and (c) some object of government expenditure. We assume also that it is optimum to tax the manufacture, and not to tax food. The optimal tax on the manufacture is in place. The strongest conceivable argument for protection arises if there is no other (direct) source of taxation, and if there are no costs of tax collection; and so this also is assumed.

In this model we can reasonably assume that there will be some rise in government revenue and expenditure if a tariff is instituted: this is

12. This has been shown by Dr. P. D. Bardhan in 'On Optimum Subsidy to a Learning Industry: an aspect of the Theory of Infant Industry Protection', M.I.T. Working Paper (in mimeo.).

because the quantity of manufactures consumed is unlikely to be much reduced, and because a switch of expenditure to manufactures will not result in any loss of taxation elsewhere.

Now consider Diagram III. The curve *PP* is the welfare gain from one rupee of government expenditure and *TT* the welfare loss from

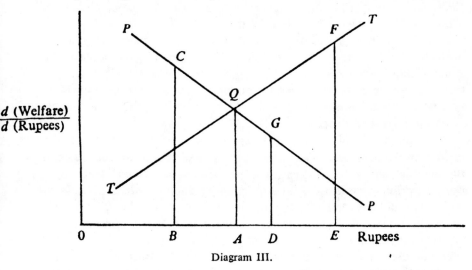

$$\frac{d\ (\text{Welfare})}{d\ (\text{Rupees})}$$

Diagram III.

raising a rupee from the public by taxing manufactures. That *PP* cuts *TT* from above is implied by the existence of an optimum. I have drawn the curves as straight lines of equal and opposite slope, for the sake of argument.

The optimum revenue and expenditure, where the welfare gain from an extra rupee of expenditure is just equal to the welfare loss of an extra rupee of revenue is at the point *Q*.[13]

The subsidy method gives a revenue and government expenditure loss of *AB* (where *AB* is analogous to *X*, in Diagram II). The welfare loss of the subsidy method is, therefore, *ABCQ*.

The tariff method increases the amount of money paid by consumers by *AE*. This amount *AE* exceeds the subsidy *AB* by the amount by which government expenditure increases, since the same quantity of

13. We neglect effects on private savings, and assume a balanced budget. One could incorporate some assumptions about private savings, but this would require an analysis through time. This would be complicated, and it is difficult to see that it would significantly alter the argument.

consumers' money goes to producers as with the subsidy method. Thus in Diagram III, if *AD* is the increase in government expenditure then $AB = DE$.[14] It is obvious that the resultant welfare loss *DEFQG* is greater than *ABCQ*.

Of course, the above result would not hold if the absolute slope of the *PP* curve were sufficiently greater than that of the *TT* curve. But I find it hard to imagine why this might be the case.

Thus far, we have asked the question whether it is better to institute protection either by raising the tariff, or by reducing the domestic tax ('subsidizing'). But inspection of Diagram III makes it clear that, in this model where manufactures are the only source of tax, a compromise is best. The tariff should be raised, at least a little, as well as the domestic tax rate reduced.

Consequently, it follows that the best policy is to have a slightly higher tariff than domestic tax—and to pay subsidies which 'go to the heart of the matter' as well. This seems to be the residual atom of truth left in the protection argument. I think it is a very small residual indeed—for our last model has tended to favour protectionism to an absurd degree. In reality, taxes on manufactures constitute only a fraction of the resources available to governments, and it is certainly not true that all manufactures deserve encouragement relative to other sectors—where externalities may often be just as, or more, important.

Everything I have said depends on domestic goods being administratively taxable, and the source of distortion being administratively subsidizable. Almost every tax or subsidy can be administratively policed at some cost. So to advance the argument further we need some hard work on the costs of administrating taxes to achieve various proportions of the theoretical revenue which should be raised if there were no evasion; and also more work on the importance of distortions of all kinds.

But, so far as the justifiability of protection is concerned, it does not follow that if a domestic good is less taxable than an import, it should be taxed at a *lower* rate. This may be the case if a high domestic tax results in a fall in 'organized' easily taxable production in favour of illicit or small scale production which evades or avoids the tax. But if this switching tendency is weak, there could be a purely revenue case for negative protection—thus if the 'organized' supply were very inelastic, it could be taxed more heavily than imports, without raising the price and

14. By analogy with Diagram II, $AB = DE = X$: and $AD = Y - Z$.

without much switching either to imports, or to a domestic supply source which evades the duty.

My own impression is that domestic production is as easily taxable as imports as soon as factory production replaces workshop and household production. The rapid increase in the relative importance of excise taxes in some developing countries supports this view. The taxability of imports may also be exaggerated. Under-invoicing and smuggling are major problems in a number of developing countries.

The next problem to consider is whether those subsidies which are appropriate for the removal of domestic distortions can be administered at reasonable cost.

The suggested list for potential subsidy includes training, research and development, and unskilled labour. We note that the first two often are to some extent subsidized. But nobody has yet taken the idea of subsidizing labour really seriously. The immediate argument usually raised is that the unions would get at it, and real wages would rise, thus making the subsidy futile. Since the intention is not to increase the profitability of industry, I do not think this is a valid argument. There is certainly no reason to suppose that the workers in an industry are likely to benefit more by its subsidization than by its protection. However, in trying to appropriate the subsidy, the unions might admittedly cause some inflation. Nevertheless I believe that even this could be avoided, and that a wage subsidy which rapidly declined to zero at a certain wage level, say Rs 300-350, could even be made part of an anti-inflationary incomes policy. But I have no time to do more than throw this out as a suggestion.

We finally note that industry's inputs, so far far from being subsidized, are often taxed, or anyway provided at more than their social cost—or there is an actual shortage of inputs. Perhaps it would be best to eliminate these created distortions, of which there are many, before trying to eliminate those which arise naturally from imperfect markets or externalities. For instance, the use of labour is taxed, even if only for social security purposes: and such important inputs as electricity and telephone calls do not always flow freely. This really brings one to the problem of how far intermediate goods can be made tax-exempt, which is the second modern fiscal guide-line I have referred to. There are many interesting administrative problems here, arising from the dual nature of quite a number of goods. There may also occasionally be an argument for taxing pure intermediates on income distribution grounds. I have, of course, the Indian fertilizer tax in mind here. But again I have no time to explore these matters in this lecture.

I have turned to the practical problems arising from modern trade and tax theory. Much of what used to be thought of as trade theory has been shown to be simply public finance: and indeed to boil down to such mundane matters as administrative costs. I cannot think that V. K. Ramaswami did not believe in the practical importance of the sort of theoretical work he did. So, if he had not been so tragically removed from the economic and Indian scene, I believe he would have been working on such matters. If, as I both hope and suspect, the 1970's prove to be a decade of greatly reduced protection in developing countries, and as a result greatly increasing exports of manufactures, both to each other and to the industrialized countries, then some of the credit will be due to him.

I. M. D. LITTLE

[13]

THE JOURNAL OF
POLITICAL ECONOMY

| *Volume LXXIV* | JUNE 1966 | *Number 3* |

THE STRUCTURE OF A TARIFF SYSTEM AND THE
EFFECTIVE PROTECTIVE RATE

W. M. CORDEN*
Australian National University

THE theory of tariff structure is concerned with the effects of tariffs and other trade taxes in a system with many traded goods. It allows for the vertical relationships between tariff rates derived from the input-output relationships between products, an aspect until recently completely neglected in the literature of international trade theory. Early contributions to the theory of tariff structure, developing the idea of the effective protective rate with respect to the policies of particular countries, have come from Barber (1955) for Canada, Humphrey (1962) for the United States, and the present author (1963) for Australia.[1] Johnson's (1965) exposition is the fullest available so far and also explores many implications. Empirical

contributions in which calculations of effective rates have been made on a large scale are by Balassa (1965) and Basevi (in press).[2] The present paper builds on this earlier work. In particular, in Part I the general equilibrium implications of the effective-protective-rate concept are spelled out, its relation to equilibrating exchange-rate adjustment is shown, and non-traded goods are introduced explicitly into the model. Part II suggests a variety of applications and extensions of the concept. The effective protective rate is a new measure which has considerable possibilities for the study of systems of protection. I have attempted here to show what it means, how it can be used, and how calculations of it must be interpreted when there is substitution between inputs.

It will be assumed in most of this paper that (1) the physical input-output coefficients are all fixed, (2) the elastici-

* This paper has benefited greatly from comments by H. W. Arndt and H. G. Johnson. I am indebted also to members of seminars at the L.S.E., Oxford, M.I.T., Yale, Brookings, Chicago, Berkeley, and Stanford, who commented on an earlier presentation of some of the main ideas.

[1] Barber's article represents the pioneering contribution on this subject. It is perhaps not surprising that the main idea can be found, treated briefly, in J. E. Meade (1955).

[2] A recent Australian official committee has made some calculations of effective protective rates and has given the concept some prominence in Australia (see *Report of the Committee of Economic Enquiry* [1965]).

ties of demand for all exports and supply of all imports are infinite, and (3) all tradable goods remain traded even after tariffs and other taxes and subsidies have been imposed, so that the internal price of each importable is given by the foreign price plus tariff. Throughout it will be assumed that (4) appropriate fiscal and monetary policies maintain total expenditure equal to full employment income and that (5) all tariffs and other trade taxes and subsidies are non-discriminatory as between countries of supply or demand. Assumption (1) is reconsidered in Part II, Section H, and assumptions (2) and (3) in Part II, Section J.

I. THE BASIC THEORY OF TARIFF STRUCTURE AND EFFECTIVE PROTECTIVE RATES

A. THE EFFECTIVE PROTECTIVE RATE

Ordinary *nominal* tariffs apply to commodities, but resources move as between economic activities. Therefore, to discover the resource-allocation effects of a tariff structure one must calculate the protective rate for each activity, that is, the *effective* protective rate. This is the main message of the new theory of tariff structures. The effective protective rate is the percentage increase in value added per unit in an economic activity which is made possible by the tariff structure relative to the situation in the absence of tariffs but with the same exchange rate. It depends not only on the tariff on the commodity produced by the activity but also on the input coefficients and the tariffs on the inputs.

Consider the simple case of an importable product, j, which has only a single input, also an importable, i. There are no taxes and subsidies affecting j and i other than the import tariffs. The formula for the effective protective rate

for the activity producing j can be derived as follows:

Let

v_j = value added per unit of j in activity j in absence of tariffs;
v_j' = value added per unit of j in activity j made possible by the tariff structure;
g_j = effective protective rate for activity j;
p_j = price of a unit of j in absence of tariffs;
a_{ij} = share of i in cost of j in absence of tariffs;
t_j = tariff rate on j;
t_i = tariff rate on i.

Then

$$v_j = p_j(1 - a_{ij}) , \qquad (1)$$

$$v_j' = p_j[(1 + t_j) - a_{ij}(1 + t_i)] , \quad (2)$$

$$g_j \equiv \frac{v_j' - v_j}{v_j} . \qquad (3)$$

From equations (1), (2), and (3),

$$g_j = \frac{t_j - a_{ij} t_i}{1 - a_{ij}} . \qquad (4)$$

This is the key formula, the implications of which can really be summarized as follows:

If $t_j = t_i$, then $g_j = t_j = t_i$.

If $t_j > t_i$, then $g_j > t_j > t_i$.

If $t_j < t_i$, then $g_j < t_j < t_i$.

If $t_j < a_{ij} t_i$, then $g_j < 0$.

If $t_j = 0$, then $g_j = -t_i \dfrac{a_{ij}}{1 - a_{ij}}$.

If $t_i = 0$, then $g_j = \dfrac{t_j}{1 - a_{ij}}$.

$$\frac{\partial g_j}{\partial t_j} = \frac{1}{1 - a_{ij}} ,$$

$$\frac{\partial g_j}{\partial t_i} = -\frac{a_{ij}}{1 - a_{ij}} ,$$

$$\frac{\partial g_j}{\partial a_{ij}} = \frac{t_j - t_i}{(1 - a_{ij})^2} .$$

Furthermore, equation (4) can be rewritten as

$$l_j = (1 - a_{ij})g_j + a_{ij}l_i . \quad (4.1)$$

This means that the nominal rate on the final good is a weighted average of its own effective rate and the tariff rate on its input.

For many importable inputs into the jth product (inputs $1, 2, \ldots, n$), but with no exportable or non-traded inputs, it can similarly be shown[3] that

$$g_j = \frac{l_j - \sum_{i=1}^{n} a_{ij}l_i}{1 - \sum_{i=1}^{n} a_{ij}} . \quad (4.2)$$

The implications are the same as above, except that in place of the single input tariff, t_i, it is necessary to write the weighted average of input tariffs

$$\frac{\sum_{i=1}^{n} a_{ij}l_i}{\sum_{i=1}^{n} a_{ij}} .$$

It is important to note that the effective protective rate for a product is not influenced by tariffs on inputs into its inputs. One need go only one step downward in the input-output structure. For example, a tariff on raw cotton, while it reduces effective protection for spinning, has no effect on the effective rate for weaving. To the weavers only the cost of yarn matters, and that is determined by the given world yarn price plus tariff.

B. INTRODUCING EXPORTABLES

So far we have been concerned with the effective protection for an importable

[3] See Johnson (1965) and Basevi (in press).

where the only inputs are importables. It is easy to encompass the discussion to include exportables. We can calculate the effective protection for an importable where some or all inputs are exportables, or for an exportable where the inputs are importables or other exportables. It needs only to be remembered that an export subsidy raises the internal price of a product and is the equivalent of a tariff, while an export tax is the equivalent of an import subsidy. In formula (4.2), g_j could be defined as the effective protective rate for any traded good, and the i's would include all inputs, whether importables or exportables. We continue to assume absence of non-traded inputs. Two examples can be given of how this method works. Suppose we have an exportable not subject to an export tax or subsidy. Its input is an importable paying a 10 per cent tariff. If the free-trade share of this input in the exportable's cost is 50 per cent, then effective protection for the exportable is negative, namely, -10 per cent. Alternatively, consider an importable which does not benefit from a tariff but which uses as an input an exportable paying a 25 per cent export tax (expressed as a percentage of the tax-free price). If the free-trade share of the exportable in the cost of the importable is 60 per cent, then the effective protection of the importable is 37.5 per cent.

C. PRODUCTION AND CONSUMPTION TAXES ON TRADABLES

So far we have allowed only for taxes and subsidies on trade. But effective protective rates are also affected by taxes and subsidies on domestic production or on domestic consumption of tradable goods—in the case of importables, taxes and subsidies which apply either to domestically produced import-competing goods alone or uniformly to these and to equivalent imports. We are concerned here only with taxes and subsidies levied specifically on tradable goods. Consumption taxes on finished goods do not affect effective protective rates. Consumption taxes on inputs have the same effect as tariffs on inputs: they raise the costs of the inputs to the using industries and therefore reduce effective protective rates for users. A production tax on any product has the same effect as an import subsidy or an export tax for that product, it reduces its effective rate. A production tax on an input, while it reduces the protection for the input, has no effect on effective protection for the using industry. Thus in our formula, t_j should be redefined to represent the net effect of the tariff or export subsidy and any production tax on industry j, while t_i nets the tariff or export subsidy on input i with any consumption tax on it.

D. THE SCALE OF EFFECTIVE RATES

Assume that the effective protective rate for each activity producing a tradable product has been calculated, taking into account tariffs, export taxes, export and import subsidies, consumption taxes, and production taxes. The next step is to order all these effective rates on a continuous scale through zero. The order is likely to be quite different from a similar scale based on nominal tariff rates and nominal export subsidies and taxes. It is quite possible that the nominal rates consist wholly of tariffs and export subsidies and hence are all *positive* nominal protective rates, and yet the scale of effective rates may include many negative rates. But whether a rate is positive or negative does not really matter for the present: all that matters is the order on the scale. The scale summarizes the total protective-rate structure. Assuming nor-

mal non-zero substitution elasticities in production, it tells us the *direction* in which this structure causes resources to be pulled as between activities producing traded goods. Domestic production will shift from low to high effective-protective-rate activities. Leaving aside for the moment a complication to be discussed below, namely, substitution between traded and non-traded goods, if four activities producing traded goods can be ordered along a scale A, B, C, D in ascending order of effective rates, we can say that output of A must fall and of D must rise and that resources will be pulled from A to B and from A and B to C; but without more precise information about production-substitution elasticities, we cannot say whether the outputs of B and C will rise or fall.

This is the production effect of the protective-rate structure and depends, thus, on the scale of effective rates and on production-substitution elasticities. In addition, the pattern of consumption will be affected by the protective-rate structure; consumption will shift from final goods with high nominal tariffs toward goods with low nominal tariffs. Thus the consumption effect still depends on the nominal tariffs of final goods as well as on consumption- (or expenditure-) substitution elasticities. Since fixed input coefficients and continued imports of all importables are assumed (assumptions (1) and (3) above), no consumption or usage effect results from tariffs on inputs.

E. THE EXCHANGE-RATE ADJUSTMENT

Now introduce into the analysis a single and only non-traded good, N. Assume that it is not an input into any tradable good, and no tradable good is an input into it. If the price of N remained constant, some resources would move from N into activities which obtain positive effective rates and toward N from activities with negative effective rates. Similarly, some consumption would be diverted toward N from products with positive nominal rates and in the reverse direction where nominal rates are negative (for example, export taxes). Assumption (4) was that aggregate expenditure is maintained equal to full employment income, so that this change in the production and expenditure patterns must lead to excess demand for or excess supply of N (internal imbalance) and a balance-of-payments surplus or deficit (external imbalance). To restore internal and external balance, a change in the price of N relative to the general internal price level of traded goods is then necessary. This could be brought about by flexible factor prices or by exchange-rate adjustment. If we assume a constant price of N, the exchange rate must alter; the function of exchange-rate adjustment in the model is to alter the price relationship between N and traded goods. This can clearly be generalized for the case where there are many non-traded goods; one must then hold constant not the price of each separate non-traded good but, rather, some kind of average price level. It should be noted that if the activities producing traded goods did not have significant production-substitution relationships with non-traded goods and if consumption-substitution relationships among traded and non-traded goods were also low, then the exchange-rate adjustment needed to maintain internal and external balance would also not be significant.

Suppose that in the first instance the protective-rate structure leads to balance-of-payments surplus and excess demand for non-traded goods as a whole.[4] Exchange-rate appreciation is then re-quired to restore internal and external balance. In relation to non-traded goods, the exchange-rate appreciation is the equivalent of a uniform ad valorem import subsidy (negative tariff) and export tax, applying to all tradables including, of course, tradable inputs. Thus it provides a uniform rate of negative effective protection for all tradables. This exchange-rate adjustment must be regarded as an integral part of the effect of a protective structure. If the appreciation were, for example, 20 per cent, all tradables with an effective rate of less than 20 per cent will, in a sense, have been taxed in relation to non-tradables, and only effective rates over 20 per cent mean protection in relation to non-tradables. If we subtract 20 per cent from all effective protective rates as previously calculated, we obtain a scale of *net effective protective rates*. Only when the net rate is positive is an activity protected relative to non-tradables. Clearly the exchange-rate adjustment implied by a protective structure must be estimated if the full effects of such a structure on resource allocation are to be understood.

F. FOUR CONCEPTS OF PROTECTION

There emerge from this analysis four distinct concepts of when an industry is really protected.

First, there is the old-fashioned approach that an industry is protected if

---

[4] Even when the protective-rate structure consists wholly of positive nominal tariffs, it is not inevitable that excess demand for non-traded goods (and hence exchange-rate appreciation) results. For the tariff structure may have yielded some negative effective rates; these draw resources from tradables into non-tradables and create a tendency toward excess supply of non-tradables. But, unless consumption-substitution elasticities are zero, positive nominal tariffs on final goods must lead at least to some shift in the demand pattern toward non-tradables. It is possible that the extra supply of non-tradables just happens to equal the extra demand, so that no exchange-rate adjustment is required.

its nominal tariff is positive. But it is the message of this article that, while the nominal tariff is relevant to the consumption effect, in itself it can tell us nothing about the production effect.

Second, there is the more sophisticated approach which emerges from the new theory of tariff structure that an industry is protected if its effective tariff is positive. It is true that, if the prices of non-traded goods are given and the exchange rate does not alter, any industry with a positive effective rate will tend to attract resources into it from non-traded goods and is thus protected relative to non-traded goods. But it clearly may not be protected relative to non-traded goods once exchange-rate adjustment is permitted.

Third, one might take into account the exchange-rate effects of a protective structure and consider an industry to be protected only when its *net* effective rate is positive, for only then is it protected relative to non-traded goods.

Fourth, one might argue that an activity is only truly protected if the net result of the protective structure combined with the appropriate exchange-rate adjustment is to raise value added in that activity. This is the concept of *total protection*. The direction of change in output or value added depends not only on protection relative to non-traded goods but also on protection relative to other traded goods. Even if we find that a particular tradable activity has a positive net protective rate and its production-substitution elasticity with the non-traded sector is positive so that there is a movement of resources into that activity from the non-traded sector, it does not follow that output of that activity must increase. For there may be substitution against it because some other tradable activities have higher effective

rates. Whether an industry is protected in this fourth sense (that is, is *totally* protected) depends not only on substitution relative to non-tradables (the direction of which is indicated by the sign of the *net* rate) but also on substitution relative to other tradables (which is influenced by its position in the scale of effective rates).

G. NON-TRADED INPUTS

So far it has been assumed that there are no non-traded inputs (for example, electricity or services) in traded goods. If there are, then the non-traded sector is affected in three ways by a protective structure, the first effect not having entered so far. First, positive total protection of traded goods leads to additional demand for non-traded inputs; those non-traded inputs intensive in the protected industries will rise in price relatively to the general price level in the non-traded sector. Second, positive nominal tariffs or export subsidies on finished traded goods will divert demand from these goods on to substitute non-traded goods. Third, primary factors will move from the non-traded sector in general into protected traded-goods industries (and also into industries producing those non-traded inputs which are indirectly protected).

Now the important question arises whether, to calculate effective protective rates of tradables, non-traded inputs should be treated in the same way as tradable inputs or whether they should be treated like primary factors. Balassa (1965) and Basevi (in press) treat a non-tradable input just like any tradable input with a zero tariff or export-tax subsidy. In defense it could be argued that the effective protective rate refers to the effect of the tariff structure on value added per unit in the industry under consideration; and to obtain value added all inputs, whether traded or non-traded, must be excluded. The alternative approach is to treat non-traded inputs in the same way as primary factors. Value added per unit in a tradable industry would then be defined as value added by primary factors plus value added by non-traded inputs. The intuitive defense is that protection for an activity producing a traded product represents not only protection for those primary factors intensive in that activity but also protection for those industries producing non-traded inputs in which that activity is intensive and thus, indirectly, protection for the primary factors intensive in these non-traded input industries. There appears, thus, to be a complete identity between primary factors and non-traded input industries.

To resolve the issue, one must ask what the purpose of the effective-protective-rate concept is. The answer is that it should shed light on the direction of the resource-allocation effects of a protective structure. If we have calculated that tradable industry X has 10 per cent effective protection and tradable industry Y has 20 per cent, we should be able to conclude that resources will be drawn from X to Y and into both from non-protected tradable industries and from those non-traded industries where prices have stayed constant.

Consider a simple model so constructed as to isolate the first of our three effects of a protective structure on the non-traded sector and, thus, to focus on the essentials of the problem. Let there be three industries producing M (importables), X (exportables), and N (non-traded goods). There are two primary factors: L, which is an input into M and X but cannot be used in N; and L_n, which is an input specific to N. Both M and X

are final consumption goods, while N is an input into M and X and is not consumed directly. All three production functions are constant returns to scale, and (departing from the fixed coefficient assumption) in M and X there is continuous substitutability between the two inputs L and N. Internal and external balance are maintained with a flexible exchange rate and appropriate monetary policy. Equilibrium can be represented in a familar manner with a box diagram, the dimensions of which are the stock of L and the output of N (depending on the stock of L_n), and a production-possibility curve in a quadrant with axes showing outputs of M and X. In free trade, the price ratio between M and X is given, and from this can be deduced outputs of M and X and inputs of L and N into each industry. Now suppose that a 10 per cent nominal tariff is imposed on M and a 10 per cent export subsidy on X, so that the price ratio remains unchanged. Our simple model tells us that outputs and resource allocation also will not change. Now suppose that we use the first method in calculating the effective rates and so treat N as we would a traded input. Assume that M is L-intensive relative to X; therefore the share of value added (defined as the cost of L) in the price of M will be greater than in the price of X. Thus the nominal protective rates of 10 per cent would yield an effective rate for M less than that for X (in both cases greater than 10 per cent). We would then conclude wrongly that resources will move from M to X. On the other hand, if non-traded inputs were treated as primary factors, we would calculate both effective rates at 10 per cent (as there are no traded inputs). Since relative effective rates would not have changed, we would conclude correctly that resources will not move as between X and M. While this model is very simple, it seems to prove conclusively that non-traded inputs should ideally be treated like primary factors and not like traded inputs.

The essence of the distinction between traded and non-traded inputs stems from our assumptions (2) and (3) (infinite foreign-trade elasticities; trade in tradable products remains after protection). Thus a tradable input is in infinite supply to an industry, and the price of each individual traded good is given (apart from the effects of taxes and subsidies). If non-traded inputs were also in infinitely elastic supply, they could indeed be treated like traded inputs. But in the absence of unemployment and excess capacity a user industry can obtain extra non-traded inputs only at increased cost, and some part of the increment in the price of the final good on account of the tariff will not increase value added per unit but will raise the price of the input. The tariff protects not only those primary factors but also those non-traded inputs (and hence their factors) which are intensive in the using industries. But the effects on the primary factors and the non-traded inputs cannot be separated out. Unless there are two inputs only and one is in infinitely elastic supply so that its price does not rise when the price of the output rises, it is impossible to distinguish the effective protective rate for different inputs. For each product one can talk only about a single effective rate for all those inputs combined which are not in infinitely elastic supply to the industry.[5]

In Section E, it was argued that if the net effective rate is positive an activity is protected relative to non-traded goods. This must now be qualified. It is protected relative to the non-traded sector as a whole, assuming that the average price level of non-traded goods stays constant. But it will not be protected relative to all non-traded goods, since the protective structure will have led to increases in the relative prices and so resource movements into those non-traded industries which produce inputs primarily for highly protected traded industries.

II. APPLICATIONS AND EXTENSIONS OF THE NEW CONCEPT

A. ESCALATION OF THE TARIFF STRUCTURE

By translating a set of nominal rates into a set of effective rates, one can understand more clearly the general characteristics of a tariff structure and of changes in it. For example, a widely noted characteristic of the tariff structures of many countries is that nominal rates tend to be low or even zero for raw materials and to rise or "escalate" with the degree of processing.[6] In an escalated structure, the nominal rate on made-up clothing is higher than that on cloth, the cloth rate is higher than the yarn rate, and at the bottom is the raw-cotton rate.

[5] If there are traded inputs in those non-traded goods which are themselves inputs in traded-goods industries, the matter becomes more complicated. Only that part of the value of the input which is value added by primary factors directly and indirectly (that is, via non-traded inputs into these non-traded inputs, and so on) should be treated like a primary factor and so included in value added in the protected industry. In other words, ideally one should go down the input-output structure until one reaches a traded input; and, to obtain value added for our formula, all direct contributions by primary factors should be summed with all indirect contributions by primary factors through non-traded inputs. In the summation process, tradable inputs (even though they may actually be produced domestically) should be treated as leakages.

[6] This is so well known that detailed substantiation is hardly needed. But see the papers by Balassa (1965) and Basevi (in press) cited earlier, and in particular W. P. Travis (1964). The subject is discussed thoroughly by Johnson (1965), but the distinction made in the present section of this paper under point (*b*) below is not made by him.

Two distinct implications follow. (*a*) Except for the basic material which has no other tradable product as an input, the effective rate is always higher than the nominal rate. This indeed is the attraction of escalated structures to protectionists: the degree of protection provided to industries is not so obvious. (*b*) It means low or zero protection for the raw material at the bottom of the chain. This is not significant when, as often, there is no potential domestic production of the material; but when there is, then an escalated structure biases trade in favor of raw materials against processed products. It is then correct to say that the escalated structures of the advanced countries encourage underdeveloped countries to export raw materials rather than to export processed products. If an advanced country replaced an escalated structure with a uniform tariff leading to the same value of imports, its production mix would include a higher proportion and its import mix a lower proportion of raw materials. On the other hand, when there is no potential production of raw materials in the advanced country, replacing the escalated structure with the uniform tariff would not raise the import of processed products. In that case, the criticism of the escalated structure is not a criticism of its effect on the pattern of protection but, rather, of the level of protection.

B. EFFECT OF REDUCTION IN TARIFF
ON AN INTERMEDIATE GOOD

Another application of the new concept concerns a country which offers to reduce the tariff on an intermediate good at international tariff negotiations and so appears to be making a "concession" that will reduce protection and increase trade. In fact, the extra imports and lower domestic production of the

intermediate good which may result must be set against the consequences of the higher effective rate for the user industry. A change in the nominal rate for an intermediate good alters at least two effective rates in opposite directions. On balance, total protected production may rise or fall, with trade moving in the opposite direction. This is clearest in the special case where the elasticity of supply of the intermediate good is zero, so that the only consequences of the tariff reduction result from the rise in the effective rate for the user industry.

C. INFANT INDUSTRIES GROWING UP

The following example suggests that historians of commercial policies and of industrialization should calculate effective rates. In a normal process of industrial development by import replacement, a country starts with importing nearly finished products free of duty, carrying out final processing or assembly behind a tariff wall, and gradually moves backward into earlier productive stages, extending the tariff at the same time. The number of nominal tariffs increases, and no nominal tariff may ever be reduced. While the historian naturally reports a growth in the tariff, effective rates are falling and infant industries are growing up. In the first stage, for example, cotton cloth pays a duty of 40 per cent, while yarn enters duty-free, the effective rate for weaving being (say) 100 per cent. In the second stage, the 40 per cent tariff is extended to yarn. So the effective rate for cloth now drops from 100 per cent to 40 per cent. Therefore, weaving has at least partially grown up. In the third stage, the effective rate for spinning might fall. It should be noted, incidentally, that an industry would be regarded as having "grown up" in the sense of the fourth meaning of protection above (total protection) not when its effective rate falls to zero but, rather, when it falls to the level when a restoration of free trade in all goods associated with the appropriate exchange-rate adjustment would leave output in this industry unchanged.

D. MULTIPLE EXCHANGE RATES

Our concept and technique of analysis can be used to analyze multiple exchange-rate systems. The first step is arbitrarily to choose any rate, say the official or the free market rate, and define it as the "base" rate. Then all rates changed on imports and paid on exports can be converted into nominal tariff rates, import subsidies, export taxes, or export subsidies. For example, if the rate applying to capital-goods imports is 9 pesos to the dollar, and 10 pesos has been chosen as the base rate, then there is an import subsidy of 10 per cent. The set of nominal rates is next converted into a set of effective rates using the procedure already described. This set is then ordered so that it can be seen in which direction resources are pulled by the multiple rate system as between traded-goods producers. Next, from the set of effective rates and a similar set of nominal tariffs and consumption taxes and from guesses or estimates of elasticities, must be estimated the single exchange rate which would achieve the same balance-of-payments result as the multiple rate system.[7] Finally, the set of effective rates must be restated in relation to this equilibrium rate. If the resulting net effective rate is negative, the multiple system has exerted a pull of resources out of that activity into the

[7] The effects of the multiple system on the capital account are ignored here. In fact, the method can readily embrace all current and capital account items.

non-traded sector; while if it is positive, it is likely to have attracted resources into it. Any rate can serve as a base to start the calculation off; the vital subsequent step is to estimate correctly the equilibrium rate in relation to which all the effective rates must finally be restated to yield the net effective rates.

E. ANALYZING THE EFFECTS OF FOREIGN TARIFFS

Let "our" country be Canada and the "foreign" country the United States. Assume that the U.S. demand curves for Canadian exports and the U.S. supply curves to Canada of U.S. exports are all infinitely elastic. Now the tariffs and other taxes and subsidies imposed by the United States provide protection or "antiprotection" for the industries of Canada, and their effect on the allocation of resources in Canada can be analyzed in the same manner as the effects of Canada's own tariffs and other taxes. For example, a U.S. tariff on furniture lowers the demand curve facing Canadian exporters and has the same effect on the allocation of resources in Canada as a Canadian export tax on furniture. The concern here is only with resource-allocation effects. The fiscal effects obviously depend on which country taxes and subsidizes, and by assumption there are no terms-of-trade effects.

A scale of effective rates can then be constructed which represents the protection or antiprotection imposed by the U.S. tax-subsidy structure on Canadian industry. The effects of this structure can be analyzed alone, holding constant Canada's own structure; the effects of the Canadian structure could be analyzed alone, this being the approach expounded in this paper so far; or the combined effects of the two structures could be analyzed, constructing a scale of combined effective rates. In any particular case, the two components of a combined effective rate (say a Canadian export subsidy combined with a U.S. import tariff) could cancel each other. The exchange-rate adjustment must again be taken into account. Even in the simple case when both the Canadian and the U.S. tax-subsidy structures consist mainly of tariffs on finished goods, the required exchange-rate adjustment could go either way and would, in any case, be less than when the effects of one of the structures alone is considered.[8]

F. LABOR AS AN INPUT

So far we have distinguished between traded inputs, assumed to be in infinitely elastic supply, and non-traded inputs plus the primary factors of production (labor, capital, etc.) where extra quantities are likely to come forth only at higher cost. The argument was that a tariff on a final good raises the returns per unit only to the non-traded inputs and primary factors and, therefore, should be related to the sum of their shares in total cost. If any non-traded input were in infinitely elastic supply, it could be grouped with the traded inputs (it would be counted among the i's in formula (4.2)). The effective rate would then describe the degree of protection (percentage increment in returns per unit) to the primary factors and any remaining non-traded inputs.

Now this principle could also be applied to any primary factors which are in infinitely elastic supply. Suppose that there are no non-traded inputs but only traded inputs and three factors of production: labor, capital, and land. If labor were in infinitely elastic supply, it could be grouped with the traded inputs; and the effective rate would be calculated in relation to the shares of capital and land, being then the effective protective rate for these two factors only. Alternatively, capital might be in infinitely elastic supply, in which case capital cost would be treated as just another input (another i in the formula); the result would be an effective rate of protection for labor and land. If labor and capital were in infinitely elastic supply, the effective rate to land would be calculated. To extend our previous method in this way, fixed physical input coefficients must be assumed for all those factors in infinitely elastic supply which are to be grouped with the tradable materials. Our earlier assumption of fixed input coefficients was necessary only for the tradable materials and not for other inputs or each primary factor separately.

The case where labor, or some types of labor, are in infinitely elastic supply may be relevant for some underdeveloped countries. While the cause is likely to be a given income or wage level in the subsistence hinterland, or perhaps in a neighboring country which supplies immigrants, the given money wage facing the protected industry need not be at the same level as that in the hinterland, the margin between them being the equivalent of the difference between the f.o.b. and the c.i.f. price of an import. Now, when labor is treated as just another input, what is the equivalent of a tariff on the input? All such "tariffs" will of course reduce the effective protection for the employing industries. One such "tariff" is a payroll tax on the use of labor, another is any tax which raises costs of transport of immigrants or costs of transfer from the hinterland. If it is

[8] This may be a defense of those discussions of the effects of the Canadian tariff which set up as the alternative to the Canadian tariff, not unilateral free trade but rather world free trade or a free-trade area with the United States, and which ignore the exchange-rate adjustment (see J. H. Young [1957]).

the real wage rather than the money wage which is fixed, then anything which raises labor's cost of living is like a tariff on this input. To give a very Ricardian example, a tariff on corn will raise money wages and reduce effective protection for labor-using weavers. In fact, corn is an input into labor, and labor is an input into cloth; we are back to the case where a tariff on a tradable input reduces effective protection for the using industry. If it is the real wage after tax which is fixed, then an income tax levied on labor employed in industry reduces effective protection. On the other hand, state provision of urban facilities which raise the real value of a given money wage spent in the city increases the effective protective rate for the employing industries.

G. CAPITAL AS AN INPUT

All calculations which treat labor as an input yield in fact effective protective rates for capital (plus land and other factors). Similarly, a calculation which treats capital as an input yields the effective protective rates for labor (plus any other factors). This calculation has been made by Basevi (in press) for the U.S. tariff.[9] But there are some conceptual problems here which must be explored. In particular, how do tariffs on capital goods enter the calculation?

First of all, at this stage fixed physical capital-output ratios must be assumed just as fixed labor-output ratios were needed before. Now let b_k be the cost of a unit of physical capital per annum to the users, just as the wage rate is the cost of a unit of labor; it is the equivalent of the

[9] Apart from his actual statistical work, Basevi's highly original contribution is this concept of the effective protective rate for labor. He does not deal with the difficulties discussed here—that is, he ignores tariffs on capital goods and the possibility of non-traded capital goods.

price of a tradable input. It is b_k which has to be constant, except when it is increased by tariffs or their equivalents. Since

$$b_k = (r + q) p_k, \qquad (5)$$

where p_k is the price of capital goods, r is the rate of interest, and q is the annual rate of depreciation on capital, it follows that p_k, r, and q must all be constant in response to changes in demand for capital from protected industries. Now q can be regarded as a fixed coefficient (dependent on the method of depreciation chosen), and r is constant if we assume (as Basevi does) that the interest rate is a given world market rate. But what about p_k? Extending our earlier analysis, this is given when the capital goods are tradables and is not given when they are non-tradables. Traded capital goods with annual cost per unit of b_{kt} must really be distinguished from non-traded capital goods with annual cost per unit of b_{kn} where

$$b_{kt} = (r + q_t) p_{kt}, \qquad (5.1)$$

$$b_{kn} = (r + q_n) p_{kn}. \qquad (5.2)$$

Only the annual service of tradable capital goods can be treated as an input, like tradable goods themselves, and only when it is legitimate to assume in addition a perfectly elastic supply of capital funds. The resulting effective rate will then be the protective rate for labor, for producers of non-tradables, whether capital goods or consumer goods, and for land. In our formula (4.2) there is needed for the capital cost (referring only to tradable capital goods) an equivalent of the tariff on an input. This must incorporate the tariff on capital goods, any other taxes or subsidies affecting the total investment cost, such as investment allowances, and any taxes or other measures which alter the rate of interest.

This equivalent is db_{kt}/b_{kt}. From (5.1), taking differentials

$$db_{kt} = rdp_{kt} + p_{kt}dr + q_t dp_{kt}. \quad (6)$$

From (6)

$$\frac{db_{kt}}{b_{kt}} = \frac{r p_{kt}}{b_{kt}} \left[\frac{dr}{r} + t_k \left(1 + \frac{q_t}{r} \right) \right] \quad (6.1)$$

where $t_k = \frac{dp_{kt}}{p_{kt}}$.

In (6.1) the percentage increase in the rate of interest resulting from the tax structure is dr/r, the tariff on capital goods minus any investment subsidies as a percentage of the capital cost is t_k, and $r p_{kt}/b_{kt}$ is the share of interest charges in the capital cost.

H. SUBSTITUTION

So far, fixed physical input ratios of material inputs to outputs have been assumed. Let us now allow for the possibility that changes in price relationships bring about substitution between material inputs and inputs of primary factors and that this substitution in turn causes changes in the input coefficients. So the tariff structure itself, through its effects on internal price relationships, may induce changes in input coefficients. Two questions then arise. The first concerns the nature of the thing which ideally we are trying to measure when we calculate an effective protective rate. The second question is to define the direction of the error, if any, which results on account of induced changes in input coefficients when certain practicable methods of calculation are used. Thus, first, we define the ideal measure and then we relate the results of measures which are practicable to the ideal.

The exposition will be in terms of a very simple model, though probably most of the conclusions would apply even when some of the constraints of the model are removed. We assume for each tradable product j a twice-differentiable linear homogenous production function $j = f_j(i, y)$, where input i is a tradable material and input y a primary factor, with positive marginal products and a diminishing marginal rate of substitution. We assume competitive pricing. Both the material input i and the primary factor y can be regarded as bundles of inputs, but we must then assume fixed ratios between inputs within each bundle. We focus, in fact, on one particular substitution relationship, that between the material inputs and the primary factors. Prices are p_j, p_i, and p_v, where p_j is a product price, p_v a factor price, and p_i is both. The only changes in prices we consider are due to tariffs or similar taxes or subsidies. When p_j, p_i, and p_v are defined as representing prices in the free-trade situation, then the tariff on the final product t_j is dp_j/p_j, and the tariff on the material t_i is dp_i/p_i. Since prices of inputs must be equal to the value of their marginal products, it follows that the marginal physical products of i and y, respectively, are p_i/p_j and p_v/p_j. We denote the physical ratio of material input i to output j in the free-trade situation as b (the input coefficient) and the physical ratio of material input i to primary factor input y in the free-trade situation as c (the factor ratio). Therefore

$$a_{ij} = b \frac{p_i}{p_j}. \quad (7)$$

We must note here the well-known relationship between input substitution and input coefficients which holds when one assumes a given linear homogenous production function with two inputs only and with continuous substitution between these inputs. The input coefficients (that is, the ratios of each input to output) depend only on the ratio between the inputs and must change when there is substitution between the inputs. In our model, the input coefficient is b, namely, the ratio of material input to output. This must rise whenever there is substitution away from y toward i, so that c rises. If c falls, b falls; and if c does not change, b does not change.

It was explained earlier that the calculation of effective rates is designed to indicate the direction in which resources will be pulled by the tariff structure. It should not incorporate the effects of these resource shifts. Therefore, the effective rate can no longer be the actual percentage rise in returns per unit to the primary factors (and non-traded inputs) resulting from the tariffs, since that depends partly on the substitution effects which have actually taken place. Thus, g_j cannot be defined as dp_v/p_v in the present model. Rather, we want to know what the rise in the rate of return to a factor is before any resources move in response to this rise. Hence, the effective rate should be the percentage rise in the return to the primary factor which would result if there were no substitution between inputs and, hence, if there were no change in the input coefficient. It follows that the ideal calculation should use the input coefficient of the free-trade situation; the formula which we have been using remains the correct one and, with or without actual substitution, the coefficient to use is b and, in value terms, a_{ij}. The difficulty is that, while previously the physical input coefficients were the same in the protection as in the free-trade situation, when there is a possibility of substitution between inputs they may be different. So starting with the protection situation, we no longer know the input coefficient required for the formula. If, nevertheless, we use the

coefficient of the protection situation, we need at least to know whether we will be understating or overstating the effective rate.

In the protection situation the information available consists of the two tariff rates t_j and t_i and the share of material input in total cost a'_{ij}:

$$a'_{ij} = b' \frac{(p_i + dp_i)}{(p_j + dp_j)}, \qquad (8)$$

where b' is the physical ratio of material input i to output j (the input coefficient) in the protection situation. Primes refer to the protection situation. Since $t_j = dp_j/p_j$ and $t_i = dp_i/p_i$, we have from (7) and (8)

$$a'_{ij} = \frac{1 + t_i}{1 + t_j} \frac{a_{ij}}{w}, \qquad (9)$$

where $w \equiv b/b'$ (that is, w is the ratio of the free trade to the protection physical input coefficients). We have

$$g_j = \frac{t_j - a_{ij}t_i}{1 - a_{ij}}. \qquad (4)$$

Substituting (9) in (4), we have

$$g_j = \frac{t_j - a'_{ij}wt_i(1 + t_j)/(1 + t_i)}{1 - a'_{ij}w(1 + t_j)/(1 + t_i)}, \qquad (10)$$

which may be rewritten as follows:[10]

$$g_j = \frac{1 - a'_{ij}w}{1/(t_j+1) - a'_{ij}w/(t_i+1)} - 1. \, (10.1)$$

The author's calculations,[11] those of the Australian committee,[12] and the calculations by Basevi (in press) of the U.S. effective rates represent an application of this formula on the assumption that $w = 1$, that is, that the input coeffi-

[10] This is my original formula (see Corden [1963], p. 197 n.).

[11] Corden (1963), pp. 208–13.

[12] *Report of the Committee of Economic Enquiry* (1965), Appendix L(4).

TARIFF SYSTEM AND EFFECTIVE PROTECTIVE RATE 235

cients in the free-trade and the protection situation are the same. They would be the same if there were a fixed ratio between inputs. Even when there are substitution possibilities, they will be the same if $l_j = l_i$, so that p_i/p_j does not change. For p_i/p_j is equal to the marginal physical product of i, which can stay constant in this model only if the input ratio also stays constant. If $l_j > l_i$, so that p_i/p_j falls, there will be substitution toward i ($c' > c$) so that the input coefficient rises ($b' > b$) and thus $w < 1$. If $l_j < l_i$, the substitution will be away from i, so that $w > 1$.

Now consider the effect if a change in w on g_j. From (10.1)

$$\frac{\partial g_j}{\partial w} = (l_j - l_i) \cdot \frac{a'_{ij}}{(l_j+1)(l_i+1)[1/(l_i+1) - a'_{ij}w^2/(l_i+1)]}. \tag{11}$$

It follows that $\partial g_j/\partial w > 0$ if $l_j > l_i$ and $\partial g_j/\partial w < 0$ if $l_j < l_i$.

Bringing all this together, we arrive at a rather surprising conclusion. Suppose that $l_j > l_i$, so that there is substitution toward i. A correct calculation of the effective rate requires then a value of $w < 1$. But the actual calculation which is made assumes that $w = 1$. Therefore, w has been overstated, and we must ask whether this leads to an understatement or overstatement of g_j. It can be seen from (11) that when $l_j > l_i$, $\partial g_j/\partial w > 0$, so that if w is too high g_j must also be too high. Therefore, by assuming $w = 1$ (no substitution), the effective rate has been *overstated*. Next we do the same exercise for the case where $l_j < l_i$, so that there is substitution against i and $w > 1$. This time, by assuming that $w = 1$, we have understated it. But it has also been seen from (11) that when $l_j < l_i$, $\partial g_j/\partial w < 0$, so that if w is too low g_j is too high. In other words, by assuming that $w = 1$, the effective rate has again been *over-*

stated. We may conclude that calculations of effective rates which use the data of the protection situation will always tend to overstate the effective rates if there is any substitution from primary inputs toward material inputs or vice versa and, of course, unless other errors are offsetting.

I. USE OF FOREIGN INPUT COEFFICIENTS

Instead of using the input coefficients in the protection situation of the country for which the effective rates are to be calculated, an alternative is to use the input coefficients of another country, the prices of which are not distorted to the same extent by tariffs. This method is used by Balassa.[13] Can one then generalize about the direction of the error?

If the production functions are the same in the country which supplies the coefficients (say, the Netherlands) as in the country for which the effective rates are required (say, Australia) and if price ratios in the Netherlands are the same as free-trade price ratios in Australia, then there will be no error. In fact, production functions do not even have to be the same; they may differ neutrally (in the Harrod, not Hicks, sense), so that the input coefficient b stays constant even though the factor ratio c varies. The assumption of similar production functions (or ones that differ only neutrally) is perhaps not unreasonable. But the existence of transport costs may cause the Netherlands price ratio to diverge from the free-trade Australian ratio. Suppose that the

[13] B. Balassa (1965), in making calculations for the United States, United Kingdom, EEC, Sweden, and Japan has "relied largely on the input-output tables for Belgium and the Netherlands."

Netherlands is the exporting country and that her exports are not differentially priced; so her internal prices are identical with Australian f.o.b. import prices, excluding duty. The Australian internal free-trade price ratio, that is, the ratio of c.i.f. prices, will then differ from the Netherlands ratio if the percentages of transport costs differ between the material and the finished good. Let us work through the implications in a special, and not implausible, case. Suppose that the transport-cost percentage is higher for materials than for finished goods, so that p_i/p_j is lower in the Netherlands than it would be in free-trade Australia; that the elasticity of substitution in the production function is less than unity, so that a_{ij} is less in the Netherlands than in free-trade Australia; and that $t_j > t_i$, so that an understatement of a_{ij} understates the effective rate g_j. It follows that the use of Netherlands coefficients understates effective rates in Australia, the answer depending in fact on a combination of three assumptions. Though each of these assumptions seems rather more reasonable than its alternative, it is clear that, in contrast to the previous case, there is no general presumption about the direction of error resulting from the method used.

J. OTHER ASSUMPTIONS

In conclusion, attention should be drawn to assumptions (2) and (3), maintained throughout this paper. Removing assumption (3), namely, that all tradable goods continue to be traded even after tariffs and other taxes have been imposed, presents few difficulties in principle. Part of a tariff can now be redundant. As is well known, many tariff structures have redundant elements in

them ("water in the tariff"), and it is these elements which trade negotiators are usually most ready to sacrifice. Since a redundant tariff has no effect of any kind other than as an insurance to protected industries against falls in import prices, all calculations should ideally be based only on the *utilized* parts of tariffs —an ideal which requires detailed price data and which may not always be practical. It should also be noted that, once imports of an input cease, further protection of the input requires the tariff on the final good to be increased (up to the point where imports of the final good cease). Thus, not only does the protection for the final product depend on both its own tariff and the tariffs on its inputs, but the protection of the inputs depends on their own tariffs and the tariff on the final good. Finally, removing assumption (2), namely, that the export-demand and import-supply elasticities are all infinite, presents considerable difficulties; and, when the elasticities for inputs are less than infinite, the effective-protective-rate concept strictly interpreted appears to break down. But perhaps if the elasticities are generally close to infinite, the calculation of effective rates and the derivation of various conclusions from the calculations are justified as reasonable approximations. The present author applied the concept in Australia, a country which, like most countries of the "periphery," faces import-supply curves which are commonly accepted to be infinitely elastic. Some export-demand curves are no doubt less than infinitely elastic, but the exportable content in protected import-competing production is fairly unimportant. So, for Australia and similar countries, no difficulty arises.

REFERENCES

Balassa, B. "Tariff Protection in Industrial Countries: An Evaluation," *J.P.E.*, LXXIII (December, 1965), 573–94.

Barber, C. L. "Canadian Tariff Policy," *Canadian J. Econ. and Polit. Sci.*, XXI, No. 4 (November, 1955), 513–30.

Basevi, G. "The U.S. Tariff Structure: Estimate of Effective Rates of Protection of U.S. Industries and Industrial Labor," *Rev. Econ. and Statis.* (in press).

Committee of Economic Enquiry. *Report of the Committee of Economic Enquiry.* Canberra: Commonwealth of Australia, 1965.

Corden, W. M. "The Tariff," in A. Hunter (ed.), *The Economics of Australian Industry.* Melbourne: Melbourne Univ. Press, 1963, pp. 162–63.

Humphrey, D. D. *The United States and the Common Market.* New York: Frederick A. Praeger, Inc., 1962, pp. 61–63.

Johnson, H. G. "The Theory of Tariff Structure with Special Reference to World Trade and Development," *Trade and Development.* Geneva: Institut Universitaire des Hautes Études Internationales, 1965.

Meade, J. E. *Trade and Welfare.* London: Oxford Univ. Press, 1955, pp. 162–63.

Travis, W. P. *The Theory of Trade and Protection.* Cambridge, Mass.: Harvard Univ. Press, 1964, pp. 187–225.

Young, J. H. *Canadian Commercial Policy.* Ottawa: Royal Commission on Canada's Economic Prospects, 1957.

Part V
Import Substituting Industrialization

[14]

The Case against Infant-Industry Tariff Protection

Robert E. Baldwin

University of Wisconsin

I

The classical infant-industry argument for protection has long been regarded by economists as the major "theoretically valid" exception to the case for worldwide free trade.[1] What controversy there is over the concept tends to center not on analytical issues but rather on empirical matters. Some writers—for example, Myrdal (1957, pp. 96–97) and Rosenstein-Rodan (1963)—maintain that the economic conditions on which the case is based apply to most manufacturing industries in less-developed countries, and they believe, therefore, that general protective measures are justified in these economies. Others—for example, Haberler (1936, pp. 281–85) and Meier (1964, pp. 302–3)—are much more skeptical about the pervasiveness of these conditions and stress the high costs of making incorrect decisions. Unfortunately, the views of both groups are based largely on casual empiricism. Careful, detailed investigations of the empirical issues involved in the infant-industry case have been rare.[2]

The purpose of this note is not to discuss these empirical matters but rather to suggest that economists have too readily accepted the theoretical arguments set forth for infant-industry protection. I will not deny that there are unique factors affecting new industries which may require market intervention by public authorities if a socially efficient allocation of resources is to be achieved. What I will question is the effectiveness of

I am especially grateful to W. M. Corden, Gottfried Harberler, Harry Johnson, Robert Mundell, Theodore Morgan, and Burton Weisbrod for valuable comments.

[1] This paper deals with the traditional "infant-industry" dogma associated with such writers as List, Hamilton, Bastable, and Mill in contrast to modern arguments for "infant-economy" protection based on the work of such writers as Rosenstein-Rodan, Scitovsky, and Dobb. See Grubel (1966) for a comprehensive analysis of the differences between the modern and traditional infant-industry arguments.

[2] Taussig's (1915) work still stands as the classic but inconclusive empirical study of the subject.

tariffs in accomplishing this result. In particular, I will argue that for some of the main conditions cited as warranting temporary tariffs, protection may well either decrease social welfare or at least fail to achieve the socially optimal allocation of resources in new industries that is the purpose of the duty.

Other writers have also recently argued that the infant-industry dogma has less generality than commonly claimed. Kemp (1960) and Grubel (1966) have pointed out, for example, that where acquired skills and knowledge are "specific" to a firm, there is no need for tariff protection as a means of encouraging socially justifiable investment in human resources. Johnson (1965) has emphasized that infant-industry protection, like other protective measures designed to correct domestic distortions, causes a relative welfare loss to consumers by raising the domestic price of the imported good above its world level.[3] The point stressed here relates to the production side. Not only is a consumption loss associated with protection but, as a general principle, one cannot be sure that a temporary tariff will result in the optimum increase in production, or, indeed, in any increase at all in the production possibility curve.

Four principal infant-industry cases will be considered in the following sections. Part II examines the case for protection based upon the point that the acquisition of knowledge involves costs, yet that knowledge is not appropriable by the individual firm. The familiar argument that infant-industry protection is needed because costs associated with on-the-job training cannot be recouped by the training firm is evaluated in Part III. The existence of static and reversible externalities as a justification for temporary protection is discussed in Part IV. This part also considers the argument for protection that imperfect information leads to systematic overestimates of investment risks or of the unpleasantness of working in particular industries. In all four cases I conclude that temporary protection by means of an import duty on the product of the industry is not likely to achieve the goal of a more efficient allocation of resources in production.

II

The essential point stressed by infant-industry proponents since Hamilton (1791) and List (1856) first wrote on the subject is that production costs for newly established industries within a country are likely to be initially higher than for well-established foreign producers of the same line, who have greater experience and higher skill levels. However, over a period of time new producers become "educated to the level of those with whom the processes are traditional" (Mill, 1909, p. 92); and their cost curves decline. The infant-industry argument states that during the temporary period

---

[3] The consumption loss referred to by Johnson (1965) can be prevented by subsidizing domestic production rather than by taxing imports.

when domestic costs in an industry are above the product's import price, a tariff is a socially desirable method of financing the investment in human resources needed to compete with foreign producers.

The first point to note about this statement is that, as Meade (1955, p. 256) has noted, the existence during early stages of production experience of higher costs than those of foreign competitors is, by itself, insufficient justification for tariff protection on grounds of economic efficiency. If, after the learning period, unit costs in an industry are sufficiently lower than those during its early production stages to yield a discounted surplus of revenues over costs (and therefore indicate a comparative advantage for the country in the particular line), it would be possible for firms in the industry to raise sufficient funds in the capital market to cover their initial excess of outlays over receipts.[4] These circumstances are no different from those in which firms go to the capital market for funds to cover the excess of expenditures over revenues incurred during their early stages because of the need to purchase indivisible units of physical capital.

As Meade (1955, p. 256) also pointed out, the key argument on which the infant-industry case must rest relates to the technological externalities frequently associated with the learning process. Consider the matter of acquiring the technological knowledge needed to compete effectively with foreign producers.[5] An entrepreneur who incurs costs in order to discover the best way to produce a particular product may face the problem that this information becomes freely available to potential competitors who can utilize it at the same time as the initial firm does. Competition then either pushes up factor prices or drives the product's price down to a point where the initial firm is unable to recover its total costs, including the sum spent on obtaining the knowledge—assuming its other costs are the same as those for competing firms entering the field. Because of this type of response, individual entrepreneurs will be reluctant to invest in knowledge acquisition unless they are sure they can easily prevent others from obtaining the knowledge or can reap a sufficiently high reward during the time it takes others to copy them. Investments in knowledge that are profitable from a social point of view may, therefore, not be undertaken in the economy.

For many types of knowledge acquisition no externality problem exists, since entrepreneurs are able to keep their knowledge about production or markets from their competitors. Thus they are able to reap exclusively the profit benefits of their investments in securing knowledge. Similarly, in

---

[4] The case in which the existence of imperfect capital markets prevents this type of response is considered in Part IV.

[5] Although it may be possible to acquire the basic technology for a new industry from foreign producers at little cost, it usually is necessary to modify this technology somewhat before production under domestic conditions has a chance of competing successfully with foreign production.

industries where there are significant economies of scale in relation to the size of the market and therefore a small number of firms, interfirm negotiations are likely to result in arrangements that offset the externality problem (see Coase, 1960; Buchanan and Stubblebine, 1962). Nevertheless, cases in which the number of firms is large and knowledge acquired by one entrepreneur becomes freely available—or available at a nominal cost—to other entrepreneurs cannot be ruled out as unlikely to be numerous or significant. The instances where these conditions hold could result in a significant divergence between private and social benefits.

A protective duty is, however, no guarantee that individual entrepreneurs will undertake greater investments in acquiring technological knowledge. A duty raises the domestic price of a product and, from the viewpoint of the domestic industry as a whole, makes some investments in knowledge more profitable. But the individual entrepreneur still faces the same externality problem as before, namely, the risk that other firms in the same industry will copy, without cost to themselves, any new technology discovered by the firm and will then drive the product's price or factor prices to levels at which the initial firm will be unable to recover the costs of acquiring the knowledge. If there were always some technologically fixed time lag between the introduction of a new, cheaper production technique and the changes in product or factor prices caused by the entry of the firms who freely copied the new production method, a duty would operate to make investment in knowledge acquisition more profitable for an individual firm in an industry. But (to make a point too often ignored in such discussions) the speed with which firms respond to market opportunities is a function of the level of profit prospects. A duty will make it worthwhile for firms to incur the costs of acquiring the knowledge discovered by other firms (if it is not completely free) faster and also to move into production more rapidly and with greater output rates (see Alchian, 1959). Setting the duty so high that both initial current production costs and the direct costs of acquiring technological knowledge can be covered from current receipts also will be ineffective. Since production under existing socially inefficient technology will be made profitable, firms which make no attempt to discover better productive techniques will enter the industry and drive out of business any firms that spend extra sums on knowledge acquisition. Thus, unless the rate of entry of new firms is relatively unresponsive to the level of profit rates of existing producers, there is no reason to assume as a general rule that any single firm will be more successful in recouping its investment in knowledge with a high duty than with none at all. A duty tends merely to encourage socially inefficient production as long as the state is willing to provide protection. A production subsidy on an industry-wide basis will have the same effect. What is needed, of course, is a subsidy to the initial entrants into the industry for discovering better productive techniques.

Only if during the period of knowledge acquisition there are no costs beyond those needed for efficient production under existing techniques would a tariff clearly accomplish its purpose—improving the long-run allocation of resources.[6] Then any firm considering the possibility of initiating domestic production in the industry need not be concerned with competition from subsequent entrants into the field who do not have to incur learning costs. However, learning through experience does involve direct costs for any firm. Unless a firm experiments on a random basis—a procedure that will not bring about the consistent decline in costs postulated under the infant-industry argument—it will be necessary for management to devote resources to analyzing previous performance before evaluating new productive practices. These are resources that could have been used to increase output (and thus lower unit costs) under existing production techniques. Consequently, as long as these learning-by-experience costs are greater than what other firms must pay to acquire the knowledge, it cannot be assumed as a general rule that firms will be prepared to incur the initial direct-learning costs even if the government imposes a tariff on the product. On the other hand, if the costs of learning by experience are actually less than the costs of acquiring known technology in the industry, all firms will follow the learn-by-experience route. A duty is still not needed in this case, since firms can borrow funds to tide them over the period during which their costs are not competitive with those of well-established foreign firms.

In many instances, the relationship among the costs of learning, the ease with which potential competitors can take advantage of newly discovered knowledge, and the benefits from this knowledge may be such that individual firms need not be concerned with recovering their learning costs. The point is that when the technological spillover flows from one firm to other firms in the same industry, protection of the entire industry—including new entrants—cannot be counted upon to induce firms to incur the volume of learning costs needed either to achieve a social optimum or to gain the knowledge possessed by foreign competitors.[7]

Recent writers on externalities have emphasized the same point in more general terms. They have shown that in order to achieve optimality when technological externalities exist, it is not enough merely to place taxes or

---

[6] In supporting the use of tariffs in the learning-by-experience case, Meade (1955, pp. 270–71) and Kemp (1960) both seem to be making this assumption. At one point in his analysis Meade (1955, pp. 256–57) does present an example in which knowledge acquisition involves costs beyond those needed for efficient current production, and at that point he states that a temporary subsidy to the *firm* may be socially desirable. But he does not distinguish between these cases in his summary of the arguments for temporary state intervention.

[7] If, however, the technological spillover affected only firms in entirely different industries, then a tariff would be effective in inducing firms within the protected industry to incur learning costs.

subsidies on an industry's output. First, as Plott (1966) illustrates with the standard smoke-diseconomy case, this type of corrective effort may actually reduce welfare. What is needed is a tax on smoke output or on the resource input from which smoke is generated. This example corresponds to the case discussed above in which an infant-industry tariff reduces welfare by being ineffective in shifting a country's production possibility curve outward, yet causing a consumption loss due to the rise in the price of the imported good above its world level.[8] Moreover, as Turvey (1963), Buchanan (1966), and Plott (1966) have noted, even if a tax is effective in raising welfare, it may not lead to the optimum set of production techniques. Specific taxes or subsidies directed toward particular types of inputs—for example, in the infant-industry case, toward research activities —may be necessary to achieve this goal. In the infant-industry context this means that a tariff is a second-best solution not only because of its consumption effects but also, even under the best of conditions, because of its effects on production.

III

Another frequently cited example of a technological spillover that creates a divergence between the private and social rates of return on investment concerns on-the-job training. If—so the argument goes—a firm could count on its workers to remain with it after they have been provided with on-the-job training, the firm could incur the costs of training and recoup them later by paying the workers wages just enough below their subsequently higher marginal productivity to cover these costs.[9] However, workers in a free market economy are not slaves, and they will be bid away by new firms after their training period if they receive less than their marginal productivity. Because of this ownership "externality" (that is, a divorce of scarcity from effective ownership) it is argued that temporary protection is justified.

Kemp (1960) has already noted an important qualification of this argument. If the learning process is internal or "specific" to the firm in the sense that the skills and experience acquired are not useful to other firms, then there are no economic-efficiency grounds for government intervention. Each firm can borrow funds to finance the costs of training and recoup these outlays by paying slightly less than the subsequent marginal productivity of the workers. The workers are still being paid at least as

[8] Terms of trade effects are being ignored in this statement.

[9] Training costs are the excess of current wage and other costs associated with the new workers over their current marginal productivity. As Haberler (1936, p. 284) has pointed out, in order for the establishment of the new industry to represent a socially desirable shift in resources, the discounted marginal productivity stream of the workers who transfer into the new industry must be higher than in the industries from which they are drawn.

much as they can earn in alternative employments, and they will not leave.

But what if the skills are not restricted to the particular firm providing the training but can be used by potential competitors in the industry? Without government intervention firms will still furnish on-the-job training, and thus a socially optimum resource allocation will be achieved. Although no firm will finance on-the-job training, the workers will. It is the workers who will benefit over their working lives from this on-the-job training, and it will be in their interest to pay for its cost. They can, for example, work during the training period at a wage rate sufficiently low that the firm's labor costs are not initially higher than foreign competitors (see Grubel, 1966; Becker, 1964). Alternatively, they can borrow on the capital market to tide them over this low-income period or even pay the firm with these borrowed funds to provide on-the-job training. This will be the rational course for workers to follow (and optimal for the economy) as long as the present value of their net income stream over their working life is greater with the training than under any other income alternatives.

If, for some reason, such as a lack of knowledge of earning opportunities, workers do not bear the costs of their own training, a protective tariff still cannot be counted upon to induce firms to pay for these training costs.[10] Competition from existing firms in the industry as well as from potential entrants will force firms to pay workers their marginal productivity both during and after their training period. Consequently, no firm undertaking the costs of training will be able to recoup them. All that a tariff can do is to raise the price of the product high enough so that production is profitable without training the workers. This merely creates an inefficient industry in the country.

IV

Static externalities can also result in divergences between private and social returns. A traditional example of such spillover effects is the increase in honey production resulting from an increase in the production of apples (and apple blossoms) near the location of beehives. How significant these sorts of spillovers are in practice is not clear. Most writers (for example, Scitovsky, 1954) do not regard them as very important. In any event, they do not constitute grounds for infant-industry protection. The infant-industry argument is a case for temporary protection, whereas duties justified because of reversible static economies will be needed on a continuing basis.

---

[10] If a monopoly price on capital funds prevented workers from borrowing to finance their training, a tariff would enable the industry to pay higher wages and thus could make it profitable for workers to pay the socially excessive interest charges. In this case a temporary duty would be socially beneficial.

Although static externalities are now generally treated as quite separate grounds for protection from those included under the infant-industry case, the same is not true for market imperfections. Popular usage suggests that the infant-industry case covers any grounds for *temporary* protection and not just those that are unique to infant industries. Thus, for example, monopolistic factor prices could make the establishment of a new industry privately unprofitable, although it would be socially beneficial. A temporary tariff can, under these conditions, move resources into the infant industry and thereby improve welfare levels in the country. Monopolistic factor markets can, of course, block socially desirable factor movements not only in new industries but also in well-established productive lines as an economy grows and taste patterns shift. Because this type of market distortion is by no means unique to new industries, it would seem more logical to consider the existence of monopolistic practices apart from the infant-industry argument for justifying tariff protection. However, if it is not treated separately, authors should at least note that the argument covers both new and old industries.

As Kafka (1962) pointed out, however, there is one type of market imperfection that tends to be particularly applicable to infant industries. In this situation a lack of knowledge about an industry causes investors to overestimate the risks of investing in the industry and causes workers to overrate the unpleasantness of moving into this line of production.[11] Whether a tariff will be effective in compensating for these imperfections depends upon (1) whether there are costs involved in knowledge acquisition other than those associated with current production, and (2) whether the knowledge that is acquired becomes freely available to others.

Suppose, for example, that a potential entrant into a new industry, if he could provide potential investors with a detailed market analysis of the industry, could borrow funds from investors at a rate that would make the project socially profitable. However, should this information become freely available to other investors and potential competitors, the initial firm might not be able to recoup the cost of making the market study. As in the earlier cases dealing with acquiring technological knowledge or training labor, under these circumstances the firm will not finance the cost of the study, and a socially beneficial industry will not be established. Suppose also that, in the absence of this market information, investors will insist upon such high interest charges that the investment will not be privately profitable. A tariff on the industry's product can overcome this unprofitability and enable firms to pay the high interest rates demanded by investors.

---

[11] Lack of perfect knowledge is also one of the major grounds used to support the modern "infant-economy" argument. For a critical view of this argument, see Haberler (1964), Baldwin (1965), and Grubel (1966).

If this high return over a period of time is all that is needed for investors to acquire sufficient knowledge about the industry for the lending rate to be bid down to a rate reflecting actual risk levels in the industry, then a temporary tariff may be socially desirable. However, while some information about earning prospects is likely to be conveyed to investors by their payments experience, it is doubtful if the full information that is socially profitable in terms of investment in knowledge acquisition will ever be conveyed to them simply by this sort of costless experience. The mere fact of tariff protection will make it difficult for investors to infer from their payments experience that they are overestimating investment risks in the industry. If this is so and the spillover problem also exists when outlays to obtain information are made, a temporary tariff cannot be relied upon to move production in the infant industry to a socially optimal level.[12] Direct subsidies to pay for the costs of knowledge acquisition will be needed. The same general point holds for providing information about working conditions to employees in a new industry. It is a gross over-simplification of the nature of the learning process to assume that all the information that is socially justifiable in terms of the return on knowledge-producing investment will eventually be provided simply by experience. Consequently, it cannot be assumed as a general rule that a tariff will be an effective device in enabling investors or workers to obtain the information needed for a socially efficient use of their factor services.

V

If the infant-industry argument for tariff protection is worthy of its reputation as the major exception to the free-trade case, it should be possible to present a clear analytical case, based upon well-known and generally accepted empirical relationships unique to infant industries, for the general desirability and effectiveness of protective duties in these industries. The contention of this paper is that such a case cannot be made.

The infant-industry case rests on the notion that a freely functioning price system will—in the absence of temporary duties—fail to bring about socially optimal levels of training, knowledge, and factor endowment in new industries. The main difficulty usually cited is the existence of technological spillover effects associated with the learning process. Learning involves costs; yet the knowledge acquired frequently becomes freely available to those who are potential competitors. The importance of these spillovers is not denied here: What is argued is that a duty cannot be relied upon to correct for these externalities and to achieve an optimal learning

---

[12] It will be necessary to maintain the duty on a permanent basis if investors do not revise their risk evaluation as they accumulate payments experience. The tariff improves the efficiency of resource allocation, but this case for protection is quite different from the argument for temporary protection of infant industries.

level. When learning involves costs other than those needed for efficient production with existing techniques and skills, as in the case of acquiring technological knowledge or training labor, a tariff may not compensate for the spillover problem at all. More generally, even though some knowledge can be obtained by production experience alone, it is highly unlikely that the socially optimal knowledge and training levels are acquired without some direct outlays for knowledge acquisition. However, when the technological spillover problem is present, imposing tariffs is no guarantee that these socially desirable kinds of expenditures will be made. What is needed is a direct subsidy devoted to knowledge acquisition.

Technological externalities, however, may not be the source of the difficulty in obtaining an optimal allocation of resources (including resources devoted to knowledge acquisition); a lack of knowledge or monopolistic prices for inputs may be the cause of the economic inefficiency. Undoubtedly a tariff-induced move of productive factors into new industries is sometimes sufficient for these factors to acquire the knowledge which will make the duty unnecessary at a later date. But there would also seem to be many cases where the knowledge that must be acquired to make the tariff subsequently unnecessary involves outlays in addition to current production costs and also becomes freely available to others. Under these circumstances, protective duties are likely either to fail completely in achieving their purpose or else to fail in directing sufficient resources into infant industries to achieve a social optimum. As far as monopolistic factor markets are concerned, it appears that these are as important impediments to efficient resource allocation in established industries as in infant industries. It would seem more logical, therefore, from a pedagogical point of view, to consider this as a protectionist argument separate from the infant-industry case.

In short, not only do infant-industry duties distort consumption—as do all duties—but they may fail to achieve a socially efficient allocation of productive resources in new industries and may even result in a decrease in social welfare. What is required to handle the special problems of infant industries is a much more direct and selective policy measure than nondiscriminatory import duties.

References

Alchian, A. "Costs and Outputs," in M. Abramovitz (ed.). *The Allocation of Economic Resources*. Stanford, Calif.: Stanford Univ. Press, 1959.

Baldwin, R. E. "Investment Policy in Underdeveloped Countries," in E. F. Jackson (ed.). *Economic Development in Africa*. Oxford: Blackwell, 1965.

Becker, G. S. *Human Capital*. New York: Nat. Bur. of Econ. Res., 1964.

Buchanan, J. M. "Joint Supply, Externality, and Optimality," *Economica*, XXXIII (November, 1966), 404–15.

Buchanan, J. M., and Stubblebine, W. C. "Externality," *Economica*, XXIX (November, 1962), 371–84.

Coase, R. H. "The Problem of Social Cost," *J. Law and Econ.*, III (October, 1960), 1–44.

Grubel, H. G. "The Anatomy of Classical and Modern Infant Industry Arguments," *Weltwirtschaftliches Archiv*, XCVII (December, 1966), 325–42.

Haberler, G. *The Theory of International Trade*. London: Hodge, 1936.

————. "An Assessment of the Current Relevance of the Theory of Comparative Advantage to Agricultural Production and Trade," *Internat. J. Agrarian Affairs*, IV (May, 1964).

Hamilton, A. *Report on Manufactures (1791)*. Reprinted in U.S. Senate Documents, Vol. XXII, No. 172. Washington: Congress, 1913.

Johnson, H. G. "Optimal Trade Intervention in the Presence of Domestic Distortions," in *Trade, Growth, and the Balance of Payments*. (Essays in Honor of Gottfried Haberler.) Chicago: Rand McNally, 1965.

Kafka, A. "A New Argument for Protection?" *Q.J.E.*, LXXVI (February, 1962), 163–66.

Kemp, M. C. "The Mill-Bastable Infant Industry Dogma," *J.P.E.*, LXVIII (February, 1960), 65–67.

List, F. *National System of Political Economy*. Translated by G. A. Matile. Philadelphia: Lippincott, 1856.

Meade, J. E. *Trade and Welfare*. New York: Oxford Univ. Press, 1955.

Meier, G. M. *Leading Issues in Development Economics*. New York: Oxford Univ. Press, 1964.

Mill, J. S. *The Principles of Political Economy*. London: Longmans, Green, 1909.

Myrdal, G. *Rich Lands and Poor*. New York: Harper, 1957.

Plott, C. R. "Externalities and Corrective Taxes," *Economica*, XXXIII (February, 1966), 84–87.

Rosenstein-Rodan, P. N. "Notes on the Theory of the 'Big Push,'" in T. Morgan, G. W. Betz, and N. K. Choudry (eds.). *Readings in Economic Development*. San Francisco: Wadsworth, 1963.

Scitovsky, T. "Two Concepts of External Economies," *J.P.E.*, LXII (April, 1954), 145.

Taussig, F. W. *Some Aspects of the Tariff Question*. Cambridge, Mass.: Harvard Univ. Press, 1915.

Turvey, R. "On Divergences Between Social Cost and Private Cost," *Economica*, XXX (August, 1963), 309–13.

[15]

Journal of Development Economics 22 (1986) 87–128. North-Holland

INDUSTRIAL STRATEGY AND TECHNOLOGICAL CHANGE

Theory versus Reality*

Howard PACK and Larry E. WESTPHAL

Swarthmore College, Swarthmore, PA 19081, USA

Received January 1985, revised version received July 1985

What are the determinants of appropriate industrial strategy under different circumstances? There is no universally accepted answer. This paper deals with two new elements in the contemporary debate, which centers around the efficacy of the neoclassically-prescribed neutral policy regime. One element is research demonstrating that market forces alone are not responsible for the purported 'market successes' of the East Asian NICs. With Korea as the case in point, this research is reviewed to draw some lessons about successful industrial strategy. The other element is an evolving conceptualization that puts technological change at the heart of industrialization. The underlying firm-level case-study research is surveyed and implications are derived regarding the nature as well as the extent of market failures affecting industrialization. It is argued throughout that industrial strategy should be seen as a matter of managing technological change to achieve dynamically efficient industrialization.

1. Introduction

Industrial strategies have many elements and many corresponding labels. One element is the part played by the state, giving rise to such labels as market-directed and centrally-planned. Another element is the role of international trade, giving rise to outward-looking and import-substituting strategies. A third element is the priority for investment, giving rise to light-

*A draft of this paper was presented at the United Nation's University Conference on 'New Directions in Development Theory', MIT Center for International Studies, Cambridge, MA, January 1985. Thanks go to Lance Taylor for comments along the way, to the conference participants for many useful reactions, and to Carl Dahlman and Morris Teubal for illuminating discussions about many of the issues covered here. Westphal's participation in writing this paper took place while he was on the staff of the World Bank and was part of a project, 'The Acquisition of Technological Capability', sponsored under the Bank's research program (ref. no. 672–48). The following disclaimer applies to the Bank's sponsorship: the World Bank does not accept responsibility for the views expressed herein which are those of the authors and should not be attributed to the World Bank or to its affiliated organizations. The findings, interpretations, and conclusions are the results of research supported by the Bank; they do not necessarily represent official policy of the Bank. The designations employed, the presentation of material, and any maps used in this document are solely for the convenience of the reader and do not imply the expression of any opinion whatsoever on the part of the World Bank or its affiliates concerning the legal status of any country, territory, city, area, or its authorities, or concerning the delimitation of its boundaries, or national affiliation.

industry and heavy-industry strategies. There also are some more general characterizations, such as capital-intensive or basic-needs focused, and so on. The elements relate to aspects of industrialization that are thought important to industrial development and to its contribution to social welfare. Since there is no unanimity about the important elements, there is no consensus about what constitutes 'industrial strategy'. Far more obviously, there also is no consensus about the industrial strategies most appropriate to the different circumstances in which countries are found.

Discussions about industrial strategy generally presume some form of intervention by the state. After all, the strategy at issue is the government's, either by explicit design or by implicit choice. The state's developmental role may thus be considered the principal element of industrial strategy. Few development analysts would argue that the proper role of government – that is, of government acting as a central agent – is to do nothing or to do everything. The efficacy of relying on free market forces nevertheless continues to be a focal point of debate.

Neoclassical practitioners argue that the government's proper role is simply to establish an economic environment in which market forces will realize the efficient allocation of resources. The appropriate instruments to create this environment are prices and price-denominated policies (e.g., taxes and subsidies). The neoclassicals advocate a neutral policy regime, 'neutral' meaning that policies should not selectively discriminate – that is, for tradeables, vis-à-vis world prices, and for non-tradeables, vis-à-vis relative scarcities – among industries except as necessary to overcome market failures. The neoclassicals allege that there are few inherent market failures and that existing market imperfections are by-and-large due to policy failures. These failures include errors of commission, licensing restrictions on production or interference in wage setting, for example; and errors of omission, which take the form of inaction to resolve institutional deficiencies – the absence of adequate capital market institutions, for example. With regard to the latter, they argue that the government's proper role is to facilitate the establishment of institutions which can and should function as market agents.

The core of the neoclassical prescription for a neutral policy regime is free trade.[1] Correspondingly, under this regime the domestic prices of traded products equal their border prices – the border price being either the import

---

[1]The prescription is for 'small countries' that have no potential monopoly power in international trade. Neoclassicals clearly recognize the possibility of monopoly power owing to inelastic demand for particular exports and prescribe specific export taxes as the first-best policy to exploit such power. But they argue that – in the relevant international markets for industrial goods and services, including technology – less developed countries typically face demand and supply conditions that correspond to perfect competition; the only notable exceptions occur on the demand side and pertain to manufactured exports subject to restrictions in developed-country markets.

price or the export price. Many neoclassicals nonetheless recognize that inherent market failures involving dynamic considerations may warrant generalized encouragement to industrialization. The prescribed, first-best means of infant-industry encouragement is a uniform and temporary subsidy to value added. But, as a practical matter, some neoclassicals [e.g., Balassa (1975)] prescribe a modest degree of uniform (and temporary) effective protection as the second-best means of generalized encouragement. Even so, all neoclassicals adamantly insist on the importance of uniform infant-industry incentives – that is, incentives that are granted equally, in overall effective terms, across industries and that are given automatically, without administrative discretion.

Some neoclassicals would also advise public provision of social overheads too large or expensive to be undertaken privately, but not with the objective of promoting specific industrial activities. And most would advocate policies to support human capital formation, but only in ways that do not discriminate among particular activities. Both forms of intervention are seen as having broad developmental objectives that extend beyond the industrial sector; in this respect they cannot be considered elements of an *industrial* strategy. In turn, other ostensibly separable elements of industrial strategy are seen simply as aspects of a neutral policy regime. For example, if it is considered another element, the appropriate trade orientation ('outward-looking'[2]) is not a separate element because it is implicit in the meaning of a neutral policy regime.

There are many other analysts, call them 'industrial strategists', who argue that there are significant choices among industrial strategies and that these choices are to some degree separable from choices among policies to achieve given strategies. For the strategists, reliance on market forces operating in a neutral policy regime is but one of a number of possibly viable strategies. They actively pursue questions about how the government should identify strategically important industries and how it should promote them through selectively targeted price-denominated policies and more direct forms of intervention. There is agreement among industrial strategists that these are meaningful and important questions. But there is disagreement about the answers and hence about which elements of industrial strategy are crucial.

The axis of intellectual dialogue about industrialization has shifted radically since the early days of 'modern' development economics. The principal contributions in the early days were made by strategists including Chenery, Hirschman, Nurkse, and Rosenstein-Rodan. They, like many later strategists, matured in an environment in which the possibility of planning was a dominant issue; they thus evinced a greater concern with allocative and

---

[2]Defined as a policy regime in which $EER_e/EER_m \approx 1$, where EER denotes the effective exchange rate for exports (e) or imports (m).

distributive issues than with policies per se. More recently, the neoclassical view, exposed by such authors as Balassa, Corden, Krueger, and Little, has become the dominant 'establishment' position. Most neoclassicals, like those just named, tend to have grown up in the tradition of international economics. They consider the principles of appropriate policy design to be quite straightforward, even if not widely understood or followed by policy makers.

Not only have the 'establishment' and its position changed, the central arguments have changed as well, from those among the strategists to those between them and the neoclassicals.[3] The neoclassicals have gained ascendance by diligently marshalling the presumed facts on their side of the debate. In particular, they have contrasted the evident success of the market-reliant, outward-looking economies with the lackluster and sometimes abysmal performance of the ostensibly more interventionist, inward-looking economies. Moreover, in doing so, they have popularized an essentially static theory of comparative advantage as the central element in the framework for analyzing industrial development.

Several new elements have recently entered the debate. One is research demonstrating that the neoclassicals don't have all their facts straight: market forces *alone* are not responsible for the purported 'market successes' of economies like Japan or Korea. This research clearly shows that a neutral policy regime is not a necessary condition for successful industrialization. The other new element is an evolving but distinct empirically based conceptualization that puts indigenous dynamic phenomena involving technological change – not simple factor accumulation and allocation – at the center of industrialization. This conceptualization implies that a neutral policy regime may not generally be a sufficient condition for rapid industrialization.[4]

Our principal purposes in this paper are to expound the new elements and to consider their implications. Here a caveat is in order. The new elements – empirical and conceptual alike – are not equally relevant to all of the issues

[3]The present-day arguments have many parallels in the on-going debate about industrial policy in the United States. Many of the issues in the latter debate have to do with government policy in circumstances of rapidly changing global technological frontiers, where first entrants may enjoy considerable advantages. The discussion in this paper focuses on a different set of circumstances – namely, those faced by countries that are at some distance from the global frontiers. Hence we are not here concerned with 'picking winners' at the leading edge of global technological change.

[4]Comparative evidence about macro industrial policy and performance is not persuasive when it comes to questions of sufficiency. (Some might argue that such evidence is not persuasive with regard to necessity either; we would argue that it is at least more persuasive.) It is impossible to determine the separate effects of a multiplicity of plausible and associated causes on the basis of the comparative experience to date. Among the NICs, Hong Kong alone stands out as having fully adhered to the neoclassical dictates. But as is widely appreciated, Hong Kong is in many respects a special case that proves very little of relevance to other less developed countries.

debated among strategists or between them and the neoclassicals. They largely pertain to what, for want of a better label, may be referred to as 'supply-side issues' that involve the responsiveness of market supply to actual and latent demand. In other words, we focus on the government's role in fostering efficient production. Distributional issues, as well as questions concerning the aggregate cum inter-sectoral balancing of supply and demand over time, are dealt with indirectly, if at all. The limitation arises in part because our empirical evidence is drawn only from countries that have followed export-oriented strategies as a way of generating employment and escaping domestic demand constraints. But the limitation also reflects our view that fostering efficient production is an overriding objective of industrial strategy.

The discussion proceeds as follows. First we consider the lessons to be learned from the hyper-successful NICs (newly industrializing – or semi-industrial, advanced developing – countries). We use the Republic of Korea as the case in point, in part because it is the country we know best. Then we go beyond these lessons to examine conceptual matters. We argue that trade considerations are secondary to technological ones in searching for an understanding of industrialization that is relevant to policy making. And we amplify on the importance of technological considerations by discussing some micro industrial policy issues. We conclude with a short summary that is in part intended to highlight the similarities and differences between the emerging conceptualization and that of the early strategists.

2. Getting the facts straight: The Korean case

Korea's industrialization is frequently cited as a powerful example of the efficacy of a neutral policy regime. Policy reforms in the early 1960s are credited with transforming the Korean economy from a 'basket case' – as it was widely perceived in the late 1950s – into a dynamic and rapidly developing economy. There can be no doubt that there were policy reforms and that they were important. But there is widespread misperception about just what those reforms entailed. Equally important, Korea was not nearly as industrially backward in the late 1950s as the 'basket case' designation would make it seem [Westphal, Rhee and Pursell (1981)].

Modern industrialization in Korea began in the colonial period (1910–1945), when the Japanese government managed the peninsula's economy as an integral part of its empire. Manufacturing growth during the period was rapid and extensive, but it depended heavily on the Japanese. Nonetheless, Koreans apparently acquired, mostly on the job, substantial knowledge about how to operate modern industries. This can be seen from the Korean ability to operate much of the existing industry just after the end of the

Second World War, notwithstanding the tremendous disruption caused by the severing of ties with Japan and the division of the peninsula into two political entities.

In what is now South Korea, manufacturing production in 1945 was substantially less than a fifth of its level in 1940. But in light of circumstances at the time, what is truly remarkable is that the Koreans were able, with relatively little foreign managerial or technical assistance, to operate nearly half the manufacturing plants that existed in 1944: there was no existing sector in which they were unable to produce at least something. By 1948, with assistance from the United States – access to raw materials, replacement parts, and technical help – the Koreans were operating facilities to produce a wide variety of manufactured goods, including shoes, textiles, rubber tires, basic steel shapes, and such engineering products as pumps, bicycles, tin cans, and ball bearings.

There is no universal agreement on just how much human capital was built up during the colonial period. But the evidence just cited – and other historical evidence that continues to accumulate – strongly suggests that Mason, Jones and Sakong [in Mason et al. (1980, p. 449)] are right in emphasizing the '"demonstration effect" of exposure to modern technology and forms of organization' and in concluding that the colonial bequest was considerable. One thing is certain, Korea's colonial experience was unlike that of most other less developed countries in that it involved considerable industrialization. It also involved substantial development of the non-industrial sectors. Korean agriculture, for example, benefitted from widespread diffusion of Japanese technology. Development during the colonial period thus contributed to creating the conditions needed to ensure satisfactory balance in the growth of output and factor use among the different sectors of the economy.

It would, however, be wrong to neglect that the departure of the Japanese meant the withdrawal of the skills that had enabled the effective operation of many businesses and institutions created by them. For the Koreans to gain these skills took time, in some cases well over a decade. But during the late 1940s and the 1950s the Koreans did more than simply work to replace the lost skills and to adapt what was left from the colonial period to conform more closely to Korean circumstances. The industrial base grew at a respectable rate owing to import substituting investments in light manufactured and non-durable consumer goods. Equally if not more significant, the human capital stock was greatly augmented through major programs that instituted universal primary education and achieved nearly universal adult literacy. Higher education was expanded and a large number of students were sent overseas for technical and advanced training.

In sum, the available evidence indicates that Korea had a comparatively strong industrial base of physical and human capital at the outset of the

1960s. This implies a difference in 'initial conditions' that raises serious doubt about the relevance of Korean experience to thinking about industrial strategies for the least industrialized countries. The conditions for supply responses to policy reforms that were present in Korea are far from being equally present in these countries.

The policy reforms in the early 1960s had two major effects [Westphal (1978)]. One was to increase the rates of savings and investment. The other – the one with which we are concerned – was to put Korea on the path of export-led industrialization. The reforms that accomplished this included the replacement – in several steps – of a complex system of multiple exchange rates by a single, unified exchange rate that was not greatly overvalued. But this was not accomplished by wholesale import liberalization. Imports destined (either directly or indirectly as inputs) for the domestic market remained subject to tariffs and quantitative controls. However, the system of controls on these imports was rationalized and thereby converted from a mechanism of socially unproductive rent-seeking into an instrument of industrial promotion. Imports of capital goods and intermediate products used to produce exports were effectively, if not administratively, freed from restriction, and they were given exemption from tariffs. Thus exporters were placed under a virtual free trade regime such that they faced world (or border) prices for both tradable inputs and exported outputs. Also very important, they were given immediate and unrestricted access to working capital finance at highly preferential rates. And a limited number of additional subsidies were instituted, the most important being a 50 percent reduction in taxes on income earned through exporting.

There have been several studies to quantify the incidence of Korean industrial policies through the estimation of effective incentives. 'Effective incentives' extends the effective protection concept to include the impact of all readily quantifiable incentive mechanisms that indirectly influence market allocations. In addition to the instruments of trade policy, these mechanisms include such things as credit preferences, direct and indirect tax preferences, and subsidies given through various means. Westphal and Kim (1982) and Nam (1981) give estimates of effective incentive rates for 1968 and 1978, respectively.[5] These studies employed a high level of disaggregation among industries and distinguished within industries between exports and domestic sales. They consequently contain a great deal of information about the degree of neutrality in Korea's industrial policy regime. This information is the basis for the statements that follow.

Taken together, Korean industrial policies after the reforms were such that producers whose costs were competitive with world prices had at least the same incentive to export as they had to sell domestically. For internationally

[5]Both sources also provide a qualitative description of the policy regime over time and give time-series estimates of effective exchange rates.

competitive production, then, the reforms came close to instituting one aspect of a neutral policy regime, that aspect being the absence of a trade-bias. [There is no trade-bias if there is no difference between the effective incentives given to export activity and to import substitution – or, more generally, to production for domestic sales (see footnote 2 on page 299).] We write 'came close' because the estimates indicate a modest pro-export bias for internationally competitive production. But, owing to the continuance of import restrictions, and the provision of additional incentives, the reforms did not establish the other aspect of a neutral policy regime, which is the absence of an industry-bias. (There is no industry-bias if there is no variance in the overall effective incentives given to different industries.) Indeed, the reforms appear to have greatly increased the effective extent of industry-bias by rationalizing the encouragement of infant industries [Westphal (1982)].

Changes made in incentive policies after the reforms have not fundamentally altered the pattern of effective incentives. The changes were largely made in response to shifts in the international competitiveness of Korean industry. Episodic import liberalization did little, if anything, to reduce the extent of industry-bias. And the withdrawal of some export incentives, including the tax preference on income from exporting, was largely to offset real exchange rate changes that made exporting comparatively more profitable. Thus there have been no major changes in pattern of industry-bias between internationally competitive industries and infant industries or in the patterns of trade-bias within each set of industries. But there have been substantial changes over time in the composition of both sets.

In short, the Korean government has not practiced neutrality in its incentive policies. Most significant, it had discriminated in its treatment between established, internationally competitive industries and new, infant industries that were deemed worthy of promotion. Something closely approximating neutrality on both counts (trade-bias and industry-bias) has characterized the government's policies affecting the established industries. Effective incentives to exports and to domestic sales have been roughly equal in these industries, and there has been little variance in effective incentive rates among these industries. But there has been substantial industry-bias in favor of the promoted infant industries. These industries have benefitted from protection, credit preferences, and various forms of tax inducements. The set of promoted infants has changed over time, but it has generally been small at any one point in time.

Also significant is the fact that the Korean government has not relied solely on tariffs to protect infant industries. It has frequently used restrictions on import quantities which, due to their nature, could be considered to afford 'absolute' protection.[6] That is, through import restrictions, selectively

---

[6]The resulting anti-export bias that is apparent in measured effective incentive rates for infant industries has been more than offset by moral suasion and more overtly persuasive encouragements – of both the carrot and stick variety – to export.

promoted infant industries were often initially granted whatever levels of effective protection were required to secure an adequate market for their output as well as a satisfactory rate of return on investment. Initial rates of effective protection were frequently in excess of 100 percent.

The preceding discussion pertains to incentive mechanisms that operate indirectly through influencing market allocations. But the Korean government has also used direct means of control and allocation to supplement and reinforce the indirect mechanisms. For some industries, competing imports were restricted through a de facto 'law of similars'; an import license would not be granted unless it could be shown that the desired product could not be obtained from domestic producers. The government also imposed 'local-content' regulations on various industries, requiring them to procure a progressively increasing share of their inputs from local sources. In some instances it even appears that imports used to produce exports were restricted under one or both mechanisms. Until recently, all long-term foreign capital inflows as well as transfers of proprietary technology were subject to licensing control and all the major domestic banks were government-owned.

The reforms in the mid-1960s included changes in monetary policy that led to greatly increased real interest rates on deposits held in the banking system. But, as Cole and Park (1983) show in their definitive study of the Korean financial system, these reforms did not lead to financial liberalization. Quite the opposite, they greatly increased government controls over financial flows by attracting deposits into the banking system, away from a large number of highly active unregulated (or 'unorganized') financial institutions.[7] The government has used its direct control over bank lending and its somewhat less pervasive control over foreign capital inflows to direct the allocation of sizable shares of both working capital and investment finance. Credit rationing has co-existed with a variety of selective preferential interest rate schemes, but it has not been limited to their administration.

The impact of credit rationing has been moderated by short-term foreign capital inflows and, more importantly, by the activities of the unregulated institutions. These institutions have provided a significant margin for the operation of market forces to channel funds flexibly. But the force of credit rationing is reflected in the large differentials that have prevailed between market-clearing interest rates on unregulated credit and non-preferential rates on bank credit. Cole and Park argue, persuasively we think, that the government's comprehensive interventions vis-à-vis the banking system were an integral and necessary part of its development strategy. But they conclude that the government's strategy could not have succeeded to anywhere near the same degree without the complementarities afforded by the unregulated

---

[7]Capital markets for bonds and securities did not exist in any substantial form until the late 1970s, when they grew in response to government incentives but nonetheless remained rather unimportant. Thus the key domestic financial agents have been the government-owned banks and an assortment of unregulated (or 'unorganized') financial institutions.

financial institutions acting in response to market forces. Similarly, the other aspect of 'getting domestic prices right', maintenance of real wages that roughly reflect labour demand and supply, was also a crucial underpinning of Korea's successful industrial performance – particularly in the (unskilled) labor intensive, less technologically advanced branches.

The Korean government has also selectively intervened to mold and even to create market agents. The most prominent objects of its molding efforts have been the *chaebol*. These are extremely large, conglomerate business groups whose activities span all sectors but are concentrated in manufacturing and construction.[8] A number of them – ten or so – regularly appear on *Fortune*'s list of the 500 largest industrial corporations outside the United States.[9] These conglomerates initially evolved through entrepreneurial responses to market opportunities. But government interventions over the past decade have significantly contributed to their present form and stature.

In the mid-1970s the government legislatively sanctioned and indeed encouraged the consolidation of the *chaebol* through the formation of integrated trading companies that were given special status and accorded special privileges. The trading companies were the government's vehicle for decentralizing the administration of export incentives. They were equally its chosen instrument for undertaking the activities needed to strengthen and expand Korea's export marketing capabilities. And the *chaebol* were also made the key agents for implementing the central thrust of Korean government planning during the 1970s, which was to develop the heavy and chemical industries. Their large-scale investments in the machinery and transport equipment sectors have been subject to government efforts, not always successful, to encourage specialization among them and to otherwise constrain the pattern of industrial organization. The automotive sector, for example, has long been a target of such efforts; the government has forced several major restructurings among the assemblers and has sometimes intervened in their decisions whether to use subcontractors to supply parts and components as well as in their choices of particular subcontractors. The principal instruments of intervention to affect market structure have been credit rationing and the licensing of both capital and technology inflows.

Moreover, the government has not always waited for market forces to respond to its direction. From the early 1960s onwards, when the incentives thought appropriate by the government failed to elicit a desired infant industry's creation, public enterprises have been established. The first producers of fertilizer, petrochemicals, and refined petroleum products, for instance, were public enterprises. A notable and somewhat more recent

---

[8]Jones and Sakong (1980) and Jones (1980) provide comprehensive information about the historical evolution of the *chaebol*.

[9]The number of Korean firms on *Fortune*'s annual list has consistently been among the highest for the non-OECD countries.

example is Korea's highly successful integrated steel mill. These firms, like all public enterprises in the industrial sector, are constrained to operate as market agents. They have been managed as autonomous profit-seeking entities and have contributed materially to government revenues.

The share of public enterprises in Korea's non-agricultural output is comparatively high, being similar to that of India.[10] There are many public enterprises that were not created to pioneer new industries. Some are utilities, but many are in mining and manufacturing. A number of the latter, including some quite large firms, started with private ownership and became public enterprises upon bankruptcy because of government debt-repayment guarantees. Upon becoming public, these firms have typically been restructured and then sold to private interests; correspondingly, the set of such enterprises has undergone continual change. Thus the government has played a major role in the regeneration of moribund firms.

In the foregoing discussion we have surveyed the principal mechanisms in the Korean government's practice of selective intervention. We will not review the various indicators typically used to gauge industrial performance. We rely instead on the widespread understanding that Korea's industrial performance has been remarkably successful. Taken together, then, the facts of Korean experience are testimony that selective intervention need not be inimical to successful industrialization. But does Korean experience show more than this, does it show that selective intervention can contribute to successful industrialization? This question cannot be addressed without counterfactual information about what would have happened in the absence of selective intervention. Hence it will probably never be answered in a way that commands the agreement of all knowledgeable observers. Our answer is that selective intervention has indeed contributed to the success, and that it has done so by accelerating the rate of industrial growth with little if any compensating loss in efficiency terms. It is not our purpose here to give an extensive argument in support of this answer.[11] Instead, we think it more useful to address a subsidiary question that assumes a positive answer: what characteristics of Korean selective intervention appear to have been most important and how have they contributed to Korea's successful industrial performance? In answering this question we focus on 'stylized facts' or 'central tendencies' as we understand them.

The most important characteristic is the consistent strategy of industrialization that lies behind the selective intervention that has been practiced by the government. The strategy treats industries that are well established in the

---

[10]Jones (1975) gives the most complete of the available discussions of Korean public enterprises.

[11]The elements of the argument can be found in Mason et al. (1980), Westphal (1982), and Rhee, Ross-Larson and Pursell (1984), which also provide more extensive and detailed discussions along the lines of that which follows in the text.

sense of being internationally competitive quite differently than it deals with the infant industries that are the particular targets of selective intervention. The objective of the strategy is to exploit the comparative advantage of the former industries while building a comparative advantage in the latter industries.

Market forces acting in response to largely neutral policies are relied upon to allocate resources in well-established industries. However, such industries can become the target of selective intervention if they are perceived to have lost competitiveness, when the government may take an active role in designing and implementing programs of rationalization cum upgrading. In turn, infant industries are developed by market agents (typically private but sometimes public) acting in response to non-neutral promotional policies and under the strong influence of direct non-price-denominated interventions in decision making and resource allocation. Other industries – suppliers of inputs and users of outputs – are affected by these measures insofar as their behavior is constrained or otherwise conditioned by the selective interventions to foster infant industries. In this limited respect, then, other industries may be subject to non-neutral policies. But the important point remains that intervention is indeed selective and is focused on industries judged to be in Korea's dynamic comparative advantage.

Thus the Korean government has not attempted either to make or to constrain most decisions about resource allocation. With respect to well-established industries, except in periods of rationalization, the government has concentrated on 'fine-tuning' its incentive policies to avoid any anti-export biases that might have resulted from costs imposed by the instruments of infant industry promotion and from periodic progressive but generally modest over-valuation of the currency. More generally, government policy toward industries not subject to selective intervention has been permissive rather than restrictive. That is, these industries are simply 'not promoted', but neither are they subject to overt restrictions through such things as investment licensing. If they have suffered discrimination, it is of the 'benign neglect' variety. For example, instead of being able to obtain credit from the banking system, they may have had to rely on the unregulated financial institutions. In turn, the government's licensing control over foreign capital inflows into these sectors by way of suppliers credits for machinery and raw materials has also been largely permissive.

The significant characteristic here is the government's general tolerance – if not covert and well reasoned use – of free market institutions to provide for flexibility in resource allocation. Korea's industrial performance owes much to this tolerance, which has resulted in many highly profitable (socially as well as privately) ventures that were either not foreseen or not actively promoted by the government. Included among these successful market outcomes are a number of industries that were infants when established by private initiative and that became relatively quite important as generators of income, employment, and foreign exchange. In turn, some highly successful, selectively promoted industries were identified by the government on the basis of – thus only after – their initial and profitable inception by private market agents.

The government's role in intervening to promote selected infant industries can be interpreted in terms of overcoming the externalities that industrial strategists have discussed in connection with industrialization. It is well appreciated – at least in theory – that such externalities can be overcome by internalizing them through organizational integration. But this is not realistically feasible: if nothing else, the externalities may flow in complex and inseparable patterns among (actual and potential) agents covering most if not all of the industrial sector. In fact, it is not organizational integration that is important, rather it is integrated (some would prefer the term coordinated) decision-making.

The Korean government can be seen as having achieved integrated decision-making by acting as a central agent mediating among market agents, forcing and facilitating information interchange and insuring the implementation of the decisions reached. The power of coercion appears to have been important to carrying out this role effectively. But coercion has typically not been absolute; it has balanced costs and benefits. Thus the Korean government can be seen as having adjudicated between suppliers and users, weighing costs and benefits from a collective standpoint and often intervening to reward cooperative players and punish uncooperative ones. Such adjudication has involved a great deal of discretionary administration.

In its decision-making about which industries to promote and how to do so, the government has almost always consulted extensively with the private agents having relevant knowledge and a possible interest in the outcome. Thus its decisions can most often be characterized as decisions reached through a process of consensus building or, if not that, of at least protracted consultation. Industry associations, which are sanctioned by the government and sometimes appear to behave in some respects like cartels, are often important elements of the process. (But one should not overstate the independent power of industry, which has been much less than in Japan.) Moreover, the process of integrated decision-making has been a highly flexible one – one that has generally been able to elicit, digest, and act on information uncovered in the process of implementing previous decisions. In other words, priorities at all levels have been established and revised through continual monitoring related to implementation. Thus, for example, initial decisions to promote or establish particular industries have been reversed or the sequential process of their implementation has been changed or delayed on the basis of market and technical information obtained along the way.

The Korean process of integrated decision-making has necessarily led the government to intervene selectively and in detail. It has been involved in the affairs of specific industries in ways that go far beyond the provision of neutral incentives on a non-discretionary basis to all comers who qualify. Acting as the central agent, the government has often been directly engaged in the search for information, in the making of decisions, and even in the implementation process.[12] In playing its role, the government can be seen as addressing problems caused by imperfect knowledge. It can also be perceived as overcoming capital market imperfections through being directly involved in investment decisions, through allocating credit as well as through establishing public enterprises. Investment decisions here encompass decisions regarding capacity creation and expansion, market creation and overseas marketing, human capital accumulation, technology acquisition, infrastructure provision, and so on.

Selective invervention has often led to successful outcomes in the sense of having fostered the rapid achievement of international competitiveness and the fast expansion of output. This, taken together with the strong overall performance of the industrial sector, is what leads us to conclude that selective intervention has contributed a great deal to Korea's industrialization. But successful outcomes have typically been observed only when the government has acted from an overriding objective of dynamic – that is, eventual, but sooner rather than later – efficiency. Export performance has been the practical yardstick for measuring progress toward the objective of international competitiveness. Infant industries have been expected to begin exporting very soon if not immediately after they began production. And established industries have likewise been monitored with respect to their export performance, with export targets and certain export subsidies having been jointly negotiated between government and industry.

There has necessarily been a great deal of ex ante uncertainty about which were the 'optimal' industries to promote and about the probable magnitude of their exports over time. This uncertainty about detailed strategy has been progressively resolved by translating information gained during implementation into its implications for expected export performance, with the comparison of actual performance against expectations being used to reformulate detailed strategy. Moreover, it has been recognized that exports per se do not necessarily imply international competitiveness if domestic sales are protected from import competition and production is given cost-reducing incentives. The government has kept close watch over the magnitude of incentives, the relationship of domestic prices to international prices, and other relevant information such as indicators of product quality. Thus, the monitoring of progress has focused on export performance but has in-

---

[12]Enos (1984) provides a detailed illustration of the extent of government involvement; Leudde-Neurath (1984) discusses the subject with general reference to direct foreign investment.

corporated the information needed to gauge international competitiveness correctly.

Because the process of successive implementation and reformulation of detailed strategy has been centered on export performance, Korea's industrial strategy can hardly be characterized as neutral with respect to its trade-bias. The primacy of the export criterion has been such that the Korean 'macro' industrial strategy cannot validly be termed 'outward-looking' in the sense of there being no trade-bias once such unquantifiables as moral suasion are recognized. The strategy has been one of export-led industrialization, but not 'at any cost'. The monitoring process has assured that exports are both privately and socially profitable – for infant industries in the medium, though not always in the short, run. The monitoring process gave this assurance because it enabled the government to change its detailed strategy in response to market signals emanating from world markets as well as other information pertaining to the costs and benefits of an industry's operations.

The foregoing should not be interpreted to suggest that selective interventions have always led to successful outcomes. Judging from a medium-run perspective, there have been some costly mistakes. Particularly serious were the mistakes made in promoting the heavy and chemical industries during the 1970s. These mistakes were largely responsible for the dramatic deterioration in Korea's industrial performance that occurred at the end of the 1970s. The effects remain even today; for example, excess capacity resulting from poorly coordinated and implemented investment continues to plague the heavy engineering industries. The mistakes stemmed from the government's initial decision to promote too many infant industries at once and from its subsequent, unprecedented reluctance to abandon or radically revise its detailed strategy on the basis of information and experience accumulated during implementation. Because there was too little selectivity, scarce technical and entrepreneurial talent was spread too thinly across too many infants. And because international competitiveness was not the overriding objective, the monitoring process described above was not effectively utilized in revising detailed strategy. The other at least coequal objective was to establish a domestic defense industry for national security reasons. It is not hard to imagine the various ways in which this objective could come into ·conflict with that of becoming internationally competitive.

That mistakes have been made is not a sufficient reason to condemn selective intervention. Given the uncertainties associated with establishing new industries, it is to be expected that mistakes would be made even under a highly effective strategy of selective intervention to foster new lines of internationally competitive industry. It is not the variance of performance that counts, it is the average in relation to what could be expected in the absence of selective intervention. Our knowledge of the evidence leads us to conclude that the average social rate of return on investments in selectively promoted infant industries has been relatively high, if the most serious mistakes made in pursuit of objectives unrelated to market performance are omitted from the evaluation. In our view, the lessons to be learned from these mistakes are lessons about how to manage selective intervention effectively. But some observers, including many Koreans, draw different lessons – lessons about why the Korean government cannot be effective in practicing selective intervention, regardless of whether it once was effective.

Korean industrial policy is currently in a state of flux. In the last several years a series of reforms have been initiated with the ostensible purpose of reducing the extent of government intervention via both incentive policies and more direct forms of control and allocation.[13] However, it is not yet clear where these reforms will ultimately lead with respect to the practice of selective intervention.

3. Toward a theory of industrial strategy

What is most significant about Korean experience is the government's operation of a dual policy structure. The duality is between industries in which Korea has a static comparative advantage and those in which it does not.[14] In the former sectors, market forces operating in response to largely neutral incentives prevail; in the latter sectors, market forces are influenced by selectively promotional incentive policies and supplemented by instruments of direct control and allocation. We see the same duality with similarly successful results in the industrial policy structures of Japan and Taiwan and suspect its presence in that of Singapore.[15] This is not to say that the details of selective intervention as practised in these East Asian countries are identical. But the central tendencies appear to be strikingly similar.

Incentive policies having a strong industry-bias together with credit rationing, import quotas, licensing controls and many other of the overt instruments of selective intervention that have been widely castigated by the neoclassicals have been used with apparently very successful results by these countries. This leads us to conclude that the neoclassical emphasis on choices among policy instruments is misplaced. The differences between Japan,

[13]The evolution of Korean industrial policy and strategy can be followed in the pages of *Business Korea*, published monthly in Seoul and distributed internationally.

[14]It should perhaps be made explicit that the latter industries have included those existing industries (textiles, for example) whose continued competitiveness in the face of changing circumstances was considered to require major rationalization.

[15]The literature on Japanese industrial policy obviously does not converge on a single view in this respect. Of the literature with which we are familiar, we consider Johnson's (1982) discussion to be particularly revealing and persuasive, though we recognize that it pays less than adequate attention to demonstrating that outcomes were successful. In turn, the majority of the literature on industrial policy in Taiwan pays far too little attention to its government's practice of selective intervention, as Wade (1985) rightly argues.

Korea, and Taiwan, on one side, and most less successful industrializing countries, on the other, are not to be found in the use of different policy instruments. The differences are to be found instead in different ways of using the same policy instruments – for example, in the scope of their application, in whether they are used promotionally or restrictively.[16] The neoclassicals are not wrong in pointing out that certain policy instruments are more likely to be subverted to rent-seeking than to be used in service of achieving dynamically efficient industrialization. But neither are the strategists wrong in saying that these same policy instruments have been used to promote industrialization, apparently very successfully.

There is no coherent theory of industrial strategy that would rationalize what we see as being the very positive contribution of selective intervention to East Asian industrialization. Certainly conventional economic theory would not lead many analysts to conclude that selective intervention as we have described its practice in Korea is a possibly optimal policy. It is not our intention to provide an adequate theory of industrial strategy here. Our purpose is rather to articulate what the central foundations of such a theory would seem to be. One is an explicit recognition that sociopolitical factors are the primary determinants of the efficacy of different forms of government intervention.[17] This recognition follows from considering the nature of selective intervention.

A great deal of uncertainty is associated with selective intervention – uncertainty about where and how to intervene and about what results to expect. This leads us to conclude that selective intervention can bring successful results only to the degree that it entails successive implementation and reformulation of detailed strategy through the accumulation of information relevant to judging progress toward an unambiguous objective. There may be many potentially relevant (or warranted) objectives that are operable in this respect. But, based on conventional economic theory and on what is known from cross-country comparative evidence, we would argue that one objective dominates in terms of both relevance and operability. This objective is the achievement of dynamic efficiency in the sense of attaining international competitiveness within an explicitly specified, medium-run time horizon. 'International competitiveness' here should be understood in terms of ability to compete – without selective interventions – in the domestic market as well as in the international market; it should not be understood simply in terms of export performance.

Social and political factors have an overwhelming importance in determining whether decision-making in pursuit of this objective can be institutionalized, which is not simply a matter of government actions but also of

---

[16]Mason (1984) brings this out very succinctly in comparing development policy and its implementation in Egypt and Korea.

[17]See Ruggie (1983) for a discussion of this issue by political scientists.

private behavior. Though many governments might claim that they selectively intervene in pursuit of dynamic efficiency (as the ultimate, if not the proximate, objective), few have in fact done so effectively. Where the claim is made without evident result, the reasons for failure lie in the internal workings of government and in the interactions between its constituent elements and the various interest and pressure groups within society. We need not belabor that governments are neither monolithic nor omnipotent – or that governments, policies, and the implementation of policies change and evolve through give-and-take among more-or-less independent parties, public as well as private.[18] Thus a government's ability to intervene selectively in pursuit of dynamic efficiency cannot be taken for granted. Indeed, most governments may lack this ability. But it appears to be a critical factor in using selective intervention to achieve faster and more successful industrialization. Hence, where this ability does not exist, the government is probably well advised to adhere rather closely to the strict neoclassical prescription for a neutral policy regime.[19]

The other foundation of an adequate theory of industrial strategy is an understanding of industrialization in terms of technological change. We will devote the rest of our discussion to developing that understanding and its implications. The role of the East Asian governments in selectively intervening to promote infant industries and to rationalize industries experiencing difficulties can be interpreted as having been intended to overcome constraints on the private sector's ability to acquire the technical, institutional, and marketing wherewithal needed to achieve and maintain international competitiveness. In other words, technological change can be seen as having been the focus of selective intervention. The concept of technology that underlies this statement is a broad one. It does not merely include the knowledge of physical processes that transform inputs into outputs (technical knowledge). It also includes the knowledge of procedural and organizational – that is, institutional – arrangements for carrying out the transformations.

Industrialization is not typically thought of in terms of technological change by development economists, though economic historians [e.g. Landes (1969) and Rosenberg (1976)] have emphasized its role in the growth of the currently-developed countries. But there is a growing body of research that shows it should be conceived in these terms.[20] Of course, most of the

---

[18]These points are often neglected in the case of Korea, whose success is incorrectly ascribed simply to the imposition of a strong government on a hard-working populace. In fact, the ingredients of Korea's success cannot be understood without an appreciation of the intricate workings of its government and of the complex interactions between the bureaucracy and the rest of society. See, for example, Cole and Lyman (1971) and Michell (1984).

[19]However, it should be noted that the factors responsible for a government's inability to intervene effectively may also preclude its following the neoclassical prescription. Rent-seekers, after all, seek not just rents but also the conditions that make for rents.

[20]Readily accessible and relatively recent compendia of representative results from this research can be found in Stewart and James (1982), Fransman and King (1984), and the

technology introduced during industrialization is transferred in one way or another from industrially more advanced countries. But because industrialization adds to the variety of products produced and processes used in a country, it does in fact involve technological change in the sense of gaining mastery over products and processes that are new to the local economy. The minor role of invention in industrialization simply means that much technological change consists of assimilating and adapting foreign technology.

The extent of indigenous effort involved in this process has been uncovered through case-study research into the technological changes that have occurred within industrial firms in less developed countries.[21] This research shows that, in all industries, 'technology is characterized by a considerable element of tacitness, difficulties in imitation and teaching, and uncertainty regarding what modifications will work and what will not' [Nelson (1979, p. 18)]. That is, important elements of the technology appropriate to particular circumstances can be acquired only through effort to apply existing knowledge to those circumstances. Effort is required in using technological information and accumulating technological knowledge to evaluate and choose technology; to acquire and operate processes and produce products; to manage changes in products, processes, procedures, and organizational arrangements; and to create new technology. This effort takes the form of investments in technological capability, which is the ability to make effective use of technological knowledge. This capability is the primary attribute of human and institutional capital, the latter being the embodiment of the know-how used to combine human skills and physical capital into systems for delivering want-satisfying products.

It has been found that firms cannot achieve or maintain international competitiveness without technological effort. Experience in production, and in investment to expand production, is necessary for gaining the capability needed for international competitiveness. But experience – or simple learning-by-doing – is not sufficient, certainly not for remaining competitive in a world of constantly improving best practice. Not all firms in less developed countries engage in the technological effort needed for international competitiveness. Those that do typically experience rapid productivity gains associated with increased mastery of the initial technology and with a wide variety of technological changes in what is produced and how it is produced. The observed technological changes are the result of various causes. Some are due to experience that uncovers unforeseen problems or possibilities in using the initial technology in the original circumstances. Some are induced

symposia contained in the November 1981 issue of *The Annals of the American Academy of Political and Social Science*, the May/June 1984 issue of *World Development*, and the September/October 1984 issue of the *Journal of Development Economics*.
    [21]See the references given in the preceding footnote, all of which contain articles which in some way report on this research.

in response to changes in circumstances; for example, changes that affect the supply of inputs of different characteristics, or changes that affect the demand for outputs of different characteristics. And others are the outcome of initiatives to accommodate or take advantage of changing circumstances by expanding and modifying the mix of processes used and products produced.

Most of these technological changes can be characterized as minor, in the sense that they do not create radically new technologies but rather adapt existing ones. But these minor changes often take place in a cumulative sequence that has a pronounced overall effect on the productivity of resource use. An increase in productivity of 100 percent or more within less than a decade does not appear to be atypical among firms that have successfully achieved international competitiveness. The successful firms have been found to complement their own efforts by extensive reliance on outside sources of information and technology. In fact, their acquisition of technological capability consists importantly of learning how most effectively to combine their own efforts with technological inputs from foreign and domestic sources. Most of these firms appear to have successively acquired a widening range of the capabilities related to their activities, but their technological development has been far from autarkic.

These findings show that industrial development is a process of acquiring technological capability in the course of continual technological change. They have important implications. The costs of achieving international competitiveness – likewise, the costs of maintaining it in the face of changed circumstances – are the costs of acquiring technological capability. These costs may be relatively high, particularly insofar as experience is a necessary element in acquiring capability. Moreover, the costs can be highly uncertain owing to the initial absence of information and knowledge. But there are important benefits. The more immediate benefits are increases in the productivity with which an economy's resources are employed. The other benefits derive from the newly acquired technological capabilities which can be deployed in further industrialization. The cumulative character of technological development implies that these benefits can be substantial. However, they are not realized automatically. In addition, the investing firm's ability to capture them is highly uncertain. Investments in human capital associated with acquiring technological capability may not be appropriable. And future benefits from being able to deploy technological capabilities in subsequent technological efforts can at best be foreseen only imperfectly. This is in part because their realization may require interactions among agents involved in interconnected activities.

What does this perspective suggest about the efficacy of selective intervention to promote internationally competitive production? Conventional economic theory has not neglected the possible significance of the learning that accompanies industrialization. The issue is discussed under the heading of 'dynamic' economies, which are economies of time that involve various forms of learning associated with experience (these economies are to be contrasted with 'static' economies of scale). Contemporary neoclassical discussions [e.g., Corden (1974, ch. 9)] in fact argue that 'dynamic' economies provide the strongest, if not the only valid, reason for promoting industrialization. But these discussions nonetheless argue against selective intervention, because dynamic economies are not seen to imply market failures that could best be overcome by using it to foster international competitiveness. We think that the evidence shows otherwise – that the magnitude and nature of dynamic economies are far more significant than is recognized. To highlight the questionable assumptions that underlie the neoclassical discussions, we will state our argument in the terms they use to assess the possibility of market failure.

The effects of dynamic economies are conventionally discussed under three categories: internal economies, pecuniary externalities, and non-pecuniary externalities.[22] The benefits of experience that accrue to the firm undergoing the experience are 'internal economies'. The benefits that accrue to other agents are 'externalities'. Of the latter benefits, those that are transmitted through market transactions are 'pecuniary' externalities, while those that are not transmitted through market transactions are 'non-pecuniary' externalities. Externalities flow via market transactions in the form of lower prices and more appropriate characteristics for the objects of the transactions.

Corden's exposition of the economics of infant industries states the neoclassical argument very well. Monopoly (monopsony) power in trade gives rise to pecuniary externalities which are best offset by specific export (import) taxes. In the absence of such market power, the only potentially significant sources of market failure are internal economies and externalities associated with human capital formation. But there can be no market failure unless it is associated with imperfect knowledge or imperfection in the capital and labor markets. Hence the neoclassical policy prescription for 'small countries' that lack market power: the government's proper roles are to facilitate the flow of information, to promote improvements in the operation of capital markets, and to ensure adequate investment in human capital formation. Later in the discussion we will argue that the government's effectiveness in carrying out these roles is greatly enhanced by the practice of selective intervention to promote the achievement of international competitiveness. But we must first evaluate the neoclassical assertion that, for small

---

[22]Conventional parlance distinguishes between 'pecuniary' and 'technological' externalities [Scitovsky (1963)]. We use the adjective 'non-pecuniary' to avoid the confusion that might result from the fact that all of the externalities with which we are concerned have their source in the nature of technology. In turn, for convenience, we omit the adjective 'dynamic' and make explicit any reference to pecuniary externalities that derive from static economies of scale.

countries, there are no important externalities other than those associated with investments by firms in human capital formation (or 'labor training').

Why do the neoclassicals consider other possible externalities to be unimportant? A careful reading does not lead us to conclude that their arguments are based on directly relevant empirical evidence. Their arguments appear instead to be grounded in the implicit assumption of perfect tradability for industrial products and technologies.[23] This assumption combines three subsidiary assumptions: that the characteristics of products and technologies are unchanging, that their import and export prices are given irrespective of the quantities traded, and that the export price of each equals its import price. The first and third are the crucial assumptions. They imply that the relative shadow prices of all tradables are fixed and invariant. Thus externalities cannot be transmitted through market transactions involving tradables. Of course, government interference in trade can lead to pecuniary externalities even if there is perfect tradability. But externalities which are the sole result of such interference have nothing to do with market failure. Thus what we are concerned with in the following discussion is the prevalence of imperfect tradability that results in externalities associated with transactions involving tradables. We will consider the tradability of technologies and of products in turn.

The notion that technologies are perfectly tradable is derived from general equilibrium theory and its assumption that technology is known, which implies that technological knowledge is freely available and costlessly assimilated. The first implication is only partially true. But the second implication is false. This ought to be obvious: knowledge in a communicable form is quite distinct from the capability to make effective use of that knowledge. As we indicated in summarizing the recent empirical research on industrial development and technological change, the assimilation of knowledge to enable its effective use – the acquisition of technological capability – requires investment that is characterized by indivisibilities quite separate from the sources of static economies of scale. Moreover, not all knowledge can be put in communicable form – at least not cost effectively. The tacitness of important elements of technology is in fact the principal reason for dynamic economies in learning to use a 'known' (somewhere else in the world) technology. In essence, experience plays a necessary part in learning to make effective use of technology – that is, in gaining technological capability. Dynamic economies may also result from the fact that the use of known elements of technology can produce new elements of technology

---

[23]This assumption is not made by careful neoclassicals who, like Corden, deal with the problems potentially raised by the fact that tradeables may be non-traded. But the arguments with which they dismiss these problems assume the prevalence of something very close to perfect tradability. Convenience of exposition is what leads us to state the assumption in an extreme form.

which are reflected in greater productivity and more appropriate product characteristics.

There is, of course, abundant trade in the elements of technology. International transactions involving these elements include foreign direct investment, turnkey plant contracts, licensing agreements, technical assistance contracts, and so on. But the elements of technology are not perfectly tradable. The tacitness of technology leads to problems in its communication over long distances and across social differences, problems which can be overcome – if at all – only at some cost. Thus the price that is paid for importing a given element from a particular location exceeds the price that would be received for exporting to the same location. Moreover, knowledge that exists (somewhere in the world) does not exist everywhere simultaneously because there are costs in advertising its mere existence or in discovering its existence through search. Only knowledge that is 'close by' is known to exist.

In addition, the tacitness of knowledge makes some of the elements of technology inherently non-tradable. Here it is not technical knowledge per se that is involved but rather knowledge of local circumstances – of peculiarities in local resources and in institutional as well as other aspects of local technological practices – that must in some way be experienced to be fully understood.[24] In turn, the combination of technical knowledge with knowledge of local circumstances can lead to innovations that would, in all likelihood, not have been forthcoming otherwise. The resultant new (differentiated, adapted, or otherwise) products or processes are non-tradable in the sense that they could not have been created without their development in the local circumstances. They are non-tradable ex ante but tradable ex post.

The foregoing discussion leads to the conclusion that dynamic economies are associated with technological elements that are either imperfectly tradable or non-tradable. The fact that technological elements are not perfectly tradable means that investments to acquire and assimilate them can generate surpluses for those undertaking the investments or for other beneficiaries. The surplus that accrues to the investor is an internal economy; it is producer's surplus. The surplus that accrues to other beneficiaries is due to externalities; we will refer to this surplus as 'users'' surplus. Of course, these surpluses are significant only to the extent that they reflect some real advantage vis-à-vis imports.[25] The two possible forms of advantage are a lower cost and a more appropriate set of characteristics.

Users' surpluses may accrue in many different ways. The recent empirical

---

[24]The literature on technology transfer contains many anecdotes that attest to the high costs of failing to adapt technology to local circumstances and to the benefits of adaptation.

[25]The expected generation of such surpluses is central to the argument for establishing infant industries that lack international competitiveness at the outset. Here we cannot but agree with Corden's (1974, p. 265 ff.) emphasis on this point in his discussion of the Mill–Bastable test.

research documents the ways but does not provide estimates of the surpluses. We will simply catalogue the modes here; we provide a more detailed discussion of several of them in the next section.

Non-pecuniary externalities associated with diffusion in the absence of market transactions are particularly hard to assess but nonetheless appear to be extremely important. These typically intra-industry externalities are due to the fact that one agent's investments to obtain information can very significantly reduce transactions costs for access by other nearby agents to the same and closely related information. If nothing else, there is an important demonstration effect from observing the use of the information. But there are other, more direct channels of diffusion, of which labor mobility is perhaps the most significant. Non-pecuniary externalities reflect the provision of a free good. Because of this, and because of the indivisibility that characterizes the investments that underlie them, these externalities are a source of market failure even in the presence of perfect capital markets.

Pecuniary externalities flow through market transactions and reflect the seller's possession of some real advantage vis-à-vis imports, part of which accrues to the buyer through a lower price or a more appropriate set of characteristics. Various forms of transactions involving the transfer of technology between local agents can give rise to pecuniary externalities. Many of the manufacturing firms studied in the recent research have sold elements of their technology or technological services to other firms in the same industry as well as in other industries. And a few of the larger firms have at some time spun off specialized technological agents, such as engineering consultants, which have in nearly all cases diversified their activities across industries. Explicit sales of technology can thus be conduits for inter-industry externalities as well as intra-industry externalities.

Another significant channel for inter-industry externalities is the exchange of technological elements in transactions involving intermediate products and capital goods. Indeed many such exchanges leading to better utilization of local resources and to improvements in the design of capital goods have been observed. A salient aspect of these exchanges is the dependence of their outcome on extensive interaction between suppliers and users in iteratively changing both process and product characteristics.[26] Here, as in other cases where cooperative technological effort is required, the return to one agent is very much affected by the capability and effort of others.

Consumers of final products can also benefit from pecuniary externalities associated with technological efforts that lead to more appropriate characteristics for final products. Here, too, the success of the outcome depends upon

---

[26]The tacitness of technology from the users' perspective means that there is uncertainty about the net benefit that can be realized by given changes in characteristics – uncertainty that can only be resolved by testing alternative designs in practice. See Teubal (1979).

the producer's being willing and able to obtain information about users' tradeoffs between price and characteristics.

Lastly, it must be recognized that users – whether other producers or consumers – can benefit from pecuniary externalities in the form of domestic prices lower than import prices. That is, products are also imperfectly tradable in that their import and export prices are not the same. Transport costs and other forms of transaction costs obviously do exist. Moreover, exports of many, if not most, industrial products involve startup costs characterized by indivisibility. The infrastructural facilities and institutions needed to support export trade are sometimes quite distinct from those utilized in import trade, and the market information relevant to exporting is not identical to that most useful when importing. Thus the export price at most establishes a lower bound on the shadow price of a tradable product. The import price sets the upper bound.

We have argued above that pecuniary externalities related to investments in technology – in acquiring technological capability and in undertaking technological effort – are ubiquitous in industrialization. We will now consider their significance. Many of them have their source in non-pecuniary externalities associated with diffusion and reflect the erosion of the initial producer's surplus through the entry of competing producers. The pecuniary externality is the most obvious manifestation of the initial producer's inability to appropriate all of the surplus arising from its innovation. Not only does the innovator provide a free good in terms of information, the innovator also suffers negative consequences as imitators emerge. As is well known, inappropriability of the returns from investments characterized by indivisibility leads to market failure regardless of whether capital markets are perfect. The failure causes underinvestment in technology as well as in its use.

Additional issues arise when the total surplus that can be generated by one agent's actions depends directly upon other agents' actions; in other words, when pecuniary externalities are reciprocal. These issues are very pertinent since many reciprocal pecuniary externalities exist owing to the multiple interconnections among industrial activities. Thus we will discuss the issues involved at some length.

Scitovsky (1963) gives the classic exposition showing that reciprocal pecuniary externalities in the presence of increasing returns lead to market failure. The result follows because market information about the present does not adequately signal the interdependence that exists among investment decisions in such circumstances. Chenery (1959) provides an illustrative example in which static economies of scale are the source of increasing returns, but he excludes the possibility of exports. With no exceptions that we are aware of, subsequent contributions to the literature have also disregarded the increasing returns associated with investments in technology. In turn, on the grounds that exports are possible, most neoclassicals seem to believe that market failure either cannot exist or may exist only in isolated and rather inconsequential cases.[27] We will therefore illustrate Scitovsky's argument with a case in which exports are possible.

Consider two potential infant industries, A and B, and suppose that industry A produces an intermediate input required in industry B. Fig. 1 gives the relevant information. For expositional convenience and to save space, we use the same cost and demand schedules to depict what each industry's circumstances would be in the other's absence. The import and export prices for the industry's (either A's or B's) output are P_m and P_e, respectively; the solid curves are its average and marginal cost schedules – the former reflects the increasing returns associated with investment in technology; the solid line cde is the schedule showing the domestic demand for its output. (Neglect the dashed line hij as well as the dashed curves mon and poq for the time being.) Using conventional analysis, we see that, if either industry were to be established in the other's absence, it would produce X_1 units, of which D_1 would be sold domestically and the remainder exported. The average cost of production would be AC_1, but the price equal to marginal cost would be P_e. The total producers' and users' surplus that would result from the industry's establishment is obtained by subtracting the area of the trapezoid defg from that of the trapezoid abcd. This surplus being negative, neither industry would be established in the other's absence. Domestic demand would be satisfied by imports and the price paid would be P_m.

But what if both industries were to be established together? The domestic demand for the output of the supplying industry (A) would be greater because some of its output would be used in industry B. The dashed line hij gives the new demand schedule for industry A.[28] In turn, the cost of production in the using industry (B) would be lower because of the difference between import and export prices for the intermediate input produced by industry A; moreover, domestic production of intermediate input could also lead to a more appropriate set of characteristics.[29] The dashed curves mon and poq, respectively, give the new average and marginal cost curves for industry B. Again using conventional analysis, we see that, if both industries were to be established: industry A's average cost would be AC_1 and its production would be X_1 units, of which D_2 would be sold domestically; industry B's average cost would be AC_2 and its production would be X_2 units, of which D_1 would be sold domestically. (To avoid confusing clutter in

[27]Corden (1974, p. 272) clearly does not hold the first view, but he appears to hold the second.

[28]The two demand schedules, cde and hij, are not parallel owing to the assumed sensitivity of industry B's demand to price.

[29]For example, if industry A were iron ore extraction and industry B were steel refining, it could be the case that local ore has distinct characteristics which can be taken advantage of through technological effort to adapt process technology in one or both industries.

H. Pack and L.E. Westphal, *Industrial strategy and technological change*   113

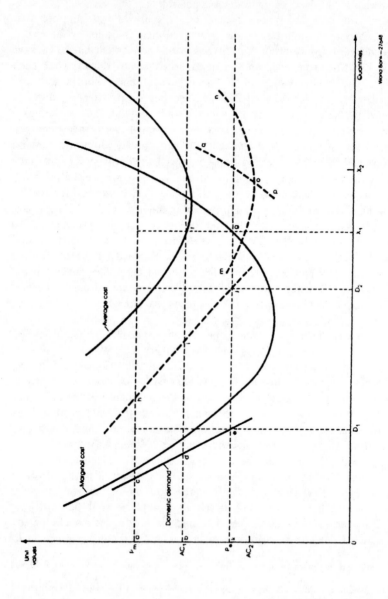

Fig. 1. Reciprocal pecuniary externalities illustrated.

the figure, we have not drawn in the vertical and horizontal lines that locate AC_2 and X_2 relative to the appropriate intersections involving the average and marginal cost curves.) The total surplus that would result from establishing both industries is equal to:

- the surplus accruing to other (i.e., not industry B or the users of its output) domestic users of industry A's output, the area of the trapezoid *akce*,
- *plus* the surplus accruing to domestic users of industry B's output, also the area of the trapezoid *akce*,
- *plus* the profits earned by industry B, the value $(P_e - AC_2)$ times X_2,
- *minus* the loss experienced by industry A, the value $(AC_1 - P_e)$ times X_1.

Though it may not be immediately obvious, this total surplus is positive.[30]

We therefore conclude that both industries should be established together. We also conclude that neither would be established without some form of explicit coordination between investment decisions – coordination to provide information that goes beyond the prices and quantities observable in the market.[31] The need for coordination stems from the fact that neither industry can realize its comparative advantage without the other. The using industry's (B's) long-run advantage in exports depends on the supplying industry's (A's) long-run advantage in production. But the realization of A's advantage requires adequate domestic demand. (Industry A has only a short-run advantage in exports: exports are warranted because they enable an efficient scale of operation, but they would disappear with the growth of demand. Industry B's advantage in exports is long-run in the sense that it can produce at an average cost less than export price.) In other words, the economy's comparative advantage in an upstream industry is inseparable from its comparative advantage in a downstream industry. Such inseparability may happen frequently as a result of transport and other transaction costs – and as a result of differences in characteristics among products and technologies.

To summarize: reciprocal pecuniary externalities can lead to market failure even if export prospects are positive.[32] Market failure causes investments to

---

[30]The value of $(P_e - AC_2)X_2$ is nearly half the value of $(AC_1 - P_e)X_1$. Thus subtracting the former from the latter gives a value somewhat less than the area of one trapezoid *akce*. Hence the total surplus is something more than the area of the other trapezoid *akce*.

[31]Note that industry A should not only produce X_1 units, it should also price them so as not to interfere with allocative efficiency. The latter requirement raises well-known issues, but they need not and will not be dealt with here.

[32]Some readers may think that our demonstration of this is contrived, because the reduction in industry B's average cost of production is pictured to be very large relative to its use of the intermediate input and to the difference between import and export prices for this input. This feature of our demonstration could be understood to reflect substantial differences in characteristics between the imported and the domestically produced input (see footnote 29 on page 112). But, more importantly, it is associated with our having not differentiated between the circumstances that would be faced by each industry in the other's absence. Such differentiation

be delayed or to be made at too small a scale.[33] Thus industrial growth is both slower and less efficient. The welfare loss is the additional cost of importing rather than producing *plus* the foregone gain from exporting. Contrary to the notion that export possibilities reduce the likelihood of market failure to nil, those possibilities increase the cost of market failure where it occurs. Why? Because profitable export opportunities are being neglected at the same time that efficient import substitution is being delayed. The likelihood (or frequency) of market failure, and its welfare cost when it occurs, depend on many things. One of them is the degree of increasing returns owing to investments in technology and to static economies of scale. But even with constant returns everywhere, the absence of perfect tradability still results in reciprocal pecuniary externalities that have the same consequences: delayed investments or investments at too small a scale [Chenery (1959)]. The consequences and attendant welfare costs are just much greater under increasing returns.

Our demonstration of the possibility of market failure due to reciprocal pecuniary externalities has focused on externalities transmitted though transactions involving products. It is important to recognize that market failure can also result from externalities transmitted through transactions involving technology. The reason is that investments in technology, even when related to production, create assets in the form of technology and technological capability, assets that are not perfectly tradable. In cataloguing the modes by which users' surpluses may accrue (see above), we indicated various ways that these assets yield returns. Here we present some additional reasons why the acquisition of technological capability, in particular, may be an important proximate objective of government intervention.

In an uncertain world of imperfect information, 'strategy' – defined as priorities determined by pitting 'initial conditions' against less perfectly understood 'future possibilities' – necessarily plays a critical part in allocating resources to technological change activities. In turn, much international trade in the elements of technology is not perfectly competitive. Many of the significant actors on the supply side do not simply seek out profitable opportunities wherever they may exist. Instead, they employ their own

---

leaves the analysis unchanged and avoids the contrivance, as the reader can easily demonstrate. [For example, note that the conclusion remains the same when, for industry B: P_m is reduced by some amount, such that P_m remains above AC_1; and P_e and AC_2 are each increased by this same amount (in the case of AC_2, by an upward shift in the dashed curves *mon* and *poq*) – everything else being taken as given in fig. 1.] In turn, by contemplating different relative values of P_m and P_e, the reader can also demonstrate that market failure can result when exports by either industry are possible but not profitable when both are established.

[33]With increasing returns, reciprocal pecuniary externalities could result in a vicious circle in which investment is not merely delayed but never takes place. But the vicious circle can be broken by the growth of the non-industrial sectors, leading to increased demands for industrial products. The statement in the text correspondingly assumes that the industrial sector is not the only possible engine of growth.

strategies that reflect their peculiar circumstances, both internal and external – strategies that constrain their search activities as well as other activities. Because knowledge about local circumstances is tacit, and because foreign agents may have their own distinct strategies, appropriate local strategies may not be identified or implemented by foreign agents. This gives a sound economic justification for favoring the development of technological capabilities by agents under local control; in other words, for controlling direct foreign investment and other means of technology transfer.

An additional justification is the asymmetry between buyer's and seller's knowledge about the value of the technology being traded [Arrow (1969)]. This asymmetry can easily result in non-competitive pricing in the sense that the price exceeds the marginal cost of providing the technology. But, the greater the local technological capability, the less the asymmetry and, when prices are established through bargaining, the lower the price. Local technological capabilities can thus have an important determining influence on the costs of technology transfers. Moreover, the benefits that can be realized are also influenced by local technological capabilities. There are strong complementarities among the elements of technology, even to the extent that some technological capability is needed to conduct efficient search for the elements of technology.

Up to this point in the discussion we have implicitly assumed that pecuniary externalities are separate from internal economies, as they indeed are conceptually. But in practice it is difficult – if not impossible – to forecast how dynamic economies will be divided between internal economies and pecuniary externalities. The reason is that individual market agents can integrate different industrial activities. Thus reciprocal pecuniary externalities among activities can become internal economies for individual agents. Correspondingly, the coordination needed to overcome market failure can – and often does – occur through organizational integration. But this obviously does not mean that such coordination must occur. Moreover, the substitution of 'internal markets' within individual agents for markets among agents can retard the achievement of dynamic efficiency. Far from internalizing dynamic economies, it can result in their being offset (eventually, if not immediately) by costly duplication of underused facilities, as frequently appears to be the case. Even if this result does not obtain, the potential gains from organizational integration must be weighed against the potential gains from specialization through subcontracting and other market arrangements.

More generally, the fact that different kinds of agents and markets exist somewhere does not imply that similar agents and markets will somehow appear locally. Local markets are likely to exist only to the degree that they are justified by the local division of labor, and vice versa. Whether markets exist is jointly determined with the organization of economic activity – that is, with the pattern of specialization and exchange among agents. That pattern results from balancing transaction costs against the gains from exploiting economies of scale and scope in production and in acquiring and using technological capability. The organization of production is by no means uniquely determined by what is being produced; it is determined more by the volumes of production. The organization of economic activity, the extent of markets (in the sense of what is traded among firms as opposed to within firms), and the structure of relative prices – all these are best seen as co-evolving through an historical process in which local circumstances are crucially important.[34]

4. Implications for tactics

The issues raised above have to do with whether generalized market forces will lead to the timely creation of the requisite agents and markets. Neoclassical theory does not squarely address this question; quite the contrary, it simply assumes that responsive agents exist. Only with this assumption does it demonstrate that selective intervention is other than first-best. And even with this assumption it cannot always demonstrate that trade restrictions are necessarily inferior to free trade, even in the absence of monopoly power in trade. Tariffs or quantitative controls are superior to free trade if the resulting immediate loss in users' surpluses is more than offset by restriction-induced future gains in users' surpluses. Thus, in the absence of perfect tradability, restrictions to promote the acquisition of technological capability can be superior to free trade, since the acquisition of technological capability can lead to lower prices and to differentiated products that would not otherwise exist [on the latter, see Snape (1977)].

Furthermore, contrary to neoclassical prescription, quantitative controls can be superior to tariffs if they are administered to balance costs and benefits to society effectively. For example, restrictions imposed through a 'law of similars' or through 'local-content' regulations may be particularly effective when the acquisition of technological capability and subsequent adaptive innovation require extensive interaction between users and suppliers. A central agent can adjudicate to maximize intertemporal welfare [see Teubal (1983)]: users for whom present costs are high (e.g., users involved in export production) or expected future benefits low can be exempted from the restrictions, and so on.

The combination of incentive policies having a strong industry-bias – together with credit rationing, import quotas, licensing controls, and other overt instruments of interference in resource allocation – may have important uses in achieving and implementing integrated decision-making, uses that have been completely overlooked by the neoclassicals. To achieve the results

[34]Stigler (1951) gives an early, classic exposition of this theme. A more recent and extensive exposition is given by Williamson (1975).

sought through selective intervention with the neoclassical first best instruments of coordination, subsidization, and capital market promotion would appear to require substantial implementation ability. That ability may exceed the administrative limits of even developed and astute bureaucracies. The instruments of selective intervention used by Korea and other East Asian countries, despite the potential disadvantages, may offer a more practicable and effective mode of intervention.[35]

Neoclassicals who recognize that products and technology are not perfectly tradable emphasize the need for facilitating the flow of information and for coordinating investment decisions. But they have not fully faced up to the question of whether information availability and investment coordination can be achieved without employing *all* the instruments of selective intervention. As should be clear, it seems to us that anyone who reflects seriously on this question will find that acquiring information and coordinating investments both require what is castigated by the neoclassicals as unwarranted selective intervention. How else to deal with the tacitness of knowledge and the indivisibilities encountered when investing in technology? How else to deal with the need to achieve meaningful exchanges of information about possibilities only imperfectly understood when trying to reach coordinated outcomes? And how else to deal with the consequent need to insure that coordinated outcomes are achieved?

Similar questions arise with regard to the neoclassical emphasis on capital market imperfections. Is it realistic to expect that capital market liberalization along the lines advocated by McKinnon and others will be sufficient to insure that capital market institutions have appropriate attitudes toward risk and the rate of discount, or that they have adequate incentives to undertake investments in obtaining the knowledge necessary for financing technological change activities?

Our answers to these and similar questions should be obvious by now. But the caveats may not be so obvious. We have already warned that selective intervention with the instruments used by Korea and other East Asian countries can 'work' only if a government is willing and able to intervene selectively in pursuit of dynamic efficiency. To this we would add several more caveats.

The first additional caveat is that selective intervention must indeed be selective. Here it is useful to distinguish between intensive and extensive technological changes.[36] 'Intensive' changes build incrementally on existing technological capabilities and take place through investments in technology

---

[35]'Effective' includes the gain from the saving of administrative resources as well as a gain from avoiding the welfare losses that accompany distortions caused by the other than lump-sum taxes that must in reality be imposed to finance subsidies. But it should be apparent that we intend the term to include far more than this insofar as we think the neoclassicals assume a world of platonic ideals.

[36]Caution: the distinction is necessarily fuzzy.

that are characterized by small indivisibilities. 'Extensive' changes result in distinctly new capabilities (for new or existing industries) and occur through investments in technology that are characterized by large indivisibilities. What is instructive about the selective intervention by Korea and the other East Asian countries is its concentration – at any one time – on a select few extensive changes. The deployment (or use) of existing capabilities has been left to market forces operating in response to largely neutral incentives. A tremendous variety of intensive changes have thereby been induced as responses to market signals.

The next caveat relates to another instructive aspect of the selective intervention practiced by these countries. Far from pursuing technological autarky, they have cleverly exploited the gains available from international trade in technology. Trade makes it both possible and efficient to acquire technological capabilities in a sequential process of cumulatively building on capabilities that have been previously obtained and deployed in industrial production. In developing their industries, these countries initially concentrated on gaining what was needed for efficient production in the simpler lines of activity. Only after mastering them did they proceed to acquire increasingly more sophisticated capabilities that were correspondingly more difficult to develop without previous learning related to experience. Though often so rapid as to appear simultaneous, the development of progressively more sophisticated capabilities has been sequential.[37] In their industrial strategies, these countries have clearly pursued the objective of rapid technological change. But as their experience shows, this objective is not attained simply by seeking technological self-sufficiency without regard to costs and benefits.

The final caveat concerns what is warranted when sociopolitical factors make the aggressive practice of selective intervention, such as that by Korea and the other East Asian countries, infeasible as a means of achieving dynamic efficiency. Market forces clearly do not always induce the seemingly intensive technological changes that are warranted. So, various policies can and should be recommended – even to countries that cannot muster the political consensus to implement a broad industrial strategy. Three examples of such policies will be presented here: stimulating the creation of appropriate technology, facilitating the transfer of technology, and improving the efficiency of existing industries. Each of them is best viewed as a technology 'tactic' that can improve the performance of the industrial sector. For many countries facing the immobility imposed by conflicting political interests, these technology tactics offer an alternative. Each of them is designed to redress one or more market failures noted in the preceding sanctions, but the benefits will be smaller than those possible from a comprehensive strategy.

[37]The sequential nature of Korea's acquisition of technological capability is discussed in Westphal, Kim and Dahlman (1985).

4.1. Appropriateness of internationally traded goods

As noted earlier, many consumer and producer goods available in international markets are not appropriate for less developed countries. Although imported consumer goods may be suitable for upper-income households, inexpensive products for the mass of low-income households are rarely traded, and the consumer surplus that could be realized from a more appropriate set of characteristics does not materialize [Stewart (1977, 1981)]. Machine designs, reflecting relative factor prices in the advanced countries, are excessively capital-intensive given relative factor prices in less developed countries. Adopting these machine designs results in lower income and employment than could be obtained from identical investment in more appropriate, labor-intensive equipment.[38] Domestic production of either type of good could eliminate the divergence between local requirements and extant foreign products and permit the realization of the relevant consumers' and users' surplus.[39]

If the situation is to be remedied by the domestic production of newly designed products or the modification of imported ones, the critical issue is whether the present discounted value of the benefits that would accrue from more suitable locally designed products exceeds the cost of the technological efforts needed to generate the designs. Any divergence between foreign and domestic production costs would also have to be considered. Notice that the unaided market cannot guide decisions because the social benefit includes the increased consumer surplus from more appropriate products – or it includes the additional national income resulting from more appropriate machinery designs – which is not reflected, assuming competitive markets, in additional profits to local innovators.

Two factors militate against the purely private provision of socially desirable levels of local adaptive effort. First, the benefits of relevant local designs might not be appropriable if the modifications are relatively simple and easily copied [Magee (1981)]. Second, at any time, the cost to a firm of undertaking technological efforts will reflect its previous efforts – the efficiency of technological effort increases with past experience. But each decision regarding technological effort may be myopic in the intertemporal context. When the dynamic benefit of learning is ignored, it always appears

---

[38]See Pack (1982) for estimates of the aggregate potential benefits from the adoption of appropriate equipment. Saxonhouse (1974) gives an account of the success of Japanese manufacturers in obtaining more labor-intensive equipment than was currently available. For evidence on current levels of induced innovation, see Pack (1981). The critical role of induced innovation in less developed countries was first emphasized by Fei and Ranis (1965).

[39]The argument here could also be phrased in terms of the identification and import of appropriate products, including producers' goods. The argument for intervention would shift to the indivisibilities in information acquisition costs and the ensuing high average but low marginal costs of information diffusion; the benefits of intervention would be smaller.

cheaper to license currently available foreign designs than to undertake one's own efforts. Local technological effort may thus be privately suboptimal and warrant subsidization because of the problems of appropriability and myopic behavior.

4.2. Transfer of technology

The international transfer of technology includes the introduction of new product lines and new proprietary methods (whether embodied in equipment or not) for producing existing products as well as the diffusion of non-proprietary know-how.[40] There is now a significant empirical literature that implies the absence of sufficient knowledge to ensure a competitive outcome in transactions related to technology purchases. Thus, some form of intervention can improve national welfare, if its administrative costs – valued at shadow prices – are less than the reduction in monopoly rents currently accruing to foreigners.

One example of the imperfection of technology markets occurs in licensing agreements, primarily with firms from developed countries, that now constitute an important source of technical information for many industrial firms in less developed countries. It can be argued that proprietary information should not loom large in the labor-intensive production in which most LDCs now have a comparative advantage. But many of the middle-income countries do compete in international markets where such knowledge is relevant. For standard products, purchasing a license and technical help from the owner of proprietary knowledge is likely to be the least cost short-run decision, certainly less expensive than attempting to replicate the technology domestically without infringing on proprietary elements.

Although licensing may be the cheaper route, developing countries often pay more than the marginal cost of the dissemination of information [Contractor (1980), Cortes and Bocock (1984)]. The fees determined in bilateral monopoly bargaining thus make a contribution to the full cost of product development in the developed countries. These 'excessive' fees are not unjust, but they reflect the fundamental imperfection of markets for technical knowledge: purchasers cannot know the true value of the information until they possess it [Arrow (1969)].[41] That is why the bargaining process is likely to favor the seller. The acquisition of domestic technological capabilities may result in improved terms for the purchasers – by increasing local capability to evaluate the commercial value of the proposed license and by providing knowledge of a greater range of suppliers.

---

[40]We ignore here the earlier point that effective technology transfer is not accomplished by passively receiving technology from abroad, but itself requires investments in understanding the principles and use of technology.

[41]Related questions are discussed by Teece (1981).

Still other problems arise in licensing. For example, restrictions accompany many licenses – sales to third markets are prohibited, and product and process improvements must revert to the licensor without payment, which reduces the incentive to engage in research and development. These restrictions permit lower licensing fees, since the licensor obtains obvious benefits, but they also limit the potential gains to the recipient, who has less freedom to alter its international trade orientation toward exporting. The aggregation of (privately warranted) restrictions accepted by individual firms may forestall a socially desirable change in policy toward exporting. This constitutes a market imperfection analogous to the one that underlies optimum tariff arguments, the difference being that national benefits are obtainable not from trade restriction but from trade encouragement achieved by the government's limitation on the freedom of firms to accept export restrictions. Because reduced restrictions may lead to higher fees for licenses, the potential gains must be compared with the additional costs.

Governments appear to have the ability to achieve favorable changes in the terms of licensing agreements and to discourage competitive concessions by individual firms – ability which reflects their capacity to limit the access of licensors to the entire domestic market.[42] The careful screening of licensing agreements by Japan and Korea seems to have a basis in the concern about exports. This concern contrasts sharply with that of other countries, such as the members of the Andean Pact, which are often far more concerned with the level of royalty payments (perceived as unfair monopoly rents) than with the limits placed on strategic options [see Chudnovsky (1981), Mytelka (1978)]. This is not surprising given the inward orientation of these countries.

4.3. Rationalization of production

The imperfect mastery of already transferred technology is another important problem in industrial development that may require some form of intervention. Recent research on productivity in developing countries highlights the problem. This research also shows that there are opportunities for significant gains in real income through greater horizontal and vertical integration. These studies use detailed microeconomic evidence and find that there is considerable intra-industry dispersion of total factor productivity (TFP), with the best firms in an industry often falling considerably short of international best-practice TFP.[43] A major source of domestic intra-industry

---

[42] A conflict may exist between obtaining a reduced price and encouraging local technological effort, as lower fees may reinforce the myopic behavior of firms with respect to innovations on standard products. There is no inexorable link, however, between the foreign exchange saved by improved negotiation and the lower effective price of foreign technology to domestic firms – a tax on royalty payments being one method of introducing a wedge.

[43] See the evidence presented by Page (1980), Kilby (1962), Hadoussa, Nishimizu and Page (1982), Nishimizu and Page (1982), and Pack (1984).

variation is the incomplete domestic diffusion of critical knowledge about production engineering. In turn, deviations from international best-practice are largely caused by inadequate product specialization among local firms producing similar products. Moreover, subcontracting is unusual even in industries where it is a dominant feature in developed countries, such as mechanical engineering [Pack (1981)].

These findings have several implications. First and very important, a narrowing of the internal dispersion of productivity, together with a movement of all firms toward the international frontier, offers a potential source of major improvement in industrial performance. Productivity can be substantially enhanced without incorporating newer technology simply by using available resources more effectively. Estimates of the potential benefits from greater technical efficiency range from 30 to 50 percent of existing production.

Second, domestic and international dispersions in productivity (apart from those attributable to different degrees of specialization) confirm that the neoclassical assumption of a freely and easily known production function is not a particularly apt description for developing countries. The dispersions of productivity are not due to vintage effects and are best viewed as implying one of two things: that there are substantial information and absorption costs for the acquisition of even non-proprietary technology, or that the assumption of cost-minimizing behavior is of limited relevance. There is an argument for government intervention when individual firms have difficulty appropriating all the benefits of investments in information gathering. Moreover, to the extent that information search has substantial fixed costs, a centralized industrywide effort has obvious advantages.[44] Where the industry consists of more than a few firms, the potential free-rider problem suggests that some government compulsion may be desirable.

Third, the inability to realize economies of vertical integration is a considerable obstacle to efficient industrialization. Pecuniary economies are foregone not because of insufficient market size but because of the failure of interfirm markets to develop. The absence of subcontracting and the consequent internalization of many production activities (such as forges in machinery-producing firms) represents a particularly debilitating form of inefficiency: each firm operates a number of facilities well below full utilization. The absence of subcontracting can thus negate potential comparative advantages from relative factor endowments and technological capability.

Fourth, government intervention can achieve a more rational division of products among firms in countries where individual firms manufacture an

---

[44]A description of the centralized information diffusion system in the early stages of Japanese industrialization and of its benefits in terms of the resultant small variations in interfirm productivity performance is given by Saxonhouse (1976).

entire range of products and thus forgo the benefits of specialization.[45] It might be argued that such intervention is necessary only where firms now receive protection – otherwise international competition will enforce the efficient pattern of specialization. But considerable evidence from the industrial countries suggests that this is not the case. In both the EEC and Japan, rationalization cartels have been sanctioned by governments to obtain greater specialization. The need for public intervention rests on the public good aspect of rationalization and on the risks that financial institutions face in lending when major structural changes are under way in an industry. Once the rationalization has been achieved, monopolistic positions in any product can be precluded by relying on international competition.

In all three areas just discussed – appropriate technology, technology transfer, and production rationalization – the governments of advanced industrial countries and of the successful NICs often selectively intervene in the market. Moreover, selective intervention in these and other technological dimensions characterizes much of the industrial history of the advanced countries. While it is possible to assert that economic performance would have been still better without such intervention, the nature of the market failures addressed suggests that ignoring them would have led to worse performance. After the considerable ingenuity economists have devoted to demonstrate the myriad failures of the invisible hand, it would be surprising if the partial redress of these failures did not improve performance, though issues of the second-best need to be kept in mind.

As emphasized earlier, however, the successful use of aggressive selective intervention requires the technical and administrative skill to implement desired strategies intelligently and the political ability to terminate intervention if there is no movement toward the desired goals.[46] Although the tactics discussed above demand fewer political and technical skills, their applicability in the least developed countries is open to serious question. In such countries, reliance on the standard neoclassical prescription probably constitutes the best policy across-the-board, even though it will probably result in far less spectacular growth than in the East Asian countries that adhered to this prescription only for well-established industries.

5. Conclusion

The understanding of industrial strategy that we have sought to convey in this paper is not entirely new. It embraces important elements of the principal contributions made in the early days by the strategists. Scitovsky (1963, pp. 305–306) put the central aspect very well: 'Market prices ... reflect

[45]See Pack (1986) for a detailed presentation.
[46]On some of the political issues, see Ruggie (1983, esp. ch. 1).

the economic situation as it is and not as it will be. For this reason, they are more useful for coordinating current production decisions ... than they are for coordinating investment decisions, which ... should be governed ... by what the future economic situation is expected to be. ... In underdeveloped countries ..., investment is likely to have a greater impact on prices, give rise to greater pecuniary external economies, and thus cause a greater divergence between private profit and social benefit.'

What needs to be added to this perspective, if only to make it explicit, is an emphasis on technological change. If we read the experience of Korea and other hyper-successful East Asian countries correctly, the crucial duality is not between production and investment decisions. It is 'more nearly' between investments in established industries where there is a static comparative advantage and investments in infant industries where there is the potential for dynamically achieving a comparative advantage. We write 'more nearly' for three reasons. Overt government promotion has not played a role in the development of some successful infant industries. Not all overtly promoted infant industries have been successful, at least not in the time frame explicit in the planning documents. And selective intervention has also been practiced to rationalize existing industries whose continued success was considered to require major restructuring.

The experience of the hyper-successful East Asian countries can also be read as testimony for the efficacy of pursuing an export-led strategy and of maintaining a factor-price regime that roughly conforms to relative factor endowments over time. There can be little question about the importance of maintaining an appropriate factor-price regime. In turn, many of the advantages of an export-led strategy are well known. But the implications of an aggressive export orientation for technological change are not well understood. Thus it is not known whether integrated decision-making centered on efficient import substitution – or, more generally, production for domestic sale – could be equally efficacious. Given the resurgence of 'export-pessimism' in the face of rising protectionism in the industrial countries, this is far from an idle question. What, then, about other possible elements of industrial strategy, such as a basic-needs focus? Where do they fit in? They are best seen as giving priorities for where to start searching for technological changes to be promoted, not as giving ultimate decision criteria meant to supplant the objective of dynamically efficient industrialization. But it has yet to be demonstrated that the incorporation of such elements into integrated decision-making can produce the expected results.

We have argued that industrial strategy is a matter of managing technological change to achieve dynamically efficient industrialization. Our argument and the policy prescriptions to which it leads are premised on several hypotheses for which there is some evidence but no conclusive proof. There are three central hypotheses: first, industrial products and the elements of technology are only imperfectly tradable, with some being inherently non-tradable. Second, the acquisition of technological capability happens neither automatically nor costlessly. Third, the organization of economic activity, the extent of markets, and the structure of relative prices for industrial products and the elements of technology evolve together, undergoing major changes as industrialization proceeds. If these hypotheses are not true, there can be only minor gains, if any, from selective intervention.

Unfortunately, the widespread acceptance of the neoclassical paradigm and the neglect of the technological change inherent in industrialization have led empirical research away from investigating the validity of these hypotheses – hypotheses that have nonetheless been around in different forms ever since the beginning of 'modern' development economics. This paper will have achieved its aim if it persuades at least some readers that there is ample reason to change the direction of much research on industrial development, away from compiling yet more evidence of the by now well understood aspects of policy failure and toward investigating the central empirical underpinnings of a theory of industrial strategy.

References

Arrow, Kenneth, 1969, Classificatory notes on the production and transmission of technological knowledge, American Economic Review 59, 29–35.
Balassa, Bela, 1975, Reforming the system of incentives in developing countries, World Development 3, 365–382.
Chenery, Hollis B., 1959, The interdependence of investment decisions, in: Moses Abramowitz et al., The allocation of economic resources (Stanford University Press, Stanford, CA) 82–120.
Chudnovsky, Daniel, 1981, Regulating technology exports in some developing countries, Trade and Development 1, 133–150.
Cole, David C. and Princeton N. Lyman, 1971, Korean development: The interplay of politics and economics (Harvard University Press, Cambridge, MA).
Cole, David C. and Yung Chul Park, 1983, Financial development in Korea: 1945–1978 (Harvard University Press, Cambridge, MA).
Contractor, Farok J., 1980, The profitability of technology licensing by U.S. multinationals, Journal of International Business Studies 11, 380–414.
Corden, W.M., 1974, Trade policy and economic welfare (Clarendon Press, Oxford).
Cortes, Mariluz and Peter Bocock, 1984, North–South technology transfer (The Johns Hopkins University Press, for the World Bank, Baltimore, MD).
Enos, John, 1984, Government intervention in the transfer of technology: The case of South Korea, IDS Bulletin 15, 26–31.
Fei, John C.H. and Gustav Ranis, 1965, Innovational intensity and factor bias in the theory of growth, International Economic Review 6, 182–198.
Fransman, Martin and Kenneth King, eds., 1984, Technological capability in the Third World (Macmillan, London).
Hadoussa, Hebra, Mieko Nishimizu and John Page, 1982, Productivity change in Egyptian industry after the opening, 1973–1979 (The World Bank, Washington, DC).
Johnson, Chalmers, 1982, Miti and the Japanese miracle: The growth of industrial policy, 1925–1975 (Stanford University Press, Stanford, CA).
Jones, Leroy P., 1975, Public enterprise and economic development: The Korean case (Korea Development Institute, Seoul).

Jones, Leroy P., 1980, Jae-bul and the concentration of economic power in Korean development: Issues, evidence, and alternatives, Consultant Paper Series no. 12 (Korea Development Institute, Seoul).

Jones, Leroy P. and Il Sakong, 1980, Government, business, and entrepreneurship in economic development: The Korean case (Harvard University Press, Cambridge, MA).

Kilby, Peter, 1962, Organization and productivity in backward economies, Quarterly Journal of Economics 76, 303–310.

Landes, David S., 1969, The unbound Prometheus (Cambridge University Press, Cambridge).

Luedde-Neurath, Richard, 1984, State intervention and foreign direct investment in South Korea, IDS Bulletin 15, 18–25.

Magee, Stephen P., 1981, The appropriability theory of the multinational corporation, The Annals of the American Academy of Political and Social Science 458, 123–135.

Mason, Edward, 1984, The Chenery analysis and some other considerations, in: Moshe Syrquin, Lance Taylor and Larry E. Westphal, eds., Economic structure and performance (Academic Press, New York) 3–21.

Mason, Edward et al., 1980, The economic and social modernization of the Republic of Korea (Harvard University Press, Cambridge, MA).

Michell, Tony, 1984, Administrative traditions and economic decision-making in South Korea, IDS Bulletin 15, 32–37.

Mytelka, Lynn, 1978, Licensing and technology dependence in the Andean group, World Development 6, 447–460.

Nam, Chong Hyun, 1981, Trade and industrial policies, and the structure of protection in Korea, in: Wontack Hong and Lawrence B. Krause, eds., Trade and growth of the advanced developing countries in the Pacific basin (Korea Development Institute Press, Seoul) 187–211.

Nelson, Richard R., 1979, Innovation and economic development: Theoretical retrospect and prospect, Working paper no. 31 (IDB/ECLA/UNDP/IDRC Research Program on Scientific and Technological Development in Latin America, Economic Commission for Latin America, Buenos Aires).

Nishimizu, Mieko and John M. Page, Jr., 1982, Total factor productivity growth, technological progress and technical efficiency change: Dimensions of productivity change in Yugoslavia, 1965–1978, Economic Journal 92, 920–936.

Pack, Howard, 1981, Fostering the capital goods sector in LDCs, World Development 9, 227–250.

Pack, Howard, 1982, Aggregate implications of factor substitution in industrial processes, Journal of Development Economics 11, 1–38.

Pack, Howard, 1984, Productivity and technical choice: Applications to the textile industry, Journal of Development Economics 16, 153–176.

Pack, Howard, 1986, Productivity, technical choice and project design (Oxford University Press, London) forthcoming.

Page, John M., Jr., 1980, Technical efficiency and economic performance: Some evidence from Ghana, Oxford Economic Papers 32, 319–339.

Rhee, Yung Whee, Bruce Ross-Larson and Garry Pursell, 1984, Korea's competitive edge: Managing the entry into world markets (The Johns Hopkins University Press, for the World Bank, Baltimore, MD).

Rosenberg, Nathan, 1976, Perspectives on technology (Cambridge University Press, Cambridge).

Ruggie, John G., ed., 1983, The antimonies of interdependence: National welfare and the international division of labor (Columbia University Press, New York).

Saxonhouse, Gary, 1974, A tale of Japanese technological diffusion in the Meiji period, Journal of Economic History 34, 149–165.

Saxonhouse, Gary, 1976, Country girls and communications among competitors in the Japanese cotton spinning industry, in: Hugh Patrick, ed., Japanese industrialization and its social consequences (University of California Press, Berkeley, CA) 97–125.

Scitovsky, Tibor, 1963, Two concepts of external economies, in: A.N. Agarwala and S.P. Singh, eds., The economics of underdevelopment (Oxford University Press, New York) 295–308.

Snape, Richard N., 1977, Trade policy in the presence of economies of scale and product variety, The Economic Record 53, 525–533.

Stewart, Frances, 1977, Technology and underdevelopment (Westview Press, Boulder, CO).

Stewart, Frances, 1981, Arguments for the generation of technology by less-developed countries, The Annals of the American Academy of Political and Social Science 458, 97–109.

Stewart, Frances and Jeffrey James, eds., 1982, The economics of new technology in developing countries (Pinter, London).

Stigler, George J., 1951, The division of labor is limited by the extent of the market, Journal of Political Economy 59, 185–193.

Teece, David J., 1981, The market for knowhow and the efficient international transfer of technology, The Annals of the American Academy of Political and Social Science 458, 81–96.

Teubal, Morris, 1979, Need determination, product type and the inducements to innovate, Discussion paper no. 791 (Falk Institute, Jerusalem).

Teubal, Morris, 1983, Market assurance policies for infant industry development: Selected issues suggested from the literature, Unpublished manuscript (Falk Institute, Jerusalem).

Wade, Robert, 1985, State intervention in 'outward-looking' development: Neoclassical theory and Taiwanese practice, in: G. White and R. Wade, eds., Developmental states in East Asia (Institute of Development Studies, Brighton) forthcoming.

Westphal, Larry E., 1978, The Republic of Korea's experience with export-led industrial development, World Development 6, 347–382.

Westphal, Larry E., 1982, Fostering technological mastery by means of selective infant-industry protection, in: Moshe Syrquin and Simon Teitel, eds., Trade, stability, technology, and equity in Latin America (Academic Press, New York) 255–279.

Westphal, Larry E. and Kwang Suk Kim, 1982, Korea, in: Bela Balassa et al., Development strategies in semi-industrial countries (Johns Hopkins University Press, for the World Bank, Baltimore, MD) 233–280.

Westphal, Larry E., Linsu Kim and Carl Dahlman, 1985, Reflections on Korea's acquisition of technological capability, in: Nathan Rosenberg and Claudio Frischtak, eds., International technology transfer: Concepts, measures, and comparisons (Praeger, New York) 167–221.

Westphal, Larry E., Yung W. Rhee and Garry Pursell, 1981, Korean industrial competence: Where it came from, World Bank Staff Working Paper no. 469 (Washington, DC).

Williamson, Oliver E., 1975, Markets and hierarchies: Analysis and antitrust implications (The Free Press, New York).

[16]

An Empirical Test of the Infant Industry Argument

By ANNE O. KRUEGER AND BARAN TUNCER*

Since World War II, many developing countries have provided high levels of protection for newly established industries. These policies have generally been followed on the grounds that new industries are "infants," and that dynamic factors will come into play to insure later economic efficiency.[1]

At a theoretical level, the infant industry exception to the proposition that free trade is optimal has always been noted.[2] Skeptics have centered their misgivings on two grounds: 1) they have questioned whether protection through the trade regime would achieve the goals of infant industry protection;[3] and 2) they have pinpointed the combination of "dynamic factors" and "externalities" that would have to arise to justify infant industry intervention and questioned the empirical likelihood of such circumstances.

*University of Minnesota and the World Bank, respectively. We wish to thank the National Science Foundation for research support, grant no SOC77-25776 We are also grateful to the Turkish Industrial Development Bank for its assistance in the project We have benefited greatly from the comments and suggestions of W M Corden and James M Henderson Ebbe Yndgaard, Claus Vastrup, Martin Paldam, and other members of the faculty at Aarhus University provided helpful comments and suggestions at an early stage of the research, as did colleagues at Bogazici University, including especially Maxwell Fry. Members of the Trade and Development Workshops at the University of Chicago made many useful comments on an earlier draft of this paper Zafar Ahmed, Roger Johnson, Inci Mubarek, Lale Tezel, and Paitoon Wiboonchutikula provided research assistance at various stages of the project

[1] The "infant industry argument" is also the basis on which developing countries are excepted from some provisions of the GATT

[2] See Paul Samuelson, (1958, ch 8), for a discussion of the history of thought with regard to the optimality of free trade. The optimum tariff argument is irrelevant to the concerns of this paper and therefore not considered here.

[3] See Robert Baldwin (1969) for an excellent statement of the reasons why, even in the presence of infant industry considerations, tariff protection might fail to correct the assumed market imperfection.

Interestingly, the debate has been entirely theoretical. There has been virtually no systematic examination of the empirical relevance of the infant industry argument. This is remarkable in light of the importance of the question, and the fact that thirty years' evidence or more has accumulated in a number of countries. Even if there are conditions under which dynamic factors and externalities in an infant industry might warrant intervention, that does not prove that those conditions are in fact met. In the last analysis, defense of infant industry protection must rest on empirical grounds: do the long-run benefits justify the short-run costs of starting up an initially high-cost infant?

It is the purpose of this paper to develop a test of whether infant industry criteria are satisfied, and then to apply the test to one developing country, Turkey. Section I sets forth the infant industry argument and necessary conditions for there to be a valid case for intervention. Section II then examines the various ways in which the necessary dynamic externalities might manifest themselves. This immediately suggests a simple empirical test. Section III then presents results of the test for Turkey. A final section contains some concluding observations and suggestions for further work. The data and details of procedures for estimation are given in the Appendix.

I. The Infant Industry Argument

It is simplest to state the infant industry case in naive form, and then to consider the conditions under which it would be valid. The basic argument, crudely put, is that:

A. Some newly established activities are initially high cost relative to established foreign enterprises and it requires time for them to become competitive.

B. It does not pay any individual entrepreneur to enter an infant industry at free trade prices; but

C. The industry, if developed, would be economic enough to permit a reasonable rate of return on the initial losses; and therefore

D. The industry requires a *temporary* period of protection or assistance during which its costs will fall enough to permit it to survive international competition without assistance.

The first proposition is essentially that costs of a new activity may initially be high. Reasons put forth as to why they might be high include learning by doing and the possibility that there are "linkages" between industries set forth by Albert Hirschman (1958). If the latter, then in the early stages of development, the absence of complementary activities or small size of the industrial sector of an economy might constitute a reason why all industrial activities would initially be high cost.

The reasons why there might be learning by doing are numerous. Workers might require a period of training. There might be an initial shake-down period as the activity became operational. Management itself might gain in experience. These possibilities have been neatly encapsulated by Kenneth Arrow (1962) in the notion that output per unit of input might increase as cumulative output within a given line of activity (the plant? the firm? the industry? the entire industrial sector?) increased.[4] Regardless of which reason is put forth, an essential feature of the infant industry notion is that a new activity will initially be high cost, but that unit costs will decline over time.

The second proposition is that, while costs will decline, they will do so in a way that individuals initially starting the activity will not reap the full rewards. Otherwise, there would be no case for protection: if start-up costs are high but the activity is economic, it would pay an individual entrepreneur to incur those costs in order to reap later benefits. For there to be a case for intervention, there must be positive externalities from the development of an infant activity which accrue to individuals other than those undertaking

the activity initially. Thus, the presence of externalities is necessary in order to show that private activity will not generate the optimal development of infant industries in a market-oriented economy. Whether the externalities are at the individual industry level, or rather at the level of the entire industrial sector is an open question, discussed further in Section II. Clearly, whatever infant industry assistance is provided should be provided to the industry, group of industries, or sector generating the externalities at a relatively uniform rate. Different levels of protection to different activities would be warranted only if the sector containing the more-protected activity were expected to experience greater cost reductions than the less-protected sector.[5]

The third proposition asserts that the losses associated with an initial period of high costs must be recovered (with interest) at a later date, although not by the individual entrepreneur starting up the activity. In essence, the costs of production of those benefiting by the development of the activity must fall enough to repay the initial losses and to provide a reasonable rate of return on those losses (since resources could otherwise have been allocated to unprotected activities with incremental international value-added).

The fourth proposition is really a logical consequence of the first three. All analysts have been willing to concede that if the first three propositions were valid, some form of assistance (and intervention with a *laissez-faire* outcome) to the externality-generating activity is warranted. However, protection would never be first best (contrasted with a production subsidy), and might not even achieve its intended purposes, as argued by Baldwin.

For the present, the important aspect of the infant industry case seems summarizable in the proposition that, in order for it to be empirically valid, a necessary (but not sufficient) condition is that costs in (temporarily)

---

[4] See Baldwin as to other mechanisms by which externalities have been said to affect profitability of start-up of new activities.

[5] It might be contended that a more-protected sector would generate greater externalities accruing to other activities The unresolved question in that case is why protection should be temporary. If it were not temporary, infant industry considerations do not apply

assisted or protected industries should have fallen over time more rapidly than costs in nonprotected or less-protected industries. This interpretation coincides with the case where it is assumed that prices in the rest of the world are given, and do not change over time due to differential rates of technical change in the rest of the world.[6] If there were also technical change in the corresponding industries abroad, the infant industry case would need to be reformulated to state that intervention would be warranted only if unit costs were expected to decline more rapidly in the infant industry than in the mature industry abroad (with the same qualifications as above regarding externalities and recovery of the initial investment with interest). For the purposes of this paper, it is assumed that world prices are given, so that a decline in costs in one industry at a more rapid rate than in another constitutes more of an infant industry case.

II. A Simple Empirical Test

There are two ways that one industry's costs per unit of output (or value-added) can change relative to another's: either its share-weighted inputs per unit of output must fall more (or rise less) than the other's, or the relative price of the factor it uses relatively intensively in production must fall.

This can readily be seen as follows. Define the total cost, C, of the ith industry as

$$(1) \qquad C_i = \sum_j W_j V_{ji},$$

where W_j is the reward to the jth factor of production and V_{ji} is the quantity of the jth factor employed in the ith industry.

[6]It might be anticipated that the world price of a particular commodity would rise over time (for reasons other than technical change), and therefore a presently uneconomic industry might become economic. This would not constitute a case for infant industry protection, however, because: (*i*) it is not clear that because the price in the future will rise, activity now is economic; and (*ii*) there is no reason for intervention since those undertaking the activity now will benefit from the higher future price.

Clearly, the change in i's costs is

$$(2) \qquad dC_i = \sum_i dW_j V_{ji} + \sum_j dV_{ji} W_j,$$

and the change in cost per unit of output is

$$(3) \qquad d\left(\frac{C_i}{X_i}\right) = \sum_j \frac{dW_j}{W_j} \frac{W_j V_{ji}}{C_i} \frac{C_i}{X_i}$$

$$+ \sum_j \frac{dV_{ji}}{V_{ji}} \frac{W_j V_{ji}}{C_i} \frac{C_i}{X_i} - \frac{dX_i}{X_i} \frac{C_i}{X_i}.$$

Denoting the share of the jth factor in total costs in industry i by α_{ij}, equation (3) can be rewritten:

$$(4)$$

$$d\frac{[C_i/X_i]}{C_i/X_i} = \sum_j \alpha_{ij} \frac{dW_j}{W_j} + \sum_j \alpha_{ij} \frac{dV_{ji}}{V_{ji}} - \frac{dX_i}{X_i}.$$

Thus, the proportionate change in costs per unit of output in the ith industry represents the share-weighted sum of changes in input prices plus the share-weighted sum of factor inputs less the rate of change of output. Let $\dot{C}_i$ represent the proportionate rate of change in costs per unit of output. Contrasting changes in costs between the ith and the kth industry yields

$$(5) \quad \dot{C}_i - \dot{C}_k = \sum_j (\alpha_{ij} - \alpha_{kj}) \frac{dW_j}{W_j}$$

$$+ \left[\sum_i \alpha_{ij} \frac{dV_{ji}}{V_{ji}} - \frac{dX_i}{X_i}\right]$$

$$- \left[\sum_j \alpha_{kj} \frac{dV_{jk}}{V_{jk}} - \frac{dX_k}{X_k}\right].$$

The first term on the right represents the change in relative costs due to changing relative input prices. Clearly, that relative input prices may change in the process of growth is not grounds for infant industry protection.[7]

If there is to be a dynamic cost reduction, it must be reflected in a difference between the two bracketed terms on the right-hand side.

We are thus led to the straightforward proposition that if there are dynamic factors warranting intervention, they will be reflected in a difference in the two right-hand terms of equation (5). Define, now,[8]

$$(6) \qquad \frac{dA_i}{A_i} = \frac{dX_i}{X_i} - \sum_j \alpha_{ij} \frac{dV_{ji}}{V_{ji}}.$$

Substituting (6) into (5), and dropping the first term as irrelevant for infant industry purposes,

$$(7) \qquad \dot{C}_i - \dot{C}_k = \frac{dA_k}{A_k} - \frac{dA_i}{A_i}.$$

In order for infant industry considerations to have warranted intervention in favor of industry *i*, costs per unit of output must have fallen more in *i* than in *k*. Equation (7) shows that a necessary condition for this to occur is that inputs per unit of output decrease more rapidly in industry *i* than in industry *k*. As formulated, this unit cost reduction could come about because of technical change, the overcoming of indivisibilities, the realization of scale economies, or for genuine infant industry reasons.

This, then, is the empirical test. Should industry *i* have been protected on infant

---

factor prices due to government intervention in the labor market, and yet the changes in costs that these could have induced seem relatively small See Table A2 for the calculations. It has also been suggested that commercial policies themselves might induce changes in relative factor prices and that this is a dynamic factor that should be considered. However, if commercial policies *caused* changes in relative factor prices, they would clearly increase costs in protected industries and thus tend to weaken whatever dynamic case there was for intervention.

[8] The dA/A is nothing other than the conventional formula for total factor-productivity growth, which is the rate of growth of output less the share-weighted rate of growth of inputs per unit of output. For present purposes, however, the assumptions necessary to justify use of dA/A as a measure are far weaker than those necessary for a total factor-productivity growth interpretation

industry grounds and its costs have fallen relative to *k*, it will be judged that there were some dynamic factors in industry *i* that *may* have warranted intervention (although there is no presumption whatsoever that intervention was optimal). Passing the test is a necessary condition for there to have been an infant industry. It is not sufficient to prove that infant industry protection was warranted because: (*i*) the industry might have developed anyway; (*ii*) the rewards may all have gone to the entrepreneurs in the industry; (*iii*) the reduction in costs might have come about for reasons other than externalities; or because (*iv*) the reduction in costs was not sufficient to provide an adequate rate of return on earlier losses. It might not have been optimal because an alternative intervention instrument or a lower level of protection might have achieved the same or better results with lower costs.

If, however, costs in industry *i* did not fall relative to industry *k*, clearly protection was not warranted.[9] It is in this sense that a contrast of rates of growth of output per unit of input between more- and less-protected industries constitutes a test for the empirical validity of the infant industry argument.

Before proceeding to the empirical results, two questions remain. A first question is the time period over which infant industry considerations might warrant intervention. The second pertains to the range of activities over which the test should be carried out.

The first is the simpler question, since all that is required is a period sufficiently long so that, if cost reductions were not incurred, it could reasonably be concluded that the costs of protection would not in all likelihood be recovered. Since the Turkish data pertain to a period of thirteen years (and longer), we note simply that with a real rate of return of 10 percent,[10] the present value of

---

[9] This does not prove that there might not have been an infant industry case It is conceivable that incentives other than those created by the forms of protection actually used might have induced entrepreneurs to engage in cost-reducing activities. See our 1981 paper for an analysis of the effects of the trade regime on incentives in Turkey

[10] Most observers would put the real rate of return in Turkey at a number substantially higher than this.

cost savings ten years' hence is less than 40 percent of the anticipated amount. It seems doubtful whether protection for a period of more than ten years, with no beginning of a reduction in costs, could conceivably come under the heading of justified infant industry protection.

The second question is the more difficult. It will be recalled that the infant industry argument presumes *both* dynamic factors *and* externalities. The test described above is straightforward in evaluating for the presence of dynamic factors, but does not indicate to which units it might apply. Since protection is granted at different rates to different industries, it seems natural to suppose that the relevant i and k to contrast would be different industries subject to different levels of protection. Having done so, a higher dA/A would be required for a more-protected industry than for a less-protected one to satisfy the infant industry test. Most proponents of the infant industry argument seem to adopt this notion that the benefits are external to the firm but internal to the industry. This would appear to imply that rates of growth of output per unit of input should be higher for the industry than for new firms (or new investments of existing firms). It is also possible, however, that externalities spread across new entrants, and do not affect more traditional firms within industries. In that event, one would expect output per unit of input to grow more rapidly in newly established firms or activities than in preexisting ones.

Both of these possible relationships imply that the relevant unit for externalities to be recaptured is somewhere within a given, protected, industry. While this seems the most plausible infant industry interpretation (and the one used here), some might argue that the benefits of new industries are spread across the entire industrial sector, and are not centered in the protected industries themselves. One might be skeptical of the argument, on the grounds that it is hard to see why different levels of temporary protection should be accorded to different industries unless their own costs would fall differentially. But if the relevant source of externalities is the entire industrial sector, the industrial sector as a whole should be observed to have experienced a relatively high rate of growth of output per unit of input in contrast to the rest of the economy (in contrast to mature industrial economies). Comparison of output per unit of input across countries is inherently difficult, but nonetheless can provide a partial check on the plausibility of this possibility.

III. Results

As already mentioned, Turkey has provided protection, on infant industry grounds, to a variety of new industries. Protection has been largely automatic because the authorities have generally prohibited imports of any good once domestic production began.[11] Rates of effective protection have been fairly high, and estimates must be based upon direct price comparisons rather than upon tariff schedules. The best available estimates are given in Table 1 below.

The details of data sources and procedures for estimating output per unit of input are given in the Appendix. Here, only three points need to be noted. First, there are two sets of estimates available: one from a sample of 92 firms and the other for two-digit manufacturing industries in the private sector of the Turkish economy. Secondly, the main thrust of import substitution activity (on infant industry grounds) in Turkey was during the early and mid-1960's. The two-digit industry data cover the period 1963–76, while data for individual firms cover at least that period when the firms were already in existence but shorter periods in some instances when the firms started operation in the late 1960's. Finally, since much of the import-substitution process consists of replacing imported inputs with domestic materials, estimates were generated for three separate inputs: labor, capital, and material inputs.[12]

Table 1 gives the main findings. The Appendix gives sources and procedures and the

---

[11] One would anticipate that, in the absence of expected monopoly power from entering a given line of activity first, the automatic protection mechanism would provide an incentive for the more economic among the import-competing industries to be developed first

[12] No data were available with which to estimate changes in skills of the labor force.

TABLE 1—EFFECTIVE RATES OF PROTECTION AND RATES OF GROWTH OF OUTPUT PER UNIT OF INPUT

Industry	ERP_1	ERP_2	DRC	Rate of Growth of Output/Input	
				Firm Sample	Industry
Food Products	13	n a	18	25	16
Fur and Leather Products	14	−24	−15	n a	−1 17
Wood and Cork Products	16	58	−13	−3 34	− 55
Furniture and Fixtures	16	n a	n a	n a	− 56
Nonmetallic Mineral Products	23	−27	1	1 61	.72
Textiles	42	−23	12	.72	84
Apparel and Footwear	42	47	n a	5.24	4 10
Metal Products	57	140	682	− 05	1 61
Chemicals	60	200	21	− 04	46
Electrical Machinery	63	113	36	5 76	1 41
Paper and Products	72	105	97	n a	1 55
Rubber Products	77	N-IVA	279	n a	4 27
Basic Metals	80	113	14	2 21	− 93
Nonelectric Machinery	142	132	36	n a	62
Petroleum Refining	n a	236	n a	n.a	−8 80
Transport Equipment	209	134	131	n a	94
All Manufacturing				1 91	1 84

Source ERP_1: Özfirat estimates given in Krueger, Table IX-2; ERP_2: Baysan estimates given in his Table 1, p. 126 *DRC*: Krueger, Table VIII-1

Notes 1) Beverages and Tobacco are not reported here due to lack of a measure of effective protection; both are traditional Estimated rates of growth of output per unit of input are 4 31 percent annually for Beverages and 5 97 percent for Tobacco. 2) All rates of growth are continuous natural rates N-IVA denotes negative international value-added

underlying data on rates of growth of outputs and inputs from which these estimates were derived.

The first three columns of Table 1 give three different estimates of sectoral protection all pertaining to the late 1960's. The first are based on sectoral averages computed by the State Planning Organization for 1968. Sectors are listed in order of increasing protection based on these estimates. The second are based on input-output tariff data adjusted for the estimated additional protection accorded by import quotas and prohibitions. The third are domestic resource-cost estimates taken from a sample of firms. While the last are most closely based on price comparisons, they suffer from the drawback that levels of protection vary so much within each sector that sampling error is probably fairly large.[13] This variability stems partly from the fact that an import-licensing regime inherently provides varying levels of protection to

the same industry at different points in time. Even more important is the consideration that there are import-substitution industries within "traditional" sectors (such as synthetic textiles), and "traditional" activities within import-substitution sectors (such as copper processing within basic metals). Thus, the variability reflects the underlying reality that levels of protection differ widely even within particular industries.[14]

Despite the wide variability, the three sets of estimates together provide a fairly good indication of the height of protection in the mid- to late 1960's, and its differential across industries. Essentially, the first seven are all regarded as traditional industries within Turkey; the last nine are regarded as the import-substitution sectors.[15] The latter are

[13]See Krueger, where the variance in the estimated sectoral means was also calculated

[14]While data in nominal terms are available for three- and four-digit industries, no appropriate price deflators or detailed estimates of effective protection rates are available

[15]The import substitution industries generally experienced more rapid growth of output See Table A1

those that were encouraged in the early 1960's, and were the focus of Turkey's import-substitution polices on infant industry grounds. The positive rates of protection for the traditional sectors probably did little more than offset currency overvaluation in the late 1960's; the Turkish lira was devalued by 66 percent in 1970.

The last two columns in Table 1 give estimated rates of growth of output per unit of input. The firm sample column gives estimated rates for the sample of firms. As can be seen, there were some industries for which no firm data were available. In some instances (such as petroleum refining) this was because the activity is undertaken primarily by one large firm; in other instances, there were simply no firms in the sample data. Rates for the industry cover the years 1963–76, the period for which State Institute of Statistics data are available.

As can be seen, there is no systematic tendency for more-protected firms or industries to have had higher growth of output per unit of input than less-protected firms and industries. Two industries—apparel and footwear and rubber products—appear to have experienced relatively rapid growth of output per unit of input. Apparel and footwear is a traditional industry in Turkey, and its medium rate of effective protection reflects currency overvaluation and the negative protection to textiles, rather than positive nominal protection directed toward apparel and footwear. Rubber products is a sector with a sizable traditional component and import-substitution activities consisting primarily of tire production. This latter activity was extremely high cost, as reflected both in Tercan Baysan's estimate that international value added was negative and in a very high *DRC* estimate. No firms producing rubber products were in the sample, so only a sectoral rate was available.

There is likewise no apparent tendency for the new activities, as reflected by the firm data, to have experienced rates of growth of output per unit of input systematically higher or lower than the industry to which they belonged. Thus, the externality argument does not seem borne out by the data: if anything, sample firms experienced a slightly

higher rate of growth of output per unit of input than their corresponding industries, but surely the difference is well within the margin of error of the calculations.

Finally, there is the question as to whether externalities could have been realized elsewhere in the manufacturing sector. Here, the only way of judging is to evaluate the estimated rate of growth of output per unit of input in the manufacturing sector as a whole. That, in turn, involves a comparison of the rate realized in Turkey with that in other countries. Because data are not entirely comparable, and because the estimates are residuals and therefore subject to fairly wide margins of error, such comparisons are necessarily extremely hazardous. Estimates typically range from 3–4 percent for developed and other developing countries.[16] Despite problems of comparability, it hardly seems plausible that differences in measurement account for the lower figure in Turkey.

To see just how low the estimated rates of growth of output per unit of input are, consider the following. Suppose a firm initially experienced a 50 percent cost disadvantage (i.e., required 50 percent effective protection). Output per unit of input would have to grow 4 percent annually more rapidly than in other industries in order for it to be able to survive without protection ten years hence.[17] This, however, would provide no return on the initial loss. It is thus an underestimate of the differential in growth of output per unit of input that would be necessary to warrant protection of the infant industry.

For the Turkish case, when all manufacturing was experiencing increased output per

---

[16] Edward Chen (1977) estimated rates of manufacturing total factor productivity growth of 2 29, 3 47, 3 50, and 3 75 percent for Hong Kong, South Korea, Taiwan and Singapore, respectively, for the 1960's. Estimated rates for developed countries include 3 5 percent for Norway (V. Ringstad, 1971), 3 66 for Japan (Mieko Nishimizu and Charles Hulten, 1978), 3 75 for Italy (Vittorio Conti and Renato Filosa, 1979), and 2.9 percent for the United States (John Kendrick, 1976) In some of these cases, quality adjustments have been made to estimated inputs. Using unadjusted data would raise those estimates, making the contrast with Turkey even sharper.

[17] This number is found by solving $I_t = I_0 (1 - r)^t$ for r when $I_t = .667$, $I_0 = 1$ and t equals 10.

unit of input at a rate of 1.8 annually, this would imply that industries experiencing 50 percent protection should increase output per unit of input at a rate of at least 5.8 percent annually. More concretely, consider rubber products, the "best" Turkish case. If the *low* estimate of the *ERP* for rubber products is accepted, the output per unit of input would have to grow at 7.34 percent annually in order for their costs to fall enough for them to become competitive in ten years. At their existing rate of growth of output per unit of input, it would require twenty-three years for them to become competitive.[18] Even that calculation takes the low estimate of the rate of protection, allows for no return on the investment over the twenty-three-year interval, and is for the two-digit industry with the highest estimated rate of growth of output per unit of input. Obviously, for "infant" industries such as paper where outputs per unit of input grew at less than the average rate of all manufacturing, there can never be a "catch up" as long as existing relative rates are maintained.

IV. Conclusions

This paper has attempted two things: to develop an empirical test for the validity of the infant industry argument; and to use that test on Turkish data. The test is simple and straightforward: input per unit of output must fall more rapidly in more protected industries if there is to be any rationale for infant industry protection. In the Turkish case, there was no such tendency over the period covered.

The fact that protected Turkish industries did not experience rapid increases in output per unit of input is sufficient to prove that protection was not warranted. It does not, however, prove that there were no infant industries. It might be that the trade regime itself provided the wrong incentives. It is at least possible that, under an alternative in-

centive structure, output per unit of input might have grown more rapidly in some, or possibly even all, Turkish industries.[19] What can be concluded is that, at least in the Turkish case, protection did not elicit the sort of growth in output per unit of input on which infant industry proponents base their claim for protection.

APPENDIX

The major thrust of import substitution into new industries occurred in the early and mid-1960's. For the period 1963–76, there are industry-level data available with which to estimate inputs and outputs. A Census of Manufacturers and Annual Survey of Industries provides detailed data on number of employees, wage bill, value of purchased inputs, value of output, investment made by firms, and number of firms for private activities within each industrial sector employing ten or more employees. These data, combined with estimates of capital stock provided by the State Planning Organization and appropriate price deflators[20] form a data set from which it is possible to infer the behavior of inputs and outputs for two-digit manufacturing industries in the private sector in Turkey.[21] Since much of the import-substitution process consists of replacing imported inputs with domestic materials, three inputs were separately estimated: labor, capital, and material inputs.

A second set of data is at the firm, rather than industry, level. It covers those firms which received loans from the Turkish Industrial Development Bank. For them, data were available on a variety of their attributes (size, date of inception, precise composition of output, etc.) and also for annual invest-

---

[18] This calculation is based on the assumption that output per unit of input in rubber products continues to grow at 4 27 percent annually while in the entire manufacturing sector it continues to grow at 1 84 percent annually

[19] See our earlier paper for an attempt to trace the links between the growth of output per unit of input and the ebbs and flows of the trade regime

[20] Wholesale price indices were available for outputs of each two-digit industry These data were then used, in conjunction with the Turkish input-output tables, to obtain a weighted input price for each sector's purchases The same price deflators were used for two-digit industries and for the firm data described below

[21] In our earlier paper the behavior of the private and public sectors is analyzed and contrasted, and a fuller description of the data is given

TABLE A1—UNDERLYING GROWTH RATES OF OUTPUT AND INPUT FOR PRIVATE
SECTOR INDUSTRIES AND SAMPLE FIRMS

	Industries' 1963–76 Growth Rate of:			Sample Firm Growth Rate of:		
	Labor	Capital	Real Output	Labor	Capital	Real Output
Food Products	4 6	14 2	7 7	7 5	13 3	9 5
Beverages	18 0	14 2	22 5	–	–	–
Tobacco	−3.3	−.3	5 7	–	–	–
Textiles	4 6	13 3	11 0	6 2	14 1	10 2
Apparel and Footwear	23 3	13 3	28 3	1 9	8 0	6 8
Wood and Cork Products	10 0	14 2	12 6	9 1	27.9	15.8
Furniture and Fixtures	4 7	14 2	6 6	–	–	–
Paper and Products	16 7	26 0	23 7	–	–	–
Chemicals	8 4	15 4	15 1	4 2	12 4	12 0
Rubber Products	5 1	13 3	16 8	–	–	–
Fur and Leather Products	7 8	17 0	8 6	–	–	–
Petroleum and Coal Products	28 1	60.5	33.7	–	–	–
Nonmetallic Minerals	8 0	16.7	15 3	5 0	7 4	7 4
Basic Metals	18.1	25 3	21 5	7 6	14 9	15 8
Metal Products	7 8	13 1	11 8	9.0	17 1	13 3
Nonelectrical Machinery	15.2	17 6	17.9	–	–	–
Electrical Machinery	12 5	20 1	19.8	–	–	–
Transport Equipment	22.7	30 5	30.1	–	–	–

Note. All rates of growth are continuous natural rates, computed by running a logarithmic regression of each variable
on time.

ments, annual labor force and wage bill, annual purchases of raw materials and intermediate goods and inventory changes, sales, profits, depreciation, and so on. Altogether, there are 91 firms for which data were available on a reliable basis for a period of more than five years.[22] Most new investments of these firms were undertaken in response to incentives provided by the trade regime, although some were in more traditional industries. Since there was credit rationing in Turkey, there is some presumption that borrowers from the Industrial Development Bank were firms of above-average quality, according to the criteria used by the Bank for its lending.

On the basis of these data, it was possible to compute an estimated capital stock for each firm using perpetual inventory techniques. Doing so was judged better than using balance sheet estimates (which were also available) since the latter made no al-

[22] Interviews were held with more than a quarter of the firms, which provided a check on the reliability of the data, and also provided additional information on characteristics of firms and their management.

lowance for price level changes in their capital stock in the context of a relatively high rate of inflation. Depreciation rates were estimated from American engineering data found in W. R. Park,[23] and then scaled to equal the State Planning Organization's estimate of the average rate for all manufacturing. Investment deflators available from the State Planning Organization were first employed to convert nominal investment into constant-price estimates of additions to capital stock. Investment in a given year was treated as becoming effective capital only at the beginning of the following year.[24] Period $t-1$'s capital stock was depreciated, and then real

[23] It is an interesting question whether one should a priori expect depreciation rates to be lower or higher in Turkey than in the United States On one hand, cheaper labor should encourage more maintenance and thus a longer economic life On the other hand, poor and irregular materials quality, irregular supplies of electric power, and workers with less experience in the care of equipment might tend to the opposite result.

[24] For some older firms, data were not available from inception. In those cases, initial balance sheet data were converted to an estimate of real capital stock based on knowledge of the firm's history and starting date.

investment in $t-1$ was added to obtain capital stock in period t.

In addition, data from the firms could be directly used for the number of workers. Purchased inputs, adjusted for inventory changes, were deflated to yield an estimate of material inputs. Finally, for some firms a physical indicator of homogeneous output (for example, tons of cement) was available and used to indicate output. For others, it proved preferable to take deflated sales adjusted for inventory change as the measure of output.

Thus, for both firms and industries, data were available on materials inputs, outputs, labor inputs, and capital stock inputs, along with the shares of the respective factors in the value of output. For purposes of estimating changes in input per unit of output, the *average* share (over the life of the firm and for the entire 1963–76 period for two-digit industries) of labor, material, and capital was used. This procedure was judged superior to employing a Divisia index because of the volatility of shares from year to year.[25]

Table A1 provides the estimates of rates of growth of labor and capital inputs and outputs. All rates are computed for the period 1963–76 at the industry level. For firms, rates were computed over the period for which data were available, and a minimum of five years. In some instances, firm data span a period of twenty years, but some newer import substitution activities did not start until the late 1960's; data on these firms are also included in the estimates.

Table A2 gives data on the wage share in each two-digit industry and computes the maximal rate of change in relative costs that could have been associated with the very steep increase in real wages that occurred in Turkey during the period. The real wage increase was the result of labor legislation and did not reflect underlying labor market conditions: urban unemployment was rising rapidly during most of the period.

[25] Initial estimates, based on Divisia indices, yielded occasionally bizarre results For example, for firms or industries suffering losses, the capital share was negative, and firms with heavy investment were calculated to have increased output per unit of input!

TABLE A2—COMPUTATION OF POSSIBLE CHANGES IN RELATIVE COSTS DUE TO CHANGES IN RELATIVE FACTOR PRICES

Industry	Wage Share of Value-Added	Rate of Cost Change
Food Products	.264	−0.4
Beverages	.101	−2.0
Tobacco	.183	−1 3
Textiles	.368	0 3
Apparel and Footwear	.521	1 7
Wood and Cork Products	.485	1.4
Furniture and Fixtures	.381	1 5
Paper and Products	.372	.4
Chemicals	319	−.1
Rubber Products	.274	−.5
Fur and Leather Products	.484	1.4
Petroleum and Coal	016	−2 8
Nonmetallic Minerals	.326	−0.0
Basic Metals	.201	−1.2
Metal Products	.384	0 5
Nonelectric Machinery	320	−0.1
Electrical Machinery	.332	0 0
Transport Equipment	562	3 7
All Manufacturing	.245	0 0

Notes: Real wages are estimated to have risen at a continuous rate of 6 percent from 1963 to 1976, based on average weekly earnings covered under social insurance. The median share of labor was 33 percent. Relative cost changes were computed be weighting these rates of change by each industry's actual (1968) shares. For the median industry's costs to have remained constant, capital costs would have had to decline at a continuous rate of 2.95 percent

REFERENCES

Arrow, Kenneth J., "The Economic Implications of Learning by Doing," *Review of Economic Studies*, June 1962, *29*, 155–73.

Baldwin, Robert E., "The Case Against Infant-Industry Tariff Protection," *Journal of Political Economy*, May/June 1969, *77*, 295–305.

Baysan, Tercan, "Economic Implications of Turkey's Entry into the Common Market," unpublished doctoral dissertation, University of Minnesota, 1974.

Chen, Edward K. Y., "Factor Inputs, Total Factor Productivity and Economic Growth: The Asian Case," *Developing Economies*, June 3, 1977, *15*, 121–43.

Conti, Vittorio and Filosa, Renato, "A Disaggregate Analysis of Accumulation, Productivity, and Labor Costs in the Manufacturing Industry" in *Economic Papers*, 2, Rome: Bank of Italy Research Department, June 1979.

Hirschman, Albert O., *The Strategy of Economic Development*, New Haven: Yale University Press, 1958.

Kendrick, John W., "Productivity Trends and Prospects," in *U.S. Economic Growth from 1976 to 1986*, Washington: Joint Economic Committee of Congress, October 1, 1976.

Krueger, Anne O., *Foreign Trade Regimes and Economic Development: Turkey*, New York: Columbia University Press, 1974.

_____ and Tuncer, Baran, "Growth of Factor Productivity in Turkish Manufacturing Industries," unpublished paper, 1981.

Nishimizu, Mieko and Hulten, Charles R. "The Sources of Japanese Economic Growth:

1955-71," *Review of Economics and Statistics*, August 1978, *60*, 351–61.

Park, W. R., *Cost Engineering Analysis*, New York: John Wiley and Sons, 1973.

Ringstad, V., *Estimating Production Functions and Technical Changes from Microdata*, Norway: Statistisk Sentralbyra, 1971.

Samuelson, Paul A., *Foundations of Economic Analysis*, Cambridge: Harvard University Press, 1958.

Turkish Republic, State Institute of Statistics, *Census of Manufacturing Industries*, Ankara, 1963; 1970.

_____,_____, *Annual Survey of Manufacturing Industries*, Ankara, various years to 1976.

_____, State Planning Organization, *Turkiye Imalat Sanayiinde Dermaye ve Isgucu* (Capital and Labor in Turkish Manufacturing Industry), Ankara, December 1977.

[17]

Indian Economic Review, Vol. XXIV, No. 1

Recent Theories of Imperfect Competition and International Trade : Any Implications for Development Strategy?

T. N. SRINIVASAN
Department of Economics, Yale University, New Haven, CT 06520-1987, USA

ABSTRACT

Application of some new results in industrial organisation to trade theory have provided a better explanation of some stylized facts by being able to recognise features such as increasing returns to scale and non-competitive market structure. Another kind of such applications have generated results favouring an active role for government intervention under certain situations. A third line of research tends to find support for the view that the optimality propositions of the neoclassical theory associated with free trade are invalid for developing countries. The purpose of this paper is to examine the new theory in relation to policies of trade liberalisation that many developing countries have recently initiated. It will be argued that the case for liberalisation is by no means weakened by the new theory.

1. INTRODUCTION

In the last decade some perceptive theorists saw an opportunity to engage in intellectual arbitrage by the application of developments in the field of industrial organization to the theory of international trade and policy. From a positive perspective, one class of applications appeared to explain better some stylized facts (such as intra-industry trade in differentiated products between countries with similar factor endowments) by taking into account a distinguishing feature of modern industrial technology, namely, increasing returns to scale and the associated non-competitive market structure, modeled as the large group Chamberlinian monopolistic competition with free entry. From a normative perspective, another class of applications based on partial equilibrium oligopoly models generated an active role for government intervention

2   T. N. SRINIVASAN

under certain circumstances. And some analysts in western developed
countries, particularly USA, saw in the latter both an explanation of the
success of the Japanese in capturing a large share of the world markets
in many products including, in particular, the so-called high-technology industries and an argument for an industrial policy in their own
countries. Some development economists (Stewart, 1984; Helleiner,
1985) and others predisposed to government intervention also saw vindi-
cation in the new theories of the view that the neo-classical proposition
that free trade is the optimal policy is invalid for developing countries.
The World Institute for Development Economics Research (WIDER)
at Helsinki even organised a conference in August 1988 on *New Trade
Theories and Industrialization in Developing Countries*. Since the new
theories apparently throw doubts about the wisdom of a policy of liberalization of foreign trade and payments that many developing countries
have begun to adopt recently after a long period of unspectacular performance under a strategy of import-substituting industrialization, it is
worthwhile to put these theories in perspective.

The purpose of the paper is expository. In Sections 2-4 the main
elements of the theory of international trade under imperfect competition
are exposited. Section 5 examines the relevance of the theory to the role
of trade policy in a develoment strategy oriented towards industrialization. It will be argued that the case for liberalization is by no means
weakened by the new theory. Section 6 concludes the paper.

2. INCREASING RETURNS AND MARKET POWER IN TRADITIONAL THEORY

Traditional trade theory is based largely on general equilibrium models
in which homogeneous commodities are produced under a convex
technology (thus ruling out increasing returns) and consumed by consumers with independent convex preferences. Other technical assumptions
sufficient for the existence of a competitive equilibrium are also part of
the theory. Such a competitive equilibrium was a Pareto Optimum
viewed either from the point of view of consumers in a nation or from
the point of view of the consumers in the trading world as a whole
(Grandmont and McFadden, 1972). Increasing returns to scale as well
as externalities were introduced in these general equilibrium models in
a way that still allowed the existence of a competitive equilibrium. This
meant that the price-taking, profit-maximizing calculus continued to be
operative in the input-output decision of individual producers. Thus,
increasing returns and other non-convexities manifest themselves at the
level of the industry as a whole (or even the economy as a whole) and
not at the level of an individual producer. Besides, the number of firms

in such an industry was assumed to be sufficiently numerous that each behaved as if it could not influence the industry-wide externality or scale effect through its own decisions. It is then easy to show that since each firm's decision will not reflect the social reality of industry or economy-wide externality or scale effects, a laissez-faire competitive equilibrium is no longer Pareto optimum. An appropriately chosen policy intervention can bring private producer behaviour to be consistent with what is needed to achieve a Pareto optimality. In the traditional terminology, the private marginal rate of transformation between any two commodities differs from the social marginal rate of transformation in a laissez-faire competitive equilibrium. The intervention brings the two into equality. Thus, in a small open economy, the intervention will make the private and social marginal rate of transformation equal to the foreign marginal rate of transformation, i.e. the relative price of one commodity in terms of the other.

The descriptive realism of increasing returns at the industry level, acting as an externality at the firm level that permits competitive market structure, is debatable. Indeed, as Helpman and Krugman (1985) point out, arguments offered in support of the traditional static external economies model are somewhat implausible, and the model is better viewed as a rough and ready approximation of a more complex reality. Be that as it may, in the traditional model of increasing returns neither the existence and uniqueness of a free trade equilibrium nor the gains from free trade are guaranteed. After all Graham (1923) pointed out long ago that the value of output at constant prices may be lower in a trading equilibrium compared to autarky if trade results in a decline of the output of increasing returns to scale industries. However, there is a strong presumption of gains. That is, the exploitation of economies of scale can provide an added incentive for trade. Indeed, small countries are almost certain to gain from trade, particularly if the economies of scale are related to the *global* rather than *domestic* output of an industry.

Analogous to increasing returns at the industry level that permits competition among firms, in traditional theory, market power in foreign trade, if it arises at all, arises at the *national level*. In such a model there are no increasing returns in production and there is atomistic competition among consumers and among producers. Thus *national* power is not perceived by the atomistic competitors, and in effect becomes *an externality* to consumer and producer decisions. Once again, laissez-faire competitive equilibrium (i e. free trade) is not Pareto optimal from the perspective of the country's consumers. An intervention in the form of an optimum tariff (i e. an export or import tax or subsidy) simply internalizes the externality so that the *national* market power is optimally

4   T. N. SRINIVASAN

exploited to maximize domestic welfare. It is usually assumed that this exploitation of market power by one trading nation does not lead to retaliation by its trading partners, although some analysis of tariff wars is also available in the literature. Instruments other than tariffs (such as quotas) for achieving maximal national welfare have also been considered. The broad conclusions of this traditional analysis are : (i) the national exercise of monopoly power in the absence of retaliation is clearly *not* Pareto optimal from a *world* or *global* perspective, (ii) an appropriate income transfer to the nation contemplating an optimal tariff in return for its desisting from imposing it will yield a Pareto superior global outcome compared to the optimum tariff equilibrium, (iii) if retaliation by its trading partners is provoked by one nation's imposition of a tariff, a tariff-war that eliminates all trade is a distinct possibility, although a (Nash) equilibrium with tariff restricted but non-zero trade is also possible and (iv) the existence of significant and exploitable power has not found much empirical support.

3. INCREASING RETURNS, IMPERFECT COMPETITION AND INTRA-INDUSTRY TRADE : RECENT MODELS

The recent theories postulate economies of scale *at the level of an individual firm* at relevant ranges of output. It is clear that equating price to its marginal cost by the firm in such a context is inconsistent with its earning of non-negative profits, and thus a competitive market structure is ruled out. Alternative market structures have to be considered. In the literature the two extremes of large group Chamberlinian monopolistic competition and a small group oligopoly have been considered. The latter opens up the possibility of strategic use of trade policy.

Krugman (1979, 1980, 1981) in a series of papers developed a set of parsimonious models which highlight the interaction of increasing returns to scale, product differentiation and Chamberlinian monopolistic competition (see Krugman (1987) for a survey of the literature). A common feature of these models is that each of the available number of differentiated products enter symmetrically in consumers' utility function. In fact, the elasticity of a consumer's demand of each of the products is constant. Given his income and the same price for each product, the maximum utility a consumer can obtain *increases* with the number of products available for consumption. In other words, each consumer prefers variety, i.e. he gets greater utility from consuming a little less of each of a larger number of products than a little more of a smaller number. Increasing returns are very simply modeled : each product is producible with the same technology that involves a *fixed* labour cost independent of the level of output and a *constant* marginal labour cost.

thus, the *average cost* per unit of output declines with output, while marginal cost is constant. Differentiating one product from another is costless Entry is free so that in equilibrium there are no excess profits.

In the simplest of the Krugman models there is a single industry producing differentiated products and all consumers are identical with the same endowment of the single factor of production, namely, labour. Thus the autarky equilibrium is easily described : each consumer consumes the *same amount* of each of a number of products, each of which sells at the same price, and this price equals the average (wage) cost of production. The number of products produced in equilibrium is an increasing function of the aggregate endowment of labour in the economy and a decreasing function of the fixed cost of production. The equilibrium *price* (or equivalently the equilibrium wage rate) depends only on the demand elasticity and the marginal labour cost and *not* on the size of the economy as represented by the size of the labour endowment. This means that as long as all countries have access to the same technology and consumer preferences are the same in all countries in autarky equilibrium *prices* and *wage* rates and the *output* of each product will be the same across countries and only the *number* of products differ between countries.

When trade opens up, its only effect is to allow consumers in each country the access to products produced in all other countries. The gain from trade is simply the welfare gain from increased product variety, with trade having no effects on production, prices and factor incomes in each country. In a variant of this model, there are *two* differentiated product industries with the same technology for each product except that the type of labour used by one industry is different from that of the other. The aggregate endowment of the two types together is normalized to 2, with the amount of labour of one of the types in the total being denoted by Z which varies from zero to one. Thus, Z is a measure of the *composition* of the labour force. When this economy trades with another economy which is its mirror image in the composition of the labour force (i.e. the foreign and home economy's endowments of the same type of labour sum to 2) but otherwise identical to it, the output of each product of each of the two industries and the number of products in each industry remain at their autarky levels as in the first model. However, since the *composition* of the labour force differs between the two economies (when $Z \neq 1$), naturally the scarce factor in the home economy is abundant in the foreign economy.

In autarky, the relative factor price (i.e. the price of one factor relative to the other) and hence the price of a typical product of one industry relative to the price of typical product of the other industry, differ between the two countries. Trade in this case has an effect on prices and

6   T. N. SRINIVASAN

wages, i.e. it equalizes factor prices and commodity prices across industries. This is because the technologies are the same in the two industries
and in the world as a whole there are an equal number (i.e. two) of
workers of each type (even though within each country the composition
of work force differs) and all products enter symmetrically in consumer
preferences. It turns out that the Grubel-Lloyd (1975) index of *intra-
industry trade* equals Z in this model.[1] It reaches a maximum of 1 when
$Z = 1$, i.e. when both countries have the same labour force composition
and reaches a minimum (i.e. *inter*-industry trade reaches a maximum)
when $Z = 0$, thereby supporting the stylized fact that intra-industry
trade is greatest among similar economies. While the abundant factor
unambiguously gains from trade in that its real wage remains unchanged
in terms of the product of the industry in which it is used and goes up in
terms of the product of the other industry, the scarce factor will also gain
if the products are sufficiently differentiated, i.e. if the elasticity of
substitution among products in consumption is low. A second variant of
the basic model considers *two* types of consumers, each consuming only
the products of one of the industries and the two trading countries being mirror images of each other in their composition of consumer types.

The model of Helpman (1981) comes closest in spirit to the traditional
Heckscher-Ohlin-Samuelson (H-O-S) model with two industries and two
factors. One of the industries produces a homogeneous product (food)
under constant returns to scale and the other produces a number of
varieties of a differentiated product (manufactures) under *increasing*
returns to scale. Both industries use two factors (capital and labour)
each of which is homogeneous and perfectly mobile between industries.

Demand for the differentiated product is modeled differentially compared to Krugman's model. Suppose there is a continuum of potential
varieties of the differentiated product that can be produced. One can
represent this continuum as points on the circumference of a circle. Each
consumer is assumed to have a most preferred variety among all varieties
of the manufactured good in the following sense : if he is asked to choose
a variety of the product given that he will receive x units of it (along
with y units of food) he will always choose the *same* variety regardless

[1]This index is $1 - \dfrac{\sum\limits_{k}(X_k - M_k)}{\sum\limits_{k}(X_k + M_k)}$ where $X_k(M_k)$ is the value of exports (imports)

of products of industry k. If all trade is inter-industry trade, then at most *one* of X_k
and M_k is different from zero for each k, thus yielding a value of zero to the index.
On the other hand, if all trade is balanced intra-industry trade, then $X_k = M_k$ for all
k so that the index takes on the value of one.

of the quantities x and y. Let us measure arc distances on the circumference in either direction from the point corresponding to the most preferred variety. The consumer is assumed to derive the *same utility* from consuming y units of food and $h(v)x$ units of a product variety that corresponds to a point located at an arc (shortest) distance v on the circumference as he does from consuming y units of food and x units of his most preferred product. The compensation function $h(v)$ depends *only* on v and *not* on x and y. It takes a value of unity when $v = 0$ and increases (at an increasing rate) as v increases from 0 to its maximum value of 1. Thus, a consumer's preferences are completely represented by a utility function $u(x, y)$ where $x(y)$ is the consumption of his most preferred variety of the manufactured good (food) and the compensation function $h(v)$.

Given the standard assumptions as in the Hecksher-Ohlin-Samuelson model, namely, identical technologies (constant returns to scale in the production of food and homothetic in the production of manufactures), identical homothetic utility functions $u(x, y)$, and identical compensation functions $h(v)$ in two trading countries and factor intensity non-reversals, Helpman shows that the Rybczynski and factor price equalization theorems can be extended to his model. Further, in a trading equilibrium in which factor prices are equalized, the country relatively better endowed with capital is a *net exporter* (importer) of the capital-intensive (labour-intensive) manufactured good (food) and if both countries have the same capital-labour endowment ratio, then *all trade* is *intra-industry* trade in varieties of the manufactured good. This result provides a nice generalization of the factor proportions theory of *inter-industry* trade a la Hecksher-Ohlin at the same time confirming the stylized facts of intra-industry trade between similar economies.

Three additional results hold in the Helpman model : first, any redistribution of world's factor endowments that increases the divergence between the factor endowment ratios of the two trading countries *without affecting* the equilibrium factor prices leads to a decline in the Grubel-Lloyd index of intra-industry trade. Second, if the above redistribution of endowments also preserves the *factor incomes* of the two countries, the volume of trade increases. Third, if starting from an initial equilibrium in which both countries have the same endowment ratio (so that there is only intra-industry trade), a redistribution of endowments that preserves the *initial endowment ratio* increases (decreases) the volume of trade if it reduces (increases) the inequality in country sizes. These there results clarify the role of divergence in factor endowments, factor incomes and country sizes in explaining the pattern as well as volume of trade.

The only important result of the traditional theory that is not easily

8   T. N. Srinivasan

generalized is the Stolper-Samuelson theorem linking relative commodity prices and relative factor prices and the related issue of using the autarky relative prices of commodities (or of factors) in the two countries to infer comparative advantage. The problem arises from the fact that a country's size affects its autarky commodity prices because of economies of scale. For instance, if two countries have the same factor endowment ratio but one is larger than the other, one may expect that in the larger country the manufactured good will have a lower relative price in autarky. But in the trading equilibria with equalized factor prices, because of identical endowment ratios *all trade* is intra-industry trade and as such, autarky relative commodity prices do not predict the pattern of inter-sectoral trade. Thus, the presumption a la standard theory, that a country with a lower (higher) relative price of manufactures (food) will export (import) manufactures (food) does not hold. However, Helpman is able to obtain a scale-adjusted commodity price ratio that provides a valid prediction of trade under the *special assumption* that preferences are represented by a Cobb-Douglas utility function, and the production function in the increasing returns to scale industry is homothetic. In summary, the Helpman analysis shows that the insights of the traditional H-O-S model hold up fairly well even in a world of differentiated products and increasing returns to scale.

4. Oligopoly, Strategic Behaviour and International Trade : Recent Theory

Unlike the Helpman and Krugman (general equilibrium) models with free entry and monopolistic competition, the recent international trade models with an oligopolistic market structure are partial equilibrium models. In some models either entry is precluded altogether by assumption or incumbent firms follow entry deterring policies if appropriate. Without free entry, excess profits are not driven to zero, i.e. incumbent firms will be earning positive profits in equilibrium. If domestic and foreign firms constitute the oligopoly, depending on the nature of the competition, government intervention in the form of suitable taxes or subsidies can raise the profits of domestic firms at the expense of the profits of foreign firms. Since in an oligopolistic equilibrium prices exceed regional costs, to the extent this wedge is reduced by intervention, such intervention can act as a substitute for domestic anti-trust policy and may even improve global welfare. In situations where marginal costs decline because of learning by doing over time, protection, by increasing the size of the market for domestic firms, can facilitate their learning faster and increase their competitive edge in other markets. While these models suggest a possible strategic use of trade policy, as Markusen and Venables (1988)

Imperfect Competition and International Trade 9

point out *"the contents of the various contributions do not . . . aggregate into a coherent 'model' in the sense we get from the factor proportions model. Different papers produce contradictory results that aggregate into confusion and disarray"* (emphasis added). The reason for this is that the results are extremely sensitive to the nature of the oligopolistic competition.

The literature on oligopolistic models is expanding at an exponential rate, though accumulation of useful knowledge through them may be expanding much more slowly if at all. A partial list of the more important contributions is included in the references. Dixit (1987) critically surveys some of them. The diversity of the conclusions can be illustrated using the eminently readable paper of Eaton and Grossman (1986). In the simplest of their models there are two firms, one domestic and the other foreign, both competing for sales in a third market with no demand for either firm in its own country. Since there is no domestic consumption of the commodity in question, considerations of consumer welfare impact of government intervention in the production and export of it are absent. Further, since any tax revenue received from the domestic firm or subsidy paid to it is merely a domestic transfer from (or to) the government, *national* objective is simply the maximization of the pre-tax profits of the domestic firm. The latter is difference between the gross revenue $r(x, x^*)$ of the domestic firm when it (the foreign firm) sells $x(x^*)$ in the third market and its total cost $c(x)$. The first order condition of a maximum of $r(x, x^*) - c(x)$ is simply $r_1 + r_2 (dx^*/dx) - c_1 = 0$ where a subscript $i (i = 1, 2)$ denotes the partial derivative of a function with respect to its ith argument. Since it is *the firm* and *not the government* which chooses the value of x, its choice need not in general satisfy the first order condition.

Clearly, the derivative dx^*/dx is the equilibrium (or actual) response of the sales of the foreign firm to changes in the sales of the domestic firm. In the absence of any intervention by the government, the firm's profit is also $r(x, x^*) - c(x)$. However, the first order condition for the maximization of this profit is $r_1 + r_2 (dx^*/dx)_{conj.} - c_1 = 0$ where $(dx^*/dx)_{conj.}$ is the response of the foreign firm as perceived or conjectured by the domestic firm. If the conjectural response and the actual response are the same (that is, the conjecture is consistent in the sense of Bresnehan (1981)), then $(dx^*/dx) = (dx^*/dx)_{conj.}$ and obviously no government intervention is called for and free trade is optimal from a national point of view, since the first order conditions for national and the private firm's optima coincide.

Suppose both firms instead behave in a Cournot-Nash fashion. Then by definition $(dx^*/dx)_{conj.} = 0$ and obviously the first order conditions for a social optimum will not be attained without intervention. Consider an output tax at the rate t (negative value of t means a subsidy instead of a tax). Of course, with no domestic sales, an output tax is equivalent to an export tax. The profits of the firm now are $(1 - t)r(x, x^*) - c(x)$. The first order condition now becomes $(1 - t) r_1 - c_1 = 0$. The value of t such that the firm's first order condition is satisfied at socially optimum value of x is the optimal value of t. Comparison of the two first order conditions yields :

$$tr_1 = - r_2 \left(\frac{dx^*}{dx} \right)$$

or substituting for r_1 from the firm's first order condition and denoting (dx^*/dx) by g, one gets the optimal tax from :

$$\frac{tc_1}{1 - t} = - r_2 g$$

The actual or equilibrium response g of the foreign firm will depend on its behaviour given any intervention of the foreign government. Given Cournot behaviour, no foreign government intervention, and that the product sold by the two firms are substitutes so that $r_2 < 0$, the sign of t can be shown to be the same as that of r_{21}^* where $r^*(x, x^*)$ is the foreign firm's gross revenue function. If demand is linear then r_{21}^* is negative, though the negative sign obtains under other demand specifications as well. In such a case, the optimal intervention involves a subsidy rather than a tax.

The above analysis is illustrated in Figure 1 in which a set of iso-profit contours for the home firm are shown (in the absence of intervention). Under Cournot behaviour the firm's optimal behaviour is depicted by its reaction curve rr (shown here as a straight line) joining the peaks of the iso-profit curve (i e. the point at which home firm's profits are maximized given the foreign firm's sales). The intersection N of rr with the foreign firm's reaction curve r^*r^* describes the Cournot equilibrium. If the firm can take r^*r^* *as given* and maximize its profits, it will choose to produce at N^* where its iso-profit curve touches r^*r^*. This is the social-optimum. But the firm cannot credibly commit itself to produce at N^* because, *given* the foreign firm's *output at* N^*, the home firm will be better off producing at the point $\overline{N}$ on its reaction curve. Since the foreign firm knows this, mere announcement by the home firm that it will operate at N^* will not be credible. What the government intervention does is to shift the home firm's reaction curve to $r'r'$ so that it passes through N^*. Now N^* is credible because *it* is the home firm's optimal choice given the foreign

Imperfect Competition and International Trade   11

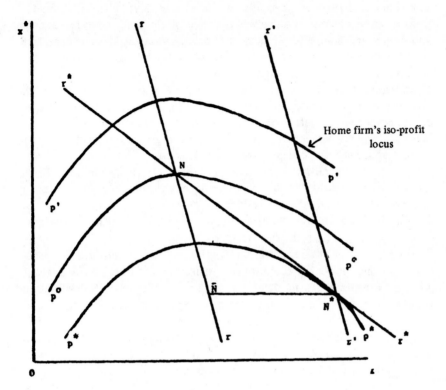

Fig. 1

firm's sale and government intervention.

Suppose now the behaviour of the two firms is price competition *a la* Bertrand. The home firm perceives a demand function $d(p, p^*)$ where p^* is the price charged by the foreign firm and it maximizes its profit $r = (1 - t) pd - c(d)$ assuming that the foreign firm keeps its price fixed. In this case the sign of the optimal value of t is the same as π^*_{21} where $\pi^*(p, p^*)$ is the foreign firms profit function, given that there is no foreign government intervention. If the two products are substitutes and marginal costs are increasing, then π^*_{21} can be shown to be *positive* (unless an increase in the rival's price has a significantly negative effect on the slope of the home firm's demand curve) so that an optimum *tax* rather than a subsidy is called for.

Eaton and Grossman also consider free entry[2], intervention by foreign

---

[2]The possibility of using entry-promoting and entry-detering strategies to ensure the success of home-country firms is analyzed by Dixit and Kyle (1985). Their analysis presumes a small group of identifiable firms and large profits in equilibrium to successful firms, thus making it largely irrelevant to developing countries.

government, multi-firm oligopoly instead of duopoly, as well allowing the product to be consumed at home. If the product sold is homogeneous and there are a sufficiently large number of identical firms in operation in a free entry equilibrium, profits are essentially zero and the profit shifting motive for intervention disappears. On the other hand, if for some reason, (say because of high fixed cost of entry), incumbent firms are earning profits while any potential entrant will earn negative profits, any intervention to shift profits will also promote entry. The entry costs incurred thereby will offset if not eliminate altogether the profits shifted. Be that as it may, for our purposes here, it is enough to note the extreme sensitivity of the policy conclusion (whether to intervene and if so, through a tax or subsidy) to the choice of assumptions regarding competition between the two firms. Besides the complexity in the real wo. ld of determining what in fact the firms assume about their rival's behaviour, (one could argue that the behaviour of oligopolistic firms is more likely to be one of implicit cooperation and collusion rather than non-cooperation as in these models), the implicit assumption in the above analysis (as in most optimal tax models) that the government has full information about each firm's (domestic and foreign) revenue and cost functions and their assumptions about each other's behaviour stretches one's credibility.

A brief reference needs to be made to the strategic use of Research and Development (R and D) expenditure in oligopolistic competition (Spencer and Brander, 1983; Dixit, 1985). The argument is illustrated in Figure 2 in which the output reaction curves of two firms (home and foreign) under Cournot behaviour are shown. The Cournot-Nash equilibrium is at N. R and D expenditure by either firm will lower its costs and shift its reaction curve outward. In the adsence of R and D expenditure by its rival, a firm will *increase its market share.* Given the foreign firm's reaction curve, the home firm's profits are maximized at N^*. But since N^* is not on its reaction curve, the home firm cannot credibly commit itself to N^*. Now subsidization of R and D by the government can shift the home-firm's reaction curve to pass through N^* and thus make it credible. R and D promotion thus shifts profits to the home firm. If entry to the industry is free but costly, as in the case of profit-shifting export taxes vs subsidies, entry may be encouraged by R and D subsidy thereby offsetting some of the shifted profits.

There is a further and perhaps more serious problem with this analysis. Dixit (1985) argues that research in high technology industries often resemble a winner-take-all race. Even, if one of the home firm wins the race with government subsidization of R and D by home firms, the resources used up by the losing firms have to be set off against the profits of the winner. Of course, if the government can pick the winner *ex ante* and exclude all others from entering the race, this loss can be avoided.

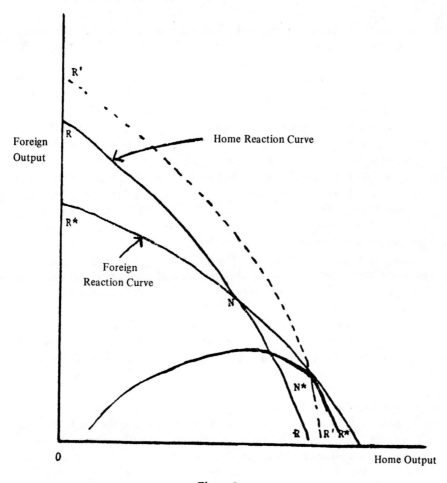

Figure 2

Even if it is politically feasible to exclude some firms, it is extremely implausible to assume that a government can pick certain winners *ex ante!*

Another avenue besides R and D expenditure, by which the domestic firm's costs can go down is through dynamic increasing returns through learning-by-doing. By limiting the sales of the foreign firm in the domestic market through tariffs or quotas, increases (reduces) the cumulative output of the domestic (foreign) firm. The result is a gain in the market share of the domestic firm, not only in the domestic markets, but also in all other markets in which the two firms compete whether or not the domestic firm enjoyed any protection in these markets. Thus, import protection, to use Krugman's words, serves as export promotion.

5. THE NEW TRADE THEORY AND DEVELOPING COUNTRIES

How relevant are the 'new' theoretical arguments of Section 2 in favour of an interventionist trade policy for the developing countries? To begin with, the traditional optimum tariff model as argued earlier is one in which a country has market power that is not perceived by price-taking domestic producers and consumers. In contrast, the oligopoly model of rent-extraction through trade policy instruments may appear relevant even if a country has no market power in the traditional sense. In other words, it can be argued that tariffs are the appropriate policy instruments even for an open economy that is 'small' in the traditional sense as long as there are some foreign firms earning rents in the home market through oligopolistic behaviour. Since most developing countries are 'small' and in many of them oligopolistic multi-national firms allegedly operate, some (e.g. Helleiner, 1985) see in this an activist role for governments in foreign trade.

The argument is illustrated in Figure 3 where, for simplicity, it is assumed that there is no home production of the importable, and the foreign firm's marginal cost curve $C_F C_F'$ is horizontal. With a downward sloping home demand curve DD (assumed to be linear for simplicity), in free trade the foreign firm will sell OQ_F (at a price OP_F) where marginal revenue equals marginal cost, thereby earning a monopoly rent equal to the area $P_F A_F B_F C_F$. Now, imposition of a specific tariff at the rate t shifts the cost curve up to $C_T C_T'$, reduces sales to OQ_T and raises prices to OP_T.

Given linearity of the demand curve, the rise in price is only $t/2$, i.e. only half the amount of the tariff, and the monopoly rent falls to $P_T A_T B_T C_T$. Thus, the tariff diverts rents to the home economy. However, the rise in price induced by the tariff cuts into the consumer surplus by increasing the wedge between marginal cost and consumer price. The home government can however achieve rent diversion as well as eliminate the wedge between marginal cost and consumer price by *subsidizing* imports by the amount s equaling $C_F C_s$, and charging the monopolist a lump sum fee (for the right to sell in home market) equaling the total subsidy cost. It can thereby ensure that the price in the home market equals the marginal cost OC_F, an outcome that occurs in a competitive market and that the entire monopoly rent is shifted to the home economy! Thus, two instruments, a lump sum tax and an import subsidy both optimally set, eliminate the wedge between marginal cost and consumer price due to monopoly as well as succeed in making the monopolist finance the subsidy he receives! While the logic of this argument is impeccable, whether many developing country governments are capable of designing and credibly implementing such a two-part tariff is open to

Imperfect Competition and International Trade   15

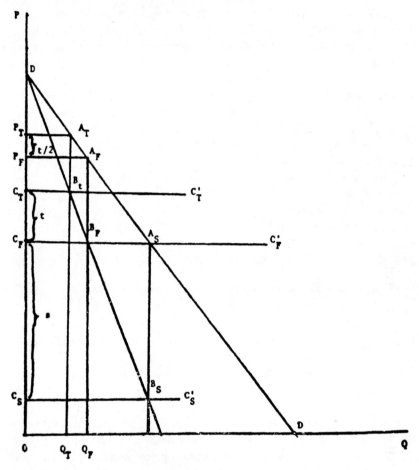

Figure 3

doubt, let alone the unrealism of the assumption that the foreign government will not respond to the home country's exercise of the two-part
tariff policy.

There are a number of other issues that arise in assessing profit shifting
arguments for trade policy (Krugman, 1986). First, even without intervention, a country that accounts only for a small share of the global
market of an oligopolistic firm may obtain concessions that the firm may
not offer to larger countries. In any case, a small country may be unable
to formulate and commit itself to a set policies specific to the market
structure in different commodities. Second, few small economies (in
terms of GNP) are home bases of multinational firms so that diversion
of rent in third markets from competitors to home firms through strategic trade policy is irrelevant.

Third, although Krugman is correct in suggesting that the new theory justifies marketing boards for centralizing purchases of *imports* so that the boards bargain with the oligopolies supplying imports to obtain price discounts that individual importers would be unable to obtain, the available evidence on the performance of such boards is not particularly encouraging. Even without the benefit of the analytical support offered by the new theory, some developing countries such as India had long ago canalized the imports of some commodities through state trading corporations. There is no strong evidence, however, that such canalization resulted in the realization of deep price discounts. Besides, as Krugman himself recognizes, the operation of such boards in the social interest presumes the existence of highly competent and honest bureaucrats at their helm. But in the real world, political patronage considerations often influence appointment of top officials of state enterprises. Instances of corruption and division of oligopolistic rents between import suppliers and the executives of the public sector trading companies are not rare either.

Apart from the issue of strategic trade policy in an environment of imperfect competition in world markets, there is the important policy question of the appropriateness of trade liberalization in the presence of increasing returns to scale and imperfect competition at home. Following Rodrick (1988a), consider the welfare impact of a small perturbation of an initial equilibrium. If $U(c_1, \ldots, c_n)$ denotes the home economy's Samuelson-type social utility function, the change in welfare dU from the perturbation equals $\Sigma U_i dc_i$ where U_i is the marginal utility of good i. Dividing by the positive marginal utility U_1 of good 1 and assuming consumer utility maximization subject to a budget constraint, one gets : $dU/U_1 = \Sigma p_i dc_i$ where p_i is the consumer price good i. By definition consumption c_i is the sum of domestic production Q_i and net imports M_i. Under balanced trade $\Sigma p_i^* M_i = 0$ where p_i^* is the world price of good i. For a small open economy p_i^* is fixed so that $\Sigma p_i^* dM_i = 0$. Now assuming the absence of scale economies, production efficiency and cost minimization, one gets $\Sigma q_i dQ_i = 0$, where q_i is the marginal cost of producing good i. Noting that $dc_i = dQ_i + dM_i$ after appropriate substitution, one obtains :

$$dU/U_1 = \Sigma(p_i - p_i^*) \, dc_i - \Sigma(q_i - p_i^*) \, dQ_i$$

From this it follows if in a protected (domestic) imperfectly competitive industry i, consumer price p_i and marginal cost q_i exceed world price p_i^*, then *expansion* of consumption c_i and *contraction* of domestic production Q_i will increase welfare, i.e. import liberalization will be welfare improving. This is an orthodox conclusion that clearly survives relaxing the orthodox assumption of pure competition at home. As has been documented in several studies, in many developing countries highly protected industries happen to be indeed the high cost ones relative to the rest of the world and as such the presence of domestic oligopolies alone is not a valid argument for ignoring the neo-classical principle of comparative advantage.

Introducing scale economies at home can alter the above conclusion since contraction of output in an industry with scale economies will increase its marginal costs thereby off-setting the gains from liberalization. The extent of this off-set is an empirical issue that depends on the precise nature of oligopolistic competition including conditions of entry and exit. Simulations by Rodrick (1988a) with data from three Turkish industries (automobile, tire and electrical appliance) under three alternative behavioural assumptions (mark-up pricing given demand elasticity, Cournot and collusion) and two entry assumptions (no entry and free entry) show that the potential for welfare-worsening trade liberalization exists only when entry and exit are precluded. Except in two of his eighteen simulations, trade liberalization in the form of a relaxation of import quota by 10% led to a *gain* in aggregate welfare (defined as the sum of consumer surplus, producer profits and quota rents). Welfare losses (of 0.3% and 0.5%) occurred in the electrical appliances industry when behaviour was not collusive and entry and exit were precluded. In all other cases welfare gain ranged from a low of 0.6% to a high of 9.2%. In computing these welfare changes it is assumed that quota rents are distributed in a lump sum fashion thereby assuming away resource using rent seeking. As Rodrick correctly notes, the rent seeking may dissipate the gains from *partial liberalization* since import quotas are being *reduced* rather than being *eliminated* in such an exercise. An important implication of the simulations is that liberalization is unlikely to be welfare worsening when nominal protection rates exceed 25%, a situation very common in developing countries. If this conclusion turns to be robust with respect to changes in modeling, parameter values, and data, conventional wisdom that trade liberalization will be welfare improving will survive the introduction of imperfect competition at home. Be that as it may, the real point, as many analysts of the traditional persuasion and Rodrick himself have noted, is that the domestic imperfect market structure is in fact the creation of domestic industrial and trade policies. Once created, if it resists removal, it limits the gains from future trade liberalization. This is an issue that has been of interest to analysts of the political economy of trade liberalization.

The neo-infant industry argument for protection[2], that is, import unlikely to have domestic markets for high technology products, large
enough for this argument for protection to be of any significance.

Even if we assume that there is a large domestic market and there is
learning by doing, it still does not necessarily follow that strategic infant
industry protection is appropriate. As Baldwin (1988) points out that
for such protection to be beneficial, the dynamic decline in marginal
costs due to learning effect must continue till the end of product life and
in his view, very few industries meet this necessary condition. Be that
as it may, it was possible for a developing country, such as Korea, to
enter late and survive in a high-technology industry (computer memory
chips without the help of any subsidy or trade restricting policy (Yoon,
1988). On the other hand, the empirical exercise in Baldwin (1988) relating to the Barzilian entry (EMB–120) in the market for 30-40 seater
aircraft in competition with a Swedish (SF–340) and Candian (Dash-8)
showed that a subsidy would be needed for the enterprise to break even
(i.e. have zero present value of profits). In order to justify the subsidy
the value of added learning by the workers in the project has to be at
least $1500 per year per worker for the twenty year project life. Baldwin
finds this figure to be high, though not totally implausible. As he readily
acknowledges, this calculation involves assigning values for several
parameters and only a market test of the worth of the learning experience of the worker will settle the issue. Thus, protection may be neither
necessary, as in the Korean semiconductor case, nor cost effective if
needed and provided, as in the Brazilian aircraft example, for a developing country to break into high-technology product exports.

Krugman (1986) suggests that while the substantial differences in factor
endowments between the developed and the developing countries will
continue to influence the pattern of trade between the two groups along
traditional lines of comparative advantage, to the extent investment in
non-traded infrastructure is necessary for engaging in *trade*, increasing
returns in the provision of infrastructure bring an element of arbitrari-
ness into the pattern of comparative advantage depending on which

---

[2]Rodrick (1988a) claims that "Indeed, by focusing on learning effects, the new
literature has provided some of the best arguments for infant-industry protection since
Alexander Hamilton and Friedrich List." This is an exaggerated claim. After all,
traditional argument for infant industry protection was based on 'market failure' due
to increasing returns arising from technology or from learning effects (for example,
see Bardhan (1970), ch. 7). In any case, the experience in many developing countries
over the last four decades suggests that the so-called infants industries rarely grow to
adulthood when they are supposed to be internationally competitive without protection
suggesting that the learning effects, if any, were exaggerated.

countries succeed in making the required investment in infrastructure. It will also open the door for the strategic use of policies to encourage such investment. A small investment subsidy by one country can tilt comparative advantage in its favour in the absence of an activist policy by other countries.

Dixit (1985a) also finds analogous "knife-edge" result in R and D expenditures : even a small policy created advantage to firms in one country can eliminate R and D expenditures altogether by its competitors. Krugman points out that in his model countries are likely to engage in a non-cooperative subsidy war that will end up in their duplicating infrastructural facilities and dissipating any profits that they could have shifted from their rivals. Dixit also cautions against the social desirability of policy created advantage to home firms pointing out that the promotion of one country's dominance through R and D will turn out to be economically costly. In any case, the R and D based argument is unlikely to be relevant for many developing countries. Even if there are any for which it is conceivably relevant, unless the government can pick the winning industries and firms *ex ante* with certainty and exclude others, such countries will gain little from intervention.

Ever since the work of Denison, Kendrick, Solow and others it is well known, though not universally accepted, that in developed countries the observed growth in total output over a long period the proportion explained by growth in inputs conventionally measured is a third or less. The unexplained residual is often called, without any independent evidence, technical progress or growth in total factor productivity (TFP). The residual has been computed for several developing countries, at the aggregate as well as at sectoral levels. Pack (1988a, 1988b) provides a useful survey and critical discussion of these estimates. Some have claimed, with some suggestive though not necessarily conclusive empirical support that an outward-oriented development strategy (i.e. a strategy that provides similar incentives for earning foreign exchange through exports or saving foreign exchange through import substitution or even a strategy biased towards export promotion will promote faster growth in TFP. More careful analysts have noted that there is no *a priori* reason why an import-substituting regime should lead to less TFP growth than an outward-oriented regime.

In their study of India's foreign trade regime, Bhagwati and Srinivasan (1975) went into this issue in some detail analytically and empirically. After pointing out why conventional methodology of estimating TFP may be particularly misleading in restrictive trading environment, they attempted to find out through a survey of firms in the chemical and engineering industries whether the export-oriented industries were characterized by greater research and development expenditures compared to the domestic-market-oriented industries. They found little support for the hypothesis that export orientation would lead to differentially higher technical change. They concluded that "(a) that the import subsitution strategy does not eliminate the incentive to conduct research and development but merely imparts a bias toward conducting it in a different direction, so that the really important question then is not whether it is eliminated by the import substitution strategy but rather whether the kind induced by such a strategy reduces or increases welfare in relation to the research and development that would otherwise be conducted; and (b) that orientation toward export markets does not in itself seem to increase the incentive to conduct research and development, so that it is difficult to sustain the argument that an export promotion strategy is superior to an import substitution strategy because it will lead to greater (and presumably welfare-increasing) research and development in the economy" (Bhagwati and Srinivasan (1975) pp. 221-222).

The determinants of technical progress are not well understood even in developed countries. Also empirical support for the Schumpeterian hypothesis relating imperfect market structure (particularly monopolistic structure) with greater innovation appears weak. It is not therefore surprising that there is inconclusive evidence from developing countries in favour of the contrary (i.e. to the Schumpeterian view) hypothesis that greater competition from imports to domestic production and from other exporters in world markets brought about through an outward oriented strategy will result in faster TFP growth. Rodrick (1988b) analyzes this issue from the perspective of the new trade theory. Unsurprisingly he concludes that "we do not have any good reason to expect that trade liberalization will generally be helpful to overall technological performance." While his observation that "the arguments for following sensible macroeconomic policies—are too often confused for arguments on behalf of trade liberalization"—is well taken, it is also the case that following fairly sensible macro policies is not a substitute for providing sensible micro incentive structures. The Indian economic policy regime is a prime example of providing terribly distorted micro incentives while pursuing cautious and sensible macropolicies.

6. CONCLUSION

The discussion in Sections 2-5 clearly suggests that the recent theories of oligopolistic competition and increasing returns do not provide unequivocal analytical support for the exercise of an interventionist trade policy by developing countries. At any rate, they do not contradict the presumption that outward-oriented policies that promote competition and efficiency will be beneficial. Indeed, given that concentration in industry and oligopolistic behaviour by *firms* in the *domestic market* have often been *created* by the set of policies pursued as part of the import-substituting industrialization, it is not profit diversion from foreign, but the promotion of competition to and improvement in the efficiency of the operation of domestic firms, that is important. Indeed, as Krugman (1986) emphasizes, "there is nothing in the theory so far that would restore intellectual respectability to the strategy of import substitution. *Import substituting industrialization strategy looks even worse in the new theory than in the standard theory*" (emphasis added). It will be a pity that the lessons learnt in a hard way from the failure of such a strategy in so many developing countries are forgotten in the vain expectation that the new theory will resurrect and improve it.

REFERENCES

Bhagwati, J. N. and Srinivasan, T. N. (1975). *Foreign Trade Regimes and Economic Development : India*, National Bureau of Economic Research, Columbia University Press, New York.

Brander, J. A. (1981). Intra-Industry Trade in Identical Commodities, *Journal of International Economics* Vol. 11, 1-14.

_____and Krugman, P. R. (1983). A Reciprocal Dumping Model of International Trade, *Journal of International Economics* Vol. 15, 313-321.

_____and Spencer, B. J. (1981). Tariffs and the Extraction of Foreign Monopoly Rents Under Potential Entry, *Canadian Journal of Economics* Vol. 14, 371-389.

_____and _____ (1985). Export Subsidies and International Market Share Rivalry, *Journal of International Economics* Vol. 18, 83-100.

Bresnahan, T. F. (1981). Duopoly Models with Consistent Conjectures, *American Economic Review* Vol. 71, 934-945.

Dixit, A. K. (1984). International Trade Policy for Oligopolistic Industries, *Economic Journal*, Supplement 1, 16.

_____(1985). The Cutting Edge of International Technological Competition, Department of Economics, Princeton University (processed).

_____(1987). Strategic Aspects of Trade Policy. *In* Truman F. Bewley (ed.), *Advances in Economic Theory*, Chapter 9, pp. 329-362, Cambridge University Press, Cambridge.

_____and Kyle, A. S. (1985c). The Use of Protection and Subsidies for Entry Promotion and Deterrence, *American Economic Review* Vol. 75, 139-152.

Eaton, J. and Grossman, G. (1986). Optimal Trade and Industrial Policy Under Oligopoly, *Quarterly Journal of Economics*, 383-406.

Graham, F. (1923). Some Aspects of Protection Further Considered, *Quarterly Journal of Economics*, Vol. 37, 199-227.

Grandmont, J. M. and McFadden, D. (1972). A Technical Note on Classical Gains from Trade, *Journal of International Economics*, Vol. 2, 109-125.

Grubel, A. G. and Lloyd, P. J. (1975). *Intra-Industry Trade*, Macmillan, London.

22   T. N. SRINIVASAN

Helleiner, G. (1985). Industrial Organization, Trade and Investment : A Selective
    Literature Review for Developing Countries, paper presented at a conference on
    Industrial Organization, Trade and Investment in North America : *Mexico,
    Canada and the USA*, Merida, Mexico.

Helpman, E. (1981). International Trade in the Presence of Product Differentiation,
    Economies of Scale and Monopolistic Competition : A Chamberlinian-Hecks-
    cher-Ohlin Approach, *Journal of International Economics*, Vol. 11, 304-340.

_____ and Krugman, P. (1985). *Increasing Returns, Imperfect Competition and the
    International Economy*, M.I.T. Press, Cambridge.

Horstmann, I. and Markusen, J. R. (1986). Up the Average Cost Curve : Inefficient
    Entry and the New Protectionism, *Journal of International Economics*, Vol.
    20, 225-248.

Kierzkowski, H., ed. (1984). *Monopolistic Competition and International Trade*,
    Oxford, London.

Krugman, P. (1979). Increasing Returns, Monopolistic Competition and Interna-
    tional Trade, *Journal of International Economics*, Vol. 9, 469-479.

_____ (1980). Scale Economies, Product Differentiation and the Pattern of Trade,
    American Economic Review, Vol. 70, 950-959.

_____ (1981). Intra-industry Specialization and the Gains from Trade, *Journal of
    Political Economy*, Vol. 89, 959-973.

_____, ed. (1986). *Strategic Trade Policy of the New International Economics*, M.I.T.
    Press, Cambridge.

_____ (1986). New Trade Theory and the Less Developed Countries. *In* G. Calvo,
    J. DeMacedo, R. Findlay and P. Kouri (eds.), *Debt, Stabilization and Develop-
    ment* : *Essays in Memory of Carlos Diaz Alejandro*, Basil Blackwell (forthcom-
    ing), London.

Krugman, P. (1987). Increasing Returns and the Theory of International Trade. *In* T.
    Bewley (ed.), *Advances in Economic Theory*, Ch. 8, 301-328, Cambridge Univer-
    sity Press, Cambridge.

Markusen, J. R. and Venables, A. J. (1986). Trade Policy with Increasing Returns
    and Imperfect Competition : Contradictory Results from Competing Assump-
    tions, Working Paper No. 8619C, The Centre for the Study of International
    Economic Relations, University of Western Ontario, London, Canada.

Pack, H. (1988a). Industrialization and Trade. *In* H. B. Chenery and T. N. Srinivasan
    (eds.), *Handbook of Development Economics*, pp. 333-380, North-Holland,
    Amsterdam.

_____ (1988b). Learning and Productivity Change in Developing Countries, paper
    prepared for the WIDER conference on New Trade Theories and Industrializa-
    tion in the Developing Countries, Helsinki, August 2-5.

Rodrick, D. (1988a). Imperfect Competition, Scale Economies, and Trade Policy in
    Developing Countries. *In* Robert E. Baldwin (ed.), *Trade Policy Issues and
    Empirical Analysis*, The University of Chicago Press, forthcoming, Chicago and
    London.

_____ (1988b). Closing the Productivity Gap : Does Trade Liberalization Really
    Help?, revised version of the paper prepared at the WIDER conference on New
    Trade Theories and Industrialization in the Developing Countries, Helsinki,
    August 2-5.

Imperfect Competition and International Trade   23

Spencer, B. and Brander, J. (1983). International R & D Rivalry and Industrial Strategy, *Review of Economic Studies* Vol. 50, 707-722.

Stewart, F. (1984). Recent Theories of International Trade : Some Implications for the South, Ch. 6 in H. Kierzkowski (1985), *op. cit.*

Yoon, C. H. (1988). International Competition and Market Penetration : A Model of the Growth Strategy of the Korean Semiconductor Industry, paper prepared for the WIDER conference on New Trade Theories and Industrialization in the Developing Countries, Helsinki, August 2-5.

[18]

Exchange Control, Liberalization, and Economic Development

By Jagdish N. Bhagwati and Anne O. Krueger*

For the past three years, the National Bureau of Economic Research (*NBER*) has been sponsoring a research project on exchange control, liberalization, and economic development. In this project, a number of country studies have been undertaken, focusing upon the quantification and analysis of individual developing countries' experiences with exchange control regimes and attempts at liberalizing those regimes, focusing equally on the interaction between the country's trade and payments regime and its economic development.

The countries studied have included Brazil (A. Fishlow), Chile (J. Behrman), Colombia (C. Diaz-Alejandro), Egypt (B. Hansen), Ghana (C. Leith), India (J. Bhagwati and T. N. Srinivasan), Israel (M. Michaely), South Korea (C. Frank, Jr.), the Philippines (R. Baldwin), and Turkey (A. Krueger). Each study has been undertaken within an analytical framework devised by us and agreed upon in advance by all participants. These studies are now completed or nearly so, and they are to be published by the National Bureau of Economic Research through 1973 and 1974. They should be of interest to students of the individual countries as well as to those concerned with trade and development issues more generally. When all the studies are final, we shall have a great deal of material for analysis on a comparable basis of different countries' experiences.

* Professors of economics at Massachusetts Institute of Technology and the University of Minnesota, respectively.

The final stage of the *NBER* project consists of our attempt to synthesize the results of the individual studies in an overall volume. This paper represents a preliminary report on some of these results. We therefore present an overview of some of the major topics in Section I. In Section II, some of the more detailed results pertaining to the effects of exchange control regimes are presented.

I. An Overview

For each country covered by the Bureau project, individual researchers were asked to trace their country's experience with a view to identifying: (1) when and why exchange control was adopted, and how the control regime was intended to relate to the country's domestic economic goals; (2) the evolution of quantitative restrictions after their initial imposition; (3) efforts, if any, to ameliorate the undesired results of the payments regime; (4) experiences with attempts at liberalization and the timing of the economy's response to those attempts; and (5) the resource-allocational, income-distributional, and growth effects of the country's experience. Within that framework, each country's author singled out for in-depth analysis a particular point in time during which the detailed working of the exchange-control regime was analyzed, and selected one liberalization effort for intensive analysis.

On the basis of the results from individual studies to date, we have been surprised at the degree of similarity among seemingly diverse countries. On each topic, certain broad conclusions have emerged.

Motivation for Quantitative Restrictions (QR)-Regimes

Initial adoption of exchange controls was generally an *ad hoc* response to external events. Rapidly, however, quantitative restrictions were perceived as a means of furthering domestic industrialization policies. Whether it was the rapid shift in international market conditions during the 1952–1954 period or memories of the Great Depression, most policy makers were pessimistic—probably to an objectively unwarranted degree—about prospects for growth through industrialization based upon export growth and diversification. The optimal resource allocation dictum—that the marginal cost of earning foreign exchange should be equated with the marginal cost of saving foreign exchange—was generally abandoned in favor of saving foreign exchange at all costs.

In the process of using exchange control to foster the growth of domestic industry, however, the internal working of the QR systems generally frustrated, at least partially, the very domestic goals they were designed to achieve. Bureaucratic allocational procedures, political pressures surrounding the administration of controls, and the private sector response to the unintended incentives created by the regimes led to frustration of the goals the QR regimes were designed to serve. We shall return to more detailed examination of the logic of QR systems in Section II.

Export Promotion Versus Import Substitution

Among the more interesting results that appear to emerge from our preliminary analysis of individual countries' experience is that countries which have had export-oriented development strategies appear, by and large, to have intervened virtually as much and as "chaotically" on the side of promoting new exports as other countries have on the side of import substitution. Yet, the economic cost of incentives distorted toward export promotion appears to have been less than the cost of those distorted toward import substitution, and the growth performance of the countries oriented toward export promotion appears to have been more satisfactory than that of the import-substitution oriented countries. If that conclusion is valid, the lesson is that policy should err on the side of allowing a higher marginal cost for earning than for saving foreign exchange.

There are several theoretical reasons which would explain such an asymmetry in outcomes, and the empirical evidence does point in their direction. In theory, there are four reasons why export promotion may be the superior strategy.

(1) Generally speaking, the costs of excess export promotion are more visible to policymakers than are those of import substitution. If there are departures from unified exchange rates, export-promoting growth can be sustained only by subsidies or other incentives costly to the government budget. Thus, there are built-in forces within the government against excessive export subsidization and promotion. The equivalent costs of import substitution are borne by firms and consumers and, hence, no obvious intragovernmental pressure group emerges as rapidly when incentives are biased toward import substitution.

(2) An export-oriented development strategy generally entails relatively greater use of indirect, rather than direct, interventions. There is considerable evidence from the individual country studies that direct intervention may be considerably more costly than is generally recognized (see Section II below). When policy makers are concerned with export promotion, direct controls cannot be as pervasive as they can be under import sub-

stitution. Price controls, distribution controls, and a host of other detailed interventions make little sense, even to bureaucrats, when firms' outputs are intended largely for overseas markets, but appear attractive when production is oriented toward the home market under import substitution. The fact that, under import substitution, government officials have power to remove or enhance domestic monopoly positions of import-competing firms implies that those firms can be induced to accept otherwise intolerable (and socially unprofitable) interventions with their decisions. By contrast, officials simply do not have the same degree of power over firms engaged primarily in the export market.

(3) Exporting firms, however much they may be sheltered on the domestic market, must face price and quality competition in international markets. Import-substituting producers, with no competition for domestic markets, are a pervasive fact of life in the developing countries where import substitution has been stressed. While there is little hard evidence on the subject, there is considerable reason to believe that sheltered monopoly positions may be important explanations of low productivity growth in the newly established manufacturing industries in developing countries. Insofar as the adverse side effects of inadequate competition are less severe under the export-oriented strategy, it may be that export promotion is superior simply because it reduces the incidence of the problem.

(4) If there are significant indivisibilities or economies of scale, an export-oriented strategy will enable firms of adequate size to realize them. When import-substituting incentives dominate the domestic market, import-substituting firms generally are confronted with powerful incentives for expansion through diversification; each new product line provides one more domestic monopoly position. If indivisibilities and/or economies to scale are important, an export-oriented strategy will provide better incentives for expansion of capacity in existing lines. As such, an export-oriented growth strategy is better suited to achieving whatever economies of scale are present than is an import-substitution strategy where firms are generally limited in their horizons by the size of the domestic market.

These and other arguments supporting the case for an asymmetrical behavior of the export-promoting *versus* import-substituting economies appear to be borne out by the contrast in the success of South Korea and the relative failure of India, for example, in the countries studied in the project. Since approximately 1960, the economic policies of South Korea have been heavily oriented toward growth through exporting. The rate of growth of exports has been almost double that of real *GNP*. Close inspection of South Korean policies indicates that the kinds of detailed and chaotic interventions which we have found in other countries are abundantly present in Korea's case as well: numerous *QR*'s, high tariffs, and physical targeting of exports and imports. The striking difference, however, is in the remarkable degree to which the government has been willing to use exchange-rate changes and to lean in favor of export promotion *via* preferential allocation of import licenses, etc. Thus, aside from other special factors, such as the high inflow of foreign resources (official and private), the one striking aspect of Korean success has clearly been the significantly less discrimination against exports than in other developing countries, and *not* (it would appear) the presence of a neoclassically efficient allocation mechanism *in toto* in the system.

Whether this asymmetry between export promotion and import substitution is important or not awaits further exploration as the final results of the country studies emerge. What is clear is that, of the countries which have stressed export promotion, none have been free from interventions of the type that economists generally identify with *QR* regimes and import-substitution strategies, and that the export-promotion strategies generally appear to have higher payoffs.

Nominal Versus Effective Devaluation

Export rebates, tariffs, surcharges, import entitlement schemes, and a host of other devices are generally employed under *QR* regimes, and they lead to a wide dispersion in effective exchange rates (the amount of domestic currency paid when a good is landed per dollar of c.i.f. value) by commodity categories. Moreover, the increasing resort to changes in surcharges and export subsidies and to alterations in effective exchange rates means that, even without a formal devaluation, there are many degrees of partial devaluation in *QR* regimes.

Usually, formal devaluation is accompanied by the partial or total removal of export incentives and surcharges upon imports. The result is that changes in the parity, as reported by the International Monetary Fund, do not necessarily provide a good indication of the economically relevant magnitude of the devaluation. Thus, in Egypt, Bent Hansen's study shows that the 1962 devaluation was little more than a tidying up operation: complicated export bonuses and import charges were replaced by across-the-board measures, so that the average local currency payments and receipts per dollar of international transactions increased by only one-fourth the amount of nominal devaluation. For Chile, Jere Behrman's study shows effective devaluations to be about two-thirds the nominal ones in 1959 and 1963. By contrast, when Chile adopted

frequent exchange-rate adjustments in the late 1960's, the effective devaluations slightly exceeded the nominal, although real devaluation was much smaller.

Determinants of Success of Liberalization

Because of the significant differences in practice between nominal and effective devaluation, we believe that it is important, under *QR*-regimes, to distinguish between devaluation and liberalization.

Liberalization may be said to occur when the official price of foreign exchange assumes an increased role in the allocation of resources, whereas devaluation occurs whenever nominal exchange rates are altered. Thus, as illustrated by Egypt's 1962 episode, it is possible to have a devaluation in which the altered nominal price of foreign exchange has little or no effect on resource allocation, and quantitative restrictions and other direct interventions maintain their importance as allocative instruments. In other cases, such as the Turkish devaluation of 1958 and the Indian devaluation of 1966, the devaluations more than offset the reductions and removals of surcharges, taxes, and export premia. In those circumstances, the official price of foreign exchange increased in importance as an allocator of scarce foreign exchange, at least in the short run.

The difference between nominal and effective devaluations has the important effect that, as happened with the 1966 Indian devaluation, the criteria by which the devaluation is judged are typically confused; and the "rationalization" implicit in shifting from a *de facto* to a *de jure* devaluation (resulting in no effective devaluation) is ignored and the nominal devaluation is assessed as though it was also the effective devaluation.

The studies also point up a number of interesting conclusions regarding the likelihood of effective devaluations leading to *continued* increases in the allocative function of the price of foreign exchange. A few vignettes are worth pointing out here. (1) Starting from the long exposure to automatic protection under the QR-regime, few industries will accept the consequence of effective devaluation and reduced reliance on QR's; namely, the need to compete or contract. As Michaely's study of Israel and the Bhagwati-Srinivasan analysis of the 1966 Indian episode show clearly, liberalization works only insofar as imports of noncompetitive goods are involved, and the degree of protection to import-using industries may even increase as imported intermediates get liberalized. (2) The effect of liberalization is often to induce a recessionary tendency rather than the traditionally feared inflationary impact. The recessionary impact follows from governments typically trying to contract monetary and fiscal policy, while ignoring the fact that the devaluation itself sets up endogenous recessionary tendencies. These come from several sources: (a.) the excess of imports over exports, thanks to influx of aid and private capital, itself implies deflation with devaluation; (b.) the increased imports of materials can lead to increased output and lowered profit margins and may adversely affect investment in the import-competing activities whereas the exporters may not push up investment in time because they expect the increased export incentives to be neutralized *or* the system remains so loaded against exports that exporters find it difficult to increase their investments sufficiently; and (c.) as in Turkey, the initial effect of an effective devaluation seems at times to be to reduce construction activity, with adverse effects (at least in the short run) on employment and income.

Payments Regimes and Economic Growth

The determinants of a developing country's overall growth rate are numerous, and the payments regime is only one such factor. The interaction between the payments regime and economic growth is complex and depends upon a host of other factors in individual countries.

That the effects of the payments regime on growth cannot be analyzed without regard to other aspects of the domestic economy cannot be stressed enough. Clark Leith's findings on Ghana provide a good illustration. Its major export, cocoa, is almost unaffected by the payments regime directly. The price paid to producers is determined by the Cocoa Board and is independent of the exchange rate. On the import side, government control over credit allocation under credit rationing, combined with severe capital market imperfections, means that the demand for imports is more a function of government policies in the credit market than it is of the price of foreign exchange. All new investment projects must be approved by the government, which has power to grant or withhold subsidies and other privileges large enough to make the difference between profit and loss on virtually all investment projects. Under such circumstances, it would be folly to analyze the payments regime as if entrepreneurs were responding in perfect markets to price signals alone. This is not to say that the payments regime does not have its own effects upon resource allocation and growth, but rather that analysis of those effects is considerably more complex than is generally assumed. The individual country studies and our forthcoming synthesis explore these interactions in some detail.

II. The Anatomy of Quantitative Restrictions

Tariffs Versus Quotas

It is always true that every quota has a nonnegative tariff equivalent at each point in time for every recipient of an import license. However, it is not always the case that there is a single tariff-equivalent for a quota for a given homogeneous import commodity, and it is generally false that the resource-allocational effects of a quota are the same as those of the tariff-equivalent even when there is a single tariff-equivalent.

The reason why there may not be a single tariff-equivalent for the import of a homogeneous commodity is that resale of imports is often illegal. In that case, there is no reason to expect a common implicit domestic price in the absence of a perfect and costless black market. Thus, the criteria for allocation and the actual detailed bureaucratic decisions as to who should receive an import license, and how much each should receive, will in general affect resource allocation.

Even when there is a single domestic price for the imported good, the method of license allocation makes an important difference to resource allocation and income distribution. It is useful to think of the differences between the c.i.f. price of the good (at the nominal exchange rate) and the domestic price as consisting of two parts: (1) the duties, surcharges, and other costs of landing paid by the actual importer, including his normal costs of foregone interest, handling, and so on; and (2) the premium accruing to the recipient of the import license. The local currency cost of the c.i.f. import plus the first item equals landed cost. Landed cost in local currency divided by the c.i.f. price in foreign currency equals the effective exchange rate. Landed cost is then the price that would prevail in the domestic market if there were no QR's upon the import. The premium, therefore, is the windfall gain accruing to the recipient of an import license.

The precise allocation of import licenses makes for important differences because it determines *who* will receive the premium; we note two here. (1) If licenses for intermediate goods imports are allocated directly to producers, these producers are

implicitly being subsidized in their production process. A devaluation would increase the costs of the manufacturers using the intermediate good. If, however, licenses are allocated to importers who then resell to the manufacturers, the premium accrues to the importers. If devaluation is then carried out, there will be no effect on manufacturers' costs unless the size of the devaluation exceeds the size of the premium. (2) The calculation of effective protection again must allow for the fact that some imports would be obtained directly by producers at premium-exclusive prices and others at premium-inclusive prices. The resulting estimates of protection can be significantly different than if no adjustment was made for the indirect allocation of imports of intermediates to producers, as illustrated for example by the Bhagwati-Srinivasan study of India.

That the distinction between premium and landed cost is important can be seen by inspection of Turkish data for 1968 presented in Krueger's study. At an official exchange rate of $TL\ 9 = \$1$, it appeared that the average landed cost of $\$1$ of imports was $TL\ 23.8$ and the premium was $TL\ 23.1$.

Logic of QR's

Once a QR regime is established, it seems to have an internal, self-contradictory logic all its own. The tariff equivalent of existing quotas tends to fluctuate widely and the unintended side effects of QR's tend to force other changes. Decision makers do not receive visible feedbacks as to the effects of their actions. Thus, one finds quota categories where the quotas are redundant and there is a zero premium side by side with quota applications exceeding the amount of the quota by exorbitant multiples. Yet these multiples provide little information to those allocating quotas, because the amount of applications is itself influenced by expectations as to the probable disparity between the amount applied for and the amount received.

But that is only a small part of the story. For, once a QR regime is established, quotas inevitably become a tool seized upon by governments to accomplish a host of purposes other than the initial one of restraining *ex ante* payments imbalances. Thus, "priorities" are established and preferential treatment is given to applicants willing to further an officially desired goal. For example, efforts are generally made to encourage capital goods imports at the expense of consumer goods imports, in the hope of accelerating the rate of investment. In turn, the newly established manufacturing capacity often has intermediate goods import "requirements" which can be met only at the cost of reducing capital goods imports, thus defeating the initial purpose of the priority. Moreover, in increasing capital goods imports, consumer goods imports are the first to go, and the production structure of the domestic economy becomes increasingly oriented toward consumer goods.

Once that happens, growth in investment becomes increasingly dependent upon expansion of imports, itself a function of export growth. Yet the protection afforded to producers in domestic markets by QR's is so great that profitability lies in expanding domestic sales and disincentives to export increase. By this point, governments are trapped: if they devalue the currency (which could have been done in the first place as an alternative to QR's), they fear that the rate of capital formation will decline as capital goods become more expensive. If they do not devalue the currency, they must resort to *ad hoc* measures such as export rebates, import entitlement schemes for exporters, and the like in order to stimulate export growth. As these "incentives" grow over time, the regime becomes increasingly piecemeal. In virtually

all the countries studied in the project which have had QR systems, governments themselves have reacted against these undesired side effects and proliferation of special regulations that seem to result from QR systems.

The tendency toward increasingly detailed, often internally inconsistent, controls and the resulting frustration of initial intentions shows up in numerous ways. In India, a major goal was the reduction of concentration in economic power, which presumably meant reducing the share of the large industrial concerns in industrial output. Yet the regulations and procedures surrounding licensing applications (for investment and for imports) became so complex that the large firms had a strong competitive advantage in satisfying license requirements: their share actually increased. In Turkey, import licenses were granted to establish assembly industries in the expectation that those (import-substitution) industries would save foreign exchange and provide incentives for domestic production of parts and components. Instead, people invested in the assembly industries in order to earn import licenses, and the value of licenses for assembly industry requirements of intermediate goods increased, rather than decreased, during the 1960's, while domestic content requirements had to be employed to induce investments in parts-and-components producing activities.

Wide Variations in Economic Costs

When producers know that they will benefit from complete protection from imports once domestic productive capacity is established, there are powerful profitability incentives to establish capacity regardless of the social opportunity costs of so doing. The drive to industrialize has been such an important goal that few of the countries covered in the Project have been able to resist using QR's to provide those incentives. In India and Turkey, goods have simply become ineligible for importation once domestic productive capacity was established. In Egypt and Ghana, the same thing happened *de facto*. In Brazil, the Law of Similars, combined with domestic content requirements, and a provision that tariff rates be doubled once domestic production started, achieved the same result.

It is easily predictable that under such systems the variation in domestic resource cost among and within industries will be great. One of the purposes of the country studies was to quantify the extent of this variation, and the results show remarkably wide differences. We do *not* find that all import-substitution firms are inefficient. On the contrary, some appear to have very low costs while others require a large multiple of all resources in order to save an equal amount of foreign exchange.

In view of this, a major defect of the QR system seems to be its inevitably indiscriminate nature. If, within such a system, low-cost activities could be differentially encouraged, the excess costs of the system should be significantly lower. Yet, the workings of the system seem invariably to result in an inability to reflect differentials in social profitability to individual decision makers.

Actual User Licensing

We have already shown that the allocation of import licenses to firms using imported goods in their production process has different resource-allocational implications from those that arise when premia on licenses accrue to individuals who then resell to actual users. One feature of most QR systems is that they have tended to become increasingly actual-user oriented, and the fraction of import licenses allocated directly to user firms has increased over time.

The motive for this method of allocation seems reasonable enough: it is designed to avoid allowing large windfall gains to accrue to persons who apparently do nothing but apply for import licenses and, in addition, it rewards those individuals who have contributed toward the industrialization goal, as well as providing an implicit subsidy for recipient firms.

Difficulty, however, arises from the fact that criteria for allocation of licenses among actual users are needed in the presence of excess demand. Without such criteria, the allocating officials are naturally accused of favoritism. The most frequently adopted criterion has been to allocate licenses to recipients in proportion to different firms' capacities, although almost all countries have made provisions whereby new entrants would be entitled to an initial allocation.

This allocational criterion has had two closely interrelated and deleterious side effects: (1) it has, predictably enough, encouraged the development of excess capacity, and (2) it has resulted in roughly proportionate expansion of all firms in a given industry with little competition between them.

Turning to excess capacity first, in many newly established industries, firms' output levels are determined, within fairly narrow limits, by the volume of imports they obtain. Hence, summing over firms within an industry, the industry's output is closely tied to the imports of intermediate goods allocated to it. The fact that there are excess profits to most firms at that level of output is reflected by the premium on import licenses: any individual firm could increase its total profit if it obtained more imports.

The only way to get more imports, however, is to expand capacity, since one's import rights are a function of his share in total capacity of the industry. Thus, even with existing excess capacity, it may pay to build more, since the return on the investment is the premium to be earned per unit of imports times the expected increment in import licenses.

When policy makers perceive this result, a natural response is to attempt to control the expansion of capacity. Then, investment licensing follows import licensing. Again, criteria are needed and the circle has one more twist: profitability cannot be used as a criterion, since it emanates from import-licensing procedures, and also is regarded with suspicion (the bureaucrats are rewarding the already rich large firms). Thus, the natural temptation is to allow expansion proportionately over all applicants or over all firms. Decisions about the relative rates at which different industries shall be expanded must then be made and private profitability departs further and further from social profitability.

This brings us to the effect of import, and investment, licensing upon competition. For those industries where a firm's imports determine its output, the firm-specific allocation of imports determines market shares. With output fixed in the short run, there is little competition among firms. If there were no investment licensing, it might be that more profitable firms would expand more, with higher equilib-

rium levels of excess capacity in the long run. In general, however, investment licensing rules out even that form of competition, perhaps diminishing excess capacity, but insuring the growth of efficient and inefficient firms alike. We spoke earlier of the asymmetries of export promotion and import substitution. It may well be that, in dynamic terms, the inability of QR systems to foster relatively more rapid growth of more efficient firms is one of the gravest drawbacks of the QR-import-substitution development pattern.

III. Concluding Remarks

We have only been able to scratch the surface of the results of the *NBER* project. Many of the statements we have made require, and indeed have, careful documentation and elaboration. Moreover, there are numerous topics on which we have been unable to touch due to space limitations—evidence on export responses to altered real exchange rates, macroeconomic considerations in exchange-rate policy, many of the factors (such as effect on R&D) involved in the trade-regime-growth interaction, and the limits to QR regimes resulting from illicit transactions.

[19]

Alternative Trade Strategies and Employment in *LDC*s

By ANNE O. KRUEGER*

The 1970's have witnessed significant changes in the trade policies and strategies of many *LDC*s. In the 1950's and 1960's most of them adhered to policies of import substitution behind highly restrictive quantitative controls, intensified by overvaluation of the exchange rate with attendant disincentives for export. In the past decade, there has been a marked reduction in the degree of bias toward import substitution. Even in countries where quantitative restrictions and tariffs continue to provide inducements for production for the domestic market much greater than incentive for sale abroad, bias is less extreme than in the past. In other countries, notably Brazil and South Korea, bias has been completely reversed, to a point where one might even claim a bias towards the foreign market and against the home market.

This shift in trade policies has resulted from a number of factors, some specific to individual countries, but chiefly because of evidence that the excesses of import substitution were detrimental to growth. The fact that there have been policy switches has enabled economists to attempt to estimate the differences in growth prospects for countries employing alternative trade strategies. Interestingly, the several studies that have been made (Constantine Michalopoulos and Keith Jay; Michael Michaely; Bela Balassa; the author, 1978) using widely different methodologies have

nonetheless reached quantitatively similar conclusions as to the increase in growth rates resulting from a switch.

Although trade policies have altered, other aspects of growth performance in *LDC*s have been increasingly questioned. Important among these is the growth of employment opportunities. It has become fashionable, especially among policymakers, to conclude that achieving a high rate of growth of *GNP* will not necessarily entail the growth of opportunity for new entrants to the labor force. Thus, the demonstration that export-oriented trade strategies results in superior growth performance may have come too late: pessimists may conclude that faster growth does not necessarily imply more employment.

In light of this view a natural question, but one that has not previously been examined systematically, is the relationship between alternative trade strategies and employment. It is possible that the observed unsatisfactory growth of employment resulted largely from the choice of an import substitution strategy, or at least that export promotion is more compatible with employment growth than is import substitution. To be sure, until recently one would have simply asserted that faster growth associated with one strategy would in itself lead to a more rapid upward shift in the demand for labor, and in all probability, the growth effects of alternative trade strategies dominate the compositional and substitution effects originating from those alternatives. However, given the prevailing skepticism about the effects of increased rates of *GNP* growth on employment and income distribution, it seems worthwhile investigating the issue in some depth.

The link between trade strategies and employment is a complex one. It involves not only trade strategies themselves and the structure of labor markets, but also entails

*Professor of economics, University of Minnesota, and senior research staff, National Bureau of Economic Research. The paper was written while I was visiting fellow at the Australian National University, and benefited from comments made during presentation of a seminar there, and also at the Development Research Centre, International Bank for Reconstruction and Development. The National Bureau's project on Alternative Trade Strategies and Employment is funded in major part by the Agency of International Development whose support is gratefully acknowledged

examination of the various factors which contribute to distorting goods and factor markets in *LDC*s. In an effort to sort out some of the issues involved in the trade strategies-employment relationship and also to obtain estimates of the quantitative significance of the links between trade strategies and employment, the National Bureau of Economic Research (*NBER*) has been conducting a research project on the topic. A major part of the *NBER* project has consisted of individual country studies, now nearing completion, undertaken by authors analyzing the situation in their particular countries. This paper represents a preliminary report on some of the findings that have emerged to date.

There are two aspects of the project which require discussion. First, there is the underlying analysis of the link between trade strategies and employment. Second, enough empirical results are available from the country studies to provide some data on some aspects of the employment-trade relationship. The countries studied and the authors are Brazil: Jose Carvalho and Claudio Haddad; Chile: Vittorio Corbo and Patricio Meller; Colombia: Francisco Thoumi; India: V.R. Panchamukhi and T.N. Srinivasan; Indonesia: Mark Pitt; Ivory Coast: Terry Monson and Jacques Pegatienan; Kenya: Peter Hopcraft and Leopold Mureithi; Korea: Wontack Hong; Pakistan: Stephen Guisinger; Thailand: Narongchai Akrasanee; Tunisia: Mustapha Nabli; Uruguay: Alberto Bension. Within a common framework of analysis and empirical methodology, all authors have attempted to estimate the trade-employment relationship for their particular country.

Before turning to the analysis of the link between trade strategies and employment, one preliminary matter must be cleared up. That pertains to the determinants of employment. After all, in a neoclassical economy, any shift in the demand curve for labor is reflected in a change in the real wage and employment changes only to the extent that the labor supply is responsive to the real wage. More generally, depending on the underlying structure of the labor market, an upward shift in the demand for labor can result in almost anything: in a Harris-Todaro world, it can even result in increased unemployment. In a world in which unions or governments are sufficiently powerful, an upward shift in the demand for labor may result in an increase in the real wage, regardless of the underlying employment situation. Thus the ways in which employment—in total and in the urban sector—responds to changes in demand for labor are functions of many variables.

For purposes of analyzing trade strategies, focus is put upon determinants of the demand for labor. The word employment is used synonymously for "demand for labor." This means that such phenomena as differences in the choice of technique or industry as a consequence of different trade strategies are evaluated in the project. However, the factors determining how much of an upward shift in the demand for labor results in greater employment and how much in higher real wages are considered to lie outside the scope of the research (see the author, 1977).

Turning to the trade strategies-employment relationship, there are three levels of linkages with simultaneity among them. First, there is the effect of the choice of trade strategy on the overall rate of growth, and therefore on the rate of growth of employment opportunities. As already indicated, experience strongly suggests that there is such a link, but it is not dealt with in the present project.

Second, there is the effect on the demand for labor *via* the influence of the trade strategy on the composition of output. If one trade strategy results in a higher proportion of *GNP* originating in labor-itensive industries, the selection of that strategy will unequivocally result in a higher demand for labor (at a given real wage) than will the selection of the alternative. It should be noted here as elsewhere that it is not only the choice of trade strategy that can matter: the degree to which the strategy is pursued will affect the composition of output. Korea's export industries, for example, form a larger fraction of her output (and therefore are more heavily weighted in determining the demand for labor) than if the emphasis upon export promotion were somewhat less.

Third, there is the effect that the trade regime has on factor prices: to the extent that, for example, import substitution results in incentives for use of capital-intensive techniques (due to overvaluation of the currency, and perhaps also to policies that discriminate in favor of applications for foreign exchange for financing imports of capital goods), it may affect the demand for labor. To be sure, such an effect must be sectoral rather than total, unless one wishes to argue that the total capital stock is different under that strategy than it would have been under the alternative.

The *NBER* project is focused upon the second and third links between trade strategies and employment. Because of space limitations this progress report is devoted simply to the second link: the different factor proportions employed in industries with differing trade orientations. At an analytical level, the underlying theory can be taken directly from the Heckscher-Ohlin-Samuelson (*HOS*) trade model, and then transformed into empirically testable hypotheses about factor proportions in importables and exportables. In practice, however, it proves useful to go beyond the usual $2 \times 2 \times 2$ framework, and to consider the predictions of an *HOS*-like model with three factors (the third presumably being a raw material), many commodities, and many countries of the type I have previously discussed (1977b).

Within that framework, commodities are partitioned, in accordance with their characteristics, into natural resource-based and *HOS* goods, and, within each of those categories, into exportables, import-competing, and noncompeting-import categories according to trade flows.[1] Where

---

[1]Noncompeting imports are those commodities which are imported for which domestic production cannot substitute within the relevant price range.

relevant, import and export data are also broken down by origin and destination, respectively. The multicountry, multicommodity trade model immediately suggests the hypothesis that the commodity composition and factor proportions of tradables with countries with significantly different factor endowments may be quite different than that with countries with similar endowments. To illustrate, one would expect that Brazil might have a comparative advantage among *HOS* goods in more labor-intensive commodities in her trade with industrialized countries than in her trade with her Latin American Common Market trading partners.

Table 1 presents some of the preliminary findings as to the labor content of trade per unit of domestic value-added (*DVA*) in domestic production of tradables. The "direct" column presents the ratio of the

TABLE 1—RATIO OF LABOR COEFFICIENTS IN EXPORTABLES TO THOSE IN IMPORT-COMPETING INDUSTRIES[a]

Country and Category	Direct Requirements	Direct plus Home Goods Indirect
Brazil[b] all trade	1.07	2.67
Chile all trade	.81	1.07
Colombia all trade	1.93	–
Indonesia		
All trade except oil	2.09	1.92
Trade excluding all raw materials	1.73	1.58
Ivory Coast *HOS* goods	1.38	1.35
Kenya all trade	.72	–
Korea all trade 1966	1.25	1.23
All trade 1973	.79	.96
Pakistan *HOS* goods	1.41	–
Thailand all trade	2.21	1.70
Tunisia *HOS* goods[c]	1.32	1.22
Uruguay *HOS* trade with developed countries	1.87	–

Sources: Individual country study manuscripts.

[a]Estimates are for different years between 1966 and 1973 depending on data availability in individual countries.

[b]Brazilian data are per unit of output rather than per unit of value-added, and therefore are not comparable with the ratios for other countries. Indirect includes agricultural indirect inputs.

[c]Unskilled labor only.

number of man-years of labor direct requirements per *DVA* in exportables to the number in import-competing industries, while the "direct plus indirect" refers to the so-called Corden measure—direct requirements, plus indirect requirements in home goods. It does not include indirect requirements of tradables, although those numbers were also computed by most country authors and do not significantly alter the results.

As can be seen from Table 1, in nearly all cases and in all cases of *HOS* goods, exports are less labor intensive than import-competing industries. Indeed, the differential in labor requirements between export and import-competing industries is quite notable in many countries—virtually 2:1 in Columbia, Indonesia, Thailand, and Uruguay. Moreover, as discussed below, Keyna's and Chile's ratios reflect a high proportion of trade with *LDC*s. In light of the Leontief Paradox findings, and also in view of the alleged importance of factor market distortions in many of the *LDC*s, it is perhaps surprising that the greater labor intensity of exports shows up so consistently across countries, even though the data pertain chiefly to all trade. The differentials in labor intensity are all the more remarkable when it is recognized that there are usually incentives for capital-intensive production of all commodities, including exportables. As such, it is likely that the "optimal" labor intensity of most activities is even greater than that indicated by the data included in the table.

The fact that exportables are more labor-intensive than import-competing industries conforms to the *HOS* model of international trade. Perhaps a somewhat more unexpected result, shown in Table 2, pertains to the differentials in labor intensity between exports to developed countries and those to other developing countries. With the exception of Thailand, all the countries for which there was enough trade to warrant the separate calculation of labor coefficients were found to have remarkably different products, and therefore factor proportions, in their trade

TABLE 2—RATIO OF LABOR REQUIREMENTS FOR EXPORTS TO DEVELOPED COUNTRIES TO THOSE FOR *LDC* TRADE

Country	Direct	Direct plus Home Goods Indirect
Chile[a]	1.40	1.31
Kenya	1.36	–
Thailand	1.10	1.03
Uruguay	1.84	–

[a] For Chile, the ratio is labor per *DVA* of exports to developed countries divided by labor per *DVA* for total trade.

with developed countries than with other developing countries. Uruguay, for example, exports products to developing countries that are less labor using than even the production competing with imports from developed countries. Likewise, Chile's exports to developed countries require almost 40 percent more labor per *DVA* than do her total exports.

A natural interpretation of this phenomenon is that the prospects for trade among the *LDC*s are indeed limited, as customs union theory forecasts. In fact, the large disparity in factor proportions between the various destinations strongly suggests that it is the high-cost import substitution industries which find their only export outlet in other developing countries.[2] Insofar as developing countries are relatively abundantly endowed with unskilled labor and relatively short of capital, trade with other *LDC*s is likely to increase the imbalance in factor availability, whereas trade with the developed countries may serve as means of exchanging abundant factors for scarce.

Another finding of considerable interest that emerges from a number of the studies is that the skill requirements in exportables

[2] Anyone familiar with the trade regimes and protectionist policies of *LDC*s will be aware that most of them erect high trade barriers against any goods which are domestically produced. To the extent that such barriers cut off any trade which would follow from "natural" comparative advantage, it would intensify the capital intensity of one *LDC*'s exports to another *LDC*.

TABLE 3—RATIO OF DIRECT SKILL COEFFICIENTS
PER *DVA* IN EXPORTABLES TO IMPORT-COMPETING
INDUSTRIES

Country	Ratio
Brazil, all industry	.98
Chile, all trade	.83
Indonesia, all trade	.81
Ivory Coast, *HOS* only	.99
Kenya	.78
Tunisia	.62

and import-competing production are virtually as disparate as the labor inputs. Data are given in Table 3. For example, Chile's exports appear to require about 83 percent as many skill units as her production of import-competing commodities. In general, exportables appear to have lower requirements of skilled man-years per *DVA*, regardless of the measure of skills used. The results appear to be fairly robust both with regard to commodity classifications and also with regard to the definition of skills. This finding lends support to the notion already prevalent elsewhere that capital-intensive industries are also industries where skill requirements are high, whereas unskilled labor-intensive industries appear to have both lower capital requirements and lower skill requirements per *DVA*.

Thus, the findings both with regard to skills or human capital, and with regard to unskilled labor, seem to reinforce the notions set forth in the neoclassical model of international trade. The Leontief Paradox results, as well as the theory underlying the analysis of trade in the presence of factor market distortions, have provided some ground for skepticism that comparative advantage in labor-abundant countries might lie in production of labor-intensive goods (as contrasted with the surely correct notion that comparative advantage lies in producing whatever one produces with relatively labor-intensive techniques). Nonetheless, the data from the countries covered by the *NBER* project indicate that,

once allowance is made for direction of trade, the labor-abundant developing countries probably would be well-advised to specialize in the export of labor-intensive products.

A paper of this length cannot possibly do justice to the scope and range of results that are emerging from the individual country studies and the other outputs of the *NBER* project. There will, however, be a volume containing the salient findings from the individual country studies which should provide considerably greater information to interested parties. What is already clear is that the findings of the country studies support the view that altering trade strategies toward a greater export orientation will certainly be consistent with the objective of finding more employment opportunities; skepticism based on Leontief Paradox or factor-market distortion considerations does not seem to be warranted.

REFERENCES

B. Balassa, "Exports and Economic Growth: Some Further Evidence," mimeo., Washington, July 1977.

M. Michaely, "Exports and Growth: An Empirical Investigation," *J. Develop. Econ.,* Mar. 1977, *4.*

C. Michalopoulos and K. Jay, "Growth of Exports and Income in the Developing World: A Neoclassical View," disc. paper no. 28, Agency Int. Develop., Washington 1973.

Anne O. Krueger, *Foreign Trade Regimes and Economic Development: Liberalization Attempts and Consequences,* Cambridge, Mass. 1978.

————, (1977a) "Alternative Trade Strategies, Growth, and Employment," in N. Akrasanee et al., eds., *Trade and Employment in Asia and the Pacific,* Honolulu 1977.

————, (1977b) *Growth, Distortions, and Patterns of Trade Among Many Countries,* in *Princeton Studies in International Finance,* No. 40, 1977.

[20]

The Political Economy of the Rent-Seeking Society

By ANNE O. KRUEGER*

In many market-oriented economies, government restrictions upon economic activity are pervasive facts of life. These restrictions give rise to rents of a variety of forms, and people often compete for the rents. Sometimes, such competition is perfectly legal. In other instances, rent seeking takes other forms, such as bribery, corruption, smuggling, and black markets.

It is the purpose of this paper to show some of the ways in which rent seeking is competitive, and to develop a simple model of competitive rent seeking for the important case when rents originate from quantitative restrictions upon international trade. In such a case 1) competitive rent seeking leads to the operation of the economy inside its transformation curve; 2) the welfare loss associated with quantitative restrictions is unequivocally greater than the loss from the tariff equivalent of those quantitative restrictions; and 3) competitive rent seeking results in a divergence between the private and social costs of certain activities. Although the analysis is general, the model has particular applicability for developing countries, where government interventions are frequently all-embracing.

A preliminary section of the paper is concerned with the competitive nature of rent seeking and the quantitative importance of rents for two countries, India and Turkey. In the second section, a formal model of rent seeking under quantitative restrictions on trade is developed and the propositions indicated above are established. A final section outlines some other forms of rent seeking and suggests some implications of the analysis.

I. Competitive Rent Seeking

A. *Means of Competition*

When quantitative restrictions are imposed upon and effectively constrain imports, an import license is a valuable commodity. It is well known that under some circumstances, one can estimate the tariff equivalents of a set of quantitative restrictions and analyze the effects of those restrictions in the same manner as one would the tariff equivalents. In other circumstances, the resource-allocational effects of import licensing will vary, depending upon who receives the license.[1]

It has always been recognized that there are *some* costs associated with licensing: paperwork, the time spent by entrepreneurs in obtaining their licenses, the cost of the administrative apparatus necessary to issue licenses, and so on. Here, the argument is carried one step further: in many circumstances resources are devoted to competing for those licenses.

The consequences of that rent seeking are examined below. First, however, it will be argued that rent-seeking activities are often competitive and resources are devoted to competing for rents. It is difficult, if not impossible, to find empirically observable measures of the degree to which rent seeking is competitive. Instead, some

* Professor of economics, University of Minnesota. I am indebted to James M. Henderson for invaluable advice and discussion on successive drafts. Jagdish Bhagwati and John C. Hause made helpful comments on earlier drafts of this paper.

[1] This phenomenon is explored in detail in Bhagwati and Krueger.

mechanisms under which rent seeking is almost certain to be competitive are examined. Then other cases are considered in which it is less obvious, but perhaps equally plausible, that competition results.

Consider first the results of an import-licensing mechanism when licenses for imports of intermediate goods are allocated in proportion to firms' capacities. That system is frequently used, and has been analyzed for the Indian case by Jagdish Bhagwati and Padma Desai. When licenses are allocated in proportion to firms' capacities, investment in additional physical plant confers upon the investor a higher expected receipt of import licenses. Even with initial excess capacity (due to quantitative restrictions upon imports of intermediate goods), a rational entrepreneur may still expand his plant if the expected gains from the additional import licenses he will receive, divided by the cost of the investment, equal the returns on investment in other activities.[2] This behavior could be perfectly rational even if, for all entrepreneurs, the total number of import licenses will remain fixed. In fact, if imports are held constant as domestic income grows, one would expect the domestic value of a constant quantity of imports to increase over time, and hence installed capacity would increase while output remained constant. By investing in additional capacity, entrepreneurs devote resources to compete for import licenses.

A second sort of licensing mechanism frequently found in developing countries is used for imports of consumer goods. There, licenses are allocated *pro rata* in proportion to the applications for those licenses from importers-wholesalers. Entry

is generally free into importing-wholesaling, and firms usually have U-shaped cost curves. The result is a larger-than-optimal number of firms, operating on the downward sloping portion of their cost curves, yet earning a "normal" rate of return. Each importer-wholesaler receives fewer imports than he would buy at existing prices in the absence of licensing, but realizes a sufficient return on those licenses he does receive to make it profitable to stay in business. In this case, competition for rents occurs through entry into the industry with smaller-than-optimally sized firms, and resources are used in that the same volume of imports could be efficiently distributed with fewer inputs if firms were of optimal size.

A third sort of licensing mechanism is less systematic in that government officials decide on license allocations. Competition occurs to some extent through both mechanisms already mentioned as businessmen base their decisions on expected values. But, in addition, competition can also occur through allocating resources to influencing the probability, or expected size, of license allocations. Some means of influencing the expected allocation—trips to the capital city, locating the firm in the capital, and so on—are straightforward. Others, including bribery, hiring relatives of officials or employing the officials themselves upon retirement, are less so. In the former case, competition occurs through choice of location, expenditure of resources upon travel, and so on. In the latter case, government officials themselves receive part of the rents.

Bribery has often been treated as a transfer payment. However, there is competition for government jobs and it is reasonable to believe that expected total remuneration is the relevant decision variable for persons deciding upon careers. Generally, entry into government service requires above-average educational at-

[2] Note that: 1) one would expect to find greater excess capacity in those industries where rents are higher; and 2) within an industry, more efficient firms will have greater excess capacity than less efficient firms, since the return on a given amount of investment will be higher with greater efficiency.

tainments. The human capital literature provides evidence that choices as to how much to invest in human capital are strongly influenced by rates of return upon the investment. For a given level of educational attainment, one would expect the rate of return to be approximately equated among various lines of endeavor. Thus, if there appear to be high official-plus-unofficial incomes accruing to government officials and higher education is a prerequisite for seeking a government job, more individuals will invest in higher education. It is not necessary that government officials earn the same total income as other college graduates. All that is necessary is that there is an excess supply of persons seeking government employment, or that highly educated persons make sustained efforts to enter government services. Competition takes place through attaining the appropriate credentials for entry into government service and through accepting unemployment while making efforts to obtain appointments. Efforts to influence those in charge of making appointments, of course, just carry the argument one step further back.

To argue that competition for entry into government service is, in part, a competition for rents does not imply that all government servants accept bribes nor that they would leave government service in their absence. Successful competitors for government jobs might experience large windfall gains even at their official salaries. However, if the possibility of those gains induces others to expend time, energy, and resources in seeking entry into government services, the activity is competitive for present purposes.

In all these license-allocation cases, there are means, legal and illegal, for competing for rents. If individuals choose their activities on the basis of expected returns, rates of return on alternative activities will be equated and, in that sense, markets

will be competitive.[3] In most cases, people do not perceive themselves to be rent seekers and, generally speaking, individuals and firms do not specialize in rent seeking. Rather, rent seeking is one part of an economic activity, such as distribution or production, and part of the firm's resources are devoted to the activity (including, of course, the hiring of expediters). The fact that rent seeking and other economic activities are not generally conducted by separate economic entities provides the motivation for the form of the model developed below.

B. *Are Rents Quantitatively Important?*

Granted that rent seeking may be highly competitive, the question remains whether rents are important. Data from two countries, India and Turkey, suggest that they are. Gunnar Myrdal believes India may " . . . on the balance, be judged to have somewhat less corruption than any other country in South Asia" (p. 943). Nonetheless, it is generally believed that "corruption" has been increasing, and that much of the blame lies with the proliferation of economic controls following independence.[4]

Table 1 presents crude estimates, based on fairly conservative assumptions of the value of rents of all sorts in 1964. One important source of rents—investment licensing—is not included for lack of any valid basis on which to estimate its value. Many smaller controls are also excluded. Nonetheless, it is apparent from Table 1 that

---

[3] It may be objected that illegal means of competition may be sufficiently distasteful that perfect competition will not result. Three comments are called for. First, it requires only that enough people at the margin do not incur disutility from engaging in these activities. Second, most lines of economic activity in many countries cannot be entered without some rent-seeking activity. Third, risks of detection (especially when bribery is expected) and the value judgments associated with illegal activities differ from society to society. See Ronald Wraith and Edgar Simpkins.

[4] Santhanam Committee, pp. 7-8.

TABLE 1—ESTIMATES OF VALUE OF RENTS: INDIA, 1964

Source of Rent	Amount of Rent (Rs. million)
Public investment	365
Imports	10,271
Controlled commodities	3,000
Credit rationing	407
Railways	602
Total	14,645

Sources:

1) Public investment: The Santhanam Committee, pp. 11–12, placed the loss in public investment at *at least* 5 percent of investment. That figure was multiplied by the average annual public investment in the *Third Five Year Plan.*

2) Imports: The Santhanam Committee, p. 18, stated that import licenses were worth 100 to 500 percent of their face value. Seventy-five percent of the value of 1964 imports was used here as a conservative estimate.

3) Controlled commodities: These commodities include steel, cement, coal, passenger cars, scooters, food, and other price—and/or distribution-controlled commodities, as well as foreign exchange used for illegal imports and other unrecorded transactions. The figure is the lower bound estimate given by John Monteiro, p. 60. Monteiro puts the upper bound estimate at Rs. 30,000 billion, although he rejects the figure on the (dubious) ground that notes in circulation are less than that sum.

4) Credit rationing: The bank rate in 1964 was 6 percent; Rs. 20.3 billion of loans were outstanding. It is assumed that *at least* an 8 percent interest rate would have been required to clear the market, and that 3 percent of bank loans outstanding would be equivalent to the present value of new loans at 5 percent. Data source: Reserve Bank of India, Tables 534 and 554.

5) Railways: Monteiro, p. 45, cites commissions of 20 percent on railway purchases, and extra-official fees of Rs. 0.15 per wagon and Rs. 1.4 per 100 maunds loaded. These figures were multiplied by the 1964 traffic volume; 203 million tons of revenue-paying traffic originated in that year. Third plan expenditure on railroads was Rs. 13,260 million. There were 350,000 railroad goods wagons in 1964–65. If a wagon was loaded once a week, there were 17,500,000 wagons of freight. At Rs. 0.15 per load, this would be Rs. 2.6 million; 100 maunds equal 8,228 pounds so at 1.4 Rs. per 100 maunds, Rs. 69 million changed hands; if one-fifth of railroad expenditures were made in 1964–65, Rs. 2652 million was spent in 1964; at 20 percent, this would be Rs. 530 million, for a total of Rs. 602 million.

import licenses provided the largest source of rents. The total value of rents of Rs. 14.6 billion contrasts with Indian national income of Rs. 201 billion in 1964. At 7.3 percent of national income, rents must be judged large relative to India's problems in attempting to raise her savings rate.

For Turkey, excellent detailed estimates of the value of import licenses in 1968 are available.[5] Data on the c.i.f. prices of individual imports, their landed cost (c.i.f. price plus all duties, taxes, and landing charges), and wholesale prices were collected for a sizeable sample of commodities representing about 10 percent of total imports in 1968. The c.i.f. value of imports in the sample was TL 547 million and the landed cost of the imports was TL 1,443 million. The value at the wholesale level of these same imports was TL 3,568 million. Of course, wholesalers incur some handling, storage, and transport costs. The question, therefore, is the amount that can be attributed to normal wholesaling costs. If one assumes that a 50 percent markup would be adequate, then the value of import licenses was TL 1,404 million, or almost three times the c.i.f. value of imports. Imports in 1968 were recorded (c.i.f.) as 6 percent of national income. On the basis of Aker's data, this would imply that rents from import licenses in Turkey in 1968 were about 15 percent of *GNP*.

Both the Indian and the Turkish estimates are necessarily somewhat rough. But they clearly indicate that the value of import licenses to the recipients was sizeable. Since means were available of competing for the licenses, it would be surprising if competition did not occur for prizes that large. We turn, therefore, to an examination of the consequences of competitive rent seeking.

[5] I am indebted to Ahmet Aker of Robert College who kindly made his data available to me. Details and a description of the data can be found in my forthcoming book.

II. The Effects of Competitive Rent Seeking

The major proposition of this paper is that competitive rent seeking for import licenses entails a welfare cost in addition to the welfare cost that would be incurred if the same level of imports were achieved through tariffs. The effects of tariffs upon production, trade, and welfare are well known, and attention is focussed here upon the additional cost of competitive rent seeking. A simple model is used to develop the argument. Initially, free trade is assumed. Then, a tariff or equivalent import restriction is introduced. Finally, an equal import restriction with competitive rent seeking is examined.

A. *The Basic Model*

Two commodities are consumed by the country under investigation: food and consumption goods. Food is produced domestically and exported. Consumption goods are imported. Distribution is a productive activity whereby food is purchased from the agricultural sector, exported, and the proceeds are used to import consumption goods which are sold in the domestic market. Labor is assumed to be the only domestic factor of production.[6] It is assumed that the country under consideration is small and cannot affect its international terms of trade. Physical units are selected so that the fixed international prices of both goods are unity.

The agricultural production function is

$$(1) \quad A = A(L_A) \quad A' > 0, \ A'' < 0$$

where A is the output of food and L_A is the quantity of labor employed in agriculture. The sign of the second derivative reflects a diminishing marginal physical product of labor in agriculture, due, presumably, to fixity in the supply of land.

The level of distribution output, D, is defined to equal the level of consumption-goods imports, M:

$$(2) \quad D = M$$

One unit of distributive services entails exchanging one unit of imports for food with the agricultural sector at the domestic terms of trade, and exporting the food in exchange for imports at the international terms of trade. Constant returns to scale are assumed for the distribution activity; one unit of distribution requires k units of labor. Total labor employed in distribution, L_D, is

$$(3) \quad L_D = kD$$

A distribution charge of p_D per unit is added to the international price of imports:

$$(4) \quad p_M = 1 + p_D$$

where p_M is the domestic price of imports. The domestic price of food is assumed to equal its unit international price.[7]

Society's demand for imports depends upon the domestic price of imports and total income generated in agriculture:[8]

$$(5) \quad M = M(p_M, A)$$

where $\partial M/\partial p_M < 0$ and $\partial M/\partial A > 0$. Demand decreases with increases in the price of imports, and increases with increases in agricultural output (income). Equation (5) is derived from micro utility maximization with the assumption that farmers, distributors, and rent seekers all have the same consumption behavior. Domestic

---

[6] Labor could be regarded as a composite domestic factor of production. Extensions to two or more factors would complicate the analysis, but would not alter its basic results.

[7] These assumptions establish a domestic numeraire. The real analysis would be unaffected by proportional changes in the domestic prices.

[8] Food and imports are consumed. But, by choice of food as the numeraire (see equation (6)) and the assumed constancy of international prices, agricultural output serves as a measure of income.

food consumption, F, is simply the quantity not exported:

(6) $$F = A - M$$

Since the fixed international terms of trade equal unity, food exports equal consumption goods imports.

Finally, it is assumed that the economy under consideration has a fixed labor supply, $\bar{L}$:

(7) $$\bar{L} = L_A + L_D + L_R$$

where L_R is the quantity of labor engaged in rent seeking.

B. *Free Trade*

Under free trade, there is free entry into both agriculture and distribution and competition equates the wage in the two activities:

(8) $$A' = p_D/k$$

Equations (1) to (8) constitute the free-trade system. These eight equations contain the eight variables A, M, D, F, L_A, L_D, p_M, and p_D. Since there is no rent seeking under free trade, $L_R \equiv 0$.

It is easily established that free trade is optimal in the sense that the domestic price ratio under free trade equals the marginal rate of transformation between food consumption and imports. The consumption possibility locus is obtained by substituting into (6) from (1) and (7)

$$F = A(\bar{L} - kM) - M$$

The locus has a marginal rate of transformation greater than one:

(9) $$\frac{-dF}{dM} = kA' + 1 > 1$$

which reflects the positive distribution cost of substituting imports for food consumption. The locus is concave:

$$\frac{d^2F}{dM^2} = k^2 A'' < 0$$

since $A'' < 0$, which follows from diminishing returns in food production. Substituting from (8) into (9),

$$\frac{-dF}{dM} = 1 + p_D$$

which establishes the aforementioned equality.

A free-trade solution is depicted in Figure 1. Domestic food consumption and import consumption are measured along OF and OM, respectively. The consumption possibility locus is $\hat{F}\hat{M}$. At the point $\hat{F}$ no imports are consumed and hence there is no distribution. If distribution were costless, society could choose its consumption point from the line $\hat{F}A$. However, to consume one unit of import requires exchanging one unit of food *and* withdrawing k workers from agriculture to provide the requisite distributive services. With diminishing marginal product of labor in agriculture, the cost of additional imports in terms of foregone food production rises. Thus, the price of distribution, and hence the domestic price of imports, increases in moving northwest from $\hat{F}$. The consump-

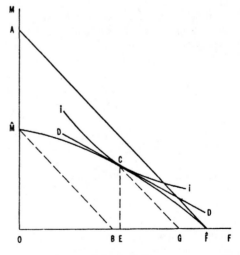

FIGURE 1. FREE TRADE

tion point $\hat{M}$ has OB food exchanged for $O\hat{M}$ of imports. The distance $\hat{F}B$ is the agricultural output foregone to distribute $O\hat{M}$ imports.

If society's preferences are given by the indifference curve *ii*, point C is optimal. The price of distribution is reflected in the difference between the slope of $\hat{F}A$ and the slope of DD at C. At the point C, OG food would be produced, with EG ($=EC$) exported, and the rest domestically consumed.

C. A Tariff or an Import Restriction Without Rent Seeking

Consider now a case in which there is a restriction upon the quantity of imports

$$(10) \qquad M = \overline{M}$$

where $\overline{M}$ is less than the import quantity that would be realized under free trade. Since entry into distribution is now limited, the competitive wage equality (8) will no longer hold. The relevant system contains (1) to (7) and (10). The variables are the same as in the free-trade case and again $L_R = 0$. The system may be solved sequentially: given (10), D follows from (2), L_D from (3), L_A from (7), A from (1), F from (6), p_M from (5), and p_D from (4). Since equations (1), (6), and (7) remain intact, the solution for this case is also on the consumption possibility locus.

It is useful to establish the directions of change for the variables following a switch from free trade to import restriction. The reduced import level will reduce the labor employed in distribution and increase the labor force in agriculture. Diminishing returns will reduce the agricultural wage. The domestic price of imports, the distributive margin, and the wage of distributors will increase. Distributors will earn a rent in the sense that their wage will exceed the wage of those engaged in agriculture.

In the absence of rent seeking, a tariff

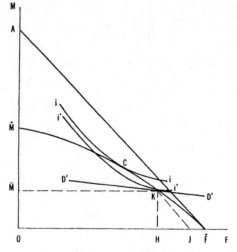

FIGURE 2. IMPORT RESTRICTION
WITHOUT RENT SEEKING

and a quantitative restriction are equivalent[9] aside from the resultant income distribution. Under a quantitative restriction the distributive wage is higher than the agricultural. If instead there were an equivalent tariff with redistribution of the proceeds, the marginal product of labor in agriculture would be unchanged, but agricultural workers would benefit by the amount of tariff proceeds redistributed to them whereas traders' income would be lower. Since the allocation of labor under a tariff and quantitative restriction without rent seeking is the same and domestic prices are the same, the only difference between the two situations lies in income distribution.

The solution under a quantitative restriction is illustrated in Figure 2, where $\hat{F}\hat{M}$ is again the consumption possibility locus and C the free-trade solution. With a quantitative restriction on imports in the amount $O\overline{M}$, the domestic prices of

[9] The change in the price of the import from the free-trade solution is the tariff equivalent of the quantitative restriction described here.

imports, and hence of distribution, rise from free trade to import restriction. Food output (OJ) and domestic consumption of food increase, and exports decline to IIJ ($=OM$). The indifference curve $i'i'$ lies below ii (and the point C), and the welfare loss may be described by the consumption and production cost measure given by Harry Johnson.

The wage rate in distribution unequivocally rises for a movement from free trade to a quantitative restriction. The total income of distributors will increase, decrease, or remain unchanged depending upon whether the proportionate increase in p_D is greater than, less than, or equal to the absolute value of the proportionate decrease of imports. For the moment, let p_D, p_M, and M represent free-trade solution values, and let p_D^*, p_M^*, and $\overline{M}$ represent import-restriction solution values. The total arc elasticity of demand for imports for the interval under consideration, η, is

$$(11) \qquad \eta = \frac{-(\overline{M} - M)}{\overline{M} + M} \cdot \frac{p_M^* + p_M}{p_M^* - p_M}$$

Total expenditures on imports will increase, decrease, or remain unchanged as η is less than one, greater than one, or equal to one. The total income of distributors will increase if

$$p_D^* \overline{M} > p_D M$$

Multiplying both sides of this inequality by $(p_M^* + p_M)/(p_M^* - p_M)$, substituting from (11), and using (4),

$$(12) \qquad 1 + 2/(p_D^* + p_D) > \eta$$

Hence, distributors' total income can increase even if the demand for imports is price elastic.[10] The smaller is the free-trade

distributive markup, the more likely it is that the distributors' total income will increase with a curtailment of imports. The reason is that an increase in the domestic price of imports results in a proportionately greater increase in the price of distribution.

D. An Import Restriction with Competitive Rent Seeking

In the import-restriction model just presented, the wage in distribution p_D/k exceeds the wage in agriculture A': Under this circumstance, it would be surprising if people did not endeavor to enter distribution in response to its higher return. Resources can be devoted to rent seeking in all the ways indicated in Section IA. This rent-seeking activity can be specified in a number of different ways. A simple and intuitively plausible specification is that people will seek distributive rents until the average wage in distribution and rent seeking equals the agricultural wage:[11]

$$(13) \qquad A' = \frac{p_D \overline{M}}{L_D + L_R}$$

One can regard all distributors and rent seekers as being partially engaged in each activity or one can think of rent seekers as entering in the expectation of receiving import licenses. In the latter case, the final solution classifies the successful seekers in L_D and the unsuccessful ones in L_R. Equation (13) implies risk neutrality in this circumstance.

The model for import restriction with rent seeking contains the same equations,

---

[10] Proof of (12) uses the step that $p_D^* \overline{M} > p_D M$ implies $(p_D^* - p_D)/(p_D^* + p_D) > -(\overline{M} - M)/(\overline{M} + M)$. Note that in the continuous case, (12) reduces to $1 + 1/p_D > \eta$.

[11] As an alternative, the distributive production function (3) can be altered to treat all persons competing for import licenses as distributors so that L_D also encompasses L_R and $A' = p_D \overline{M}/L_D$. Another alternative is to introduce a rent-seeking activity distinct from distribution with a wage determined from total rents $(p_D - A'k)\overline{M}/L_R$, and require that this wage equal the wages in distribution and agriculture. These specifications give results equivalent to those that follow from (13).

(1) to (7) and (10), and the same variables as the model for import restrictions without rent seeking. In addition, the new model contains (13) and the introduction of L_R as a variable. The essential factor of rent seeking is that L_R becomes positive.

Let us start with a solution for an import restriction without rent seeking and ask what happens to the values of the variables when rent seeking is introduced. By assumption $M = \bar{M}$ is unchanged, so that L_D is unchanged. Therefore, $dL_A = -dL_R$, because the labor that enters rent seeking can only come from agriculture. Substituting into the total differential of (1) and using (6),

$$(14) \qquad dF = dA = -A'dL_R < 0$$

Agricultural production and food consumption are reduced by the introduction of rent seeking. Since the import level remains unchanged, rent seeking entails a welfare loss beyond that for an import restriction without rent seeking. The concavity of the agricultural production function results in a food loss that is less than proportional to decrements in L_A. Differentiating (5) totally,

$$(15) \qquad 0 = M_1 dp_M + M_2 dA$$

where M_1 and M_2 are the partial derivatives of (5) with respect to p_M and A, respectively. Solving (15) for dp_M, and substituting from (4) and (14),

$$(16) \qquad dp_D = dp_M = \frac{M_2}{M_1} A'dL_R < 0$$

since $M_1 < 0$ and $M_2 > 0$. The domestic cost of imports will be lower under rent-seeking competition. This follows from the decrease in the consumption of food relative to imports.

The results of (14) and (16) are not dependent upon the particular form of the equilibrium of the labor market. They hold for any specification of competitive

rent seeking. Equation (13) serves to determine particular values for L_R and other variables of the system. The mere existence of competitive rent seeking is enough to determine the directions of change of the variables.

The above results are sufficient to indicate that, for any given level of import restrictions, competition among rent seekers is clearly inferior to the tariff equivalent of the restrictions, in that there could be more food consumed with no fewer imports under the latter case than the former. To the extent that rent seeking is competitive, the welfare cost of import restrictions is equal to the welfare cost of the tariff equivalent *plus the additional cost of rent-seeking activities.* Measurement of that excess cost is considered below.

The tariff-equivalent and rent-seeking equilibria are contrasted in Figure 3. Equilibrium under rent seeking will be at some point such as L, with the same consumption of imports, but smaller production and consumption of food than occurs under a tariff. The points K and C are the tariff-equivalent and free-trade equilibria, respectively. The line $D'D'$ cor-

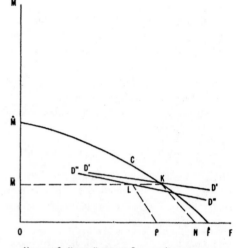

FIGURE 3. RENT-SEEKING IMPORT RESTRICTION

responds to the domestic price of imports in Figure 2, and the steeper line $D''D''$ corresponds to the lower domestic price of imports under competitive rent seeking.

So far, it has been shown that for any given level of import restriction, a tariff is Pareto-superior to competitive rent seeking, and the properties of rent-seeking equilibrium have been contrasted with those of the tariff-equivalent case in the absence of competition for the rents. A natural question is whether anything can be said about the properties of rent-seeking equilibrium in contrast to those of a free-trade equilibrium, which is, after all, the optimal solution. It has been seen that the number of persons engaged in distribution declines from free trade to import restriction without rent seeking, and increases as one goes from that situation to competition for import licenses. Likewise, agricultural output increases between free trade and the tariff-equivalent case, and declines between that and rent seeking. The question is whether any unambiguous signs can be placed on the direction of these changes between free trade and rent seeking and, in particular, is it possible that society might produce and consume less of both goods under rent seeking than under free trade?

The answer is that if inequality (12) is satisfied, the absolute number of persons $(L_D + L_R)$ in distribution will increase going from a free-trade to a rent-seeking equilibrium. If import demand is more elastic, the number of persons in distribution will decline. Contrasted with a free-trade equilibrium, there would be less agricultural output *and* fewer imports when inequality (12) holds. If, with import restriction, the income from distribution $p_D^* \overline{M}$ is greater than distributors' income at free trade, more persons will be employed in distribution-cum-rent seeking with import restriction than are employed under free trade.

E. *Measuring the Welfare Loss from Rent Seeking*

A tariff has both production and consumption costs, and it has already been shown that rent seeking entails costs in addition to those of a tariff. Many forms of competition for rents, however, are by their nature difficult to observe and quantify and one might therefore question the empirical content of the result so far obtained.

Fortunately, there is a way to estimate the production cost of rent seeking. That cost, in fact, is equal to the value of the rents. This can be shown as follows. The rent per import license, r, is:

$$(17) \qquad r = p_D - kA'$$

This follows because the labor required to distribute one unit of imports is k, which could be used in agriculture with a return A'. Note that at free trade r equals zero. A distributor could efficiently distribute an import and earn his opportunity cost in agriculture with zero rent. The total value of rents, R, with competitive rent seeking is thus the rent per unit of imports times the amount imported.

$$(18) \qquad R = r\overline{M} = (p_D - kA')\overline{M}$$

Using (3) and (13),

$$(19) \qquad R = \left(p_D - \frac{k p_D \overline{M}}{L_D + L_R} \right) \overline{M}$$

$$= p_D \left(1 - \frac{L_D}{L_D + L_R} \right) \overline{M}$$

$$= \frac{p_D \overline{M} L_R}{L_D + L_R}$$

Thus the total value of rents reflects the agricultural wage (A') times the number of rent seekers.

The value of rents reflects the value (at current prices) of the domestic factors of production which could be extracted from the economy with no change in the final goods and services available for society's utilization. Thus, if the value of rents is known, it indicates the volume of resources that could be transferred out of distribution and into other activities, with no loss of distributive services from an initial position of rent-seeking activity. The estimates of rents in India and Turkey, therefore, may be interpreted as the deadweight loss from quantitative restrictions in addition to the welfare cost of their associated tariff equivalents if one believes that there is competition for the rents.

The value of the rents overstates the increase in food output and consumption that could be attained with a tariff to the extent that the marginal product of labor in agriculture is diminishing, since the equilibrium wage will rise between the tariff and the competitive rent-seeking situation. In the case of a constant marginal product of labor in alternative uses, the value of rents will exactly measure foregone output.

F. *The Implications of Rent Seeking for Trade Theory*

Recognition of the fact of rent seeking alters a variety of conclusions normally obtained in the trade literature and examination of such cases is well beyond the scope of this paper. A few immediately derivable results are worth brief mention, however.

First, an import prohibition might be preferable to a nonprohibitive quota if there is competition for licenses under the quota. This follows immediately from the fact that a prohibition would release resources from rent seeking and the excess cost of domestic production might be less than the value of the rents. Second, one could not, in general, rank the tariff-equivalents of two (or more) quotas, since the value of rents is a function of both the amount of rent per unit (the tariff equiva-

lent) and the volume of imports of each item.[12] Third, it has generally been accepted that the more inelastic domestic demand the less is likely to be the welfare cost of a given tariff. For the quota-cum-rents case, the opposite is true: the more price inelastic is demand, the greater will be the value of rents and the greater, therefore, the deadweight loss associated with rent seeking. Fourth, it is usually believed that competition among importers will result in a better allocation of resources than will a monopoly. If rent seeking is a possibility, however, creating a monopoly position for one importer will generally result in a higher real income if not in a preferable income distribution for society. Finally, devaluation under quantitative restrictions may have important allocation effects because it diminishes the value of import licenses, and hence the amount of rent-seeking activity, in addition to its effects upon exports.

III. Conclusions and Implications

In this paper, focus has been on the effects of competition for import licenses under a quantitative restriction of imports. Empirical evidence suggests that the value of rents associated with import licenses can be relatively large, and it has been shown that the welfare cost of quantitative restrictions equals that of their tariff equivalents plus the value of the rents.

While import licenses constitute a large and visible rent resulting from government intervention, the phenomenon of rent seeking is far more general. Fair trade laws result in firms of less-than-optimal size. Minimum wage legislation generates equilibrium levels of unemployment above the optimum with associated deadweight losses, as shown by John Harris and

---

[12] I am indebted to Bhagwati for pointing out this implication.

Michael Todaro, and Todaro. Ceilings on interest rates and consequent credit rationing lead to competition for loans and deposits and/or high-cost banking operations. Regulating taxi fares affects the average waiting time for a taxi and the percent of time taxis are idle, but probably not their owners' incomes, unless taxis are also licensed. Capital gains tax treatment results in overbuilding of apartments and uneconomic oil exploration. And so on.

Each of these and other interventions lead people to compete for the rents although the competitors often do not perceive themselves as such. In each case there is a deadweight loss associated with that competition over and above the traditional triangle. In general, prevention of that loss can be achieved only by restricting entry into the activity for which a rent has been created.

That, in turn, has political implications. First, even if they *can* limit competition for the rents, governments which consider they must impose restrictions are caught on the horns of a dilemma: if they do restrict entry, they are clearly "showing favoritism" to one group in society and are choosing an unequal distribution of income. If, instead, competition for the rents is allowed (or cannot be prevented), income distribution may be less unequal and certainly there will be less appearance of favoring special groups, although the economic costs associated with quantitative restrictions will be higher.

Second, the existence of rent seeking surely affects people's perception of the economic system. If income distribution is viewed as the outcome of a lottery where wealthy individuals are successful (or lucky) rent seekers, whereas the poor are those precluded from or unsuccessful in rent seeking, the market mechanism is bound to be suspect. In the United States, rightly or wrongly, societal consensus has been that high incomes reflect—at least to some degree—high social product. As such, the high American per capita income is seen as a result of a relatively free market mechanism and an unequal distribution is tolerated as a by-product. If, instead, it is believed that few businesses would survive without exerting "influence," even if only to bribe government officials to do what they ought in any event to do, it is difficult to associate pecuniary rewards with social product. The perception of the price system as a mechanism rewarding the rich and well-connected may also be important in influencing political decisions about economic policy. If the market mechanism is suspect, the inevitable temptation is to resort to greater and greater intervention, thereby increasing the amount of economic activity devoted to rent seeking. As such, a political "vicious circle" may develop. People perceive that the market mechanism does not function in a way compatible with socially approved goals because of competitive rent seeking. A political consensus therefore emerges to intervene further in the market, rent seeking increases, and further intervention results. While it is beyond the competence of an economist to evaluate the political impact of rent seeking, the suspicion of the market mechanism so frequently voiced in some developing countries may result from it.

Finally, all market economies have some rent-generating restrictions. One can conceive of a continuum between a system of no restrictions and a perfectly restricted system. With no restrictions, entrepreneurs would seek to achieve windfall gains by adopting new technology, anticipating market shifts correctly, and so on. With perfect restrictions, regulations would be so all-pervasive that rent seeking would be the only route to gain. In such a system, entrepreneurs would devote all their time and resources to capturing windfall rents.

While neither of these extreme types could ever exist, one can perhaps ask whether there might be some point along the continuum beyond which the market fails to perform its allocative function to any satisfactory degree. It will remain for further work to formalize these conjectures and to test their significance. It is hoped, however, that enough has been said to stimulate interest and research on the subject.

REFERENCES

J. Bhagwati, "On the Equivalence of Tariffs and Quotas," in his *Trade, Tariffs and Growth*, London 1969.

—— and P. Desai, *Planning for Industrialization: A Study of India's Trade and Industrial Policies Since 1950*, Cambridge 1970.

—— and A. Krueger, *Foreign Trade Regimes and Economic Development: Experience and Analysis*, New York forthcoming.

J. R. Harris and M. P. Todaro, "Migration, Unemployment, and Development: A Two-Sector Analysis," *Amer. Econ. Rev.*, Mar. 1970, *60*, 126–42.

H. G. Johnson, "The Cost of Protection and the Scientific Tariff," *J. Polit. Econ.*, Aug. 1960, *68*, 327–45.

A. Krueger, *Foreign Trade Regimes and Economic Development: Turkey*, New York 1974.

J. B. Monteiro, *Corruption*, Bombay 1966.

G. Myrdal, *Asian Drama*, Vol. III, New York 1968.

M. P. Todaro, "A Model of Labor Migration and Urban Employment in Less Developed Countries," *Amer. Econ. Rev.*, Mar. 1969, *59*, 138–48.

R. Wraith and E. Simpkins, *Corruption in Developing Countries*, London 1963.

Government of India, Planning Commission, *Third Five Year Plan*, New Delhi, Aug. 1961.

Reserve Bank of India, *Report on Currency and Finance*, 1967–68.

Santhanam Committee, *Report on the Committee on Prevention of Corruption*, Government of India, Ministry of Home Affairs, New Delhi 1964.

[21]

European Economic Review 24 (1984) 291–307. North Holland

DUP ACTIVITIES AND ECONOMIC THEORY*

Jagdish N. BHAGWATI

Columbia University, New York, NY 10027, USA

Richard A. BRECHER

Carleton University, Ottawa, Ont., Canada K1S 5B6

T.N. SRINIVASAN

Yale University, New Haven, CT 06520, USA

Received October 1983, final version received January 1984

This paper considers the theory of Directly Unproductive Profit Seeking (DUP) activities, examining its implications for economic theory. Two classes of DUP activities are distinguished: one where the DUP activity is triggered by policy which is itself exogenously specified (e.g., tariff-revenue seeking resulting from pre-specified tariff); the other where DUP activity endogenises policy fully (e.g., tariff seeking). Implications for both positive and normative argumentation in economic theory are considered in depth for both these classes of DUP activity.

1. Introduction

Recently, several economists have directed their talents to examining the impact of what have been christened [Bhagwati (1982a)] as Directly-Unproductive Profit-seeking (DUP) activities. Among the more prominent such contributors, distinguished by different 'schools' of thought, are (i) Buchanan, Tullock and other important members of the public-choice school, with their major work now conveniently collected in Buchanan, Tullock and Tollison (1980) and reviewed well in Tollison (1982); (ii) Bhagwati, Findlay, Hansen, Krueger, Magee, Srinivasan, Wellisz and other international economists, whose work is reviewed and systematized in Bhagwati (1982a); (iii) Becker (1983), Peltzman, Posner, Stigler and other members of the Chicago school, whose notable work is variously available; and (iv) Lindbeck (1976), whose influential work on 'endogenous politicians' is widely known.

While considerable progress has been made in formally analyzing indi-

*Bhagwati's research has been supported by the National Science Foundation. This paper was presented, in an earlier version, at a conference at Middlebury College, and will appear in selected proceedings of the conference: David Colander, ed., *Neoclassical Political Economy: The Analysis of Rent-seeking and DUP Activities* (Ballinger & Co., Cambridge, MA) in Fall 1984.

vidual DUP phenomena (e.g., revenue seeking, tariff seeking, monopoly seeking, etc.) in recent works that integrate them into properly specified general equilibrium models, attempts at synthesizing them have begun only
recently: among them are Buchanan (1980) and Bhagwati (1982a). In this
paper, we propose to examine a somewhat different but equally general and
ambitious question: how serious for economic theory, as conventionally
practiced, is the systematic integration of DUP phenomena into our analysis?

Section 2 defines DUP activities and lays out a suitable taxonomy of DUP
categories or types which will serve our later analysis. Section 3 then
considers the implications of different DUP categories for positive analysis.
Section 4 addresses welfare or normative implications.

2. DUP activities: Concept and taxonomy

The essential characteristic of the phenomena which this volume addresses,
and which the many 'schools' of thought distinguished above analyze, is that
they represent ways of making a profit (i.e., income) by undertaking activities
which are directly unproductive; that is, they yield pecuniary returns but
produce neither goods and services that enter a conventional utility function
directly nor intermediate inputs into such goods and services. Insofar as such
activities use real resources, they result in a contraction of the availability set
open to the economy. Thus, for example, tariff-seeking lobbying, tariff
evasion, and premium seeking for given import licenses are all privately
profitable activities. However, their direct output is simply zero in terms of
the flow of goods and services entering a conventional utility function. For
example, tariff seeking yields pecuniary income by changing the tariff and
hence factor rewards; evasion of a tariff yields pecuniary income by
exploiting the differential price between legal (tariff-bearing) imports and
illegal (tariff-evading) imports; and premium seeking yields pecuniary income
from the premia on import licenses. [Krueger's (1974) analysis of what she
christened 'rent-seeking' activities relates to a subset of the broad class of
these DUP activities: she is concerned with the lobbying activities which are
triggered by different licensing practices of governments.[1]]

From the viewpoint of the analysis presented below, DUP activities can be
subdivided into two generic types.[2] The distinction is between introducing
policy-related DUP activity in models where the policy itself is *endogenously*
determined by the interplay of the DUP activity with the otherwise orthodox

---

[1]Her focus is on licensing/quantity restrictions and the rents thereon, and her generic set of
rent-seeking activities excludes from its scope other DUP activities such as price-distortion-
triggered DUP activities or distortion-triggering DUP activities For a fuller analysis of the
relationship, analytical and terminological, between DUP and 'rent seeking' activities, the reader
should consult Bhagwati (1983).

[2]Other classifications, addressed better to other purposes, are also possible, as in Bhagwati's
(1982a) synthesis of the welfare effects of DUP activities.

economic specification of the 'pure' economic system, and where the activity is embedded in a model where the policy is *exogenously* specified while the DUP activity is endogenous to that policy. Examples of the former, using tariff theory, are models where the tariff is endogenously determined; examples of the latter are models where a tariff exogenously specified to be in place leads to seeking for the revenues resulting from the tariff, and models where the tariff is evaded. The former class of DUP activities raises deeper questions for economic analysis than the latter, as we will contend below.

3. DUP activities and positive analysis

3.1. Exogenous policy

When the policy which induces DUP activity is exogenously specified, the implications of such DUP activity for positive analysis are tantamount to introducing an essentially non-traded sector into the formal model. Thus, depending on the problem and the model, the analytical conclusions derived, on which policy intuitions are based, will change. We illustrate this by briefly considering two recent DUP-theoretic analyses in tariff and transfer theory: revenue seeking in Bhagwati and Srinivasan (1980) and transfer seeking in Bhagwati, Brecher and Hatta (1982).

3.1.1. Revenue seeking and the Metzler paradox

Conventional trade theory tells us that, provided suitable convexity assumptions are satisified, a small country will find that a tariff will necessarily increase the domestic price and hence the output of the protected good. The Metzler paradox is that, for a large country (i.e., one that can influence its terms of trade), the tariff leads to such an improvement in the international terms of trade that the tariff-inclusive domestic price of the importable good falls and hence the importable good is paradoxically deprotected. We thus have the Metzler *price* and hence, what we can christen, the Metzler *production* paradox, in the conventional 2×2 model of trade theory.

But introduce now revenue seeking. Then, as Bhagwati and Srinivasan (1980) have shown, even if the Metzler price paradox were eliminated by assuming a small country, the Metzler production paradox can obtain. Thus, consider fig. 1. $F_y F_x$ is the production possibility curve. With free trade, this small economy would produce at P^*. With a tariff, production shifts to $\hat{P}$, implying that production of the importable good Y has increased, and consumption is at $\hat{C}$. However, if the tariff leads to DUP lobbying for the tariff revenues, then the production of goods will decline as some resources must be diverted towards revenue seeking. The equilibrium shown must therefore reflect this. If we make the so-called 'one-on-one' assumption, i.e.,

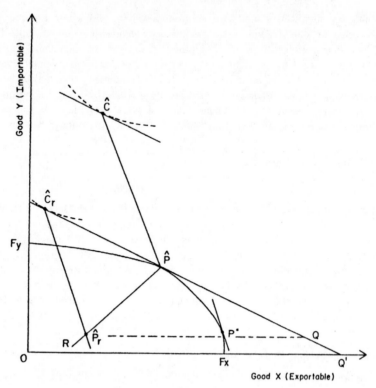

Fig. 1

that competitive revenue seeking leads to diversion of one dollar worth of resources for every dollar worth of revenue, then the equilibrium will shift in Fig. 1 such that consumption is at $\hat{C}_y$ on the national-income-at-market-price budget line $\hat{P}\hat{C}_y$, and production is at $\hat{P}_y$ where the world price line $\hat{C}_y\hat{P}_y$ intersects the generalized Rybczynski line $\hat{P}R$ (which reflects successive withdrawals of resources for revenue seeking, at the given tariff-inclusive prices). Trade is defined by $\hat{C}_y$ and $\hat{P}_y$, tariff revenue is equal to the dashed distance $\hat{P}_yQ$ which, in turn, exactly equals (given the one-on-one assumption) the value of resources diverted to revenue seeking since it is equal to the value of reduced output of goods as measured by the difference between $\hat{P}$ and $\hat{P}_y$ at domestic prices. Revenue seeking, in this depiction, takes the form analytically of a non-traded activity that pays market-determined wages and rentals to factors (equal to those in goods production) and whose 'output' is simply the revenue that is 'sought' by the lobby. While therefore the value of goods production reduces thanks to it, it is fully offset by the *revenue* in equilibrium, and hence national income/expenditure at domestic market prices is determinate as $\hat{P}\hat{C}_y$, with earned income in goods production being determined at $\hat{P}_y$ and earned income in revenue seeking being equal to the revenue and both adding up to OQ' as the national expenditure or budget.

Note then that Fig. 1 (as drawn) shows the production of the imported good Y at $\hat{P}_y$ as less than at P^*: the Metzler production paradox obtains. The conventional 'substitution' effect of the tariff does protect, taking production from P^* to $\hat{P}$; but this is more than offset by the 'income' effect of the induced revenue seeking that shifts production again, to $\hat{P}_y$, given that the (generalized) Rybczynski line is positively sloped in the present example.

3.1.2. Transfer seeking and the terms-of-trade-change criterion

An application of this analysis to the transfer problem can again be shown to change dramatically the conventional criterion for change in the terms of trade — as in the recent work of Bhagwati, Brecher and Hatta (1982).

Thus, consider the case where the transfer, instead of being received directly by consumers or given to them as a lump-sum gift as in conventional analysis, goes into the governmental budget and then leads to transfer-seeking lobbying. [In principle, we could also assume symmetrically that the donor country experiences reduced lobbying when it makes the transfer: a case we discuss later.] Also consider again the one-on-one assumption such that the transfer-seeking lobbying uses up a value of domestic primary factors *equal* in total to the amount of the transfer. This situation is analyzed in fig. 2.

Initially, the recipient country produces on its production-possibility frontier $F_y F_x$ at point P, consumes on its social indifference curve $V_y V_x$ at point C, and trades with the donor country (the rest of the world) along price line PC from point P to point C. For starters, consider the case where the terms of trade can not change.

In the small-country case, the transfer has of course no impact on the goods–price ratio. The transfer-seeking activity of lobbyists, however, causes output in the recipient to move down the generalized Rybczynski line PR until production reaches $\hat{P}$, where the value of national output has fallen by the amount of the transfer to the level represented by the price line (parallel to PC) through point $\hat{P}$. Since this value of output plus the transfer equals national expenditure, consumption remains at point C. Thus, the transfer has paradoxically failed to enrich the recipient.

In the case of a large country, the recipient's welfare could actually decline, if the marginal propensity to consume good X (along the income–consumption curve) in the donor is less than the (analogous) marginal propensity to produce this good along the (generalized) Rybczynski line PR in the recipient. In this case, the transfer at initial prices would create an excess world demand for good X, and (given stability) the relative price of

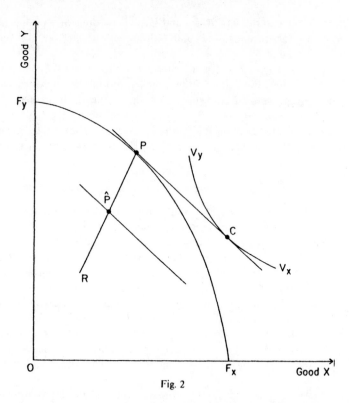

Fig. 2

this commodity would rise to clear world markets. As the equilibrium price line steepens from the initial position PC, the recipient must reach a lower indifference curve, provided that the relative price of X does not rise above the autarkic level (where an indifference curve would touch curve F_yF_x). By similar reasoning, the opposite ranking of marginal propensities would lead to a fall in the world price of good X, and hence enrichment of the recipient.

Bhagwati, Brecher and Hatta (1982) have analyzed also the *symmetric case* where the transfer-seeking DUP activity in the recipient country is matched by identical effects of DUP activity in the donor. To make the symmetry complete, they assume that the donor was initially disbursing domestically a given amount of revenue, resulting in equivalent utilization of resources in competitive subsidy-seeking lobbying; and that the subsequent international transfer payment simply reduces by an equivalent amount the subsidies subject to domestic lobbying and hence also reduces the resource-use on such lobbying equivalently. As they then show, given market stability and the above-mentioned proviso about the autarkic level of relative prices, national welfare will then improve (worsen) for the donor and worsen (improve) for the recipient *if and only if* the recipient's marginal propensity to produce its own importable is greater (less) than the donor's marginal propensity to produce this good.

3.2. Endogenous policy

The endogenization of policy *via* DUP activity is also subversive of traditional intuitions. Traditionally, economists are trained to think of governments as 'neutral' in positive analysis and of economic agents to compete, perfectly or imperfectly, in alternative types of market environments. Once policy is endogenized, this tradition must necessarily be undermined. For, some or all economic agents may now also operate to have policy defined in their favour; there is a non-economic, or non-traditional, marketplace, as it were, in which economic agents can simultaneously conduct their profitmaking activities.[3] We thus have *two* components of the overall model: the orthodox 'economic' specification and the 'political' specification where profit motivation may equally extend and where the economic returns accrue through induced-policy changes influencing economic returns in the traditionally 'economic' sphere of the model.

While we will deal later with the critical implication of this transformation in modelling policy for orthodox welfare-theoretic analysis, we mention here simply that, as with the exogenous-policy DUP activities analyzed earlier, the results in positive analysis are sensitive to this basic change in the way the total economic system is modelled. For example, the customary view is that, given an exogenously-specified tariff, an improvement in the terms of trade will reduce the domestic production of the importable good in an economy with given resources, well-behaved technology and perfect markets. But this conclusion need not follow, or may be seriously weakened, if the effect of the terms of trade change is to trigger tariff-seeking lobbying successfully.

While there is indeed a vast literature on 'political economy' models which endogenise policy through DUP-activity specification in a variety of contexts, several efforts of a general-equilibrium type have emerged recently in trade-theoretic literature in particular. We will give an indication here of the nature of these models by drawing on two of the early papers on tariff seeking:[4] Findlay and Wellisz (1982), and Feenstra and Bhagwati (1982). These papers may be characterized in the following way.

(i)   Economic *agents* are defined, which will engage in lobbying. In the Findlay–Wellisz model, these are the two specific factors in the two activities in the specific-factors model and their interests are in conflict since goods price changes affect them in an opposite manner. In

---

[3]Of course, this is also true of DUP lobbying and policy-evading models we considered in the case where the policy *causing* the DUP activity was specified exogenously.
[4]The earliest, pioneering work is that of Brock and Magee (1978, 1980).

Feenstra–Bhagwati, there is only one economic agent (that hurt by import competition) which engages in lobbying, in the 2×2 Heckscher–Ohlin–Samuelson model.

(ii) The agents lobby to have a *policy* adopted or to oppose it. In both Findlay–Wellisz and Feenstra–Bhagwati, that policy is uniquely defined to be a tariff.

(iii) The 'government', as an economic agent, is not explicit in Findlay–Wellisz. The cost-of-lobbying functions which postulate the tariff as a function of the lobbying resources spent in proposing and opposing a tariff are *implicitly* assuming a government which is subject to these opposing lobbying efforts and whatever preferences the government has are reflected implicitly in the postulated function. On the other hand, in Feenstra–Bhagwati, there is a 2-*layer* government: the lobbying process interacts with one branch of government (e.g., the legislature) to enact a *Lobbying Tariff* whereas another branch of the government (e.g., the President in the U.S.) then comes into the picture to use the tariff revenues generated by the lobbying tariff to bribe the lobby into accepting a different, welfare-superior *Efficient Tariff* which yields to the lobby, from both the revenue bribe *plus* the earned income from the market place at the efficient tariff, the same income as from the lobbying tariff.[5]

These papers then define rather well how the theoretical analysis of endogenous policymaking can be approached in the conventional manner of economic theory. By taking a simple set of political-cum-economic assumptions, they manage to get a neat, simple model working. In fact, from a pedagogic viewpoint, the extension of the traditional $2 \times 2 \times 2$ HOS-type trade theory model to an augmented $2 \times 2 \times 2 \times 2$ model, where there are 2 lobbies and capitalists and workers engage in tariff-seeking lobbying, would be a splendid exercise. It would imply combining, suitably and easily, elements from the Findaly–Wellisz and Feenstra–Bhagwati models.

These models can also be enriched in different directions. Of particular theoretical interest is the role of the government itself. Recall that the Feenstra–Bhagwati model postulates a 2-layer view of the government, building in *both* the view (taken exclusively in Findlay–Wellisz) that the government is 'acted upon' by political lobbies and that the tariff becomes then a function of the resources expended (presumably in financing re-election) by the respective lobbies, *and* the view that the government acts so as to maximize a conventional social welfare function. Instead, one could well take for example the view, sometimes propounded, that the government will maximize its *revenue*, since that will maximize its patronage. If so,

[5]Feenstra and Bhagwati note that the efficient tariff may paradoxically exceed the lobbying tariff if the shadow price of lobbying activity is negative.

Johnson's classic analysis of maximum-revenue tariff yields, of course, in a conventional world where other economic agents are not engaged in lobbying, the politically-endogenous tariff.

Again, the analysis can be extended instead rather on the dimension of the *policy instruments* for which the economic agents can lobby in response to import competition. Thus, as a supplement to tariffs, one can consider policy instruments in regard to international factor and technological flows. Without formally incorporating them into a model that endogenously yields the equilibrium choice or policy-mix of instruments in response to import competition, Bhagwati (1982a, b), Sapir (1983), and Dinopoulos (1983) have analyzed the *preferences* that different economic agents could have between these instruments when faced by import competition (i.e., improved terms of trade). Such analyses throw light on the incentives for lobbying for different policy adoptions by the government and hence yield the necessary insights into why certain policy options rather than others emerge as actual responses to import competition.

4. DUP activities and welfare analysis

Again, we will consider exogenous and endogenous policies successively.

4.1. Exogenous policies

The welfare effects of specific policies, and of parametric changes in the presence of exogenously specified policies, can be extremely sensitive to whether induced DUP activities are built into the model or not. Again, we take two telling instances.

(i)   Bhagwati and Srinivasan (1982), following on Foster's (1981) work, have shown that shadow prices for primary factors in a small, tariff-distorted open economy are different, depending on whether the tariff has or has not resulted in revenue seeking. In fact, the shadow prices can be shown to be the market prices when revenue seeking obtains.

(ii) We will also show here that, while the conventional rank-ordering of an arbitrary $t\%$ tariff vis-à-vis a production tax or a consumption tax in a small open economy at the same rate implies that the tariff is inferior to each of the other two policies since the tariff imposes both a production *and* a consumption cost, this rank-ordering gets reversed if the different policies also result in revenue seeking!

4.1.1. Shadow prices in a tariff-distorted, small economy in cost–benefit analysis

The shadow prices for a small, tariff-distorted economy are known from the cost–benefit literature to be derivable as the duals to the world goods prices at the distorted techniques. On the other hand, it is obvious from the fact that if revenue seeking is present, as in fig. 1, the economy operates on the national-expenditure, social-budget line defined at the market, tariff-inclusive prices. Therefore, a marginal withdrawal of factors from the distorted, DUP equilibrium will evidently imply an opportunity cost reflecting the market prices.[6] To put it another way, with the entire revenue sought away, the consumer expenditure on goods equals income at market prices for factors. And these factor prices and goods prices do not change (as long as incomplete specialization continues), as we vary factor endowments, thanks to the tariff. As such, the value of change in the labour (capital) endowment by a unit is its market reward: hence the shadow factor prices in this DUP-activity-inclusive model are the market prices.[7] The invisible hand strikes again!

4.1.2. Policy rankings with revenue seeking

Recall that, for a small economy, a consumption tax on the importable (production tax on the exportable) is welfare superior to a tariff at the same *ad valorem* rate since it avoids the additional production (consumption) loss associated with the tariff. It turns out that once full revenue seeking *a lá* Bhagwati and Srinivasan (1980) is unleashed by the imposition of any tax, this welfare ranking is reversed. This is seen as follows.

With tariff at an *ad valorem* rate t, let the output vector of the economy be (X', Y') under no revenue seeking. Let the free-trade (i.e., zero-tariff) output vector be (X^0, Y^0). With full revenue seeking under the tariff, consumers maximize utility given a relative price of $(1+t)$ of the importable good Y (with the world relative price normalized at unity) and income Y equal to $[X' + (1+t)Y']$. They thus derive utility $v(1+t, X'_1 + (1+t)Y')$ expressed in terms of their indirect utility function $v(p, Y)$. On the other hand, with a consumption tax at an *ad valorem* rate t and full revenue seeking, they face the same price $(1+t)$ but an income of $(X^0 + Y^0)$, thus obtaining utility: $v(1+t, X^0 + Y^0)$. From the fact that (X', Y') maximizes the value of output given the tariff t, we get $\{X' + (1+t)Y'\} \geqq \{X^0 + (1+t)Y^0\} \geqq \{X^0 + Y^0\}$. Hence $v(1+t, X' + (1+t)Y') > v(1+t, X^0 + Y^0)$, i.e., a tariff with full revenue seeking is superior to a consumption tax with full revenue seeking.

The foregoing argument can be readily illustrated in fig. 3.[8] Without any

---

[6]Thus, as Anam (1982) has shown, Johnson's (1967) type of immiserizing growth in the presence of a tariff is impossible when all tariff revenues are sought.

[7]If not all of the tariff revenues are subject to seeking, the shadow prices would be differently defined, as noted by Anam (1982).

[8]For an important diagrammatic analysis of a consumption tax with revenue seeking, see Anam (1982), who showed that such a tax might be welfare-inferior to a tariff in achieving a given level of consumption for one good.

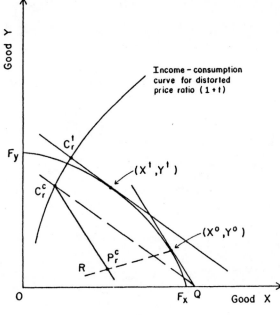

Fig. 3

seeking and free trade, equilibrium production is at (X^0, Y^0). With a tariff, production shifts at relative price ratio $(1+t)$ to (X', Y'). With tariff-revenue seeking, consumption is at C_r^t, as shown in fig. 1 also. Shift, however, to a consumption tax on good Y with attendant revenue-seeking. Production then remains at (X^0, Y^0) and the income, measured in terms of good X, is OQ, and is spent at the consumption-tax-inclusive price ratio $(1+t)$ along QC_r^c, taking consumption to C_r^c. Fig. 3 also shows production in the consumption-tax-cum-seeking equilibrium. It is given at P_r^c by the intersection of the world price line from C_r^c and the R-line which is the Rybczynski line for the world price ratio (unity) at (X^0, Y^0). Evidently, welfare at C_r^c dominates that at C_r^t: the tariff is superior to the consumption tax.

Consider now a comparison between a tariff at rate t and a production tax on good X yielding the same domestic relative good price as the tariff, both with attendant full revenue seeking. Under the tariff, equilibrium consumption is then at C_r^t in fig. 4. But shift now to the production tax. Income, in terms of good Y, will then be OQ as with the tariff but consumers will face the world price ratio (unity) and consumption will be at C_r^p. The production equilibrium will then be at P_r^p, the intersection between the expenditure line QC_r^p and the R-line from (X', Y') at the tax-distorted price $(1+t)$. Evidently, C_r^t dominates C_r^p: welfare under the tariff exceeds that

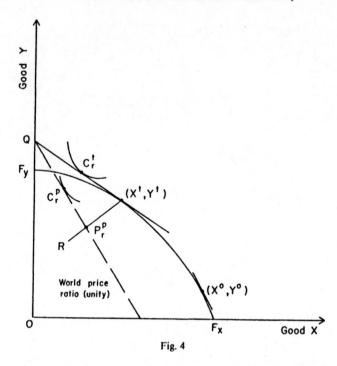

Fig. 4

under an indentical production tax, when full revenue seeking obtains in each case.

The intuitive explanation of these results is evidently that, with no revenue seeking, a consumption (production) tax generates more revenue than a tariff at the same rate,[9] the reason being that the offsetting production (consumption) subsidy effect of a tariff is absent. In effect, what we are getting into is a situation where there are *two* distortions, rather than one, associated with each of the policies being ranked: the direct distortion implied by the policy itself and the indirect distortion implied by the (induced) DUP activity. What is interesting in the specific policyrankings considered here is that these rankings are still possible, and in fact get reversed, when the indirect DUP effect is considered!

From a welfare-theoretic viewpoint, therefore, the analyst has to be alerted to the possibly critical role that (policy-induced) DUP activities can play in analyzing policies and hence in determining desirable policy intervention. This conclusion is also dramatically highlighted by the welfare-theoretic analysis of transfers. Thus, revert to our discussion of the DUP-theoretic transfer problem in section 3 and to fig. 2. Recall that, in the traditional 2×2

[9]See also Anam (1982) on this point.

(non-DUP) framework, exacting a reparation payment will always be enriching for the recipient of the resulting transfer in a Walras-stable market. Once, however, full transfer seeking is permitted, this is no longer so! Thus, take the case of a 'large' recipient country, as discussed above in fig. 2. If the terms of trade worsen in this DUP-activity-inclusive 2×2 model, that is *sufficient* to immiserize the recipient in a Walras-stable market whereas by contrast such deterioration in the terms of trade cannot ever be large enough to offset the primary gain from the transfer in a Walras-stable market in the orthodox non-DUP-activity 2×2 model.

We therefore need to re-examine a number of policy intuitions if policies induce DUP activities in the real world, as they indeed do. The world lies somewhere along the continuum defined by two end points: one where no DUP activity is induced and the other where DUP activity is induced fully (on a one-to-one basis).[10] But while we have charted reasonably in depth the former end, we are only beginning to understand and sketch the latter end. An agenda for research to map out the latter landscape clearly awaits a new generation of researchers in all branches of economic theory.

4.2. Endogenous policy

A far more critical question is raised, however, once you fully endogenise policy in DUP-theoretic models. Exploiting our comparative advantage, we may consider again a trade-theoretic example to raise and probe this issue.

Take a tariffseeking model of any species that you prefer. The endogenous tariff that emerges then in such a model may be illustrated in fig. 5. $F^{ex}F^{ex}$ is the production possibility curve when all resources are deployed for producing X and Y and an *exogenous* tariff leads this small economy from P^* at given world prices to $\hat{P}^{ex}$ under protection. But now the model is augmented to endogenise the tariff and, in equilibrium, resources are used up in tariff-seeking DUP activity and the tariff-inclusive equilibrium is at $\hat{P}^{en}$. The production possibility curve $F^{en}F^{en}$ is a hypothetical construct, taking the endowment of factors as *net* of those used up in tariff seeking *equilibrium:* the tariff-inclusive goods price ratio must therefore be tangent to it at $\hat{P}^{en}$. It is assumed, of course, that revenue-seeking-induced DUP activity is not simultaneously present here.[11]

Now, as Bhagwati (1980) has shown, if we wish to measure the cost of protection in this endogenous-tariff model, the appropriate way to do it would be to put the world price ratio tangent to $F^{en}F^{en}$ at $\hat{P}^*$ and then, using the Hicksian equivalent-variational measure, to take the move from $\hat{P}^{en}$

---

[10]The latter end point may even be more drastic if, as Tullock (1981) has suggested, seeking leads to more resources being spent on chasing a prize than the value of the prize itself, depending on how you model the terms and conditions of such a chase.

[11]See Tullock (1981) and Bhagwati (1982b) for analysis of the case where however this DUP activity is simultaneously present.

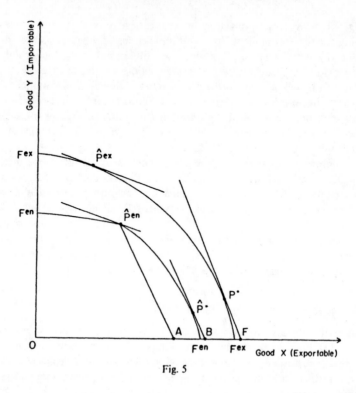

Fig. 5

to $\hat{P}*$ as the standard production cost of protection (reflecting the distortion of prices faced by producers) and the further move from $\hat{P}*$ to P* as the added cost of tariff-seeking lobbying (reflecting the loss due to resource diversion to lobbying). Hence the *total* cost of protection in an endogenous-tariff model would be AF, reflecting the comparison between the free-trade-equilibrium position at P* and the endogenous-tariff-equilibrium position at $\hat{P}^{en}$. In turn, it is decomposed then into AB , the conventional 'cost of protection', and BF, the 'lobbying cost'. It might be appropriate perhaps to christen the total cost as the cost of the 'protectionist process', to avoid confusion between AF and AB.[12]

While this analytical innovation to extend the traditional cost-of-protection analysis to the case where the tariff is endogenous may be applauded, it raises the deeper question that we now wish to address.

---

[12]Bhagwati (1980) also shows that it is incorrect to argue that the cost of an endogenous tariff at $t\%$ always exceeds the cost of an exogenous tariff at $t\%$. This proposition involves comparing $\hat{P}^{ex}$ with $\hat{P}^{en}$; and, since this is a second-best comparison, the endogenous tariff can be less harmful than the exogenous one. This is also at the heart of the problem with the Buchanan–Tollison definition of DUP activities, as discussed in Bhagwati (1983).

Once the tariff is endogenised, it will generally be determined uniquely as at $\hat{P}^{en}$ (though, of course, multiple equilbria can be introduced as readily as in conventional 'strictly-economic' models). To compare this outcome with a hypothetical free-trade policy leading to $P*$ is to compare a policy choice that is made as a solution to the entire, augmented economic-cum-policy-choice system with a wholly hypothetical policy that descends like manna from heaven! Such a comparison makes obvious sense, of course, when we take policies as exogenous: we are then simply varying them, given the conventional economic system, and reading off their welfare consequences. But, with only one policy outcome determined endogenously, the comparison between it and another hypothetical policy arrived at by exogenous specification, while of course possible, is not compelling. It is virtually as if we had wiped out one (the 'political') side of our model for our point of reference!

It would appear therefore that we need to *change* the way we pose welfare-theoretic questions once policies are endogenised critically, as in the foregoing analysis. Thus, it is not particulary meaningful to rank-order policies as in traditional analysis, once policies are endogenous. Nor is it appropriate to compare them vis-à-vis a reference point (such as $P*$ in fig. 3) which reflects an exogenously-specified policy.

Rather, it would appear that the analyst must now shift focus and concentrate on *variations around the endogenous equilibrium* itself (i.e., around $\hat{P}^{en}$ in fig. 3). Thus, it is customary to ask what happens, given a policy, to welfare when accumulation comes about, or when technical knowhow changes, etc. We can rephrase these questions as follows, keeping in mind that there are now two parts of the overall economic system: 'economic' and 'political': what will happen to welfare if, on the economic side of the model, these changes such as accumulation, technical progress etc. occur; and what happens if changes occur instead on the political side such as an increased cost of lobbying for a tariff if there is an exogenous shift in attitudes against protection?[13] In short, the overall system must be solved for endogenous policy change and for final welfare impact for parametric changes that can occur now *either* in the 'economic' *or* equally in the 'political' side of the overall, augmented system. An interesting way to decompose the overall welfare impact of such parametric changes in either the 'economic' or the 'political' side of the system could be to assume first that policy does remain exogenous and then, in the next stage, to allow it to change to its endogenous value. The first stage should capture the essence of what we have come to think of as the customary impact of a parametric change in the system; the second stage can be taken to correspond to the fact that policy is endogenous.

[13]On this point, see Brecher (1982).

5. Concluding remark

Evidently, therefore, the integration of DUP activities into theoretic analysis is a serious business. We hope that we have raised the issues sufficiently sharply to stimulate the response of our fellow economists in the shape of future research on what promises to be an extremely important innovation in economic theorising.

References

Anam, Mahmudul, 1982, Distortion-triggered lobbying and welfare: A contribution to the theory of directly-unproductive profit-seeking activities, Journal of International Economics 13, no. 1/2, Aug., 15–32.

Becker, Gary S., 1983, A theory of competition among pressure groups for political influence, Quarterly Journal of Economics 93, Aug., 371–400.

Bhagwati, J.N., 1980, Lobbying and welfare, Journal of Public Economics 14, Dec., 355–363.

Bhagwati, J.N., 1982a, Directly-unproductive, profit-seeking (DUP) activities, Journal of Political Economy 90, Oct., 988–1002.

Bhagwati, J.N., 1982b, Lobbying, DUP activities and welfare: A response to Tullock, Journal of Public Economics 19, Dec., 395–401.

Bhagwati, J.N., 1983, DUP activities and rent seeking, Working paper (Columbia University); abbreviated version in Kyklos 36, 634–637.

Bhagwati, J.N. and T.N. Srinivasan, 1980, Revenue seeking: A generalization of the theory of tariffs, Journal of Political Economy 88, Dec., 1069–1087.

Bhagwati, J.N. and T.N. Srinivasan, 1982, The welfare consequences of directly-unproductive profit-seeking (DUP) lobbying activities: Prices versus quantity distortions, Journal of International Economics 13, 33–44.

Bhagwati, J.N., R.A. Brecher and T. Hatta, 1982, The generalized theory of transfers and welfare: Exogenous (policy-imposed) and endogenous (transfer-induced) distortions, Mimeo., July, forthcoming in Quarterly Journal of Economics.

Brecher, Richard A., 1982, Comment, in: Jagdish N. Bhagwati, ed., Import competition and response (University of Chicago Press, Chicago, IL).

Brock, William and Steven P. Magee, 1978, The economics of special interest politics: The case of tariff, American Economic Review 68, May, 246–250.

Brock, William A. and Steven P. Magee, 1980, Tariff formation in a democracy, in: J. Black and B. Hindley, eds., Current issues in international commercial policy and diplomacy (Macmillan, New York) 1–9.

Buchanan, J., 1980, Rent seeking and profit seeking, in: J. Buchanan, G. Tullock and R. Tollison, eds., Towards a general theory of the rent-seeking society (Texas A & M University Press, College Station, TX).

Buchanan, J., G. Tullock and R. Tollison, eds., 1980, Towards a general theory of the rent-seeking society (Texas A & M University Press, College Station, TX).

Dinopoulos, E., 1983, Import competition, international factor mobility and lobbying responses: The Schumpeterian industry, Journal of International Economics 14, May.

Feenstra, R. and J.N. Bhagwati, 1982, Tariff seeking and the efficient tariff, in: J.N. Bhagwati, ed., Import competition and response (The University of Chicago Press, Chicago, IL) 245–258.

Findlay, R. and S. Wellisz, 1982, Endogenous tariffs, the political economy of trade restrictions, and welfare, in: J.N. Bhagwati, ed., Import competition and response (The University of Chicago Press, Chicago, IL) 223–233.

Foster, E., 1981, The treatment of rents in cost-benefit analysis, American Economic Review 71, March, 171–178.

Johnson, Harry G., 1967, The possibility of income losses from increased efficiency or factor accumulation in the presence of tariffs, Economic Journal 77, March, 151–154.

Krueger, A.O., 1974, The political economy of the rent-seeking society, American Economic Review 64, June, 291-303.

Lindbeck, Assar, 1976, Stabilization policies in open economies with endogenous politicians, Richard Ely Lecture, American Economic Review 66, May, 1-19.

Sapir, Andre, 1983, Foreign competition, immigration and structural adjustment, Journal of International Economics 14, May, 381-394.

Tollison, R.D., 1982, Rent seeking: A survey, Kyklos 35, 575-602.

Tullock, Gordon, 1981, Lobbying and welfare: A comment, Journal of Public Economics 16, 391-394.

[22]

FOREIGN TRADE REGIMES AND ECONOMIC GROWTH IN DEVELOPING COUNTRIES

Deepak Lal
Sarath Rajapatirana

The static case for free trade is as simple as it is powerful. The removal of barriers to foreign trade expands the feasible set of consumption possibilities. It does so by providing, in effect, an indirect technology for transforming domestic resources into the goods and services that yield current and future utility for consumers. This static case does not involve any commitment to laissez-faire;[1] the law of comparative advantage, as well as the gains from trade it underpins, applies to both socialist and capitalist economies. The dynamic version of the law incorporates investment in line with a country's changing comparative advantage, which minimizes the present value of the resource costs of its future demands. By widening the market, foreign trade also allows a country to exploit economies of scale. Furthermore, the competitive pressures exerted by imports prevent the emergence of welfare-reducing domestic monopolies and induce domestic producers to improve quality and reduce costs. To the extent the static gains are saved and invested efficiently, they will grow over time, while the introduction of new goods and (more important) new technology through foreign trade can affect an economy's rate of technical progress.

Apart from this last factor, the result of moving toward free trade is a higher level of per capita income, not a permanently faster rate of growth. This is one argument currently being used to denigrate the case for free trade as a means of enhancing growth (see Lucas 1985); it will be discussed in the last section of this paper. Longer-standing skepticism includes, first, the claim that the static gains are fairly small for even large reductions in tariffs and, second, that dirigiste foreign trade regimes (which in 1945–65 encouraged import substitution and then, after 1965, export promotion) are likely to do more to boost a country's growth rate.

This article surveys empirical studies that seek to demonstrate the limited static gains from freer trade and then reviews studies of the dynamic effects of growth of exports on that of per capita income. The following section summarizes the results of comparative studies of developing countries undertaken in the 1960s and early 1970s, which show fairly conclusively that "outward orientation" seems to be positively associated with faster growth and greater equity. The article then examines whether the conclusions of these studies hold for the more volatile conditions since then. It considers the various arguments that cast trade as an "engine of growth." The final section introduces certain insights of the classical writers—in particular Adam Smith—which have reemerged in the neo-Austrian, as well as the more recent neoclassical "new political economy" schools, which might explain the stylized facts about the links between trade and growth. These emphasize the importance of the nonquantifiable aspects of a free trade regime in creating (in an irreducibly uncertain world) an economic framework that encourages entrepreneurship, productivity, and thrift. We argue that free trade is thus the handmaiden of growth, as it indirectly constrains the state from going beyond the bounds of providing those public goods essential for development.

The Static Gains from Trade

Early studies of the costs of protection measured the static gains from trade in terms of the familiar welfare triangles associated with complete or partial trade liberalization (as in the case of customs unions). Harberger (1959) estimated that the cost of protection in Chile amounted to "no more than 2½ percent of the national income" (p. 135). Scitovsky (1958) estimated the gains to the European Community from increased specialization at "less than one-twentieth of one percent of the gross social product of the countries involved" (p. 67). Johnson (1958) estimated the gain to Britain from the formation of a free trade area as at most 1 percent of national income.

Recently, several models have been developed to examine the general equilibrium effects of trade liberalization (*AB* in figure 1).[2] These estimates are based on the standard Heckscher-Ohlin model with constant returns to scale. The gains are estimated as Hicksian-equivalent variations as percentages of gross domestic product (GDP) in a base period. The gains from trade liberalization appear to be small: Whalley (1984) estimates a global *net* gain of about 0.3 percent of world GDP in 1977, and the maximum for any region or country is 0.5

190

percent of GDP (see Srinivasan 1986a, 1986b). Moreover, in Whalley's model, with a move to world free trade, the developing countries *lose* 4 percent of their GDP.

As Srinivasan (1986a) has argued, however, the results of these models are not credible, partly because of how they manipulate data to make an internally consistent equilibrium set (when the data themselves come from nonequilibrium situations) and partly because of how they specify some crucial elasticity parameters. In particular, they all make use of estimated trade elasticities (see Stern and others 1976), which have a well-known bias to underestimation (see Orcutt 1950, Kemp 1962, Kakwani 1972).[3] Most of these models also do not take account of scale economies and imperfect competition. An exception is a model for Canada by Harris (1983), which shows that a multilateral reduction of all tariffs yields welfare gains of more than 5 percent of GDP.

Furthermore, most of these models do not take account of the "rent seeking" and "directly unproductive" activities triggered by protectionism (see Tullock 1967, Krueger 1974, Bhagwati 1980). In the case of rent seeking, the deadweight loss associated with, for instance, a tariff, is not merely

Figure 1

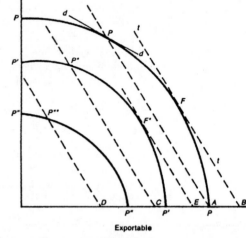

Note PP is the production possibility frontier. *F* is the free trade output when world prices are given by *tt*. With a tariff and no lobbying or rent seeking, the production point is *P*, with the domestic price ratio being given by *dd* and the welfare cost by *AB* With lobbying for the tariff, the production possibility curve shifts to *P'P'*, the production point to *P**, and the welfare loss is *CB*. To avoid various "immiserizing paradoxes" (which depend on the relative slopes of the Rybczynski line between *P* and *P**, and the world price ratio *tt*), which could imply a welfare gain from the lobbying equilibrium at *P** as compared with *P*, it is better to decompose the welfare loss *CB* into the loss due to the tariff *CE* (this is the usual triangle estimate) and that due to lobbying *EB* (see Bhagwati 1980). With rent seeking, the production possibility curve shifts inward to *P"P"*, the production point to *P"*, and the welfare loss at world prices is *DB*.

the conventional net change in the consumer and producer surplus triangles, but also the spending by lobbies for and against the tariff and by those who aim to capture the rent for themselves. Thus in figure 1 the lobbying costs shift the production possibility (*PP*) curve inward, with an associated welfare cost of protection *CB*.[4] If there is a struggle over the rents associated with the tariff, the welfare costs rise to *DB*, as the *PP* curve shifts further inward (see Srinivasan 1986b). One study by Grais and others (1984) has attempted to estimate the costs of rent seeking (but not lobbying) associated with quotas in Turkey. It found that if tariffs were removed but quotas maintained, there was little effect on real GDP; if quotas were also eliminated, real GDP rose between 5 and 10 percent.

So far we have excluded the deadweight losses of domestic monopoly and X-inefficiency associated with protection (see Leibenstein 1966, Corden 1974, Krueger 1984). Thus "a reduction in tariff levels might be expected to result in a downward shift in industry supply curves. The welfare costs of protection would then consist of the conventional production cost, plus an inefficiency cost and possibly a monopoly cost" (Krueger 1984, p. 544). The only attempt to measure all these costs is by Bergsman (1974). He found that the costs of protection as a proportion of GNP, consisting of the conventional allocative inefficiency costs (A), the X-inefficiency combined with monopoly costs (X), and the total costs $(T = X + A)$ were as follows for four developing countries:

	A	X	T
Brazil	0.3	6.8	7.1
Mexico	0.3	2.2	2.5
Pakistan	0.5	5.4	5.9
Philippines	1.0	2.6	3.6

The static welfare gains from trade liberalization could therefore be quite substantial. But these would still affect only the level of income, not its rate of growth. They do not explain why the growth rates of free-trading countries should be higher on a sustainable basis, as seems to have been the case.

Statistical Tests of Exports and Growth

The links between trade and growth have many statistical studies, which are summarized in tables 1 and 2. Michalopoulos and Jay (1973) estimated an aggregate neoclassical production function for thirty-nine countries. Exports were found to be highly significant, and GNP growth was significantly correlated to the growth rate of exports.

By studying the change in the proportion of exports to GNP relative to the rate of GNP growth in forty-one countries during 1950–73, Michaely (1977) found a significant relationship at the 1 percent level for the Spearman rank correlation. The study attempted to avoid autocorrelation between exports and GNP by using the change in the share of exports in GNP to represent the growth of exports which was then regressed against the rate of change of per capita income (Michaely 1977, p. 50).

In her study for the National Bureau of Economic Research (NBER) on foreign trade regimes and economic development, Krueger (1978)

Table 1. *Estimated Spearman Rank Correlation Coefficients between Export Growth and Output Growth in Developing Countries*

Author	Average annual change in export GNP ratio vs. average annual per capita GNP growth	Export growth vs. GNP growth	Incremental export GNP ratio vs. GNP growth	Increments in export GNP ratios vs. GNP growth
Michaely				
For 41 observations, 1950–73	0.380**	—	—	—
For 23 middle-income countries, 1950–73	0.523**	—	—	—
For 18 low-income countries, 1950–73	−0.04	—	—	—
Balassa: for 11 semi-industrial countries, 1960–73	—	0.888**	0.813**	0.776**

**indicates 1 percent level of significance.
Source: Michaely 1977, pp. 51–52, and Balassa 1978, p. 184.

regressed GNP growth for each of ten countries against the rate of export growth. She found a positive and significant relationship between the two. Similarly, Balassa (1978), by reestimating Michaely's equations and incorporating the Michalopoulos-Jay factors, noted a robust relationship between exports and GNP growth for eleven countries. He recognized that it understated the effects of export growth. And Feder (1983) not only found a positive correlation between exports and GNP growth, but also provided evidence to support the hypothesis that export-oriented policies both led the economy to an optimal allocation of resources and generally enhanced productivity.[5]

All these studies confirm a statistical relationship between export and income growth. But at best this provides a stylized fact, not a theory. As in most statistical matters however, even this association is disputed—a reflection of the emerging "law" that all econometric evidence is equivocal. Thus Helliner (1986) in a study of low-income countries heavily weighted toward Sub-Saharan Africa, concluded that the results for 1960–80 "show no statistically significant link between the change in export share of GDP and growth. Indeed, the sign on this relationship is consistently negative" (p. 146). Similar results were also reported by Michaely (1977): "the positive association of the economy's growth rate with the growth of the export share appears to be particularly strong among the more developed countries, and not to exist at all among the least developed ... This seems to indicate that growth is affected by export performance only once countries achieve some minimum level of development" (p. 52).

Table 2. Estimated Relationship between Export Growth and Output Growth in Developing Countries

Author	Dependent variable,[a] $\left(\dfrac{\Delta Y}{Y_1}\right)$	Independent variables[b]								
		$\dfrac{\Delta K_d}{Y_1}$	$\dfrac{\Delta K_f}{Y_1}$	$\dfrac{\Delta L}{L_1}$	$\dfrac{\Delta X}{\Delta Y}$	$\dfrac{\Delta X}{X_1}$	$\dfrac{\Delta X}{Y_1}$	$D_{i1}t$	$D_{i2}t$	R^2
Michalopolous and	—	0.25	0.20	0.66	—	—	—	—	—	0.53
Jay: for 39		(7.81)	(3.35)	(2.44)						
observations,	—	0.24	0.12	0.60	0.04	—	—	—	—	0.71
1960–66		(9.62)	(2.33)	(2.81)	(4.82)					
Balassa: for 10	—	0.18	0.30	1.09	—	—	—	—	—	0.58
observations,		(3.23)	(2.42)	(1.74)						
1960–73	—	0.15	0.23	0.97	0.04	—	—	—	—	0.77
		(3.33)	(2.40)	(1.99)	(3.57)					
Feder: for 31	—	0.284		0.739	—	—	—	—	—	0.37
observations,		(4.311)		(1.990)						
1964–73[c]	—	0.178		0.747	—	—	0.422	—	—	0.689
		(3.542)		(2.862)			(5.454)			
	—	0.124		0.696	—	0.131	0.305	—	—	0.809
		(3.009)		(3.399)		(4.239)	(4.571)			
Krueger: for 10	—	—		—	—	0.11	—	0.08	0.16	0.99
observations,						(4.29)		(0.85)	(1.70)	
1950–70[d]										

Note: Numbers in parentheses are *t* values.

a. The dependent variable ($\Delta Y/Y_1$) is the GNP growth in Michalopoulos and Jay, Balassa, and Krueger. In the Feder study, it refers to GDP growth.

b. The independent variables are $\Delta K_d/Y_1$, domestically financed investment as a proportion of the GNP in the initial period; $\Delta K_f/Y_1$, foreign-financed investment as a proportion of GNP in the initial period; $\Delta L/L_1$, increase in population as a proportion of the population in the initial period; $\Delta X/\Delta Y$, incremental export-GNP ratio; $\Delta X/X_1$, increase in exports as a proportion of the exports in the initial period; $\Delta X/Y_1$, increase in exports as a proportion of GNP in the initial period; D_{i1} a dummy variable which takes the value of 1 during Phases 1 and 2 of the trade regimes; D_{i2}, a dummy variable which takes the value of 1 during Phases 3 and 4 of trade regimes; and *t* which is a time variable.

c. The export variables in Feder are $(\Delta X/X)(X/Y) = (\Delta X/Y)$ and $(\Delta X/X)$.

d. In Krueger's study log refers to a pooled sample of ten countries in which log GNP is regressed on a time trend and log X, a dummy variable for the country's Phases 1 and 2 trade regime (that is, $D_{i1}t$), and another dummy variable for Phases 3 and 4 trade regime.

Source: Michalopoulos and Jay 1973; Balassa 1978, p. 186; Feder 1983, pp. 65, 68; Krueger 1978, p. 273.

As most of the low-income countries in the sample used by Helliner (using data from the *World Development Reports*[e]) can hardly be classified as having followed outward-oriented policies, the failure to find a link between exports and growth is not surprising. We would expect, however, that in the turbulent decade after the first oil shock of 1973, even among these dirigiste low-income countries, the *relatively* more outward-oriented would have had a better growth record. Using data from the *World Development Report 1986*, on GDP, labor force growth, and the growth of export and investment shares in GDP,

we estimated the following regression for eighteen low-income countries for which statistics were available:

$$\text{GDP growth rate, 1973–84} = 2.251 + 0.225 \; \text{Investment share of GDP, 1984} - 0.963 \; \text{Growth of labor force, 1973–84} + 0.152 \; \text{Growth of export share of GDP, 1965–73}$$

$$(0.064) \qquad\qquad (0.786) \qquad\qquad (0.079)$$

$$r^2 = 0.30; \; F = 3.2$$

The figures in brackets are standard errors. This equation shows
that there was a positive and statistically significant association between income growth rates in the turbulent decade after the oil shock
and the growth of exports in GDP in the preceding period (1965–73).

All the studies reviewed above use conventional statistical tests for
establishing an association between exports and growth. Following
classical statistical methodology, these correlations by themselves reveal nothing about causation. To make causal inferences, an underlying theoretical model is required, whose validity is then tested by
standard econometric techniques. Recently, however, a new school of
econometrics has sought to make causal statements purely on the
basis of a particular statistical technique called vector auto regression
(VAR) and of a Granger-Sims causality test, which seeks to establish
whether over time a particular variable regularly precedes another.
Jung and Marshall (1985) have applied the Granger causality test to
data for thirty-seven developing countries in 1950–81 to determine
whether exports "Granger-cause" growth, or vice versa. They find
that only Costa Rica, Ecuador, Egypt, and Indonesia provide evidence
in favor of export promotion; "more interestingly, many of the countries most famous for the miraculous growth rates that appeared to
arise from export promotion policies (e.g. Korea, Taiwan, Brazil)
provide no statistical support for the export promotion hypothesis"
(p. 10). Darrat (1986) has also applied the Grangercausality test to the
time series for exports and growth between 1960 and 1982 for Hong
Kong, Korea, Singapore, and Taiwan and finds that for the first three
"neither exports cause economic growth nor economic growth causes
exports." For Taiwan he finds that "economic growth unidirectionally
causes exports" (p. 697).

Several points need to be made against this recent counterrevolu-
tion. First, even within the atheoretical Grangercausality framework,
the results showing that output growth causes export growth are not
inconsistent with the export-growth link found by the more conventional studies. Consider this comment by Darrat: "The economic

growth that Taiwan enjoyed during the estimated period (1960–82) appears to be an internal process perhaps due to domestic technological advancement and enhanced accumulation of human capital (Jung and Marshall 1985). *Given the country's limited market capacity, Taiwan's producers were probably compelled to turn to foreign markets for exports.* It seems therefore, that economic growth (generated internally) has caused higher exports in Taiwan, contrary to the implication of the export-led growth hypothesis" (p. 697–98, emphasis added). However, it is obvious that, if a small country is developing efficiently in line with its comparative advantage, it will specialize and hence be "compelled to turn to foreign markets for exports" of goods that use its most abundant factor of production most intensively. The statistical establishment of this fact hardly disproves the validity of the outward-oriented development strategy; in fact, it supports it. Thus in the Jung and Marshall (1985) study if the cases in which output growth causes export growth are also included as supporting the outward orientation theory (as they should be on the above argument), the list of countries rises to fourteen and also includes Bolivia, Greece, Iran, Israel, Kenya, Korea, Pakistan, Peru, South Africa, and Thailand.

Second, it is clear from the test of precedence (which is what the the Grangercausality test amounts to) that the statistical counterrevolutionaries are testing for the growth-enhancing effects of a development strategy that *biases* incentives toward exports. They are not concerned with the neutral free trade equilibrium point—*F* in figure 1—whereas (as we argue below) most proponents of outward orientation do not favor this biased export-led growth. The same criticism applies to Fishlow's (1985) interpretation of the case for outward orientation as identical with that for export-led growth. To test this hypothesis, he rightly argues, "requires calculation of the relationship between aggregate performance and the extent to which the rate of growth of exports *exceeds* overall growth"; not surprisingly, he finds that "with such a specification, there is no statistically significant relationship" (p. 139). But again, it is clearly unwarranted to identify the case for outward orientation (or, more precisely, for neutral trade policies) with that for an export bias.

Third, the statistical studies based on Granger causality, which test for the precedence of one variable over another, do not in fact reveal anything about causation as the term is normally understood. Leamer (1985), in a review of the new econometric fashion that uses vector autoregressions alone for causal inferences, rightly notes that: "this concept should be called 'precedence'. . . We can all think of contexts in which precedence is suggestive of causation and also contexts in which it is not . . . It is altogether clear that precedence is not sufficient for causality. Weather forecasts regularly precede the weather,

196

but few of us take this as evidence that the forecasts 'cause' the weather" (pp. 259, 283).[7]

There is one other, more compelling reason why judgments based solely on statistical tests (both conventional and novel) of dynamic effects of trade regimes must remain inconclusive. Economics, as Hicks (1979) has put it, "is on the edge of science and of history" (p. 38). The historical aspects are particularly important for what he terms "sequential causality"—which is the relevant notion of causality for analyzing the dynamic effects of trade regimes. But in studying such dynamic historial processes, techniques of statistical inference may not be very useful, because "when we cannot accept that the observations along the time series available to us are independent or cannot by some device be divided into groups that can be treated as independent, we get into much deeper water. For we have then, in strict logic, no more than one observation, all of the separate items having to be taken together. We are left to use our judgment, making sense of what has happened as best we can, in the manner of the historian. Applied economics does then come back to history after all" (p. 126).[8]

This section looks at five comparative studies of particular developing countries' trade regimes undertaken in the 1960s and 1970s (Little and others 1970, Balassa 1971, Donges 1976, Bhagwati 1978, and Krueger 1978). The studies provide fairly firm evidence that countries that adopted or moved toward an export-promoting (EP) strategy did much better in growth of per capita income and equity than those with an import-substituting (IS) strategy. These terms, EP and IS, have caused some confusion. The most common definition now is that a movement from the neutral free trade position is IS, and a movement toward it (that is, from *P* to *F* in figure 1) is EP. Thus the EP strategy does not imply any subsidization of exports beyond the level that restores equality between the effective exchange rates on imports and exports.[9]

Evidence on Trade Regimes

For our purpose we need only note that the five comparative studies have established that IS regimes produce a misallocation of resources. Although there are analytical doubts about the use of domestic resource cost (DRC) measures as indicators of static efficiency in some of these studies, the general conclusion is reinforced by more appropriate indicators of allocative efficiency: the divergences between Little-Mirrlees (LM) shadow prices and market prices for several developing countries.[10] More significantly, these studies (in particular the NBER study) showed that countries that reduced or removed the bias against exports had accelerated their growth rates of per capita incomes; those with an IS strategy did not.

In this context it is important to distinguish between the degree and pattern of protection. It has been argued that the existence of some highly protected industries in an economy whose trade regime *on average* shows little IS bias (for example, Korea) invalidates drawing any inferences from its experience in favor of neutral trade (see Wade 1985). Jagdish Bhagwati (1986) has given the correct response to this argument:

> Thus, within the broad aggregates of an FP country case, there may well be activities that are being import-substituted (i.e., their EER_m exceeds the average EER_x) [where EER_m is the effective exchange rate for imports, and EER_x is the effective exchange rate for exports]. Indeed there often are. But one should not jump to the erroneous conclusion that there is therefore no way to think of FP versus IS and that the distinction is an artificial one—any more than one would refuse to acknowledge that the Sahara is a desert, whereas Sri Lanka is not, simply because there are oases (p. 93).

Tables 3 and 4 summarize the divergence between market and IM shadow prices for traded goods in India and Korea.[11] Though there are highly protected activities in both countries, even casual inspection shows that Korea's trade regime is much more neutral than India's, and the dispersion of its protection is lower.[12]

Of the five studies, only the one from the NBER explicitly sought to quantify the possible effects of alternative trade regimes on savings rates, technical progress, and entrepreneurship—the dynamic factors that affect a country's growth rate. The evidence (surveyed in Bhagwati 1978) on entrepreneurship, innovation, and technical change is inconclusive, though none of these factors is shown to benefit from IS regimes. On savings, Bhagwati concludes that the evidence does not support the view that restrictionist exchange control regimes "will or are likely to contribute to increased domestic savings, and/or to augmented capital formation. If anything, much of our evidence—at least on the domestic savings issue—suggests an opposite relationship" (p. 174).

The NBER study also emphasized the importance of appropriate macroeconomic and exchange rate policies to maintain a realistic real exchange rate. As Krueger (1978) put it:

> It seems a fair conclusion that one of the policy mistakes of the two decades covered by the country studies was using devaluation to a new fixed exchange rate as an instrument designed to attain both domestic price stabilisation and a liberalised trade regime (p. 297).

Exogenous Shocks in the 1970s and 1980s

The 1970s and 1980s produced two oil shocks, the worst recession since the Great Depression, and a huge switch in real interest rates (low or negative for most of the 1970s, unprecedentedly high in the 1980s). These shocks were common to all developing countries, yet the relative performance of the FP countries was far superior (see Lal and Wolf 1986).

Table 3. *Accounting Ratios for Traded Commodities in India, 1973*

Sectoral code number	Commodity	Accounting ratio
T1	Electrical equipment	0.36
T2	Nonelectrical equipment	0.65
T3	Transport equipment	1.28
T4	Metal products	0.29
T5	Iron and steel	1.00
	Pipes and tubes	1.00
	Pig iron	1.00
T6	Cement	0.66
T7	Nonferrous metals	0.59
T8	Other minerals	0.61
T9	Rubber	0.60
T10	Leather	0.50
T11	Other leather products	0.50
T12	Leather footwear	0.81
T13	Animal husbandry	0.37
T14	Sugar	0.52
T15	Gur and khandsari	1.08
T16	Vegetable oils	1.14
T17	Vanaspati	0.65
T18	Starch	0.87
T19	Milk products	0.29
T20	Breweries and soft drinks	0.68
T21	Confectionery	0.60
T22	Cigarettes and cigars	0.39
T23	Other tobacco products	0.39
T24	Fruits and vegetables	0.32
T25	Cashew nut processing	0.27
T26	Cotton	0.51
T27	Cotton yarn	2.04
T28	Cotton textiles	0.46
T29	Jute	0.57
T30	Jute textiles	0.44
T31	Woolen yarn	0.60
T32	Woolen textiles	0.61
T33	Raw silk	0.71
T34	Silk textiles	0.50
T35	Man-made fiber (rayon)	0.13
T36	Artificial silk	0.43
T37	Other textiles	0.44
T38	Tobacco	0.43
T39	Fertilizers	1.00
T40	Ceramics and bricks	0.44
T41	Glass and glassware	0.72
T42	Wood products	0.97
T43	Timber	0.80
T44	Chinaware, pottery	0.50
T45	Wood, others	0.56
T46	Other forest products	0.27
T47	Petroleum products	0.65
T48	Rubber footwear	0.73

(Table continues on next page)

Table 3 *(continued)*

Sectoral code number	Commodity	Accounting ratio
T49	Synthetic rubber	0.73
T50	Other rubber products	0.48
T51	Paper and paper products	0.44
T52	Plastics	0.47
T53	Dyestuff	0.39
T54	Paints and varnishes	1.35
T55	Insecticides and pesticides	0.91
T56	Drugs and pharmaceuticals	0.32
T57	Soaps and glycerine	0.57
T58	Perfumes and cosmetics	0.39
T59	Miscellaneous chemicals	0.53
T60	Coal and coke	0.72
T61	Matches	0.76
T62	Plantations	1.00
T63	Aluminum primary product	0.80
T64	Zinc	0.61
T65	Lead	0.58
T66	Tin	0.57
T67	Manganese	1.00
T68	Sulfur	0.65
T69	Sulfuric acid	0.65
T70	Rock phosphate	0.87
T71	Salt	1.00
T72	Wheat	0.87
T73	Soda ash	0.76
T74	Dry cells	0.52
T75	Ball bearings	0.40
T76	Electric fans	1.00
T77	Radio receivers	0.52
T78	Nonferrous metal alloys	0.69
T79	By-products of foodgrains	0.87
T80	Gypsum	1.00
T81	Limestone	1.00
T82	Iron ore	1.00
T83	Bauxite	1.00

Note: The accounting ratio is the ratio of the social price to the market price; see note 11 to the text for a fuller definition. The unweighted means of these accounting ratios is 0.675, with a standard deviation of 0.294.

Source: Lal 1980.

The starting point for explaining this conclusion is a simple one: all countries need some foreign trade. In dealing with external shocks, the more inward-looking countries face greater costs of output forgone through compressing imports (which are mainly capital goods), and they have more difficulty in expanding exports because of a smaller proportion of their output is tradable. For these reasons, IS countries have not only had slower growth but also more serious debt

Table 4. *Accounting Ratios for Traded Commodities in Korea, 1973*

Sector number	Commodity	Accounting ratio
1	Rice, barley, and wheat	0.84
2	Vegetables, fruits	0.79
3	Industrial crops	0.84
4	Livestock breeding	0.87
5	Forestry products	0.88
*6	Fishery products	1.27
7	Coal	0.85
8	Metallic ores	0.95
9	Nonmetallic minerals	0.87
10	Slaughtering, dairy products	0.85
11	Canning and processing	0.81
12	Grain polishing and milling	0.81
13	Other food preparations	0.80
14	Beverages	0.47
*15	Tobacco	0.95
*16	Fiber spinning	1.16
*17	Textile fabrics	1.08
*18	Apparel and fabrications	1.08
*19	Leather and leather products	1.04
*20	Lumber and plywood	1.03
*21	Wood products and furniture	1.00
22	Paper and paper products	0.67
23	Printing and publishing	0.93
24	Inorganic chemicals	0.77
25	Organic chemicals	0.68
26	Chemical fertilizers	0.93
27	Drugs and cosmetics	0.80
28	Other chemical products	0.68
29	Petroleum refining	0.80
30	Coal products	0.91
31	Rubber products	0.69
32	Nonmetallic minerals	0.77
33	Iron and steel	0.86
34	Primary iron and steel manufactures	0.76
35	Nonferrous metal manufactures	0.79
*36	Fabricated metal products	1.05
37	Nonelectrical machinery	0.84
38	Electrical machinery	0.76
39	Transportation equipment	0.83
40	Measuring, medical	0.67
*41	Miscellaneous manufactures	1.33
*56	Unclassifiable	1.33

Note: These ratios have been derived as described in Lal (1978b). The asterisked items were taken to be export sectors. The unweighted mean of these ratios is 0.883 with a standard deviation of 0.178.

problems than EP countries: witness the contrast between the newly industrializing countries (NICs) in Southeast Asia and the Latin American Southern Cone countries.

201

Deepak Lal and Sarath Rajapatirana

For comparative purposes, three groups of economies have been selected. Group A consists of Hong Kong, Korea, Singapore, and Taiwan, which have followed EP strategies as defined in the Bhagwati-Krueger studies.[13] Group B includes the Southern Cone countries—Argentina, Chile, Uruguay—plus a South Asian country, Sri Lanka. They are referred to as moderately IS countries, which made some effort to liberalize their trade regimes in the late 1970s.[14] Group C consists just of India, an IS country in which the effective exchange rate for imports markedly exceeds that for exports.

Group A: Export-Promoting Countries

The four economies in this group have been the most dynamic exporters in the world. During 1970–79, their exports grew at an annual average rate of 25 percent, with manufactured exports growing at 30 percent. During 1978–81 their exports grew at 19 percent a year; then, with the world recession of the early 1980s, they actually declined. But they recovered more rapidly than the exports of any other group, despite experiencing greater external shocks than most other developing countries. The shocks were equal to 18 percent of GNP for Singapore, 10 percent for Taiwan, and 9 percent for Korea; for developing countries as a whole, the shock was 6 percent of GNP (Balassa 1984). By 1983, the GDP growth rates of all four economies were back to the 1970–82 average; so were their trade balances and export growth.

The four EP economies adjusted in two ways. First, they expanded exports by raising their market shares even when world demand was depressed. Second, they raised domestic savings. Korea was an exception to this rule, because its financial market was repressed. It financed part of the temporary loss in income by increasing its external borrowings—but, unlike most heavily indebted countries, it was able to service its debt without cuts in domestic output.[15]

Group B: Moderately Import-Substituting Economies

The countries in this group tried to liberalize their trade regimes between the mid-1970s and the early 1980s. They are the Southern Cone countries of Argentina, Chile, and Uruguay and one South Asian country, Sri Lanka. All were initially successful in liberalizing their trade regimes. They speeded up their GDP and export growth and improved their external accounts. In the 1980s, however, they ran into crises of macroeconomic stabilization.

The Southern Cone countries shared a common path up to the mid-1970s. By that stage, Argentina's GDP growth was slow (averaging 0.5

percent a year during 1965–73), and its trade heavily protected. Inflation was high—around 180 percent in 1975—so was unemployment. Effective rates of protection ranged from 111 percent for manufacturing to −13 percent for agriculture. Since the 1930s it had followed an IS strategy.

For Chile, too, the initial conditions were very difficult. GDP shrunk by 5.6 percent in 1973 on the eve of the reforms. Inflation had reached 1,000 percent. In trade, rates of protection averaged 217 percent, varying from 1,140 percent for petroleum and coal products to −7 percent for agriculture.

Uruguay had experienced prolonged stagnation during 1950–70. In 1965–73, GDP growth averaged 2.0 percent a year. Inflation had reached 97 percent, capital flight was substantial, and the currency was overvalued. By 1970 its IS strategy had hit the limits of the small domestic market.

All three countries undertook substantial economic reforms during 1975–80, of which a principal feature was trade liberalization. In Argentina, taxes on exports were reduced;[16] so were import tariffs, thus lowering both the average level of effective protection and the variance. Following these reforms GDP growth averaged nearly 4 percent a year between 1978 and 1980. Manufactured exports increased by 216 percent in 1975–80. In 1978 the government started to preannounce exchange rates (the *tablita*). But it had failed to curb the fiscal deficit. The ensuing domestic inflation, coupled with a slowly adjusting nominal exchange rate, led to a rise in the real exchange rate, capital flight, and the collapse of the banking system (Calvo 1986). Because of this stabilization crisis, by 1982 the trade reforms had been reversed.

The Chilean trade reforms were the most far-reaching. All quotas were eliminated except those on motor vehicles. All tariffs were reduced to a uniform 10 percent by 1979. By 1977–78, the budget was balanced. The exchange rate was first put on a crawling peg, and then in 1979 fixed against the U.S. dollar. Also by 1979 the capital account was liberalized. The results of these reforms were dramatic. During 1976–81 GDP grew by 8 percent a year and manufactured exports by 30 percent a year. However, the opening of the capital account and the fixing of the nominal exchange rate led to a large appreciation in the real exchange rate. As in Argentina, this was followed by a balance of payments crisis, capital flight, and the collapse of the domestic banking system. In 1982 GDP declined by 14 percent, and unemployment reached 22 percent of the labor force.

In Uruguay, taxes on traditional exports were lowered in the mid-1970s. Nontraditional exports were given additional incentives. Price controls were reduced sharply, and restrictions on the inflow of private capital were eliminated. The results of these reforms were impressive. Having averaged 1.0 percent a year in 1955–73, GDP growth rose to an average of 4.5 percent during 1974–80. In 1982, however, the worldwide rise in interest rates, combined with an appreciation in the real exchange rate (because of its tablita) and an increase in the fiscal deficit, led to a balance of payments crisis. GDP declined by nearly 10 percent in 1982.

The Southern Cone experience provides several lessons. The trade reforms were successful in raising export and GDP growth, particularly in Chile and Uruguay. But the overall attempt at economic liberalization failed eventually, because of unsustainable macroeconomic and real exchange rate policies (Corbo and de Melo 1985, de Melo and Tybout 1986). Compared with the Southeast Asian NICs, the Southern Cone countries faced more difficult conditions initially and made errors in macropolicy when it came to dealing with external shocks.

In Sri Lanka, the trade liberalization of 1977 reversed a long-standing IS strategy. By that stage, the economy was highly distorted—but not subject to the inflationary instability of the Southern Cone. For many years the economy was sluggish: in 1965–77, for example, GDP growth averaged 2.9 percent a year. The country's share of world trade declined, as did its volume of exports—by 1.5 percent between 1970 and 1977.

The wide-ranging reforms of 1977 mainly involved the trade regime and led to a dramatic economic recovery. Sri Lanka's GDP grew by 6 percent a year in 1978–85, and unemployment fell from 24 percent of the labor force in 1973 to 12 percent in 1981 (Bhalla and Glewwe 1986). By 1983, however, macroeconomic imbalances forced the government to slow down its reform program. Heavy public expenditure and a reluctance to close loss-making public enterprises proved to be incompatible with the trade reforms (Lal and Rajapatirana 1987). As in the Southern Cone, macroeconomic imbalances—in this case brought about by the financing of public expenditure by capital inflows—led to a real appreciation of the rupee and to a balance of payments and fiscal crisis.

The experience of this group of countries points to three lessons for trade liberalization. First, appropriate macroeconomic policies are vital to maintaining a more liberal trade regime. Second, an appropriate real exchange rate plays a bigger role in trade reform than was realized in the five comparative studies. Third, the order in which the various repressed markets are reformed seems to be important. In both Chile and Uruguay the liberalization of financial markets was destabilizing. It is still an open question whether this was due to the structure of the domestic financial market, or to poor macroeconomic and exchange rate management, or is an inherent property of financial liberalization itself.

Group C: Import-Substituting Countries

India's relative immunity to the external shocks of the 1980s is often used to suggest that, over the long haul and despite the acknowledged productive inefficiencies of the country's trade regime, India's "delinking" from the world economy has allowed it to maintain much steadier growth in the past two turbulent decades.[17] This view is mistaken, because any stability of domestic incomes achieved by delinking can also mean that average income is lower than if the international roller coaster is ridden efficiently.

India proves this point. Its trend rate of GDP growth has been 3–4 percent a year for three decades—much lower than the growth that could have been obtained by integration into a world economy, which boomed for two decades. To illustrate this loss, in 1960 the absolute size of Korea's manufacturing industry was a quarter of India's; in 1980 it was almost two-thirds of the size. Korean manufactured exports rose from virtually nothing in 1960 to more than $15 billion in 1980. In the same period India's manufactured exports rose from $600 million to only $4.1 billion. "Even tiny Singapore has managed to export more manufactures in value terms ($11.7 billion in 1981) than India! India's share in world exports has declined steadily from 2.4 percent in 1968 to a minuscule 0.41 percent in 1981" (Srinivasan 1986). Since labor-intensive manufacturing is a major means of providing employment and alleviating poverty in countries with a rapidly growing labor force and a scarcity of land, India's inward-looking policies have done long-term damage to both growth and equity.

Though it is now fashionable to castigate Latin American countries for having followed "debt-led" growth in the late 1960s and 1970s, the subsequent income losses they may have suffered to service their debts have to be set off against the enormous previous gains in real incomes that debt-financed growth entailed (see Bhagwati 1986).

Two of the most influential development economists, Nurkse (1961) and Lewis (1980) have adduced a link between trade and growth in terms of the transmission of rapidly growing world demand to an open developing country: "trade as the engine of growth."[18] Nurkse (1961) argued that in the nineteenth century, trade had been such an engine for white settler communities, but predicted that it would no longer be so for developing countries in the second half of the twentieth century.

Nurkse's historical analysis and his forecasts both proved false. The view that international trade assisted the growth of the countries of new settlement in the nineteenth century has been questioned by Kravis (1970). Essentially, he argues that economic growth is deter-

Income Effects of Trade and Growth

mined by internal factors. Foreign trade provides an extension of the domestic opportunities available for converting resources into goods and services. Furthermore, by widening the market, it enables a country to produce goods with decreasing costs of production. Probably most important of all, exposure to international competition is the best antimonopoly policy—and thereby prevents the development of high-cost industries.

Most of these benefits concern the efficient use of available resources and hence the supply side of an economy. The demand factors that preoccupied Nurkse and others cannot be as influential, because the countries that shared in the nineteenth century expansion of trade developed in such different ways. For instance, Australia seemed to develop whereas Argentina did not, despite similar natural resource, "white" populations (Argentina had none of the problems of assimilation posed for other countries in Latin America by an indigenous population), and a similar stimulus from the rise in foreign demand for their primary products. Thus, as Kravis emphasizes, though strong external demand for a country's exports may be helpful,

> it is neither a necessary nor sufficient condition for growth or even trade to play a helpful role in growth . . . The term "engine of growth" is not generally descriptive and involves expectations which cannot be fulfilled by trade alone; the term "handmaiden of growth" better conveys the role that trade can play (p. 869).

More recently, Lewis (1980) has presented another model in which trade serves as an engine of growth. He bases his theory on the following empirical regularity:

> The growth rate of world trade in primary products over the period 1873 to 1913 was 0.87 times the growth rate of industrial production in the developed countries; and just about the same relationship, about 0.87, also ruled in the two decades to 1973. World trade in primary products is a wider concept than exports from developing countries, *but the two are sufficiently closely related for it to serve as a proxy.* We need no elaborate statistical proof that trade depends on prosperity in the industrial countries (p. 556, emphasis added).

The italicized words contain by no means an innocuous assumption: whereas manufactures accounted for only 10 percent of developing countries' nonfuel exports in 1955, their share had risen to over 40 percent by 1978. Primary product exports can no longer serve as a proxy for developing country exports, as Lewis asserts. Nor, except for Sub-Saharan Africa, does the picture change much when the figures are disaggregated. There are big differences in the export structures of developing countries: manufactures now account for 75 percent of the exports of the four East Asian superperformers, for example. But most countries in South Asia plus Brazil, Egypt, Mexico, Tunisia, and some smaller Latin American countries (together accounting for about two-thirds of the population of the developing world) have also raised the share of manufactures in their exports (on a trade weighted basis) from an average of 15 percent in 1950 to above 50 percent in 1978.

Disaggregation also greatly weakens Lewis's link coefficient of 0.87 between the rate of growth of industrial production in industrial countries and developing country exports (see Riedel 1984). Broadly speaking, Lewis's hypothesized link is unstable over time, and the only commodities to which it seems to apply are tea and sugar. For manufactures, the dominant and growing element in developing country exports, Riedel concludes that "the evidence . . . suggests that supply rather than demand factors have principally determined LDC export performance in manufactures." This is also the conclusion of the numerous historical studies of the trade and industrialization policies of developing countries cited earlier (Little and others 1970, Balassa 1971 and 1982, Bhagwati 1978, and Krueger 1978). Despite creeping protectionism and the slowdown in industrial countries, Reidel noted that

> whereas in the 1960s LDC exports of manufactures grew almost twice as fast as DC [industrial country] real GDP . . . in the 1970s, despite a general slowdown of growth after 1973, LDC exports maintained their rapid pace, growing four times as fast as DC real GDP. (p. 67).

Thus the view of trade as the engine of growth cannot adequately explain the link between neutral or liberal trade regimes and growth.

Other studies (Streeten 1982, Cline 1982) have argued that there is a fallacy of composition in generalizing the example of the East Asian NICs to the rest of the world. They claim that if all developing countries were to switch to export promotion, the industrial countries would become protectionist in an effort to stave off a surge in developing country exports. Ranis (1985) provides a thorough critique of these views (see also Havrylyshyn 1987). Ranis writes that, with the adoption of an EP strategy, "the much more substantial growth of per capita income resulting in the exporting countries would enable them to increase their imports from the North as well as each other" (p. 544). Unless developing countries were to run continual and massive trade surpluses, the industrial countries would boost their exports to them—a powerful counterweight to any protectionist lobbies. Despite the fears expressed about the "new protectionism" in industrial countries, the fact is that protectionism has by and large been kept at bay during the deepest recession since the 1930s.

Level
and Growth
Effects

It seems to be as firm a stylized fact as any in the economics of developing countries: a sustained movement to an outward-oriented trade regime leads to faster growth of both exports and income. How can this be explained? Krueger (1978) argues that mere neutrality of the trade regime is not enough:

> There are numerous countries where incentives for export and import substitution have been about equal, and the results have not been spectacular ... Although economic theory suggests that incentives for exports and for import substitution should be equated at the margin, in fact neither Brazil nor South Korea did so; during the rapid growth years [Korea after 1964 and Brazil after 1968] the bias in their regimes was toward exports (p. 282–83).

Krueger then compares two activist policies to encourage growth ("the alternative of a strictly laissez-faire regime is not explored") and argues that "a growth strategy oriented toward exports entails the development of policies that make markets and incentives function better, while an import-substitution strategy usually involves policies designed to frustrate individuals' maximizing behaviour under market incentives" (p. 284).

These statements have misled some economists (see Streeten .1982 and the riposte by Henderson 1982) to suggest that an outward-oriented strategy necesssarily involves an export bias. Of course, export promotion can be as inefficient and chaotic as protection, as India has shown (Lal 1979c). The liberal position on trade and growth (which we support) is different. As a first step it entails a neutral trade regime. The fact that such a regime does not necessarily lead to growth merely underlines the Kravis view of "trade as the handmaiden of growth," which sees internal factors as the biggest determinants of growth, with trade a helpful though not dominating influence.

However, a liberal trade regime (and an export-biased one) can help more directly than Kravis allowed to create a domestic economic system conducive to growth. This was one of Tumlir's insights developed in a series of papers in the late 1970s and early 1980s but unfortunately not consolidated into the book he was planning to write when his life was so tragically cut short. Analytically, he accepted that the case for government intervention in foreign trade can be separated from that in the domestic economy—so that, whatever view one takes of the latter, the former is unjustifiable (except for the optimal tariff case). But he argued that the analytical separation in this "management economics for governments" was misguided (Tumlir 1981). Though it mitigated some of the irrational dirigisme of governments, it nevertheless implied that market failure was ubiquitous. The canons

208

of second-best welfare economics then allowed benevolent, omniscient, and omnipotent governments to intervene in the social interest.

There is another, clearer view of government motives and foresight. It is associated with Adam Smith and the classicists, whose modern votaries are the so-called neo-Austrians, and it recognizes the ubiquitousness of government failure. The case for a liberal trade regime then becomes part of the general case for markets against mandarins. The ideal balance between the two is discussed in Lal (1986), not in this article. But, if one accepts the need for restraints on the natural and often irrational dirigisme of mandarins in most developing countries, then the adoption of a liberal trade regime (irrespective of the ensuing gains from trade, static and dynamic) becomes an important means to this end.

This line of thought can be developed by making use of some ideas attributable to Maurice Scott on investment and growth (see Scott 1976). They also provide an antidote to the criticism by Lucas that static gains from free trade merely affect the level of income, not its rate of growth.

In the standard neoclassical growth model (Solow 1956, Swan 1956), the steady state growth of an economy—its "natural rate of growth"—is determined by the exogenously given growth rate of population (n), plus the rate of labor-augmenting (Harrod-neutral) technical progress (t) which falls like manna from heaven. Several authors, starting with Kaldor (1957), Kaldor and Mirrlees (1962), and including Arrow (1962),[19] have argued that this exogeneity of productivity growth does not explain one of the mainsprings of economic growth. In various forms they have sought to introduce the rate of investment (which in the neoclassical model only affects the level and not the rate of growth) as an endogenous determinant of technical progress. In the standard neoclassical framework, an improvement in allocative efficiency in economy A compared with (otherwise identical) economy B leads to a higher level of income per person in A; it is as if A had saved more. But income does not grow faster. This result also holds in the Arrow (1962) and Kaldor-Mirrlees (1962) type of growth models, which seek to endogenize technical progress through a technical progress function that assumes a direct link between the growth of capital per person and the rate of labor-augmenting technical progress. However, as Eltis (1973) has argued,[20] it is more plausible in endogenizing technical progress to include in the technical progress function the saving ratio instead of the rate of growth of capital. In that case an increase in allocative efficiency, which is equivalent to an increase in savings, will raise the growth rate.[21]

These ideas have been further developed by Scott (1976). He argues that "investment is ... by definition ... the cost of *change*, and so will cover all activities associated with growth" (p. 317) and that "growth due to capital and technical progress are *both* the result of investment" (p. 330) in the sense of "the cost, in terms of consumption forgone, of propelling the economy forward instead of leaving it in a stationary state" (p. 318). "Incurring capital expenditure leads to a rearrangement of the things of this world. It does not lead to there being any more of some substance 'capital'.... There is then simply *change* which is due to investment, and to population growth. We cannot separate change which is 'more capital' from change which is 'technical progress.' We must abandon the attempt to distinguish between movements along a production function whose arguments are labor, land and *all* capital, and a shift in that function due to technical progress" (p. 331). Within his proposed framework, "the rate of increase of static income is a function of only two variables: total savings and labor force growth. There is no independent technical progress" (p. 331).

The key aspect of Scott's analysis is its emphasis on "the importance of allocation" for the growth rate. Unlike the conventional framework, which views allocative improvements as providing "a once-and-for-all increase in output and a temporary boost to the growth rate while it is occurring," Scott argues that "if, however, investment is essentially a matter of incurring costs to reallocate resources, then the efficiency with which this is done must affect the yield of investment, and so the *proportionate* rate of growth in the *long run*. So long as investment is occurring, reallocation is occurring. It is *not* once-and-for-all, but a continuing process, and, indeed, the principal source of growth in many countries" (p. 332–33).

Moreover, argues Scott, "investment at any given time is undertaken in a state of ignorance about the future. We make changes whose consequences we cannot wholly foresee, and, simultaneously, others are making changes of which we can only become aware after they are made. In the light of these changes we are then in a better position to make the next round of changes." This implies "that there is an externality to investment" (p. 334).[22] But "if the externality exists just because we are *ignorant* of the future effects of investment, it may be impossible to discover very much about the characteristics of investment that produce the externality" (p. 325).

This argument needs to be extended. It suggests the importance of an economic environment that is conducive to this ignorance-based, externality-creating form of investment. This is the place for the neo-Austrian insights concerning the role of the entrepreneur in an economic environment characterized by *ignorance* (see Lal 1986 for references and a fuller discussion). The entrepreneur is redundant in neo-classical economics, which assumes an environment of purely actuarial Knightian risk. But he is at the center of the neo-Austrian stage—creating and searching out investment opportunities and gambling on the future. Like the speculator and middle man, the entrepreneur is an economic agent who lives by making money out of irreducible Knightian uncertainty. This entrepreneurial function must, for reasons to do with incentives and information, be decentralized. To the extent that an EP strategy has to rely on this entrepreneurial function (as export markets cannot be ensured by local mandarins), it will induce the creation of that economic framework in which Scott's externality-creating investments will lead to faster growth.

The case for a free trade regime (or, as a second best, an export biased one) is thus close to that argued by the classical and neo-Austrian economists. As Keynes emphasized, the classical case against mercantilism was *not* based on laissez-faire, but rather on limiting state action to areas where such action was indispensable. These, broadly speaking, are to provide the public goods essential for the efficient functioning of market processes—law and order, stable money—and those infrastructural activities that affect public goods. The modern variant of the classical case, while accepting the need for an activist state, would seek to limit its activities. The state would be prevented from creating those policy-induced distortions that supposedly are there to cure endogenous distortions in the working of the price mechanism but which merely aggravate the level of distortions in the economy. Such distortions have led to large, though unquantifiable, losses, through diverting energies and resources from productive activities into the wasteful lobbying and rent-seeking activities so common in most developing countries. In this task of confining public action to its proper place, a free trade regime could be an important component. It would help to create an economic framework that provides the necessary incentives for entrepreneurship, productivity, and thrift. In a formal sense, these qualities are only dimly understood by economists. But they are, at bottom, the mainsprings of sustained and sustainable economic growth.

Abstract

This article surveys empirical studies of the static gains from a movement toward free trade and studies of the dynamic effects of growth in exports on per capita income. It also summarizes comparative studies of the trade regimes of developing countries undertaken in the 1960s to 1970s, which show fairly conclusively that "outward-orientation" is associated with better economic performance. The conclusions of these studies are then tested for the more volatile global environment of the 1970s and 1980s. Various arguments are weighed about the dynamic income effects of the growth in world income and trade on a free-trading country's economic growth rate—the "trade as an engine of growth" view. The closing section introduces insights of the classical writers that have reemerged in the neo-Austrian and the more recent neoclassical "new political economy" schools, which might explain the links between trade and growth performance. These emphasize the importance of the nonquantifiable aspects of a free trade (as compared with a protectionist) regime in creating a general economic framework conducive to individual entrepreneurship, productivity, and thrift. In this context we argue that free trade is the "handmaiden of growth," as it indirectly constrains the state

Deepak Lal and Sarath Rajapatirana

from going beyond the bounds of necessary public action for the provision of those domestic public goods that are essential for development.

Notes

The authors wish to thank Jagdish Bhagwati and Soogol Young for valuable comments on the draft of this article and Sophie Kim, Fayez Omar, and John Wayem for research assistance. This is a revised and considerably expanded version of a paper prepared for the conference on "Free Trade in the World Economy" organized by the Institute for World Economics, Kiel. This article is dedicated to the memory of Jan Tumlir.

1. Thus it is recognised that endogenous domestic distortions may require appropriate domestic public interventions for their correction; where the country has monopoly (monopsony) power in trade and can feasibly influence its terms of trade, taxes or subsidies on trade may be justified.

2. See Srinivasan and Whalley (1986) for a comprehensive discussion and evaluation of the principal models in this genre. Also see Srinivasan (1986a, 1986b, and 1987).

3. Also see Krueger (1984), Taylor and Black (1974), and de Melo (1978), for other model-based estimates of these static gains.

4. But see the note to the figure for the decomposition of this loss into that due to the tariff and lobbying.

5. See also Tyler (1981), Heller and Porter (1978), Michaely (1979).

6. The World Bank's *World Development Report* is published annually by Oxford University Press.

7. Leamer is also quite caustic about Granger's defense that: "provided I define what I personally mean by causation, I can use the term." Leamer rightly castigates Granger for misusing common language and for misleading persuasive definitions. He writes: "I detect a certain lack of concern for the human capital that is invested in our language. If I were to continue in that tradition I would propose that we henceforth refer to this notion of precedence by the word pair: fool's causation. This substitutes a loaded word 'fool' for the neutral 'Granger' just as 'causation' has replaced the neutral 'precedence.' Moreover, 'fool' is decidely simpler than 'Granger'—it contains only four letters, one of which is repeated—and, like 'cause,' it is rather difficult to define precisely. One man's fool is another man's genius. My definition of a 'fool' would be a friend of mine living in San Diego" (Leamer 1985, p. 284). But, as Leamer is at pains to emphasize, this does not mean to imply that the atheoretical statistical technique of vector autoregressions underlying the new econometrics cannot be useful as a descriptive and perhaps a forecasting device.

8. See also McKloskey (1983) who rightly argues that the evidence adduced in support of particular economic propositions must be ecclectic and cannot be confined to the positivist statistical testing that is currently so fashionable. As Hicks argues, "the usefulness of 'statistical' or 'stochastic' methods in economics is a good deal less than is now conventionally supposed. . . Thus it is not at all sensible to take a small number of observations (sometimes no more than a dozen observations) and to use the rules of probability theory to deduce from them a 'significant' general law. For we are assuming, if we do so, that the variations from one to another of the observations are random, so that if we had a larger sample (as we do not) they would by some averaging tend to disappear. But what nonsense this is when the observations are derived, as not infrequently happens, from different countries, or localities, or industries—entities about which we may well have relevant information, but which we have deliberately decided by our procedure to ignore. By all means let us plot the points on a chart and try to explain them; but it does not help in explaining them to suppress their names. The probability calculus is no excuse for forgetfulness" (p. 122).

9. See Lal (1981), and for an emphatic reassertion of this point see Bhagwati (1986). This point is also emphasized in the last chapter of Bhagwati (1978).

In this context it may also be useful to distinguish a liberal trade regime from a neutral one. A failure to do so has caused some confusion about the nature of what different developing countries have done to liberalize their trade. A neutral trade regime is one where incentives for import substitution do not outweigh those for export promotion; but it does not rule out (essentially offsetting) trade interventions. A liberal trade regime ensures this neutrality of trade incentives, because of the absence of trade intervention. We owe this point to Soogil Young's comment on our paper at the conference.

10. For these I M shadow price estimates see the references in Little and Scott (1976); in addition see Little and others (1979) for Pakistan, Lal (1978a) for the Philippines, Lal (1978b) for Korea, Lal (1979a) for Jamaica, Lal (1980) for India, and Lal (1979c) for Sri Lanka.

11. These I.M accounting ratios are the commodity-specific ratio of the domestic to border price (c.i.f./f.o.b.) of the traded good, with the dollar value of the border price converted into local currency at the official exchange rate. The effective exchange rate on exports (imports) is the units of domestic currency that can be obtained for a dollar's worth of exports (imports). Thus the rates are weighted averages of the relevant accounting ratios of traded commodities, where the weights are the actual shares in exports (imports) of the relevant commodities.

12. Wade in a private communication has stated that we have misrepresented his position, which he says is from Wade (1985): "In the comparison between Taiwan and Korea, on the one hand, and India and Latin America, on the other, the first important fact about trade regimes is that the East Asia type is more 'liberal' in the sense that the average level of protection is much lower. But the second important fact, which the neoclassical argument has tended to ignore, is that dispersion around the average is much higher in East Asia, because selective promotion of some industries requires high protection to a small number" (p. 27). However, as can be seen from tables 3 and 4, the dispersion around the average protection is also lower in Korea than India, as measured by the respective standard deviations of the accounting ratios in the two countries.

13. This is in relation to the effective exchange rates for exports and imports.

14. These countries attempted to move from Phase II to Phase III of the restrictive trade regimes in the Bhagwati-Krueger sense. See Krueger (1978).

15. Balassa's studies (1981, 1982, 1984) of forty-three countries subject to shocks in 1974–76 and 1979–81 confirm the superior response of the NICs to external shocks.

16. The export tax on wheat was reduced from 56 percent to 5 percent, on corn from 46 percent to 16 percent, and for wool from 33 percent to 16 percent from July 1976 to July 1977 (Nogues 1981).

17. The external shock to India was 2.1 percent of GNP in the 1974–78 period. See Balassa (1981).

18. Much of this is based on Lal (1983).

19. See Hahn and Matthews (1965) for a more complete survey.

20. See Dixit (1976, p. 81 and following) for a lucid discussion of the models that seek to endogenize technical progress. See also Hahn and Matthews (1965).

21. Formally in the standard Solow-Swan model, the determinants of the steady state growth rate are:

$$g_y = g_k = s/v = n + t$$

where g_y = growth rate of output
  g_k = growth rate of capital
  s = savings rate
  v = capital output ratio
  n = rate of population growth
  t = rate of Harrod neutral (labor-augmenting) technical progress.

With $n + t$—the natural rate of growth—determined exogenously, changes in the savings ratio will not effect the steady state growth rate of output or capital, but through countervailing changes in the capital output ratio (v) merely lead to changes in the *levels* of capital and output per capita.

In the Eltis framework, the exogenously given technical progress term t, is replaced by an endogenously determined term whose argument is savings (s), hence in this alternative framework,

$$g_y = g_k = s/v = n + \phi(s)$$

where ϕ is an increasing concave function (see Dixit 1986, ch. 4) Actual and "as if" increases in savings because of improved efficiency will now lead to a rise in the growth *rates* of output and capital (y and k).

22. Lucas (1985) presents a neoclassical model of economic development in which a central element is an externality in human capital investment. Many of his insights would seem to complement those of Scott, except that he draws unwarranted dirigiste implications from them.

References

Arrow, K. J. 1962. "The Economic Implications of Learning by Doing." *Review of Economic Studies* 29, no. 3: 155–73.

Balassa, B. 1971. *The Structure of Protection in Developing Countries*. Baltimore, Md.: Johns Hopkins University Press.

_____. 1978. "Exports and Economic Growth: Further Evidence." *Journal of Development Economics* 5, no. 2 (June): 181–89.

_____. 1981. "The Newly Industrializing Development Countries after the Oil Crisis." *Weltwirtschaftliches Archiv* 117, no. 1: 142–94.

_____. 1982. *Development Strategies in Semi-Industrial Economies*. Baltimore, Md.: Johns Hopkins University Press.

_____. 1984. *Adjustments to External Shocks in Developing Countries*. World Bank Staff Working Paper 472. Washington, D.C.

Bergsman, J. 1974. "Commercial Policy, Allocative and 'X-Efficiency.'" *Quarterly Journal of Economics* 58 (August): 409–33.

Bhagwati, J. 1978. *Foreign Trade Regimes and Economic Development Anatomy and Consequences of Exchange Control Regimes*. Cambridge, Mass.: Ballinger.

_____. 1980. "Lobbying and Welfare." *Journal of Public Economics* 14, no. 3 (December): 355–64.

_____. 1986. "Rethinking Trade Strategy." In J. P. Lewis and V. Kalleb, eds. *Development Strategies Reconsidered*. Washington, D.C.: Overseas Development Center.

Bhalla, S., and P. Glewwe. 1986. "Growth and Equity in Developing Countries: A Reinterpretation of the Sri Lankan Experience." *World Bank Economic Review* 1, no. 2: 35–63.

Calvo, G. A. 1986. "Fractured Liberalism: Argentina under Martinez de Hoz." *Economic Development and Cultural Change* 34, no. 3: 511–34.

Cline, W. R. 1982. "Can the East Asian Model of Development Be Generalised?" *World Development* 10, no. 2: 81–90.

Corbo, V., and J. de Melo. 1985. "Overview and Summary: Liberalization and Stabilization in the Southern Cone of Latin America." *World Development* 13, no. 8: 863–66.

Corden, W. M. 1974. *Trade Policy and Economic Welfare*. Oxford: Oxford University Press.

Darrat, A. F. 1986. "Trade and Development: The Asian Experience." *Cato Journal* 6, no. 2: 695–700.

de Melo, J. 1978. "Protection and Resource Allocation in a Walrasian Trade Model." *International Economic Review* 19, no. 1: 25–44.

de Melo, J., and J. Tybout. 1986. "The Effects of Financial Liberalization on Savings and Investment in Uruguay." *Economic Development and Cultural Change* 34, no. 3: 561–88.

Dixit, A. K. 1976. *The Theory of Equilibrium Growth.* Oxford: Oxford University Press.

Donges, J. 1976. "A Comparative Study of Industrialisation Policies in Fifteen Semi-Industrial Countries." *Weltwirtschftliches Archiv* 112, no. 4: 626–59.

Eltis, W. A. 1973. *Growth and Distribution.* London: Macmillan.

Feder, G. 1983. "On Exports and Economic Growth." *Journal of Development Economics* 12, no. 1/2 (February/April): 59–74.

Fishlow, A. 1985. "The State of Latin American Economics." In Inter-American Development Bank. *Economic and Social Progress in Latin America: Annual Report.* Washington, D.C.

Grais, W., and others. 1984. "A General Equilibrium Estimation of the Reduction of Tariffs and Quantitative Restrictions in Turkey in 1978." In T. N. Srinivasan and J. Whalley, eds. *General Equilibrium Trade Policy Modelling.* Cambridge, Mass.: Cambridge University Press.

Hahn, F. H., and R. C. U. Matthews. 1965. "The Theory of Economic Growth: A Survey." In American Economic Association. *Surveys of Economic Theory*, vol. 2. London: Macmillan.

Harberger, A. C. 1959. "The Fundamental of Economic Progress in Underdeveloped Countries: Using the Resources at Hand More Effectively." *American Economic Review* 49, no. 42: 134–46.

Harris, R. 1983. *Trade, Industrial Policy and Canadian Manufacturing.* Toronto: Ontario Economic Council.

Havrylyshyn, O. 1986. "Penetrating the Fallacy of Export Composition." Background paper to the *World Development Report 1987.* Washington, D.C.: World Bank, Economics and Research Staff.

Heller, P. S., and R. C. Porter. 1978. "Exports and Growth: An Empirical Re-Investigation." *Journal of Development Economics* 5, no. 2: 191–94.

Helliner, G. 1986. "Outward Orientation, Import Instability and African Economic Growth: an Empirical Investigation." In S. Lall and F. Stewart, eds. *Theory and Reality in Development.* London: Macmillan.

Henderson, P. D. 1982. "Trade Policies and 'Strategies': Case for a Liberal Approach." *World Economy* 5, no. 3: 291–302.

Hicks, J. R. 1979. *Causality in Economics.* Oxford: Blackwell.

Johnson, H. G. 1958. "The Gain for Free Trade with Europe: An Estimate." *Manchester School* 26, no. 3: 241–55.

Jung, W. S., and P. J. Marshall. 1985. "Exports, Growth and Causality in Developing Countries." *Journal of Development Economics* 18, no. 1: 1–12.

Kakwani, N. C. 1972. "On the Bias in Estimates of Import Demand Parameters." *International Economic Review* 13, no. 2: 239–44.

Kaldor, N. 1957. "A Model of Economic Growth." *Economic Journal* 67, no. 268: 591–624.

Kaldor, N., and J. A. Mirrlees. 1962. "A New Model of Economic Growth." *Review of Economic Studies* 29, no. 3: 174–92.

Kemp, M. C. 1962. "Errors of Measurement and Bias in Estimates of Import Demand Parameters." *Economic Record* 38, no. 83: 369–72.

Kravis, I. B. 1970. "Trade as a Handmaiden of Growth—Similarities between the 19th and 20th Centuries." *Economic Journal* 80, no. 320: 850–72.

Krueger, A. O. 1974. "The Political Economy of the Rent-Seeking Society." *American Economic Review* 64, no. 3: 291–303.

———. 1978. *Foreign Trade Regimes and Economic Development: Liberalization Attempts and Consequences.* Cambridge, Mass.: Ballinger.

———. 1984. "Trade Policies in Developing Countries." In R. W. Jones and P. B. Kenen, eds. *Handbook of International Economics*, vol. 1. New York: North Holland.

Lal, D. 1978a. *Men or Machines.* Geneva: International Labour Office.

———. 1978b. *Estimates of Shadow Prices for Korea.* Discussion Papers in Public Economics 10. London: University College, Department of Political Economy.

———. 1979a. "Accounting Prices for Jamaica." *Social and Economic Studies* 28, no. 3: 534–82.

———. 1979b. "Estimates of Accounting Prices for Sri Lanka." London: University College, Department of Political Economy.

———. 1979c. "Indian Export Incentives." *Journal of Development Economics* 6, no. 1: 103–17.

———. 1980. *Prices for Planning.* London: Heinemann.

———. 1981. Review of Bhagwati (1978). *Journal of Political Economy* 89, no. 4: 826.

———. 1983. *The Poverty of Development Economics.* London: Institute of Economic Affairs.

———. 1986. "Markets, Mandarins and Mathematicians." Paper prepared for Cato Institute Conference in Honor of Lord Bauer, May 1986. To be published in *Cato Journal*, forthcoming.

Lal, D., and S. Rajapatirana. 1987. *Impediments to Trade Liberalization in Sri Lanka.* Thames Essay No. 51. London: Gower for the Trade Policy Research Centre.

Lal, D., and M. Wolf, eds. 1986. *Stagflation, Savings and the State: Perspectives on the Global Economy.* Oxford: Oxford University Press.

Leamer, E. E. 1985. *Vector Autoregressions for Causal Inference?* Carnegie Rochester Series on Public Policy 22. Amsterdam: North Holland.

Leibenstein, H. 1966. "Allocative Efficiency vs. X-Efficiency." *American Economic Review* 56, no. 3: 392–415.

Lewis, W. A. 1980. "The Slowing Down of the Engine of Growth." *American Economic Review* 70, no. 4: 555–64.

Little, I. M. D., and others. 1970. *Industry and Trade in Some Developing Countries.* Oxford: Oxford University Press.

Little, I. M. D., and M. F. Scott. 1976. *Using Shadow Prices.* London: Heinemann.

Little, I. M. D., and others. 1979. "Shadow Pricing and Macro Economic Analysis: Some Illustrations from Pakistan." *Pakistan Development Review* 18, no. 2: 89–112.

Lucas, R. E., Jr. 1985. "The Mechanics of Economic Development." University of Chicago, Department of Economics.

Mckloskey, D. 1983. "The Rhetoric of Economics." *Journal of Economic Literature* 21, no. 2: 481–517.

Michaely, M. 1977. "Exports and Growth an Empirical Investigation." *Journal of Development Economics* 4, no. 1: 149–53.

———. 1979. "Exports and Growth: A Reply." *Journal of Development Economics* 6, no. 1: 141–43.

Michalopoulos, C., and K. Jay. 1973. "Growth of Exports and Income in the Developing

World: A Neoclassical View." Discussion Paper 28. Washington, D.C.: U.S. Agency for International Development.

Nogues, J. 1981. "Politica Comercial y Cambiaria: Una Evaluacion Cuantitativa de la Politica Argentina Durante 1961–1981." Technical Study 52. Buenos Aires: Banco Central de la Republica Argentina.

Nurkse, R. 1961. *Equilibrium and Growth in the World Economy*. Cambridge, Mass.: Harvard University Press.

Orcutt, G. H. 1950. "Measurement of Price Elasticities in International Trade." *Review of Economics and Statistics* 32, no. 2: 117–32.

Ranis, G. 1985. "Can the East Asian Model of Development be Generalised?" *World Development* 13, no. 4: 543–45.

Riedel, J. 1984. "Trade as the Engine of Growth in Developing Countries, Revisited." *Economic Journal* 94, no. 373: 56–73.

Scitovsky, T. 1958. *Economic Theory and Western European Integration*. London: Allen and Unwin.

Scott, M. F. 1976. "Investment and Growth." *Oxford Economic Papers* 28, no. 3: 317–63.

Solow, R. M. 1956. "A Contribution to the Theory of Economic Growth." *Quarterly Journal of Economics* 70, no. 1: 65–91.

Srinivasan, T. N. 1986a. "Development Strategy: Is the Success of Outward Orientation at an End?" In S. Guhan and M. Shroff, eds. *Essays on Economic Progress and Welfare*. New Delhi: Oxford University Press.

———. 1986b. "International Trade and Factor Movements in Development Theory, Policy and Experience." Twenty-fifth Anniversary Symposium on The State of Development Economics, April 11–13, 1986, Yale University, New Haven, Conn.

———. 1987. "Structural Change, Economic Interdependence and World Development." In J. Dunning and M. Usui, eds. *Economic Independence*. London: Macmillan (forthcoming).

Srinivasan, T. N., and J. Whalley, eds. 1986. *General Equilibrium Trade Policy Modeling*. Cambridge, Mass.: MIT Press.

Stern, R. M., and others. 1976. *Price Elasticities in International Trade: An Annotated Bibliography*. London: Macmillan for the Trade Policy Research Centre.

Streeten, P. 1982. "A Cool Look at 'Outward-looking' Strategies for Development." *World Economy* 5, no. 1: 159–70.

Swan, T. W. 1956. "Economic Growth and Capital Accumulation." *Economic Record* 32, no. 2: 334–61.

Taylor, L., and S. L. Black. 1974. "Practical General Equilibrium Estimation of Resource Pulls under Trade Liberalisation." *Journal of International Economics* 4, no. 1: 37–58.

Tullock, G. 1967. "The Welfare Costs of Tariffs, Monopolies and Theft." *Western Economic Journal* 5, no. 3: 224–32.

Tumlir, J. 1981. "The Contribution of Economics to International Disorder." Second Harry G. Johnson Memorial Lecture. Trade Policy Research Centre, London.

Tyler, W. 1981. "Growth and Export Expansion in Developing Countries: Some Empirical Evidence." *Journal of Development Economics* 9, no. 1: 121–30.

Wade, R. 1985. "The Role of Government in Overcoming Market Failure: Taiwan, South Korea and Japan." In Helen Hughes, ed. *Explaining the Success of East Asian Industrialisation*. Cambridge: Cambridge University Press.

Name Index

Abramovitz, M. 76
Aker 339
Akrasanee, N. 332
Alchian, A. 238
Amin, S. 153
Arrow, K. 275, 280, 289, 386
Ashley 31

Balassa, B. 215, 220, 229, 248, 249, 331,
  370, 374, 379, 384
Balasubramanyan, V.N. 126
Baldwin, R.E. 126, 131, 235–45, 289, 316,
  322
Barber, C.L. 215
Basevi, G. 215, 220, 226, 228
Baysan, T. 294
Becker, G.S. 241, 349
Behrman, J. 322, 325
Bension, A. 332
Bensusan Butt, D. 201
Bergsman, J. 369
Bertrand, T.J. 4, 10
Bhagwati, J. 193–9, 201, 203, 317–18,
  322–30, 322, 326, 327, 337, 349–65, 368,
  374–5, 382, 384
Bhalla, S. 381
Bickerdike, C.F. 201
Bocock, P. 280
Brander, J. 310
Brecher, R.A. 349
Bronfenbrenner, M. 184–90
Buchanan, J.M. 238, 240, 349, 350

Cairncross, A.K. 52, 57
Calvo, G.A. 380
Cannan 30
Carvalho, J. 332
Castree, J.R. 150
Caves, R.E. 3, 5
Chan, L. 134, 164
Chenery, H.B. 175, 248, 270, 274
Chudnovsky, D. 281
Cline, W.R. 384
Coase, R.H. 238
Cole, D.C. 254
Contractor, F.J. 280
Corbo, V. 332, 381

Corden, W.M. 215–31, 249, 266, 369
Cortes, M. 280

Darrat, A.F. 372
Deardorff, A.V. 9, 10, 13–28
de Melo, J. 381
Denison 317
Desai, P. 337
Diamond, P. 205
Diaz-Alejandro, C. 322
Dickey, D.A. 134
Dinopoulos, E. 357
Dixit, A.K. 307, 310, 317
Donges, J. 374

Easterlin, R.A. 57
Eaton, J. 307, 309
Ellsworth, P.T. 126
Eltis, W.A. 386
Emmanuel, A. 153

Feder, G. 370
Feenstra, R. 355–6
Findlay, R. 84–5, 349, 355–6
Fishlow, A. 322, 373
Flanders, M.J. 103–24
Frank, C. Jr. 322
Ford, A.G. 57
Foster, E. 357
Fuller, W.A. 134

Glewwe, P. 381
Graham, F.D. 111, 301
Grais, W. 368
Grandmont, J.M. 300
Greer, D.F. 153
Grilli, E.R. 125–71
Grossman, G. 307, 309
Grubel, A.G. 304
Grubel, H.G. 236, 241
Guisinger, S. 332
Gujarati, D. 134, 164

Haberler, G. 52, 193–5, 235
Haddad, C. 322
Hagen, E.E. 193, 197, 203
Hamilton, A. 203, 236

The International Library of Critical Writings in Economics

1. Multinational Corporations
   Mark Casson

2. The Economics of Innovation
   Christopher Freeman

3. Entrepreneurship
   Mark Casson

4. International Investment
   Peter J. Buckley

5. Game Theory in Economics
   Ariel Rubinstein

6. The History of Economic Thought
   Mark Blaug

7. Monetary Theory
   Thomas Mayer

8. Joint Production of Commodities
   Neri Salvadori and Ian Steedman

9. Industrial Organization
   Oliver E. Williamson

10. Growth Theory (Volumes I, II and III)
    R. Becker and E. Burmeister

11. Microeconomics: Theoretical and Applied (Volumes I, II and III)
    Robert E. Kuenne

12. The Economics of Health (Volumes I and II)
    A.J. Culyer

13. Recent Developments in Macroeconomics (Volumes I, II and III)
    Edmund S. Phelps

14. Urban and Regional Economics
    Paul C. Cheshire and Alan W. Evans

15. Modern Public Finance (Volumes I and II)
    A.B. Atkinson

16. Exchange Rate Economics (Volumes I and II)
    Ronald MacDonald and Mark P. Taylor

International Trade
J. Peter Neary

The Theory of Inflation
Michael Parkin

Evolutionary Economics
Ulrich Witt

Post-Keynesian Theory of Growth and Distribution (Volumes I and II)
Carlo Panico

The Theory of Inflation
Michael Parkin

The Foundations of Public Finance
Peter Jackson